FOU

Psychology A Level Year 2

The Complete Companion Student Book

Cara Flanagan • Mike Cardwell

OXFORD
UNIVERSITY PRESS

OXFORD
UNIVERSITY PRESS

Great Clarendon Street, Oxford, OX2 6DP, United Kingdom

Oxford University Press is a department of the University of Oxford. It furthers the University's objective of excellence in research, scholarship, and education by publishing worldwide. Oxford is a registered trade mark of Oxford University Press in the UK and in certain other countries

© Oxford University Press 2016

The moral rights of the authors have been asserted

First published in 2016

All rights reserved. No part of this publication may be reproduced, stored in a retrieval system, or transmitted, in any form or by any means, without the prior permission in writing of Oxford University Press, or as expressly permitted by law, by licence or under terms agreed with the appropriate reprographics rights organization. Enquiries concerning reproduction outside the scope of the above should be sent to the Rights Department, Oxford University Press, at the address above.

You must not circulate this work in any other form and you must impose this same condition on any acquirer

British Library Cataloguing in Publication Data
Data available

ISBN 978-0-19-833868-0

10 9 8 7 6 5 4 3 2

Paper used in the production of this book is a natural, recyclable product made from wood grown in sustainable forests. The manufacturing process conforms to the environmental regulations of the country of origin.

Printed in China by Golden Cup

Acknowledgements

Typesetting & project management: GreenGate Publishing Services
Design: Fiona MacColl
Cover design: Fiona MacColl & Chris Cardwell
Cover illustrations: Chris Cardwell

Credits

The publishers would like to thank the following for permissions to use copyright material:

ACTagainstviolence.apa.org: p.238; **Icek Ajzen:** p.313; **Alamy:** © AF archive/Alamy Stock Photo pp.137, 230, 247, © Bubbles Photolibrary/ Alamy Stock Photo p.175, © David Grossman/Alamy Stock Photo p.242, © IanDagnall Smartphones/Alamy Stock Photo p.302, © MARKA/Alamy p.82, © Pictorial Press Ltd/Alamy p.65, © Photos 12/Alamy p.71, © Trinity Mirror/Mirrorpix/Alamy Stock Photo p.231, © US Navy Photo/Alamy Stock Photo p.196, © WENN Ltd/Alamy p.83, © YAY Media AS/Alamy Stock Photo p.297, © Steve Skjold p.246; **Associated Press:** p.166; **Nathan Azrin:** p.153; **Rennee Baillargeon:** pp.122, 123; **Daryl Bem:** p.93; **Patricia Briggs:** pp.20, 128; **Cartoonstock:** pp.53, 167, 205, 233, 257, 273, 281, 308; **Professor Napoleon Chagnon:** p.233; **Corbis:** pp.95, 104, 116, © Bettmann/CORBIS pp.233, 294, © Image Source/Corbis p.210, © The Print Collector/Corbis p.299; **Dan Piraro:** Reprinted by permission of Dan Piraro, bizarro.com p.215; **Dreamstime:** Loveliestdreams p.106, Rawpixelimages p.281; **Steve Duck:** p.79; **Getty Images:** p.96; © AFP PHOTO/WANG ZHAO p.178, © AHMAD AL-RUBAYE p.315, © Alessandro Albert p.262, © Boyer p.262, © De Agostini Picture Library p.100, © Hans Casparius/Stringer p.101, © Peter Dazeley p.313, © Popperfoto p.267, © Universal History Archive p.258; **Mark Griffiths:** p.305; **Harvard University Press:** Fetus into Man: Physical Growth from Conception to Maturity by J.M. Tanner, Cambridge, MA: Harvard University Press © 1978, 1989 by J.M. Tanner. p.49; **iStock:** p.Skip Odonnell p.104; **Janice Kiecolt-Glaser:** p.194; **Suzanne Kobasa:** p.207; **Kurume University:** image courtesy of the Institute of Life Science, Kurume University p.168; **Library of Congress:** p.105; **Olivier Hess Photography:** p.260; **Rex:** REX Shutterstock p.69; **Science Photo Library:** ALFRED PASIEKA p.171; CORDELIA MOLLOY p.306; Cheryl Power p.94;

Dedication
To Mike Stanley – Our friend

Acknowledgements
The authors would like to thank the hardworking and enthusiastic team behind the production of this book. Rob Bircher for helping us develop the idea and for managing the opening stages of the project and Alison Schrecker at OUP for taking us to the finish line with her customary cheerful efficiency. Fiona MacColl provided the initial design inspiration, and we were delighted that the wonderful Carrie Baker at GreenGate could once again make our words actually look good on the page. We'd like to thank Mark Billingham for carrying out the arduous task of writing all the sample exam material and the valuable comments of Sally Morris, Gill Ries, Jackie Stanbury and Jane Williams on the material in this text. Writing a book like this isn't an easy task, lots of hard work, frustration and the occasional sleepless night. Therefore we'd like to say thank you to Sarah Flynn and the rest of the publishing team at OUP for making us feel more like family than jobbing writers!

EYE OF SCIENCE p.194; Graphic Equinox p.129; SCIENCE SOURCE p.192; WILL & DENI MCINTYRE p.212; **Dr Richard Rahe:** p.196; Robert Selman: p.125; **Shutterstock:** alxhar p.106, View Apart p.68, 1000 Words p.15, 240, Aaron Amat p.244, Adam Gregor p.211, Agencia Boxx p.178, Aleutie p.176, Alexei Zinin p.190, Alila Medical Media p.195, altanaka p.77, Andrea Danti p.230, Andrey Burmakin p.69, Andrzej Wilusz p.193, angelo gilardelli p.169, Antonio Guillem p.140, ArtFamily p.29, auremar pp.215, 219, 295, Belushi p.171, bibiphoto p.6, BlueSkyImage p.214, Brian A Jackson p.182, Brocreative p.237, ChameleonsEye p.139, Charlie Hutton pp.23, 35, CREATISTA pp.183, 270, Creativa Images p.54, Darryl Brooks p.268, Daxiao Productions p.299, DeiMosz p.16, Diego Schtutman p.182, DM7 p.7, dolphfyn p.217, Dooder p.114, Dragon Images pp.151, 156, Drop of Light p.66, EDHAR p.52, Edyta Pawlowska p.207, eldeiv p.271, erichon p.164, fabiodevilla p.102, Fer Gregory p.290, file404 p.266, Forewer p.24, frechtoch p.309, Gladskikh Tatiana p.154, glenda p.99, Goodluz p.43, GrandeDuc p.226, GryniuK p.96, hartphotography p.314, Hasselnott p.176, hecke61 p.299, Helga Esteb p.216, HieroGraphic p.200, Hirurg p.19, Hopeful.ya p.136, Image Point Fr p.306, indira's work p.174, ISchmidt p.98, Jerry-Rainey p.274, Jessica Bethke p.229, John Gomez p.213, Jorg Hackemann p.296, Joseph Sohm p.277, Kamil Macniak pp.66, 183, Kateholms p.165, KieferPix p.201, Kjetil Kolbjornsrud p.209, kudla p.45, 56, kurhan p.227, Kuzma p.153, lassedesignen p.203, leungchopan p.71, lipik p.279, Lisa F. Young p.72, Lithiumphoto p.291, LittleMiss p.167, LoloStock p.206, Luis Molinero pp.264, 283, Malyugin p.70, marcogarrincha pp.18, 35, Marcos Mesa Sam Wordley p.155, 301, Mary_L p.24, Marzolino p.263, Matthew Cole p.276, maximino p.245 (x3), Melinda Varga p.144, 157, meunierd p.265, Michael C. Gray p.311, Mikhail Kolesnikov p.272, Minerva Studio p.208, Monkey Business Images pp.14, 73, 153, 172, 198, nasruleffendy p.300, Nejron Photo p.275, Nick Fox p.13, Oleg Golovnev p.83, Oleksiy Mark pp.256, 282, ostill p.261, 283, PAISAN HOMHUAN pp.193, 219, PathDoc p.204, paulista p.90, Pavel L Photo and Video p.107, Peter Hermes Furian p.304, Photographee.eu pp.74, 148, 235, PhotoStock10 p.239, plavevski p.163, Podlesnyak Nina p.17, Pressmaster pp.212, 220, racorn p.68, rangizzz p.259, Rawpixel p.103, rmnoa357 pp.236, 303, Ron Leishman p.310, runzelkorn p.99, rvlsoft p.20, salajean p.237, Scott Leman pp.124, 131, Sergey Nivens p.278, Serhiy Kobyakov p.127, sheff p.26, Shi Yali p.254, Shutter_M p.259, Siberia - Video and Photo p.217, Sign N Symbol Production p.245, Sonsedska Yuliia pp.31, 34, StockLite p.293, studiostoks p.40, studioVin p.50, Sundraw Photography p.23, suns07butterfly pp.47, 57, Surrphoto p.91, Suzanne Tucker p.183, Syda Productions p.79, Tanya Puntti p.232, Thinglass p.63, veleknez p.138, victoriaKh p.162, View Apart p.234, Volt Collection p.129, Voyagerix p.10, wavebreakmedia pp.26, 34, 44, 62, 64, 79, 199, zadirako p.92, Ziga Camernik p.75; **Texas A&M College of Veterinary Medicine & Biomedical Sciences:** p.49; **theonion.com:** p.80; **Topfoto:** p.120; **UC Berkeley:** p.198 Saxon Donnelly photo; **University of Chicago Press:** p.21; **Professor Philip Zimbardo:** p.240; **Wiley:** reproduced with permission from John Wiley and Sons p.97.

Although we have made every effort to trace and contact all copyright holders before publication this has not been possible in all cases. If notified, the publisher will rectify any errors or omissions at the earliest opportunity.

Links to third party websites are provided by Oxford in good faith and for information only. Oxford disclaims any responsibility for the materials contained in any third party website referenced in this work.

CONTENTS

How to use this book **4**

The examination **6**

Types of exam question **8**

How to use this book

The contents of this book are designed to follow the AQA Year 2 specification as closely as possible. The book is divided into 11 chapters matching the topics in the specification. These chapters, together with 'Approaches to psychology', 'Biopsychology' and 'Research methods', which you will have studied last year, constitute the content for Paper 2 and Paper 3 of your A level examination.

- For Paper 2 (Psychology in context), we have added a new chapter on 'Issues and Debates in psychology' and have revisited 'Research Methods' to supplement the content that you will have studied in your first year.
- The remaining 9 chapters cover Paper 3 (Issues and options in psychology). There are three options in this paper. You select a minimum of one chapter from each option. For Option 1, this means one from 'Relationships' (Chapter 3), 'Gender' (Chapter 4) or 'Cognition and development' (Chapter 5). For Option 2, you select one from 'Schizophrenia' (Chapter 6), 'Eating behaviour' (Chapter 7) or 'Stress' (Chapter 8). Finally, for Option 3 you select one from 'Aggression' (Chapter 9), 'Forensic psychology' (Chapter 10) or 'Addiction' (Chapter 11).

In the top left of each spread there is an **Introduction** to the topic. This explains what it is about and may identify some key issues or links to previous topics.

Each chapter begins with a list of the topics covered in that chapter.

The full details of the specification content to be covered by each chapter are presented on the chapter's opening page.

We have included an activity for you to try to get you thinking about the chapter content.

The main **descriptive** (AO1) content is on the left side of each spread, and usually in the central column. We sometimes include an **extra information** feature for any interesting (but not essential) information to extend your understanding of the topic. You will recognise these features by the pale yellow border around the text.

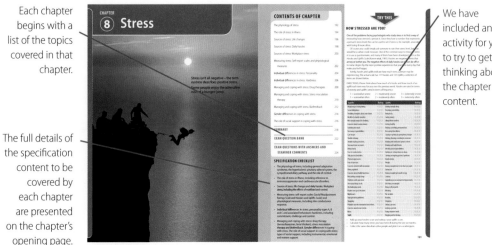

The content of each chapter consists of a series of double-page spreads. The features of these double-page spreads are illustrated on the two sample spreads on the right.

Each chapter ends with some useful features, consisting of:

Each chapter has a particular colour scheme to help you locate it easily. This is reflected in the topic heading and throughout the chapter.

A diagrammatic summary of the chapter

Example examination questions to give you an idea of how the chapter contents might be assessed in an exam.

Key terms are defined and explained when named in the specification so that you are able to define these terms when required to do so.

We have occasionally included definitions of other terms and concepts, even if they aren't named in the specification, if we consider them 'key' for a particular topic.

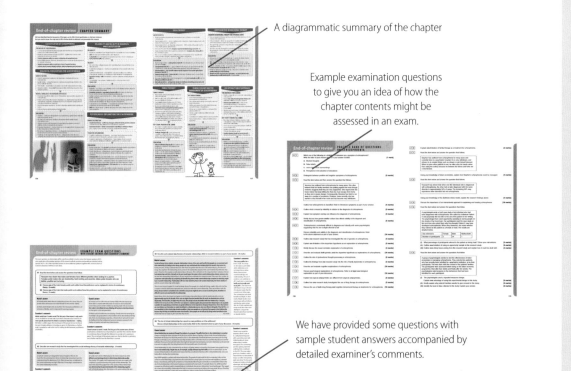

We have provided some questions with sample student answers accompanied by detailed examiner's comments.

The spread heading tells you what this topic is about.

We sometimes invite you to **Meet the researcher** if he or she has made a particularly significant contribution to the topic covered on the spread.

Sometimes there is a helpful comment to enhance understanding (**Aside**) or to offer valuable exam advice (**Insider tip**).

On some spreads we have an **Apply your knowledge** feature so you can hone your application (AO2) skills. These are usually a bit lengthier than the questions you will face in the exam, but serve the same purpose.

On the right-hand side of each spread there is the **Evaluation** (AO3). We thought it helpful to separate AO1 and AO3 material clearly in this way.

Evaluation comes in many different forms, e.g. limitations, research support, applications. We have aimed for five AO3 points for each topic.

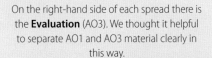

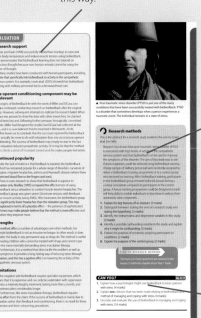

On some spreads we have included a **research methods** scenario linked to the topic, with some sample questions for you to try.

On other spreads we have included an **Upgrade** feature with valuable advice on how you might boost your exam performance when answering exam questions on a particular topic.

On each spread we ask you some **Can you…?** Questions to help focus you on the level of knowledge and understanding that you will need for the exam. We have tried to ask questions that will be useful for your exam. You will not be required to reproduce the amount of detail on the spreads, but to select just enough to be effective in answering each question.

The examination

There are three examinations that make up your A Level in psychology, and which you will take at the end of your second year – Papers 1, 2 and 3. We have covered most of the content for Paper 1 (Introductory topics in psychology) and most of the content for Paper 2 (Psychology in context) in our 'Psychology A Level Year 1 and AS' book.

This Year 2 book focuses on Paper 3 (Issues and Options in psychology), as well as including some of the research methods content for Paper 2 that is not included in the AS specification.

The questions on all three of these papers will be a mixture of multiple choice, short answer and extended writing questions. Many of these questions will be parted. On this spread we'll look at what's involved in these three examinations, and then take a closer look at the all important assessment objectives (i.e. AO1, AO2 and AO3).

Paper 1: Introductory topics in psychology

Written exam: 2 hours

33.3% of your A Level marks

Paper 1 contains four sections, each worth 24 marks. You must answer all questions. The content of the four sections is as below:

Section A:	Social influence
Section B:	Memory
Section C:	Attachment
Section D:	Psychopathology

Paper 2: Psychology in context

Written exam: 2 hours

33.3% of your A Level marks

Paper 2 contains three sections, two worth 24 marks each and the third worth 48 marks. You must answer all questions. The content of the three sections is as below:

Section A:	Approaches in psychology
Section B:	Biopsychology
Section C:	Research methods

Examinations arouse all sorts of different emotions, ranging from anxiety and despair through to excitement and a sense of triumph when you do well. Being prepared for what might come will help you feel more positively about your exam and, dare we say, a tad excited about the prospect?

Paper 3: Issues and options in psychology

Written exam: 2 hours

33.3% of your A Level marks

Paper 3 contains four sections, each worth 24 marks. Section A is compulsory. For Sections B–D, you choose one topic (e.g. for Section C you choose either Schizophrenia or Eating behaviour or Stress) and answer all the questions on that particular topic. The content of the four sections is as below:

Section A:	Issues and debates in psychology
Section B:	Relationships
	Gender
	Cognition and development
Section C:	Schizophrenia
	Eating behaviour
	Stress
Section D:	Aggression
	Forensic psychology
	Addiction

Assessment objectives

Assessment objective 1 (AO1)

Questions linked to this objective will be testing your ability to identify, outline, describe or explain (although this last term may also imply some evaluation). They are a chance to show off your knowledge of a particular area, with the different terms usually being associated with different numbers of marks available. Hence, 'Identify' tends to be used for 1 mark questions, 'Outline' and 'Explain' for slightly higher tariff questions and 'Describe' for the highest tariff AO1 questions (usually 6 marks). This is not a hard and fast rule, but it helps to recognise what you are being asked to do and to respond accordingly.

DESCRIBE IT

Assessment objective 2 (AO2)

AO2 questions assess your ability to *apply* your knowledge in some way. This is your chance to show evidence of your knowledge of a particular topic but within a specific scenario, i.e. *in context*. These appear on all three papers, but are particularly prominent on Paper 2, where the majority of the marks awarded on 'Research methods' are for AO2 because of the need for answers to be within the specific context of the stimulus material. Elsewhere these questions may assess your ability to explain a particular behaviour, your maths or research methods skills in the context of a particular topic or your ability to incorporate some specific stimulus material into your response to an extended writing question.

APPLY IT

Assessment objective 3 (AO3)

Although we have labelled this skill as 'evaluation', this is not restricted to pointing out the limitations of a particular theory, explanation or study. It can include *strengths* (e.g. showing research support for something or that it applies across different cultures) and *limitations* (e.g. pointing out that there are gender differences which reduces its universal application or that it lacks research support). AO3 can also include *applications* (which show its value through its application in therapy, more general application or just in terms of increasing our understanding of an area). We have included a variety of different types of AO3 in this book.

EVALUATE IT

Responding to the different assessment objectives

When asked about assessment objectives, AQA tend to give the sensible suggestion that students should not worry too much about the divisions between AO1, AO2 and AO3, but should just answer the question. This is useful advice up to a point as it prevents the anxious search for the different types of question in what is already a highly anxious situation (the examination). However, being aware of the differences between these different objectives and responding accordingly is still a useful skill. In practice, the differences between the three can be quite subtle, as it is more a case of what you *do* with the material that makes it AO1, AO2 or AO3 rather than any inherent properties of the material itself.

Lets look at a (completely fictional) example from a galaxy far, far away:

> *Solo (2016) found that space travel could be particularly stressful. In his study, Solo found that the chronic stress of having to deal with mechanical problems in hyperspace while battling with superior galactic forces led to a number of psychological problems, including depression, delusional behaviour and substance abuse.*

Now lets look at how this material can be used as a way of responding to three very different types of question. Note that the underlying material is more or less the same in all three cases, but has been 'tweaked' so that it is being used in either a descriptive (AO1), application (AO2) or evaluative (AO3) way.

An AO1 question

Outline the findings of one psychological study of the relationship between stress and space travel. (3 marks)

Solo (2016) found that space travel could be particularly stressful. In his study, Solo found that the chronic stress of having to deal with mechanical problems in hyperspace while battling with superior galactic forces led to a number of psychological problems, including depression, delusional behaviour and substance abuse.

An AO2 question

Rey is considering a career as a space freighter pilot but is put off by claims it is very stressful. Using your knowledge of the relationship between stress and space travel, what advice would you offer her? (3 marks)

Solo (2016) found that the chronic stress associated with space travel led to a number of psychological problems, including depression and substance abuse. Based on this finding, I would tell Rey that if she were to continue with this choice of career, she should take steps (e.g. by learning stress management techniques) to deal with the potential problems she will face.

An AO3 question

Explain one critical point concerning the relationship between stress and space travel. (3 marks)

The claim there is a relationship between stress and space travel is supported by research by Solo (2016), who found that the chronic stress of having to deal with mechanical problems in hyperspace while battling with superior galactic forces led to a number of psychological problems, including depression, delusional behaviour and substance abuse. This research provides evidence demonstrating that space travel can be particularly stressful.

Types of exam question

Question type	Example	Advice
Multiple choice questions	Which **one** of the following pairs of hormones is associated with aggression? Write the letter of your chosen answer in your answer booklet. *(1 mark)* **A** cortisol and dopamine **B** cortisol and serotonin **C** dopamine and testosterone **D** serotonin and testosterone	Questions such as this should be straightforward enough, so the trick is making sure you have selected the right answer and not ticked more than the correct number of boxes. If you aren't sure which answer is the right one, try crossing through those that are obviously wrong, thus narrowing down your options before making your final choice.
Description questions (e.g. *Describe, Outline, Identify, Explain*).	Briefly outline theory of mind as an explanation of autism. *(2 marks)* Give **two** examples of human reproductive behaviour and explain how each one can be related to sexual selection. *(4 marks)* Describe Wundt's contribution to the development of psychology. *(6 marks)*	These AO1 description questions can come in a variety of different forms, but will never be more than 6 marks for any one part of a question. To judge how much to write in response to a question, simply look at the number of marks available and allow about 25 words per mark. However, where the sole command word is 'Name' or 'Identify', there is no need to develop a 25 word per mark response, simply identifying or naming (as required by the question) is enough. Sometimes the phrasing of a question (such as the second question) is a prod to get students to go beyond just naming or identifying something and to offer additional detail to flesh it out.
Differences/Distinguish between	Distinguish between a Type I error and a Type II error. *(2 marks)* Using an example, distinguish between physical and psychological dependence in addiction. *(3 marks)* Distinguish between the top-down and bottom-up approach to offender profiling. *(4 marks)*	Students often ignore the instruction to 'distinguish between' or 'identify differences' and simply outline the two terms or concepts named in the question. This is not what is required, and would not gain full credit. You should be guided by the number of marks allocated as well as any specific instructions in the question. For example, the first question requires one difference (with elaboration), the second one difference and an example, and the third question would require 2-3 differences.
Applying knowledge	Read the item below and then answer the question that follows. Sarah was unhappy in her first serious relationship. Looking back, she now realises that Matthew was much more successful and much more confident than she was, and she did not fit in with his wide circle of friends. Sarah is much happier with her new partner, Karl, because their jobs are very similar and they come from the same kind of family background. Using your knowledge of the matching hypothesis, explain Sarah's experiences of her two relationships. *(4 marks)* Read the item below and answer the question that follows. Niamh has anorexia nervosa. Even though she is clearly underweight, when she looks in the mirror she perceives that she is overweight. This really upsets her as she thinks that nobody is going to want to socialise with someone who is so unattractive. Distinguish between distortions and irrational beliefs. Use the case of Niamh as part of your response. *(4 marks)*	In these (AO2) questions, you will be provided with a scenario (the question 'stem') and asked to use your psychological knowledge to provide an informed answer. You must make sure that your answer contains not only appropriate psychological content, but that this is set explicitly within the context outlined in the question stem. In the first example on the left, some students would ignore the question stem and simply provide a description of the matching hypothesis. Other students might ignore the underlying psychology completely and simply engage with the material in the stem in some other way. Neither approach is appropriate, and would result in a disappointingly low mark. The same warning applies to the second example question on the left. There is a temptation to either ignore Niamh's symptoms or just mention them in passing. Examiners will be looking for total engagement with the question stem, so ignore it at your peril! We have included a number of 'Apply your knowledge' features throughout the book so you can practice your skills in this area. The scenarios in these features tend to be lengthier than in actual exam questions, but the skill in answering them is the same.
Research methods questions	Read the item below and then answer the questions that follow. A group of psychologists conducted a covert observation to investigate if men displayed more aggressive behaviours in the presence of women rather than if there were no women present. They observed men in a number of contexts including nightclubs, leisure centres, shopping centres and parks. Each time, a different group of males were observed as all situations were naturally occurring. (i) Outline **one** advantage and **one** disadvantage of using a covert observation in this study. *(4 marks)* (ii) Identify an inferential test that could be used to analyse the data from this study. Give **two** reasons for your choice of test. *(3 marks)* (iii) State why the study could be said to have 'high ecological validity'. *(1 mark)*	Most research methods questions are set within the context of a hypothetical research study. This means that your answers must also be set within the context of that study. If you don't set your answers within the specific context of the study, you cannot receive full marks. We have included a large number of sample research methods questions throughout the book. The more you practice these, the better you will become at them, and with mastery comes increased confidence. With practice, you should be able to unpack the specific requirements of each question and plan your response accordingly. For example, identifying an advantage and disadvantage in question (i) would bring 1 mark each, but adding detail to each would bring the other 2 marks. Likewise, in (ii), correct identification of an appropriate test would give you the first mark, and identification of two reasons for your choice the other 2 marks. Finally, in (iii), a brief statement (e.g. 'the observations were carried out in natural environments rather than artificial lab settings') would be sufficient.

Question type	Example	Advice
Maths questions	Read the item below and then answer the questions that follow. A psychologist did a content analysis of a TV drama targeted at adolescents. She was interested in the ways that the media influences eating behaviour and whether it was different for males and females. The main female and male characters were categorised in terms of whether they were average weight or below or above. The findings are shown below. |	Above average	Average	Below average
---	---	---	---
Female	1	3	5
Male	1	5	2 | (i) What percentage of female characters were categorised as below average weight? Show your calculations. *(3 marks)* (ii) What was the modal category for the characters' weight? *(1 mark)*	'Maths' questions can appear anywhere on the paper, and can assess your ability to carry out simple calculations, construct graphs and interpret data. For example, in the first question, a correct answer and appropriate working are necessary for the full 3 marks. It is easy to become flustered and give the wrong answer even when you probably have the requisite knowledge to give the right answer. For example, you probably know what a 'mode' is but may not recognise what a 'modal category' means. If the mode is the most frequently occurring score then the weight category that is observed most often (i.e. the 'modal' category) is 'Average'.
Evaluation questions	Briefly explain **one** limitation of the dispositional explanation for institutional aggression. *(2 marks)* Explain **one** limitation of the dopamine hypothesis as an explanation of schizophrenia. *(3 marks)* Evaluate the use of drug therapy as a way of reducing addiction. *(6 marks)*	AO3 'evaluation' questions come in many different forms, but the most common are worth 2, 3 or 4 marks. The 2 and 3 mark questions tend to ask for one critical point, with the marks awarded being determined by the level of elaboration. With 6-mark questions, two or three elaborated points would be expected. We have shown you how to achieve this all important elaboration in some of the Upgrade features throughout this book.
Mixed description and evaluation questions	Briefly outline how family therapy is used to treat schizophrenia and explain one limitation of using family therapy to treat schizophrenia. *(4 marks)* Briefly outline and evaluate **one** research study into genetic factors in aggression. *(4 marks)* Discuss sources of workplace stress. *(8 marks)*	Not all questions are straightforward 'description only' or 'evaluation only', but may be mixed. The command words (e.g. outline, evaluate) will tell you that description and evaluation are required, or sometimes (as in the third question here) the word 'discuss' is used instead to indicate the same need for both AO1 and AO2 in your answer. In A Level essays there are usually more marks for AO3 than AO1.
Extended writing questions	Describe and evaluate **both** genetics **and** the dopamine hypothesis as explanations of schizophrenia. *(16 marks)* Read the item below and then answer the question that follows. Patricia and Marilyn were both obese when they joined a slimming club six months ago. Patricia followed her diet and has now met her target weight. Marilyn kept over-eating at weekends and now weighs more than she did when she started the club. Discuss explanations of obesity **and** dieting. Refer to both Patricia and Marilyn as part of your answer. *(16 marks)*	Although the distinction between this and the previous category is somewhat arbitrary, questions worth more than 8 marks are usually referred to as extended writing questions. The most common of these is the 16-mark question. As a rough guide, you should aim for 25-30 words per mark. So, for a 16-mark answer, between 400-500 words would be appropriate. Five well-developed AO3 points are the target for a 16-mark question, and that is the approach we have taken throughout this book. As more marks are allocated for AO3 in these questions (10/16) than for AO1 (6/16), this means that the amount of evaluation should be proportionately greater than the description. Some questions, such as the second one here, have additional requirements. The second sentence ('Refer to. . .') means that there is an application component to the question, so your response plan would be slightly different. In this case (and for similar questions), the marks for description would stay the same at 6, but there would be fewer marks for AO3 (6 instead of the usual 10), with 4 marks being allocated to AO2. Complicated? Perhaps, but with all the different types of question on this spread, you'll soon get used to it!

CONTENTS OF CHAPTER

SPECIFICATION CHECKLIST

- Content analysis and coding. Thematic analysis.

- Case studies.

- Reliability across all methods of investigation. Ways of assessing reliability: Test–retest and inter-observer; improving reliability.

- Types of validity across all methods of investigation: face validity, concurrent validity, ecological validity and temporal validity. Assessment of validity. Improving validity.

- Features of science: objectivity and the empirical method; replicability and falsifiability; theory construction and hypothesis testing; paradigms and paradigm shifts.

- Probability and significance: use of statistical tables and critical values in interpretation of significance; Type I and Type II errors.

- Levels of measurement: nominal, ordinal and interval.

- Factors affecting the choice of statistical test, including level of measurement and experimental design. When to use the following tests: Spearman's rho, Pearson's r, Wilcoxon, Mann-Whitney, related t-test, unrelated t-test and Chi-Squared test.

- Analysis and interpretation of correlation, including correlation coefficients.

- Reporting psychological investigations. Sections of a scientific report: abstract, introduction, method, results, discussion and referencing.

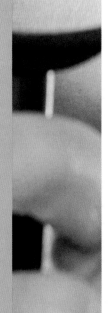

TRY THIS

This is the most important chapter in this book. Why? Because **at least 25%** of the marks across your whole A level qualification will be questions related to research methods. There is one section on Paper 2 devoted to research methods, but there will also be questions on Papers 1 and 3 on research methods.

Here is a checklist that also contains the AS/year 1 content. Tick the statements you feel confident about.

	Page in Year 1 book	Tick if you feel confident
I know the difference between an aim and a hypothesis.	178	
I can identify an independent variable and a dependent variable in an experimental hypothesis.	178	
I can write operationalised hypotheses, and both directional and non-directional.	178, 182	
I know the difference between laboratory, field, natural and quasi experiments.	186, 188	
I know the strengths and limitations of each of these.	189	
I know three types of experimental design and their strengths and weaknesses.	184	
I know when and how random allocation and counterbalancing are used.	185	
I know about control in experiments including extraneous and confounding variables.	180	
I can give examples of demand characteristics and investigator effects.	190	
I understand why standardisation is important.	178	
I can design a well-controlled experiment.	180, 184, 190, 191	
I can name the five sampling techniques in the specification and how they are used.	192	
I know the strengths and limitations of each of them.	192	
I can explain how bias and generalisability are important in relation to sampling.	193	
I can explain how and why to use a pilot study and I know the aims of piloting.	183	
I can name six types of observational study.	198	
I know the strengths and limitations of each of them.	199	
I can explain what behavioural categories are.	200	
I can distinguish between time and event sampling.	200	
I can design an observational study.	200	
I know what a self-report (questionnaires and interviews) technique is.	202	
I know the differences between structured and unstructured interviews and between questionnaires and interviews.	202	
I know the strengths and limitations of questionnaires and structured/unstructured interviews.	203	
I know how to use closed and open questions.	204	
I know how to design a questionnaire and an interview.	204, 205	
I know the difference between correlations and experiments.	207	
I can design a correlational study to analyse the relationship between co-variables.	206	
I can identify and explain positive, negative and zero correlations.	206	
I can identify ethical issues in the design and conduct of psychological studies.	194, 195	
I can suggest ways to deal with these issues.	196, 197	
I can distinguish between quantitative and qualitative data.	216	
I can distinguish between primary and secondary data.	217	
I know the strengths and limitations of each of them.	216, 217	
I know what a meta-analysis is.	208	
I can name and calculate three measures of central tendency and know their strengths/limitations.	212, 213	
I can name and calculate two measures of dispersion and know their strengths/limitations.	212, 213	
I can calculate percentages, fractions, decimals, standard form, significant figures and decimal places, and can estimate answers and substitute values in a formula.	211	
I can present quantitative data in tables, graphs, scattergrams, bar charts and histograms.	214, 206	
I know about normal distributions and skewed distributions (positive and negative).	215	
I can calculate the sign test.	218, 219	
I can discuss the role of peer review in the scientific process.	220, 221	
I can discuss the implications of psychological research for the economy.	222, 223	

A Level:

I know about correlation coefficients and how to interpret them.	30	
I know about content analysis, thematic analysis and coding.	12, 13	
I know about case studies.	14	
I know the strengths and limitations of content analysis and case studies.	12, 15	
I know about reliability, and how to assess it and how to improve it.	16, 17	
I can explain four kinds of validity, and I know how to assess and improve them.	18, 19	
I know the features of science, how theories are constructed and understand paradigm shifts.	20, 21	
I know about probability and significance, including Type I and II errors.	22, 23	
I know seven statistical tests and can select and calculate the appropriate one and report significance.	24, 25–32	
I know how psychological investigations are reported.	33	

Content analysis

Most of this chapter is concerned with statistical testing, but we begin with two research methods not included in the Year 1 course. First up is content analysis.

Content analysis is what it says it is – a researcher looks at the content of something and analyses it. For example, you might look at what is in a book and identify patterns – the way men and women are portrayed, the way the characters interact, and so on. These patterns might be called different behavioural categories or different themes – so content analysis may also involve **thematic analysis**.

CONTENT ANALYSIS

The process involved in conducting a content analysis is similar to any observational study, but instead of observing actual people a researcher usually makes observations indirectly through books, films, advertisements and photographs – any artefact people have produced.

As in an observational study the researcher has to make design decisions about the following:

Sampling method
The researcher has to decide the following:
- If analysing the content of books, does the researcher look at every page or just, say, every fifth page (a kind of time sampling)?
- If comparing the content in various books, does the researcher select books randomly from a library or identify certain characteristics (e.g. look at books that are biographies or romantic fiction)?
- If analysing ads on TV, does the researcher sample behaviours, say, every 30 seconds, and note whenever certain behaviours occur?

Coding the data
The process of **coding** basically means that the researcher uses behavioural categories. For example, if the researcher wishes to look at the way men and women are portrayed in books, they create a list of behavioural categories (such as the example from Manstead and McCulloch on the right) and then count instances.

Decisions about behavioural categories may involve a thematic analysis – described on the facing page.

Method of representing data
Data can be recorded in each behavioural category in two different ways. Consider the example of performing a content analysis of paintings. First you identify the behavioural categories (e.g. abstract art, landscape, etc.). Then you record instances in each category:
- You can count instances = a quantitative analysis.
- You can describe examples in each category = a qualitative analysis.

EVALUATION

Strengths
Content analysis tends to have high ecological validity because it is based on observations of what people actually do – real communications that are current and relevant, such as recent newspapers or the books that people read.

When sources can be retained or accessed by others (e.g. back copies of magazines or videos of people giving speeches), the content analysis can be replicated, and therefore the observations can be tested for reliability.

Limitations
Observer bias reduces the objectivity and validity of findings because different observers may interpret the meaning of the behavioural categories differently.

Content analysis is likely to be culture biased because interpretation of verbal or written content will be affected by the language and culture of the observer and the behavioural categories used.

KEY TERMS

Coding The process of placing quantitative or qualitative data in categories.

Content analysis A kind of observational study in which behaviour is usually observed indirectly in visual, written or verbal material. May involve either qualitative or quantitative analysis, or both.

Thematic analysis A technique used when analysing qualitative data. Themes or categories are identified and then data is organised according to these themes.

A quantitative content analysis

Anthony Manstead and Caroline McCulloch (1981) were interested in the way men and women are portrayed in TV ads. They observed 170 ads over a one-week period, ignoring those that contained only children or those with animals. In each ad they focused on the central adult figure and recorded frequencies in a table like the one on the right. For each ad there might be no ticks, one tick or a number of ticks.

	Male	Female
Credibility basis of central character		
Product user		
Product authority		
Role of central character		
Dependent role		
Independent role		
Argument spoken by central character		
Factual		
Opinion		
Product type used by central character		
Food/drink		
Alcohol		
Body		
Household		

A qualitative content analysis

A Finnish study considered the role of the family in adolescents' peer and school experiences. Katja Joronen and Päivi Åstedt-Kurki (2005) conducted semi-structured interviews with 19 adolescents aged 12–16, using questions such as 'What does your family know about your peers?' and 'How is your family involved in your school activities?' These interviews produced 234 pages of notes which were analysed using a qualitative content analysis.

1. All answers to the same question were placed together.
2. Each statement was compressed into a briefer statement and given an identifier code.
3. These statements were compared with each other and categorised so that statements with similar content were placed together and a category (or theme) identified.
4. The categories were grouped into larger units, producing eight main categories; for example:
   - Enablement, e.g. 'Yeah, ever since my childhood we've always had lots of kids over visiting.' (Girl, 15 years)
   - Support, e.g. 'They [family members] help if I have a test by asking questions.' (Boy, 13 years)
   - Negligence, e.g. 'My sister is not at all interested in my friends.' (girl, 16 years)

One of the conclusions drawn from this study is that schools should pay more attention to the multiple relationships that determine an adolescent's behaviour.

THEMATIC ANALYSIS

One problem with qualitative data is that it is difficult to summarise. Quantitative data can be readily summarised with measures of central tendency and measures of dispersion, and also with the use of graphs. None of these options are possible with purely descriptive findings. Instead, qualitative data is summarised by identifying repeated themes in the material to be analysed.

The material to be analysed might be a book, advertisements on TV or the transcript from interviews (all examples from the facing page), or a researcher might wish to analyse graffiti or analyse videotaped play sessions with children.

Thematic analysis is a very lengthy process because it is painstaking and iterative – every item is carefully considered and the data are gone through repeatedly. The main intentions are:

- To impose some kind of order on the data.
- To ensure that the 'order' represents the participants' perspective, i.e. fits in with how they see the phenomenon.
- To ensure that this 'order' emerges from the data rather than any preconceptions.
- To summarise the data so that hundreds of pages of text or hours of videotapes can be reduced.
- To enable themes to be identified and general conclusions drawn.

There is no one method to use, but the following table gives a general picture of what is done.

▲ The psychology of graffiti.

How can we summarise the way that people express themselves through graffiti? Psychologists use thematic analysis and content analysis to do this.

	General principles	Applied to the analysis of graffiti	Applied to the analysis of videotaped play sessions with various children
1	Read and reread the data transcript dispassionately (or do the same with a video), trying to understand the meaning communicated and the perspective of the participants. No notes should be made.	Study a photographic or written record of a wide range of graffiti.	Watch videos of play sessions or read a transcription of what happened (the transcription should include details of what was said and also describing facial expressions and body movements.
2	Break the data into meaningful units – small bits of text which are independently able to convey meaning. This might be equivalent to sentences or phrases.	In the case of graffiti it would be each item of graffiti.	Each verbal and non-verbal movement would constitute a unit.
3	Assign a label or code to each unit. Such labels/codes are the initial categories that you are using. You will have developed some ideas when initially reviewing through the data in step 1. Each unit may be given more than one code/label.	Each unit of graffiti is given a code to describe its meaning, such as 'humour', 'advice', 'love' or 'power domination'.	Each unit is coded, for example 'playing with toy', 'sadness expressed' or 'request made'.
4	Combine simple codes into larger categories/themes and then instances can be counted or examples provided.	Larger order categories are developed which combine units, such as 'interpersonal concerns'.	Larger categories developed such as 'negative emotion'.
5	A check can be made on the emergent categories by collecting a new set of data and applying the categories. They should fit the new data well if they represent the topic area investigated.		

APPLY YOUR KNOWLEDGE

1. A university department was given funding to investigate the stereotypes presented in children's books (age stereotypes, gender stereotypes, etc.). They were to compare books that children read today with those from 20 years ago to see how and if stereotypes had changed.
   a) Suggest **three** items that could be used as behavioural categories in this study. (3 marks)
   b) Write an operationalised definition for **one** of these items. (2 marks)
   c) Explain how you would use these categories to code the data. (3 marks)
2. Select a source item. This might be a wall with graffiti, a novel, a film, letters to an agony aunt – or any form of human communication.
   a) Explain what you would do to perform a thematic analysis of your source item. (4 marks)
   b) Give an example of **one** theme that might emerge and how you would use this to code the data. (3 marks)
   c) Is the original data qualitative or quantitative? Explain your answer. (2 marks)

CAN YOU? No. 1.1

1. Explain what is meant by *content analysis*. (2 marks)
2. Explain how observer bias might affect the findings of a content analysis. (3 marks)
3. Briefly outline what is involved in thematic analysis. (3 marks)
4. Give **one** strength and **one** limitation of content analysis. (2 marks + 2 marks)

Case studies

You probably remember the case study of HM as part of your Year 1 memory studies, and may also remember the case study of Little Hans described by Sigmund Freud. Some more case studies are described on this spread.

People are fascinated by such **case studies**. Is it because of the rich detail that provides interesting insights into human behaviour? Psychologists turn to case studies for the same reason – they provide rich details of what people do and think. In addition they often are a good antidote to the more superficial collection of statistics from, for example, experiments and questionnaires.

CASE STUDIES

A case study involves the detailed study of a single individual, institution or event. It is an example of evidence-based research – psychologists turn to individual cases partly to look at unusual behaviours, and partly to look in greater detail at any kind of behaviour.

The case study is a scientific research method and thus aims to use objective and systematic methods.

Case studies use information from a range of sources, such as from the person concerned and also from their family and friends.

Many techniques may be used – the people may be interviewed or they might be observed while engaged in daily life. Psychologists might use IQ tests or personality tests or some other kind of questionnaire to produce psychological data about the target person or group of people. They may use the experimental method to test what the target person/group can or can't do.

The findings are organised into themes to represent the individual's thoughts, emotions, experiences and abilities. The data therefore may be presented in a qualitative way, though quantitative data may also be included, such as scores from psychological tests.

Case studies are generally *longitudinal*; in other words, they follow the individual or group over an extended period of time.

Individuals – case studies you may know

Henry Molaison (HM), whose hippocampus was removed to reduce epileptic seizures, resulting in an inability to form new memories (see Hilts, 1995); and another case study concerning memory: Clive Wearing, whose memory was damaged by an infection (see his wife's account: Wearing, 2005).

Freud's study of Little Hans to illustrate the principles of psychoanalysis (Freud, 1909). Not to be confused with Watson's study of Little Albert, which is not a case study because it was not a detailed record of the individual – just a record of several classical conditioning trials (Watson and Rayner, 1920).

You can also read about David Reimer, the boy raised as a girl (see page 95).

The case of a teenage addict

Mark Griffiths (1993) sought to gain a greater understanding of fruit machine addiction through the in-depth study of one individual. Data was collected through interviews with 'David', aged 18, and his mother. Initially David's parents put his problems down to adolescence. Once when his mother followed him discreetly, she saw that he went into an amusement arcade. It seemed he was just occupied with 'harmless fun'. Then his mother and sister began to find money missing. The more rows David had with his parents, the more he shut himself away.

Why did he continue? 'I always got the feeling of being "high" or "stoned" . . . Although winning money was the first thing that attracted me to playing fruit machines, this gradually converted to light, sounds and excitement.' Such information offers different insights into behaviour than just looking at quantitative data about addiction.

▼ Phineas Gage, the skull of the man who survived an iron rod passing through his brain.

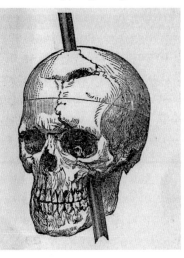

The case of Phineas Gage

In 1848 Phineas was working on the construction of the American railway. An explosion of dynamite drove a tamping iron right through his skull (see artist's impression on left). He survived and was able to function fairly normally, showing that people can live despite the loss of large amounts of brain matter. However, the accident may have affected Phineas' personality. A record was kept of events in the rest of his life and people he knew were interviewed. After the accident his friends said he was no longer the same man, though more recent analyses have concluded that such changes were temporary.

This case was important in the development of brain surgery to remove tumours because it showed that parts of the brain could be removed without having a fatal effect.

EVALUATION

Strengths

The method offers rich, in-depth data information. Such data can provide insights into the complex interaction of many factors, in contrast with experiments where variables are held constant. This means that insights overlooked using other methods are likely to be identified.

Case studies can be used to investigate instances of human behaviour and experience that are rare, for example investigating cases of children locked in a room during their childhood (see case study of Genie, e.g. Rymer, 1993). Such cases enable researchers to see what effects such disruption of attachment have on emotional development. It would not be ethical to generate such conditions experimentally.

Limitations

It is difficult to generalise from individual cases. Each one has unique characteristics. For example, the case study of HM told us a great deal about the effects of his operation on his memory, but we don't know to what extent his epilepsy rather than the brain damage may have affected aspects of his behaviour.

There are important ethical issues such as confidentiality and informed consent. Many cases are easily identifiable because of their unique characteristics, even when real names are not given. Many individuals, such as HM or Little Hans (see right), are not able or not asked to give informed consent. Psychological harm may also be an issue when an individual such as HM is tested repeatedly over decades.

Events

Psychologists have studied the psychological effects of many important events, such as the attack on the World Trade Towers in September 2011, the causes of the London riots in August 2011, or the mass suicide of a cult group.

Mob behaviour, London riots 2011

Psychologists have always been interested in mob behaviour, so this case of the London riots provided an opportunity to re-examine some of the explanations for the apparently unruly behaviour of 'mobs'.

One such study was produced by Steve Reicher and Clifford Stott (2011), where they argued that their data showed that mob behaviour was not unruly. Mobs 'don't simply go wild but actually tend to target particular shops and particular types of people. The patterns of what they attack and don't attack reveals something about the way they see the world and their grievances about the world' (Furlong, 2011).

Mass suicide of a cult group

The study of obedience includes the behaviour of cult groups, such as the People's Temple Full Gospel Church led by the charismatic Reverend Jim Jones. He convinced members of his congregation to give him all of their money and property. He eventually came to see himself as a god, and demanded that everyone else see him as one too. If people refused, they were publicly humiliated and even beaten.

The US government began to have serious questions about the conduct of the church, so Jones moved it to South America in the 1970s, where he created Jonestown. However, he became more paranoid and eventually ordered his 900 followers, including children, to commit suicide by drinking a combination of poison mixed with Kool-Aid.

The case study was used to reflect on social processes in groups and the effect of leaders – both conformity and obedience.

🐾 APPLY YOUR KNOWLEDGE

1. The case study of HM was used to provide insights into memory.
   a) Suggest **two** strengths of using case studies rather than experiments to collect data about memory. (2 marks + 2 marks)
   b) Suggest **two** limitations of using case studies rather than experiments to collect data about memory. (2 marks + 2 marks)
2. A hospital is interested to find out why some patients with head injuries recover faster than others. Why would you recommend using a case study? (3 marks)
3. Consider the case study of the London riots below left.
   a) Who do you think would be the participants in this case study? (2 marks)
   b) Consider **one** possible research method that might be used in this case study. What information would probably be collected? (3 marks)
   c) How could this data be analysed? (3 marks)
   d) Identify **one** possible ethical issue in this case study and suggest how it might be dealt with. (3 marks)
4. Two famous studies discussed in the Year 1 course were those of Little Hans and Little Albert. Little Hans was a case study of phobia and gender development; Little Albert's study was used to demonstrate the conditioning of emotional responses to a white furry rat. Explain why Little Hans is a case study while Little Albert probably isn't (there are no hard and fast rules!). (4 marks)

▲ Police and rioters in London, March 2011.

CAN YOU?   No. 1.2

1. Explain what is involved in a case study. Use examples in your answer. (3 marks)
2. Outline **one** strength and **one** limitation of using case studies to investigate behaviour. (2 marks + 2 marks)

Reliability

There are two very important concepts that run across research – **reliability** and validity. This spread is concerned with reliability, which is basically about *consistency*.

Reliability refers to how much we can depend on any particular measurement, for example the measurement of a desk, the measurement of a psychological characteristic such as IQ, or the findings of a research study. In particular we want to know whether, if we repeat the same measurement/test/study, we can be sure that we would get the same result, i.e. the measurement is consistent. If not, our measurement is unreliable.

▲ Means you expect the same thing every time.

RELIABILITY OF OBSERVATIONAL TECHNIQUES

Observations are a form of measurement. A researcher is recording (i.e. measuring) what people (or animals) are doing. The researcher will keep a record of events observed using a set of behavioural categories such as the example on the right.

Assessing reliability

It is important that this record is a reliable measurement of behaviour, and the way this is assessed is for the observer to repeat the observations a second time (e.g. by watching a video recording). If the observations are reliable then the second set of observations should be more or less the same as the first set.

Except there's a problem. What if our observer was biased? The observer might have believed that young girls were not very aggressive and therefore the observer tended to ignore aggressive behaviour in the girls.

Therefore a better way to assess accuracy is to have two or more observers making separate recordings and then compare these records.

The extent to which the observers agree on the observations they record is called **inter-observer reliability**.

This can be calculated as a correlation coefficient for pairs of scores (see 'Assessing reliability' below). A result of .80 or more suggests good inter-observer reliability.

Improving reliability: Behavioural categories

If the score for inter-rater reliability is low, there are ways to improve this.

- It may be that the behavioural categories were not operationalised clearly enough, so one observer interpreted an action as 'hitting' whereas another interpreted it as 'touching'. So behavioural categories need to be clearer.
- It may be that some observers just need more practice using the behavioural categories so they can respond more quickly.

▼ Observations made of a young girl in a video.

One observer watched a video of a young girl playing with friends in her garden. The observations were an example of event sampling.

Hits	III
Touches	⧻ II
Cuddles	III
Sits next to	II
Talks	⧻ IIII

KEY TERMS

Inter-observer reliability The extent to which there is agreement between two or more observers involved in observations of a behaviour.

Reliability is consistency – the consistency of measurements. We would expect any measurement to produce the same data if taken on successive occasions.

Test–retest reliability The *same* test or interview is given to the *same* participants on two occasions to see if the *same* results are obtained.

Insider tip…
You will find it easier if you simply think of reliability in terms of measurement, as we have done on this spread.
When considering the consistency of a study, getting the same results tends to be more about validity than reliability.

Assessing reliability

The agreement between observers is worked out by calculating a correlation coefficient. Later in this chapter we will look at how these are calculated using statistical tests (see pages 30 and 31).

The table below shows data from two observers. The data is plotted in the scattergram.

The correlation coefficient for this data (calculated with a statistical test) = +.470

This is low inter-observer reliability.

	Observer A	Observer B
Hits	3	7
Touches	7	6
Cuddles	3	2
Sits next to	3	5
Talks	2	3
Running about	2	2
Crying	1	1
Laughing	5	2
Smiling	3	4

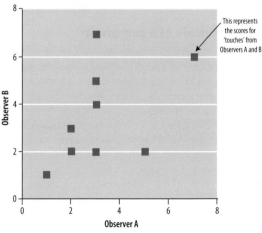

Scattergram showing correlation between observations from two observers

This represents the scores for 'touches' from Observers A and B

RELIABILITY OF SELF-REPORT TECHNIQUES

Questionnaires and interviews are self-report techniques, i.e. research methods where the individual tells a researcher what they think or feel. Psychological tests such as IQ tests or personality tests are similar to self-report techniques and their reliability is particularly important.

We are measuring an aspect of a person and want to ensure that the measurement is reliable, i.e. we would obtain the same set of answers or the same score on a personality test every time we took the test.

In fact your score might vary. For example, let's say you were taking a psychological test that measures mood. You score 20 on the test this week, showing you are very happy, but score 8 the next week suggesting your mood is lower – but wait, … is your mood lower or is the test just unreliable? We need to be sure that any change is due to the person and not the test.

Assessing reliability: Test-retest reliability

Test–retest reliability is used to assess the reliability of a psychological test or other self-report measure. The test/questionnaire designer gives the test to a group of people and then gives the same people the same test a second time. Usually there is a short interval between the tests, such as a week or two, so that people don't remember their answers. If the measure is reliable the outcome should be the same every time.

The scores for each person are compared using correlation (see facing page).

Assessing reliability: Inter-interviewer reliability

In the case of interviews, a researcher could assess the reliability of one interviewer by comparing answers on one occasion with answers from the same person with the same interviewer a week later. Or, the researcher might want to assess the reliability (consistency) of two interviewers using the same method as with two observers.

Improving reliability: Reduce ambiguity

Low reliability in a psychological test may be because some test items are ambiguous so people give different answers. For example, a question might be: 'What are your thoughts about dieting?' Some people might interpret this as being a question asking for factual information, and provide facts about dieting, whereas others might think the question was about emotions and respond with their own feelings about their efforts at dieting.

In such cases test items (or questions on a questionnaire) need to be re-examined and rewritten.

RELIABILITY OF EXPERIMENTS

The dependent variable in an experiment is often measured using a rating scale or behavioural categories; for example:
- The study by Bandura *et al.* (1963) on aggression using a Bobo doll (see Year 1 book and also page 238 in this book). In this study the dependent variable was the aggressive behaviour of the children. This was assessed by observing their behaviour in a room full of toys and using behavioural categories such as verbal imitation.
- The study by Rutter and Sonuga-Barke (2010) on Romanian orphans (see Year 1 book) used IQ scores as one of their dependent variables.

So, reliability in an experiment may be concerned with whether the method used to measure the dependent variable is consistent, i.e. the observations or the self-report method. (The same is true of how co-variables in correlations are measured.)

Improving reliability: Standardisation

Another aspect of reliability that is an issue in experiments (and any research study) concerns the procedures. The procedures are often repeated for different participants. It is important that the procedures are exactly the same each time (i.e. reliable) because otherwise we can't compare the performance of participants. For this reason procedures are standardised.

If another researcher wishes to repeat the experiment, they also need to use exactly the same procedures.

▲ A reliable friend.

🐾 APPLY YOUR KNOWLEDGE

1. In each of the following studies suggest how reliability could be assessed. (2 marks each)
   a) A psychologist intends to use a repeated measures design to test participants' memories in the morning and afternoon. He uses two tests of memory.
   b) A psychologist uses a questionnaire to find out about teenage girls' attitudes about their dieting.
   c) A psychologist decided to observe the non-verbal behaviours between two people having a conversation. (Non-verbal behaviours are those that don't involve language, such as smiling, touching, etc.)
2. In each of the examples above, suggest how reliability could be improved. (2 marks each)
3. Some psychology students plan to conduct an observational study on the effects of different dress styles to see if men look more at girls dressed casually or smartly.
   a) Identify **two** ways you could operationalise being dressed 'casually'. (2 marks)
   b) Identify **one** way in which you could ensure reliability among the different observers and explain how to do this. (2 marks)
   c) Describe what sampling technique you might use for making the observations. (2 marks)
4. A group of students wishes to study mobile phone use in people aged 14–18. They plan to do this using a questionnaire.
   a) Write **one** open question and **one** closed question that might appear on this questionnaire. (2 marks + 2 marks)
   b) The students plan to assess whether their questionnaire is reliable. Explain how they could do this. (3 marks)

CAN YOU?   No. 1.3

1. Explain what is meant by *reliability*. (1 mark)
2. Explain how you can assess whether a set of data from a questionnaire is reliable. (3 marks)
3. Explain how inter-observer reliability is calculated. (3 marks)
4. Explain how inter-observer reliability can be improved if it is low. (3 marks)

Validity

In our Year 1 book we looked at the concept of **validity**. Validity concerns legitimacy. In other words, it concerns whether the data collected in a study represents 'reality' – do the results really reflect how people behave in their everyday lives or are the results an artefact of the research in some way (for example, due to demand characteristics)?

On this spread we continue to explore the meaning of the concept of validity and look at some of the ways it is assessed.

▼ Field experiments aren't always high in ecological validity.

INTERNAL VERSUS EXTERNAL VALIDITY

Validity can be separated into concerns about what goes on within a study (internal validity) and concerns about what goes on after the study (external validity). Examples of internal validity include:

- Investigator effects – anything that an investigator does that has an effect on a participant's performance other than what was intended. For example, encouraging participants to try harder.
- Demand characteristics – cues that inadvertently communicate the aims of the study to participants, such as the Bobo doll in Bandura's study 'inviting' an aggressive response.
- Confounding variables – a variable in an experiment that varies systematically with the independent variable, and therefore conclusions cannot be drawn about what caused changes in the dependent variable.
- Social desirability bias – in a questionnaire, the tendency for participants to provide answers that do not reflect reality because people prefer to show themselves in a good light and don't always answer questions honestly.
- Poorly operationalised behavioural categories – observers can't record reality because the categories are not clear.

External validity concerns generalising the findings of a study to other people (population validity), historical periods (historical or **temporal validity**) and settings (**ecological validity**). Ecological validity may be the most important of these and the one that students often misunderstand.

ECOLOGICAL VALIDITY

Ecological validity refers to being able to generalise the findings from one study to other situations, most particularly to be able to assume that the finding applies to 'everyday life'.

The term natural in 'natural experiment' leads people to think that such studies must be high in ecological validity.

The fact that a laboratory is an artificial contrived environment leads people to assume that a laboratory experiment is low in ecological validity.

The issue of 'naturalness' is more subtle than that. Consider some of the examples on this page.

Example of a natural experiment

In Year 1 you studied the effects of institutionalisation on Romanian orphans. In such studies the independent variable (IV) is whether the children were adopted before or after the age of six months. This variable was not controlled by the researchers, and is sometimes described as varying 'naturally'. However, this 'naturalness' does not make the study high in ecological validity.

The key feature to consider is the dependent variable (DV), not the IV. In the Romanian orphan study one DV was intellectual development, assessed using IQ tests. Such tests are conducted in a controlled environment and may be quite 'artificial' measures of intellectual development. *This* is what we should consider when assessing the ecological validity of the findings from these studies. We need to consider the method used to assess the DV rather than the 'naturalness' of the IV. The IV is actually irrelevant to the ecological validity of the findings.

Example of a field experiment

Field experiments are conducted in a natural environment, but that is not what matters when considering ecological validity. The DV may be important in terms of the task that was used to measure the DV.

Consider this example. In Year 1 you studied context-dependent forgetting and learned about Godden and Baddeley's (1975) experiment with deep-sea divers. Divers learned a set of words either on land or underwater and then had to recall the word list either on land or underwater.

Here are some questions that will help you think about the ecological validity of this study:

- *What environment was the study conducted in?*

  It was either on land or underwater. When underwater the participants might have felt relaxed and acted as 'normal' because they were divers.

- *How was the DV measured?*

  It was measured by learning word lists. This is a rather contrived way to test memory. It has low **mundane realism**, i.e. low similarity to everyday life.

- *Were the participants aware their behaviour was being studied?*

  Yes, this means they may not behave 'naturally'. They may want 'to look good' (social desirability bias) or they may try to behave in line with the researcher's expectations.

Another field experiment

Godden and Baddeley (1980) did a further study. This time they didn't use word lists; instead participants were trained to do a task that is commonly required of deep-sea divers – they had to learn how to transfer nuts and bolts from one brass plate to another.

We might consider that this study had higher ecological validity than their first study because the task had greater mundane realism. However, the participants were still aware of being studied and this may have affected their behaviour.

So ... what is ecological validity?

It is not easy to decide whether a study has high or low ecological validity. You must think about different aspects of the study, all of which contribute to the question of whether an observed effect can be generalised to other settings, especially 'everyday life'.

It is much less about the environment where people are studied and more about:

- How the DV was measured.
- Whether participants knew their behaviour was being assessed.

ASSESSING AND IMPROVING VALIDITY

Assessing validity

Let's consider an example: A researcher decides to test whether men or women are more stressed at work. In order to do this he decides to measure stress using a questionnaire. We can assess the reliability of his measurements as discussed on the previous spread. The questionnaire may be reliable – but is it valid? Does it actually measure stress?

There are a number of ways to assess the validity of this stress questionnaire. Two methods are described below:

Face validity concerns the issue of whether a self-report measure *looks* like it is measuring what the researcher intended to measure; for example, whether the questions on a stress questionnaire are obviously related to the stress. Face validity only requires intuitive measurement.

Concurrent validity involves comparing the current method of measuring stress with a previously validated one on the same topic. To do this, participants are given both measures at the same time and then their scores are compared. We would expect people to get similar scores on both measurements, thereby confirming concurrent validity of the current questionnaire.

Improving validity

If the questionnaire is judged to have poor face validity then the questions should be revised so they relate more obviously to the topic.

If concurrent validity is low then the researcher should remove questions which may seem irrelevant and try checking the concurrent validity again.

In the case of internal and external validity issues described on the facing page, improvements should come from better research design. For example, double blind can be used to prevent participants guessing research aims (neither the person running the study nor the participant knows the aims of a study).

▲ Reliability and validity.

The psychomeasure of intelligence: It has been suggested that the circumference of a person's head could be used as a measure of intelligence. This is likely to be a fairly *reliable* measure of intelligence because adult head size is consistent from one year to the next.

You may even feel this is a *valid* measure of intelligence. After all, if you have a bigger brain, then you might have more intelligence. However, research doesn't always bear this out. Intelligence is not always related to brain or head size. This means this measure of intelligence is likely to lack *validity*.

🐾 APPLY YOUR KNOWLEDGE

1. You have been asked to write a questionnaire about obedience.
   a) Give an example of an item that might lack face validity, and explain why. (2 marks)
   b) Once you have created your questionnaire, describe how you might assess it in terms of concurrent validity. (3 marks)
2. A research team receive funding to assess the effectiveness of a new drug. They intend to give one group of participants a placebo (a substance that has no physiological effect) and the other group will receive the actual drug. Effectiveness will be assessed by comparing the severity of the patients' symptoms before and after the study to see if there has been any improvement.
   a) Describe how you could collect information about the patients' symptoms. (2 marks)
   b) This study is an experiment. Explain why it is an experiment and explain what kind of experiment you think it is. (3 marks)
   c) Write a non-directional hypothesis for this experiment. (2 marks)
   d) Explain whether this study would be high or low in ecological validity. (2 marks)
   e) Discuss **one** other issue of validity that might arise in this study. (3 marks)
   f) Suggest how the researcher might deal with this issue. (2 marks)
3. In each of the following studies describe **two** features of the study that might affect the validity of the data being collected and how the validity could be improved.
   a) A psychologist conducts interviews with mothers about their attitudes towards day care. (4 marks)
   b) A psychologist conducts a study to see if students do more homework in the winter or spring term. To do this he asks students to keep a diary of how much time they spend on homework each week. (4 marks)

CAN YOU?   No. 1.4

1. Explain what is meant by *face validity* and *concurrent validity*. (2 marks + 2 marks)
2. Explain the term *ecological validity* using an example from a research study. (3 marks)
3. Explain why temporal validity may be a problem in research. (2 marks)
4. Explain how validity can be assessed in a questionnaire. (3 marks)
5. Explain how validity can be improved in a research study. (3 marks)

Features of science

The word 'science' comes from the Latin word for 'knowledge'. Science is essentially a systematic approach to creating knowledge. The fact that it is systematic and controlled means we can rely on it in order to predict and control the world (e.g. build dams, create vaccines, treat schizophrenia).

People quite often make the mistake of thinking that the only scientific method of research is the experiment. Observations, questionnaires, interviews, case studies and so on are all scientific methods – they are systematic methods where researchers are concerned about reliability, validity and control.

▲ Being empirical.

On the left is a picture of a burger from a well-known fast-food outlet. This is what you are led to expect you will get. But what about reality? You may think you know something, but unless you test this empirically you cannot know if it is true. On the right is the empirical evidence of what the burgers are really like. 'Empirical' refers to information gained through direct observation. Science uses empirical methods to separate unfounded beliefs from real truths.

You should always ask: 'Where's the evidence?' Take no one's word for it (*nullius in verba*).

Thanks to Professor Sergio della Sala of Edinburgh University for this tasty and memorable example of empiricism.

The scientific method

Science is a process. It is a process by which we can obtain information that is valid. The method used to gain scientific knowledge is the scientific method.

We looked at a version of the scientific method in our Year 1 book. A more detailed version is described here. The scientific method starts with observations of phenomena in the world. In the *inductive model* this leads scientists to develop hypotheses. Hypotheses are then tested empirically which may lead to new questions and new hypotheses. Eventually such data may be used to construct a theory.

The *deductive model* places theory construction at the beginning, after making observations. In both cases the process is repeated over and over again to refine knowledge.

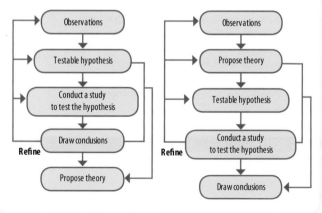

FEATURES OF SCIENCE

Scientific knowledge is based on five key features:

Empirical methods

Information is gained through direct observation or experiment rather than from unfounded beliefs or reasoned argument. There have been times in human history when scientific evidence has come from reasoned argument, but scientists now look for empirically based facts.

This is important because people can make claims about anything (such as the truth of a theory, the benefits of a treatment or the taste of a hamburger), but the only way we know such things to be true is through direct testing, i.e. **empirical** evidence.

Objectivity

An important aspect of empirical data is that it should be objective, i.e. not affected by the expectations of the researcher. Systematic collection of measurable data is at the heart of the scientific method.

In order to be objective the ideal is to carefully control conditions in which research is conducted, i.e. in a laboratory. Such controlled environments are used for observational studies as well as experiments.

Replicability

One way to demonstrate the validity of any observation, questionnaire or experiment is to repeat it. If the outcome is the same, this affirms the truth of the original results.

In order to achieve such replication it is important for scientists to record their procedures carefully so someone else can repeat them exactly and verify the original results.

This may sound like reliability but it is actually about validity. In order to test reliability we would test the same people in exactly the same way, but, for replication, psychologists usually test a different group of people and often use a slightly different task to see if similar behaviour is observed.

Theory construction

Facts alone are meaningless. Explanations or theories must be constructed to make sense of the facts. A theory is a collection of general principles that explain observations and facts. Such theories can then help us understand and predict the natural phenomena around us.

Scientists use both inductive and deductive methods (see left), so sometimes theory comes before hypothesis testing and sometimes it comes after.

Hypothesis testing

Theories are modified through the process of hypothesis testing. This is another essential characteristic of science where the validity of a theory is tested. A good theory must be able to generate testable expectations. These are stated in the form of a hypothesis (or hypotheses). If a scientist fails to find support for a hypothesis, then the theory requires modification, as shown in the diagrams on the left.

Hypothesis testing as we know it only developed in the twentieth century, as described in the box on falsification (facing page). Science as a method for discovering reliable knowledge and the process itself is constantly evolving and improving.

FALSIFIABILITY

Science is a process that is constantly evolving as people realise that it can be done better. Up until the 1930s (which is less than 100 years ago) scientists believed that their task was to find examples that would *confirm* their theories.

Karl Popper, a philosopher of science, brought about a major change in the way scientists thought about proof. He argued that it was not possible to confirm a theory; it was only possible to *disconfirm* it. He gave the following example:

'No matter how many instances of white swans we may have observed, this does not justify the conclusion that all swans are white.' (Popper, 1934)

No number of sightings of white swans can prove the theory that all swans are white, whereas the sighting of just one black one will disprove it.

This proposition led to the realisation that the only way to prove a theory correct was actually to seek *disproof* (falsification) – i.e. look for those black swans. Therefore, we start research with what is called a *null hypothesis*: 'Not all swans in the world are white, i.e. there are black swans.' We then go looking for swans and record many sightings, but if we see no black swans this leads us to be reasonably certain (we can never be absolutely certain) that the null hypothesis is false. We therefore can reject the null hypothesis (with reasonable certainty). If the null hypothesis isn't true this means that the alternative is true. The alternative to the null hypothesis is 'All swans are white' – called the alternative hypothesis. We can now accept the alternative hypothesis, with reasonable certainty!

Falsifiability refers to being able to prove a hypothesis wrong. In any study it is necessary to be able to make a statement (a hypothesis) that can be proved wrong, i.e. a hypothesis that is falsifiable. One of the criticisms of some scientific approaches, such as Freudian psychoanalysis, is that they lack falsifiability.

PARADIGMS

In 1962 Thomas Kuhn published an enormously influential book called *The Structure of Scientific Revolutions*. He proposed that scientific knowledge about the world develops through revolutions, rather than the process suggested by Popper's theory of falsification, whereby theories are fine tuned by a successive series of experiments.

Kuhn proposed that there are two main phases in science. One is called 'normal science', where one theory remains dominant despite occasional challenges from disconfirming studies. Gradually the disconfirming evidence accumulates until the theory can no longer be maintained and then it is overthrown. This is the second phase – a revolutionary shift. Kuhn didn't use the term 'theory', he spoke of a **paradigm**. He said that a science (like physics or biology) has a unified set of assumptions and methods.

Paradigm shift

A classic example of a paradigm shift was the revolution in our understanding of the universe due to the work of the Polish astronomer Copernicus in the sixteenth century. He overthrew the belief held for almost 2,000 years that the earth was the centre of the universe. Such changes are not as logical as Popper's view of science might suggest. According to Kuhn, scientific progress is more like a religious conversion and is related to social factors (e.g. what other people are saying).

Kuhn's view itself is potentially an example of a paradigm shift in the sciences – a change of view from seeing science as logical to science as a social construction (i.e. built through dialogues with other people) – though this view is still hotly debated (Jones and Elcock, 2001).

A crew member from an oil rig took a nap during the middle of his shift and didn't reappear. His work mates went searching for him and came upon a python who had clearly eaten a very large meal. When they cut the python open, they found their friend.

What goes through your mind when you read this?

A good scientist is a skeptic. He or she always asks, where is the evidence?

How good is the evidence? Is there other evidence?

The photograph is fake, as is the case with many pseudoscientific beliefs (such as ghost photos) – yet people frequently take such things as good evidence. Scientists always ask questions and want direct proof.

KEY TERMS

Empirical   A method of gaining knowledge which relies on direct observation or testing, not hearsay or rational argument.

Falsifiability   The possibility that a statement or hypothesis can be proved wrong.

Paradigm   'A shared set of assumptions about the subject matter of a discipline and the methods appropriate to its study' (Kuhn, 1962).

🐾 APPLY YOUR KNOWLEDGE

1. Dr Thomas notices that many of his seriously ill patients have experienced several distressing events in the months before they became ill and wonders if the distressing events may contribute to the illness. Dr Thomas asks a colleague to rate the severity of each patients' illness and the severity of each event. He can therefore see if there is a correlation between the severity of the events and the illness.
    Explain why these research findings could be accepted as scientific evidence. Refer to some of the features of science in your answer. (6 marks)

2. Harriet's mother is always telling her that blondes have more fun. Harriet is studying psychology and explains to her mother that something isn't true just because you believe it to be so.
    Outline how Harriet could use her knowledge of the features of science to explain what is wrong with her mother's argument. (6 marks)

3. Five key features of science are listed on the facing page. For each one try to think of your own examples from research you have studied.

CAN YOU?   No. 1.5

1. Explain what is meant by *replicability* and *falsifiability*. (2 marks + 2 marks)
2. Explain how theory construction is a feature of science. (3 marks)
3. Explain how paradigm shifts contribute to scientific understanding. (3 marks)
4. Explain what is meant by the *empirical method*. Refer to an example of psychological research in your answer. (3 marks)

Probability

You may have heard the phrase 'statistical tests' – for example you might read a newspaper report that claims 'statistical tests show that women are better at reading maps than men'. If we wanted to know if women are better at reading maps than men we wouldn't be able to test this by measuring the map reading abilities of all the women and men in the world, so we just measure a small group of women and a small group of men. If we find that the sample of women are indeed better with maps than the sample of men, then we *infer* that the same is true for all women and men. However, it isn't quite as simple as that because we can only make such inferences using statistical (or inferential) tests. Such statistical tests are based on probabilities, so we will start the topic of statistical tests by looking at **probability**.

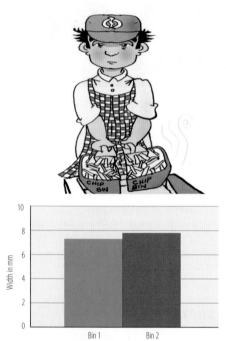

▲ Graph showing the mean width for both bins.

PROBABILITY

On the previous spread we looked at the concept of falsifiability. If we want to know whether men or women are better map readers, what we actually do is test whether men and women are the *same* in terms of their map reading abilities and seek to falsify the **null hypothesis**. For map reading the null hypothesis would be:

'There is no difference between men and women in terms of map reading ability.'

We then collect some data from a sample of men and women, let's say 20 of each. The question we seek to answer is 'What is the probability that the data collected came from a population where men and women have the same map reading abilities?' (i.e. the null hypothesis is correct).

Consider this example

The psychologist and statistician Hugh Coolican (2004) tells this story:

At my local chip store I am convinced that they save money by giving some people rather thin chips (because they then can get more chips from each potato).

There are two chip bins under the counter – the owner of the chip store claims the two bins contain the same kind of chips but I suspect they are different. So I (sadly) tried an experiment. I asked for one bag of chips from each of the chip bins, and I measured the width of the chips in each bag.

- Belief 1 is 'The two bins contain chips of an equal average width'.
- Belief 2 is 'One bin has thinner chips on average than the other'.

In fact I found a very small difference between the average width of the chips in each bag (as you can see in the bar chart on the left).

We would expect small differences between samples (bags of chips) just because things do vary a little – this is simply random variation or 'chance'. What we are looking for is a sufficiently large difference between the samples to be sure that the bins (the total population) are actually different. Otherwise we assume the bins are the same, i.e. the samples are drawn from a single population rather than from two different populations.

- The *bins* contain the populations – in the earlier example about gender differences in map reading, the population is the map reading abilities of all the men and women in the world.
- The *bags* of chips are samples – in our other example, the 20 women and 20 men comprise our samples.
- The belief that the two bins contain chips of the same width or the belief that there is no gender difference in map reading is called the null hypothesis (H_0). This is a statement of *no effect* – the samples are not different.
- The alternative belief is that one bin has thinner chips or that women are better than men – this is called the **alternative hypothesis** (H_1). This is a statement that there is an effect – the populations are different.

Ultimately we are interested in making a statement about the population(s) from which the samples are drawn rather than just stating something about samples themselves. Therefore the alternative hypothesis should be stated in terms of people rather than participants.

CAN YOU? No. 1.6

1. Briefly explain what is meant by *probability*. (2 marks)
2. Distinguish between a Type I and a Type II error. (3 marks)
3. Explain the difference between the alternative hypothesis and the null hypothesis. Use examples to help you. (3 marks)
4. Explain what is meant by $p \leq 0.05$. (2 marks)

Null hypothesis

The null hypothesis is a statement of no difference or no correlation. It is a statement that 'nothing is going on'. The null hypothesis isn't as strange as it sounds. Consider this example:

It's late at night and on your way home you happen to see your best friend's boyfriend with another girl, and he's doing more than talking. You think to yourself, '*How likely is it that he would be kissing her if there is nothing going on between them?*'

- Null hypothesis: 'There is nothing going on, there is no relationship between them.'
- Alternative hypothesis: 'There is something going on between them.'

It isn't very likely that he would be kissing her if there was nothing going on; therefore you reject the null hypothesis and accept the alternative hypothesis – and tell your friend you are fairly certain that he is cheating on her.

🐾 APPLY YOUR KNOWLEDGE

1. Write an alternative hypothesis and a null hypothesis for each of the following research aims. (2 marks each)
   a) To see if blondes have more fun than brunettes.
   b) To investigate whether arts students are less clever than science students.
2. Identify which of the following is a null hypothesis:
   a) There is no correlation between time of day and tiredness.
   b) There is a correlation between time of day and tiredness.
3. A psychologist uses a 5% level of significance. What is the likelihood of making a Type I error in this study? Explain your answer. (2 marks)

MORE ON PROBABILITY

In the example above, you might have worked out the *likelihood* that the cheating was real (e.g. you might have felt 'fairly certain'). In research we need to be a bit more precise than that. In order to work out whether a difference is or is not significant, we use statistical tests. Such tests permit us to work out how *probable* it is that a pattern in research data could have arisen by chance or how probable it is that the effect occurred because there is a real difference/correlation in the populations from which the samples were drawn.

What do we mean by 'chance'?

Chance refers to something with no cause. It just happens. We decide on a probability that we will 'risk'. You can't be 100% certain that an observed effect was not due to chance, but you can state how certain you are. In the kissing example you might say to your friend that you are 99% sure her boyfriend is cheating. This means you are fairly confident that you are right but nevertheless have a little bit of doubt.

Probability levels

In general, psychologists use a level of **probability** of 95%. This expresses the degree of uncertainty. It means that there is a 5% chance (probability) of the results occurring if the null hypothesis is true (i.e. there is nothing going on). In other words, a 5% probability that the results would occur even if there was no real difference/correlation between the populations from which the samples were drawn. This probability of 5% is recorded as $p = 0.05$ (where p means probability). In fact the probability is 5% or less which is written as $p \leq 0.05$.

In some studies psychologists want to be more certain – such as when they are conducting a replication of a previous study or considering the effects of a new drug on health. Then, researchers use a more stringent probability of 1% or less, which is written as $p \leq 0.01$. This chosen value of 'p' is called the significance level, which we will discuss on the next spread.

Type I and Type II errors

Psychologists generally use the 5% probability level because this is a good compromise between being too strict or too lenient about accepting the null hypothesis – or, more formally, a good compromise between a **Type I error** and a **Type II error**.

Consider this scenario: You are a juror and have to decide whether the criminal being tried is guilty or innocent. The table below expresses the four possible outcomes:

Test result		Truth (which we will never know)	
		Guilty	Not guilty
Test result	Guilty verdict	True positive	False positive (guilt reported, i.e. positive) **TYPE I ERROR**
	Not guilty verdict	False negative (guilt not detected, i.e. negative) **TYPE II ERROR**	True negative

The same can be applied to a research study:

Test result		Truth (which we will never know)	
		Alternative hypothesis H_1 true	Null hypothesis H_0 true
Test result	Reject null hypothesis	True positive	False positive **TYPE I ERROR**
	Accept null hypothesis	False negative **TYPE II ERROR**	True negative

▶ We all have an intuitive sense of probability. Would you like to buy a £50 raffle ticket to win this car? If the promoter is only selling 10 tickets your answer would probably be 'yes' because your chances of winning would be fairly high, whereas, if he is selling 1,000 tickets, you might think again. Probability is about chance – how probable is it that you would win if 1,000 tickets are sold? You have a 1 in 1,000 chance of winning or 0.10% probability (one divided by a thousand = 0.10%).

Statistical tests

There are two kinds of statistics: descriptive statistics (such as averages and graphs, covered in the Year 1 book) and inferential statistics.

Inferential tests are designed by statisticians who work out the probabilities of certain results so we can decide whether to accept or reject a null hypothesis. They are called 'inferential' because the statisticians make an inference (deduction) about whole populations based on smaller samples.

We may find a difference or correlation between our samples, but is this big enough to infer there is a real difference/correlation in the population from which they were taken (think of the chip shop on the previous spread)? To answer this we use inferential statistical tests and then find out if the result is **significant** using tables of critical values. You did this in Year 1 with the sign test.

▲ As easy as eating pie.

Exam questions on statistical tests are very easy marks; for example: *State an appropriate statistical test to use with this data. Give reasons for your choice. (3 marks)*

SELECTING WHICH STATISTICAL TEST TO USE

There are a large number of statistical tests that are used by psychologists. These are divided into parametric and non-parametric tests. Parametric tests are preferred to non-parametric tests because they are more *powerful* (a concept explained below). However, they can only be used if certain criteria are met (see table at bottom of page).

The tests required in the specification are shown in the decision tree below, along with the criteria to make your choice:

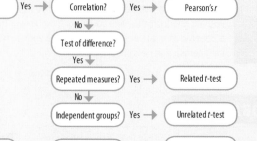

NB matched pairs design counts as a repeated measures (related) design because the two groups of participants are related.

PARAMETRIC CRITERIA

Criterion	Explanation	How to decide
The **level of measurement** is interval or better.	Levels of measurement were covered in the Year 1 book.	Are the data in categories (nominal) or ordered in some way (ordinal) = non-parametric statistics. Are the intervals between the data truly equal interval = parametric statistics.
The data are drawn from a population that has a normal distribution.	Note that it is not the sample that must be normally distributed but the population. A normal distribution (which was described in your Year 1 book) is when most items cluster around the mean with an equal number of items above and below the mean.	We expect many physical and psychological characteristics to be normally distributed, such as height, shoe sizes, IQ and friendliness. Therefore you can justify the use of a parametric test by saying that the characteristic measured is assumed to be normal. You could also check the distribution of scores to see if they are skewed or not.
The variances of the two samples are not significantly different.	The variance is a measure of how spread out a set of data is around the mean. It is the square of the standard deviation.	In the case of repeated measures (related samples) any difference in the variances should not distort the result (Coolican, 1996). For independent groups you can check the variances. The variance of one sample should not be more than four times the variance of the other.

Note: parametric tests are quite robust and therefore they can be used, unless the parametric assumptions are met quite poorly.

▲ What does 'powerful' mean?

Parametric statistical tests make calculations using the mean and standard deviation of a data set, whereas non-parametric tests use ranked data, thus losing some of the detail.

The end result is that parametric tests can detect significance in some situations where non-parametric tests can't.

USING STATISTICAL TESTS

On each spread that follows we explain how to calculate each of the tests listed on the facing page (except the sign test, which was included in the Year 1 book).

Calculated and critical values

Each statistical test involves taking the data collected in a study and doing some arithmetical calculations which produce a single number called the **test statistic**. For example, in the case of Spearman's correlation test, that test statistic is called *rho*, whereas for the Mann-Whitney test it is *U*. The *rho* or *U* value calculated for any set of data is called the **calculated value** (because it is based on the calculations made).

To decide if the calculated value is significant, this figure is compared to another number, found in a statistical table. The value in the statistical table is called a **critical value** because this is the value that a test statistic must reach in order for the null hypothesis to be rejected.

Using statistical tables

There are different statistical tables for each different statistical test. To find the appropriate critical value in a table you need to know:

1. **Significance level** selected, usually $p \leq 0.05$.
2. **Kind of hypothesis** It must be determined whether a **one-tailed** or **two-tailed test** is required – If the hypothesis was a directional hypothesis, then you use a one-tailed test; if it was non-directional, you use a two-tailed test.
3. **Value of N** is the number of participants in the study (N). In studies using an independent groups design, there are two values for N (one for each group of participants), which are called N_A and N_B. In the case of some tests, such as *t*-tests and Chi-Squared, you calculate **degrees of freedom** (*df*).

Tables of critical values: importance of R

Some tests are significant when the calculated value is equal to or greater than the critical value; for others it is the reverse. You need to know which, and you will find it is stated underneath each table.

One way to remember is to see if there is a letter R in the name of the test. If there is an R, then the calculated value should be greater than the critical value (e.g. for Spearman's, Pearson's, Chi-Squared and related and unrelated t-test). If there is no R (e.g. sign test, Mann-Whitney and Wilcoxon), then the calculated value should be less than the critical value.

🐾 APPLY YOUR KNOWLEDGE

1. Identify the level of measurement in the examples below:
   a) Rating how stressful certain experiences are.
   b) Counting the days a person has had off school.
   c) Asking people to indicate their reasons for days off school.
2. With the following designs and data, which statistical test should you use? In each case justify your choice.
   a) Ordinal data on both measures in a study to see if two variables are associated.
   b) Interval data collected from an experiment with a matched pairs design.
   c) An experiment with an independent groups design in which the DV is measured on an interval scale.
   d) A study using a correlational technique in which one measure is ordinal and the other is ratio.
   e) A field experiment producing nominal data with an independent groups design.
   f) A study testing a correlation using a nominal level of measurement.
   g) A study using a correlational technique in which one co-variable is interval and the other is ordinal.

CAN YOU? No. 1.7

1. Briefly outline the criteria used to decide if a parametric statistical test can be used with a set of data. (3 marks)
2. Give an example of nominal data. (2 marks)
3. Explain the difference between ordinal and interval data. (3 marks)
4. Suggest why a researcher may choose to use $p \leq 0.01$ in preference to $p \leq 0.05$. (Try to give **two** reasons.) (2 marks)
5. Explain the relationship between the calculated value and the critical value. (3 marks)
6. Identify the **three** pieces of information used to find the critical value. (3 marks)
7. Answer the following: if a hypothesis is directional, should you use a one-tailed or a two-tailed test? (1 mark)
8. Answer the following: when using the Wilcoxon test, is the calculated value greater than or less than the critical value? (1 mark)

Non-parametric tests of difference

A test of difference is used in an experiment to see if one set of data is significantly different to another set of data.

- In a repeated measures design the two sets of data are *related* (they come from the same person).
- In a matched pairs design the two sets of data are *related* (they come from matched pairs).
- In an independent groups design the two sets of data are *unrelated* (they come from separate groups).

The Wilcoxon test is used for related samples, and the Mann-Whitney test is used for unrelated (or independent) samples.

▼ Calculation table

Column A Most frequent face	Column B Less frequent face	Difference	Rank
5	2	3	9.5
4	3	1	3
3	3	0mit	
6	4	2	6.5
2	3	−1	3
4	5	−1	3
5	2	3	9.5
3	4	−1	3
6	3	3	9.5
4	6	−2	6.5
5	2	3	9.5
3	4	−1	3
N = 12			

▼ Frequency count table for calculating ranks

Score	Frequency	Ranks	Final rank
1	IIIII	1, 2, 3, 4 and 5	3
2	II	6 and 7	6.5
3	IIIII	8, 9, 10 and 11	9.5

▼ Mr and Mrs Wilcoxon are related by marriage. Mr Mann and Ms Whitney are not married – they are unrelated.

WILCOXON TEST FOR RELATED DESIGNS

Investigation

Research has found that people like things that are familiar. In one study Zajonc (1968) told participants that he was conducting a study on visual memory and showed them photographs of 12 different men (face only), each for two seconds only. At the end, participants were asked to rate how much they liked the 12 different men on a scale from 0 to 6. Some photos were shown more often than others; for example, one photo appeared 25 times, whereas another appeared only once.

Step 1. State the hypotheses

Alternative hypothesis: People rate the more frequently seen face as more likeable than the less frequently seen face. (Directional hypothesis)

Null hypothesis: There is no difference in the likeability score for more and less familiar faces.

> **Reasons for choice of test**
> - The hypothesis states a *difference* between two sets of data.
> - The two sets of data are pairs of scores from one person = *related*.
> - The data are *ordinal* because there are not equal intervals between ratings.

Step 2. Place raw data in table

The raw data (collected by a group of students) are the rating scores for each condition. There are two items for each participant (see calculation table on left).

Step 3. Find the differences and rank

Calculate the difference between each score.

If the difference is zero, omit this from the ranking and reduce N accordingly.

Rank the differences from low to high. When ranking, you ignore the signs. The lowest number receives the rank of 1, the next lowest number is rank 2 and so on.

If there are two or more of the same number (tied ranks), calculate the final rank by working out the mean of the ranks that would have been given. In our case, 1 occurs five times and would have had ranks of 1, 2, 3, 4 and 5, so gets a rank of 3.

(You may find it easier to write the numbers down somewhere else and place them in order and then rank them, or use a frequency count table as on the left.)

Step 4. Find calculated value of T

T is the sum of the ranks of the less frequent sign.

The less frequent sign is minus, so we add 3 + 3 + 3 + 6.5 + 3 = 18.5

Step 5. Is the result in the right direction?

The predicted direction was that the more frequent face would be more likeable, so the result is in the right direction.

Step 6. Find critical value of T

- Significance level: 5% (0.05)
- Kind of hypothesis: Directional, therefore one-tailed test.
- N value (total number of scores ignoring zero values). In our case N = 11 (1 score omitted).
- Locate the row in the statistical table on the right that begins with our N value. The critical value of T = 13

Step 7. Report the conclusion

If the calculated value is equal to or less than this critical value, our result is significant. In our case it is not significant.

As the calculated value is not significant (at $p \leq 0.05$), we must accept the null hypothesis and conclude that there is no difference in the likeability score for more and less familiar faces ($p \leq 0.05$).

▼ Table of critical vales for the Wilcoxon test.

Level of significance for a one-tailed test	0.05	0.01
Level of significance for a two-tailed test	0.10	0.02
N = 5	0	
6	2	0
7	3	2
8	5	3
9	8	5
10	11	8
11	13	10
12	17	13
13	21	17
14	25	21
15	30	25
16	35	29
17	41	34
18	47	40
19	53	46
20	60	52
25	100	89
30	151	137

Observed value of T must be EQUAL TO or LESS THAN the critical value in this table for significance to be shown.

Source: R. Meddis (1975). *Statistical handbook for non-statisticians*. London: McGraw Hill.

Note that both statistical tests on this spread involve ranking data – which loses some of the detail, making them less powerful than parametric tests at detecting differences.

MANN-WHITNEY TEST FOR UNRELATED DESIGNS

Investigation

One explanation offered for why people fall in love is that it is physiological arousal that gets mislabelled as love. To test this, White *et al.* (1981) created high and low arousal by asking men to run on the spot for 2 minutes or 15 seconds respectively, and then showed the men a short video of a young woman. Participants were asked to rate the young woman's attractiveness.

Step 1. State the hypotheses

Alternative hypothesis: People who run for 2 minutes (high arousal) rate a woman as more attractive than people who run for 15 seconds (low arousal). (Directional hypothesis)

Null hypothesis: There is no difference in the attractiveness rating scores for the high and low arousal conditions.

Reasons for choice of test
• The hypothesis states a *difference* between two sets of data.
• The two sets of data are from separate groups of participants = *unrelated*.
• The data are *ordinal* because there are not equal intervals between ratings.

Note that this justification must always be tailored as far as possible to the particular features of the study, such as explaining why the data are ordinal.

Step 2. Place raw data in table

The raw data (collected by a group of students) are the rating scores from each group of participants, see calculation table on right.

Step 3. Rank each data set

Rank all data items jointly, following the steps on the facing page for ranking. As there are so many tied ranks it may be best to work out a frequency count as shown on the facing page.

Step 4. Add each set of ranks

Total for Column A is R_A and for Column B is R_B

Step 5. Find calculated value of *U*

U is calculated using whichever total is smaller. In our case the smaller value is the total for Column B: $N_B = 14$

$$U_2 = R_B - [N_B (N_B + 1)]/2$$
$$= 121.5 - (14 \times 15)/2 = 16.5$$

Step 6. Is the result in the right direction?

The predicted direction was that higher arousal would cause higher ratings, so the result is in the right direction.

Step 7. Find critical value of *U*

- Significance level: 5% (0.05)
- Kind of hypothesis: Directional, therefore one-tailed test.
- N_A = Number in Column A = 10
- N_B = Number in Column B = 14
- Locate the point in the statistical table on right where our N_A and N_B value intersect. The critical value of U = 41

Step 8. Report the conclusion

If the calculated value is equal to or less than this critical value, our result is significant. In our case it is significant.

As the calculated value is significant (at $p \leq 0.05$) we can reject the null hypothesis and conclude that people with high arousal rate a woman as more attractive than people with low arousal ($p \leq 0.05$).

🐾 **APPLY YOUR KNOWLEDGE**

For each of the studies below decide which test you would do and explain why. Invent some data and check the significance.

1. A researcher tested whether participants had a better short-term memory in the morning or afternoon.
2. A psychologist investigated happiness by asking one group of participants to rate cartoons with a pencil clenched between their teeth (feels like smiling). Another group of participants had no pencil. The hypothesis is 'Participants rate cartoons as funnier when they are smiling than if they are not smiling.'

▼ Calculation table

Column A (High arousal)	Rank	Column B (Low arousal)	Rank
7	16	4	4.5
10	23.5	6	12.5
8	18.5	2	1
6	12.5	5	8
5	8	3	2.5
8	18.5	5	8
9	21	6	12.5
7	16	4	4.5
10	23.5	5	8
9	21	7	16
		9	21
		3	2.5
		5	8
		6	12.5
$N_A = 10$	$R_A = 178.5$	$N_B = 14$	$R_B = 121.5$

▼ Table of critical values for the Mann-Whitney test for a one-tailed test ($p \leq 0.05$)

N_B \ N_A	2	3	4	5	6	7	8	9	10	11	12	13	14	15
2					0	0	0	1	1	1	1	2	2	3
3		0	0	1	2	2	3	3	4	5	5	6	7	7
4			1	2	3	4	5	6	7	8	9	10	11	12
5	0	1	2	4	5	6	8	9	11	12	13	15	16	18
6	0	2	3	5	7	8	10	12	14	16	17	19	21	23
7	0	2	4	6	8	11	13	15	17	19	21	24	26	28
8	1	3	5	8	10	13	15	18	20	23	26	28	31	33
9	1	3	6	9	12	15	18	21	24	27	30	33	36	39
10	1	4	7	11	14	17	20	24	27	31	34	37	41	44
11	1	5	8	12	16	19	23	27	31	34	38	42	46	50
12	2	5	9	13	17	21	26	30	34	38	42	47	51	55
13	2	6	10	15	19	24	28	33	37	42	47	51	56	61
14	2	7	11	16	21	26	31	36	41	46	51	56	61	66
15	3	7	12	18	23	28	33	39	44	50	55	61	66	72

▼ Table of critical values for the Mann-Whitney test for a two-tailed test ($p \leq 0.05$)

N_B \ N_A	2	3	4	5	6	7	8	9	10	11	12	13	14	15
2							0	0	0	0	1	1	1	1
3			0	1	1	2	2	3	3	4	4	5	5	5
4		0	1	2	3	4	4	5	6	7	8	9	10	
5	0	1	2	3	5	6	7	8	9	11	12	13	14	
6	1	2	3	5	6	8	10	11	13	14	16	17	19	
7	1	3	5	6	8	10	12	14	16	18	20	22	24	
8	0	2	4	6	8	10	13	15	17	19	22	24	26	29
9	0	2	4	7	10	12	15	17	20	23	26	28	31	34
10	0	3	5	8	11	14	17	20	23	26	29	33	36	39
11	0	3	6	9	13	16	19	23	26	30	33	37	40	44
12	1	4	7	11	14	18	22	26	29	33	37	41	45	49
13	1	4	8	12	16	20	24	28	33	37	41	45	50	54
14	1	5	9	13	17	22	26	31	36	40	45	50	55	59
15	1	5	10	14	19	24	29	34	39	44	49	54	59	64

For any N_A and N_B observed value of U must be EQUAL TO or LESS THAN the critical value in this table for significance to be shown.

Source: R. Runyon and A. Haber (1976). *Fundamentals of behavioural statistics* (third edition). Reading, Mass: McGraw-Hill.

Parametric tests of difference

Where possible, researchers prefer to use parametric statistical tests because they are more powerful. The tests on this page would be used instead of the Wilcoxon test or the Mann-Whitney test when looking at differences between two samples of data – however, the two samples must meet the criteria for using a parametric test described on page 24.

▼ Calculation table

Column A Deep processing	Column B Shallow processing	Difference (d)	d²
21	18	3	9
18	19	−1	1
25	22	3	9
12	16	−4	16
16	13	3	9
8	9	−1	1
18	16	2	4
24	20	4	16
21	14	7	49
16	17	−1	1
Mean = 17.9	Mean = 16.4	Σ d = 15	Σ d² = 115

▼ Table of critical values for the *t*-test.

Level of significance for a one-tailed test	0.05	0.01
Level of significance for a two-tailed test	0.10	0.02
$df = (N - 2)$		
1	6.314	12.706
2	2.920	4.303
3	2.353	3.182
4	2.132	2.776
5	2.015	2.571
6	1.943	2.447
7	1.895	2.365
8	1.860	2.306
9	1.833	2.262
10	1.812	2.228
11	1.796	2.201
12	1.782	2.179
13	1.771	2.160
14	1.761	2.145
15	1.753	2.131
16	1.746	2.120
17	1.740	2.110
18	1.734	2.101
19	1.729	2.093
20	1.725	2.086
25	1.708	2.060
30	1.697	2.042

Observed value of *t* must be EQUAL TO or GREATER THAN the critical value in this table for significance to be shown.

Source: abridged from R.A. Fisher and F. Yates (1982). *Statistical Tables for Biological, Agricultural and Medical Research*. (6th edition). London: Longman. Reproduced with permission by Pearson Education Limited.

Investigation

Craik and Tulving (1975) demonstrated that memory for words is better if participants are required to process the words semantically (e.g. FLAME: Does the word mean something hot? Yes/No) rather than just in terms of its physical structure (e.g. FLAME: Is the word in capital letters? Yes/No). Semantic processing is considered 'deep' processing, whereas processing in terms of physical structure is called 'shallow' processing.

Step 1. State the hypotheses
Alternative hypothesis: People remember more words that are semantically processed (deep condition) than words that are processed in terms of physical structure (shallow condition). (Directional hypothesis.)
Null hypothesis: There is no difference in the number of words remembered in the deeply processed or shallowly processed conditions.

> **Reasons for choice of test**
> - The hypothesis states a *difference* between two sets of data.
> - The two sets of data are pairs of scores from one person = *related*.
> - The data are *interval* because there are equal intervals when counting frequency.
> - The data fit the criteria for a parametric test: the data are interval, the population is assumed to have a normal distribution and the variances of the samples are the same because they come from the same participants.

Step 2. Place raw data in table
The raw data (collected by a group of students) are the number of words recalled for each condition. There are two items for each participant (see calculation table above left).

Step 3. Find calculated value of *t*
The number of participants (N) was 10

$$t = \frac{\Sigma d}{\sqrt{(N\Sigma d^2 - (\Sigma d)^2)/N - 1)}}$$

$$= \frac{15}{\sqrt{(10 \times 115 - (15 \times 15)/9)}}$$

It is possible that you will be asked to substitute data values in this formula in an exam and use your calculator to work out the value of t. You don't have to memorise the formula. Any formula would be provided in the exam.

Step 4. Is the result in the right direction?
The predicted direction was that deep processing would produce a higher score, so the result is in the right direction (you can see this by looking at the means for each group in the calculation table above left).

Step 5. Find critical value of *t*
- Significance level: $p \leq 5\%$ (0.05)
- Kind of hypothesis: Directional, therefore one-tailed test.
- *df* value = N − 1 = 9
- Locate the row in the statistical table on left that begins with our *df* value. The critical value of *t* = 1.833

Step 6. Report the conclusion
If the calculated value is equal to or greater than this critical value, our result is significant. In our case it is not significant.

As the calculated value is not significant (at $p \leq 0.05$), we must accept the null hypothesis and conclude that there is no difference in the number of words remembered in the deeply processed or shallowly processed conditions ($p \leq 0.05$).

UNRELATED *T*-TEST

Investigation

Piliavin *et al.* (1969) investigated helping behaviour, and looked specifically at whether people were quicker at offering help in an emergency situation to a man with a cane or a man who appeared drunk. The emergency situation was when a person appeared to collapse on an underground train. Participants were randomly assigned to condition A (man with cane collapses) or condition B (man who appears drunk collapses).

Step 1. State the hypotheses

Alternative hypothesis: The speed of offering help in an emergency situation is faster when the victim is carrying a cane than when appearing drunk. (Directional hypothesis.)

Null hypothesis: There is no difference in the speed of offering help to victims with a cane or appearing drunk.

> **Reasons for choice of test**
> - The hypothesis states a *difference* between two sets of data.
> - The two sets of data are pairs of scores from separate groups of participants = *unrelated*.
> - The data are *interval* because there are equal intervals when counting frequency.
> - The data fit the criteria for a parametric test: the data are interval, the populations are assumed to have a normal distribution and the variances of the samples are assumed to be the same, as the participants were randomly assigned to conditions.

Step 2. Place raw data in table

The raw data are the number of seconds it took for help to be offered (see calculation table below right).

Step 3. Find calculated value of *t*

The formula for the unrelated *t* test is very complex and would not be used in an exam. There are many online calculators that will calculate this for you, for example www.socscistatistics.com/tests/studenttest/

The result of this calculation is $t = 1.882$

Step 4. Is the result in the right direction?

No, the results are not in the predicted direction.

Step 5. Find critical value of *t*

- Significance level: 5% (0.05)
- Kind of hypothesis: Directional, therefore one-tailed test.
- *df* value = $(N_A + N_B) - 2 = 20$
- Locate the row in the statistical table on the facing page that begins with our *df* value. The critical value of $t = 1.725$

Step 6. Report the conclusion

If the calculated value is equal to or greater than this critical value, our result is significant. In our case it is significant.

As the calculated value is significant (at $p \leq 0.05$), we should be able to reject the null hypothesis... but, as the result was actually in the wrong direction, we can't accept the alternative hypothesis. We therefore can't draw any conclusion. And no, we can't change the hypothesis at this point.

In fact, once we spotted that the data is in the wrong direction, there was no point calculating the statistic.

◀ Just to put the record straight, Piliavin *et al.* actually found that men with a cane were offered help more quickly.

🐾 APPLY YOUR KNOWLEDGE

1. A group of psychology students repeated the investigation about the matching hypothesis on the facing page using 19 participants. They placed their data in a calculation table and calculated the following values:
   The sum of the differences: $\Sigma d = 24$
   The sum of the squared differences: $\Sigma d^2 = 236$
   Substitute these values in the formula on the facing page and work out whether their result is significant.

2. State what test would be suitable for the following studies and justify your choice.
   a) Comparing a person's reaction time before and after drinking coffee.
   b) Giving participants word lists to see how many words can be remembered. One group is given the words in categories and another group gets them in a random order.
   c) One group of participants are given a test before lunch and another group are given the same test after lunch to see if time of day affects performance. Participants are matched on intelligence.

3. Write an alternative and a null hypothesis for each of the studies in question 2.

4. A researcher conducts study (b) above with 17 participants in Group A and 10 in Group B.
   a) Calculate degrees of freedom for this number of participants.
   b) The critical value calculated is 1.65. Is this significant for a two-tailed test at $p \leq 0.02$?

▼ Calculation table

Column A Time for man with cane to be helped	Column B Time for man appearing drunk to be helped
56	74
34	96
49	83
74	80
61	40
30	22
52	97
83	121
110	92
43	73
	93
	85
$N_A = 10$	$N_B = 12$
Mean = 59.2	Mean = 86.75

Tests of correlation

Tests of correlation are used to determine whether the *association* (rather than a difference) between two co-variables is significant or not.

A correlation can be positive or negative, as shown in the scattergrams on the facing page. The closer the dots are to forming a diagonal line, the stronger the correlation. This 'strength' can be assessed by calculating a **correlation coefficient**. A perfect positive correlation will have a correlation coefficient of +1.0, and a perfect negative correlation will have a correlation coefficient of −1.0.

It is important to realise that +.65 and −.65 are equally strong correlations – the sign simply indicates a positive or negative correlation, i.e. the direction of the relationship.

KEY TERMS

Correlation coefficient A number between −1 and +1 that tells us how closely the co-variables in a correlational analysis are related.

▼ Calculation table

Column A Finger length ratio	Rank A	Column B Numeracy score	Rank B	Difference between Rank A and Rank B (d)	d²
1.026	10	8	2.5	7.5	56.25
1.000	5.5	16	9	−3.5	12.25
1.021	9	10	5	4.0	16.0
0.991	4	9	4	0	0
0.984	3	15	8	−5.0	25.0
0.975	1	14	7	−6.0	36.0
1.013	7	12	6	1.0	1.0
1.018	8	8	2.5	5.5	30.25
0.982	2	17	10	−8.0	64.0
1.000	5.5	5	1	4.5	20.25
					$\Sigma d^2 = 261.0$

▼ Table of critical values for Spearman's *rho*.

Level of significance for a one-tailed test	0.05	0.01
Level of significance for a two-tailed test	**0.10**	**0.02**
$N = 4$	1.000	
5	.900	1.000
6	.829	.886
7	.714	.786
8	.643	.738
9	.600	.700
10	.564	.648
11	.536	.618
12	.503	.587
13	.484	.560
14	.464	.538
15	.443	.521
16	.429	.503
17	.414	.485
18	.401	.472
19	.391	.460
20	.380	.447
25	.337	.398
30	.306	.362

Observed value of *rho* must be EQUAL TO or GREATER THAN the critical value in this table for significance to be shown.

Source: J.H. Zhar (1972). Significance testing of the Spearman rank correlation coefficient. *Journal of the American Statistical Association, 67*, 578–80. (Reproduced with kind permission of the publisher.)

Investigation

A study by Brosnan (2008) found that boys with a smaller finger length ratio between their index and ring fingers were more likely to have a talent in maths. The explanation is related to the effects of testosterone which is associated with reduced finger length ratio and increased numeracy skills.

Step 1. State the hypotheses

Alternative hypothesis: The finger length ratio between index finger and ring finger is negatively correlated to numeracy skills in boys. (Directional hypothesis)
Null hypothesis: There is no correlation between finger length ratio and numeracy in boys.

> **Reasons for choice of test**
> * The hypothesis states a *correlation* between two sets of data.
> * The two sets of data are pairs of scores from one person = *related*.
> * The data are *ordinal* because numeracy skills are measured using a test and may not have equal intervals between scores.

Step 2. Place raw data in table

The raw data (collected by a group of students) are the finger length ratio and numeracy score for each person (see calculation table on left).

Step 3. Find calculated value of *rho*

The formula is shown below. In order to use this formula you need to:
* Rank data in Column A from low to high and do the same for data in Column B.
* Find the difference between each pair of ranks.
* Square this difference and add the column up (Σd^2).

$$rho = 1 - \frac{6\Sigma d^2}{N(N^2 - 1)} = 1 - \frac{6 \times 261.0}{10 \times (100 - 1)}$$

$$= 1 - \frac{1566}{990} = 1 - 1.58 = -0.58$$

Step 4. Is the result in the right direction?

The predicted direction was a negative correlation, so the result is in the right direction.

Step 5. Find critical value of *rho*

* Significance level: 5% (0.05)
* Kind of hypothesis: Directional, therefore one-tailed test.
* *N* value = 10
* Locate the row in the statistical table on right that begins with our *N* value. The critical value of *rho* = .564

Step 6. Report the conclusion

If the calculated value is equal to or greater than this critical value, our result is significant. In our case it is significant.

As the calculated value is significant (at $p \leq 0.05$), we can reject the null hypothesis and conclude that finger length ratio between index finger and ring finger is negatively correlated to numeracy skills in boys ($p \leq 0.05$).

A PARAMETRIC TEST: PEARSON'S *R*

Investigation

On page 16 we looked at inter-rater reliability, and how correlational tests are used to determine the degree to which observations from two observers are related.

Step 1. State the hypotheses

Alternative hypothesis: The observations from observer A are positively correlated to the observations from observer B. (Directional hypothesis.)

Null hypothesis: There is no correlation between observations made by observer A and observer B.

Reasons for choice of test
- The hypothesis states a *correlation* between two sets of data.
- The two sets of data are pairs of scores that are *related*.
- The data are *interval* because they are counting the number of observations.
- The data fit the criteria for a parametric test: the data are interval, the populations are assumed to have a normal distribution and the variances of the samples are assumed to be the same, as the participants are related.

Step 2. Place raw data in table

The observations from two observers (A and B) are placed in a raw data table (see right).

Step 3. Find calculated value of *r*

The formula for Pearson's *r* is very complex and would not be used in an exam. There are many online calculators that will calculate this for you, for example www.socscistatistics.com/tests/pearson

The result of this calculation is $r = .470$

Step 4. Is the result in the right direction?

The predicted direction was a positive correlation, so the result is in the right direction.

Step 5. Find critical value of *rho*

- Significance level: 5% (0.05)
- Kind of hypothesis: Directional, therefore one-tailed test.
- *df* value = N − 2 = 7
- Locate the row in the statistical table on right that begins with our *df* value. The critical value of $r = .582$

Step 6. Report the conclusion

If the calculated value is equal to or greater than this critical value, our result is significant. In our case it is not significant.

As the calculated value is not significant (at $p \leq 0.05$), we must accept the null hypothesis and conclude that there is no correlation between observations made by observer A and observer B ($p \leq 0.05$).

▼ Raw data from page 16

	Observer A	Observer B
Hits	3	7
Touches	7	6
Cuddles	3	2
Sits next to	3	5
Talks	2	3
Running about	2	2
Crying	1	1
Laughing	5	2
Smiling	3	4

▼ Table of critical values for Pearson's *r*.

Level of significance for a one-tailed test	0.05	0.01
Level of significance for a two-tailed test	0.10	0.02
df = (N − 2)	0.10	0.02
2	.9000	.9500
3	.805	.878
4	.729	.811
5	.669	.754
6	.621	.707
7	.582	.666
8	.549	.632
9	.521	.602
10	.497	.576
11	.476	.553
12	.475	.532
13	.441	.514
14	.426	.497
15	.412	.482
16	.400	.468
17	.389	.456
18	.378	.444
19	.369	.433
20	.360	.423
25	.323	.381
30	.296	.349

Observed value of *r* must be EQUAL TO or GREATER THAN the critical value in this table for significance to be shown.

Source: F.C. Powell (1976). *Cambridge Mathematical and Statistical Tables*. Cambridge: Cambridge University Press.

The two scattergrams below show a strong positive correlation (+.95) and a moderate negative correlation (−.41). There are online sites that allow you to play around with scattergrams, so you can see how correlation coefficients increase and decrease by changing data items. You can also use Excel to do this. Highly recommended.

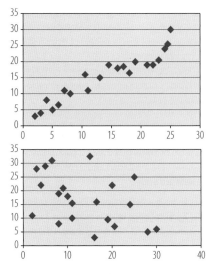

🐾 **APPLY YOUR KNOWLEDGE**

1. A researcher conducts a study to see if age at time of taking GCSEs and mean GCSE grade are associated (mean GCSE grade is calculated by assigning a number to each grade).
   a) Identify a suitable test to use to analyse this data and justify your choice.
   b) The researcher calculates the correlation coefficient for 15 participants, using a non-directional hypothesis. What calculated value would be significant at the 2% level?

2. A researcher conducts a study looking at the correlation between twins in terms of height.

   a) Identify a suitable test to use to analyse this data and justify your choice.
   b) The researcher calculates the correlation coefficient for 25 participants, using a directional hypothesis. What calculated value would be significant at the 1% level?

Chi-Squared test (χ^2)

Chi-Squared is a strange test because it can be a test of difference or a test of association – see the hypotheses for this study; you can either state a difference or an association.

It is also one of the few tests that deals with nominal (categorical) data. For each category you count up the number of people or items in that category (a frequency count).

These data must be independent – in other words, no person or item can appear in more than one of the cells.

▼ Contingency table

The table below is called a 2×2 contingency table because there are 2 rows and 2 columns in which the data are put.

You can have any number of rows and columns. A 3×2 contingency table would have 3 rows and 2 columns (the first number is always the number of rows).

	Female	Male	Totals
Ethic of justice	5 (cell A)	12 (cell B)	17
Ethic of care	10 (cell C)	9 (cell D)	19
Totals	15	21	36

▼ Table of critical values for the Chi-Squared (χ^2) test

Level of significance for a one-tailed test	0.10	0.05	0.025	0.01
Level of significance for a two-tailed test	0.20	0.10	0.05	0.02
df				
1	1.64	2.71	3.84	5.41
2	3.22	4.60	5.99	7.82
3	4.64	6.25	7.82	9.84
4	5.99	7.78	9.49	11.67

Observed value of χ^2 must be EQUAL TO or GREATER THAN the critical value in this table for significance to be shown.

Source: abridged from R.A. Fisher and F. Yates (1974). *Statistical tables for biological, agricultural and medical research* (sixth edition). Longman.

Investigation

Gilligan and Attanucci (1988) found that women were more likely to make moral decisions based on an ethic of care than an ethic of justice, whereas men made moral decisions based the other way round.

Step 1. State the hypotheses

Alternative hypothesis: There is an association between gender and the kind of moral decisions made (based on care or justice). (Non-directional hypothesis)

OR

There is a difference between men and women in terms of the basis for making moral decisions. (Non-directional hypothesis)

Null hypothesis: There is no association/difference between men and women in terms of the basis for making moral decisions.

> **Reasons for choice of test**
> - The hypothesis states a *difference/association* between two sets of data.
> - The data in each cell are *independent*.
> - The data are *nominal* because each person belongs to one of the four categories.

Step 2. Place raw data in contingency table

The raw data (collected by a group of students) have been placed in a 2×2 contingency table (see left). The number of people in each cell is recorded and then totals for each row and column are calculated.

Step 3. Find observed value of χ^2

The expected frequencies are calculated following the steps in the table below. This may look complicated but isn't.

Add all the values in the final column to get the observed value of $\chi^2 = 2.9839$

	row × column / total = expected frequency (E)	Subtract expected value from observed value (O), ignoring signs $\lvert(E-O)\rvert$	Square previous value $(E-O)^2$	Divide previous value by expected value $(E-O)^2 / E$
Cell A	17 * 15 / 36 = 7.08	5 – 7.08 = 2.08	4.3264	0.6110
Cell B	17 * 21 / 36 = 9.92	12 – 9.92 = 2.08	4.3264	0.4361
Cell C	19 * 15 / 36 = 7.92	10 – 7.92 = 2.08	4.3264	0.5463
Cell D	19 * 21 / 36 = 11.08	9 – 11.08 = 2.08	4.3264	1.3905

$\Sigma (E-O)^2 / E$ (means add up all the values of $(E-O)^2 / E$) = 2.9839

Step 4. Find critical value of χ^2

- Significance level: 5% (0.05)
- Kind of hypothesis: Non-directional, therefore two-tailed test.
- *df* value = (number of rows – 1) × (number of columns – 1) = 1
- Locate the row in the statistical table on left that begins with our *df* value. The critical value of $\chi^2 = 3.84$

Step 5. State the conclusion

If the calculated value is equal to or greater than this critical value, our result is significant. In our case it is not significant.

As the calculated value is not significant (at $p \leq 0.05$), we must accept the null hypothesis and conclude that there is no association between men and women in terms of the basis for making moral decisions ($p \leq 0.05$).

Reporting investigations

JOURNAL ARTICLES

Throughout this book you have read about research studies, such as Gilligan and Attanucci on the facing page. These studies are written up and published in peer-reviewed academic journals for everyone to read. You can access many original reports online and you will see that they are almost always organised into the following sections:

Abstract

A summary of the study covering the aims, hypothesis, the method (procedures), results and conclusions (including implications of the current study). This is usually about 150–200 words in length and allows the reader to get a quick picture of the study and its results.

Introduction

The introduction begins with a review of previous research (theories and studies), so the reader knows what other research has been done and understands the reasons for the current study. The focus of this research review should lead logically to the study to be conducted so the reader is convinced of the reasons for this particular research. The introduction should be like a funnel – starting broadly and narrowing down to the particular research hypothesis. The researcher states their aims, research prediction and/or hypothesis.

Method

This section contains a detailed description of what the researcher did, providing enough information for replication of the study.
- Design, e.g. 'repeated measures' or 'covert observation'. Design decisions should be justified.
- Participants – Information about sampling methods and how many participants took part and their details (e.g. age, job, etc.).
- Apparatus/materials – Descriptions of any materials used.
- Procedures, including standardised instructions, the testing environment, the order of events and so on.
- Ethics – Significant ethical issues may be mentioned, as well as how they were dealt with.

Results

Details are given about what the researcher found, including:
- Descriptive statistics – Tables and graphs showing frequencies and measures of central tendency and dispersion.
- Inferential statistics (statistical tests) are reported, including calculated values and significance level.
- In the case of qualitative research, categories and themes are described along with examples within these categories.

Discussion

In this section the researcher aims to *interpret* the results of the study and consider their implications for future research as well as suggesting real-world applications.
- Summary of the results – The results are reported in brief and some explanation given about what these results show.
- Relationship to previous research – The results of the study are discussed in relation to the research reported in the introduction and possibly other research not previously mentioned.
- Consideration of methodology – Criticisms may be made of the methods used in the study, and improvements suggested.
- Implications for psychological theory and possible real-world applications.
- Suggestions for future research.

References

The full details of any journal articles or books that are mentioned in the research report are given, just like we have provided full references at the end of this book.

The format for journal articles generally is: Author's name(s), date, title of article, *journal title, volume (issue number)*, page numbers.

If it is a book: Author's name(s), date, *title of book*, place of publication, publisher.

Do it yourself

In the past, Psychology A Level involved producing a file of coursework which was marked and counted towards your final grade. Students had to design, conduct and report their own studies. The reporting part required using the conventions described on the left.

Here are some ideas for studies you can try for yourself and then write the report.
- Names are more difficult to remember than remembering what people do (James, 2004); for example, people remember if you are a farmer better than if someone's name is Farmer.
- Are women more conformist than men? Some studies have found this to be true, although Eagly and Carli (1981) suggest that this is only the case for male-oriented tasks. Try different types of conformity tasks and see whether females conform more in some than others. For example, ask questions on a general knowledge test which are related to male or female interests and see if females conform more where female interests are involved rather than when male interests are involved. The answers from previous female 'participants' should be shown so you can see if your real participant conforms to the majority answer.
- People are more willing to comply with a request if you touch them lightly on their arm. Brockner *et al.* (1982) arranged for a confederate to approach participants as they left a phone box and ask for some money which had been left behind in the phone box. In one condition the confederate touched the participant lightly on their arm when making the request. In the 'no touch' condition the request was made without any touch.
- Laughter increases the pain threshold (Dunbar *et al.*, 2011). Pain can be created by putting your hand in a bucket of ice cold water. People also feel less pain when they swear rather than when they say a neutral word (Stephens *et al.*, 2009).

🐾 APPLY YOUR KNOWLEDGE

1. Draw a contingency table to show the following data: old and young participants are asked whether they sleep more or less than eight hours per night on average. Of the older people, 11 said they sleep more and 25 said they sleep less. Of the younger participants, 31 said they sleep more than eight hours and 33 said they sleep less.
2. State an appropriate non-directional alternative hypothesis and null hypothesis for this investigation.
3. Calculate the value of Chi-Squared for the above study and report whether it is significant.
4. A researcher conducts a study and places the data in a 3×2 contingency table. What will the degrees of freedom be?
5. The research calculates a value of Chi-Squared of 4.7. Is this significant at the 5% level for a two-tailed test?
6. Select a study you know well and write an abstract for the study following the guidance given at the top of this page.

End-of-chapter review | CHAPTER SUMMARY

We have identified here the key points of the topics on the AQA A level specification, i.e. the bare minimum that you need to know. You may want to fill in further details to elaborate and personalise this material.

CONTENT ANALYSIS

CONTENT ANALYSIS

- A kind of observational study, which is usually indirect.
- Involves decisions about sampling, coding the data (deciding on behavioural categories) and deciding on methods of representing the data (quantitative or qualitative).
- Thematic analysis is an iterative process of identifying themes from a large amount of qualitative data. The themes are then used to represent the data either by counting instances or providing descriptive examples.

EVALUATION

- High ecological validity – based on what people have actually done.
- Replication possible to check reliability of observations.
- Observer bias reduces validity.
- Cultural bias due to personal interpretation.

CASE STUDIES

CASE STUDIES

- Study of one person, institution or event, often over a long period of time (longitudinal).
- Objective and systematic methods used e.g. observation, interviews and psychological testing.
- The target person or people may be involved and also friends and family.
- Detailed information collected in terms of depth and breadth.

EVALUATION

- Rich, in-depth data may provide new insights.
- Instances of unusual behaviour can be investigated.
- Complex interaction of many factors studied.
- Difficult to generalise from unique instances.
- Data may lack validity because recollection involved and researchers may lack objectivity.
- Ethical issues with confidentiality and over-testing.

RELIABILITY

RELIABILITY

- Consistency of measurements.
- Reliability of observations assessed with inter-observer reliability, which should be > .80.
  - Improved by better operationalisation of behavioural categories and by training observers.
- Reliability of self-report assessed with test–retest: repeat test with same participants over a short interval of a few weeks.
  - Improved by reducing ambiguity in questions.
- Reliability in experiments may relate to how the DV is measured (e.g. using observations or self-report).
  - Improved using standardisation of procedures in order to be able to repeat method with all participants.

VALIDITY

VALIDITY

- Internal validity, e.g. investigator effects, demand characteristics, confounding variables, social desirability bias, poorly operationalised behavioural categories – all mean that a researcher may not be recording how people really think and behave.
- External validity
  - Population validity – generalising from one sample to all people.
  - Ecological validity – generalising a research effect from one setting to another. It is affected by how the DV is measured (which may lack mundane realism) and whether participants are aware they are being studied.
  - Temporal validity – generalising a research effect from one historical period to another.
- Assessing validity
  - Face validity – whether test/questionnaire items look like they are measuring what they claim to be measuring.
  - Concurrent validity – checking if a test correlates well with existing validated measures.
- Improving validity
  - Revise questions so they look more relevant, or revise and check concurrent validity again.
  - Improve design, e.g. use double blind or more realistic task.

FEATURES OF SCIENCE

FEATURES OF SCIENCE

- Empirical methods – evidence gained through direct observation rather than rational argument or hearsay.
- Objectivity – not affected by personal expectations.
- Replicability – repeating a study in order to verify the findings, usually with a different group of participants and slightly different task.
- Theory construction – a set of principles to explain facts and enable predictions to be made and tested.
- Hypothesis testing – conducting research studies to assess the validity of a hypothesis.
- Falsifiability (Popper) – seeking to disconfirm a null hypothesis in order to demonstrate with some certainty that the alternative may be correct.
- Paradigm shift (Kuhn) – scientific progress occurs through revolutions and social construction rather than fine tuning.

INFERENTIAL STATISTICS

PROBABILITY

PROBABILITY

- A numerical measure of the likelihood or chance that certain events will occur.
- Null hypothesis – a statement of no relationship. How probable is the research result if there is actually 'nothing going on'?
- Chance is something without any cause. Is a result due to chance or a real effect?
- Psychologists use the 95% level: $p = 0.05$ means 5% possibility that a result is due to chance, 95% possibility that it is a real effect (there is something going on).
- In research concerning e.g. life and death matters, probability level (p) is 0.01 or 1%.
- Type I error – rejecting a null hypothesis that is true.
- Type II error – accepting a null hypothesis that is false.

STATISTICAL TESTS

STATISTICAL TESTS

- Parametric tests are more powerful; data must:
  - Have an interval or ratio level of measurement.
  - Be drawn from population with normal distribution.
  - Both samples have equal variances.
- Statistical tests produce a calculated value. To determine significance this is compared to a critical value found in a statistical table. Need to know:
  - Significance level (usually $p = 0.05$).
  - One- or two-tailed test (directional and non-directional hypotheses respectively).
  - Value of N or df.

NON-PARAMETRIC TESTS OF DIFFERENCE

WILCOXON TEST FOR RELATED DESIGNS

- Hypothesis states difference between two sets of data.
- Related design (repeated measures or matched pairs).
- Data is ordinal.

MANN-WHITNEY TEST FOR UNRELATED DESIGNS

- Hypothesis states difference between two sets of data.
- Unrelated design (independent groups).
- Data is ordinal.

SIGN TEST (covered in Year 1 book)

- Hypothesis states difference between two sets of data.
- Related design (repeated measures or matched pairs).
- Data is nominal.

CHI-SQUARED TEST

- Hypothesis states difference/association between two sets of data.
- Data in each cell is independent.
- Data is nominal.

TESTS OF CORRELATION

NON-PARAMETRIC: SPEARMAN'S *RHO*

- Hypothesis states correlation between two sets of data.
- Related design.
- Data is ordinal.

PARAMETRIC: PEARSON'S *r*

- Hypothesis states correlation between two sets of data.
- Related design.
- Data is interval.
- Criteria for parametric test met.

PARAMETRIC TESTS OF DIFFERENCE

RELATED *t*-TEST

- Hypothesis states difference between two sets of data.
- Related design (repeated measures or matched pairs).
- Data is interval.
- Criteria for parametric test met.

UNRELATED *t*-TEST

- Hypothesis states difference between two sets of data.
- Unrelated design (independent groups).
- Data is interval.
- Criteria for parametric test met.

REPORTING INVESTIGATIONS

JOURNAL ARTICLES

- Abstract – summary of study in about 150 words covering aims, hypothesis, method, results.
- Introduction/aim – literature review, research aims/hypothesis(es).
- Method – includes decisions about research method and design, participants and sampling methods, apparatus/materials, procedures and ethics.
- Results – descriptive and inferential statistics; where appropriate, details of qualitative analysis.
- Discussion – outcomes in relation to other research, criticisms and implications of study.
- References cited and given in full using standard format.

0 1 Read the item below and answer the questions that follow.

> A psychologist was interested in how female body image has changed over time. One part of his research involved looking at the waist to hip ratio (WHR) of shop dummies over a period of five decades. He predicted that the ratio would decrease over time.

(i) The most common waist and hip measurements in the 1970s were 62cm and 89cm. Calculate the WHR for this decade to 2 decimal places. Show your calculations. **[3 marks]**

(ii) Identify and explain the level of data used in this investigation. **[3 marks]**

(iii) The psychologist analysed his data using $p \leq 0.01$. Outline what is meant by this significance level. **[2 marks]**

(iv) After analysing his data, the psychologist was concerned that he had made a Type II error.

Explain what is meant by a *Type II error* with reference to this investigation. **[3 marks]**

0 2 Read the item below and answer the questions that follow.

> A psychologist designed a questionnaire to measure how aggressive individuals are. Initial tests showed that the questionnaire had face validity, but the psychologist also wanted to assess its reliability before using it for her research project.

(i) Outline what is meant by face validity in relation to this study. **[2 marks]**

(ii) Describe how the psychologist could assess the reliability of the questionnaire. Refer to a statistical test as part of your answer. **[5 marks]**

0 3 Read the item below and answer the questions that follow.

> A group of psychologists were concerned about the temporal validity of an experiment they had carried out. To assess the validity, the researchers replicated the original experiment.

(i) Outline what is meant by temporal validity. **[2 marks]**

(ii) Explain the role of replication in science. **[2 marks]**

(iii) In the original experiment, the researchers had used the related t-test to analyse the data. In the second experiment, they needed to use the unrelated t-test.

Using this information, state what had changed about the design of the experiment. **[1 mark]**

0 4 Which one of the following is a definition of a paradigm? Write the letter of your chosen answer in your answer booklet. **[1 mark]**

A. a common perspective on how a subject should be investigated

B. a piece of evidence collected through direct observation

C. a set of principles used to explain a phenomenon

D. a statement that predicts the outcome of an investigation

0 5   Name **two** sections of a scientific report and explain their purpose in reporting psychological investigations.   **[4 marks]**

0 6   Which one of the following is an example of nominal data? Write the letter of your chosen answer in your answer booklet.   **[1 mark]**

   A. deciding whether a child recognises an object or not

   B. rating a child's exploratory play

   C. scoring a child's intelligence

   D. timing how long it takes for a child to complete a task

0 7   Read the item below and then answer the questions that follow.

> A psychologist carried out an investigation into criminal facial features by measuring the height of the foreheads of convicted criminals and comparing this measure with that taken from people not convicted of a crime. The mean measurements and standard deviations from this investigation are shown below.
>
> | | Mean (cm) | Standard deviation |
> |---|---|---|
> | Convicted criminals | 7.5 | 0.5 |
> | Non-criminals | 9 | 0.7 |

   (i) What conclusion would the researcher draw from the means? Refer to the data in your answer.   **[2 marks]**

   (ii) Explain what the standard deviations show in this investigation.   **[2 marks]**

   (iii) Explain why the measurement of foreheads is seen as an objective measure.   **[2 marks]**

   (iv) Name **one** statistical test that could be used to analyse the data from the investigation. Justify your choice of test.   **[4 marks]**

0 8   Read the item below and answer the questions that follow.

> A psychologist conducted a piece of research to test the concurrent validity of a questionnaire designed to rate how masculine an individual is. This questionnaire was tested against a well-established questionnaire that also scored masculinity.

   (i) Explain how concurrent validity is used to assess validity.   **[2 marks]**

   (ii) The questionnaire was tested using Spearman's rho. Give **two** reasons for this choice of test.   **[2 marks]**

   (iii) The correlation coefficient from the test was 0.55.

Significance level	$p=0.05$	$p=0.02$	$p=0.01$
$N=16$	0.503	0.582	0.635

State the significance level that gives evidence for concurrent validity.   **[1 mark]**

The exam questions on research methods will be varied but are likely to involve some short answer questions (AO1), some application of knowledge questions (AO2) and some are evaluation (AO3). We've provided answers to some additional questions together with comments from an examiner about how well they've each done.

---

01 Read the item below and answer the questions that follow.

> A psychologist investigated how schizophrenia was presented in the media across ten different countries to investigate the effect of culture on perception of the disorder. To do this, she carried out a thematic analysis to identify similarities and differences in presentation.

(i) Outline what is meant by thematic analysis. *(2 marks)*

(ii) With reference to **two** features of science, explain why this investigation may be considered unscientific. *(6 marks)*

Maisie's answer

(i) A thematic analysis is a process where a researcher looks through qualitative data to see if there are any themes. The themes are a bit like behavioural categories.

(ii) One feature of science is objectivity and this study lacks objectivity because individual researchers are likely to pick out different themes concerning media representations of schizophrenia because of their expectations about what these themes might be. These expectations mean that the researcher is being subjective instead of being objective in their analysis. Another feature of science is replicability, i.e. other researchers should be able to repeat the study in the same way to see if they get the same results. Because the different themes emerge as a direct result of the interviewer's questions, it would be unlikely that another researcher would ask the same questions in the same way, thus failing to replicate the exact conditions of the previous interview.

Examiner's comments

(i) Although Maisie's response is quite simplistic, it is good enough for both marks. 1 mark for recognising the thematic analysis is applied to qualitative data and 1 mark for suggesting it can result in behavioural categories.

(ii) Maisie has dealt effectively with the demands of this question. She has identified two appropriate features of 'science' that may be absent in this study (for the first 2 marks) and explained each of these features in turn for the second 2 marks. To gain full marks, however, these features need to be applied to the specific study described in the question stem. Maisie does this well for both features so 6 marks in total.

Ciaran's answer

(i) When you have qualitative data one way to analyse this is using something called a thematic analysis. The researcher goes through the data and identifies themes that recur in the data and then can summarise the data using these themes. The researcher might give some examples of particular themes.

(ii) Objectivity is really the main issue because this method is quite subjective. Each person reads through the data and selects what they see as the key themes. So each person is likely to do this differently which makes it subjective instead of objective. Another feature of science here is replication which is a bit related to objectivity. If each person does it slightly differently then it is difficult to replicate what you have done. Replication is important to demonstrate validity and reliability.

Examiner's comments

(i) Ciaran earns 2 marks. 1 mark for recognising that thematic analysis is used on qualitative data. The second mark is for the explanation – although Ciaran uses the word 'themes' quite frequently (which is a bit obvious for credit), it is in the context of other relevant ideas such as 'identifies', 'recur' and 'summarise'.

(ii) Ciaran would earn 2 of the 4 marks. He identifies two relevant features of science and it does not matter that they are linked – we would expect that if they both contribute to a scientific approach. Each one of these is worth a mark, especially with a bit of explanation behind them. However, when explaining the features, Ciaran does not really seem to have the study in the item in mind. There is no indication that more than one researcher is involved yet both of his examples assume this is the case.

---

02 Read the item below and answer the questions that follow.

> A psychologist was interested in how female body image has changed over time. One part of his research involved looking at the waist to hip ratio (WHR) of shop dummies over a period of five decades. He predicted that the ratio would decrease over time. The most common waist and hip measurements in the 1970's were 62cm and 89cm.

(i) Calculate the WHR for this decade to 2 decimal places. Show your calculations. *(3 marks)*

(ii) Identify and explain the level of data used in this investigation. *(3 marks)*

(iii) The psychologist analysed his data using $p \leq 0.01$. Outline what is meant by this significance level. *(2 marks)*

(iv) After analysing his data, the psychologist was concerned that he had made a Type II error. Explain what is meant by a Type II error with reference to this investigation. *(3 marks)*

Maisie's answer

(i) 89:62 = 0.8414

(ii) The data is interval level because it is numbers with equal intervals.

(iii) The significance level is 10% which means there is less than a 10% chance that the results would have occurred by chance.

(iv) A Type II error is when the null hypothesis is accepted when it should have been rejected. In this study this means that the researcher would accept that body image doesn't change over time when in fact it does.

Examiner's comments

(i) 1 mark awarded. The answer is right because Maisie has divided 62 by 89 but she has got the numbers the wrong way round in her working. The answer is not to 2 decimal places as required.

(ii) 1 mark for identifying that it is interval data. The definition needs to be more precise by stating that it is the *scale* that numbers are measured that has equal intervals. The final mark would rely on Maisie then relating this to length to show how centimetres are always the same distance from each other.

(iii) 1 mark for knowing what significance levels refer to i.e. the chance of results occurring by chance. However, no further marks as 0.01 has been incorrectly interpreted as 10% rather than 1%.

(iv) Maisie would be awarded 1 mark for knowing what a Type II error is. In her case, she gets a further mark for relating it to the hypothesis (rather than the significance level itself).

Ciaran's answer

(i) 62 ÷ 89 = 0.84146341463

WHR = 0.84 (to 2 dec pl)

(ii) This is interval level because it is using a public scale of measurement. In other words, it does not matter who measures the waists or hips, the measure will be the same as centimetres do not need to be interpreted.

(iii) 0.01 means 1% which is quite a stringent level as it means that there is equal to or less than a 1% chance that the results occurred by chance

(iv) A Type II error is a false negative when the research erroneously accepts a null hypothesis that is false and is more likely to happen when the significance level is stringent as in this case.

Examiner's comments

(i) 1 mark for the working i.e. 62 ÷ 89. 1 mark for a correct answer to this. 1 mark for rounding to 2 decimal places correctly.

(ii) 1 mark for identifying the data as interval. 1 mark for a definition of what interval data is. 1 mark for applying this definition to the measurement used in the item.

(iii) Ciaran did not need to comment on the stringency of this significance level necessarily but he gets a mark for equating 0.01 to 1% and then a further mark for relating this to the occurrence of chance results. It is good that he has been precise and picked up on the 'equal to or less than' chance factor.

(iv) Ciaran gets 1 mark for correctly identifying what a Type II error is and then a further mark for considering this in the context of the study – in his case by linking it to the stringency of the significance level which is relevant in this particular answer. Ciaran would have earned the third mark if he had explained how a stringent significance level leads to the error.

---

03 Read the item below and answer the questions that follow.

> A psychologist designed a questionnaire to measure how aggressive individuals are. Initial tests showed that the questionnaire had face validity but the psychologist also wanted to assess its reliability before using it for her research project.

(i) Outline what is meant by face validity and explain how it could have been tested in this investigation. *(4 marks)*

(ii) Describe how the psychologist could assess the reliability of the questionnaire. Refer to a statistical test as part of your answer. *(5 marks)*

Maisie's answer

(i) Face validity is a way of assessing the validity of a questionnaire by considering if it looks like what it should be measuring. In this investigation the researchers would have looked at the questionnaire and decided whether the questions did seem to be about aggression.

(ii) To assess reliability you could use test-retest. This means that you give a group of participants the questionnaire and then ask them to answer it again about 2 weeks later. The answers should be fairly similar if the questionnaire is reliable. I would use a test of correlation to assess this by correlating the answers on both occasions.

Examiner's comments

(i) Maisie earns 2 marks for knowing what 'face validity' measures. 1 mark is for 'validity' (what it should be measuring) and the other for 'face' more specifically ('it looks like'). She earns a further mark for applying it to the study in the item where she suggests the researchers would check the questions are about aggression. However, it would have been better to suggest that a questionnaire should actually be piloted and then respondents could judge whether their scores had face validity.

(ii) 1 mark for an appropriate technique to assess reliability (test-retest). 1 mark for an outline of the technique. 1 mark for the desired outcome to show reliability. 1 mark for a general way of testing this (through correlation). What is missing from Maisie's answer is the name of a specific test for correlation (e.g. Spearman's rho) so four out of 5 marks in total.

Ciaran's answer

(i) You can check the validity or 'trueness' of a test using face validity. This shows that it is measuring what it intends to measure because it looks like it does.

(ii) A good way to check the reliability of a questionnaire is to give the questionnaire to the same person on two separate occasions, then you can correlate how similar their answers are using a test of correlation.

Examiner's comments

(i) 2 marks here. Ciaran can earn a mark for the idea of 'trueness' or for the idea of 'measuring what it intends to measure' but both are related to validity. He also gets a mark for identifying that face validity is specifically about what a measure 'looks like' it is measuring. However, because there is no obvious reference to the item, there are no further marks.

(ii) 1 mark for the general idea of testing retesting but it is a little naïve to think it would be enough to do this with only one person. 1 mark for the use of a correlation. However it is not enough to say that the researcher looks for 'how similar their answers are' – Ciaran needs to be clear that answers *should* be similar for reliability to be established. So, Ciaran earns 2 marks in total.

CONTENTS OF CHAPTER

SPECIFICATION CHECKLIST

- Gender and culture in psychology – universality and bias. Gender bias, including androcentrism and alpha and beta bias; cultural bias, including ethnocentrism and cultural relativism.

- Free will and determinism: hard determinism and soft determinism; biological, environmental and psychic determinism. The scientific emphasis on causal explanations.

- The nature–nurture debate: the relative importance of heredity and environment in determining behaviour; the interactionist approach.

- Holism and reductionism: levels of explanation in psychology. Biological reductionism and environmental (stimulus-response) reductionism.

- Idiographic and nomothetic approaches to psychological investigation.

- Ethical implications of research studies and theory, including reference to social sensitivity.

TRY THIS

This chapter focuses on the important issues and debates that are a concern for all psychology theories and research. Some of these issues and debates also reflect the thoughts that people have about their behaviour. For example, people wonder whether they are who they are because of genes they have inherited or because of parental influences (the issue of nature or nurture). People also wonder about their capacity to be self-determining or, for example, being determined by the environment they grew up in (the issue of free will versus determinism). Maybe they can explain their behaviour simply in terms of the way their parents rewarded things that they did.

Determinism is the view that something other than your own conscious decisions has guided your behaviour, i.e. that your genes, your hormones or your past experiences 'make' you behave in particular ways. The alternative – free will – is the view that at any moment you can make a conscious decision to act according to your own principles or wishes.

There is a middle ground, described as 'soft determinism'. One version of soft determinism is that behaviour is always determined – it just sometimes *appears* to be less determined: behaviour that is highly constrained by a situation appears involuntary, whereas behaviour that is less constrained by a situation appears voluntary.

An investigation

This version of soft determinism was investigated in a study by Malcolm Westcott (1982), who asked students to say how free they felt in 28 different situations. Here are some of them:

For each statement consider how free you feel in the situation using a 5-point scale:

5 = very much   4 = quite a lot   3 = somewhat   2 = very little   1 = not at all

		Write your rating in this column
1	As the end of term approaches I am up-to-date with all my work. I plan to spend the rest of term in both study and relaxation. I am in the process of setting my own priorities and making a schedule for myself which will include both.	
2	Sometimes I am not actively engaged in any particular activity, and I have nothing to do.	
3	All day long I have had a nagging headache, and I have just realised that it is gone.	
4	Getting all 'A' marks on my report is something I would really like to achieve. With some difficult courses this seems a very unlikely outcome. A 'B' average does seem reasonable and within my reach. By lowering my aims I go for the more certainly attainable goal.	
5	It's 12.00 and I've gone to the local cafeteria for lunch. I'm standing in line looking at the array of sandwiches, soups and salads. I am deciding what to buy for lunch.	
6	An ad in the paper advertises a holiday to a place I'd like to visit. The offer is open for the next year. I have the time and money but haven't taken any action to pursue it yet.	
7	Working at the Hel-Repair organisation I have become very good at fixing broken furniture and repairing clothing. Now, when faced with the task of repair, I am able to manage well and efficiently.	
8	Sometimes I restrict or reduce my desires to fit in with what I believe a situation allows and to what I believe my abilities to be.	

Add up your rating for questions 1, 2, 3 and 7, and then add up ratings for 4, 5, 6 and 8. (You might like to combine answers from your whole class.) The first group of scores should be higher than the second group according to Westcott's findings because he found that students reported feeling most free when they were in situations with little responsibility or when their behaviour would result in escape from an unpleasant situation, i.e. there would be little to stop them behaving like that (least constraint). They felt least free in situations when they recognised that there were limits on their behaviour, for example having to take their abilities into account when selecting course options, i.e. most constraint.

This suggests that behaviour is more to do with constraints on behaviour. People can exercise free will when there are less constraints.

Gender in psychology: Gender bias

In your studies of psychology you have learned about how there are gender differences in behaviour; for example, in your Year 1 studies you learned about possible gender differences in obedience. Such differences raise important questions about the value of any explanation because it may not be universal (i.e. apply to everyone). But perhaps most importantly differences may lead to a bias – a distorted view of the world. In the case of **gender bias** it is a distorted view of what behaviours may be typical and atypical for men and/or women.

Because if you say men and women are the same and if male behaviour is the norm, and women are always expected to act like men, we will never be as good at being men as men are.

Dee Dee Myers, Former White House Press Secretary
(source: izquotes.com)

KEY TERMS

Alpha bias A tendency to exaggerate differences between men and women. The consequence is that theories devalue one gender in comparison to the other.

Androcentrism Centred or focused on men, often to the neglect or exclusion of women.

Beta bias A tendency to ignore or minimise differences between men and women. Such theories tend either to ignore questions about the lives of women, or assume that insights derived from studies of men will apply equally well to women.

Gender bias The differential treatment or representation of men and women based on stereotypes rather than real differences.

Universality The aim to develop theories that apply to all people, which may include real differences.

Moral reasoning research

Lawrence Kohlberg (1969) produced a very influential theory of moral development, suggesting that the moral decisions we make are based on an ethic of justice. He based his theory on research with boys and men where he asked them to describe what behaviour would be right in certain situations that were related to fairness. This is an example of beta bias because he assumed the male responses would apply to all people.

Carol Gilligan (1982) pointed out that, aside from the biased sample, the dilemmas used by Kohlberg were also biased – they had a male orientation because they were concerned with justice rather than being concerned with, for example, hurting someone else's feelings (a moral of care). When Kohlberg tested women, he found that they were less morally developed than men – a classic outcome of alpha bias. In other words, his original beta bias meant that he now exaggerated the differences between men and women.

Gilligan's own theory and research showed that women favoured a care orientation, whereas men favoured a justice orientation. Gilligan's approach showed that men and women are different, but it was not biased because neither kind of moral reasoning was considered as 'better' – they are just different.

GENDER BIAS

Rachel Hare-Mustin and Jeanne Marecek (1988) proposed that there are two different ways that theories may be biased. **Alpha bias** refers to theories that assume there are real and enduring differences between men and women. **Beta bias** refers to theories that ignore or minimise gender differences. They do this by assuming that all people are the same and therefore it is reasonable to apply the same theories/methods with both men and women. The aim is to produce theories that can claim to have **universality**.

Androcentrism

For most of its life psychology (and society in general) has been very much male-dominated. Almost all psychologists were and are men, and therefore the theories they produce tend to represent a male world-view. This is described as **androcentrism** and may result in either an alpha or a beta bias.

Alpha bias

An alpha bias exaggerates the difference between men and women and, as a consequence of this, theories that are alpha biased devalue one gender in comparison to the other.

An example from Freud's research
Sigmund Freud's theories reflected the culture in which he lived. In the nineteenth century, men were more powerful and more educated, and regarded as superior to women. In his alpha-biased theory of psychoanalysis Freud viewed femininity as failed masculinity – he exaggerated the difference between men and women.

As Josselson (1988) points out: 'In this theory, women are seen as being inferior to men because they are jealous of men's penises (penis envy) and because they cannot undergo the same Oedipus conflict as boys do (which involves castration anxiety). Because the superego develops from the Oedipus conflict, women therefore must be morally inferior because they have a weaker identification with their mothers.'

Beta bias

Androcentrism can also result in people assuming that what is true for men is also true for women, thus mistakenly minimising the differences between men and women. The consequence is that the needs of one gender (usually women) are ignored.

An example from stress research
A good example of beta bias is research on the fight-or-flight stress response. Biological research is usually conducted with male animals because in females the variations in hormone levels would make the research more difficult. It is assumed that such male-only samples wouldn't matter because what is true for males would be true for females. In stress research it was assumed that the fight-or-flight response was universal – until Shelley Taylor and colleagues (2000) challenged this. They provided evidence that females produce a tend-and-befriend response at times of stress which is adaptive because it ensures the survival of their offspring.

The beta-biased approach of ignoring the possibility of a difference meant that female behaviour went undiscovered and meant that the stress response was not fully understood. The beta bias meant that a real difference was ignored.

Universality

It would be wrong to try to eradicate gender differences as a way to resolve the gender bias issue. That approach is in itself a beta bias. The solution lies in recognising differences but not the superiority of one gender over another. See 'Moral reasoning research' on the left.

Feminist psychology

One way to counter androcentrism is to take a feminist perspective – as Carol Gilligan did (facing page). Feminist psychology argues that 'difference' psychology arises from biological explanations of behaviour. The alternative, the social constructionist approach, aims to understand behaviour in terms of social processes and thus find a way to greater equality.

Feminist psychology agrees that there are real biologically based sex differences, but socially determined stereotypes make a far greater contribution to perceived differences. Therefore feminist psychology takes the view that a prerequisite to any social change with respect to gender roles must be a revision of our 'facts' about gender. Whether such facts are true or not, they perpetuate our beliefs about women. Feminist psychology is a branch of psychology that aims to redress the imbalances in theory and research in psychology.

One way to redress the balance is, perhaps surprisingly, to use evidence that women may be inferior to provide women with greater support. For example, Eagly (1978) acknowledged that women may be less effective leaders than men, but this knowledge should be used to develop suitable training programmes and therefore create a future with more women as leaders.

Bias in research methods

If psychological theories and studies are gender-biased, one consequence is that research may find differences between genders. It may not be the genders that differ, but the methods used to test or observe them are biased, so males and females *appear* to be different.

Another issue is the gender of the researcher. Rosenthal (1966) found that male experimenters are more pleasant, friendly and encouraging to female participants than to male participants. The result was that the male participants appeared to perform less well on the tasks assigned.

Feminists argue that lab experiments disadvantage women because findings created in the controlled world of the lab tell us very little about the experiences of women outside of these settings. For example, a meta-analysis by Eagly and Johnson (1990) noted that studies in real settings found women and men were judged as more similar in styles of leadership than in lab settings.

Reverse alpha bias

Another approach is to develop theories which show the differences between men and women but that emphasise the value of women. This can be seen in feminist research which shows instances where women are better. For example, research shows that women are better at learning because they are more attentive, flexible and organised (Cornwell *et al.*, 2013).

Such research challenges the stereotype that in any gender differences the male position must be better, and changes people's preconceptions.

Avoiding a beta bias

Beta bias, or minimising differences, has consequences for women. On the positive side, equal treatment (a beta bias) under the law has allowed women greater access to educational and occupational opportunities.

However, Hare-Mustin and Marecek point out that arguing for equality between men and women draws attention away from women's special needs and from differences in power between men and women. In a society where one group holds most of the power, seemingly neutral actions end up benefiting the group with the power. For example, equal parental leave ignores the biological demands of pregnancy, childbirth and breastfeeding, and the special needs of women, therefore disadvantaging women.

Assumptions need to be examined

Examples of gender bias continue unchallenged in many theories. For example, Darwin's theory of sexual selection portrays women as choosy and males as the ones who compete to be chosen. It pays, in terms of ultimate reproductive success, for females to be more selective because the costs (to produce eggs) are high. This has been used to explain female 'coyness' as a means of masking their interest in males when they are making choices. (In contrast, males are more explicit in pursuit of the opposite sex because they are in competition.)

This view has recently been challenged as being rooted in Victorian ideas that women are coy and males are aggressive with other male competitors. It has been recognised that women are equally competitive and aggressive when the need arises. For example, DNA evidence supports the idea that it is a good adaptive strategy for females to mate with more than one man. This puts females in competition with other females (Vernimmen, 2015).

▲ If you assume that men and women are equal (a beta bias) the consequence is that one gender might be misrepresented.

If you assume there are differences (an alpha bias), one gender may be devalued.

⬆ UPGRADE

Fitting your answer to the question set

Many students appear to read all questions as 'tell me something about…' regardless of the actual wording (and therefore the specific requirements) of the question. Let's look at some of the questions in the 'Can you…?' feature on this page.

1. *Explain what is meant by gender bias in psychology. (2 marks)*
   The term 'explain' requires you to go a little bit further than a brief definition in order to show the examiner that you really understand this concept. You might do this by including an example, in this case an example of gender bias within psychology. There are lots on this page, for example Freud's theory of psychoanalysis or androcentrism in stress research.

2. *Explain how androcentrism has affected psychological research. (3 marks)*
   This question is surprisingly similar to the previous one (although on a different topic) but is worth one mark more. The astute among you will have noticed those extra words '…how androcentrism has affected…', which means considering how this has impacted on research. For example, in the section on stress research, we make the point that androcentrism prevents us from fully understanding the stress response in females as research has concentrated on males alone.

We'll return to this theme of fitting your answer to the question in later exam features in this chapter.

Insider tip…
The topic of gender bias, as well as all the issues and debates in this chapter, are quite theoretical – your task is to relate these theoretical considerations to theories and studies with which you are familiar.

CAN YOU?   No. 2.1

1. Explain what is meant by *gender bias in psychology*. (2 marks)
2. Explain how androcentrism has affected psychological research. (3 marks)
3. Explain the difference between alpha bias and beta bias. (4 marks)
4. Outline an example of gender bias in psychological research. (3 marks)
5. Discuss gender bias in psychology. (16 marks)

Culture in psychology: Cultural bias

Much of traditional psychology represents a Western bias, which is hardly surprising because most of the world's psychologists are trained in the West and most of the participants in psychological research are from Western cultures. This means that most psychological theories and research techniques have a basis in a Western world view. When this knowledge base is applied to members of other **cultures** it reflects a **cultural bias**. However, as developing countries also increase their involvement in psychological theory and research, this bias is slowly being addressed.

KEY TERMS

Cultural bias The tendency to judge all people in terms of your own cultural assumptions. This distorts or biases your judgement.

Cultural relativism The view that behaviour cannot be judged properly unless it is viewed in the context of the culture in which it originates.

Culture The rules, customs, morals and ways of interacting that bind together members of a society or some other collection of people.

Ethnocentrism Seeing things from the point of view of ourselves and our social group. Evaluating other groups of people using the standards and customs of one's own culture.

Our concern is with bias rather than difference. Many studies have found differences between human cultural groups; for example, some cultures are described as individualist and focus on independence and self-achievement, whereas other cultures are described as collectivist because of a greater emphasis on group goals.

Cultural bias is not concerned with these differences; it is concerned with the distorted view that psychologists have because of their own cultural affiliations and how this bias affects their theories and studies.

If psychological theories and studies are culture-biased, this may explain why differences are found between cultures. It may not be the cultures that differ, but the methods used to test or observe them that are biased so that some cultural groups appear different.

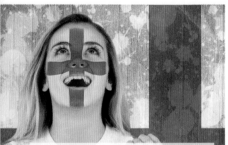

▲ Supporting your own team is an example of ethnocentrism. The end result of ethnocentrism is that we feel better about ourselves. If you overestimate the value of the group you belong to and underestimate the value of all other groups, you increase your self-esteem. Ethnocentrism is a psychological inevitability.

CULTURAL BIAS

Rachel Hare-Mustin and Jeanne Marecek (1988) suggested that before being able to decide if there are cultural differences one must consider the extent to which any research (theory or study) is biased. Only then can the 'truth' be disentangled from the way psychological research has found it.

As we discussed on the previous spread, Hare-Mustin and Marecek proposed that there are two different ways that theories may be biased – alpha and beta bias. We can apply this to culture as well as gender.

Alpha bias refers to theories that assume there are real and enduring differences between cultural groups. An example of alpha bias is the distinction that is often made between individualist and collectivist cultures (e.g. the US and Japan respectively). For instance, we would expect members of individualist cultures to be less conformist because they are less oriented towards group norms. To assess the validity of this view, Takano and Osaka (1999) reviewed 15 studies that compared the US and Japan in terms of individualism/collectivism. Surprisingly, 14 of the 15 studies did not support the common view about differences in conformity.

This finding suggests that the individualism/collectivism dimension may not be a real distinction, suggesting that the distinction between 'individualist' and 'collectivist' cultures is no longer a useful one.

Beta bias refers to theories that ignore or minimise cultural differences. They do this by assuming that all people are the same and therefore it is reasonable to use the same theories/methods with all cultural groups.

One example of this is intelligence testing. Psychologists use IQ tests devised by Western psychologists to study intelligence in many different cultures. The psychologists assume that their view of intelligence applies to all cultures equally. For example, Western societies see intelligence as something *within* the individual. In contrast, a collectivist culture such as Ugandan society sees intelligence as a functional relationship depending on shared knowledge between the individual and society (Wober, 1974). The result is that, when such Western IQ tests are used on non-Western cultures, non-Western people may appear less intelligent. Such tests are described as an *imposed etic*, where a research method or psychological test that is developed by one group is imposed on other groups of people (an 'etic' being the belief that perceptions, behaviours, etc. are shared by all cultural groups).

Ethnocentrism

Ethnocentrism refers to the use of our own ethnic or cultural group as a basis for judgements about other groups. There is a tendency to view the beliefs, customs and behaviours of our own group as 'normal' and even superior, whereas those of other groups are 'strange' or deviant.

Alpha bias Ethnocentricism is an example of alpha bias because one's own culture is considered to be different and better, and the consequence of this is that other cultures and their practices are devalued. An example of this is individualist attitudes towards attachment where independence is valued and dependence is seen as undesirable. In collectivist cultures, dependence tends to be more highly valued.

Beta bias Ethnocentrism can also lead to a beta bias, if psychologists believe their world view is the only view. For example, the case of IQ testing above results from ethnocentrism where it was believed it was appropriate to use American IQ tests all over the world because there was an assumption that the American standard was universal.

Cultural relativism

In a way the opposite of ethnocentrism in psychology is **cultural relativism** – the idea that all cultures are worthy of respect and that in studying another culture we need to try to understand the way that a particular culture sees the world.

Alpha bias Cultural relativism can also lead to an alpha bias where the assumption of real differences leads psychologists to overlook universals. For example, Margaret Mead's research in Papua New Guinea (see page 104) where she initially concluded that there were significant gender differences due to culture, but later recognised that there were universals (probably related to biology) – that the men in all cultures were more aggressive than the women.

Beta bias Cultural relativism is often discussed in the context of defining mental disorder. In the case of the statistical infrequency definition of abnormality (part of your Year 1 studies), behaviours that are statistically infrequent in one culture may be statistically more frequent in another. For example, one of the symptoms of schizophrenia is claiming to hear voices. However, this is an experience that is common in some cultures.

By assuming that the same rules apply universally (a beta bias), we may diagnose some people as mentally ill, but that diagnosis is relative to our culture.

Indigenous psychologies

One way to counter ethnocentrism in psychology is to encourage indigenous psychologies – the development of different groups of theories in different countries. For example, Afrocentrism is a movement whose central proposition is that all black people have their roots in Africa and that psychological theories concerning such people must, therefore, be African-centred and must express African values. Afrocentrism disputes the view that European values are universally appropriate descriptions of human behaviour that apply equally to Europeans and non-Europeans alike. It suggests that the values and culture of Europeans at worst devalue non-European people, and at best are irrelevant to the life and culture of people of African descent.

The emic–etic distinction

The approach described above is an 'emic' approach, one which emphasises the uniqueness of every culture by focusing on culturally specific phenomena. The problem with such approaches is that the findings tend to be significant only to the understanding of behaviour within that culture.

On the other hand, an 'etic' approach seeks universals of behaviour. One way to achieve this, while at the same time avoiding cultural bias, is to use indigenous researchers in each cultural setting. This is what David Buss and co-workers did in their classic study of mate preferences (see page 64). The data for the study was collected from people in 37 different cultures in order to look at universal behaviour. In each cultural setting there were three local researchers – one translated the questionnaire from English into the native language, a second translated the answers back into English and the third one resolved any discrepancies.

Bias in research methods

Cultural bias in psychology can also be dealt with simply by using studies with samples from different cultural groups. This was not the situation at the end of the last century. For example, in 1998, Smith and Bond surveyed research in one European textbook on social psychology. They found that 66% of the studies were American, 32% European and 2% came from the rest of the world.

Sears (1986) reported that 82% of research studies used undergraduates as the participants in psychology studies and 51% were psychology students. A more recent study (Henrich et al., 2010) found that 67% were American psychology students. The researchers calculated that a randomly selected American student was 4,000 times more likely to be a participant in a psychology study than a random non-Westerner. This suggests that a considerable amount of psychology is based on middle-class, academic, young adults who incidentally are often male – these represent different cultural groups. Psychology findings are not only unrepresentative on a global scale, but also within Western culture.

Consequences of cultural bias

One of the most infamous examples of the damage done by psychologists through cultural bias was the US Army IQ test (see examples on right), used just before the First World War. The tests showed that European immigrants fell slightly below white Americans in terms of IQ, and African-Americans were at the bottom of the scale with the lowest mental age. The data from these tests had a profound effect on the attitudes held by Americans towards certain groups of people – black people and people from southeastern Europe. The data led to enduring stereotypes concerning certain ethnic groups and their IQ (Gould, 1981).

The worldwide psychology community

Researchers in psychology, like most people, travel much more now than they did 50 years ago. This means they have an increased understanding of other cultures at a personal level but also at a professional level. Academics hold international conferences where researchers from many different countries and cultures regularly meet to discuss and exchange ideas. In fact this is how David Buss (above) found his researchers in 37 different cultures.

This means there is a much greater exchange of ideas, which should reduce ethnocentrism in psychology, enable an understanding of cultural relativism and mean that real differences are identified and valued.

🐾 APPLY YOUR KNOWLEDGE

Professor Randolph Harley-Bagel is an American academic with a particular interest in conformity research. He and his colleagues at the University of West Texas have developed a psychological scale to measure the likelihood of someone being able to resist this type of social influence (the RC, or 'Resisting Conformity', score). They try it out on students at their university, and get a mean RC score of 14.9 out of 20, where the higher the score the more a person is able to resist conformity.

Professor Harley-Bagel is then given the opportunity to try the questionnaire out on students in the UK and in North Korea, finding RC scores for these two cultures of 15.2 and 8.1 respectively. From this he concludes that people in North Korea are far more conformist than people in the US and UK.

Using your knowledge of cultural bias, identify and explain two biases that are evident in Professor Harley-Bagel's work.

▼ The US Army IQ test.

It's hard to believe that anyone thought the test items in the US Army IQ tests were a fair way to assess intelligence. Look at the cultural bias in the items below:

> 1 'Washington is to Adams as first is to…'
> 2 'Crisco is a: patent medicine, disinfectant, tooth paste, food product?'
> 3 'What item is missing in this picture?'

Answers
1 Second, because Washington was the first US president and Adams was the second.
2 It is a food product.
3 A ball is missing from the man's right hand.

CAN YOU?   No. 2.2

1. Explain what is meant by *cultural bias in psychology*. (2 marks)
2. Explain the terms *ethnocentrism* and *cultural relativism*. (3 marks)
3. Outline an example of cultural bias in psychological research. (3 marks)
4. Discuss cultural bias in psychology. (16 marks)

Free will and determinism

Determinism is the view that an individual's behaviour is controlled by either internal or external forces. This means that behaviour should be predictable.

Free will is used to refer to the alternative end of the spectrum where an individual is seen as being capable of self-determination. According to this view, individuals have an active role in controlling their behaviour, i.e. they are free to choose and are not acting in response to any external or internal (biological) pressures.

However, it is important to realise that free will does not mean randomness, and determinism may not necessarily lead to predictability.

The eighteenth century author Samuel Johnson had an easy solution: 'We know the will is free; and there's an end to it.'

KEY TERMS

Determinism Behaviour is controlled by external or internal factors acting upon the individual.

Free will Each individual has the power to make choices about their behaviour.

Hard determinism The view that all behaviour can be predicted and there is no free will. The two are incompatible.

Soft determinism A version of determinism that allows for some element of free will.

Reconciling free will and determinism

One solution to the debate is to claim free will and determinism are not incompatible, a position called **soft determinism** (the opposite view is **hard determinism**). For example, it can be argued that everything is determined by your biology and past experiences, but this still leaves a person with some choices that can be made.

This was the view of Nick Heather (1976), who proposed that behaviour may be predictable but this doesn't make it inevitable. Individuals are free to choose their behaviour, but this is usually from within a fairly limited repertoire.

William James (1890) suggested that we should separate behaviour into a physical and mental realm. The former is determined, whereas the latter is subject to free will.

Elizabeth Valentine (1992) claimed that behaviour is always determined – it just sometimes appears to be less determined: behaviour that is highly constrained by a situation appears involuntary, whereas behaviour that is less constrained by a situation appears voluntary. This was supported by Westcott's study described at the beginning of the chapter (see page 41).

DETERMINISM

There are many examples of determinism in psychology – explanations or approaches which are based on the concept that human behaviour is caused by factors not under an individual's personal control.

Biological determinism

Research into the human genome is producing increasing evidence of genetic influences on behaviour. The more we discover, the more it appears that our behaviours (not just our physical characteristics) are determined by our genes. For example, research on intelligence has identified particular genes found in people with high intelligence, such as the IGF2R gene (Hill *et al.*, 1999).

Genes, in turn, influence brain structure and neurotransmitters such as serotonin and dopamine that are often implicated in behaviour. For example, see the dopamine hypothesis of schizophrenia (page 142).

Environmental determinism

Behaviourists believe that all behaviour is caused by previous experience, through the processes of classical and operant conditioning (which may be direct or indirect). For example, in your Year 1 studies you learned how phobias may develop as a consequence of conditioning – a new stimulus response relationship can be learned if the item 'dog' is paired with being bitten. Such a phobic response is also unlearned through conditioning (e.g. systematic desensitisation).

The principles of learning theory have been applied to many areas of behaviour, such as aggression (page 238) and eating behaviour (page 166).

Psychic determinism

Freud's psychoanalytic theory of personality suggests that adult behaviour is determined by a mix of innate drives and early experience, i.e. both internal and external forces. Behaviour is driven by the libido, which focuses sequentially on erogenous zones, such as the mouth or anus. If a child is frustrated or overindulged (external forces) at any stage during development, then the libido remains tied to the relevant erogenous zone and the individual is thus fixated on that zone. The method of obtaining satisfaction that characterised the stage will dominate their adult personality.

Scientific determinism: emphasis on causal explanations

Scientific research is based on the belief that all events have a cause. An independent variable is manipulated to observe the causal effect on a dependent variable. For example, in your Year 1 studies you learned about Harlow's (1959) research on attachment involving an independent variable (wire mother with milk or cloth covered) and a dependent variable (attachment formed). The result demonstrated that contact comfort, not food, determined the formation of an attachment.

FREE WILL

At a subjective level we each have a sense of free will, as the quote above from Johnson (top left) suggests.

Humanistic approach

Humanistic psychologists, such as Abraham Maslow and Carl Rogers, argued that self-determination was a necessary part of human behaviour. Without it, healthy self-development and self-actualisation are not possible. Rogers (1959) claimed that as long as an individual remains controlled by other people or other things, they cannot take responsibility for their behaviour and therefore cannot begin to change it. Things which are outside a person's sense of self remain beyond personal control. For example, a person who says 'I lied but that isn't like me' does not admit that they are a liar and therefore will not seek to change the behaviour. Only when an individual takes self-responsibility (i.e. self-determination) is personal growth possible, resulting in psychological health.

Moral responsibility

The basis of moral responsibility is that an individual is in charge of their own actions, i.e. can exercise free will. The law states that children and those who are mentally ill do not have this responsibility, but otherwise there is the assumption, in our society, that 'normal' adult behaviour is self-determined. In other words, that humans are accountable for their actions, regardless of innate factors or the influences of early experience.

EVALUATION OF DETERMINISM

Genetic determinism

It is doubtful that 100% genetic determination will ever be found for any behaviour. For example, studies that compare identical twins (individuals who have an identical genetic make-up) find about 80% similarity on intelligence or about 40% for depression. In other words, if one twin has a high IQ, there is only a 80% chance that the other twin will be the same. Therefore genes do not entirely determine behaviour.

Environmental determinism

The concordance rates referred to above equally show that environment cannot be the sole determining factor in behaviour; there is at least some genetic input. Therefore environmental explanations cannot solely determine behaviour.

Scientific determinism

Dennett (2003) argues that, in the physical sciences, it is now accepted that there is no such thing as total determinism. Chaos theory proposes that very small changes in initial conditions can subsequently result in major changes, sometimes called 'the butterfly effect'. The conclusion is that causal relationships are probabilistic rather than determinist, i.e. they increase the probability of something occurring rather than being the sole determinant.

Determinist explanations tend to oversimplify human behaviour. They may be appropriate for non-human animals (e.g. explaining mating behaviour in a peacock in terms of biological factors), but human behaviour is less rigid and influenced by many factors – for example, cognitive factors such as thinking about what you intend to do, which can override biological impulses. This means that the idea of ever finding a simple determinist formula from psychological research is unrealistic.

Does it matter?

There have been attempts, in criminal cases in the US, for murderers to claim that their behaviour was *determined* by inherited aggressive tendencies and therefore they should not be punished with the death penalty. Stephen Mobley, who killed a pizza shop manager in 1981, claimed this happened because he was 'born to kill', as evidenced by a family history of violence. The argument was rejected, and Mobley was sentenced to death. In practice, therefore, a determinist position may be undesirable because it would allow individuals to 'excuse' their behaviour.

Determinism is also an issue in the treatment of mental disorder. If we take the view that disorders such as schizophrenia and depression are determined by an individual's biology (genes and neurotransmitters), then it follows that treatment should target their genes or neurotransmitters. However, such determinist treatment may then block the consideration of other treatments that might be beneficial, such as cognitive behavioural therapy.

EVALUATION OF FREE WILL

The illusion of free will

Just being able to decide between different courses of action is not free will, but it may give us the *illusion* of having free will, an argument put forward by the behaviourist B.F. Skinner. His point was that a person might 'choose' to buy a particular car or see a particular film, but in fact these choices are determined by previous reinforcement experiences.

Culturally relative

The idea of self-determination may be a culturally relative concept, appropriate for individualist societies only. Collectivist cultures place greater value on behaviour determined by group needs.

Research challenge to free will

The free will position received a significant blow from research conducted by Benjamin Libet *et al.* (1983). They recorded activity in motor areas of the brain *before* the person had a conscious awareness of the decision to move their finger. In other words, the decision to move the finger (a conscious state) was simply a 'read out' of a pre-determined action. Follow-up research confirmed the findings; for example, Chun Siong Soon *et al.* (2008) found activity in the prefrontal cortex up to 10 seconds before a person was aware of their decision to act.

However, other researchers have conducted similar studies and reached a different conclusion. For example, Trevena and Miller (2009) showed that the brain activity was simply a 'readiness to act' rather than an intention to move. For the moment it seems that neuroscience still supports free will.

▲ Chaos theory or the 'butterfly effect': A butterfly flapping its wings in Bristol can, in theory, produce a tornado in Kansas. One small change may lead to a series of other unpredictable changes.

⌕ Research methods

In Chapter 1 we discuss the features of science, including the nature of hypothesis testing.

Consider the experiment by Loftus and Palmer (1974) on eyewitness testimony, which was part of your Year 1 studies. In this study participants were asked to estimate the speed of a car in a film. There were five groups of participants, each given a different verb in the key question; for example, 'How fast was the car travelling when it *hit* the other car?'

1. Explain why this study is described as an experiment. (2 marks)
2. In what way is the experimental approach a determinist approach, compared to other research methods in psychology? (3 marks)
3. Name **one** research method in psychology, which is not determinist. (1 mark)
4. In the Loftus and Palmer study which variable was the one doing the 'causing' i.e. which variable determined the behaviour of the other? (1 mark)
5. Explain how confounding variables may challenge the determinist nature of Loftus and Palmer's research. (3 marks)
6. Explain **one** strength and **one** limitation of this kind of determinist approach to research in psychology. (4 marks)

LINK TO RESEARCH METHODS

Features of science page 20.

CAN YOU? No. 2.3

1. Briefly explain the concept of free will. (3 marks)
2. Explain what is meant by *biological determinism* and *environmental determinism*. (2 marks + 2 marks)
3. Explain the difference between hard determinism and soft determinism. (3 marks)
4. Explain why science places an emphasis on causal explanations. (3 marks)
5. Discuss free will and determinism in psychology. (16 marks)

The nature–nurture debate

This is a debate we all engage in – am I like this because I was born that way or is it down to life experience? Is it my **nature** or my **nurture**?

At one time nature and nurture were seen as largely independent and additive factors; however, for many years now no one has supported this view. It is accepted that the two processes do not just interact but are inextricably entwined. It is no longer really a **nature–nurture debate** at all but a new understanding of how genetics works – an **interactionist approach**.

The interdependence of nature and nurture makes adaptive sense – hardwired systems that are passed on through **heredity**, such as areas of the brain for memory and language, are necessary, because without genes for these systems it would not be possible to learn and recall. But a flexible system that responds to the **environment** ensures that each individual makes maximum use of their innate qualities.

KEY TERMS

Environment Everything that is outside our body, which includes people, events and the physical world.

Heredity The process by which traits are passed from parents to their offspring, usually referring to genetic inheritance.

Interactionist approach With reference to the nature–nurture debate, the view that the processes of nature and nurture work together rather than in opposition.

Nature Behaviour is seen to be a product of innate (biological or genetic) factors.

Nature–nurture debate The argument as to whether a person's development is mainly due to their genes or to environmental influences.

Nurture Behaviour is a product of environmental influences.

A political debate

Underlying the nature–nurture debate is a subtext relating to politics. The contrasting concepts of human nature have tended to correlate with contrasting political ideals.

On the one side, 'nature' has been linked with twentieth-century *eugenics* (enforced selective breeding) as advocated, for example, by the Nazis. If nature determines behaviour, then the human stock can be improved by selective breeding. Many countries (particularly the US) have practised selective breeding by sterilising thousands of people deemed 'feeble-minded'.

On the other side, the 'environment is all' idea is popular with people who believe that any human trait can be altered with the appropriate changes in social institutions. This has led to equally brutal regimes under leaders such as Stalin (in the former Soviet Union) and Pol Pot (in Cambodia) who believed that you could engineer the behaviour of others through conditioning so that they behaved as you wished them to behave.

Such political agendas mean that arguments for or against nature (or nurture) may be as much founded on political beliefs as on scientific evidence (Pinker, 2003).

NATURE AND NURTURE

Innate influences are referred to as 'nature'. This does not simply refer to abilities present at birth but to any ability determined by genes, such as secondary sexual characteristics which appear at puberty or a condition like Huntingdon's disease which is usually only apparent in adulthood.

Environmental influences, or 'nurture', are acquired through interactions with the environment. This includes both the physical and the social world, and may be more widely referred to as 'experience'. It includes effects on an infant before birth, such as a mother who smokes.

On this side of the spread we will consider a few examples of the influence of nature and for the influence of nurture.

Examples of the influence of nature

Genetic explanations

Family, twin and adoption studies show that the closer two individuals are genetically, the more likely that both of them will develop the same behaviours. You can read about such research in relation to schizophrenia (page 138), addiction (page 294) and criminal behaviour (page 264).

For example, the concordance rate for a mental disorder such as schizophrenia is about 40% for MZ twins (who have identical genes) and 7% for DZ twins (who, on average, share 50% of their genes) (Joseph, 2004 – see page 143). This closer similarity for individuals with the same genes shows that nature has a major contribution to the disorder.

Evolutionary explanations

Any evolutionary explanation is based on the principle that a behaviour or characteristic that promotes survival and reproduction will be naturally selected. This is because such behaviours/characteristics are adaptive and thus the genes for that behaviour/characteristic will be passed on to subsequent generations.

For example, Bowlby (1969) proposed that attachment was adaptive because it meant an infant was more likely to be protected and therefore more likely to survive. In addition, attachment promotes close relationships which would foster successful reproduction. Therefore attachment behaviours are naturally selected, which can only be done through genetic mechanisms.

Examples of the influence of nurture

In the seventeenth century, the philosopher John Locke described the newborn infant as a *tabula rasa*, a blank slate on which experience is written. This was the view adopted by the behaviourists.

Behaviourism

Behaviourists assume that all behaviour can be explained in terms of experience alone. B.F. Skinner used the concepts of classical and operant conditioning to explain learning.

For example, behaviourists suggested that attachment could be explained in terms of classical conditioning (food is the mother who feeds the baby) or operant conditioning (food reduces the discomfort of hunger and is therefore rewarding).

Social learning theory

Bandura's view was a little less extreme than traditional behaviourism. He too proposed that behaviour is acquired through learning, adding the new dimension of indirect (vicarious) reinforcement. But Bandura did also allow that biology had a role to play; for example, he acknowledged that the *urge* to behave aggressively might be biological, but the important point was that the way a person learns to *express* anger is acquired through environmental influences (direct and indirect reinforcement).

Other explanations

There are a number of other psychological explanations that are not behaviourist or social learning but are basically nurture. For example, the double bind theory of schizophrenia (Bateson *et al.*, 1956 – see page 144) suggests that schizophrenia develops in children who frequently receive contradictory messages from their parents; for example, if a mother tells her son that she loves him, yet at the same time turns her head away in disgust. Such conflicting messages about her feelings prevent the child developing an internally consistent construction of reality, which may lead to symptoms of schizophrenia.

On this side of the spread we look at explanations of how nature and nurture interact as a means of evaluating the approach of either using nature or using nurture to explain behaviour.

Nature and nurture cannot be separated

When asked whether nature or nurture was more important, the psychologist Donald Hebb said that was the same as asking whether the length or width of a rectangle was more important when working out the area of a rectangle. It is a meaningless question – they both contribute.

A classic example of this is the disorder *phenylketonuria*, an inherited disorder that prevents the amino acid phenylalanine being metabolised, resulting in brain damage. However, if the condition is detected at birth, an infant can be given a diet devoid of phenylalanine and thus brain damage is averted. If prevention can be achieved through environmental manipulation, is this condition due to nature or nurture?

Diathesis-stress

One conceptualisation of the interaction between nature and nurture is the diathesis-stress model. This is often used to explain mental disorders such as phobia (Year 1 studies) or schizophrenia (see page 154). A diathesis is a biological vulnerability, such as being born with certain genes that predispose a person to developing a disorder. However, research has shown that not everyone with those genes does develop the disorder. Expression of the gene or genes depends on experience in the form of a 'stressor' which triggers the condition. Thus a person's nature is only expressed under certain conditions of nurture.

Nature affects nurture

Genes may exert an *indirect* effect in a number of ways. First, genetic factors create an infant's microenvironment. For example, a child who is genetically more aggressive might provoke an aggressive response in others. This response becomes part of the child's environment and affects the child's development. Robert Plomin *et al.* (1977) called this *reactive* gene–environment interaction because the child is reacting to genetically influenced behaviour.

Plomin *et al.* identified a second kind of interaction – *passive* influence. Parents' genes determine aspects of their behaviour. For example, a parent with a genetically determined mental illness creates an unsettled home environment. In this case a child's mental disorder could be due to indirect, passive effects.

The third kind of interaction is *active* influence, or what Scarr and McCartney (1983) call *niche picking*. As children grow older they seek out experiences and environments that suit their genes. Research has shown that the influence of genes *increases* as children get older, which is due to niche picking.

Nurture affects nature

Your Year 1 study of neural plasticity has taught you how life experiences shape your biology. For example, Maguire *et al.*'s (2000) study of London taxi drivers (see Year 1 book) showed that the region of their brains associated with spatial memory was bigger than in controls. This is not because they were born this way but because their hippocampi had responded to increased use.

Blakemore and Cooper's (1970) work with kittens shows how experience affects innate systems. The kittens were given large collars from when they were born to restrict what they could see and they were raised in a circular drum with either only vertical or horizontal stripes. When they were introduced to the real world at age 5 months, they no longer had the ability to see lines of the opposite orientation. Their innate visual system had been altered through experience.

Epigenetics

Epigenetics refers to the material in each cell of your body that acts like a set of 'switches' to turn genes on or off. Life experiences, such as nutrition or stress, control these switches, and most importantly these 'switches' are passed on to subsequent generations. Therefore, the twins depicted at the top of the page might produce children who would differ in weight even though their children had identical diets – because of the epigenetic material they inherited, which was derived from an environmental effect.

This explains why cloning doesn't produce identical copies. Cloning involves placing the genetic material from one individual into an egg that has no nucleus. The egg should then grow into an identical copy of the cloned individual. However, that doesn't happen, as you can see in the pictures on the right. Genes from the parent cat, Rainbow, were cloned to produce the kitten CC (Carbon Copy) – except the clone isn't identical. The reason is that there is epigenetic material in the donor egg cell. This epigenetic material was produced by environmental effects in the donor's lifetime.

What does it all mean? It means that genetics and environment are much less separate than was previously thought.

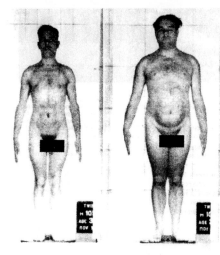

▲ The above photos show identical twins separated at birth; the one on the left was very malnourished through childhood. It's a clear demonstration of how the environment can modify the expression of our genes.

🐾 APPLY YOUR KNOWLEDGE

Pharrel is in the first year of his GCSEs but he spends more time on report than in his classes. He frequently gets into fights with the other children in his class and has recently been excluded after it was discovered he was bullying other children and stealing from them.

When teachers look into his family background they discover that his father is currently in prison for aggravated burglary and his two brothers both have a history of violent assault charges.

Using your knowledge of the nature–nurture debate, explain as many possible reasons for Pharrel's violent behaviour at school.

▲ Rainbow (on left) was cloned to produce a kitten called CC (on right). They have identical genes but look quite different.

CAN YOU? No. 2.4

1. Explain the terms *nature* and *nurture*. (4 marks)
2. Outline **one** example of an interactionist approach to the nature–nurture debate. (3 marks)
3. Discuss the relative importance of heredity and environment in determining behaviour. (16 marks)
4. Describe and evaluate the nature–nurture debate in psychology. (16 marks)

Holism and reductionism

Reductionism involves breaking a complex phenomenon down into more simple components. It also implies that this process is desirable because complex phenomena are best understood in terms of a simpler level of explanation. Psychologists (and all scientists) are drawn to reductionist explanations and methods of research because reductionism is a powerful tool, which has led to major discoveries.

The alternative to reductionism is **holism**, the view that simple components do not express the essence of a behaviour or experience – the sum of the parts does not equal the whole.

▲ When you look at this heap of parts, does that represent a 'car' to you?

REDUCTIONISM

Levels of explanation

The reductionist approach in psychology suggests that explanations begin at the highest level and progressively look at component elements:
- Highest level: cultural and social explanations of how our social groups affect our behaviour.
- Middle level: psychological explanations of behaviour.
- Lower level: biological explanations of how hormones and genes etc. affect our behaviour.

We can consider any behaviour in terms of all three levels. For example, memory can be explained at a social level in terms how cultural expectations affect what we remember. It can be explained at a psychological level in terms of episodic memories (memories of events in a person's life). It can be explained at a biological level in terms of the areas of the brain where the memories are stored (hippocampus and temporal lobe) and the neurotransmitters involved in forming memories (e.g. acetylcholine).

Biological reductionism

Since all animals are made up of atoms, then human behaviour must be explainable at this level, i.e. can be reduced to a physical level. Biological psychologists reduce behaviour to the action of neurons, neurotransmitters, hormones and so on. A popular way to explain mental illness is in terms of such units. For example, it has been suggested that schizophrenia is caused by excessive activity of the neurotransmitter dopamine because drugs that block this neurotransmitter reduce the symptoms of this disorder.

Environmental (stimulus-response) reductionism

Behaviourist explanations suggest that all behaviour can be explained in terms of simple stimulus-response links, i.e. behaviour can be reduced to a simple relationship between behaviour and events in the environment. Examples of such explanations include the behaviourist explanation offered for attachment (Year 1 studies). The complex emotion of attachment is reduced to a set of probabilities: the mother is likely to provide food which is reinforcing (reduces discomfort). Hence, she is a rewarding individual and so becomes a 'loved one'.

Experimental reductionism

Reducing complex behaviours to isolated variables is a useful strategy for conducting research. It underlies the experimental approach where behaviours are reduced to operationalised variables that can be manipulated and measured to determine causal relationships.

HOLISM

This approach focuses on systems as a whole rather than on the constituent parts, and suggests that we cannot predict how the whole system will behave just from a knowledge of the individual components. This means that reductionist explanations would only play a limited role in understanding behaviour.

Gestalt psychology

The word 'Gestalten' means 'the whole' in German and was an approach favoured by a group of German psychologists in the first part of the twentieth century. They focused especially on perception, arguing that explanations for what we see only make sense through a consideration of the whole rather than the individual elements, as illustrated by the illusion on the right.

Humanistic psychology

Humanistic psychologists believe that the individual reacts as an organised whole, rather than a set of stimulus-response (S-R) links. What matters most is a person's sense of a unified identity; and thus a lack of identity or a sense of 'wholeness' leads to mental disorder.

Cognitive psychology

Memory is a complex system which in recent years has been understood in terms of connectionist networks. The idea of a network is that each unit (such as a neuron) is linked to many other units (other neurons). These links develop through experience and, with each new experience, the links are strengthened or weakened. Connectionist networks are described as holist because the network as a whole behaves differently than the individual parts; linear models (where one item links only to the next in a sequence) assume that the sum of the parts equals the whole.

Insider tip…

There is some debate over whether reductionism refers solely to moving to the lowest level of analysis, which in psychology usually means the biological approach. Or whether it also means reducing an explanation to a simpler set of components, as in environmental reductionism. Some people accept both as examples of reductionism.

There is no debate over whether reductionism refers to a limited theory or approach which is focused on only one kind of explanation. It doesn't refer to this. For example, the cognitive approach is not reductionist because it ignores emotional and biological factors.

▲ The kind of visual illusion Gestalt psychologists used to illustrate that the whole is not simply a sum of its parts.

The danger of lower levels of explanation

Lower levels are indeed part of any account of behaviour, but offering accounts at different levels creates problems. First, if lower levels (e.g. biological or behavioural explanations) are taken in isolation, then the *meaning* of behaviour may be overlooked. This may lead to fundamental errors of understanding.

For example, Wolpe (1973), who developed the therapy of systematic desensitisation, treated one woman for a fear of insects. He found no improvement from this behavioural method of therapy. It turned out that her husband, with whom she had not been getting along, was given an insect nickname. So her fear was not the result of conditioning but a means of representing her marital problems; to focus on the behavioural level and ignore meaning would have been an error.

The danger of lower levels of explanation is that they may distract us from a more appropriate level of explanation. For example, the administration of the amphetamine *Ritalin* to hyperactive children may miss the *real* causes of a child's hyperactive behaviour (e.g. family or emotional problems).

Biological reductionism

One consequence of biological explanations has been the development of drug therapies. The strength of such treatments is that they have led to a considerable reduction in institutionalisation since the 1950s. It is also a more humane approach to the treatment of mental illness insofar as it does not blame the patient, which may, in turn, lead to greater tolerance of the mentally ill.

On the other hand, drug therapies are fraught with difficulties. Their success rates are variable and they treat the symptoms and not the causes, and thus may not have lasting effects. Reducing mental illness to the biological level ignores the context and function of such behaviour. Psychological explanations take more account of these and have produced many successful therapies.

Environmental reductionism

The behavioural approach was developed as a result of experiments with non-human animals. It may be appropriate to explain their behaviour in terms of simple components, but such explanations may not be appropriate for more complex human behaviour. Humans are not scaled-up versions of other animals – their behaviour is influenced by social context, intentions and so on. Even in non-human animals, reductionist explanations ignore other possible influences such as cognitive and/or emotional factors.

Experimental reductionism

Reducing behaviour to a form that can be studied is productive and may be a necessary part of understanding how things work. Experimental research in psychology has produced a huge array of findings about behaviour, but the question is how much such findings actually tell us about everyday life.

Consider, for example, research into eyewitness testimony. The findings from laboratory experiments such as Loftus and Palmer have not always been confirmed by studies of real-life eyewitnesses where memories have been found to be highly accurate (e.g. Yuille and Cutshall, 1986). The operationalisation of variables, such as eyewitness memory, may result in something that is measurable but bears no resemblance to the real thing. Also in real life there are other factors that motivate performance which cannot be recreated in an experiment – therefore findings often do not reflect the real world.

The mind–body problem – an interactionist approach

One of the issues arising from a reductionist perspective is the mind–body problem – the problem of describing the relationship between the mind and body/brain. One solution to this problem (materialism) suggests that ultimately everything is reducible to the physical world. The problem with this kind of reductionism is that it assumes that the physical basis of behaviour has a causal link to the higher levels, whereas we can only observe that certain physical events are *associated* with mental events. For example, certain electrical activity in the brain (during REM sleep) is associated with subjective reports of dreaming. Psychologists often make the mistake of leaping to the assumption that one causes the other.

There is another alternative way to deal with the mind–body problem as well as dealing with reductionism, which is to analyse how the different levels of explanation *interact*. Dualists believe there is a physical brain and a non-physical 'mind' which interact with each other. Research has shown that the mind can affect our biology. For example, Martin *et al.* (2001) found that depressed patients who received psychotherapy experienced the same changes in levels of serotonin and norepinephrine in the brain as those receiving drugs. Kandel (1979) points out that such physiological changes should not be surprising because we know that learning creates new neuronal connections.

▲ Occam's razor expresses the principle of parsimony. Suppose there exist two explanations for an occurrence. According to Occam's razor the simpler one is usually right – and that's often the one at the lowest level. The razor is named after William of Occam, a fourteenth-century Franciscan friar and philosopher.

⬆ UPGRADE

On page 43 we emphasised the importance of working your answers around the specific demands of the questions set. We can follow through on that advice here with an analysis of two more question types.

3. *Discuss biological reductionism in psychology. (6 marks)*

The term 'discuss' in AQA questions is more usually used in essay questions but can also crop up in lower tariff questions such as this. The rule is still the same, i.e. it requires AO1 description and AO3 evaluation. However, unlike the 16-mark essay questions, which assign 6 marks for the description and 10 marks for the evaluation, in these lower value questions there is usually an equal split of AO1 and AO3. So, you would write about 75 words of description and 75 words of evaluation (both restricted to biological reductionism).

4. *Give an example of environmental (stimulus-response) reductionism from an area of psychology that you have studied. (3 marks)*

On the previous page we gave you an example (from attachment theory) for the first mark, followed with an explanation of why this might be considered an example of environmental reductionism (for the second mark), then elaborated this for the third mark. You could try this with your own example.

CAN YOU?　No. 2.5

1. Explain what is meant by *holism*. (3 marks)
2. Explain what is meant by *levels of explanation* in relation to reductionist explanations. (3 marks)
3. Discuss biological reductionism in psychology. (6 marks)
4. Give an example of environmental (stimulus-response) reductionism from an area of psychology that you have studied. (3 marks)
5. Discuss holism and reductionism in psychology. (16 marks)

Idiographic and nomothetic approaches to psychological investigation

The **idiographic approach** is an approach to psychological research that focuses on the individual case as a means of understanding behaviour, rather than aiming to formulate general laws of behaviour (the **nomothetic approach**).

'Nomos' means 'law' in Greek, whereas 'idios' means 'own'. Mainstream psychology has tended to be nomothetic in its approach, but throughout the last century a number of psychologists made significant contributions using idiographic techniques.

▲ Which should be the focus of psychology – the generalisations we can make about all people, or the unique insights gained from the study of a few individuals?

KEY TERMS

Idiographic approach focuses on individuals and emphasises uniqueness; favours qualitative methods in research.

Nomothetic approach seeks to formulate general laws of behaviour based on the study of groups and the use of statistical (quantitative) techniques. It attempts to summarise the differences between people through generalisations.

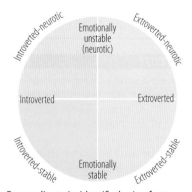

▲ Personality traits identified using factor analysis of data collected using Eysenck's personality test, a nomothetic approach.

THE IDIOGRAPHIC APPROACH

The idiographic approach involves the study of individuals and the unique insights each individual gives us about human behaviour.

Qualitative methods

The idiographic approach is qualitative because the focus is on gaining insights into human behaviour by studying unique individuals in depth rather than gaining numerical data from many individuals and determining average characteristics. The focus is on the quality of information rather than quantity.

It is also qualitative because it employs qualitative methods such as unstructured interviews, case studies and thematic analysis.

Examples of the idiographic approach

Sigmund Freud used case studies of his patients as a way to understand human behaviour, such as the case of Little Hans. This case consists of almost 150 pages of verbatim quotes recorded by Hans' father and descriptions of events in Hans' life, plus Freud's own interpretations of the events (Freud, 1909). Freud did produce generalisations from his case studies, but these are still idiographic because they are drawn from unique individuals.

Humanistic psychologists also favour the idiographic approach as they are concerned with studying the whole person and seeing the world from the perspective of that person. What matters is the person's subjective experience and not something that someone else might observe of their behaviour.

Another example is given in the Research Methods activity on the facing page – the study of Jenny by Gordon Allport was used by him as a way to support his theory of personality (Allport, 1961). Allport believed that this idiographic perspective could tell us more about human behaviour and personality than could the use of personality tests, which only provide statistical information. In fact he called his approach the 'psychology of the individual'.

THE NOMOTHETIC APPROACH

The nomothetic approach involves the study of a large number of people and then seeks to make generalisations or develop laws/theories about their behaviour. This is also the goal of the scientific approach.

Quantitative research

Quantitative research is based on numbers – measures of central tendency and dispersion, graphs and statistical analysis. Such calculations require data from groups of people rather than individuals. Research studies may only involve 20 people, but normative research, such as establishing norms for IQ tests, involves thousands of participants.

Examples of the nomothetic approach

The biological approach seeks to portray the basic principles of how the body and brain work. As we saw earlier in this chapter, this approach has sometimes mistakenly just studied men and assumed that the same processes would occur in women, e.g. the stress response.

Behaviourist psychologists produced general laws of behaviour – classical and operant conditioning. Their research may not have involved thousands of *human* participants, which is the more typical nomothetic approach, but they were seeking one set of rules for all animals – humans and non-humans.

Cognitive psychology is also a nomothetic approach in its aim to develop general laws of behaviour which apply to all people, such as understanding typical memory processes. The cognitive approach does use case studies (such as HM, the man with no short-term memory), but these are required because, in order to understand the working of the normal mind, it is often necessary to look at rare abnormal cases.

Finally, as a comparison with Allport's research on personality, we can consider Hans Eysenck's (1947) psychometric approach to personality. Psychometrics literally means measuring psychological characteristics such as personality and intelligence. Large groups of people are tested, and the distribution of their scores informs us about what is normal and abnormal. In the case of personality, the Eysenck Personality Questionnaire (EPQ) was used to collect large amounts of data which used factor analysis to produce the personality types shown on the left. (Factor analysis is a statistical technique that reduces data to a smaller set of component variables.)

Focus on the individual level

Humanistic psychologists and qualitative psychologists in the latter half of the last century felt that there was too much emphasis on measurement and that psychologists had lost sight of what it was to be human. Allport, who was the first to use the terms idiographic and nomothetic, argued that a drastic reorientation was needed and that's precisely what the idiographic approach did. Allport argued that it is only by knowing the person as a person that we can predict what that person will do in any situation.

Thus the great strength of the idiographic approach has been to focus psychology back on the more individual level.

Scientific basis

A criticism that is made of the idiographic approach is that it is not scientific. In fact this is one of the reasons for the recent growth in positive psychology whose view is that humanistic psychology was not sufficiently evidence-based and therefore any 'findings' were essentially meaningless. The positive approach aims to be more evidence-based.

The same criticisms can't be made about other idiographic approaches (e.g. case studies or qualitative research) which do use an evidence-based approach and also seek to be objective (another important criterion of science). For example, qualitative approaches use reflexivity to identify the influence of any biases. Reflexivity refers to the process where the researcher reflects or thinks critically during the research process about the factors that affect the behaviour of both researchers and participants.

Being able to make predictions

The idiographic approach may be scientific, but the inability to produce general predictions about behaviour is limiting. Such general predictions can be useful, for example in producing drugs to treat mental illness. It would be far too time consuming to produce personal therapies for unique individuals and therefore we need to make predictions about the most likely therapeutic solutions.

However, Allport argued that the idiographic approach does enable predictions. Once a researcher has built up extremely detailed observations of a few individuals, this can be used to make generalisations and formulate theories.

Hall and Lindzey (1970) argue that this stance makes Allport's approach basically nomothetic rather than idiographic!

Time consuming

The idiographic approach is more time consuming. Both approaches are based on large amounts of data, but one is in terms of collecting large amounts of data about one person (idiographic) and the other is in terms of number of people (nomothetic). Collecting large amounts of data from a group of people takes time but, relatively speaking, is quicker because, once you have devised a questionnaire or psychological test, data can be generated and processed quickly.

Combined methods

Holt (1967) argued that the idiographic/nomothetic distinction is a false separation because inevitably generalisations are made. Holt claimed that there is no such thing as a unique individual and what idiographic approaches actually do is generate general principles. In other words the idiographic approach actually ends up being nomothetic (as Hall and Lindzey concluded regarding Allport's approach).

Millon and Davis (1996) suggested that research should start with the nomothetic approach and, once 'laws' have been produced, they can then focus on a more idiographic understanding. In fact the future for drug therapies will probably entail just that – individualised 'recipes' for what is effective based on a mix of genetic and environmental insights.

A number of approaches actually combine the two approaches. Freud used idiographic methods to study people, but also used those insights to produce general laws about human development in his theory of personality.

Finally, uniqueness can be produced using the nomothetic approach – it depends how we define uniqueness. For Allport, only individual traits capture a person's uniqueness, whereas for Eysenck each individual is unique insofar as they have a unique combination of extraversion, introversion and neuroticism. Therefore uniqueness can be explained through nomothetic laws.

You're UNIQUE ... Just like everyone else.

Reynolds

🔎 Research methods

Gordon Allport was a major figure in the study of personality from the early part of the twentieth century. Together with his students he analysed 301 letters from a middle-aged woman given the name Jenny Masterson. The letters were written to Allport and his wife over a period of 12 years (Allport, 1965). The method used in the analysis was similar to thematic analysis.

1. In what way is Allport's approach to research a qualitative one? (2 marks)
2. Think about the possible contents of Jenny's letters (which were about her everyday life). Identify **two** behavioural categories that a researcher might use in analysing these letters. (2 marks)
3. Explain how Allport and his students might have used thematic analysis with the letters from Jenny. Give details of the steps in their analysis. (6 marks)
4. Explain in what way thematic analysis might or might not be considered to be a scientific approach. (4 marks)
5. Identify **one** ethical issue in this research and suggest how Allport should have dealt with this. (3 marks)
6. Another of Allport's students, Jeffrey Paige, used factor analysis (a statistical technique) to analyse the letters leading to the identification of eight factors which were very similar to the themes that emerged from Allport's qualitative analysis. Explain what this shows about Allport's more qualitative approach. (3 marks)

LINK TO RESEARCH METHODS

Thematic analysis on page 13.
Scientific processes on page 20.

CAN YOU? No. 2.6

1. Explain what the terms *idiographic* and *nomothetic* mean. (4 marks)
2. Describe the nomothetic approach to psychological investigation. (4 marks)
3. Evaluate the nomothetic approach to psychological investigation. (6 marks)
4. Discuss idiographic and nomothetic approaches to psychological investigation. (16 marks)

Ethical implications of research studies and theory

You studied ethical issues in psychological research as part of your Year 1 course. So you understand that matters such as deception and privacy are issues because there are no straightforward ways of dealing with them – research has a duty to balance the rights of individual participants against the need for psychologists to produce research that will be useful to all of us.

The ethical implications of psychological research concern the way that research impacts on those who take part in research and also on the way the findings are communicated to the public and how the findings are used. Psychologists have focused particularly on the implications of findings that are socially sensitive.

Socially sensitive research refers to '*studies in which there are potential social consequences or implications, either directly for the participants in research or the class of individuals represented by the research*' (Sieber and Stanley, 1988).

KEY TERMS

Socially sensitive research Any research that might have direct social consequences for the participants in the research or the group that they represent.

All Trials Campaign

Psychologists rely on research into drug therapies to inform ways of treating mental disorders such as depression. Much if not all of research on drug therapies is funded by pharmaceutical companies who have been accused of selective publication of data from such research. For example, it is likely that companies do not publish data that may be harmful to their sales.

The *All Trials Campaign*, spearheaded by medical doctor Ben Goldacre, has called for all research to be made public and, in addition, that all research should actually be pre-registered. Such pre-registration would include stating the intended statistical analysis so that researchers cannot process data in a way which makes the outcome look more favourable to the drug.

Other issues include the fact that researchers often have to agree that institutional sponsors can censor the data produced.

The association PhRMA (Pharmaceutical Research and Manufacturers of America) has defended itself by saying such disclosures would reduce patients' privacy and result in the production of fewer new drugs.

ETHICAL IMPLICATIONS: SOCIAL SENSITIVITY

Part of the process of scientific research is the responsibility that scientists have for the way their research is used. Joan Sieber and Eve Stanley (1988) produced a landmark paper on the issues related to research that has social consequences. They pointed out that the ethical guidelines produced by the American Psychological Association referred to the social implications of research but offered no advice about how such ethical issues might be resolved. Their paper offered a way forward.

The research process

Sieber and Stanley identified four aspects in the research process at which ethical issues with social consequences may occur:

- **The research question** Simply asking a research question (such as 'are there racial differences in IQ?' or 'is homosexuality inherited?') may be damaging to members of a particular racial group or sexual orientation because it appears to add scientific credibility to the prevailing prejudice.
- **Conduct of research and treatment of participants** The main concern is the confidentiality of the information collected (e.g. if a participant confesses to a crime, should confidentiality be maintained?).
- **The institutional context** Research may be funded and managed by private institutions who may misuse the data or may misunderstand the data that is produced (see 'All Trials Campaign' below left). The media may obtain reports of such research and misreport the findings.
- **Interpretation and application of findings** Research findings may be used for purposes other than originally intended. For example, the development of IQ tests by psychologists was subsequently used to demonstrate the inferiority of certain groups of people (see page 45) and was also used to identify the 'feeble-minded' who could then be sterilised (a practice in the US in the early twentieth century).

Ethical issues in socially sensitive research

Sieber and Stanley also identified 10 types of ethical issue that relate especially to socially sensitive research:

- **Privacy** During the research process, a skilled investigator may extract more information from participants than they intended to give. Some research (e.g. AIDS research) may lead to social policies that are an invasion of people's private lives (e.g. through compulsory testing).
- **Confidentiality** Participants may be less willing to divulge information in the future if confidentiality is breached and further related research would be compromised.
- **Valid methodology** In cases of poor methodology (and therefore invalid findings), scientists may be aware of these problems, but the media and the public may not, and thus poor studies might shape important social policy to the detriment of those groups represented by the research.
- **Deception** includes self-deception whereby research may lead people to form untrue stereotypes (e.g. believing that women are less good at maths), which then affects one's own performance.
- **Informed consent** Potential participants may not always comprehend what is involved.
- **Equitable treatment** All participants should be treated in an equitable manner, and resources which are vital to the participants' well-being (e.g. educational opportunities) are not withheld from one group whilst being available to another.
- **Scientific freedom** The scientist has a duty to engage in research but at the same time has an obligation not to harm participants as well as institutions in society.
- **Ownership of data** Some of the problems with determining ownership involve the sponsorship of the research (e.g. a university department or commercial organisation) and the public accessibility of the data.
- **Values** Psychologists differ in their orientation towards subjective (idiographic) approaches and more objective (scientific) approaches. Sensitive issues arise when there is a clash in such values between the scientist and recipient of the research.
- **Risk/benefit ratio** Risks or costs should be minimised, but problems arise in determining risks as well as benefits.

Insider tip…

The specification says 'Ethical implications of research studies and theory, including reference to social sensitivity'. This means that you could be set an essay on ethical implications of research studies and theory. The content for such an essay could draw on what you know about ethical issues in psychological research from your Year 1 course OR you could focus solely on socially sensitive research. Alternatively you could be set an essay on socially sensitive research. Therefore the material on this spread satisfies both possible essays.

EVALUATION

The wider impact of research

There are always some social consequences to participation in research, but with socially sensitive research there is also the increased potential for a more indirect impact on the participant's family, their co-workers, or maybe even the group that the participant represents (e.g. addicts, women, the elderly and so on).

It does not seem sufficient, therefore, to simply safeguard the interests of the individual in research – there must also be some consideration of the likely impact of the research on the larger group of which the participant is a member.

The inadequacy of current ethical guidelines

Psychologists typically deal with ethical issues in research by the development of strict guidelines for the conduct of their studies. Ethical guidelines may protect the immediate needs of research participants, but may not deal with all the possible ways in which research may inflict harm on a group of people or section of society.

For example, at present ethical guidelines don't ask researchers to consider how their research might be used by others, as recommended by Sieber and Stanley. Therefore the considerations outlined some time ago have not yet permeated into professional practice.

May disadvantage marginalised groups

Many groups in society have suffered the consequences of having been excluded from research or being misrepresented when they have been included. It might be argued that our understanding of human behaviour has been lessened by our misinterpretations of, or our failure to include, representative samples of persons with disabilities, the elderly, the disadvantaged and members of minority cultures.

The failure to accurately represent and research such groups carries with it an additional ethical issue – the fact that these groups then miss out on any of the potential benefits of research.

Should socially sensitive research just be avoided?

It might be tempting to think that the solution to the problem of handling socially sensitive research might be to try to avoid it; for example, to avoid research on homosexuality, race, gender, addiction, etc. because the findings may have negative consequences for the participants, for the section of society they represent or indeed for the whole of society. However, this would probably leave psychologists with nothing to examine but unimportant issues.

Sieber and Stanley's view is that to simply ignore sensitive research is not a responsible approach to science. They suggest that avoiding controversial topics, simply because they are controversial, is also an avoidance of responsibility. Therefore psychologists have a duty to conduct such research.

Engaging with the public and policymakers

This research has important applications. In order to reduce the likelihood of misuse of data, psychologists should be energetic in taking responsibility for what happens to their findings. They should be aware of the possibility that the results of their research might lead to abuse and discrimination or, as Sieber and Stanley (1988) suggest, offer 'scientific credibility to the prevailing prejudice'.

The British Psychological Society has a press centre which aims to promote evidence-based psychological research to the media. But it is really a matter for individual researchers to see it as part of the research process to promote their research in a socially sensitive way, as opposed to the neutral position that some scientists wish to take.

⬆ UPGRADE

In the final Upgrade feature for this chapter we continue our analysis of exam questions with two more from the 'Can you…?' section below.

1. *Explain what is meant by 'socially sensitive research.'* (3 marks)

   Although we dealt with this type of question earlier, it is worth emphasising again the importance of doing enough to deserve the full 3 marks available. Students frequently fall into the trap of just dropping in a brief definition (e.g. the 'Key term' definition on the facing page) and then expecting 3 marks. However, you need to help convince the examiner that your answer is worth all 3 marks. A rule of thumb here is, for 3 marks, say three things. For example, define (1), elaborate (2) and give an example (3).

2. *Outline **one** piece of research that is socially sensitive.* (3 marks)

   This is another 3-marker, so the same 'say three things' rule applies. Don't just outline a piece of research, but make sure you explain why that research would be considered socially sensitive. So, (1) identify a piece of research, (2) explain what aspect of the research might be considered 'socially sensitive' and (3) then elaborate on this by considering the ethical implications of this. You could use the examples on this spread (e.g. IQ testing), but you will come across many others throughout your course, so keep this question in the back of your mind!

▶ In their controversial book *The Bell Curve*, Herrnstein and Murray (1994) used psychological research to argue it was a waste of resources to improve the educational opportunities for disadvantaged groups because these groups are genetically destined to be low achievers. Should psychologists just stop doing research that has the potential to be used in this way?

Insider tip…

It is important to link the points made here to examples of research you have studied, which could include research described on the spreads related to gender and cultural bias.

CAN YOU? No. 2.7

1. Explain what is meant by *socially sensitive research*. (3 marks)
2. Outline **one** example of research that is socially sensitive. (3 marks)
3. Discuss the ethical implications of research studies and theory, including reference to social sensitivity. (16 marks)

End-of-chapter review | CHAPTER SUMMARY

We have identified here the key points of the topics on the AQA A level specification, i.e. the bare minimum that you need to know. You may want to fill in further details to elaborate and personalise this material.

GENDER IN PSYCHOLOGY: GENDER BIAS

GENDER BIAS

- Androcentrism – psychology and society is male-dominated, so our world view tends to be focused on men.
- Alpha bias exaggerates the differences and results in one gender (usually women) being devalued.
  - For example, Freud's psychoanalytic theory viewed femininity as failed masculinity; women had penis envy and were morally inferior.
- Beta bias minimises differences, so women's needs are ignored.
  - For example, stress research was based on male responses and it was assumed women responded in the same way; Taylor *et al.* argued for a different tend-and-befriend response.
- Universality can be achieved by acknowledging differences without superiority, such as ethic of care versus justice, or fight-or-flight versus tend-and-befriend.

EVALUATION

- Feminist psychology – there are real differences, but social stereotypes cause more damage than any real biological differences; by identifying such stereotypes the balance can be redressed.
- Bias in research methods – poor methodology (single-sex samples, male-only experimenters) may disadvantage one gender.
- Reverse alpha bias – change preconceptions with research that over-values women, e.g. women are better learners (Cornwell *et al.*).
- Avoiding a beta bias – equal rights may disadvantage women because they do have different needs, e.g. equal parental leave ignores special biological demands on women.
- Assumptions need to be examined – Darwin's theory of sexual selection has been challenged as rooted in Victorian ideas about female coyness.

CULTURE IN PSYCHOLOGY: CULTURAL BIAS

CULTURAL BIAS

- Bias produces differences that don't exist (Hare-Mustin and Marecek).
- Example of alpha bias – individualist versus collectivist cultures; difference not found in meta-analysis of conformist behaviour (Takano and Osaka).
- Example of beta bias – Western-based IQ tests used to measure other cultural groups who then appear less intelligent (an imposed etic).
- Ethnocentrism – assuming one's own beliefs are the correct ones.
  - Alpha bias because difference leads to devaluing the other group (e.g. seeing attachment as related to independence, a Western preference).
  - Beta bias because of assumptions that there are no differences in intelligence and therefore it is acceptable to use Western IQ tests.
- Cultural relativism – relating the behaviour of cultural groups to their own standards.
  - Beta bias because may mistakenly assume symptoms of mental disorder are universal (e.g. hearing voices); results in misdiagnosis.
  - Alpha bias if psychologists assume there are differences and overlook universals.

EVALUATION

- Indigenous psychologies, each rooted in their own culture, such as Afrocentrism that seeks to understand the culture of Africans.
- The emic–etic distinction – indigenous psychology is an emic approach; an etic (universal) approach can use indigenous researchers for data collection (e.g. Buss *et al.*).
- Bias in research methods – samples in textbooks mainly American (Smith and Bond) and mainly middle-class, young adults (Sears, Henrich *et al.*).
- Consequences of cultural bias – US Army IQ tests led to enduring and damaging stereotypes about black and immigrant populations (Gould).
- The worldwide psychology community meets much more now than 50 years ago, which should reduce ethnocentrism and cultural bias.

FREE WILL AND DETERMINISM

DETERMINISM

- Hard determinism – all behaviour is determined, there is no free will.
- Soft determinism – biological factors and past experience present a range of choices; we feel more free in situations with little constraint.
- Biological determinism – individual genes (e.g. IGF2R role in IQ, Hill *et al.*) or neurotransmitters (dopamine hypothesis of schizophrenia).
- Environmental determinism – all behaviour caused by previous experiences, as in classical and operant conditioning. Stimulus-response can explain phobias, aggression and gender development.
- Psychic determinism – adult personality is caused by a mix of innate drives (libido) and early experience (frustration or indulgence).
- Scientific determinism – science seeks causal relationships by manipulating an IV and observing the effect on a DV, e.g. Harlow's attachment experiment.

EVALUATION

- Genetic determinism – twin studies do not show 100% concordance even with identical genes.
- Environmental determinism – twin studies also show that there is some genetic contribution; therefore experience is not sole determinant.
- Scientific determinism – even in the physical sciences relationships are regarded as probabilistic (chaos theory); determinist research in psychology oversimplifies human behaviour.
- Does it matter? A determinist position suggests criminals might excuse their behaviour on genetic grounds or that mental disorder must be treated using drugs or conditioning.

FREE WILL

- Humanistic approach – self-determination is required for mental health (Rogers), otherwise can't take control of negative behaviours.
- Moral responsibility – adults are accountable for their behaviour regardless of innate factors or poor early environment.

EVALUATION

- The illusion of free will – being able to make choices does not mean you are free.
- Culturally relative – free will may be less important in collectivist cultures.
- Research to challenge free will – Libet *et al.* found brain activity before a decision was made; however, Trevana and Miller found it is a readiness potential, not an intention to move.

THE NATURE–NURTURE DEBATE

NATURE–NURTURE

- Nature – innate influences which may appear at any stage of life.
  - Genetic explanations – MZ twins more likely to both develop schizophrenia than DZ twins (Joseph).
  - Evolutionary explanations – attachment is adaptive because it aids survival and reproduction (Bowlby); it relies on genetic transmission.
- Nurture – the social and physical environment/experiences; we are born as a blank slate.
  - Behaviourism – classical and operant conditioning can explain the formation of attachment.
  - Social learning theory – the urge to be aggressive may be biological, but we learn how to express this through direct and indirect reinforcement (Bandura).
  - Other explanations, e.g. Bateson's double bind theory of schizophrenia is based on experience.

EVALUATION

- Nature and nurture cannot be separated – like the length and width of a rectangle (Hebb), or phenylketonuria which is genetic but not expressed if given the right diet.
- Diathesis-stress – a person's nature (diathesis) is only expressed under certain conditions of nurture (stressor).
- Nature affects nurture – indirect genetic influences: reactive (one's behaviour changes the environment), passive (parents influence the home environment) or active (niche picking).
- Nurture affects nature – neural plasticity, as in Maguire *et al.*'s study of spatial memory in taxi drivers, or Blakemore and Cooper's study of perception in kittens.
- Epigenetics – material in each cell that acts as switches to turn genes on and off, which is passed on to subsequent generations. Explains why MZ twins and clones are not identical.

HOLISM AND REDUCTIONISM

HOLISM

- Cannot predict behaviour of whole system from individual parts.
- Gestalt psychology – concerned with perception; the whole does not equal the sum of the parts. ·
- Humanistic psychology – we react as a whole rather than a set of S-R links.
- Cognitive psychology – connectionist networks for memory behave as a whole.

REDUCTIONISM

- Levels of explanation – highest = cultural/social, middle = psychological, lowest = biological.
- Biological reductionism – behaviour explained in terms of hormones, neurotransmitters, brain (e.g. dopamine hypothesis of schizophrenia).
- Environmental (stimulus-response) reductionism – behaviour such as attachment explained in terms of a stimulus (food/mother) causing a response (pleasure).
- Experimental reductionism – use of operationalised variables in experimental research.

EVALUATION

- Danger of lower levels of explanation – the real meaning of behaviour may be overlooked, e.g. prescribing drugs for hyperactivity which might be due to family problems.
- Biological reductionism – drug therapies have only had partial success and may block possibility of more successful psychological therapies.
- Environmental reductionism – may be appropriate for non-human animals but ignores influence from higher levels, e.g. emotion.
- Experimental reductionism has been productive but may not represent real life, e.g. research on eyewitness testimony by Yuille and Cutshall didn't support experimental research.
- The mind–body problem – materialism assumes that physical states (e.g. REM electrical activity) cause mental events (dreams); alternatively dualists suggest mind and body interact in both directions; the mind can cause physical changes.

IDIOGRAPHIC AND NOMOTHETIC APPROACHES TO PSYCHOLOGICAL INVESTIGATION

THE IDIOGRAPHIC APPROACH

- Focus on individuals and their unique characteristics as a way to understand human behaviour.
- Qualitative research – focuses on depth (details) of one individual; use of qualitative methods (e.g. unstructured interviews, thematic analysis).
- Examples – Freud's case studies (e.g. Little Hans), humanistic research into subjective experience, Allport's letters from Jenny.

THE NOMOTHETIC APPROACH

- Study of large numbers of people to establish laws about behaviour.
- Quantitative research – large data sets used to work out averages and conduct statistical tests, producing normative data about behaviour.
- Examples – biological approach (general principles, e.g. stress response), behavioural approach (laws of conditioning), cognitive psychology (case studies have to be used for abnormal behaviour), Eysenck's personality theory.

EVALUATION

- Focus on the individual level – humanistic and qualitative psychologists felt that nomothetic psychology had lost sight of what it was to be human.
- Scientific basis – humanistic psychology may not be evidence-based but idiographic approaches do seek to be systematic and objective.
- Being able to make predictions – Allport argued that predictions can be made from individual cases, but that makes his approach nomothetic.
- Time consuming – nomothetic techniques can produce large data sets and then analyse them more quickly.
- Combined methods – the idiographic approach ends up being nomothetic (Holt); start with a nomothetic approach and then focus on idiographic (Millon); combine approaches, e.g. Freud.

ETHICAL IMPLICATIONS OF RESEARCH STUDIES AND THEORY

SOCIAL SENSITIVITY

- The research process may have social consequences (Sieber and Stanley):
  - Research question may damage some groups.
  - Conduct of research, especially confidentiality.
  - Institutional context may lead to data misuse or misunderstanding.
  - Interpretation and application of findings, e.g. IQ tests used to promote black stereotypes.
- Ethical issues in socially sensitive research; for example:
  - Privacy – participants may reveal more than they intended.
  - Valid methodology – poor methods omitted from media reports.
  - Values – scientists seek general laws, whereas participants interested in individuals.
  - Risk/benefit ratio – hard to determine.

EVALUATION

- The wider impact of research – family, co-workers, etc. may be affected and need safeguarding.
- Inadequacy of current ethical guidelines, e.g. researchers not required to consider the use of their research.
- May disadvantage marginalised groups who are not included as research participants and then research findings can't be applied to them.
- Can't avoid socially sensitive research – psychologists have a responsibility to tackle difficult topics.
- Engaging with the public and policymakers – individual psychologists should actively promote the benefits of their research.

| 0 1 | Explain what universality means in psychology. | [3 marks] |

| 0 2 | Which **one** of the following types of bias occurs when the differences between females and males is understated? Write the letter of your chosen answer in your answer booklet. | [1 mark] |

A. alpha bias

B. androcentrism

C. beta bias

D. cultural bias

| 0 3 | Outline **one** example of androcentrism in psychological theory. | [3 marks] |

| 0 4 | Describe **one** example where cultural bias has affected research findings. | [3 marks] |

| 0 5 | Explain the difference between androcentrism and ethnocentrism in psychology. | [3 marks] |

| 0 6 | Briefly discuss the view that cultural relativism is a type of cultural bias. | [6 marks] |

| 0 7 | Read the case below and then answer the question that follows. |

> Ruth: I am hopeless at maths – I was born to fail my GCSE, and there is nothing I can do about it.
> Theo: I disagree. You need to find the motivation to want to do better and then you will.

With reference to the above conversation, outline what is free will and determinism. **[6 marks]**

| 0 8 | (i) Name **one** psychological approach which supports the idea of psychic determinism. | [1 mark] |

(ii) Name **one** psychological approach which supports the idea of environmental determinism. **[1 mark]**

| 0 9 | Explain why biological determinism is an example of hard determinism. | [4 marks] |

| 1 0 | Explain the role of free will in psychology. Refer to **one** topic or behaviour you have studied to support your answer. | [6 marks] |

| 1 1 | Distinguish between the terms nature and nurture. | [2 marks] |

| 1 2 | Read the following case and answer the question that follows. |

> Tony and Clive both play tennis to a high standard. Tony believes that his skill is innate, whereas Clive explains his in terms of the effort he has put into training since his childhood.

With reference to the above case, outline what is meant by the nature–nurture debate in psychology. **[4 marks]**

| 1 3 | Outline **one** research study that shows the relative importance of heredity in determining human behaviour. | [3 marks] |

| 1 4 | Choose **one** psychological approach and explain how it supports the relative importance of the environment in determining human behaviour. | [4 marks] |

| 1 5 | Discuss the view that heredity is more important than the environment in determining human behaviour. Refer to **one** behaviour you have studied as part of your response. | [8 marks] |

| 1 6 | Briefly discuss the value of taking an interactionist approach in psychology. | [6 marks] |

| 1 7 | Outline **two** levels of explanation that could be used to explain a behaviour you have studied in psychology. | [6 marks] |

| 1 8 | Describe **two** limitations of using a holistic approach to explain human behaviour. | [4 marks] |

| 1 9 | Outline **one** strength and **one** weakness of taking a reductionist approach in psychology. | [4 marks] |

2 0 Read the case below and answer the question that follows.

> Some researchers believe that people have no choice over their sexuality and that it is genetically determined. Others accept there is a genetic component but say we cannot ignore the influence of upbringing on people's sexual behaviour, and how this interacts with the norms and values of society.

Briefly discuss **both** biological determinism **and** biological reductionism. Refer to the case above as part of your discussion. **[8 marks]**

2 1 Outline what is meant by stimulus-response psychology and explain how this is an example of environmental reductionism. **[4 marks]**

2 2 Which **two** of the following are features of the nomothetic approach? Write the letters of your chosen answers in your answer booklet. **[2 marks]**

    A. analysis of quantitative data

    B. emphasis on subjective experience

    C. making generalisations

    D. recognising the role of free will

    E. use of the case study method

2 3 Outline **one** strength and **one** limitation of using the idiographic approach to study human behaviour. **[4 marks]**

2 4 Describe **one** research study that has taken an idiographic approach in psychology. **[3 marks]**

2 5 Read the case below and answer the question that follows.

> A psychologist surveyed a large sample of students and found that males were more likely to be addicted to computer gaming than females. However, she was interested in carrying out a follow-up interview with one of the females whose addiction levels were much higher than anyone else's.

Discuss the value of adopting both a nomothetic and idiographic approach in psychology. Refer to the case above as part of your discussion. **[8 marks]**

2 6 Using an example, explain how a theory can be socially sensitive. **[4 marks]**

2 7 Briefly discuss **two** ethical implications that can arise in psychological research. **[6 marks]**

2 8 Read the case below and answer the questions that follow.

> A psychologist used a stratified sample of 100 participants in order to investigate the reasons why people lie. He used a questionnaire with a series of statements that participants had to strongly agree, agree, disagree or strongly disagree with.

    (i) Explain how the sample in this study supports a nomothetic approach. **[4 marks]**

    (ii) Explain the level of data used in this study. **[3 marks]**

2 9 Read the case below and answer the questions that follow.

> A psychologist used a covert observation to record how males and females behave differently when out on a date. She used behavioural categories in order to collect quantitative data. However, when the report on the investigation was published, critics said the results were unreliable due to the psychologist's cultural bias.

    (i) Outline **one** strength and **one** weakness of using a covert observation in this investigation. **[4 marks]**

    (ii) Explain how behavioural categories may have been used in this investigation. **[3 marks]**

    (iii) Outline what is meant by cultural bias in psychological investigations. **[2 marks]**

    (iv) Outline how the reliability of this study could have been improved. **[3 marks]**

The exam questions on issues and debates will be varied but are likely to involve some short answer questions (AO1), some application of knowledge questions (AO2), research methods questions and possibly an extended writing question (AO1 + AO3). We've provided answers to some additional questions together with comments from an examiner about how well they've each done.

---

01 Briefly explain why gender bias is a concern in psychology. *(4 marks)*

Maisie's answer

Gender bias is a concern in psychology because a lot of research is by male researchers using male participants and this means that the outcome doesn't represent women very well. For example Milgram conducted his original studies of obedience using men only and generalised this to all people. Kohlberg constructed a theory about moral development and used all boys and also wrote a theory from a male perspective of what morals are about – he thought it was only about justice whereas Gilligan suggested that an ethic of care was also important and a more female orientation.

Examiner's comments

This response earns 2 of the 4 marks available. It focuses on one type of gender bias and then explains why it is an issue in terms of generalisability. The examples do not really add to the answer, especially when they make the same kind of point.

Ciaran's answer

There are two kinds of bias – an alpha bias and a beta bias. With an alpha bias, there is tendency to exaggerate differences between men and women. The consequence is that theories devalue one gender in comparison to the other. With a beta bias there is a tendency to ignore or minimise differences between men and women. Such theories tend either to ignore questions about the lives of women, or assume that insights derived from studies of men will apply equally well to women. Both of these are concerns for psychology because they result in genders being misrepresented.

Examiner's comments

This is a 4-mark response. It helps that Ciaran has included two types of gender bias as this gives him more to write about. The issues around both types are explained as required and, indeed, his final point takes the explanation further and is a good place to end.

---

02 Read the item below and answer the question that follows.

> Helen and Heather are identical twins who were raised very similarly. As children, they used to score more or less the same on intelligence tests. Now they are adults, Helen consistently scores much higher than Heather. Researchers have explained this in terms of Helen's much better diet and fitness regime.

Explain what is meant by an interactionist approach in the nature–nurture debate. Refer to the case of Helen and Heather as part of your answer. *(4 marks)*

Maisie's answer

An interactionist approach is one that mixes both nature and nurture explanations and suggests that taken together they offer an explanation of behaviour. In the scenario you can see that the differences between Helen and Heather can be explained in an interactionist way. If it was just nature then they would have remained similar even as adults because they share identical genes. But they had different environmental influences (Helen had a better diet and fitness regime) and these interact with their nature.

Examiner's comments

This answer is worth 2 marks. 1 mark is for a weak but creditworthy definition of interactionism, and there is a further mark for linking this to the stem. Application would have been better if there had been a clearer focus on intelligence and how this manifests itself.

Ciaran's answer

According to the nature approach we are determined by innate factors, i.e. genes that we have inherited. According to the nurture approach (e.g. behaviourists) we are entirely determined by life experiences and the environment we live in. The interactionist approach says it isn't one or the other but they combine to produce what we become. In the case of the identical twins their ultimate behaviour is not just a product of their identical genes but differences in their environment as they have got older.

Examiner's comments

This answer is worth 2 marks. Both marks are for a relatively accurate outline of the concept of interactionism. However, there is no explicit reference to the stem (apart from mentioning identical twins) and this is not enough for the AO2 marks on offer.

---

03 Explain the difference between holism and reductionism in psychology. *(4 marks)*

Maisie's answer

Holism refers to seeing behaviour as a whole. Reductionism means reducing a behaviour to constituent parts such as environmental reductionism or biological reductionism. For example, a complex condition such as schizophrenia can be investigated holistically by looking at the factors that interact to cause it or the disorder can be reduced to the behaviour of parts of the brain or action of neurotransmitters which are both biological elements of a person.

Examiner's comments

Maisie would earn 3 marks here. She has shown she understands what holism and reductionism are, by dealing with each separately. Her example of schizophrenia is then useful in helping her to begin to draw out a distinction between the two. She could have elaborated on this, for example, by focusing on a broader distinction between being more or less scientific.

Ciaran's answer

The difference between these terms is that holism emphasises the whole whereas reductionism focuses on splitting a behaviour into smaller parts which can then be used to understand the target behaviour. Gestalt psychologists believed that the whole is greater than the sum of the parts (a holist approach). In contrast experimental psychologists prefer to operationalise behaviours into separate variables that can be tested in an experiment and produce useful scientific data.

Examiner's comments

This answer would earn Ciaran 3 marks. He clearly knows what holism and reductionism are and his use of words and phrases such as 'whereas' and 'in contrast' allow him to make a more explicit distinction. However, the distinction is not always obvious – for example, in the first statement it would be more useful if Ciaran wrote 'emphasises the whole *behaviour*' to make more sense of what follows.

04 Briefly discuss the extent to which soft determinism can support the scientific emphasis on causal explanations. *(8 marks)*

Maisie's answer

Soft determinism is an attempt to explain determinism in a way that allows for some free will. For example Heather suggested that everything is determined but this produces a range of possible behaviours and people are free to choose within this range. Therefore there is some free will. A totally free will position makes scientific research difficult because it is looking for cause and effect. However, the soft determinism approach means we can investigate the kind of decisions that people make.

In fact there is research on soft determinism that shows that people do exercise free will when in situations with little constraint but feel less free when in situations with more constraint, i.e. where there are few choices. Westcott did research asking students to indicate when they felt most free and they select situations where there was less constraint.

The scientific emphasis on causal explanations can be seen within this framework. The ideal of science is to demonstrate that an independent variable invariably causes a dependent variable. However, more recent approaches to science are more probabilistic, allowing for increasing (or decreasing) likelihood of something happening and this can be related to constraints in a situation.

Examiner's comments

Maisie demonstrates sound knowledge and understanding of both soft determinism and the scientific emphasis on causal explanations easily securing AO1 credit. There is also some good discussion around the extent to which soft determinism allows science to happen in psychology. Maisie tends to focus on the idea that soft determinism is still largely determinist, whereas a more balanced answer would look at the free will elements and how these challenge science. Overall, though, the answer is still worth 7 marks given the insight shown.

05 Read the item below and answer the question that follows.

> A psychologist surveyed a large sample of students and found that males were more likely to be addicted to computer gaming than females. However, she was interested in carrying out a follow-up interview with one of the females whose addiction levels were much higher than anyone else's.

Discuss the value of adopting both a nomothetic and idiographic approach in psychology. Refer to the case above as part of your discussion. *(16 marks)*

Ciaran's answer

There are two opposing approaches to research in psychology. The nomothetic approach aims to produce general laws of behaviour based on the study of groups of people and the use of quantitative techniques. In the scenario the first kind of research is nomothetic as a large sample of students was used and came to a general conclusion about male and female behaviour.

In contrast the idiographic approach focuses on individuals – so the researcher in the scenario then went on to conduct an interview with just one person which meant she would have collected qualitative data. She would find out things like why the girl was addicted and would ask follow-up questions which would supply deeper insights into the experiences of girls and computer gaming.

Both approaches are trying to understand why people do what they do, but some psychologists think that the problem with studying just one person or a few people is that they may have special characteristics and therefore it is important to look at large numbers. In particular the aim of science is to discover general laws about the world, so this approach means that you can discover general principles. The objection is that knowing about averages doesn't really reveal what people are like because people are different.

The solution is probably to use a combination of both approaches and that is what is suggested in the scenario. The scenario describes a researcher who firstly does a large-scale study about computer gaming and gender differences in addiction but then focuses on the micro level, looking in detail at what the experience is like and why this one person might have become addicted. Furthermore Holt argued that there is not really such a clear distinction between the two approaches. Even the idiographic approach ultimately seeks to make generalisations from the detailed information collected. Holt said people aren't unique and so you can draw conclusions and see if it fits other cases. Furthermore Millon says that the approach in the scenario is the one to take – start with nomothetic research and then fine tune the understanding with idiographic approaches.

One disadvantage of this is that idiographic approaches are time-consuming – it takes time to interview individuals and then more time to analyse the data collected by looking for trends and themes in the data. Collecting large amounts of data and doing statistical analyses is quicker and researchers also use meta-analysis to combine the results of many studies.

Examiner's comments

Ciaran has produced a high scoring Level 3 response here. He demonstrates he understands the difference between the two approaches – not just through definition but also as the discussion develops. He has made reference to the item as required, and made the connection between the information provided and what he knows about the idiographic and nomothetic approaches. Ciaran's essay has a good discursive style where he goes backwards and forwards between the two sides of the debate, considering relevant strengths and limitations. There could have been more focus on the strengths of an idiographic approach to offer more balance. It would also have been better if he had made more reference to the item when doing this. The essay would also benefit from a clearer conclusion – indeed, the point about combining approaches may have been more effective at the end of the essay. This suggests that Ciaran could have planned the structure of his essay more carefully.

CONTENTS OF CHAPTER

SPECIFICATION CHECKLIST

- The evolutionary explanations for partner preferences, including the relationship between sexual selection and human reproductive behaviour.

- Factors affecting attraction in romantic relationships: self-disclosure; physical attractiveness, including the matching hypothesis; filter theory, including social demography, similarity in attitudes and complementarity.

- Theories of romantic relationships: social exchange theory, equity theory and Rusbult's investment model of commitment, satisfaction, comparison with alternatives and investment. Duck's phase model of relationship breakdown: intra-psychic, dyadic, social and grave dressing phases.

- Virtual relationships in social media: self-disclosure in virtual relationships; effects of absence of gating on the nature of virtual relationships.

- Parasocial relationships: levels of parasocial relationships, the absorption addiction model and the attachment theory explanation.

Mate selection and lonely hearts ads

Cast a glance at the personal ads in your local newspaper and you get the impression that men and women adopt broadly distinct strategies and that these conform to predictions from evolutionary theory. According to evolutionary theory, because women have a greater biological investment in their offspring (nine months of pregnancy followed by years of care), they tend to be particularly choosy in the type of mate they require. To an ancestral female, *resources* would have been everything, as resources were associated with safety and security for her and her offspring. Males offering resources, or traits indicating the potential for resources, such as ambition or industriousness, would have been particularly attractive to a woman looking for a mate. Ancestral males, on the other hand, would have valued *fertility* in a mate, i.e. the potential to bear him lots of children. Characteristics such as youth and physical attractiveness would have indicated greater fertility and health, so these would be important for males when choosing a mate.

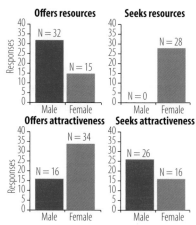

It is easy enough to imagine that these considerations would have been important millions of years ago, when our ancestors faced a very harsh environment and a high infant mortality rate. What is particularly interesting is that these same trends still operate today. Researchers such as Thiessen *et al*. (1993) and Waynforth and Dunbar (1995) have found evidence of these same gender differences operating in the personal ads today. The personal ads (or lonely hearts ads as they are sometimes called) act as a sort of mate selection arena, where males and females offer certain characteristics in an attempt to attract a mate, whilst at the same time requesting qualities they would like in return. Thiessen *et al*.'s study, summarised above, showed that men typically offer resources and seek attractiveness, while for women it is the other way round.

TRY THIS

Much of the research in this area is now over 20 years old, and it is distinctly possible that the trends identified by researchers such as Thiessen have changed and a GSOH (great sense of humour) is more important than ambition and industriousness. However, if our partner preferences really are driven by evolutionary forces, then we should expect to find males still offering resources and seeking attractiveness and females still offering attractiveness and seeking resources.

To find out, head for the personal ads in your local paper or on websites (only the free ones, and avoid the 'adult' ones!). Look for any mention of attractiveness (e.g. 'pretty', 'handsome' or a reference to some feature that might be considered attractive, such as 'youthful' or 'slim') and any mention of resources (e.g. 'company director', 'graduate' or a reference to some characteristic related to resources, such as 'ambitious' or 'hardworking'). Keep a record of whether it is a male or female, and whether they are offering or seeking the characteristic in question. If you combine your data with other people's, you will end up with graphs like the ones above.

Some questions to ask:

1. Are these gender differences still apparent, i.e. what do your graphs actually tell you?
2. What other reasons are there for these gender differences other than evolutionary forces?
3. Is this an appropriate way to assess gender differences in mate preferences? Can you think of a more valid way to do this?

Evolutionary explanations for partner preferences

Reproductive success is at the very heart of the evolutionary process. Among early humans, those who failed to mate also failed to become ancestors. For our ancestors, successful mating was a complex business, involving selecting the right mate, out-competing rivals and then engaging in all the right behaviours to ensure successful conception and child-rearing. **Evolutionary explanations** for partner preferences are important because they give us some insight into who is likely to be excluded from and included in mating. Those favoured mate characteristics that are, to some degree at least, inherited (such as physical attractiveness and intelligence) will then be represented more frequently in subsequent generations. This process is referred to as **sexual selection**.

'Sexual selection depends not on a struggle for existence in relation to other organic beings or to external conditions, but on a struggle between the individuals of one sex, generally the males, for possession of the other sex.' (Darwin, 1871)

The power of sexual selection

It becomes clear why sexual selection is such a powerful influence on mate selection when we consider the impact on future generations. Individuals who manage to mate pass on their genes to their children, who pass on these genes to *their* children and so on. On the other hand, an individual who doesn't mate never gets to pass on their genes. Even if they live to a ripe old age, those genes never get passed on to anyone. When viewed from this perspective, we are all the result of successful sexual selection, when our ancestors either outcompeted other individuals or possessed the right characteristics for selection as a mate.

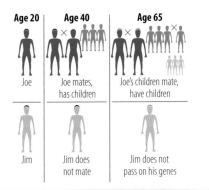

Age 20	Age 40	Age 65
Joe	Joe mates, has children	Joe's children mate, have children
Jim	Jim does not mate	Jim does not pass on his genes

You might consider why youth and physical attractiveness are indicators of reproductive capacity in women, and why the potential to provide resources is so important for women when choosing a male mate.

Key study: Buss (1989)

David Buss explored what males and females looked for in a long-term partner.

Procedure   The study involved over 10,000 people from 37 different cultures. Participants were asked to rate each of 18 characteristics (e.g. physical attractiveness, good financial prospect) on how important they would be in choosing a mate. A four-point scale was used, ranging from '3' (indispensable) to '0' (irrelevant).

Findings   Among the main results were the following:
- **Resources**: Women more than men desired mates who were 'good financial prospects'. This translated into a desire for men with resources, or qualities such as ambition and industriousness.
- **Physical attractiveness**: Men placed more importance on physical attractiveness. This provides cues to a woman's health and hence her fertility and reproductive value.
- **Youth**: Men universally wanted mates who were younger than them – an indication that men valued increased fertility in potential mates.
- **Other important characteristics**: Both sexes wanted mates who were intelligent (linked to skill at parenting) and kind (linked to an interest in long-term relationships).

THE NATURE OF SEXUAL SELECTION

In 1871, Charles Darwin developed his less well-known (after natural selection) theory of evolution – the theory of sexual selection. This theory explains the evolution of characteristics that confer a *reproductive* advantage as opposed to a *survival* advantage. In sexual selection, an individual's survival is not at stake, but rather it is their ability to leave more descendants.

Intrasexual selection

Sexual selection operates in two main ways. In *intrasexual selection*, individuals of one sex (usually males) must outcompete other members of their sex in order to gain access to members of the other sex. Successful individuals are able to mate and so are able to pass on their genes. The losers are not able to mate and so are not able to pass on their genes. Whatever characteristic leads to success in these same-sex contests (e.g. greater size and strength, cunning, etc.) becomes more widespread in the gene pool by virtue of the reproductive advantage this gives to the winners.

Intersexual selection

In *intersexual selection*, members of one sex evolve preferences for desirable qualities in potential mates. Members of the opposite sex who possess these characteristics (e.g. attractiveness, status, resources) will then gain a mating advantage over those who do not. The preferences of one sex, therefore, determine the areas in which the other sex must compete.

Sexual selection and long-term mate preferences

Why do mechanisms for mate choice evolve? Being choosy requires time and energy, and the costs of mate choice can even impair survival in some cases. The rationale behind sexual selection is that random mating is essentially stupid mating. It pays to be choosy, as the genetic quality of a mate will determine half the genetic quality of any offspring. Low-quality mates (e.g. those who are unattractive and unhealthy) will be more likely to produce unattractive, unhealthy offspring. By joining forces with an attractive, high-quality mate, offspring are higher quality and an individual's genes are much more likely to be passed on.

For females, this means being attracted to males who (i) are able to invest resources in her and her children, (ii) are able to physically protect her and her children, (iii) show promise as a good parent and (iv) are sufficiently compatible to ensure minimal costs to her and her children (Buss, 2003). However, males do not give away their resources indiscriminately – therefore males would be most attracted to females who display signals of fertility, an indication of their reproductive value. Buss's research (see left) explored sex differences in long-term mate choice and found universal trends in male and female preferences.

▲ Females are attracted to males who show promise as a good parent

Cultural traditions may be just as important as evolutionary forces

Bernstein (2015) points out that gender differences in mate preference patterns might stem from cultural traditions rather than being the result of evolved characteristics. For example, the fact that women have been denied economic and political power in many cultures might account for their tendency to rely on the security and economic resources provided by men. An analysis of 37 cultures (Kasser and Sharma, 1999) showed that women valued potential mates' access to resources far more in those cultures where women's status and educational opportunities were sharply limited. This suggests that although findings such as those in Buss's study (see facing page) may show evidence of evolutionary forces at work in mate selection, we should not underestimate the role of social and economic factors in establishing mate preference patterns.

Female preferences for high-status men may not be universal

Buller (2005) claims that evolutionary psychologists are mistaken in their claims of a universal female preference for high-status men as mates. He argues that the majority of studies attempting to determine female mate preferences have been carried out on female undergraduate students. These women expect to achieve high educational status and so have expectations of high income levels. The fact that these women prefer high-status men might be explained by a general preference for high-status men, or it may be better explained in terms of a preference for men with similar interests, education and prospects to their own. As a result, Buller concludes that the evidence for a universal female mating preference for high-status men is weak or non-existent.

Mate choice in real life

Studies such as Buss's survey of mate choice might suffer from a serious problem of validity – i.e. they give us an indication of expressed preferences rather than being a reflection of what actually happens in real life. However, many real-life studies also support these mate-choice hypotheses. For example, a study of actual marriages in 29 cultures (Buss, 1989) confirmed that men do choose younger women. In addition, some critics suggest that questionnaires such as the ones used in Buss's study are *more* valid measures of partner preference than real-life marriage statistics, particularly in cultures where arranged marriages are the *norm*.

Mate choice and the menstrual cycle

Research by Penton-Voak *et al.* (1999) suggests that, far from being constant, female mate choice varies across the menstrual cycle. They found that women chose a slightly feminised version of a male face as 'most attractive' for a long-term relationship. However, for a short-term sexual relationship, during the high conception risk phase of the menstrual cycle, the preferred face shape was more masculinised. Sexual selection may well have favoured females who pursue a mixed mating strategy under certain conditions. A female might choose a main partner whose feminised appearance suggests kindness and cooperation in parental care, but might also copulate with a male with a more masculine appearance when conception is most likely. Such males are likely to have higher levels of the sex hormone testosterone, which suppresses the immune system. A male who is healthy despite this must, therefore, have a highly efficient immune system – a very valuable characteristic to pass on to offspring.

Is there a human equivalent of the peacock's tail?

Research supports the view that some human traits that serve no survival purpose have evolved purely as a result of sexual selection. For example, a preference for highly creative partners has been a characteristic of mate choice throughout evolutionary history. Nettle and Clegg (2006) compared a sample of contemporary British poets and artists and a control group of males in the non-creative professions. They found that males in the creative professions tended to have significantly more sexual partners, and the amount of their creative output was positively correlated with the number of sexual partners. This suggests that females are motivated to choose creative males because of the potential adaptive value of creativity and ingenuity that would be passed on to their offspring.

◄ Prolific Spanish artist Pablo Picasso was married twice and had four children by three different women. He also had affairs with dozens, perhaps hundreds, of women throughout his adult life, until he died at the age of 91.

UPGRADE

Boosting your AO1 marks

Extended writing questions (okay, let's call them essays…) are typically worth 16 marks each. Although AQA do not award separate marks for AO1 (description) and AO3 (evaluation), they do nominally assign a certain number of marks for each in their marking schemes. Of the 16 marks available for an essay question, 6 are assigned to AO1 and 10 to AO3, so it pays to be aware of this when structuring your essays. Assuming most students would write about 480 words in response to a 16-mark question, that would mean writing about 180 words of AO1, 30 words each for the 6 points.

To gain a mark in the top mark level for an essay question, the descriptive (AO1, remember…) content should be 'accurate and generally well detailed'. But how do you achieve this? First of all, don't waste time with pointless introductions and definitions – they won't get you any marks. Then pick six things you want to say that cover the AO1 part of the question. To make your answer more 'detailed', think about fleshing out a study or explanation, going a bit deeper and perhaps giving an example to push each point up to the 25-word target. Of course, the content also has to be accurate, but that's down to you!

KEY TERMS

Evolutionary explanations focus on the adaptive nature of behaviour, i.e. modern behaviours are believed to have evolved because they solved challenges faced by our distant ancestors and so became more widespread in the gene pool.

Sexual selection A key part of Darwin's theory explaining how evolution is driven by competition for mates, and the development of characteristics that ensure reproductive success.

CAN YOU?   No. 3.1

1. Explain what is meant by *sexual selection*. (2 marks)
2. Outline the sexual selection explanation of partner preferences. (4 marks)
3. Explain **one** limitation of the sexual selection explanation of partner preferences. (2 marks)
4. Briefly outline and evaluate the findings of **one** research study into evolutionary explanations for partner preferences. (4 marks)
5. Discuss evolutionary explanations for partner preferences. (16 marks)
6. Discuss the relationship between sexual selection and human reproductive behaviour. (16 marks)

Physical attractiveness

Research on partner preferences suggests that men in particular place great importance on physical attractiveness when choosing a mate. Physical appearance is an important cue to a woman's health and hence her fertility and reproductive value. Although the nature of physical attractiveness may vary across cultures, its importance in attraction does not. As well as physical attractiveness, a number of other variables determine attraction, and ultimately how satisfied a person is with their relationship. On this spread we look at the importance of physical attractiveness in determining attraction, and introduce the idea of 'matching', the tendency for people to choose partners of similar attractiveness to themselves.

Darwin was fascinated by the flamboyant tail of the peacock. It appears to serve no purpose in terms of survival and may actually be a handicap as it makes it more difficult for the bird to escape from predators. The sexual selection explanation is that, for some reason, peahens are attracted to it, possibly because it signals the male's ability to survive *despite* the large cost imposed by his fancy plumage. As a result, males with longer, more brightly coloured tails would be more likely to mate and would then pass this characteristic on to the next generation. Over many generations, peacocks' tails would become more and more flamboyant because of this female preference. Thus, the peacock's tail gives an advantage in terms of mating success despite being a disadvantage in terms of general survival.

PHYSICAL ATTRACTIVENESS

Buss's research on partner preferences in different cultures (Buss, 1989) demonstrated that men in particular place great importance on physical attractiveness when choosing a mate. Physical appearance is an important cue to a woman's health and hence her fertility and reproductive value. Despite the long-standing belief that partner physical attractiveness is more important to men, more recent research (e.g. Eastwick *et al.*, 2011) suggests that it may be just as important to women as it is to men when choosing a romantic partner. However, these researchers suggest that whereas women may rely on physical attractiveness when choosing males for short-term relationships (i.e. for 'one-night stands'), physical attractiveness was less important in what they describe as 'serious relationships'. Men were more likely than women to rely on physical attractiveness in long-term relationships.

The 'matching hypothesis'

The **matching hypothesis** (Walster and Walster, 1969) claims that, when initiating romantic relationships, individuals seek out partners whose social desirability approximately equals their own. According to this view, when choosing a partner, individuals must first assess their own 'value' in the eyes of a potential romantic partner and then select the best available candidates who would be most likely to be attracted to them. Although both individuals would theoretically be attracted to the most socially desirable potential partners, by opting for partners of similar social desirability to themselves (i.e. who are 'in their league') they can maximise their chances of a successful outcome.

Matching and physical attractiveness

Although the matching hypothesis initially proposed that people would pair up with someone as 'socially desirable' as themselves in terms of a wide range of 'assets', over time it has come to be associated specifically with matching on physical attractiveness alone. We would expect, therefore, to find that people tend to pair up with those who are similar in terms of physical attractiveness. Walster *et al.* referred to these mating choices as 'realistic' choices, because each individual is influenced by the chances of having their affection reciprocated. Realistic choices must consider a number of different factors, including what the person desires (i.e. their ideal choice), whether the other person wants him or her in return, and whether other desirable alternatives are available for one or both of them. In real life, therefore, people have to settle for mating 'within their league' whether they want to or not.

▼ The matching hypothesis claims that, when choosing a partner, we look for someone whose level of physical attractiveness matches our own.

Key study: Walster *et al.* (1966)

Procedure In order to test the matching hypothesis, Walster *et al.* advertised a 'computer dance' for new students at the University of Minnesota. From the large number of students who purchased tickets, 177 males and 170 females were randomly selected to take part in the study. When they came to pick up their tickets, four student accomplices surreptitiously rated each of them for physical attractiveness. The participants were then asked to complete a lengthy questionnaire (e.g. to assess personality, intelligence, etc.) and told that the data gathered from these questionnaires would be used to allocate their ideal partner for the evening of the dance. In fact the pairing was done completely randomly. During the intermission part of the dance, participants were asked to complete a questionnaire about their dates, with a follow-up questionnaire distributed six months after the dance.

Findings The findings from this study did not support the matching hypothesis. Once participants had met their dates, and regardless of their own physical attractiveness, they responded more positively to physically attractive dates and were more likely to subsequently try to arrange dates with them if they were physically attractive. Other factors, such as personality and intelligence, did not affect liking the dates or any subsequent attempts to date them.

Speed dating and the challenge to traditional views of attraction

Eastwick and Finkel (2008) claim that although men may value physical attractiveness more than women do when stating their ideal partner preferences, these differences may not predict real-life partner choice. They used evidence from speed dating and backed this up with longitudinal follow-up procedures 30 days later. Prior to the speed-dating sessions, participants showed traditional sex differences when stating the importance of physical attractiveness (men) and earning prospects (women) in an ideal partner. However, their ideal preferences failed to predict what inspired their actual behaviour at the event. No significant sex differences emerged in the degree to which judgements of targets' physical attractiveness or earning prospects influenced speed daters' romantic interest in those targets. Participants' actual partner preferences were more likely to reflect their evaluation of a specific speed-dating partner's characteristics and their romantic attraction to him or her (across 17 different measures of romantic attraction).

Complex matching

Sprecher and Hatfield (2009) suggest a reason why research often fails to find evidence of matching in terms of physical attractiveness. People come to a relationship offering many desirable characteristics, of which physical attractiveness is only one. A person may compensate for a lack of physical attractiveness with other desirable qualities such as a charming personality, kindness, status, money and so on. Sprecher and Hatfield refer to this tendency to compensate for a lack of physical attractiveness by offering other desirable traits as 'complex matching'. In this way people are able to attract partners far more physically attractive than themselves by offering compensatory assets, for example an older, wealthy man may pair with a younger, attractive woman.

Research support for sex-differences in the importance of physical attractiveness

If physical attractiveness in long-term partners is more important for males, then research should show that males with physically attractive partners are more satisfied with their relationship. Meltzer et al. (2014) provided support for this claim. They found that objective ratings of wives' attractiveness were positively related to levels of husbands' satisfaction at the beginning of the marriage and remained that way over at least the first four years of marriage. In contrast, and supporting the lower importance that females attach to physical attractiveness in a mate, objective ratings of husbands' physical attractiveness were not related to wives' marital satisfaction, either initially or over time.

Matching may not be that important in initial attraction

Taylor et al. (2011) cast doubt on the value of the matching hypothesis in attraction. In a study of online dating patterns, they found no evidence that daters' decisions were driven by a similarity between their own and potential partners' physical attractiveness. Instead they found evidence of an overall preference for attractive partners, suggesting that people do not take their own physical attractiveness into account in the initial stages of attraction, but instead aim for someone more desirable than themselves. Although the matching hypothesis did not predict who was initially attracted to whom, the researchers did find that those individuals who specifically targeted similarly attractive others were more likely to receive responses to their messages.

Implications of sex-differences in the importance of physical attractiveness

Meltzer et al. (2014) claim that if physical attractiveness plays a stronger role in men's long-term relationship satisfaction than in women's, then women may experience increased pressures to maintain their physical attractiveness in order to successfully maintain a long-term relationship. However, physical attractiveness is not the only predictor of marital satisfaction for a man. Both men and women also desire partners who are supportive, trustworthy and warm, and those with partners who demonstrate these qualities tend to be more satisfied with their relationships (Pasch and Bradbury, 1998). Accordingly, less physically attractive women who possess these qualities do not tend to have less satisfied partners.

Research methods

Elaine Walster and William Walster (1969) conducted a further study to look at the matching hypothesis. This time participants met before the computer dance and were given a choice of who to partner to the dance. This made the circumstances more similar to everyday life where people have more control over who is their partner. The findings this time *did* support the matching hypothesis, as participants did prefer someone who matched their own perceived physical attractiveness.

1. This second study has been described as having greater ecological validity than the original. Explain what is meant by *ecological validity*, referring to features of this study that may have increased its ecological validity. (3 marks)
2. In the original study the pairing was done randomly. Explain how participants might have been paired randomly. (3 marks)
3. Suggest how the researchers could have determined the physical attractiveness of each participant. (3 marks)
4. Give **one** strength of the method you described in question 3. (2 marks)
5. How could the researchers have assessed the reliability of the measurement used in question 3? (2 marks)

LINK TO RESEARCH METHODS

See reliability on pages 16–17. The other topics in these questions are covered in the research methods chapter of our Year 1 book.

CAN YOU? No. 3.2

1. Explain what is meant by the *matching hypothesis*. (2 marks)
2. Outline the role of physical attractiveness in attraction. (4 marks)
3. Outline the matching hypothesis as it applies to attraction. (2 marks)
4. Briefly outline and evaluate the findings of **one** research study of the matching hypothesis. (4 marks)
5. Outline and evaluate the role of physical attractiveness in attraction. (8 marks)
6. Discuss **one or more** factors affecting attraction in romantic relationships, for example physical attractiveness and self-disclosure. (16 marks)

Self-disclosure

One variable that is related to attraction and ultimately relationship satisfaction is **self-disclosure**, the voluntary sharing of private aspects of the self with another person. Through self-disclosure, an individual lets himself or herself be known to the other person, thus 'reducing the mystery' between them.

SELF-DISCLOSURE

The term self-disclosure was first used by clinical psychologist Sidney Jourard (1971). It refers to the extent to which a person reveals personal information about themselves – their intimate thoughts, feelings and experiences to another person. Self-disclosure is an important process in the development of romantic relationships, with greater disclosure leading to greater feelings of intimacy. People tend to prefer those who disclose intimate details to those who disclose themselves to a lesser extent. Furthermore, people reveal more intimate information to those they like and also tend to like those to whom they have revealed intimate information (Collins and Miller, 1994).

Research on self-disclosure

Research on self-disclosure makes a distinction between self-disclosure *given* (i.e. disclosing one's own personal thoughts, feelings and experiences) and self-disclosure *received* (i.e. information disclosed by the other). Research (e.g. Sprecher *et al.*, 2013) has typically shown that the level of self-disclosure received in a romantic relationship was a better predictor of liking and loving than the level of self-disclosure that is given. Sprecher's research also found that self-disclosure was positively related to relationship stability. In a study of 50 dating couples, Sprecher found that the amount of overall disclosure in the relationship was predictive of whether the couples stayed together for longer than four years.

Different types of self-disclosure

The relationship between self-disclosure and relationship satisfaction is not straightforward because self-disclosure takes many different forms. For example, disclosing one's taste in music and disclosing one's inner fears and fantasies are quite different. Researchers have found that it is not self-disclosure per se that predicts relationship satisfaction, but the type of self-disclosure. Sprecher (1987) found that disclosure of, for example, experiences of personal disappointments and accomplishments, and information about previous sexual relationships, have a greater influence on relationship satisfaction than more 'neutral' types of self-disclosure.

▲ Self-disclosure is important in the development of romantic relationships, with greater disclosure leading to greater feelings of intimacy.

Norms of self-disclosure

There are norms about self-disclosure. For example, there is the norm that people should engage in only a moderately personal level of self-disclosure in the early stages of a relationship. Derlega and Grzelak (1979) suggest that these should be neither so personal that the discloser appears indiscriminate for disclosing them to a relative stranger, nor so impersonal that the listener is unable to know the discloser better as a result. The norm of reciprocity governs much of our social behaviour, i.e. people expect others to return the services they provide, be it money, favours or, in romantic relationships, self-disclosure. There is considerable evidence (e.g. Berg and Archer, 1980) that people possess a norm of reciprocity concerning self-disclosure. The more one person discloses to another, the more disclosure is expected in return.

Key study: Sprecher *et al.* (2013)

Sprecher *et al.* were interested in whether reciprocal self-disclosure was more influential in determining attraction than one-sided self-disclosure and listening.

Procedure Participants were 156 undergraduate students at a U.S. university paired into two-person dyads. Approximately two-thirds of these dyads were female–female and one-third male–female. Each dyad of unacquainted individuals engaged in a self-disclosure task over Skype. In the reciprocal condition, dyad members immediately took turns asking questions and disclosing. In the non-reciprocal condition, one person asked questions in the first interaction while the other person disclosed. Then the two switched roles for the second interaction (i.e. extended reciprocity). After each interaction, the researchers assessed liking, closeness, perceived similarity, and enjoyment of the interaction.

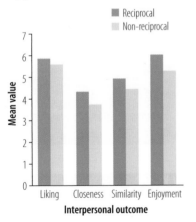

Findings Individuals in the reciprocal condition dyads reported more liking, closeness, perceived similarity, and enjoyment of the interaction than did those in the non-reciprocal dyads after the first interaction. This difference remained after participants in non-reciprocal dyads switched disclosure roles during the second interaction. This showed that turn-taking self-disclosure reciprocity is more likely to lead to positive interpersonal outcomes than is extended reciprocity.

Research support for the importance of self-disclosure

A meta-analysis by Collins and Miller (1994) supports the central role that self-disclosure plays in the development and maintenance of romantic relationships. They found that people who engage in intimate disclosures tend to be liked more than people who disclose at lower levels, and people like others as a result of having disclosed to them. Collins and Miller also found that the relationship between disclosure and liking was stronger if the recipient believed that the disclosure was shared only with them rather than being shared indiscriminately with others.

Self-disclosure on the Internet: The 'boom and bust' phenomenon

Some researchers have suggested that relationships formed over the Internet involve higher levels of self-disclosure and attraction than in face-to-face relationships. Because individuals communicating over the Internet are often anonymous, the greater psychological comfort that comes with such anonymity may lead them to reveal more information about themselves. Cooper and Sportolari (1997) refer to this as the 'boom and bust' phenomenon. When people reveal more about themselves earlier than they would in a face-to-face interaction, relationships get intense very quickly (*boom*). However, because the underlying trust and true knowledge of the other person are not there to support the relationship, it becomes difficult to sustain (*bust*). Cooper and Sportolari highlight instances where people who are certain they have found their 'soulmate' online have left an established relationship to meet people who do not turn out to be what they first seemed.

The norms of self-disclosure run deep

Tal-Or and Hershman-Shitrit (2015) showed that the relationship between gradual self-disclosure and attraction applies not only to real-life romantic relationships, but also to liking reality TV contestants. Reality TV shows such as *Big Brother* tend to be characterised by the very intimate self-disclosure of contestants early on in the shows. This rapid self-disclosure appears to conflict with what happens in everyday interactions, where such intimate self-disclosure is welcomed only when it evolves gradually. Tal-Or and Hershman-Shitrit discovered that although viewers *liked* characters who make early intimate disclosures, they still preferred this disclosure to evolve gradually and become more intimate, as in real relationships.

Self-disclosure may be greater in face-to-face than online relationships

Research by Knop *et al.* (2016) challenges the assumption that people self-disclose more in offline relationships than in face-to-face relationships. Their study revealed that members of a social group disclose personal information more often in face-to-face than online interactions and also disclose more intimate information. It appears that individuals do not seize the opportunity to reveal personal information online as much as expected, contrary to the belief that people disclose too much personal information via the Internet. The authors suggest that this may be due to the relative lack of intimacy of the Internet as a context for personal self-disclosure. A person who is disclosing appreciates non-verbal cues such as eye contact and the attentive silence of someone they are disclosing to, both absent in the online environment.

Cultural differences in patterns of self-disclosure

Cultures differ in the extent to which various topics are considered appropriate for conversation. In the West, people typically generally engage in more intimate self-disclosure than do non-Westerners. Americans, for example, disclose more than do Chinese or Japanese (Chen, 1995). Cultural norms also shape how comfortable men and women are in self-disclosing. For example, Nakanishi (1986) found that Japanese women prefer a lower level of personal conversations than do Japanese men. This is opposite to the self-disclosure patterns typically found in the West, where women prefer more disclosure than do men. This suggests that the importance of self-disclosure as an aspect of attraction is moderated by the influence of culture.

🐾 APPLY YOUR KNOWLEDGE

Paul and Jane are out on their first date, a meal together. During the meal, Paul tells Jane all about his previous partners, particularly the intimate details of these relationships. He dominates the conversation with more and more personal revelations, while Jane talks only about more neutral topics such as the restaurant, films she has seen and so on. The next day, each discusses the date with friends. Jane tells her friends he made her feel uncomfortable and she has no desire to see him again. Paul tells his friends he didn't think she was interested in him so he won't be contacting her again.

Using your knowledge of the role of self-disclosure in attraction, explain why Paul and Jane are not attracted to each other.

▲ Our preference for gradual self-disclosure appears to stretch even to liking contestants on reality TV shows such as *Big Brother*.

CAN YOU?   No. 3.3

1. Explain what is meant by *self-disclosure*. (2 marks)
2. Outline research into self-disclosure and its importance in attraction. (4 marks).
3. Outline and evaluate the role of self-disclosure in attraction. (16 marks)

Attraction: Filter theory

Early theories of relationship development proposed that couples move through a sequential series of stages characterised by increasing levels of commitment and involvement. Based upon a longitudinal study of the experiences of dating couples, Alan Kerckhoff and Keith Davis discovered that various filtering factors were prominent at different stages of the partner selection process as potential partners tried to find the best 'fit' between themselves and a future romantic partner. Rather unsurprisingly this theory became known as the **filter theory** of relationships.

KEY TERMS

Complementarity of needs refers to how well two people fit together as a couple and meet each other's needs.

Filter theory We choose romantic partners by using a series of filters that narrow down the 'field of availables' from which we might eventually make our choice.

Similarity in attitudes If people share similar attitudes, values and beliefs, communication is easier and so a relationship is likely to progress.

Social demography refers to variables such as age, social background and location, which determine the likelihood of individuals meeting in the first place.

Key study: Kerckhoff and Davis (1962)

Procedure Kerckhoff and Davis carried out a longitudinal study of 94 dating couples at Duke University in the US. Each partner in the couple completed two questionnaires assessing the degree to which they shared attitudes and values (the Index of Value Consensus test) and also the degree of need complementarity (the Fundamental Interpersonal Relations Orientation or FIRO-B test). Seven months after the initial testing, the couples completed a further questionnaire assessing how close they felt to their partner compared to how they felt at the beginning of the study. The researchers believed that this would indicate 'progress toward permanence' in the relationship.

Findings In the initial analysis of the results, only similarity appeared to be related to partner closeness. However, when the researchers divided the couples into short-term (those who had dated for less than 18 months) and long-term (those who had dated for more than 18 months), a difference emerged. For those couples that had been seeing each other for less than eighteen months, similarity of attitudes and values was the most significant predictor of how close they felt to their partner. For those who had been dating for more than 18 months, only complementarity of needs was predictive of how close each individual felt to their partner.

FILTER THEORY

Kerckhoff and Davis's 'filter theory' of attraction (Kerckhoff and Davis, 1962) suggests that we choose romantic partners by using a series of filters that narrow down the 'field of availables' from which we might eventually make our choice. According to this theory, different filters are prominent at different stages of partner selection. During the early stages of courtship, demographic similarities (e.g. class, religion, where they live) are likely to be the most important factors in initiating a relationship. As the relationship develops, a similarity of attitudes and underlying values becomes more important in determining whether or not the relationship continues. Finally, partners are assessed in terms of whether they are compatible, for example whether their personality traits complement the individual's own traits.

Social demography

Social demography refers to variables such as age, social background and geographical location, which determine the likelihood of individuals meeting in the first place. Social circumstances reduce the range of people that are realistically available for us to meet. This range is already fairly restricted as we are more likely to come into contact with people from our own ethnic, social and educational groups, and those who live geographically close to us. These are the people we feel similar to and so more at ease with. As a result, we find them more attractive precisely because we have more in common with them. In this first filtering stage, attraction has more to do with social rather than individual characteristics.

Similarity in attitudes

The second filter involves individuals' psychological characteristics, specifically their agreement on attitudes and basic values. Kerckhoff and Davis found that **similarity in attitudes** and values was of central importance at the start of a relationship and was the best predictor of the relationship becoming stable. Through their disclosures to each other, individuals are able to weigh up their decisions about whether to continue or terminate their relationship. Partners who are very different to the individual in terms of their attitudes and values are not considered suitable for a continuing relationship, and so are 'filtered out' from the field of possible long-term partners.

Complementarity of needs

The final filter involves an assessment of the **complementarity of needs**. People who have different needs (e.g. the need to be caring and the need to be cared for) like each other because they provide each other with mutual satisfaction of these opposed needs. This is important, because finding a partner who complements them ensures that their own needs are likely to be met. For example, young women who lack economic resources may feel attracted to older men who are a good financial prospect and therefore may be good providers. Winch's investigation of 25 married couples in the US (Winch, 1958) suggested that 'social needs' (such as dominance and deference) should be complementary rather than similar if marriages are to work. If one partner was low in a particular attribute then the other should be high. This is not the same as suggesting that 'opposites attract', but rather that in long-term relationships people are attracted to others whose needs are 'harmonious' with their own rather than conflicting with them.

Lack of research support for filter theory

Levinger *et al.* (1970) failed to replicate the results of the Kerckhoff and Davis study. In their study, 330 couples who were 'steadily attached' went through the same procedures as in Kerckhoff and Davis's study. There was no evidence that either similarity of attitudes and values or complementarity of needs influenced progress toward permanence in relationships. They also found no significant relationship between the length of the couples' relationships and the infuence of these different variables. In an attempt to explain why their research failed to replicate Kerckhoff and Davis's findings, Levinger *et al.* suggest that the questionnaires used in the original Kerckhoff and Davis study (the FIRO-B and the Index of Value Consensus) would not have been appropriate given the changes in social values and courtship patterns that had occurred in the intervening years between the two studies.

The real value of the filtering process

Duck (1973) suggests that the real value of the filtering process is that it allows people to make predictions about their future interactions and so avoid investing in a relationship that 'won't work'. Each person conducts a series of explorations, disclosing bits of information about themselves, and making enquiries about the other person. Duck claims that people use a variety of different strategies to gather information about each other, including encouraging a partner's self-disclosure through questioning, through to provoking disagreement about a topic in order to cut through the polite front in order to 'get at' the other person's real feelings. Based on these exchanges, partners may decide to continue with a relationship or make a decision that it will not work and so end the relationship before becoming too deeply involved with the other person. Filtering, therefore, stops people making the wrong choice and then having to live with the consequences.

Perceived similarity may be more important than actual similarity

Research has generally supported the importance of attitudinal similarity in attraction, e.g. finding that individuals are more likely to become attracted to another person with whom they share many common attitudes than to someone with whom they share only a few (Byrne *et al.*, 1970). Consistent with the assumptions of Kerckhoff and Davis's second stage of the filtering process, some researchers have found that *perceived* similarity predicts

▲ People are attracted to each other because they *perceive* similarity in a potential partner.

attraction more strongly than does *actual* similarity (Hoyle, 1993). Tidwell *et al.* (2013) tested this claim in the context of a speed-dating event, where decisions about attraction must be made over a much shorter time span. After measuring actual and perceived similarity using a questionnaire, the researchers found that perceived but not actual similarity predicted romantic liking for these couples.

Complementarity of needs may not be that important

Although studies have consistently found support for the 'similarity-attraction' aspect of Kerckhoff and Davis's theory, support for the importance of the complementarity of needs is much scarcer. For example, research by Dijkstra and Barelds (2008) studied 760 college-educated singles (476 women, 284 men) on a dating site who were looking for a long-term mate. Participants' own personalities were measured and they were then asked to rate personality characteristics they desired in an ideal mate. The researchers found that although initially participants indicated that they desired a complementary partner rather than a similar one, there were strong correlations between individual's own personality and their ideal partner's personality. This lent support to the similarity-attraction hypothesis rather than the complementarity of needs hypothesis.

A problem for filter theory

Kerckhoff and Davis's filter theory assumes that relationships progress when partners discover shared attitudes and values with their partner and the possession of needs that complement their own. However, most problematic for this assumption is that these are constantly changing over time and, in many instances, people are not aware of their partners' values, needs or role preferences. For example, Thornton and Young-DeMarco (2001) found evidence of changed attitudes toward relationships in young American adults over a period of a few decades. This included a weakening of the normative imperative to marry, to stay married and to have children, a more relaxed attitude towards cohabitation and more egalitarian attitudes toward gender roles in marriage.

 APPLY YOUR KNOWLEDGE

Pohan and her family have just moved to the UK from Hong Kong, as both her parents have relocated to jobs in the North of England. She is an only child, and in Hong Kong she led a rather sheltered life, being encouraged to help look after her grandmother as her parents worked full time. Pohan and her grandmother became very close and she misses her grandmother, as she would always give her advice when Pohan was growing up.

Pohan would dearly like a romantic relationship so that she isn't so lonely since the move. She telephones her grandmother back in Hong Kong to ask her advice about what she should do. Her grandmother suggests that she should join the young person's group at her local church because that would help her to 'meet the right sort of person'. The more she gets to know the boys within the group, the better she will get an idea of who might be right for her. Pohan's grandmother tells her that whoever she picks, if she wants it to last, she should make sure he is the sort of boy that will always look after her properly.

Using your knowledge of the filter theory of romantic relationships, explain how Pohan's grandmother's advice fits the claims of this theory and why this is good advice. (4 marks)

CAN YOU? No. 3.3

1. Outline the filter theory of attraction in romantic relationships. (6 marks)
2. Briefly outline the role of demography, similarity in attitudes and complementarity as they apply to attraction in romantic relationships. (3 marks each)
3. Briefly evaluate the filter theory of attraction in romantic relationships. (4 marks)
4. Outline **one** study of the filter theory of attraction in romantic relationships. (6 marks)
5. Discuss the filter theory of attraction in romantic relationships. (16 marks)

Social exchange theory

Psychologists are not only interested in why relationships form, but also what keeps them going. Some relationships never seem to flourish, while others are extremely successful and long-lasting. Maintaining a relationship is not a one-way process, but involves an interaction between the two partners, each with their own needs and expectations. **Social exchange theory** explains this process by focusing on the rewards that partners obtain from being in a relationship weighed against the costs that they incur. Individuals who receive favourable reward/cost outcomes are more likely to be satisfied with their relationship and so are less likely to leave it.

KEY TERMS

Social exchange theory The likelihood of a person staying in a relationship is determined by an assessment of what they get out of the relationship compared to what they put in, and how the relationship measures up against what they expect and what they might achieve in a different relationship.

Key study: Kurdek and Schmitt (1986)

Procedure Kurdek and Schmitt investigated the importance of social exchange factors in determining relationship quality in 185 couples. These comprised 44 heterosexual married couples, 35 co-habiting heterosexual couples, 50 same-sex male couples and 56 same-sex female couples. Each couple lived together and did not have children living with them. Each couple completed a questionnaire without discussing their answers with each other.

Findings For each of the four different types of couple, greater relationship satisfaction was associated with:

a. The perception of many benefits of the current relationship (CL).

b. Seeing alternatives to the current relationship as less attractive (CLA).

These findings show that the factors that predict satisfaction in same-sex relationships are the same ones that predict satisfaction in heterosexual relationships.

▲ Social exchange factors are associated with relationship satisfaction in same-sex relationships as well as in heterosexual relationships.

SOCIAL EXCHANGE THEORY

Profit and loss

At the centre of social exchange theory (Thibaut and Kelley, 1959) is the assumption that all social behaviour is a series of exchanges – individuals attempt to maximise their rewards and minimise their costs. In our society, people exchange resources with the expectation (or at least the hope) that they will earn a 'profit', i.e. that rewards will exceed the costs incurred. Rewards that we may receive from a relationship include companionship, being cared for, and sex. Costs may include effort, financial investment and time wasted (i.e. missed opportunities with others because of being in that particular relationship). Rewards minus costs equal the outcome (i.e. either an overall profit or a loss) for that relationship. Social exchange, in line with other 'economic' theories of human behaviour, stresses that commitment to a relationship is dependent on the profitability of this outcome.

Comparison level

In order to judge whether one person offers something better or worse than we might expect from another, Thibaut and Kelley proposed that we develop a comparison level – a standard against which all our relationships are judged. Our comparison level (CL) is a product of our experiences in other relationships together with our general views of what we might expect from this particular exchange. If we judge that the potential profit in a new relationship exceeds our CL, then that relationship will be judged as worthwhile and the other person will be seen as attractive as a partner. If the final result is negative (i.e. the profit is less than our CL), then a relationship with that person will be seen as less attractive.

Someone who has previously had unpleasant or unsatisfying relationships may well have a very low CL, and as a result they may be perfectly happy in a relatively poor relationship. In contrast, someone who has previously had very rewarding relationships (and therefore a high CL) would have high expectations for the quality of any future relationships. As a result, they would most likely exit any relationship that did not meet these high expectations. A romantic relationship is likely to have a greater degree of solidarity if both partners' outcomes or perceived profits are above their comparison level.

Comparison level for alternatives

Although an individual's satisfaction with a relationship depends on the assessed profit received from that relationship relative to the comparison level, this is not the only factor that determines the likelihood of them staying in that relationship. A related concept is the comparison level for alternatives (CLA), where the person weighs up a potential increase in rewards from a different partner, minus any costs associated with ending the current relationship. A new relationship can take the place of the current one if its anticipated profit level is significantly higher.

An individual will be committed to their current relationship when the overall benefits and costs are perceived as being greater than what might be possible in an alternative relationship (or perhaps even having no relationship). If these alternative options are more appealing, there will be a temptation for the individual to leave their current relationship and start a new one elsewhere. The more rewarding a partner's alternatives (e.g. another man or woman, friends, a career), the less is that individual's dependence on their current relationship. Relationships may then become less stable if one (or both) of the partners has a low level of dependence on that relationship (Kurdek, 1993). As a result, partners who differ in their degree of dependence may experience distress because one or both of them lacks commitment to that relationship.

Evidence for the influence of comparison level for alternatives

Sprecher (2001), in a longitudinal study of 101 dating couples at a US university, found that the exchange variable most highly associated with relationship commitment was partners' comparison level for alternatives. Sprecher's study showed that the presence of alternatives was consistently and negatively correlated with both commitment and relationship satisfaction for both males and females. In other words, in relationships where the comparison level for alternatives was high, commitment to, and satisfaction, with the current relationship tended to be low. Sprecher suggests this is not surprising as those who lack alternatives are likely to remain committed (and satisfied), but also those who are satisfied and committed to their relationship are more likely to devalue alternatives.

The problem of costs and benefits

A problem for social exchange theory is the confusion of what constitutes a *cost* and a *benefit* within a relationship. What might be considered rewarding to one person (e.g. constant attention and praise) may be punishing to another (e.g. it may be perceived as irritating). In addition, what might be seen as a benefit at one stage of the relationship may be seen as a cost at another juncture as partners may redefine something they previously perceived as rewarding or punishing (Littlejohn, 1989). This suggests that it is difficult to classify all events in such simple terms as 'costs' or 'benefits', and challenges the view that all romantic relationships operate in this way.

The problem of assessing value

Nakonezny and Denton (2008) argue that, for social exchange to be relevant to personal relationships, individuals must have some way of quantifying the *value* of costs and benefits in order to assess whether benefits received outweigh costs incurred. They point out that not only is value difficult to determine but so is the relative value of costs and benefits (given that they tend to be different in many ways). This tends not to be the case in commercial and economic relationships, where social exchange theory is more typically applied, but the vagueness of terms such as costs and benefits and the difficulty in assessing their relative value suggests that this theory is less comfortable explaining more personal relationships.

Overemphasis on costs and benefits

A reliance on profitable outcomes as an indication of relationship satisfaction ignores other factors that play some role in this process. An individual's own relational beliefs may make them more tolerant of a relatively low ratio of benefits to costs within their relationship. They may, for example, have the belief that 'If you have committed yourself to a relationship, you live with what it brings' or 'It is selfish to focus on one's own needs'. Although they may recognise an unfavourable ratio of benefits to costs, their relationship standard means that they continue to provide benefits to their partner and simply put up with the costs. Thus, social exchange alone cannot explain relationship satisfaction without also considering individual differences in relational standards and beliefs.

▲ For some people, their personal relational beliefs are more influential in determining satisfaction than the level of benefits they receive in the relationship.

Real-world application – Relationship Therapy

Individuals in unsuccessful marriages frequently report a lack of positive behaviour exchanges with their partner and an excess of negative exchanges. Gottman and Levenson (1992) found that, in successful marriages, the ratio of positive to negative exchanges was around 5:1, but in unsuccessful marriages this ratio was much lower, at around 1:1 or less. A primary goal of Integrated Behavioural Couples Therapy (IBCT) is to increase the proportion of positive exchanges within a relationship and decrease the proportion of negative exchanges. IBCT helps partners to break the negative patterns of behaviour that cause problems, thus making each other happier. Christensen *et al.* (2004) treated over 60 distressed couples using ICBT and found that about two-thirds reported significant improvements in the quality of their relationships as a result.

Research methods

Simpson *et al.* (1990) asked young adults (men and women, median age 19.3 years) to rate their liking for 16 advertisements, some of which contained pictures of opposite-sex individuals. Afterwards participants were asked to complete a range of questions including details of their current dating status. Simpson *et al.* found that participants involved in ongoing dating relationships rated the opposite-sex photos as less attractive.

1. Explain how this study supports social exchange theory. (2 marks)
2. Age of participants was reported in terms of the median. Explain why researchers may have used the median instead of the mean as a measure of central tendency. (2 marks)
3. Data about dating (and other personal information) was collected using a questionnaire. Give **one** limitation of using this research technique in this study. (2 marks)
4. Participants rated liking for advertisements using a rating scale. Would this be regarded as an open or closed question? Explain your answer. (2 marks)
5. This is an experimental study. Identify the independent and dependent variables and the experimental design. (3 marks)
6. Identify a suitable statistical test that could be used to analyse the data in this study. Justify your choice. (3 marks)

LINK TO RESEARCH METHODS

See statistical tests on page 24. The other topics in these questions are covered in the research methods chapter of our Year 1 book.

CAN YOU? No. 3.4

1. Explain what is meant by the term *social exchange* as it applies to romantic relationships. (2 marks)
2. Outline research into the social exchange theory of relationships. (6 marks)
4. Outline and evaluate the social exchange theory of romantic relationships. (16 marks)

Equity theory

According to social exchange theory, relationship satisfaction is largely a function of each individual's overall costs and benefits in the relationship. This rather selfish way of looking at relationships doesn't really match experiences in real life where people tend to report greater satisfaction if what they get out of a relationship is broadly equivalent to what they put in. According to **equity theory**, developed in the 1970s by Elaine Hatfield and colleagues to accommodate this finding, an individual would be equally happy in a relationship in which they give little to their partner and receive little in return and one in which they give a lot and receive a lot, as in both cases the equity between the two partners is equivalent.

KEY TERMS

Equity theory claims that people are most comfortable when what they get out of a relationship (i.e. the benefits) is roughly equal to what they put in (i.e. the costs).

Key study: Stafford and Canary (2006)

Procedure Stafford and Canary were interested in how equity and satisfaction predicted the use of maintenance strategies typically used in marriage. They asked over 200 married couples to complete measures of equity and relationship satisfaction. In addition each spouse was asked questions about their use of relationship maintenance strategies such as assurances (emphasising affection and commitment to the relationship), sharing tasks (sharing in household responsibilities and chores) and positivity (communicating in an upbeat and optimistic manner).

Findings Findings revealed that satisfaction was highest for spouses who perceived their relationships to be equitable, followed by over-benefited partners and then under-benefited partners. In particular, under-benefited husbands reported significantly lower levels of relationship maintenance strategies compared to equitable or over-benefited husbands. The relationship between equity and marital happiness appeared to be complementary. Spouses who were treated equitably tended to be happier and so were more likely to engage in behaviours that contributed to their spouse's sense of equity and happiness.

CAN YOU?   No. 3.5

1. Explain what is meant by the term *equity* as it applies to romantic relationships. (2 marks)
2. Outline research into the equity theory of romantic relationships. (6 marks)
4. Outline and evaluate the equity theory of romantic relationships. (16 marks)
5. Outline and evaluate the social exchange **and/or** equity theory of romantic relationships. (16 marks)

EQUITY THEORY

Inequity and dissatisfaction

In social exchange theory, we learned that all social behaviour is a series of exchanges, with individuals attempting to maximise their rewards and minimise their costs. Equity theory is an extension of that underlying belief, with its central assumption that people are most comfortable when they perceive that they are getting roughly what they deserve from any given relationship. An equitable relationship should, according to the theory, be one where one partner's benefits minus their costs equals their partner's benefits less *their* costs.

Relationships that lack equity are associated with distinct types of dissatisfaction. If people feel over-benefited, they may experience pity, guilt and shame; if under-benefited, they may experience anger, sadness, and resentment. The greater the inequity, the greater the dissatisfaction and stress, and the more they are motivated to do something about it.

▲ Inequitable relationships are associated with dissatisfaction and a greater motivation to do something about it.

A timetable of equity and inequity in marriages

Schafer and Keith (1980) surveyed hundreds of married couples of all ages, noting those who felt their marriages were inequitable because of an unfair division of domestic responsibilities. During the child-rearing years, wives often reported feeling under-benefited and husbands over-benefited. As a result, marital satisfaction tended to dip. In contrast, during the honeymoon (when newly married) and empty-nest stages (after children have left home), both husbands and wives were more likely to perceive equity and to feel satisfaction with their marriages.

Hatfield and Rapson (2011) suggest that how couples are concerned with reward and equity depends on the stage of their relationship. When couples are in the initial stages of a relationship, considerations of reward, fairness and equity are important. However, once individuals become deeply committed to each other, they become less concerned about day-to-day reward and equity. Happily married people, they suggest, tend not to keep score of how much they are giving and getting. Couples in equitable relationships are also less likely to risk extramarital affairs than their peers, and their relationships are generally longer lasting than those of their peers (Byers and Wang, 2004).

Dealing with inequity

If people perceive inequity in their relationships, then they are motivated to restore it. Hatfield and Rapson (2011) suggest that this can be achieved in three different ways:

1. **Restoration of actual equity** – Individuals can restore equity by voluntarily setting things right or by urging their partners to do so.
2. **Restoration of psychological equity** – Couples in inequitable relationships can distort reality and convince themselves that things are perfectly fair just the way they are.
3. **If couples are unable to restore equity in their relationship, they can leave it** – This can be physically (i.e. divorce) or emotionally (i.e. no longer having feelings for their partner).

Equity sensitivity

Equity theory is based on the 'norm of equity', which assumes that everyone is equally sensitive to equity and inequity. This also means that each individual experiences the same level of tension when they perceive inequity. However, this isn't always the case. Huseman *et al.* (1987) developed the idea of equity sensitivity, which determines the extent to which an individual will tolerate inequity. Huseman identified three categories of individuals: *benevolents*, *equity sensitives* and *entitleds*. Benevolents are 'givers' and tend to be more tolerant of under-rewarded inequity. Equity sensitives behave in accordance with equity theory, experiencing tension when faced with inequity. Entitleds prefer to be over-rewarded, having the attitude that they are owed and thus are entitled to receive benefits. As a result, they are dissatisfied when in an under-rewarded *or* an equitable situation.

Gender differences in the importance of equity

DeMaris *et al.* (2010) point out that men and women are not equally affected by inequity in romantic relationships. Women tend to perceive themselves as more under-benefited and less over-benefited in relationships, compared to men. Women are also more disturbed by being under-benefited than are men. Sprecher (1992) has also found that women feel more guilt than men in response to being over-benefited. DeMaris *et al.* suggest several reasons

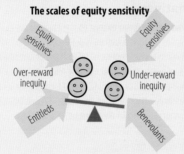

The scales of equity sensitivity

▲ Not everyone is sensitive to inequity in the same way. Some people perceive inequity even in equitable relationships, while others fail to perceive inequity even when it exists.

for these gender differences. These include the fact that women's greater relationship focus may make them more sensitive to injustices and more likely to react negatively to being exploited. An increased emphasis on gender equality in modern marriage may lead women to be more vigilant about, and reactive to, relationship inequity.

Cultural differences in the importance of equity

There is a possibility that the concept of equity is not as important in non-Western cultures given that most research on equity theory has been carried out in the US and in Western Europe. Aumer-Ryan *et al.* (2006) investigated this possibility. They found that, in all the cultures they studied, people considered it important that a relationship or marriage should be

equitable. However, people in the different cultures differed markedly in how fair and equitable they considered *their* relationships to be. Both men and women from the US claimed to be in the most equitable relationships, and both men and women (but especially women) from Jamaica claimed to be in the least equitable relationships.

Supporting evidence from the study of non-human primates

Further evidence for the importance of equity and fairness in relationships comes from studies of other primates. In a study with capuchin monkeys, Brosnan and de Waal (2003) found that female capuchin monkeys became very angry if they were denied a highly prized reward of grapes in return for playing a game. If another monkey (who had played no part in the game) received the grapes instead, the

▲ Don't try and cheat a capuchin monkey – you might end up getting food thrown at you!

capuchins grew so angry that they hurled food at the experimenter. In a later study, Brosnan *et al.* (2005) found that chimpanzees were more upset by injustice in casual relationships than in close, intimate relationships, where injustice 'caused barely a ripple'. These studies echo what researchers have found in human relationships and suggest that the perception of inequity has ancient origins.

A problem of causality

Although research has established that inequity and dissatisfaction are linked, the *nature* of the causal relationship itself is not clear. For example, Clark (1984) argues that, in most relationships, couples do not think in terms of reward and equity. If they do, she claims, it is a sign that their marriages are in trouble. According to this perspective, dissatisfaction with a relationship is the *cause*, not the consequences of inequity. However, a study of married couples (Van Yperen and Buunk, 1990) found that people in inequitable marriages became less satisfied over the course of a year, with no evidence for the converse. Hatfield and Rapson (2011) suggest that in failing marriages both processes might be operating. When marriages are faltering, partners become preoccupied with the inequities of the relationship, and this can then lead to relationship dissolution.

 UPGRADE

On page 65 we explained that, for essays such as question 4 opposite, 10 of the 16 marks are assigned to AO3 (evaluation). There is no specific requirement as to the *number* of AO3 points that you would use in your answer (i.e. three well-elaborated points *could* be enough to get you in the top mark band) but we have worked on the assumption that five AO3 points (each of approximately 60 words) would be ideal in an essay question.

The absolutely essential quality of any AO3 point is that you make it *effective*. Most teachers have their own technique for this (the 'three-point rule', the 'hamburger technique', SEEL, PEEL and so on). They all involve more or less the same thing in that a critical point is identified, evidence is given to support the point, and then some sort of conclusion is offered. If we take the evaluative point above regarding equity sensitivity, this could be made into an effective AO3 point as follows:

Not everyone responds to inequity in the same way... Huseman et al. *developed the idea of equity sensitivity to explain this... 'Benevolents' are more tolerant of under-rewarded inequity. 'Entitleds' are dissatisfied when under-rewarded or in an equitable situation... Therefore, only one type of individual ('equity sensitives') behave as predicted by equity theory.*

Insider tip...
Because social exchange theory and equity theory are so closely associated, exam questions may ask for either one on its own, or offer an 'and/or' alternative. It is usually better to stick to the 'or' choice, as that gives you the opportunity to write a much more detailed answer (and earn higher marks).

The investment model of relationships

Caryl Rusbult's **investment model** of relationships (Rusbult, 1980) was developed as a way of understanding why people persist in some romantic relationships but not in others. Relationships persist not just because of the positive qualities that attract one person to another (their satisfaction with that relationship), but also because of the ties that bind partners to each other (their investments in that relationship) and the absence of a better option beyond that particular relationship (lack of alternatives). These three factors provide the explanatory framework by which we might predict the chances of someone being committed to the relationship they are currently in.

The AQA specification uses the term 'comparison with alternatives', but Rusbult uses a different term, 'quality of alternatives', so we have stuck with that here.

MEET THE RESEARCHER

Caryl Rusbult (1952–2010) received her PhD in Psychology from the University of North Carolina in 1978. She returned to North Carolina in the 1980s to work on her investment model of relationships and more recently what she referred to as the 'Michelangelo effect' (the way in which close partners 'sculpt' each other in ways that help them attain valued goals). In 2004, she moved to the Netherlands, where she became Professor of Social Psychology at the Free University in Amsterdam. She died in 2010 at the age of 57.

THE INVESTMENT MODEL

Satisfaction level

Satisfaction level refers to the positive versus negative emotions experienced within a relationship and is influenced by the extent to which the other person fulfils the individual's most important needs. For example, a partner may feel satisfied to the degree that the other partner gratifies their domestic, companionate and sexual needs.

Quality of alternatives

Quality of alternatives refers to the extent to which an individual's most important needs might be better fulfilled *outside* the current relationship. Perceiving that an attractive alternative might provide superior outcomes to those experienced in the current relationship might lead an individual toward that alternative and away from their current relationship. However, if alternatives are not present, an individual may persist with a relationship because of a lack of better options. Attractive alternatives are not necessarily other people, as in some cases having no relationship may be seen as a more attractive option than staying in the current relationship.

Investment size

Rusbult proposed that **investment** size also contributes to the stability of a relationship. Investment size is a measure of all the resources that are attached to the relationship, and which would diminish in value or be lost completely if the relationship were to end. For example, partners invest time and energy in the relationship, they share each other's friends, take on shared possessions or give things of value to each other. Partners make these sorts of investments expecting that in doing so it will create a strong foundation for a lasting future together. Investments increase dependence on the relationship because they increase connections with the partner that would be costly to break. As a result, investments create a powerful psychological inducement to persist with a relationship.

Commitment level

The term **commitment** is used to describe the likelihood that an involvement will persist. Commitment is high in romantic partners who are happy with their relationships (i.e. they have high levels of satisfaction) and anticipate very little gain and high levels of loss if they were to leave the relationships (i.e. the quality of alternatives is low and the investment is high). Conversely, commitment is low when satisfaction levels and investment in the relationship are both low and the quality of alternatives is high. When people are satisfied with their relationship, feel tied to it because of their investments or have no suitable alternatives, they become dependent on that relationship. Commitment, therefore, is a consequence of increasing dependence.

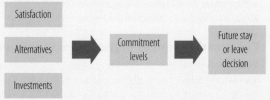

Key study: Le and Agnew (2003)

Procedure Le and Agnew carried out a meta-analysis of 52 studies conducted between the late 1970s and the late 1990s. Each of these studies had explored the different components of the investment model and the relation between them. This produced a total sample of over 11,000 participants (54% male and 46% female) from five countries (USA, UK, Netherlands, Israel and Taiwan).

Findings Across all the studies, satisfaction level, quality of alternatives and investment size were highly correlated with relationship commitment. The correlation between satisfaction level and commitment (.68) was found to be significantly stronger than either quality of alternatives (−.48) and investment size (.46) and commitment. The correlation between commitment and stay or leave behaviours was also significant at .47, with individuals showing higher levels of commitment being more likely to stay in a relationship and those with lower levels more likely to leave.

Research support for the investment model

The importance of commitment as an indicator of relationship stability is supported by a meta-analysis by Le *et al.* (2010). They analysed data from nearly 38,000 participants in 137 studies over a 33-year period to discover the key variables that predicted 'staying or leaving' behaviour in non-marital romantic relationships. In line with predictions from Rusbult's investment model, commitment (or lack of it) was a particularly strong predictor of whether a relationship would break up. Other relational variables that make up the model, namely satisfaction, quality of alternatives and investments, were modest predictors of the likelihood of staying in a relationship or breaking up.

Problems in measuring the variables of the investment model

A particular problem for the investment model is that it is difficult to measure commitment and the other variables (i.e. satisfaction level, investment size and quality of alternatives) that lead to commitment in the relationship. Rusbult *et al.* have developed the 'Investment Model Scale' to overcome this problem (Rusbult *et al.*, 1998). They have shown this scale to be high in both reliability and validity in the measurement of these variables, and have shown it to be suitable for a wide variety of different populations. One potential problem is that the scale relies on self-report measures, which often have problems with respondents wishing to present themselves in a good light. Although this raises the possibility of biased findings from the use of such methods, it would be extremely difficult to measure such a subjective state as commitment in any other way.

Real-world application: Explaining abusive relationships

The investment model is able to explain why individuals may persist in a relationship with an abusive partner. Victims of partner abuse experience low satisfaction, which would lead us to predict that they would leave the abusive partner, yet many stay. The investment model highlights features of the relationship that would explain why a victim of abuse might remain in the relationship. They may, for example, lack alternatives to the relationship and may have too much invested with that partner, making dissolution too costly. Rusbult and Martz (1995) revealed that alternatives and investments were a strong indication of whether battered women at a shelter remained committed to and returned to their partner.

Investment in the future is also important

Goodfriend and Agnew (2008) have elaborated on the original investment model. They suggest that the notion of 'investment' should include not only things that have already been invested in the relationship, but also any *plans* that partners have made regarding the relationship. In ending a relationship, an individual would not only lose investments made to date, but also the possibility of achieving any of the future plans they had made with that partner. As a result, claim Goodfriend and Agnew, some relationships persist, not because of the current balance of investments made, but because of a motivation to see cherished future plans come to fruition. Their research provided evidence that future plans were strongly predictive of commitment in romantic relationships, over and above past investments.

The wide application of the investment model

A strength of Rusbult's investment model is that its main claims (e.g. that commitment is positively associated with satisfaction level and investment size and is negatively associated with quality of alternatives) have been shown to be true across many different populations and in many different types of relationship. For example, research has supported the relevance of the investment model across different cultures (e.g. the US, the Netherlands and Taiwan), in a variety of different participant populations (e.g. marital and non-marital relationships, gay and lesbian relationships, friendships and abusive relationships).

Research methods

Rusbult (1980) conducted two experiments to test her theory. In one of them male and female students were asked to read a four-page essay (Robert for male participants, Sarah for females) and imagine how they would feel and behave in the situation described if they were the person in the essay. The essay had four variables: relationship cost (high or low), alternative outcome value (poor or good), investment size (high, medium or low) and sex of participant. Participants then answered a questionnaire.

Rusbult's findings are shown in the table below. The values in the table represent the mean for the three dependent measures – the likelihood of leaving the relationship (the less likely, the higher the number), commitment (the higher the number, the greater the commitment) and attachment (the higher the number, the greater the commitment).

Insider tip...

Occasionally an exam question may ask for a 'limitation' of a particular theory or model. To choose an appropriate point with which to answer such a question, simply select one that suggests a problem (e.g. lack of research support or difficulties of measurement), and introduce that as a 'limitation'.

| | | High cost | | Low cost | |
		Poor alternative	Good alternative	Poor alternative	Good alternative
Investment size	Low	17.13	15.14	18.29	15.87
	Medium	18.15	16.36	19.69	15.79
	Large	18.93	17.43	19.80	18.15

1. The data is given to how many decimal places? (1 mark)
2. Draw a suitable graph displaying the findings in the table. (4 marks)
3. Outline **two** conclusions you can draw from the table of data (and your graph). (4 marks)
4. Identify **two** independent variables in this study. (1 mark)
5. The participants in this study were university students. Suggest **one** limitation of this sample. (2 marks)

LINK TO RESEARCH METHODS

The topics in these questions are covered in the research methods chapter of our Year 1 book.

CAN YOU? — No. 3.6

1. Briefly outline the role of 'satisfaction', 'investment', 'quality of alternatives' and 'commitment' within the investment model of relationships. (3 marks each)
2. Outline **one** study that has investigated the investment model of relationships. (4 marks)
3. Briefly explain **two** criticisms of the investment model of relationships. (4 marks)
4. Outline and evaluate the investment model of relationships. (16 marks)

Relationship breakdown

Some relationships flourish, some survive in name alone and some fail completely. Relationships are considered 'successful' if partners stay together, and those relationships that end prematurely are considered 'failures'. Most models of relationship breakdown have depicted relationship breakdown as a 'relentless tragedy unfolding in a sequence of predictable and unavoidable steps' (Duck, 2005). The theory we discuss on this spread suggests that the real story of breakdown is somewhat more complex and perhaps less tragic than we might imagine.

There is a more recent version of this model by Stephanie Rollie and Steve Duck (2006), but AQA have specified Duck's earlier (1982) version instead. We have, therefore, covered that one here and referred to what is offered in the updated (2006) model as an evaluative point on the page opposite.

A PHASE MODEL OF RELATIONSHIP BREAKDOWN

Breakdown

The first phase of **Duck's model of relationship breakdown** (Duck, 1982) begins when one of the partners becomes distressed with the way the relationship is conducted. As we saw on page 74, inequitable relationships are more likely to create dissatisfaction than equitable relationships, so this realisation that the person is no longer willing or able to stand this dissatisfaction may be the first step in the eventual breakdown of the relationship.

The intrapsychic phase

These feelings of dissatisfaction lead to the **intrapsychic phase**, characterised by a brooding focus on the relationship and a consideration of whether they might be better off out of this relationship. The individual feels burdened by feelings of resentment and a sense of being under-benefited.

During this phase, the individual may not say anything about their dissatisfaction to their partner, but they may express their discontentment in other ways, e.g. in a personal diary entry or through social withdrawal while they take stock of their partner and the relationship. Some people will end relationships without ever discussing their dissatisfaction with their partner. The promises of 'I'll call you' or 'Let's stay friends' often disguise a deeper dissatisfaction with the other person as a romantic partner.

The dyadic phase

In the **dyadic phase**, individuals confront their partners and begin to discuss their feelings, their discontentment and the future of the relationship. Feelings of guilt and anger are likely to surface as part of these discussions. They may well discover that the partner also has concerns to air. At this point, couples may become aware of the forces that bind them together (e.g. children and other investments made in the relationship) and the costs that would be incurred (e.g. the social and economic costs) should the relationship be terminated.

At this stage, the relationship might be saved if both partners are motivated to resolve the issues and so avoid a breakup. It is at this point that many couples seek marital therapy in the hope that it may save their relationship. Alternatively, the partners begin to involve others in their dissatisfaction with the relationship.

The social phase

Up to this point, partners might have kept their dissatisfaction fairly private, but now it spills over to a network of friends and family as it reaches the **social phase** of the breakdown. This is a crucial psychological moment, as the distress experienced by one or both partners is now made public. This makes it harder for the two partners to deny that there really is a problem with their relationship and also harder for them to subsequently bring about a reconciliation.

Others may take sides, offer advice and support, or may help in mending any disputes between the two sides. The involvement of others may even speed the partners toward dissolution through revelations about one or other of the partners' behaviour.

The grave-dressing phase

Having left a relationship, partners attempt to justify their actions. This **grave-dressing phase** is important, as each partner must present themselves to others as being trustworthy and loyal – key attributes if they are to attract a new partner. Partners strive to construct a representation of the failed relationship that does not paint their contribution to it in unfavourable terms. La Gaipa (1982) makes the point that every person who leaves a relationship has to leave with their 'social credit' intact for future use, i.e. they must leave in such a way that they are not debarred from future relationships.

At this point, individuals may also strategically reinterpret their view of the partner. For example, they may have initially been attracted to their 'rebellious' nature, but now label that characteristic as 'irresponsible'. Topics in grave-dressing are likely to be stories about the betrayal of one partner by the other, or perhaps tell the story of two people who worked hard on a relationship but eventually found that it simply wasn't worth the effort.

BREAKDOWN
Dissatisfaction with relationship
Threshold: I can't stand this anymore

INTRAPSYCHIC PHASE
Social withdrawal; 'rumination' resentment
Brooding on partner's 'faults' and relational 'costs'
Re-evaluation of alternatives to relationship
Threshold: I'd be justified in withdrawing

DYADIC PHASE
Uncertainty, anxiety, hostility, complaints
Discussion of discontents
Talk about 'our relationship'; equity, roles
Reassessment of goals, possibilities, commitments
Threshold: I mean it

SOCIAL PHASE
Going public; support seeking from third parties
Denigration of partner, alliance building
Social commitment, outside forces create cohesion
Threshold: It's now inevitable

GRAVE-DRESSING PHASE
Tidying up memories; making relational histories
Stories prepared for different audiences
Saving face
Threshold: Time to get a new life

◀ A summary of Duck's model of relationship breakdown.

Steve Duck (1946–) was brought up in Keynsham, Bristol, and attended Bristol Grammar School. After completing his PhD at the University of Sheffield, he taught at Glasgow and Lancaster Universities before moving to the US and becoming Professor of Psychology at the University of Iowa in 2000. He has written or edited more than 60 books on relationships. In his spare time he likes to research the Duck family history, discovering that its origins can be traced back to Viking times ('Duck' apparently means 'hunchback' in old Norse).

EVALUATION

Fails to reflect the possibility of personal growth

Duck (2005) acknowledged that his 1982 model had failed to reflect the possibility of relational growth following breakdown. By introducing a new model with a final phase of 'resurrection processes' (Rollie and Duck, 2006), Duck stressed that, for many people, this is an opportunity to move beyond the distress associated with the ending of a relationship and instead engage in the process of personal growth. There is research support for the existence of this new phase. Tashiro and Frazier (2003) surveyed 92 undergraduates who had recently broken up with a romantic partner. Respondents typically reported that they had not only experienced emotional distress but also personal growth, as predicted by Rollie and Duck's updated model.

The impact of the social phase varies by type of relationship

Duck (2005) suggests that the nature and impact of the social phase experienced during breakup depends on the sort of relationship that is involved. For example, for teenagers and young adults, romantic relationships are seen as more unstable than long-term adult relationships, and are largely recognised by others as being 'testing grounds' for future long-term commitments. As a result, individuals may receive sympathy but no real attempt at reconciliation from their confidants as there are 'plenty more fish in the sea'. Older people in longer-term relationships, however, have lower expectations of being able to find a replacement for the present partner (Dickson, 1995). The consequences of a breakup in such cases are more significant – therefore the social processes phase may be characterised by more obvious attempts by others to rescue the current relationship.

Benefits of the grave-dressing phase

Research supports the importance of the grave-dressing phase in dealing with the after-effects of relationship breakdown. The end of a romantic relationship can be a very stressful event. For example, Monroe *et al.* (1999) found that students who experienced the end of a romantic relationship in the previous year had a greater risk of developing a major depressive disorder for the first time. However, Tashiro and Frazier (2003) found that individuals are able to feel better about ending a relationship when they focus on how the *situation*, rather than their own flaws, was responsible for the breakup. The benefit of grave-dressing, therefore, is that the individual is able to create stories that play down their role in the breakup and so do not threaten their psychological well-being.

Ethical issues in breakdown research

Carrying out research in this sensitive area raises particular issues of vulnerability (participants may experience distress when revisiting the issues that led to breakdown), privacy (many such issues are of an intensely personal nature) and confidentiality (particularly for victims of an abusive relationship). A guiding principle in all psychological research is that the benefits of undertaking the research must outweigh the risks, most notably the impact of the research on the participants involved. This is a particularly difficult issue when dealing with vulnerable individuals attempting to  cope with the trauma and emotional distress associated with a relationship breakup. Psychologists must ask themselves whether they truly have the interests of the participants in mind when exploring their research question.

Real-world application: Implications for intervention

Duck's model stresses the importance of *communication* in relationship breakdown. Paying attention to the things that people say, the topics that they discuss and the ways in which they talk about their relationship offers both an insight into how they are thinking about their relationship and also suggests appropriate interventions by friends and family. If the relationship was in the intrapsychic processes phase, repair might involve re-establishing liking for the partner, perhaps by re-evaluating their behaviour in a more positive light. In the later phases of the model, different strategies of repair are appropriate. For example, in the social processes phase, people outside the relationship (such as family members) may help the partners to patch up their differences.

🐾 APPLY YOUR KNOWLEDGE

Kaya is going through a breakup from her long-term partner, Jack. She tried talking to Jack about why she was so unhappy and her fears about where the relationship was going. However, nothing changed as a result of this discussion, and now she finds herself confiding in her friend Leila, who tells her she deserves better and should think about dumping him.

Which two of Duck's phases of relationship breakdown is Kaya demonstrating here? Give reasons for your answer. (4 marks)

KEY TERMS

Duck's phase model of relationship breakdown A model of relationship breakdown that describes the different phases that people go through during the dissolution of a romantic relationship.

Dyadic phase An individual confronts their partner and discusses with them their feelings, their discontentment and the future of the relationship.

Grave-dressing phase Partners strive to construct a representation of the failed relationship that does not paint their contribution to it in unfavourable terms.

Intrapsychic phase An individual broods over their current relationship and considers whether they might be better off out of it.

Social phase Discontentment spills over to friends and family, as the distress experienced by one or both partners is made public.

CAN YOU?   No. 3.7

1. Explain what is meant by the terms *intrapsychic phase*, *dyadic phase*, *social phase* and *grave-dressing phase*. (2 marks each)
2. Give **two** criticisms of Duck's phase model of relationship breakdown. (3 marks each)
3. Outline and evaluate Duck's phase model of relationship breakdown. (16 marks)

Virtual relationships in social media

Social networking sites have thrived in recent years. Sites such as Facebook, Twitter and Instagram offer a way for online users to interact with each other and to make and maintain interpersonal relationships. In 2015, Facebook had over 1.39 billion users worldwide, with more than 890 million of these logging on every day. Research has shown that there are differences in the way that people conduct these **virtual relationships** and how they conduct face-to-face relationships. On this spread we look at two of these differences: the higher levels of **self-disclosure** typically found in virtual relationships and the removal of the **gates** that would, for some people, make offline relationship formation more difficult.

'Strangers on a train'

Internet interactions with others might be considered analogous to the encounters one sometimes has with complete strangers when travelling. In the 1970s, psychologist Zaik Rubin carried out a series of studies where confederates disclosed personal information about themselves (varying in level of intimacy) to a complete stranger on trains, in airport lounges or when standing at bus stops. He discovered that when confederates disclosed intimate details of their lives to the stranger in the next seat or next to them in a queue, this was often met with a reciprocal self-disclosure from the stranger.

SELF-DISCLOSURE IN VIRTUAL RELATIONSHIPS

Jourard (1971) proposed the concept of 'broadcasting self-disclosure' to explain the difference between disclosure to a romantic partner and the sharing of personal information in a public situation. Jourard claimed that self-disclosure in the public domain involves the individual presenting an 'edited' version of the self to others. Individuals using social networks such as Facebook exercise different levels of self-disclosure depending on whether they are presenting information publically or privately. People feel more secure about disclosing intimate and sensitive information in private (including private messaging) because of the increased control over disclosure to a selected individual. In contrast, when sharing self-disclosures in more visible ways with a wider audience (e.g. on a Facebook wall), people are more selective over the content, revealing information that is less private and less intimate. People may, therefore, compensate for the lack of control over the target audience (i.e. who has access to the information) by exercising increased control over what information this audience has access to.

Why do people self-disclose more on the Internet?

Most explanations for the relatively high levels of self-disclosure in Internet relationships compared to face-to-face relationships have focused on the psychological effects of anonymity. Individuals do not usually engage in self-disclosure with one another until they are confident that what they disclose remains confidential, and would not be leaked to mutual acquaintances. The dangers of this type of self-disclosure in face-to-face interactions are that confidentiality might be violated or the other person might respond negatively to the disclosure, leading to ridicule or rejection.

The relative anonymity of Internet interactions greatly reduces the risks of such disclosure because people can share their inner thoughts and feelings with much less fear of disapproval and sanction from the other person. In this way, self-disclosures with online acquaintances are similar to the 'strangers on a train' phenomenon (Rubin, 1975). Rubin explained that we are more likely to disclose personal information to people we don't know and probably will never see again (see left). Also, because a stranger does not have access to an individual's social circle, the confidentiality problem is less of an issue.

ABSENCE OF GATING IN VIRTUAL RELATIONSHIPS

Gating in face-to-face relationships

In face-to-face relationships, personal factors such as physical appearance and mannerisms tend to determine whom we approach, and whom we develop romantic relationships with. We use available features such as attractiveness, age or ethnicity to categorise potential partners before making a decision about whether we would like a relationship with that person. In online relationships there is an absence of these barriers or 'gates' that normally limit the opportunities for the less attractive, shy or less socially skilled to form relationships in face-to-face encounters.

Absence of gating and its consequences

Because of the relative anonymity of the Internet, these barriers to interaction are not initially in evidence and so are less likely to stop potential relationships from getting off the ground. A consequence of removing the traditional gating features that dominate initial liking and relationship formation is that a person's true self is more likely to be active in Internet relationships than it is in face-to-face interactions. This is made possible by the absence of the traditional gating features that dominate initial liking and relationship formation, and is a contributor to the establishment of close relationships over the Internet.

Zhao *et al.* (2008) found that online social networks such as Facebook can empower 'gated' individuals to present the identities they hope to establish but are unable to in face-to-face situations. The reduction of gating obstacles in the online environment also enables people to 'stretch the truth a bit' in their efforts to project a self that is more socially desirable than their real 'offline' identity. Yurchisin *et al.* (2005) interviewed 11 online daters, and found that these individuals tended to give accounts of both their real *and* better selves in dating profiles as a way of attracting potential partners. Some interviewees even admitted that they would steal other daters' ideas or copy other people's images, as a way of making themselves more popular. Yurchisin did, however, find that most online identities were still close to a person's true identity in order to avoid unpleasant surprises in a possible real-life encounter.

The importance of the Internet for romantic relationships

Rosenfeld and Thomas (2012) demonstrated the importance of the Internet and of social media in helping individuals to form and maintain relationships. In a study of 4,000 US adults, they found that individuals with Internet access at home were far more likely to be partnered, and less likely to be single. Of these 4,000 individuals, 71.8% of those who had Internet access at home had a spouse or romantic partner. For individuals who did not have Internet access, this figure was much lower at 35.9%. Even after controlling for other important variables such as age, gender, education, sexual preference and religion, individuals with Internet access were still almost twice as likely to have a partner compared to those without Internet access. Their research suggests that the Internet may be displacing rather than simply complementing the traditional ways of meeting a romantic partner.

Virtual relationships can be as strong as offline relationships

It is often claimed that the nature of Internet communication is such that it can only lead to superficial relationships that cannot compare with the richness of face-to-face relationships (Putnam, 2000). For example, it is believed that relationships formed online are of lower quality and more temporary than relationships formed in more traditional ways. However, Rosenfeld and Thomas (2012) found no evidence to support this claim. In their research they found no difference in the quality of online and offline relationships, nor did they find that online relationships were more fragile than relationships formed offline.

A biological basis for self-disclosure on Facebook

Tamir and Mitchell (2012) found evidence of a biological basis for the motivation to self-disclose on social media. They found increased MRI activity in two brain regions that are associated with reward, the nucleus accumbens and the ventral tegmental area. These areas were strongly activated when people were talking about themselves, and less so when they were talking about someone else. Tamir and Mitchell also found that participants in their study experienced a greater sensation of pleasure when sharing their thoughts with a friend or family member, and less pleasure when they were told their thoughts would be kept private. These findings suggest that the human tendency to share our personal experiences with others over social media may arise from the rewarding nature of self-disclosure.

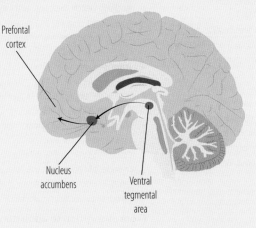

Prefontal cortex

Nucleus accumbens

Ventral tegmental area

Facebook helps shy people have better quality friendships

Baker and Oswald (2010) argue that virtual relationships are particularly helpful for shy people. Through social media sites like Facebook, shy people are able to overcome the barriers they face when trying to form relationships in real life. To test whether shy people really do benefit from Internet use, Baker and Oswald surveyed 207 male and female students about their shyness, Facebook usage and the quality of their friendships. For students who scored high for shyness, greater use of Facebook was associated with higher perceptions of friendship quality. In contrast, for those who scored low for shyness, Facebook usage was not associated with perception of friendship quality. This demonstrated that shy individuals find particular value in virtual relationships.

Virtual relationships have consequences for offline relationships

Zhao et al. (2008) claim that we should not think of the online world and the offline world as being completely separate, as relationships formed online do have consequences for people's offline lives. For example, the development of virtual relationships online allows some individuals to bypass gating obstacles and create the sort of identity that they are unable to establish in the offline world. Zhao et al. claim that these 'digital selves' can then enhance the individual's overall self-image and as a result may increase their chances to connect to others in their offline world.

UPGRADE

A particular feature of AQA psychology examinations is the 'Application' question. You should be familiar with these questions, but it's worth revisiting the general rules about answering them. Let's illustrate these in the context of the following question:

Declan is a shy 18-year-old. He always seems to get tongue-tied when talking to members of the opposite sex, and finds that his social awkwardness means that girls don't really want to spend time with him. However, he finds it much easier to chat to girls when using social networking sites, and as a result is much more popular.

Using your knowledge of the effects of absence of gating on the nature of virtual relationships, explain why Declan finds it easier to conduct his relationships online. (4 marks)

For a 4-mark question there would be two mark bands. For the top band you would need to display a 'clear and accurate' knowledge of the specific psychology related to the scenario (in this case the effects of 'absence of gating' on relationships). However, having a good understanding of the psychology is not enough on its own – it must be used 'appropriately' to explain the scenario (here it is why Declan finds it easier to conduct relationships online). The marks awarded reflect how effectively you have used the former to explain the latter. Ignore either of these and you simply won't get any marks.

KEY TERMS

Gates are the barriers that limit opportunities for the less attractive, shy or less socially skilled to form relationships in face-to-face encounters.

Self-disclosure is when a person reveals intimate personal information about themselves to another person.

Virtual relationships are relationships that are conducted through the Internet rather than face to face, for example through social media.

CAN YOU? No. 3.8

1. Explain what is meant by the term *virtual relationship*. (2 marks)
2. Outline the nature of self-disclosure in virtual relationships. (4 marks)
3. Outline the effect of absence of gating in virtual relationships. (4 marks)
4. Outline and evaluate the nature of virtual relationships in social media. (16 marks)

Parasocial relationships

Parasocial relationships (PSRs) are one-sided relationships, where one person expends considerable emotional energy, interest and time, although the other person (usually a celebrity) is completely unaware of their existence. Parasocial relationships typically develop with television celebrities, but they can also occur between individuals and their favourite bloggers, social media users and gamers. The pervasiveness of mass media such as television and the Internet gives the viewer the illusion of having a face-to-face relationship with a particular celebrity. This association is so strong that the celebrity becomes a meaningful figure in the individual's life, and can produce a much more complex set of responses than just simple imitation.

AN ATTACHMENT THEORY EXPLANATION

Attachment behaviours in parasocial relationships

Parasocial relationships may function similarly to 'real-life' relationships in terms of attachment behaviours, as relationships with TV personalities exhibit to some degree the three fundamental properties of adult attachment as identified by Weiss (1991).

- **Proximity seeking** – A key component of **attachment theory** is proximity seeking as individuals attempt to reduce the distance between themselves and their attachment figure. Fans exhibit many proximity-seeking behaviours as part of their PSR. For example, research has shown that people like to stay informed about their favourite celebrities – they collect trivia about them, will rearrange schedules to see them on TV and will even attempt to contact them through fan letters or in person (Leets *et al.*, 1995).
- **Secure base** – The presence of the attachment figure provides a sense of security for the individual, a 'safe haven' that allows them to explore the world. With a PSR, where there is little or no chance of rejection from the attachment figure, the individual is able to create a secure base from which they can explore other relationships in a safe way. An example can be seen in a fan's story about Michael Jackson (see right).
- **Protest at disruption** – The best marker of an attachment may be the presence of prolonged distress following separation or loss of the attachment figure. BBC's axing of Jeremy Clarkson from *Top Gear* in 2015 was met by the sort of raw emotion that is typical of the loss of an attachment figure. On the petition site to 'Bring back Clarkson', one fan wrote, 'I want to cry. . .', while others lamented the loss, saying how Clarkson and the rest of the *Top Gear* team had 'given their lives purpose'.

Attachment style

Cole and Leets (1999) explain why some people are more likely to develop PSRs through the concept of attachment style. In their research, they found that a person's willingness to form a parasocial bond with his or her favourite TV personality is related to their attachment beliefs. Individuals with an insecure-avoidant attachment were most likely to enter into PSRs with their favourite TV personalities. Avoidant attachment is characterised by a concern that others will not reciprocate one's desire for intimacy. Cole and Leets argued that individuals with an insecure-avoidant style turn to TV characters as a means of satisfying their 'unrealistic' and often unmet relational needs. They suggest that the parasocial bonds these individuals form with media figures simply reflect another manifestation of their desire for intimacy, even if this intimacy is with a TV character. Avoidant individuals were the least likely to enter into PSRs with TV personalities. People with an avoidant attachment style find it difficult to develop intimate relationships and therefore are less likely to seek real-life relationships *or* PSRs. They appear to avoid not only relational intimacy but imagined intimacy as well.

THE ABSORPTION ADDICTION MODEL

The nature of parasocial relationships

The reasons why people form PSRs are as varied as the reasons for forming face-to-face relationships in real life. For example, people may form PSRs because of a lack of real relationships in their own life. Shyness and loneliness create a void in a person's life that can be filled by a PSR. Such relationships, common among celebrities and their fans, might be particularly appealing to some individuals because the relationship makes few demands. Because a fan does not usually have a 'real' relationship with the celebrity, they do not run the risk of criticism or rejection, as might be the case in a real relationship (Ashe and McCutcheon, 2001). Parasocial relationships are more likely to form with characters who are considered attractive by the viewer (the perception of *attractiveness*) and are viewed as similar to the viewer (the perception of *homophily*).

According to the **absorption addiction model** and levels of PSR (McCutcheon *et al.*, 2002), most people never go beyond admiring celebrities because of the celebrities' entertainment or social value. However, some go much further than that. Using the Celebrity Attitude Scale (CAS), Giles and Maltby (2006) identify three levels in this process:

- **Entertainment-social** – Fans are attracted to a favourite celebrity and will watch, keep up with, read and learn about that celebrity for the purposes of entertainment and gossip. For example, on the CAS they would agree with statements such as 'Learning the life story of my favourite celebrity is a lot of fun.'
- **Intense-personal** – This level involves a deeper level of involvement and reflects intensive and compulsive feelings about the celebrity, akin to the obsessive tendencies of fans often referred to in the literature; for example: 'I love to talk to others who admire my favourite celebrity.'
- **Borderline-pathological** – This level is typified by, on the one hand, empathy with the celebrity, as individuals at this level identify with the celebrity's successes and failures. However, it is also characterised by overidentification with the celebrity and uncontrollable behaviours and fantasies about their lives; for example: 'If I walked through the door of my favourite celebrity's house, he or she would be happy to see me.'

From absorption to addiction

Lange *et al.* suggest, however, that, for some adolescents, an introverted nature, an especially difficult set of social circumstances and a lack of meaningful relationships may lead them to become increasingly 'absorbed' by the lives of these 'parasocial friends'. Absorption involves an 'effortless focusing of attention' which leads fans to believe they have a special relationship with that celebrity, motivating them to learn more about the object of their attention.

If the level of absorption is high enough, the person may move on to higher levels of parasocial interaction, where the motivational forces driving this absorption may eventually become addictive, leading the person to more extreme (and even delusional) behaviours in order to sustain satisfaction with the parasocial relationship they have developed with the celebrity. At the borderline-pathological level, the PSR becomes 'addictive' because of the progressively stronger involvement that is now required to remain 'connected' with the celebrity. Lange *et al.* suggest that initially interest in celebrities and the development of a PSR is via absorption; this interest is subsequently maintained by means of psychological addiction.

▶ An 18-year-old Michael Jackson fan reported that after her father left her family, Jackson became a substitute source of comfort for her. This fan found a secure base and source of personal comfort in Jackson and his music. This became a safe haven for her as she dealt with the abandonment of her father (cited in Stever, 2009).

Research support for factors involved in parasocial relationships

Schiappa *et al.* (2007) carried out a meta-analysis of studies that had explored factors that were instrumental in the formation of PSRs. They found support for the assumption that people with higher levels of parasocial relationships also watched more television. Their analysis also showed that there was a significant positive relationship between the degree to which a person perceives television characters as being real and their tendency to form PSRs. Finally, they found evidence to support the claim that the likelihood of forming a PSR with TV characters was linked to those characters' perceived attractiveness and their similarity to the viewer.

Are parasocial relationships linked to loneliness?

PSRs were initially believed to be a substitute for 'real' social relationships and therefore linked to feelings of social isolation and loneliness. Although some research (e.g. Greenwood and Long, 2009) has shown that individuals may develop PSRs as a way of dealing with feelings of loneliness or loss, other research (e.g. Chory-Assad and Yanen, 2005) has found no relationship between *intensity* of loneliness and intensity of PSRs. Eyal and Cohen (2006) did find evidence of a link between PSRs and intensity of loneliness experienced in a parasocial 'breakup'. In a sample of 279 students who were fans of the popular TV series *Friends*, the intensity of their PSR with their favourite character was the strongest predictor of their feelings of loneliness following broadcast of the final episode. This suggests that PSRs may not only compensate for feelings of loneliness, but their loss can also *create* feelings of loneliness.

The absorption addiction model: Links to mental health

Maltby *et al.* (2003) used the *Eysenck Personality Questionnaire* (EPQ) to assess the relationship between parasocial relationship level and personality. They found that whereas the *entertainment-social* level was associated with extraversion (i.e. sociable, lively, active), the *intense-personal* level was associated with neuroticism (i.e. tense, emotional, moody). As neuroticism is related to anxiety and depression, this provides a clear explanation of why higher levels of parasocial relationship are associated with poorer mental health. Maltby *et al.* suggest that future research might explore the implications of a reported connection between the *borderline-pathological* level and psychoticism (i.e. impulsive, anti-social, egocentric), as measured by the EPQ.

Loss of a parasocial relationship is linked to attachment style

An Israeli study (Cohen, 2004) lends support to the claim that viewers would show the same negative response to loss of a *parasocial* relationship as they would to the loss of a *real* relationship. A sample of 381 adults completed questionnaires, including questions about their relationships with their favourite TV characters, how they would react if those characters were taken off the air, and their attachment styles. Viewers expecting to lose their favourite characters anticipated negative reactions (e.g. feelings of sadness, anger and loneliness) similar to those experienced after the loss of close personal relationships. These reactions were related both to the intensity of the PSR with the favourite character *and* to the viewers' attachment style, with anxious-ambivalently attached participants anticipating the most negative responses.

Cultural similarities in parasocial relationships

When watching a film or reading a book, viewers (or readers) must interpret and evaluate the content based on their own cultural background. Schmid and Klimmt (2011) investigated whether there would be differences in the PSRs formed with the fictional character *Harry Potter* in two contrasting cultures. They studied Germany, an individualist culture that stresses individuality over loyalty to the group, and Mexico, a collectivist culture where the individual is more deeply involved in social groups. Despite the differences between these cultures, the researchers found fans from Mexico and fans from Germany displayed very similar patterns of PSRs with Harry Potter and the other characters in the franchise. Their online survey revealed that fans from both cultures admired Harry Potter and found commonalities between their own lives and relationships and those portrayed in the films and books, demonstrating the universal influence of mainstream media characters.

Jasmine is a huge fan of the singer Rihanna. Her interest in Rihanna began when she was at school, as Jasmine and her friends would constantly talk about Rihanna's music, sing her songs and swap celebrity gossip about the singer. Now Jasmine has left school and started work, she doesn't really have the same opportunities for talking about Rihanna. However, she finds that her interest in the singer hasn't waned in the slightest. In fact, it seems to have got even worse. Jasmine misses her friends, but she misses the opportunity to talk about Rihanna even more. She spends most of her day, when she should be working, on social media reading about Rihanna and talking about her with people she doesn't even know. Her preoccupation with the singer has now almost taken over her life as Jasmine spends most of her wages trying to copy the way that Rihanna dresses, the cosmetics she uses and so on. She eventually loses her job because she doesn't concentrate on her work any more.

Using the absorption addiction model of relationships, explain Jasmine's parasocial relationship with Rihanna. (3 marks)

► Robyn Rihanna Fenty, known professionally as Rihanna, is a Barbadian singer-songwriter.

KEY TERMS

Absorption addiction model Individuals can become psychologically absorbed with a celebrity to establish a sense of fulfilment. The motivational forces driving this absorption might then take on an addictive component, leading to more extreme behaviours in order to sustain the parasocial relationship.

Attachment theory An explanation of the formation of an emotional bond between two people (especially caregiver and child). It is a two-way process that endures over time. It leads to certain behaviours such as clinging and proximity-seeking.

Parasocial relationship An individual is attracted to another person (usually a celebrity), who is usually unaware of the existence of the person who has created the relationship.

CAN YOU?   No. 3.9

1. Explain what is meant by the term *parasocial relationship*. (2 marks)
2. Outline the levels of parasocial relationships. (4 marks)
3. Outline the absorption addiction model of parasocial relationships. (4 marks)
4. Outline the attachment theory explanation of parasocial relationships. (4 marks)
5. Outline and evaluate explanations of parasocial relationships. (16 marks)

End-of-chapter review / CHAPTER SUMMARY

We have identified here the key points of the topics on the AQA A level specification, i.e. the bare minimum that you need to know. You may want to fill in further details to elaborate and personalise this material.

EVOLUTIONARY EXPLANATIONS FOR PARTNER PREFERENCES

THE NATURE OF SEXUAL SELECTION
- Intrasexual selection – individuals compete with other members of their sex.
- Intersexual selection – individuals evolve preferences for desirable qualities in potential mates.

SEXUAL SELECTION AND LONG-TERM MATE PREFERENCES
- Females most attracted to males who can provide resources.
- Males most attracted to females who display signals of fertility.

KEY STUDY: BUSS (1989)
- Procedure: Male and females from 37 cultures asked to rate 18 characteristics that they looked for in a mate.
- Findings: Women looked for men who were 'good financial prospects'. Men looked for physical attractiveness and youth.

EVALUATION
- Cultural traditions just as important as evolutionary forces – Bernstein.
- Buller claims evidence for a universal female mating preference for high-status men is weak.
- Studies of mate-selection in real-life also support these mate-choice hypotheses (Buss).
- Females choose creative mates because of the potential adaptive value of creativity and ingenuity.
- Female mate choice is not consistent but varies across the menstrual cycle.

ATTRACTION: FILTER THEORY

FILTER THEORY
- We choose partners by using a series of filters that narrow down the 'field of availables'.
- Different filters prominent at different stages.
- Social demographic variables important in initial stages; similarity in attitudes important for next stage.
- Complementarity of needs – people are attracted to others whose needs are 'harmonious' with their own.

KEY STUDY: KERCKHOFF AND DAVIS (1962)
- Procedure: Couples completed questionnaires of shared attitudes and values and degree of need complementarity.
- Findings: Dating for less than 18 months – similarity the most significant predictor of closeness. More than 18 months, only complementarity of needs predictive of closeness.

EVALUATION
- Lack of research support for filter theory-Levinger et al. failed to replicate predictions.
- Filtering process allows people to avoid investing in a relationship that 'won't work' (Duck).
- Perceived similarity predicts attraction more than *actual* similarity (Hoyle).
- Complementarity of needs not as important as similarity of attitudes (Dijkstra and Barelds).
- Many people are not aware of their partners' values, needs, etc. (Thornton and Young-DeMarco).

PHYSICAL ATTRACTIVENESS

PHYSICAL ATTRACTIVENESS
- Men place great importance on physical attractiveness in a mate.
- Matching hypothesis – individuals seek out partners whose social desirability approximately equals their own.

KEY STUDY: WALSTER AND WALSTER (1966)
- Procedure: Male and female students completed questionnaires and rated for physical attractiveness.
- Allocated partner as random although students believed they were matched in terms of personality and intelligence.
- Findings: Participants responded more positively if their dates were physically attractive than 'matched'.

EVALUATION
- Speed dating and the challenge to traditional views of attraction – Eastwick and Finkel found no gender differences in importance of physical attractiveness.
- Value for physical attractiveness may not predict real-life partner choice.
- Complex matching – person may compensate for a lack of physical attractiveness with other desirable qualities.
- Research support for sex differences in the impprtance of physical attractiveness – Meltzer.
- 'Matching may not be that important in initial attraction – Taylor et al.
- Implications of sex differences in the importance of physical attractiveness (Meltzer et al.).

SELF-DISCLOSURE

SELF-DISCLOSURE
- Greater disclosure leads to greater feelings of intimacy.
- Self-disclosure received is a better predictor of liking and loving than level of self-disclosure given.
- Norms include appropriate rate of self-disclosure and reciprocity.

KEY STUDY: SPRECHER *ET AL.* (2013)
- Procedure: Students paired in either reciprocal or non-reciprocal dyads and assessed for liking the other person.
- Findings: Those in reciprocal dyads showed higher levels of liking than those in non-reciprocal dyads.

EVALUATION
- Research support for importance of self-disclosure – Collins and Miller meta-analysis.
- Self-disclosure on the Internet: the boom or bust phenomenon – Cooper and Sportolari.
- The norms of self-disclosure run deep – Tal-Or and Hershman-Shitrit.
- Self-disclosure greater in face-to-face than online relationships – Knop et al.
- Cultural differences in patterns of self-disclosure, e.g. Americans disclose more than Chinese (Chen).

SOCIAL EXCHANGE THEORY

SOCIAL EXCHANGE THEORY
- Individuals attempt to maximise their rewards within a relationship.
- Commitment to a relationship is dependent on its profitability.
- Comparison level – experiences with previous relationships set standards for current relationship.
- Comparison level for alternatives – person considers potential increase in rewards from a different partner.

KEY STUDY: KURDEK AND SCHMITT (1986)
- Procedure: Investigated importance of social exchange factors in heterosexual and same-sex couples.
- Findings: Satisfaction for all couples determined by perception of many benefits (CL), and alternatives seen as less attractive (CLA).

EVALUATION
- Sprecher – support for influence of comparison level for alternatives.
- Limitations – difficult to determine what is a cost and what is a benefit.
- Limitations – the problem of assessing the relative value of costs and benefits.
- Limitations – overemphasis on costs and benefits rather than relational standards.
- Real-world application – use of Integrated Behavioural Couples Therapy.

EQUITY THEORY

EQUITY THEORY
- Equity when one partner's benefits minus their costs equals their partner's benefits less *their* costs.
- Being under- or over-benefited = inequity, leading to distress.
- Schafer and Keith – inequity more likely to be perceived during child-rearing years.
- Hatfield and Rapson – concern with inequity dependent on stage of relationship.
- Dealing with inequity – restoration of actual equity, psychological equity or leaving relationship.

KEY STUDY: STAFFORD AND CANARY (2006)
- Procedure: 200 married couples completed measures of equity and relationship satisfaction.
- **Findings**: Satisfaction highest when relationships perceived to be equitable.

EVALUATION
- Not all individuals experience inequity in the same way (equity sensitivity).
- Gender differences in importance of equity – e.g. women feel more guilt than men when over-benefited.
- Aumer-Ryan *et al.* – all cultures considered equity important in relationships, although cultural differences in how equitable actual relationships were.
- Supporting evidence from non-human primates – capuchin monkeys became angry at lack of fairness (Brosnan and de Waal).
- A problem of causality – perception of inequity may lead to dissatisfaction, or dissatisfaction can lead to perception of inequity (Clark).

VIRTUAL RELATIONSHIPS IN SOCIAL MEDIA

SELF-DISCLOSURE IN VIRTUAL RELATIONSHIPS
- People present 'edited' version of self over social media (broadcasting self-disclosure).
- Different levels of self-disclosure dependent on whether it is a public or private presentation.
- Confident to self-disclose on the Internet because of anonymity and 'strangers on a train' effect.

ABSENCE OF GATING IN VIRTUAL RELATIONSHIPS
- Barriers that limit opportunities for less attractive individuals to form face-to-face relationships absent in virtual relationships.
- Online social networks empower 'gated' individuals to present identities they are unable to in face-to-face situations (Zhao *et al.*).
- Online environment enables people to project a more socially desirable self than 'offline' identity (Yurchisin *et al.*).

EVALUATION
- Rosenfeld and Thomas found individuals with Internet access far more likely to be partnered.
- Rosenfeld and Thomas found no evidence to support the claim that virtual relationships were of lower quality.
- Tamir and Mitchell found evidence of a biological basis for motivation to self-disclose on social media.
- Virtual relationships helpful for shy people (Baker and Oswald), allowing for higher quality friendships.
- Positive consequences for offline relationships by enhancing individual's self-image (Zhao *et al.*).

THE INVESTMENT MODEL OF RELATIONSHIPS

THE INVESTMENT MODEL
- Satisfaction level = positive versus negative emotions experienced within a relationship.
- Quality of alternatives – assessment of whether these needs are better fulfilled outside the relationship.
- Investment size – a measure of all the resources that are attached to the relationship and which would be lost.
- Commitment level – describes the likelihood the relationship will persist.
- High levels of satisfaction plus high investment = increasing dependence on relationship = high commitment.

KEY STUDY: LE AND AGNEW (2003)
- Procedure: Meta-analysis of 52 studies of different components of investment model.
- Findings: All three components highly correlated with relationship commitment with satisfaction level most correlated.

EVALUATION
- Research support for importance of commitment as indicator of relationship stability (Le *et al.*).
- Difficult to measure variables of model, including reliance on self-report measures.
- Real-world application – can explain abusive relationships.
- 'Investment' should also include plans made, i.e. notion of *future* investment as well as past investment.
- Main claims shown to be true across different cultures and types of relationship.

RELATIONSHIP BREAKDOWN

A PHASE MODEL OF RELATIONSHIP BREAKDOWN
- Breakdown – first phase begins when one partner feels dissatisfied with the relationship.
- Intrapsychic – individual broods over the relationship and re-evaluates alternatives.
- Dyadic – individual confronts their partner to discuss their dissatisfaction.
- Social – dissatisfaction is shared with network of family and friends.
- Grave-dressing – partners construct a representation of the failed relationship that does not paint their contribution to it in unfavourable terms.

EVALUATION
- Model fails to reflect possibility of personal growth, hence development of updated model.
- Impact of social processes varies by type of relationship. Less advice about reconciliation in younger relationships.
- Benefits of grave-dressing phase – stories protect person's psychological well-being.
- Ethical issues in breakdown research due to vulnerability of the potential participants.
- Suggests that different phases can be identified and appropriate interventions offered.

PARASOCIAL RELATIONSHIPS

PARASOCIAL RELATIONSHIPS
- PSRs are appealing because they make few demands and the person does not risk rejection.
- PSRs more likely to form with characters considered *attractive* and with characters considered *similar* to the viewer (*homophily*).

THE ABSORPTION ADDICTION MODEL AND LEVELS OF PSR
- Absorption may become addictive, leading the person to extreme behaviours to sustain satisfaction with the PSR.
- Giles and Maltby identify three levels of PSR.
- Entertainment-social; Intense-personal; Borderline-pathological.

AN ATTACHMENT THEORY EXPLANATION OF PARASOCIAL RELATIONSHIPS
- PSRs exhibit the same properties of adult attachment identified by Weiss.
- Proximity seeking; Secure base; Protest at disruption.
- Individuals with insecure-avoidant attachment most likely to develop PSR and avoidant individuals least likely.

EVALUATION
- Research support for factors involved in parasocial relationships (Schiappa *et al.*).
- Parasocial relationships linked to loneliness (Greenwood and Long), but other research suggests not (Chory-Assad and Yanen).
- Absorption addiction model may be linked to mental health (Maltby *et al.*).
- Impact of loss of parasocial relationship linked to attachment style (Cohen).
- Research (Schmid and Klimmt) found cultural similarities in parasocial relationships.

0 1 Give **two** examples of human reproductive behaviour and explain how each one can be related to sexual selection.   **[4 marks]**

0 2 Describe **one** evolutionary explanation for partner preferences.   **[4 marks]**

0 3 Explain **one** criticism of using evolutionary explanations for partner preferences.   **[3 marks]**

0 4 Identify **two** factors affecting attraction in romantic relationships.   **[2 marks]**

0 5 Which one of the following is a definition of complementarity in romantic relationships?
Write the letter of your chosen answer in your answer booklet.   **[1 mark]**

  A. The extent to which partners find each other attractive.

  B. The extent to which partners match on social desirability.

  C. The extent to which partners meet each other's needs.

  D. The extent to which partners share values and beliefs.

0 6 Read the item below and then answer the question that follows.

> Sarah was unhappy in her first serious relationship. Looking back, she now realises that Matthew was much more successful and much more confident than she was, and she did not fit in with his wide circle of friends. Sarah is much happier with her new partner, Karl, because their jobs are very similar and they come from they same kind of family background.

Using your knowledge of the matching hypothesis, explain Sarah's experiences of her two relationships.   **[4 marks]**

0 7 Which one of the following sequences shows the order of stages in the filter theory of attraction? Write the letter of your chosen answer in your answer booklet.   **[1 mark]**

  A. complementarity, similarity in attitudes, social demography

  B. complementarity, social demography, similarity in attitudes

  C. similarity in attitudes, social demography, complementarity

  D. social demography, similarity in attitudes, complementarity

0 8 Briefly evaluate the filter theory of attraction in romantic relationships.   **[4 marks]**

0 9 Briefly discuss the role of self-disclosure in attraction in romantic relationships.   **[6 marks]**

1 0 *'Physical attraction is the most important ingredient for an intimate relationship to be successful.'*

Discuss factors affecting attraction in romantic relationships. Refer to the above statement as part of your discussion.   **[16 marks]**

1 1 Describe **one** research study that has investigated the social exchange theory of romantic relationships.   **[4 marks]**

1 2 Discuss the social exchange theory of romantic relationships. Refer to equity theory as part of your discussion.   **[16 marks]**

1 3 Explain **one** criticism of using equity theory to explain romantic relationships.   **[3 marks]**

1 4 Explain the concept of commitment with reference to Rusbult's investment model of relationships.   **[3 marks]**

1 5 Read the item below and answer the question that follows.

> Colin and Peter have been in a relationship for over 20 years. They are not as happy as they used to be but also recognise that it would be difficult for both of them to find someone that they feel so comfortable with. They also recognise how long they have spent building a home together, and how close they have become to each other's families. This is not something that they could easily sacrifice.

Using your knowledge of Rusbult's investment model, explain why Colin and Peter's relationship is likely to last.   **[6 marks]**

1 6 Distinguish between the intrapsychic and dyadic phases of relationship breakdown with reference to Duck's model. **[3 marks]**

1 7 Read the following item and answer the questions that follow.

> Frances's relationship has recently broken down and she is keen for her friends to know that her partner is primarily to blame for not trying hard enough.
>
> George is dissatisfied with his relationship and has taken the day off work to talk this through with his girlfriend.
>
> Ayesha has told her future husband that she is not sure that their relationship is right for her, and has also started to share her concerns with her family.

    (i) Name the person who is in Duck's social phase of relationship breakdown. **[1 mark]**
    (ii) Name the person who is in Duck's grave dressing phase of relationship breakdown. **[1 mark]**

1 8 Describe and evaluate **two** theories of romantic relationships. Refer to research evidence as part of your answer. **[16 marks]**

1 9 Briefly discuss the findings from **one** research study into the role of self-disclosure in virtual relationships. **[4 marks]**

2 0 Outline **two** effects of the absence of gating on the nature of virtual relationships. **[4 marks]**

2 1 *'The rise of virtual relationships has caused as many problems as it has addressed.'*
Discuss virtual relationships in the social media. Refer to the statement above as part of your discussion. **[16 marks]**

2 2 Explain how virtual relationships differ from parasocial relationships. **[3 marks]**

2 3 Identify and outline **one** level of parasocial relationships. **[3 marks]**

2 4 Explain **one** criticism of the absorption addiction model of parasocial relationships. **[3 marks]**

2 5 Discuss psychological explanations of parasocial relationships. **[16 marks]**

2 6 Read the item below and answer the questions that follow.

> A psychologist investigated relationship breakdown by using unstructured interviews with three couples who were in the process of splitting up. She had selected them when they responded to an advertisement on the Internet. She used the interviews to investigate whether there are patterns in the relationship breakdown.

    (i) The psychologist collected qualitative data in this study.
       With reference to the study, outline **one** strength and **one** weakness of this type of data. **[4 marks]**
    (ii) Identify the sampling technique used by the psychologist and outline **one** limitation of using the technique in this study. **[3 marks]**
    (iii) Outline **one** ethical issue that the psychologist would need to consider in this study. **[2 marks]**

2 7 Read the item below and then answer the questions that follow.

> A psychologist was interested in the personality types that engaged in parasocial relationships. To investigate this, he used a questionnaire which was completed by a sample of college students. He used open questions to establish whether they had experienced parasocial relationships or not, and then used closed questions to assess personality type. He found that students that had experienced parasocial relationships scored significantly higher on scales measuring anxiety, isolation and obsession.

    (i) Give **one** advantage of using open questions to establish whether a participant had experienced parasocial relationships or not. **[1 mark]**
    (ii) Give **one** advantage of using closed questions to assess personality. **[1 mark]**
    (iii) The psychologist used a Mann-Whitney test to analyse his findings. With reference to the study, give **three** reasons why this test was used. **[3 marks]**

The exam questions on relationships will be varied but are likely to involve some short answer questions (AO1), some application of knowledge questions (AO2), research methods questions and possibly an extended writing question (AO1 + AO3). We've provided answers to some additional questions together with comments from an examiner about how well they've each done.

---

01 Read the item below and answer the questions that follow.

> Research has shown that males and females have different priorities when looking for a partner. Females prefer males who are trustworthy, hard-working and assertive. Males prefer females who are faithful, youthful and nurturing.

(i) Choose **one** of the traits females prefer and outline how this preference can be explained in terms of evolutionary theory. (3 marks)

(ii) Choose **one** of the traits that males prefer and outlined how this preference can be explained in terms of evolutionary theory. (3 marks)

Maisie's answer

(i) Females prefer males who are hardworking because this means they can provide them with resources to make life better for her and her children.

(ii) Males prefer females who are youthful. This is because youthfulness is an indication of fertility, which is important for passing on genes.

Examiner's comments

Maisie would earn 3 marks overall. The first part of her answer is only worth one as she links her chosen trait to provision of resources but needs to be more specific about how this relates to survival or reproduction – making life better is a little vague. Her second part of the answer is more technical because it makes reference to 'passing on genes'. In this instance, a further mark is awarded as well as the one for making the link between youthfulness and fertility.

Ciaran's answer

(i) Females look for males who are assertive. Males who are assertive are better able to compete with other males for resources and to physically protect their partner and her children. By selecting males who are assertive, this makes it more likely that any offspring will survive to maturity and pass on their genes to the next generation.

(ii) Males look for females who are nurturing. Females who are nurturing are more likely to be good mothers to their children and to show better parenting skills. From an evolutionary perspective, a female who is nurturant increases the likelihood that their children will survive to maturity compared to the children of mothers who lack these characteristics.

Examiner's comments

Ciaran's answer is worth 5 marks. The first part of his answer earns all three: assertiveness is related to two clear behaviours and then this is further related to evolutionary theory through the reference to survival and to passing on genes. The second part of the answer earns two. One for the link to parenting and a further mark for how this then links to survival.

---

02 Describe one research study that has investigated the social exchange theory of romantic relationships. (4 marks)

Maisie's answer

(i) Sprecher carried out a longitudinal study of couples in the US. She found that the most important factor in relationship commitment was the comparison level for alternatives (CLA). When this was low, commitment to the current relationship was high. When the CLA was high, commitment to the current relationship was lower.

Examiner's comments

Although brief, Maisie's answer gives a good overview of the study. 1 mark for some detail on procedure (type of study, sample). 1 mark for a conclusion. 1 mark for a set of findings. 3 marks in total.

Ciaran's answer

(i) Kurdek and Schmitt (1986) looked at the relative importance of the different social exchange factors in determining relationship quality. They studied 185 couples, both heterosexual and same-sex couples, who completed a questionnaire about the quality of their relationships. The researchers found that judgements of the quality of these relationships was determined by the perceived benefits of the relationship, together with individuals judging that alternatives to the current relationship were considered less attractive.

Examiner's comments

This answer also scores 3 marks. The opening statement is a little obvious given the question so the response earns marks after this. There is some detail on procedure (sample, method). Then the findings can be read in two distinct parts, each worth 1 mark.

03 Describe and evaluate **two** theories of romantic relationships. Refer to research evidence as part of your answer. (16 marks)

Maisie's answer

Social exchange theory explains romantic relationships in terms of the costs and benefits that people see as associated with their relationship. According to this theory, people are more satisfied with their relationship if the benefits they receive (e.g. having resources, having someone who looks after them) are greater than the costs of the relationship (e.g. the time and energy they expend in the relationship). Each partner in the relationship compares their current relationship with what they expect (based on their experience with relationships in the past). This is referred to as the comparison level. Someone who has had relationships with lots of benefits in the past would expect the same in their current relationship, whereas someone who has had very unrewarding relationships in the past would have a relatively low comparison level. They must also consider the comparison with alternatives by comparing the benefits they have in their current relationship compared to what they might have in another relationship. If alternatives offer less than what they have in the current relationship, then their satisfaction with the current relationship will be higher.

There is some research support for social exchange theory. For example, in a study with dating couples, those who had low comparison level for alternatives expressed more satisfaction with their current relationship. There are problems with this theory, because what is considered to be a benefit to one person might be seen as a cost to another person, therefore it is difficult to assess costs and benefits of a relationship.

Equity theory claims that people are happier in relationships when what they put into the relationship (the costs) are approximately equal to the benefits. If the costs are higher than the benefits then this results in dissatisfaction with the relationship. If the benefits are higher than the costs, then people are also dissatisfied with their relationship. A study by Stafford and Canary found that satisfaction was highest in married couples who perceived their relationships to be equitable. A problem for equity theory is that there are gender differences in the importance of equity. Research has shown that women are more likely to see themselves as under-benefitted in a relationship and are also more likely to feel guilty if they feel they are over-benefitted in their relationship. Another problem is that some people are not bothered by inequity in their relationship because they feel they are entitled to receive more benefits. Other people are not affected by being under-benefitted in their relationship and are happy to give more than they receive.

421 words

Examiner's comments

This essay qualifies for a level 2 mark. It is strong on description, particularly when addressing social exchange theory where Maisie demonstrates sound knowledge and understanding. The use of evidence can contribute to AO1 marks but is covered quite briefly and not really used to any effect. The main issue with Maisie's essay is the lack of evaluation given that this is worth most of the marks. The commentary lacks both breadth and depth. In other words, Maisie needs to raise more issues with each theory and develop points where she can. A more sophisticated essay would also make some attempt to compare the theories rather than treat them as separate entities.

04 'The rise of virtual relationships has caused as many problems as it has addressed.'

Discuss virtual relationships in the social media. Refer to the statement above as part of your discussion. (16 marks)

Ciaran's answer

Virtual relationships are conducted through the medium of a computer. They differ from face-to-face relationships in a number of ways, including the nature and speed of self-disclosure and the absence of gating. A characteristic of virtual relationships is that people self-disclose more than they would in a face-to-face relationship. Individuals feel more secure about self-disclosing through social media such as Facebook because they are better able to control how much (or how little) they disclose to another individual. Disclosure of intimate information that might be important when developing a romantic relationship can be restricted to private messaging rather than being broadcast in the more public areas of social media.

Virtual relationships are also characterised by an absence of gating, barriers to interaction that prevent some people forming face-to-face relationships. People who are, for example, socially awkward may find it difficult to form relationships, but the removal of these barriers in the online world means that they are able to be their true self in a virtual relationship, and so are better able to develop close relationships.

Ling (2000) highlights a problem with virtual relationships. The growth of social media has led to a reduction in face-to-face contact in social relationships. Ling claims that this means that we no longer spend as much time with neighbours, extended family or close friends, preferring the convenience of virtual relationships through social media. A second problem linked to the rise of virtual relationships is the increase in jealousy associated with social media. For example, Muise et al. (2009) found that increased use of Facebook predicts increased jealousy in individuals who monitor their partners' social media pages. They suggest this is due to the accessibility of information that leads to increased monitoring and jealousy for many people. Because 'friendship' status on social media lacks context and can be ambiguous, jealousy can be a result of misunderstandings.

However, virtual relationships can also have positive consequences for people's offline relationships. For example, shy or awkward people are less likely to experience the same gating obstacles when forming virtual relationships that they would in the offline world. Zhao et al. (2008) claim that this can increase their self-confidence and so increase their chances of connecting to others in their offline world. Baker and Oswald (2010) provided evidence to support the claim that virtual relationships were good for shy people. Students who used Facebook rated their friendships as being of higher quality than those who did not. This demonstrated that shy people find virtual relationships particularly valuable in forming and maintaining relationships. The reasons why many people find virtual relationships so rewarding may also be explained by the pleasure that people experience when they self-disclose online. Tamir and Mitchell (2012) found that when people self-disclose, they experience increased MRI activity in the brain areas associated with reward. This suggests that the desire to share personal experiences over social media may be a consequence of the rewarding nature of self-disclosure.

490 words

Examiner's comments

Ciaran's essay would be awarded a level 3 mark. It is a well planned response with a good discursive style. Understanding of virtual relationships is evident throughout the commentary and the opening statement outlining them contributes to the AO1. The essay makes good use of evidence which is important here as these kinds of essays can often end up being quite anecdotal. The discussion is balanced, looking at both the advantages and disadvantages of virtual relationships. Ciaran could have improved the response by using the quote in his essay – indeed this was a requirement of the question. The content would not have to change but its structure would. It would also have been useful to end the essay with a clear conclusion which made some judgement on the overall value of virtual relationships.

CONTENTS OF CHAPTER

SPECIFICATION CHECKLIST

- Sex and gender. Sex-role stereotypes. Androgyny and measuring androgyny, including the Bem Sex Role Inventory.

- The role of chromosomes and hormones (testosterone, oestrogen and oxytocin) in sex and gender. Atypical sex chromosome patterns: Klinefelter's syndrome and Turner's syndrome.

- Cognitive explanations of gender development: Kohlberg's theory; gender identity, gender stability and gender constancy; gender schema theory.

- Psychodynamic explanations of gender development: Freud's psychoanalytic theory; Oedipus complex; Electra complex; identification and internalisation.

- Social learning theory as applied to gender development. The influence of culture and media on gender roles.

- Atypical gender development: gender identity disorder; biological and social explanations for gender identity disorder.

TRY THIS

Bem Sex Role Inventory

In this chapter you will learn about how some people embrace being both male and female rather than the more traditional male/female divide. One of the early expressions of this idea was Sandra Bem's concept of androgyny. Some people feel comfortable incorporating characteristics of both genders into their own personality, whereas other people prefer to be clearly male or female.

To assess sex roles, Sandra Bem created the Bem Sex Role Inventory (BSRI). It characterises your personality as masculine, feminine, androgynous or undifferentiated. The 60 different attributes are listed below. For each of them you should rate yourself on a scale of 1 to 7, where 1 means never or almost never true and 7 means almost always true.

1. self-reliant	21. reliable	41. warm
2. yielding	22. analytical	42. solemn
3. helpful	23. sympathetic	43. willing to take a stand
4. defends own beliefs	24. jealous	44. tender
5. cheerful	25. leadership ability	45. friendly
6. moody	26. sensitive to others' needs	46. aggressive
7. independent	27. truthful	47. gullible
8. shy	28. willing to take risks	48. inefficient
9. conscientious	29. understanding	49. acts as a leader
10. athletic	30. secretive	50. childlike
11. affectionate	31. makes decisions easily	51. adaptable
12. theatrical	32. compassionate	52. individualistic
13. assertive	33. sincere	53. does not use harsh language
14. flatterable	34. self-sufficient	54. unsystematic
15. happy	35. eager to soothe hurt feelings	55. competitive
16. strong personality	36. conceited	56. loves children
17. loyal	37. dominant	57. tactful
18. unpredictable	38. soft spoken	58. ambitious
19. forceful	39. likable	59. gentle
20. feminine	40. masculine	60. conventional

To score yourself, add up ratings for all masculine items and add up all feminine items. Ignore the neutral items.

> Masculine items: 1, 4, 7, 10, 13, 16, 19, 22, 25, 28, 31, 34, 37, 40, 43, 46, 49, 52, 55, 58
> Feminine items: 2, 5, 8, 11, 14, 17, 20, 23, 36, 29, 32, 35, 38, 41, 44, 47, 50, 53, 56, 59
> Neutral items: 3, 6, 9, 12, 15, 18, 21, 24, 37, 30, 33, 36, 39, 42, 45, 48, 51, 54, 57, 60

In other words, if you rated 'self-reliant' as 3 you add that to your masculine score as that is a masculine item. If you rated 'yielding' as 5 then you add that to your feminine score as that is a feminine item. You ignore 'helpful' as that is neutral. 'Defends own beliefs' is masculine again and so on.

If the number of masculine and feminine items are roughly equal, you are undifferentiated (if both totals are low) or androgynous (if both totals are high).

If the two scores are quite different then you are either classed as masculine or feminine (depending which score is bigger).

Sex-role stereotypes and androgyny

If we ask 'who are you?', one of your first answers might be to say 'a boy' or 'a girl'. Your sex is a key aspect of your sense of who you are. In fact psychologists distinguish between **sex** and **gender**. Sex is a biological fact – whether a person is a genetic male or female. Gender refers to a person's sense of maleness or femaleness. In this chapter we are concerned with the development of gender, which is due in part to biology (nature) and in part to life experiences (nurture).

We begin by looking at maleness and femaleness.

▲ Androgyny seems fairly natural now but wasn't in the 1960s.

KEY TERMS

Androgyny Formed from the two words 'andro', meaning male, and 'gyny', meaning female. The word means a combination of male and female characteristics.

Gender A person's sense of maleness or femaleness, a psychological/social construct.

Sex Being genetically male (XY) or female (XX).

Sex-role stereotypes A set of shared expectations within a social group about what men and women should do and think.

SEX-ROLE STEREOTYPES

Whether you are a male or a female is a biological fact (and discussed on the next spread), but the way we behave is related to **sex-role stereotypes** (sometimes also called *gender stereotypes*).

The concept of 'roles' is to do with how we behave – we take on various roles such as 'friend' or 'student' or 'shop assistant', and our behaviour is related to social norms associated with this role. There are expectations, for example, about how students behave, and your behaviour within that role is considerably influenced by these expectations.

This applies to your behaviour as a male or a female. Society has expectations about how boys and girls, and men and women, should behave. Such expectations are referred to as 'stereotypes' – a fixed belief about a particular group of people.

A sex-role stereotype is learned from birth as children are exposed to the attitudes of their parents and others in their society who tell them 'Little boys don't cry' or 'Little girls don't like climbing trees'. Learning about sex-role stereotypes is implicit (i.e. not directly expressed) as well as explicit because we model the behaviour of individuals of the same sex (social learning theory).

ANDROGYNY

Sandra Bem introduced the concept of psychological **androgyny** in the 1970s, proposing that a person can be both masculine *and* feminine, an idea that contrasted with the traditional view that masculine and feminine behaviours are two separate clusters.

Furthermore, Bem argued that the traditional view was that rigid sex roles were important for mental health, whereas her view was that the opposite was true – that it was actually psychologically more healthy to *avoid* fixed sex-role stereotypes. Instead, she argued, men and women should feel free to adopt a variety of masculine- and feminine-type behaviours as suits their personality. For example, a man who likes cooking or being gentle should not have to stifle his personal inclinations because it isn't 'manly behaviour'. Stifling personality in this way has a psychological cost which can lead to mental disorder.

Measuring androgyny – the BSRI

Bem tested her ideas by creating a psychological test to measure androgyny, the Bem Sex Role Inventory (BSRI). This inventory was developed by asking 100 American undergraduates which personality traits they thought were desirable for men or women. The original list of 200 items was narrowed down to 40 (20 masculine and 20 feminine traits), and 20 neutral items were added as distractors. The inventory items are shown on the previous spread.

Each person rates themselves on a 7-point Likert scale ranging from never or almost never true to almost always true. Numerical scores for all masculine items are added up and the same for all feminine items, and then a person is given a score for femininity, masculinity and androgyny.

Bem designed the inventory to make it possible to test for masculinity and femininity independently rather than setting them against each other. In traditional tests, if you selected a masculine item you couldn't select a feminine one.

Using the original scoring method, individuals were categorised as masculine (high masculine score, low feminine), feminine (low masculine score, high feminine) and androgynous (high ratio of masculine to feminine traits).

A fourth category of undifferentiated (low scores for both masculine and feminine) was added after criticisms by Spence *et al.* (1975), who pointed out that Bem had not distinguished between persons who are androgynous (high in both masculine and feminine traits) and a different kind of androgyny, where a person is neither masculine nor feminine (low in both). This is the undifferentiated type.

Gender schema theory

Bem (1983) reformulated her approach in terms of what she called 'gender schema theory' (which is discussed further on page 98). She suggested that the difference between an androgynous and a traditionally sex-typed person is one of cognitive style. An androgynous person, when faced with a decision as to how to behave in a particular situation, responds independently of any gender concepts. In contrast, a traditionally sex-typed person determines what would be appropriate for their gender using gender schemas. Bem's argument was that a person who has a 'freer' cognitive style will be psychologically healthier.

EVALUATION

Support for parental influence

Smith and Lloyd (1978) showed that mothers do treat boy and girl babies differently, in line with sex-role stereotypes. The mothers (sample size 32) were videotaped playing for 10 minutes with a baby (not their own child). The baby was six months old and dressed and named as a boy or a girl. Two were actually boys and two were girls but the clothes/names were not always consistent with sex. Seven toys were present: a squeaky hammer and stuffed rabbit in trousers (masculine); a doll and squeaky Bambi (feminine); and a squeaky pig, a ball and a rattle (neutral).

If a mother thought she was playing with a boy, she verbally encouraged more motor activity and offered gender-appropriate toys. In other words, mothers responded to the perceived sex of the infant, in line with typical gender expectations.

More research on the effect of culture on gender development is described on page 104.

Support for the relationship between androgyny and psychological health

Research has found a positive correlation between androgyny and psychological health, as Bem predicted. For example, Prakash et al. (2010) tested 100 married females in India on masculinity/femininity and a range of outcome measures related to health: physical health, depression, anxiety and perceived stress. Masculinity/femininity was measured using the personal attribute scale (another test used to assess androgyny). Females with high masculinity scores had lower depression scores, etc., whereas those with high femininity scores had higher depression scores, etc. This supports the view that androgyny has a psychoprotective effect, because those with masculinity and feminity were better off in terms of their health.

Real-world applications

If androgyny is better for physical and psychological health then the obvious application is to encourage parents to raise children free to assume characteristics of either gender and free of sex-role stereotypes. There are a few individual cases of parents who have done this. One British couple (Time magazine, 2012) raised their son in a gender-neutral manner. The child knew he was a boy (because it is not possible to hide biological facts) but in every other way he did not identify with either gender.

Surprisingly there was a storm of protest about the parents' actions by people who felt it amounted to child abuse. This reveals how strongly people feel about sex-role stereotypes and the persisting belief that such stereotypes are important to healthy development. For those who agree with Bem's views, this means there is still work to do in promoting the benefits of androgyny.

Reliability of the BSRI

Research has demonstrated high test–retest reliability for the BSRI over a four-week period; correlations range from .76 to .94 (Bem, 1981).

A short form of the scale has been developed using just 30 items and has a good correlation of .90 with the original. Having a shorter form improved the internal reliability of the test because the less socially desirable terms were removed, such as 'gullible' and 'childlike'.

Validity of the BSRI

The link between androgyny and psychological health may be explained in terms of an intervening variable – self-esteem. Most of the adjectives in the BSRI are socially desirable – therefore someone who scored high on both masculine and feminine traits (i.e. androgynous) would also be higher in self-esteem than someone who chose only male or female items. This suggests that androgyny doesn't explain psychological healthiness at all.

The validity of the inventory has also been criticised in terms of response bias. Liberman and Gaa (1986) analysed the data from 133 graduate students and found that those students classed as androgynous simply had higher overall scores than those classed as either masculine or feminine. This happens because some individuals have a tendency to select answers at the higher end of the Likert scale and thus become classed as androgynous. Therefore the scores may be an artefact of the measurement rather than representing a true difference.

Finally the temporal validity of the scale can be questioned. The adjectives used in the BSRI were selected back in the 1970s and people's attitudes have changed since then, so it is questionable whether it is still appropriate. Hoffman and Borders (2001) asked a group of almost 400 undergraduates to rate the items on the BSRI as masculine or feminine. The results were that only two terms were still endorsed as masculine and feminine – and these were the adjectives *masculine* and *feminine*. All other terms failed to reach a 75% agreement level. This suggests that the BSRI is no longer relevant (lacks temporal validity).

MEET THE RESEARCHER

Sandra Bem (1944–2014). When Sandra Lipsitz first married fellow psychologist Daryl Bem, they decided they wanted an equalitarian marriage, sharing parenting roles and responsibilities and career commitments, as many couples do today – but in the 1960s gender roles were much more clearly demarcated. Her contribution went beyond the women's lib movement – Bem argued that both women *and* men were constrained by sex-role stereotypes.

Recently Sandra Bem was diagnosed with Alzheimer's disease and decided that she would end her own life before the disease took hold. She died in 2014, aged 69, after four years of fighting the disease.

⬆ UPGRADE

Extended writing questions (okay, let's call them essays…) such as question 4 in the 'Can you?' box below are typically worth 16 marks each. Although AQA do not award separate marks for AO1 (description) and AO3 (evaluation), they do nominally assign a certain number of marks for each in their marking schemes. Of the 16 marks available for an essay question, 6 are assigned to AO1 and 10 to AO3, so it pays to be aware of this when structuring your essays. A total of 400 words in response to the time available for a 16-mark question (6 marks AO1 and 10 marks AO3) would mean writing about 150 words of AO1, or 25 words each for the 6 points.

To gain a mark in the top mark level for an essay question, the descriptive (AO1, remember…) content should be 'accurate and generally well detailed'. But how do you achieve this? First of all, don't waste time with pointless introductions and definitions – they won't get you any marks. Then pick six things you want to say that cover the AO1 part of the question. To make your answer more 'detailed', try to include technical terms or specific words that fine tune what it is you are trying to say. This means you are going a bit deeper. Perhaps add an example to demonstrate your understanding and push each point up to the 25-word target. Of course, the content also has to be accurate, but that's down to you!

CAN YOU?  No. 4.1

1. Distinguish between the terms *sex* and *gender*. (2 marks)
2. Describe **one** study related to sex-role stereotypes. (4 marks)
3. Describe the Bem Sex Role Inventory. (4 marks)
4. Discuss the concept of androgyny. Refer to the Bem Sex Role Inventory in your answer. (16 marks)

The role of chromosomes and hormones in sex and gender

At the moment of conception your genetic makeup is fixed. Genes determine whether you are male or female, i.e. they determine your biological sex.

Genes also determine the production of various **hormones**, and these hormones affect your sense of maleness and femaleness, i.e. affect your gender.

The role of **chromosomes** and hormones (testosterone, oestrogen and oxytocin) is important in sex and gender.

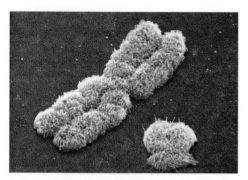

▲ Genetic males have a pair of chromosomes described as XY, which are shown here. The picture has been taken using an electron microscope.

KEY TERMS

Chromosomes The X-shaped bodies that carry all the genetic information (*DNA*) for an organism.

Hormones The body's chemical messengers. They travel through the bloodstream, influencing many different processes, including mood, the stress response and bonding between mother and newborn baby.

Intersex is the term used to describe an individual who is neither distinctly male nor female because of a mismatch between, for example, chromosomes and genitals.

THE ROLE OF CHROMOSOMES

Typical chromosome patterns

Each person has 23 pairs of chromosomes (in each cell of their body). Each of these chromosomes carries hundreds of genes containing instructions about physical and behavioural characteristics, such as eye colour and predisposition to certain mental illnesses.

One pair of chromosomes are called the sex chromosomes because they determine an individual's sex. In the case of a female this pair is called XX because both chromosomes are shaped like Xs. The male chromosome pair is described as XY. The Y chromosome carries very little genetic material, although it does determine the sex of a child.

There is usually a direct link between an individual's chromosomal sex (XX and XY) and their external genitalia (vagina or penis) and internal genitalia (ovaries or testes). During prenatal development all individuals start out the same – a few weeks after conception both male and female embryos have external genitalia that look essentially feminine. When the foetus is about three months old, if it is to develop as a male, the testes normally produce the male hormone testosterone which causes external male genitalia to develop.

Genetic transmission explains how individuals acquire their sex. It may also explain some aspects of gender (a person's sense of whether they are male or female) because of the link between genes and genitalia and hormones.

Atypical sex chromosome patterns

There are a variety of well-recognised atypical patterns of sex chromosomes.

Klinefelter's syndrome is due to an XXY configuration. The individual is born with a penis and develops as a fairly normal male. Approximately 1 in 1,000 males have this condition. Such individuals tend to be taller than average and may have less muscular coordination than average. Physically they look less masculine because of reduced levels of testosterone, e.g. less facial hair, broader hips and possible breast tissue. Such individuals are often infertile.

Turner's syndrome is due to an XO configuration, meaning the second sex chromosome is partly or completely missing. This occurs in about 1 in 2,000 females at birth. Such individuals are born with a vagina and womb. The characteristics include being shorter than average and having a lack of monthly periods due to underdeveloped ovaries. There are a wide range of other symptoms such as small lower jaw, webbed neck, narrow hips, misshapen internal organs and so on – no two XO females have the same characteristics.

THE ROLE OF HORMONES

Genes/chromosomes initially determine a person's sex and they also determine which hormones are produced. The hormone testosterone is produced in much greater quantities in males, and the hormones oestrogen and oxytocin are mainly female hormones. Most gender *development* is actually governed by hormones.

Testosterone

Testoserone is produced prenatally (before a baby is born) and affects the development of genitalia. However, some XY individuals have an insensitivity to such hormones, i.e. their bodies' tissues do not respond to the effects of the hormone. In extreme cases the consequence is that no external male genitalia develop. Such individuals are usually identified as females at birth (because no penis developed) and raised as girls, although some are identified as XY and raised as boys.

Testosterone also affects brain development both prenatally and later in childhood. For example, XX females exposed prenatally to relatively large doses of male hormones (because their pregnant mothers had been given drugs containing male hormones) later showed more tomboyish behaviour and greater interest in male-type activities (Berenbaum and Bailey, 2003).

The surge of testosterone during puberty is responsible for secondary sexual characteristics such as facial hair and deepening voice.

Oestrogen

The default gender is female; a genetic male will develop as a female unless exposed to testosterone. So females do not need hormones to direct *prenatal* genital development. However, there is some evidence of other prenatal effects. For example, some recent research found that oestrogen may actually lead to smaller brain size (Shi *et al.*, 2015).

Oestrogen plays a major role from puberty onwards promoting secondary sexual characteristics (such as breast development) and directing the menstrual cycle (increasing the blood supply to the uterus in preparation for pregnancy and maintaining it during pregnancy).

Oxytocin

Oxytocin has been called the 'love' hormone as it promotes feelings of bonding in both men and women. Oxytocin is produced in the pituitary gland and evokes feelings of contentment and calmness.

In women the hormone is important in breastfeeding because it causes milk to flow in a lactating mother. In men and women oxytocin is related to orgasm and faster wound healing.

At times of stress, oxytocin dampens the *fight-or-flight response*. In females the alternative *tend and befriend response* is triggered (Taylor *et al.*, 2000). This evolved response ensures that females protect their young (tending) and form protective alliances with other women (befriending). The same does not happen in men because testosterone dampens the effects of oxytocin.

◀ David Reimer (also called 'Bruce'), born a boy, was raised as a girl because of a botched circumcision. This case is described below.

Challenging biological determinism

John Money (Money and Ehrhardt, 1972) claimed that biological sex was not the main factor in gender development. He argued that sex of rearing was much more important and recommended that **intersex** individuals such as David Reimer (right) could be successfully raised as either a boy or a girl. Initially the case study supported his views, but ultimately David showed a strong male identity despite being raised as a girl.

This outcome has been further supported by subsequent research, for example that of Reiner and Gearhart (2004), who studied 16 genetic males born with almost no penis. Two were raised as males and remained as males. The remaining 14 were raised as females, and of these, eight re-assigned themselves as males by the age of 16. Such research suggests that biological factors have a key role in gender development.

The importance of other factors

However, genes and hormones are not the whole story either. Genetic sex does not match external genitalia in cases of abnormal hormone exposure, and even hormones do not produce a simple formula for establishing gender. The eventual outcome for each individual is what appears to be a complex and unpredictable combination of genes, hormones, sex of rearing and socialisation. The outcome is described as 'unpredictable' because there do not appear to be any simple rules.

For example, congenital adrenal hyperplasia (CAH) occurs when XX females have prenatally high levels of male hormones resulting in varying degrees of external male genitalia. Research appears to indicate that whatever gender is assigned at birth seems to be accepted by some individuals but not others (see studies on page 106). Thus gender development is in part biologically determined (nature), but experience, personal qualities and socialisation (nurture) also have a key role.

The role of culture and social influences

One of the classic cases of abnormal gender development illustrates the role of culture (and also the effect of testosterone). The case concerns the Batista family from the Dominican Republic (Imperato-McGinley *et al.*, 1974). Four children were born with external female genitalia and raised as girls. The large amounts of testosterone produced during puberty caused their male genitalia to appear externally. These children were genetically XY, but the external male genitalia had not appeared because of an inherited gene that caused testosterone insensitivity. It is said the 'girls' accepted their new male role without any difficulty.

It has been suggested that the ease of transition from female to male highlights the importance of culture – in a community prepared to accept more fluidity in gender roles it seemed to be relatively easy to move between roles, something which is much more difficult in Western culture.

Real-world applications

In the past the general practice for intersex conditions (such as CAH, described above) has been to perform surgery to make the individual look more normal. The Intersex Society of North America recommends that babies with such conditions should be assigned a gender, but no surgery should be conducted until the individual can make an informed decision themselves. It is important for certain individuals, such as those with Turner's syndrome, to be identified early because then they can be given hormone supplements. Usually Turner's is only detected in puberty when they fail to develop secondary sexual characteristics, and this is too late. Obviously genetic testing can be used to help early detection.

An interesting slant on the issue of biological determinism is shown in a dilemma faced by the International Olympics Committee. Since 1968 it has tested the genetic sex of all athletes and excluded all but XX females and XY males, which meant that individuals with genetic abnormalities couldn't compete – for example, XY individuals who had been sex-typed as females (see above). In 1991 there was a ruling that genetic sex would no longer determine entry to the Games; individuals are now excluded from women's events only if they are obviously physically male (Bown, 1992). In other words, genetic sex no longer determines gender.

The effect of hormones on brain development

The effects of testosterone on brain development have been confirmed in experimental work with non-human animals. For example, Quadagno *et al.* (1977) found that female monkeys who were deliberately exposed to testosterone during prenatal development later engaged in more rough-and-tumble play than other females and were more aggressive. Of course there are issues generalising from non-human animal studies because human behaviour is governed (at least to some extent) by expectations and deliberate choice. In one study Eisenegger *et al.* (2010) observed women playing a bargaining game. Those women who believed they had been given a dose of testosterone behaved in a more unfair manner than those given who believed they were given a neutral placebo. This demonstrates the effect of expectations which would mean that there is not a simple relationship between hormones and behaviour in humans.

Research methods

Dr John Money used the case study of David Reimer as evidence to support his theory. David started life as Bruce Reimer and had an identical twin, Brian. When the twins were 6 months old they were circumcised to cure a urination problem. Tragically the operation on Bruce was botched and Bruce's penis was all but burned off. Bruce's parents sought advice from Dr Money, who said that Bruce should have his penis and testes removed so he looked like a girl and he should be raised as Brenda.

Over the next 10 years the twins, now Brian and Brenda, visited Money regularly because the case provided a unique natural experiment, a normal XY male raised as a female with an identical twin brother as a control. Money regularly reported on the twins, claiming that the gender assignment had been a success and advising that this was the way forward for intersex individuals.

However, it turned out that David was by no means happy and, when he was told his true sex in his teen years, he decided to change and live as a man. He said: 'Suddenly it all made sense why I felt the way I did. I wasn't some sort of weirdo' (Colapinto, 2000). Unfortunately he never recovered from the events of his early life and and he committed suicide in 2004.

1. Use this study to discuss the advantages and limitations of case studies. (6 marks)
2. Consider the ethics of this study. Focus particularly on John Money's role in the study. (4 marks)
3. One of the ways to analyse a case study like this is using thematic analysis. Describe **two** themes you might examine. (4 marks)

LINK TO RESEARCH METHODS

Case studies on page 14.
Thematic analysis on page 13.

CAN YOU?   No. 4.2

1. Outline the role of chromosomes in sex and gender. (6 marks)
2. Outline the role of hormones in sex and gender. (6 marks)
3. Describe Klinefelter's syndrome. (4 marks)
4. Explain the role of testosterone in sex and/or gender. (4 marks)
5. Discuss the role of chromosomes and hormones in sex and gender. Refer to atypical sex chromosome patterns in your answer. (16 marks)

Cognitive explanations of gender development: Gender schema theory

This spread concerns a second cognitive approach to explaining gender development. Both gender schema theory and Kohlberg's gender constancy theory take a cognitive approach, emphasising the role of a child's *thinking* in their gender development.

It was Sandra Bem who first introduced gender schema theory, as described on page 92. The later version of the theory, which is described here, was developed by Carol Martin and Charles Halverson. Like Kohlberg, they believed that the key to gender development lies in seeking to acquire information about one's own gender.

What is a schema?

Think of a bank robbery and write down all the words that come into your mind associated with it.

These words represent your *schema* of a bank robbery.

A schema is a mental representation of an aspect of the world. It's a cluster of related items that together represent a concept. The term 'stereotype' is often used instead of schema. However, a schema involves more than a stereotype, being more complex and generating inferences and expectations.

🐾 APPLY YOUR KNOWLEDGE

Milo's parents are both psychologists who specialise in developmental psychology. They are determined that Milo should not grow up with narrow 'male' gender schema so have ensured that he is not exposed to anything (either at home or in the media) that would result in this. They have encouraged him to engage in many activities that are seen as stereotypically 'female' and he seems happy with this. All is well until his first week at pre-school when he comes home and says he doesn't want to help his dad make cakes because that would be 'girly'. His parents are disappointed because all their efforts appear to have been in vain.

Using your knowledge of gender schema theory, explain why Milo has suddenly started acting in this way. (4 marks)

GENDER SCHEMA THEORY

Martin and Halverson (1981) propose two key factors that differentiate their theory from Kohlberg's. First, they argue that the process of acquiring gender-relevant information happens *before* gender constancy is achieved. They claim that basic gender identity (gender labelling) is sufficient for a child to identify him/herself as a boy/girl and take an interest in what behaviours are appropriate for their gender. Kohlberg claimed this did not happen until after gender constancy was achieved.

Second, Martin and Halverson go further than Kohlberg in suggesting how the acquisition of stereotypes/**schemas** affects later behaviour, especially in terms of memory and attention.

Schemas

The main concept in gender schema theory (GST) is the concept of a schema (see left). Children learn schemas related to gender from their interactions with other children and adults, as well as from television programmes or videos. Such schemas are therefore very much related to cultural norms.

Gender schemas (or stereotypes) have the function of organising and structuring other information that is presented to children. They learn about what toys are appropriate for each gender, what clothes to wear and so on. In a sense, these gender schemas are like 'naïve' theories (i.e. personal rather than scientific) about appropriate behaviour for men and women.

Ingroup and outgroup schemas

The term ingroup refers to the groups with which a person identifies. Being a girl means that you identify yourself with that ingroup. A girl will also identify with many other groups (such as the town she comes from, the football team she supports, the boy bands she likes and so on). The same is true for boys. Once a child has identified with any group(s), this leads them to positively evaluate their own group and negatively evaluate the outgroup. People do this because it enhances their self-esteem – it means you can say 'I belong to groups that are successful/well liked and therefore I share these qualities'.

In turn, this evaluation motivates a child to be like their own group and avoid the behaviours of the other group. It also leads them to actively seek information about what their ingroup does, i.e. to acquire ingroup schemas. According to GST, from an early age, before gender constancy, children focus on ingroup schemas and avoid behaviours that belong to outgroup schemas.

Resilience of gender beliefs

An important aspect of GST is that it can explain the power of gender beliefs. Gender beliefs lead children to hold very fixed gender attitudes because they ignore any information they encounter that is not consistent with ingroup information. For example, if a boy sees a film with a male nurse, this information is ignored because the man is not behaving consistently with the boy's ingroup schema. Therefore, the boy does not alter his existing schema. In this way gender schemas have a profound effect on what is remembered and our perceptions of the world around us.

Peer relationships

Play with other children leads children to believe that all girls share the same interests and all boys share the same interests, and to avoid children of the opposite sex because they are 'not like me' and therefore less fun to play with. Same-sex peers, on the other hand, are 'like me', and therefore more fun to play with whatever they are doing.

Children also develop knowledge of the potential *consequences* associated with different social relationships – for example, they may come to realise that their peers will tease them if they play with members of the other sex, and so avoid this type of interaction. Gender schemas, therefore, influence children's likelihood of developing social relationships with same- and opposite-sex peers (Martin, 1991).

Gender schemas without constancy

GST predicts that children begin acquiring information about gender schemas before they reach gender stability, around the age of three. Martin and Little (1990) found that children under the age of four showed no signs of gender stability, let alone signs of constancy (which, according to Kohlberg, appears around the age of six). Despite a lack of constancy, the children did display strong gender stereotypes about what boys and girls were permitted to do. This shows that they have acquired information about gender roles before Kohlberg suggested, in line with GST.

Gender identity even earlier

Zosuls *et al.* (2009) provided evidence that children can label their gender group earlier than indicated in previous studies. They recorded samples of children's language and observed them at play in order to identify when they first started labelling themselves as a boy or girl. They concluded that children were using gender labels by the age of 19 months.

However, there is more recent evidence that children show gender-typed preferences even earlier than this (i.e. before gender identity), which was seen as a challenge to gender schema theory (Bandura and Bussey, 2004).

Gender schemas organise memory

If gender schemas are important in acquiring information about ingroup gender stereotypes then we would expect children to pay greater attention to information consistent with gender schemas and to remember this information better. Indeed, Martin and Halverson (1983) found that when children were asked to recall pictures of people, children under six recalled more of the gender-consistent ones (such as a male firefighter or female teacher) than gender-inconsistent ones (such as a male nurse or female chemist).

Furthermore, children appear to pay greatest attention to ingroup rather than outgroup schemas. Bradbard *et al.* (1986) told 4–9-year-olds that certain gender-neutral items (e.g. burglar alarms, pizza cutters) were either boy or girl items. Participants took a greater interest in toys labelled as ingroup (i.e. a boy was more interested in a toy labelled as a boy's toy). Also, one week later, they were able to remember more details about ingroup objects. This shows how gender schemas are related in particular to memory (organisation of information).

Gender schemas may distort information

Aside from not remembering inconsistent information, gender schemas may also lead children to actually distort such inconsistent information. This was shown in Martin and Halverson's study. When children were shown consistent or inconsistent (counter-stereotypical) pictures, they distorted the information. For example, when shown a boy holding a gun (consistent) or a boy holding a doll (inconsistent), children then described what they saw as a girl holding the doll. Such distorted memories search to maintain ingroup schemas and support GST because they show how behaviour can be explained in terms of schema-related behaviour.

Resilience of children's gender stereotypes

GST explains why children are frequently highly sexist despite the best efforts of parents (insisting on Barbie dolls for their sons and toy guns for their daughters). It is because children actively seek to acquire gender-appropriate schemas and prefer to ignore counter-stereotypes. However, Hoffman (1998) reports that children whose mothers work have less stereotyped views of what men do, suggesting that children are not entirely fixed in their views but are receptive to some gender-inconsistent ideas.

The fact that gender schemas lead to misremembering or even distorting information has important implications for efforts to reduce gender stereotypes. It means that even when children are exposed to counter-stereotypes they don't remember them accurately. This suggests that the use of counter-stereotypes may not be the best way to reduce children's gender schemas.

▶ Research suggests that if children see a gender-inconsistent picture they just remember it incorrectly – they are more likely to recall this as a man. This memory bias makes it difficult to change gender stereotypes using counter-stereotypes.

Schema A cognitive framework that helps organise and interpret information in the brain. A schema helps an individual to make sense of new information.

◀ Seems to be ignoring his ingroup schema.

CAN YOU?
No. 4.4

1. Outline gender schema theory as an explanation of gender development. (6 marks)
2. Give **one** criticism of gender schema theory. (4 marks)
3. Explain in what way gender schema theory is an example of the cognitive approach in psychology. (3 marks)
4. Explain **one** difference between Kohlberg's theory of gender development and gender schema theory. (3 marks)
5. Discuss **two** cognitive explanations of gender development. (16 marks)

Psychodynamic explanation of gender development

The first two psychological explanations for gender were cognitive. We now turn to a further psychological explanation – Freud's psychoanalytic theory, the most common example of a psychodynamic explanation. There continue to be some cognitive elements in this theory – the concepts of **identification** and **internalisation**. These concepts also appear in Bandura's social learning theory and also in explanations of conformity. Freud used them first.

▲ The name Oedipus is taken from a Greek myth. King Laius and his wife were told that he would be killed by his son, so when his wife gave birth to a son he mutilated the boy's feet and left him to die atop a mountain. The boy was rescued and called Oedipus because of his deformed feet ('Oedipus' literally means 'swollen foot' in Greek). Many years later Oedipus travelled to the city of Thebes not knowing that this was where his real parents lived. On the way he had an encounter with a small group of men, in which he killed them – one of them being his father King Laius. He then married King Laius's wife and, when it was discovered that she was in fact his mother, Oedipus gouged out his own eyes.

FREUD'S PSYCHOANALYTIC THEORY

Sigmund Freud's theory of personality development (psychoanalysis) includes an explanation of gender development. This theory was described in the Year 1/AS book as an example of the psychodynamic approach. The theory includes the structure of the personality (id, ego and supergo) and defence mechanisms such as repression – these mechanisms are required to protect the ego (the conscious self) from anxiety-provoking thoughts. Such thoughts are repressed into the unconscious mind.

Freud also described psychosexual stages when the life force (libido) is focused on different body parts. According to Freud, gender development occurs during the third stage – the phallic stage when a child is between the ages of three and six years. At this time a child's libido is focused on his/her genitals. The child's gender identity is resolved during this stage either through the Oedipus complex (in boys) or the Electra complex (in girls).

The Oedipus complex

Freud (1905) proposed that, during this genital stage, boys experience the **Oedipus complex** which has three key components:

1. Boys desire their mothers. At the age of three or four, a young boy becomes aware of his sexuality and desires his mother, wanting her sole attention.
2. Boys then see their fathers as a rival for their mother's love and, as a result wish their father were dead. This wish creates anxiety and a fear of castration. Such fears are repressed.
3. The complex is eventually resolved because the boy begins to identify with his father. It is through *identification* with the father that a boy *internalises* his father's gender identity and takes this as his own gender identity.

This gender identity and identification leads to masculine behaviour as young boys take on the attitudes and expectations of their fathers.

The Electra complex

The idea of the **Electra complex** was proposed by Carl Jung (1913), a neo-Freudian (i.e. Jung's ideas were based in part on psychoanalytic theory). Like Oedipus, the name 'Electra' is drawn from Greek myth. Also, like the Oedipus complex, the Electra complex is concerned with a conflict between a child and same-sex parent because they are in competition for the opposite-sex parent.

Freud proposed a similar idea, which he called the *feminine Oedipus attitude*. The basic concept is:

1. A young girl is initially attracted to her mother but this ends when the girl discovers that her mother doesn't have a penis. The girl blames her mother for her own lack of a penis, believing she was castrated, and so as a result she experiences penis envy.
2. The girl's sexual desires are transferred to the father.
3. The complex is resolved when the girl converts her penis envy to a wish to have a baby, and this reduces her anger towards her mother. The girl can now identify with her mother and take on gender behaviours.

The end resolution is less satisfactory for girls because their identification with the same-sex parent is less strong – Freud believed there was little reason for anyone to identify with a woman because women had a lower status so why would anyone want to identify with them.

Unresolved phallic stage

In Freudian theory each psychosexual stage is resolved through conflict. Successful resolution leads to a healthy psychological outcome – in the case of the genital stage the healthy outcome is identification with the same-sex parent and internalisation of an appropriate gender identity and sex-role stereotypes.

Both frustration and overindulgence (or any combination of the two) may lead to what psychoanalysts call fixation at a particular psychosexual stage. Fixation on the genital stage results in a phallic character who is afraid of or not capable of close love. Freud also claimed fixation could be a root cause of amoral behaviour and homosexuality.

General criticisms of Freud's theory of personality development can be used to evaluate this account.

Support from case studies

The only support Freud gave for his Oedipus complex was the case study of a five-year-old boy growing up in Vienna, referred to as 'Little Hans' (Freud, 1909). Hans developed a fear of horses which Freud interpreted as a result of repressing his desires for his mother: (1) Hans developed a love for his mother and wished his father dead. This led Hans to fear that his father would castrate him and also fear castration because his mother said she would have his penis chopped off because he asked her to touch it. (2) Hans associated this 'touching' with words he overheard when a man told his daughter not to touch a horse because it might bite her. This led Hans to associate his fear of castration with touching horses. He was thus able to express the repressed fear of castration as a fear of horses. (3) The final resolution came when Hans came to identify with his father and no longer wished him dead and didn't fear castration.

Levin (1921) reported on the cases of 32 mental patients who were diagnosed with manic depression (bipolar disorder). Psychoanalysis revealed that 22 appeared to be suffering from an unresolved Electra complex or penis envy, and 12 had regressed to earlier stages of psychosexual development. This suggests a link with an unresolved stage of gender development and later mental health problems.

Such case studies are fraught with problems of subjective interpretation and selective reporting. Nevertheless, it is interesting to note the similarities between Freud's concepts and gender schema theory. Freud's critical age is closer to gender schema theory than Kohlberg's gender constancy, and Freud suggested that identification with the ingroup (same-sex parent) was important in taking on gender attitudes.

Child sexual awareness

Both complexes depend on the child having an awareness of genitals. On page 97 we reported a study by Bem who found that many children aged 3–5 didn't know what opposite-sex genitalia looked like, which would make it impossible for the Oedipus/Electra complex to develop.

However, other research does support the notion that parental sex is an issue for children in this age group. For example, a longitudinal study by Okami *et al.* (1998) followed 200 children from age 6 to age 18. When they were younger, the children had been exposed to scenes of parental nudity and/or sexual activity. At age 18 a few significant effects were found: the girls were more likely to become pregnant or infected with a sexually transmitted disease than others, and the opposite was true for the boys.

This finding suggests an association between sexual experiences during the phallic stage and later sexual behaviour. However, it does not indicate a causal effect on gender development.

Lacks predictive validity

According to the Oedipus complex, children would have difficulty acquiring a gender identity if they live in one-parent families or where both parents are of the same sex. There is no evidence for this. For example, Patterson (2004) reports from a review of research that sexual identities (including gender identity, gender-role behaviour and sexual orientation) develop in much the same way among children of lesbian mothers as they do among children of heterosexual parents, and that children of lesbian and gay parents have normal social relationships with peers and adults.

Alternative psychodynamic explanations

There have been a number of alternative psychodynamic explanations. Nancy Chodorow (1994) proposed that mothers and young daughters are closer precisely because they are the same sex, whereas sons are able to become more independent because they are different to their mothers. Research (e.g. Goldberg and Lewis, 1969) supports this, with observations that mother–daughter pairs show greater physical closeness when playing. Both boys and girls attempt to identify with the father, but because fathers treat sons and daughters differently, only sons succeed.

The advantage of this account is that it does not involve sexual desire for the opposite-sex parent and also does not predict problems where parents are both the same sex.

Reinterpretation

Not surprisingly many people have objected to the idea that children are sexually active at an early age (at least mentally), and feminists in particular dismiss Freud's idea of inferior female development due to having penis envy. It simply seems to be a case of gender bias – in fact Freud claimed he didn't really understand women.

However, Freud's ideas do not have to be taken literally. The French psychoanalyst Jacques Lacan (1966) suggested that penis envy is a symbolic envy of male power in a male-dominated society, which perhaps makes better sense.

MEET THE RESEARCHER

Sigmund Freud (1856–1939) lived most of his life in Vienna, teaching at the university there and having a private practice. In his apartment he held weekly evening meetings with people interested in his theory of psychoanalysis, one of whom was the father of Little Hans.

People are very critical of his theories because they lack falsifiability and are very sexually oriented – but they continue to have a profound effect.

UPGRADE

On page 93 we explained that for essays such as Q4 in the 'Can you?' box on this page, 10 of the 16 marks are assigned to AO3 (evaluation). There is no specific requirement as to the *number* of AO3 points that you can use in your answer, but we have worked on the assumption that five AO3 points (each of approximately 50 words) would be ideal in an essay question.

The absolutely essential quality of any AO3 point is that you make it *effective*. Most teachers have their own technique for this (the 'three- or four-point rule', the 'hamburger technique', SEEL, PEEL and so on). They all involve more or less the same thing in that a critical point is identified, evidence is given to support the point, perhaps some further elaboration, and then a conclusion is offered. If we take the evaluative point on this page regarding predictive validity, this could be made into an effective AO3 as follows:

Freud's theory of gender development lacks predictive validity... The Oedipal complex concept suggests children would have difficulty acquiring a gender identity if both parents are of the same sex... However, Patterson's (2004) research did not support this claim... finding that gender development was the same regardless of whether parents were same-sex or opposite-sex.

CAN YOU? | No. 4.5

1. Outline the Oedipus complex. (4 marks)
2. Outline the Electra complex. (4 marks)
3. Explain how both identification and internalisation are part of Freud's psychoanalytic account of gender development. (4 marks)
4. Discuss Freud's psychoanalytic theory of gender development. (16 marks)

Social learning theory as applied to gender development

Albert Bandura proposed **social learning theory** in the 1960s to explain how children and adults acquire new behaviours. His view of development is not purely social – he acknowledged that biology (nature) had a role to play, but his focus has been on nurture, how we learn through both direct and indirect conditioning. His particular contribution was the indirect nature of learning, learning by observing and imitating others. The 'social' in social learning theory is about what we learn from other people by modelling their behaviour.

Insider tip…

The first thing that comes into most people's mind when they think of social learning theory is Bandura's Bobo doll studies (described on page 238). This study showed how aggressive behaviour was learned through modelling. This means it has some relevance to gender development (it shows that people learn through vicarious reinforcement) but that relevance is limited (because the study was about aggression). When discussing social learning theory and gender development, it is important to keep your focus on gender.

▲ Modelling

Modelling has two meanings – a model can model clothes (as above) or behaviours, and a child can model this behaviour by imitating it. So 'modelling' refers to the behaviour of a role model and the behaviour of the person doing the imitating.

SOCIAL LEARNING THEORY

Social learning theory was described in the approaches chapter of our Year 1 book. Traditional learning theory (or behaviourism) proposed that organisms learn new behaviours through classical and operant conditioning. This involves association and reinforcement respectively. However, Bandura pointed out that association and direct reinforcement alone could not explain the complexity of human behaviour. Bandura (1991) proposed that gender role development is the result of learning from social agents who model and reinforce gender role behaviours.

Indirect reinforcement

Children observe the behaviour of others and learn the consequences of the behaviour (vicarious reinforcement). Children witness many examples of gender behaviour at home and at school, as well as on television and in films. By observing the consequences of such gender behaviours, children gradually learn something about what is appropriate behaviour in the world around. Thus they learn the behaviours (through observation), and they also learn whether and when such behaviours are worth repeating (through vicarious reinforcement).

This vicarious reinforcement is vital. Although boys and girls may observe the characteristic behaviours of both sexes, they are only likely to repeat behaviours of people they identify with. Therefore girls are more likely to perform behaviours they see performed by other girls and women. Boys may learn a great deal about the homemaking role through repeated observation of their mothers but they are less likely to repeat such behaviour.

The role of mediational processes

Information about reinforcements is stored as an expectancy of future outcome. Thus Bandura's theory moved from behaviourism to a kind of cognitive behaviourism because mental representations are involved (he later called his explanation 'social cognitive theory').

When appropriate opportunities arise in the future, children will display behaviours they have observed *provided* that the expectation of reward is greater than the expectation of punishment. This display of such behaviours is called imitation or modelling – but it depends on indirect reinforcement and opportunity.

Maintenance through direct reinforcement

If a child is rewarded (i.e. gets what he or she wants or is praised by others) for certain gender-related behaviours, they are likely to repeat the same action in similar situations in the future. This direct reinforcement then influences the usefulness of that behaviour for that child.

This direct reinforcement is also vital because a child may see a same-sex individual behaving in a particular way and being rewarded for it – for example, a boy might see another boy dressing as a girl and getting a lot of attention. But if the boy tries it himself he may be 'punished' by disparaging remarks, which reduces the likelihood that this behaviour will be repeated.

Direct tuition

Children learn through indirect and direct reinforcement but also learn through explicit (direct) instructions about appropriate gender behaviour. Direct tuition begins when children acquire linguistic skills. It serves as a convenient way of informing children about appropriate or inappropriate styles of conduct.

Self-direction

Bandura believes that people are not just shaped by environmental forces but also have the capacity to direct themselves, a process he called *environmental determinism*. This means that once children have internalised gender-appropriate behaviours, their own behaviour is no longer dependent on external rewards or punishments. They then direct their own behaviour. This is regarded as a key element of the social learning approach – the active role of children in their observational learning.

Evidence to support modelling

Bandura's initial source of evidence for both learning and modelling was the Bobo doll studies (Bandura *et al.*, 1961), which demonstrated the effects of an adult model on children's aggressive behaviour. These effects have also been demonstrated for gender. For example, a study by Perry and Bussey (1979) showed film clips to children aged eight and nine. In the film boys and girls were seen selecting an apple or pear, both gender-neutral items. Later the children were given a choice of fruit. Boys selected the fruit they had seen another boy selecting, and the same for girls. This shows that children model gender behaviours they have observed in gender-appropriate models.

However, in this study the children only modelled same-sex behaviour as long as the behaviour was not counter to gender stereotypes (e.g. a man wearing a dress). So it seems that the effects of modelling are limited by existing stereotypes.

Direct tuition may be more effective than modelling

Research has shown that children do not always model the behaviour of a same-sex model and that direct tuition may be more important. For example, Martin *et al.* (1995) found that preschool boys played with toys labelled 'boys' toys' (a kind of 'direct tuition' because they were told the toy was for boys). They did this even if they saw girls playing with them. However, they didn't play with toys labelled 'girls' toys' even when they saw boys playing with them (i.e. they didn't model same-sex behaviour when 'told' that it was a girl's toy). This suggests that direct instruction is more important than modelling, at least in preschool children.

However, 'instructors' (such as parents and teachers) do not always practise what they preach, and the impact of this tuition is weakened when what is being taught is contradicted by what is modelled (Hildebrandt *et al.*, 1973).

Peers as gender influences

Some psychologists (e.g. Maccoby, 1998) take the view that peers are the prime socialising agency of gender development. However, peers are unlikely to be important in early childhood when important aspects of gender development are taking place.

Later on in childhood it is likely that peer behaviour does not create gender-role stereotypes but simply reinforces existing ones. For example, Lamb and Roopnarine (1979) observed preschool children at play and found that when male-type behaviour was reinforced in girls the behaviour continued for a shorter time than when male-type behaviour was reinforced in boys. This suggests that peer reinforcement mainly acts as a reminder.

Self-direction

The increasing importance of self-regulation was demonstrated in a study by Bussey and Bandura (1992) involving children aged 3–4 years old. They were shown videotapes of other children playing with masculine and feminine toys and asked to comment on the children in the video. In particular they were asked to comment on situations where children were playing with gender-inconsistent toys (e.g. a boy playing with a doll) and also asked to rate how they would feel when playing with gender-consistent and gender-inconsistent toys. The younger children disapproved of others but did not disapprove of themselves for gender-inconsistent behaviour, whereas the older children disapproved of both. These self-evaluations were confirmed when the children actually played with the toys (i.e. the younger children did play with the gender-inconsistent toys, whereas the older children didn't). This shows how self-regulation increases with age.

Too much emphasis on social process

Social learning theory acknowledges the role of innate, biological behaviours but doesn't incorporate them into the account. Earlier in this chapter (page 94) we looked at the role of hormones in masculine and feminine behaviour – for example, testosterone during prenatal development creates a more 'masculine' brain and a tendency to certain types of behaviour.

Cross-cultural research also indicates there are some universals in the way that men and women behave which in turn supports the role of biology. For example, Margaret Mead's (1935) classic research with people in Papua New Guinea found that men were more aggressive in all the groups she studied despite some large variations in gender roles. Research by Buss (1989) showed that what men and women desire in a partner is very similar world-wide (e.g. men seek physical attractiveness and women seek resources).

Such universal similarities suggest that biology plays an important role in shaping gender behaviour, and perhaps social factors merely refine it.

🐾 APPLY YOUR KNOWLEDGE

Arpad's parents, who have been trying to raise their child without him having a narrow male gender schema, were appalled when he came home from play school declaring that baking was 'girly'. As they are both psychologists specialising in this area, they decide to have a word with the preschool workers to see if they can do anything to stop activities being branded 'boyish' or 'girly'. They decide to use social learning theory as a way to achieve this.

Using your knowledge of social learning theory, explain what Arpad's parents might suggest to the preschool workers to achieve their aim of a 'gender-free' zone. (4 marks)

Comparison with gender schema theory

All three explanations just covered – social learning theory (SLT), gender schema theory (GST) and Freud's theory – relate gender development to gender stereotypes that children learn. All three include the role of identification as part of the process – in SLT, children are more likely to imitate role models with whom they identify. In GST, identity is the key turning point in gender development – once a child has identified themselves as male or female, they then identify with the ingroup. However, SLT does not explain why children identify with same-sex role models – it is just stated that they do.

The particular strength of SLT is that it highlights the active role of children in their observational learning and regulating their own behaviour.

CAN YOU?   No. 4.6

1. Outline social learning theory as applied to gender development. (4 marks)
2. Give **one** criticism of social learning theory as applied to gender development. (4 marks)
3. Discuss social learning theory as applied to gender development. Refer to an alternative explanation for gender development as part of your evaluation. (16 marks)

Cultural and media influences on gender roles

As we have seen, social learning theory was concerned with the role of social factors in gender development, and now we turn to two sources of socialisation – **culture** and **media**, and focus on gender *roles*, i.e. the different behaviours, jobs, tasks, duties etc. that men and women take.

▲ **Cultural indoctrination** In 1993 the Barbie Liberation Organization (BLO) was horrified to find that American Barbies had been programmed to say 'Math is hard!' and 'I love shopping!' Such comments reinforce gender stereotypes, so the BLO operated on some 300 'GI Joes' and Barbies so that the Barbies said 'Eat lead, Cobra' and 'Dead men tell no lies'. The GI Joes were full of their love of shopping.

▲ Some cultures recognise a third sex. For example, it is estimated that there are over 5 million *hijras* in India – individuals who are neither male nor female. In 2005 the Indian passport system changed to allow people to class themselves as M, F or E (for Eunuch).

Native Americans use the term 'two spirit' to refer to people who have both a male and a female spirit. Gender (male, female or two spirit) is decided by each child at puberty, and at that time they chose what clothing to wear to physically display their gender choice (Lang, 1998).

CULTURAL INFLUENCES

When we say 'culture', what are we referring to? It is the rules, customs, morals, childrearing practices and so on that bind a group of people together. Throughout the chapter we have been looking at factors that influence gender roles – such as genes, hormones, stereotypes, parental reinforcement and peer reinforcement. All of the psychological factors are in turn influenced by the gender rules of the culture.

Cultural differences

The effect of culture can be seen in the way gender expectations vary from one culture to another. For example, across cultures there is a general belief that women are more conformist than men. However, this difference varies considerably with culture. Berry *et al.* (2002) report that conformity is highest in tight, sedentary societies (i.e. groups that aren't nomadic), with a correlation of +.78 between this sex difference and an ecocultural index (a measure of the kind of environment people live in).

We can also include historical changes when considering cultural differences in gender roles. In the UK, women continue to perform more domestic duties than men and to occupy less powerful positions. However, this gender gap has been decreasing, which supports the role of changing cultural influences (Alleye, 2011).

One of the classic studies of cultural difference was conducted by Margaret Mead (1935) looking at social groups in Papua New Guinea. She provided evidence of cultural role differences. She found the *Arapesh* men and women to be gentle, responsive and cooperative. The *Mundugumor* men and women were violent and aggressive, seeking power and position. By contrast the *Tchambuli* exhibited gender role differences: the women were dominant, impersonal and managerial, whereas the men were more emotionally dependent.

THE INFLUENCE OF THE MEDIA

Culture also expresses itself through the media. The results of a natural experiment demonstrating the effects of the media are described on the facing page.

Role models in the media

The media generally portrays males as independent and directive, and pursuing both engaging occupations and recreational activities. By contrast, women are usually shown as acting in dependent, unambitious and emotional ways (Bussey and Bandura, 1999). Men are also more likely to be shown exercising control over events, whereas women are frequently shown to be more at the mercy of others (Hodges *et al.*, 1981). A more recent analysis looked at gender portrayals in advertisements and found that women were shown as more flawless and passive than men (Conley and Ramsey, 2011).

Not surprisingly, those who have a higher exposure to these differential gender representations tend to display more stereotypic gender role conceptions than do light viewers. McGhee and Frueh (1980) conducted a longitudinal study over 15 months and found that children aged 6–12 who watched more than 25 hours a week held more sex-stereotype perceptions than those who watched 10 or less hours. This was especially true for male stereotypes.

Vicarious reinforcement

The media does more than simply model gender-typical behaviours, as it also gives information about the likely outcomes of those behaviours for males and females. Seeing similar others succeed raises a person's beliefs in their own capabilities (self-efficacy), whereas the failure of similar others produces self-doubt about a person's own ability to master similar activities.

Counter-stereotypes

The media is responsible for perpetuating gender stereotypes, but it is also a means of changing such stereotypes by presenting men or women in unusual roles (counter-stereotyping). Pingree (1978) found that stereotyping was reduced when children were shown commercials with women in non-traditional roles. This has led to pressure on programme makers to try to use this knowledge to alter such attitudes.

EVALUATION OF CULTURAL INFLUENCES

Cultural similarities

The evidence for cultural differences shows how culture influences gender roles, but there is contrasting evidence that shows that biology is at least as important. For example, social role theory (Eagly and Wood, 1999) argues that the biologically based physical differences between men and women allow them to perform certain tasks more efficiently. Childbearing and nursing of infants mean that women are well placed to care for young children but are less able to take on roles which require extended absence from home, such as commuting to work. Men's greater speed and upper-body strength facilitate their efficient performance of tasks that require intensive bursts of energy and strength.

In addition, according to social role theory, in societies where strength is not required for occupational roles outside the home and/or societies where there is alternative care for children, gender roles will be more similar between men and women, and psychological differences are reduced – but this is still a biological account.

Criticisms of Mead (and cross-cultural research)

Evidence about cultural differences may be flawed, which challenges the conclusions of such research. For example, observers from one culture may record behaviours in another culture and 'see' things differently to the indigenous population. Another problem is that indigenous people may tell researchers what they want to hear. In fact this was the criticism Freeman (1984) made of Mead's research, suggesting that the data was not valid. Freeman himself worked with native Samoans who told him that they had created a false picture of their behaviour – but his version has also been criticised for being inaccurate (e.g. Appell, 1984)!

We should add that Mead subsequently changed her conclusion and decided that there were more similarities between males and females than there are differences – though it does not detract from the fact that there *are* differences.

▲ Margaret Mead with people from Samoa.

EVALUATION OF MEDIA INFLUENCE

Demonstrating media influence

It is difficult to demonstrate the effects of media stereotypes because almost all children watch some television and therefore there are no control groups for comparison – except for the rare cases of communities that have no television, as in the study by Williams described on the right. This study shows that exposure to the media can have significant effects on gender attitudes.

Media effects may be insignificant

Another study that looked at the effects of TV on a community previously without it (Charlton *et al.*, 2000) found no changes in aggressive behaviour and concluded that this was because of pre-existing community values that reduced the effect of exposure to the media.

This latter study did concern aggression rather than gender but does suggest that simply exposing children to stereotypes is not sufficient to change attitudes. In general, it seems that the media's effect is simply to reinforce the status quo. For example, Signorelli and Bacue (1999) examined the effects of over 30 years of TV programming and found very little change in gender stereotypes.

Backlash to counter-stereotyping

There is research that has shown that exposure to non-stereotypical information in the media can change expectations. However, not all research has supported the effectiveness of this approach. Pingree (facing page) also found that pre-adolescent boys displayed *stronger* stereotypes after exposure to the non-traditional models. It is possible that this 'backlash' occurs because boys of this age want to take a view that is counter to the view held by the adults.

There is also the issue, raised by Martin and Halverson (see page 99), that gender-inconsistent messages are mis-remembered and therefore have no effect.

Research methods

In the 1970s, a valley in Canada which was surrounded by high mountains had never been able to receive a television signal. This community, code-named *Notel*, offered Tannis Williams (1985) an opportunity to study the effects of exposure to TV.

The behaviour and attitudes of children in these towns were assessed in various ways, including questionnaires about their gender stereotypes (e.g. asking them what characteristics were more typical of boys or girls).

A further analysis was made of the children in *Notel* before the introduction of TV and again two years after the introduction of TV. It was found that their views had become significantly more sex-typed.

1. Identify the independent variable in this study.
2. Explain why this study is an example of a natural experiment. (2 marks)
3. Identify the experimental design used in this study. (1 mark)
4. Data was collected using questionnaires. Discuss **one** issue with using questionnaires to collect this data. (4 marks)

In addition to *Notel* there were two further towns that were studied – *Unitel* was a town with only one Canadian TV channel (CBC), whereas *Multitel* had access to a number of American channels.

Williams found that children in *Notel* and *Unitel* had weaker sex-typed views than the children in *Multitel*. This was especially true for the girls.

5. What were the aims of this part of the study? (2 marks)
6. Identify **one** possible confounding variable and explain why it might have been confounding. (2 marks)

LINK TO RESEARCH METHODS

The topics in these questions are covered in the research methods chapter of our Year 1 book.

CAN YOU?　　No. 4.7

1. Outline the influence of culture on gender roles. (4 marks)
2. Outline the influence of media on gender roles. (4 marks)
3. Describe and evaluate the influence of culture and/or media on gender roles. (16 marks)

Atypical gender development

Atypical gender development can include some of the conditions we looked at earlier in this chapter, such as CAH or AIS (see page 95). Such conditions arise where abnormal chromosomes and/or abnormal hormone exposure lead to a mismatch between gender identity and certain sexual characteristics. These conditions are referred to as intersex.

The focus of this spread is on **gender identity disorder** (GID), a psychiatric condition where a person feels uncomfortable with the gender assigned to them at birth. Terms such as gender dysphoria, transgender and transsexual are alternative descriptions. GID does not include intersex conditions.

None of these classifications are related to homosexuality where both men and women are content with their sex assignments.

Gender dysphoria affects both males and females – males to females (MtF) outnumber females to males (FtM) by about 5 to 1 (NHS, 2012).

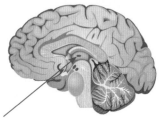

▲ The brain-sex theory suggests that the BSTc is abnormally enlarged in transsexual men. The BSTc is located in the thalamus.

KEY TERMS

Gender identity disorder is a psychiatric condition listed in DSM-V. Individuals experience a sense of gender dysphoria (confusion) because they have strong, persistent feelings of identification with the opposite gender and discomfort with their own. It is only diagnosed where there is no physical intersex condition.

▼ GID is probably much more common than most people realise. *The Gender Identity Research and Education Society* (GIRES) estimates that about 1 in 4,000 of the British population is receiving medical help for GID – to get a sense of the meaningfulness of this, compare this to rates of about 1 in 1,000 for autism.

BIOLOGICAL EXPLANATIONS OF GID

Transsexual gene

One study (Hare *et al.*, 2009) looked at the DNA of 112 MtF transsexuals and found they were more likely to have a longer version of the *androgen receptor gene* than in a 'normal' sample. The effect of this abnormality is reduced action of the male sex hormone testosterone, and this may have an effect on gender development in the womb (e.g. under-masculinising the brain).

The brain-sex theory

This theory is based on the fact that male and female brains are different and perhaps transsexuals' brains do not match their genetic sex. One region of the brain that has been studied is the BSTc (*bed nucleus of the stria terminalis*), which is located in the thalamus (see diagram on left). On average, the BSTc is twice as large in heterosexual men as in heterosexual women and contains twice the number of neurons.

The explanation offered for GID is that the size of the BSTc correlates with preferred sex rather than biological sex. Two Dutch studies (Zhou *et al.*, 1995; Kruijver *et al.*, 2000) found that the number of neurons in the BSTc of MtF transsexuals was similar to that of the females. By contrast, the number of neurons in a FtM transsexual was found to be in the male range.

Phantom limb and cross-wiring

The neuroscientist Vilayanur Ramachandran (2008) suggested that gender dysphoria is an innate form of phantom limb syndrome. People who have a limb amputated often report they feel as if the limb was still there, for example they feel itches in the limb or even try to pick things up with the missing limb. Ramachandran *et al.* (1995) demonstrated that this occurs because the brain is 'cross-wired'. The part of the brain that received input from the amputated limb is taken over by a different part of the body, such as the cheek.

In the case of gender dysphoria it is proposed that the image of the sex organs is innately hardwired in the brain in a manner opposite to the person's biological sex (Ramachandran and McGeoch, 2007). Such cross-wiring means that some males feel they should not have a penis and some females feel they should have one. For example, it is estimated that two-thirds of FtM transsexuals report the sensation of a phantom penis from childhood onwards, including phantom erections.

Environmental effects – pesticides

Not all biological causes are internal or genetic. One external possibility is that environmental pollution may be causing problems. For example, the pesticide DDT contains oestrogens which may mean that males are prenatally exposed to unduly high levels of these female hormones causing a mismatch between genetic sex and hormone influences. Vreugdenhil *et al.* (2002) found that boys born to mothers who were exposed to dioxins (which can promote oestrogen) displayed feminised play.

SOCIAL EXPLANATIONS OF GID

Social explanations relate to how a child is socialised. There are different explanations for boys and girls.

Mental illness

A number of psychologists have proposed that GID is related to mental illness, which in turn is linked to some childhood trauma or maladaptive upbringing. For example, Coates *et al.* (1991) produced a case history of a boy who developed GID, proposing that this was a defensive reaction to the boy's mother's depression following an abortion. The trauma occurred when the boy was three, a time in development when a child is particularly sensitive to gender issues. Coates *et al.* suggest that the trauma may have led to a cross-gender fantasy as a means of resolving the ensuing anxiety.

Mother–son relationships

Stoller (1975) proposed that GID results from distorted parental attitudes. In clinical interviews with individuals diagnosed with GID, Stoller observed that they displayed overly close and enmeshed mother–son relationships. This would be likely to lead to greater female identification and confused gender identity.

Father–daughter relationships

In the case of FtM transsexuals, Zucker (2004) has suggested that females identify as males because of severe paternal rejection in early childhood. Unconsciously, they think that, if they became males, they might gain acceptance from their father.

Criticisms of the brain-sex theory

The theory was seriously challenged by Chung et al. (2002) who noted that the differences in BSTc volume between men and women does not develop until adulthood, whereas most transsexuals report that their feelings of gender dysphoria began in early childhood (e.g. Lawrence, 2003). This suggests that the difference found in the BSTc could not be the cause of transsexualism but might perhaps be an effect.

In addition, Hulshoff Pol et al. (2006) found that transgender hormone therapy does influence the size of the BSTc and the individuals in the Dutch studies (see facing page) had been receiving hormone therapy. Therefore, it may be the hormones that caused the difference in transsexuals such that their brain sex was more similar to their gender identity rather than their biological sex.

However, there is other evidence that does continue to support transsexualism as a sexual differentiation disorder. For example, Rametti et al. (2011) studied the brains of FtM transsexuals before they started transgender hormone therapy. In terms of amounts of white matter in their brains, the FtM individuals had a more similar pattern to individuals who share their gender identity (males) than those who share their biological sex (females).

Support for cross-wiring

Ramachandran and McGeoch (2007) have provided support for their explanation with reference to comparisons between GID patients and 'normal' individuals who have had surgery to remove sex organs (e.g. for cancer). Around 60% of non-GID men who have to have penile amputation experience a phantom penis, but only 30% of GID men have such experiences, suggesting that there was no wiring to a 'penis representation' in their brain in the first place.

Similarly, only 10% of FtM patients experience phantom breast sensations after surgery to remove breasts (Ramachandran and McGeoch, 2008).

Support for social explanations

Zucker et al. (1996) studied 115 boys with concerns about their gender identity and their mothers. Of the boys who were eventually diagnosed with GID, 64% were also diagnosed with separation anxiety disorder, compared to only 38% of the boys whose symptoms were subclinical. This points to some kind of disordered attachment to a mother as a factor in GID, but it does only explain MtF transsexuals.

Zucker was also involved in another study (Owen-Anderson et al., 2010) that found high levels of emotional over-involvement in mothers of boys with GID, supporting the view of some family psychopathology underlying the condition.

However, not all research supports the role of pathological family relations in the development of GID. For example, Cole et al. (1997) studied 435 individuals experiencing GID and reported that the range of psychiatric conditions displayed was no greater than found in a 'normal' population, which suggests that GID is generally unrelated to trauma or pathological families.

More than one explanation needed

With regards to MtF transsexuals, Blanchard (1985) has proposed two distinct groups: 'homosexual transsexuals', who wish to change sex because they are attracted to men, and 'non-homosexual transsexuals', who wish to change sex because they are autogynephilic (sexually aroused by the thought or image of themselves as a woman).

Furuhashi (2011) concluded, from a study of 27 Japanese male patients with GID, that there were two types – those who have had a longing to be female since childhood (the 'core' group) and those whose discomfort did not appear until adolescence (the 'periphery' group).

Such research suggests that there are likely to be different explanations for different types of GID.

Socially sensitive research

Research on GID has potential social consequences for individuals represented by the research. The question is whether they are better off with or without the research. If a biological cause is identified, this may help other people to be more accepting about the needs of transsexuals (it is not their 'fault', it is simply in their biology).

On the other hand, if a biological cause is identified this might harm individuals born with the abnormality because it might be assumed (wrongly) that transsexualism is inevitable. The evidence, for example from CAH cases, is that a simple cause and effect (determinist) relationship is unlikely.

Either way, the outcome of research has social consequences for individuals represented by this research.

⬆ UPGRADE

A particular feature of AQA psychology examinations is the 'Application' question. You should be familiar with these questions, but it's worth revisiting the general rules about answering them. Let's illustrate these in the context of the following question:

Max is an 11-year-old boy. At school he has problems interacting with the other boys in his year, preferring to spend time either on his own or with the girls in his class. He feels much more comfortable interacting with girls and sometimes he will play-act being a girl while in their company. His parents are increasingly concerned about his overly feminine behaviour, particularly when his head of year suggests to them that he may be suffering from 'gender identity disorder'.

Explain why Max's head of year believes Max has gender identity disorder and outline one possible explanation of why he may have developed this disorder. (4 marks)

For a 4-mark question there would be two mark levels. For the top level you would need to display a 'clear and accurate' knowledge of the specific psychology related to the scenario (in this case it would be the explanation of the development of gender identity disorder). However, having a good understanding of the psychology is not enough on its own – it must be used 'appropriately' to explain the scenario (here it is why Max may have developed this disorder). The marks awarded reflect how effectively you have used the former to explain the latter. Ignore either of these and you will get half marks at best.

CAN YOU?   No. 4.8

1. Explain what is meant by *gender identity disorder*. (3 marks)
2. Outline **one or more** social explanations for gender identity disorder. (4 marks)
3. Give **one** criticism of biological explanations of gender identity disorder. (3 marks)
4. Describe and evaluate research related to gender identity disorder. Refer to both biological and social explanations in your answer. (16 marks)

We have identified here the key points of the topics on the AQA A level specification, i.e. the bare minimum that you need to know. You may want to fill in further details to elaborate and personalise this material.

SEX-ROLE STEREOTYPES AND ANDROGYNY

SEX-ROLE STEREOTYPES

These tell us what is appropriate for male and female behaviour.

- Learned from birth, related to cultural norms.
- Implicit modelling, explicitly taught.

ANDROGYNY

Being masculine and feminine is psychologically more healthy (Bem).

- BSRI – personality traits identified by 200 undergraduates; 20 masculine, 20 feminine, 20 neutral adjectives.
- Femininity and masculinity measured independently; total score shows masculine, feminine, androgynous or undifferentiated type.
- Bem's gender schema theory – androgynous person has a different cognitive style, freer to choose behaviours.

EVALUATION

- Support for parental influence – choice of gender-matched toys made by mothers (Smith and Lloyd).
- Androgyny and psychological health – masculinity scores negatively correlated with e.g. depression and anxiety, femininity scores positively correlated except if score was high (Prakash et al.).
- Real-world applications – parents adopt gender-neutral child-rearing, still regarded as unhealthy by some.
- Reliability (Bem) – test–retest high, split-half improved by removing socially undesirable items (e.g. gullible).
- Validity – correlation may be due to self-esteem rather than androgyny, or due to response bias to select higher ratings (Liberman and Gaa), and adjectives may have low temporal validity (Hoffman and Borders).

THE ROLE OF CHROMOSOMES AND HORMONES IN SEX AND GENDER

THE ROLE OF SEX CHROMOSOMES

- Usually genetic sex determines external genitalia – all foetuses start off with female genitalia.
- Genes determine genitalia and also which hormones, in turn leads to gender behaviours.
- Atypical sex chromosomes – Klinefelter's syndrome (XXY), low levels of testosterone mean less body hair and infertility, taller than average, less muscular co-ordination.
- Turner's syndrome (XO) – underdeveloped ovaries, short stature, no monthly period, may have other unusual physical characteristics, e.g. small lower jaw.

THE ROLE OF HORMONES

Hormones govern gender development.

- Testosterone effects – XYs insensitive to testosterone and then born with no penis (classed as females) and in XXs exposed prenatally to testosterone who show masculine behaviour (Berenbaum and Bailey).
- Oestrogen – not required to direct prenatal genital development, may lead to smaller brain size (Shi et al.), important for female secondary sexual characteristics, e.g. breast development.
- Oxytocin – contentment and bonding, released when breastfeeding and at orgasm, moderates stress response (tend and befriend, Taylor et al.).

EVALUATION

- Challenging biological determinism – Money's sex-of-rearing view important but evidence shows genetic sex most significant (case studies: David Reimer and males born with no penis – Reiner and Gearhart).
- Importance of other factors – no simple formula, e.g. CAH individuals are XX but exposed to male hormones, many content with gender assigned at birth.
- Role of culture – Batistas (Imperato-McGinley et al.), boys sex-typed as girls but adjusted to male role when male genitalia appeared because culture had more fluid notion of gender.
- Real-world applications – avoid early surgery (Intersex Society), give hormone supplements, e.g. for Turner's syndrome, Olympic Games Committee uses physical characteristics (Bown).
- Effects of hormones on brain development: female monkeys showed more rough-and-tumble play when exposed to testosterone (Quadagno et al.) but Eisenegger et al. showed expectations might explain human behaviour better.

COGNITIVE EXPLANATIONS OF GENDER DEVELOPMENT

KOHLBERG'S THEORY

DESCRIPTION

- Cognitive-developmental – emphasises the role of thinking in development.
- Development occurs in stages due to changes in biological maturity.
- Stage 1: Gender labelling (about 2–3 years) – gender based on appearance, can change if appearance changes, linked to Piaget's pre-operational thinking (conservation).
- Stage 2: Gender stability (about 4–5 years) – gender stays same over time, children lack ability to conserve and still swayed by appearance, e.g. dress worn, even if genitals showing (McConaghy).
- Stage 3: Gender constancy (about 6 years) – gender constancy across time and situations, now ready to learn gender-appropriate stereotypes.

EVALUATION

- Research support – gender labelling (Thompson, gender identification improves by 3 years), gender stability (Slaby and Frey, children didn't recognise stability of traits over time at age 4) and gender constancy (Slaby and Frey, high scores on stability/constancy correlated with interest in gender-appropriate models).
- Methodological criticisms – children judge using appearance because most salient cue (Bem), children answering in 'pretend' mode (Martin and Halverson).
- Gender constancy may appear at age 5, possibly related to availability of gender information in media (Slaby and Frey).
- Gender difference – boys show gender constancy earlier, explained by social learning theory (male models more powerful), needs to be incorporated into Kohlberg's theory.
- Gender constancy not required for learning gender behaviour – learned earlier than predicted (Martin and Little).

GENDER SCHEMA THEORY

DESCRIPTION

- Martin and Halverson's theory differs from Kohlberg's: (1) information about gender-appropriate behaviour acquired before gender constancy, (2) describes how schemas are processed.
- Gender schemas organise and structure information presented to children, form 'naïve' theories.
- Gender ingroup schema acquired because child identifies with group and actively seeks information about ingroup.
- Desire to negatively evaluate outgroup to strengthen positive feelings of belonging to ingroup (increased self-esteem).
- Gender attitudes resilient because affect what children perceive and what they remember.
- Peers have strong influence – children seek same-sex friendships because 'like me', avoid teasing for behaving like opposite sex.

EVALUATION

- Gender schemas without constancy – children age 4 acquired schema, supports GST (Martin and Little).
- Gender identity even earlier – Zosuls et al. found gender identity at 19 months; however, Bandura and Bussey argue gender concepts acquired even before this.
- Gender schemas organise memory – gender-consistent pictures recalled best (Martin and Halverson, Bradbard et al.).
- Gender schemas distort information – children misremember inconsistent information, maintains ingroup stereotypes (Martin and Halverson).
- Resilience of gender stereotypes – children of working mothers have less fixed stereotypes so can change, but generally exposure to counter-stereotypes not effective (Hoffman).

PSYCHODYNAMIC EXPLANATION OF GENDER DEVELOPMENT

DESCRIPTION

- Freud's psychoanalytic theory of personality development – ego represses anxiety-provoking thoughts to unconscious mind.
- Psychosexual stages – libido attached to body parts, 3rd stage is phallic stage (age 3–6), libido attached to genitals, gender development occurs.
- In both genders attraction to opposite-sex parent resolved when child identifies with same-sex parent and internalises gender identity and gender concepts.
- Oedipus complex in boys – attraction to mother leads to wish that father was dead, guilt leads to repression, eventual resolution through identity with father.
- Electra complex in girls (Jung) – disenchantment with mother due to lack of penis and penis envy, resolved through desire to have a baby.
- Unresolved phallic stage leads to fixation, phallic character not capable of close love, may be associated with amoral behaviour and homosexuality.

EVALUATION

- Support from case studies – Little Hans wanted his mother and repressed fears of castration until he came to identify with his father; Levin reported link between bipolar patients and Electra complex.
- Child sexual awareness – children aged 4 not aware of genitals (Bem); however, Okami et al. found link between early sexual awareness and later sexual activity.
- Lacks predictive validity – children from one parent or same-sex families should have difficulty with gender development but they don't (e.g. Patterson).
- Alternative psychodynamic explanations – Chodorow focused on mothers only, closeness with daughters (supported by Goldberg and Lewis) and greater independence for sons.
- Reinterpretation – Lacan suggested penis envy symbolised male power.

CULTURAL AND MEDIA INFLUENCES ON GENDER ROLES

CULTURAL INFLUENCE

- From parents, peers and related to social learning theory.
  - Women more conformist than men in tight, sedentary societies (Berry et al.).
  - Women's roles changing, women still do more domestic duties but cultural attitudes changing.
  - Mead's research in Papua New Guinea showed cultural role differences, e.g. Mundugumor men and women both aggressive.

MEDIA INFLUENCE

- Males portrayed as more independent and in control, women as emotional (Hodges et al.).
  - Those who watch more TV display more stereotypic gender role conceptions (McGhee and Frueh).
  - Vicarious reinforcement – media provides gender role models but also provides information about likely outcomes, raises or lowers self-efficacy.
  - Counter-stereotypes were effective in advertising (Pingree).

EVALUATION

- Cultural similarities – social role theory (Eagly and Wood) explains how biologically based physical differences dictate roles.
- Cross-cultural research (e.g. Mead) flawed because of observer bias and inaccurate information provided by indigenous population (Freeman).
- Demonstrating media influence – Williams showed gender effects in study of Notel.
- Media effects insignificant – may simply reinforce status quo.
- Backlash to counter-stereotyping – adolescents may wish to take opposite view to one promoted by adults.

SOCIAL LEARNING THEORY AS APPLIED TO GENDER DEVELOPMENT

SOCIAL LEARNING THEORY

- Social learning theory (SLT) emphasises learning from others (social) who model and reinforce gender behaviours (Bandura).
- Indirect (vicarious) reinforcement – children learn consequences of behaviour through observation but only imitate people with whom they identify (same-sex models).
- Mediational processes – cognitive theory because expectancies of future outcomes determine likelihood of imitation.
- Maintenance through direct reinforcement – children may learn gender-inappropriate behaviour but are punished for imitating it.
- Direct tuition – once children acquire language, people (e.g. parents) can explicitly tell them what to do and not do.
- Self-direction – once gender-appropriate behaviours internalised, a child can direct own behaviour.

EVALUATION

- Evidence to support modelling – children imitate behaviour of same-sex models but not if counter-stereotypical (Perry and Bussey).
- Direct tuition may be more effective than modelling – children played with toys labelled for their sex even if same-sex child observed playing with opposite-sex toy (Martin et al.).
- Peers not gender influences – either too young to be relating to peers or peers simply reinforce existing stereotypes (Lamb and Roopnarine).
- Self-direction – younger children disapproved of others engaging in gender-inappropriate play but not themselves; older children disapproved of themselves too (Bussey and Bandura).
- Too much emphasis on social processes – cross-cultural research shows universals in gender behaviour, e.g. what men and women desire in a partner is similar (Buss).

ATYPICAL GENDER DEVELOPMENT

BIOLOGICAL EXPLANATIONS OF GID:

- Transsexual gene (androgen receptor) more common in MtF transsexuals (Hare et al.).
- The brain-sex theory – BSTc smaller in normal females and transsexuals (e.g. Zhou et al.).
- Innate form of phantom limb syndrome – FtM transsexuals have a phantom penis, MtF transsexuals feel they should not have a penis (Ramachandran and McGeoch).
- Environmental cause – DDT contains oestrogen, feminises boys.

SOCIAL EXPLANATIONS OF GID:

- Mental illness – cross-gender fantasy to resolve maternal anxiety issues (Coates et al.).
- Mother–son – enmeshed relationships leading to female identification (Stoller).
- Father–daughter – seek male role to overturn paternal rejection (Zucker).

EVALUATION

- Criticisms of the brain-sex theory – BSTc size difference appears in adulthood so cannot be cause of dysphoria (Chung et al.); however, Rametti et al. found support.
- Support for cross-wiring – 'normal' individuals with penis/breasts removed more likely to experience phantom sensation than transsexuals (Ramachandran and McGeoch).
- Support for social explanations – high levels of separation anxiety in MtF individuals (Zucker et al.) and of emotional over-involvement (Owen-Anderson et al.).
- More than one explanation needed for e.g. homosexual and non-homosexual transsexuals (Blanchard) and core and peripheral people with GID (Furuhashi).
- Socially sensitive research – evidence for biology may make people feel more accepting of GID but also make people wrongly believe that GID is inevitable.

0 1   Outline **two** differences between sex and gender.   **[4 marks]**

0 2   Which one of the following statements about gender is **false**? Write the letter of your chosen answer in your answer booklet.   **[1 mark]**

     A. Gender can be identified through physical characteristics.

     B. Gender describes whether someone is masculine, feminine or androgynous.

     C. Gender is a set of behaviours.

     D. Gender is a subjective concept.

0 3   Using an example, outline what is meant by androgyny.   **[3 marks]**

0 4   Explain **two** limitations of using Bem's Sex Role Inventory as a measure of androgyny.   **[4 marks]**

0 5   Describe and evaluate research into sex-role stereotypes.   **[16 marks]**

0 6   Give **one** psychological difference between males who have Klinefelter's syndrome and males with typical sex chromosome patterns.   **[1 mark]**

0 7   Name **one** sex hormone and outline the influence that it might have on an individual's behaviour.   **[4 marks]**

0 8   Read the item below and then answer the question that follows.

> Chi is a four-year-old girl who looks different from her female peers. She is shorter than average, and has a webbed neck and a shield chest. Medical tests have revealed that Chi has the sex chromosome pattern XO.

     (i) Name the syndrome that Chi has.   **[1 mark]**

     (ii) State how Chi's sex chromosome pattern differs from that of most females.   **[1 mark]**

     (iii) Give **one** psychological trait associated with the sex chromosome pattern XO.   **[1 mark]**

     (iv) Explain how studying people like Chi can contribute to psychologists' understanding of the way that gender develops.   **[3 marks]**

0 9   Briefly outline and discuss **one** research study that investigated the influence of hormones on gender related behaviour.   **[5 marks]**

1 0   Identify and briefly explain **one** limitation of the argument that chromosomes determine gender.   **[3 marks]**

1 1   Read the item below and then answer the questions that follow.

> Kian is three years old. He is looking through a fashion magazine, and tells his dad, 'When I grow up, I am going to be a lady like her.'
>
> Matilda is five years old. She is looking through a newspaper when she sees a picture of a female pop star dressed in a suit and tie. She asks her dad, 'Is Rita a man now?'

     (i) Outline what is meant by gender stability. Use Kian's comment as part of your answer.   **[2 marks]**

     (ii) Outline what is meant by gender constancy. Use Matilda's comment as part of your answer.   **[2 marks]**

1 2   Describe the findings of **one** research study into gender schema theory.   **[3 marks]**

1 3   Briefly describe gender schema theory as an explanation of gender.   **[4 marks]**

1 4   Discuss Kohlberg's theory of gender development. Refer to **at least one other** explanation of gender as part of your answer.   **[16 marks]**

1 5   With reference to Freud's psychoanalytic theory of gender, explain the difference between identification and internalisation.   **[3 marks]**

1 6   **(i)**   Briefly describe Freud's concept of the Oedipus complex.   **[3 marks]**

         (ii)   Outline **one** limitation of Freud's concept of the Oedipus complex.   **[2 marks]**

1 7   Read the item below and then answer the question that follows.

> Sadie is six years old and enjoys spending time with her mother, doing activities such as shopping and cooking. Her brother, Tom, is four years old and also wants to join in with their activities. When Tom's father tries to spend time with his son, Tom is not interested and often runs away from him.

With reference to psychodynamic theory, explain both Sadie's and Tom's behaviours.   **[4 marks]**

1 8   Outline and discuss both a psychodynamic explanation and the social learning theory of gender development.   **[16 marks]**

1 9   Read the item below and then answer the question that follows.

> Martin has a five-year-old son called Freddie. Martin says Freddie has turned into his 'little shadow' – following him everywhere, trying to copy what his dad is doing. The other day, Freddie tried to mow the lawn alongside Martin but using a toy shopping trolley! Freddie also says he really wants to learn to head a football like Martin does, as he thinks it's really cool.

Discuss social learning as an explanation of gender development. Refer to the case of Freddie as part of your answer.   **[16 marks]**

2 0   Describe **one** research study which investigates the influence of the media on gender roles.   **[4 marks]**

2 1   Evaluate the view that culture influences gender roles.   **[4 marks]**

2 2   Read the item below and answer the question that follows.

> Nina is 12 years old. Ever since she can remember, she has much preferred socialising with boys rather than girls. Most of her hobbies are typically masculine, and she is often mistaken for a boy because of the way that she dresses. She has recently told her parents that she wants to rename herself Nathan, and wants to be referred to as 'he'.

Discuss both biological **and** social explanations of gender identity disorder. Refer to the case of Nina as part of your answer.   **[16 marks]**

2 3   Read the item below and answer the questions that follow.

> A psychologist carried out a content analysis of children's toy adverts, comparing those aimed at boys and those aimed at girls. She recorded a total of 10 hours of adverts shown across a two-week period on one TV channel. She then sampled from these recordings by watching the middle 10 minutes from each 30-minute segment. Key findings included the following:
>
> - adverts aimed at boys presented nearly twice as much active play compared to adverts aimed at girls
> - the slogans used for girls' adverts had a median of eight words compared to a median of five for adverts aimed at boys
> - adverts aimed at girls were described as emphasising development in adulthood and glamorising the role of women in society
> - adverts aimed at boys were described as emphasising adventure through exploration of the world.

     (i)   Outline what is meant by content analysis.   **[2 marks]**

     (ii)   Explain **one** strength of using content analysis when researching gender.   **[2 marks]**

     (iii)   Identify whether the psychologist was using time or event sampling in their research. Justify your decision.   **[2 marks]**

     (iv)   Explain how this research uses both quantitative and qualitative data.   **[4 marks]**

The exam questions on gender will be varied but are likely to involve some short answer questions (AO1), some application of knowledge questions (AO2), research methods questions and possibly an extended writing question (AO1 + AO3). We've provided answers to some additional questions together with comments from an examiner about how well they've each done.

---

01 Read the item below and then answer the question that follows.

> Adam was given a toy toolkit for his sixth birthday. His younger sister, Evie, said she wanted one too because when she grew up she wanted to be a builder. Adam laughed at Evie and said, 'You can't be a builder. You're a girl.'

Explain what is meant by a sex-role stereotype. Refer to Adam and Evie as part of your answer. *(4 marks)*

Maisie's answer

This scenario illustrates sex-role stereotypes because Adam thinks Evie can't be a builder because that is what boys do. So Adam has a fixed idea about what girls and boys can do and this is called a stereotype. Children learn about sex-role stereotypes from their parents and peers as they grow up. For example a study by Smith and Lloyd showed that mothers selected boys' type toys if they thought they were playing with a boy baby (it was either a boy or girl dressed up as a boy). Children learn these stereotypes once they have a gender identity, though the age at which this happens is debated by psychologists. Some think it is earlier than others.

Examiner's comments

Maisie's response starts well, as she is clearly considering the item. She earns an AO2 mark, just, for identifying Adam's stereotyped view and a further mark (AO1) for knowing something about stereotypes, which occurs in the second line. Thereafter, the answer loses focus. The content is still addressing sex-role stereotypes but not in a way that meets the demand of the question.

Ciaran's answer

A sex-role stereotype is a set of shared expectations within a social group about what men and women should do and think. The society we live in teaches us expectations about how men and women should behave, such as expectations that men are doctors and women are nurses. Adam has a fixed sex-role stereotype about girls because he thinks they can't be builders. These expectations can be quite fixed and are learned from people around you. Evie does not hold the same stereotypes as her brother. She is more flexible in her thinking about what boys and girls can do. This may be because she has had different experiences from Adam, or it may be that her stereotypes are still forming as she is younger.

Examiner's comments

This is a full mark answer. Ciaran easily earns 2 marks by starting with a detailed outline of stereotyping which also has a clear focus on sex roles too. Both Adam and Evie are explicitly referred to in the second part of answer. Ciaran doesn't just identify the examples of stereotyping but also makes a decent attempt to explain why they may (or may not) occur in this scenario.

---

02 Discuss the extent to which chromosomes and hormones can be used to explain the development of gender in human beings. *(16 marks)*

Maisie's answer

The genetic gender of most people is XX or XY. These represent 2 of our 46 chromosomes. A person who is XX is a female and XY is a male. If you are XY this leads to the production of certain hormones, mainly testosterone, which then has an effect on which genitals develop. However, in some cases this doesn't happen. For example in a person who is testosterone insensitive the male genitals may not develop and then that person may be sex-typed at birth as a female. So in this case chromosomes don't correctly determine gender.

There are cases of abnormal chromosomes such a Klinefelter's and Turner's syndrome. In Klinefelter's syndrome a person is XXY in terms of their chromosomes. This produces a male baby who grows up with certain abnormal characteristics such as being less hairy than usual and possibly having breasts. In Turner's syndrome a person just has one X chromosome and this leads to a female child who may have ovaries but may not. They often have other abnormalities such as a webbed neck and being small. Hormone supplements early on can help – and this is an advantage of this research because it shows how we can treat these problems.

In normal XX females there is less effect of hormones on development as basically all embryos develop externally into females unless testosterone instructs otherwise. Female hormones do have an effect on the development of internal organs such as ovaries and also on the menstrual cycle later. Testosterone has an effect on the developing brain and masculinises, which may explain why men think differently to women.

The case of David Reimer is used to show the importance of chromosomes rather than sex of rearing. David was born as a normal male. His penis was accidentally damaged in an operation and then surgically removed and he was raised as a girl. However, he was not a happy child and eventually was told that he was biologically male and he chose to return to his actual sex. The strong feelings he had show that biological is more important than social factors. It shows that gender is more about biology.

This research has been important in sports where it is important to prevent men taking part in female events because they are stronger and more muscular. The problem is that some people think they are women but have abnormal chromosomes and are actually men. Sports federations have to find ways to decide who can compete. There are no clear answers in some cases. Being male or female is not a clear cut thing and, in fact, in some countries this is no longer an official question to ask on e.g. passports.

Examiner's comments

Maisie demonstrates a good understanding of the biology behind gender with accurate references to chromosome patterns and sex hormones. However, throughout the description, her focus is on the physical effects rather than the psychological effects – so it is an essay much more about sex than gender development. For example, Maisie could have written about the impact testosterone has on behaviour, or the absence of testosterone on mental processes. In the case of atypical chromosome patterns, Maisie should have identified how individuals act and think differently from normal rather than how they appear. When Maisie does begin to consider gender – as in the case of David Reimer or the issues around categorising people for the purposes of sport – it is all rather vague, e.g. what were his 'strong feelings'? In short, the terms 'masculine' and 'feminine' are rarely used. They are just a couple of attempts to include discussion at the end of the essay, but this is not enough given the balance of marks (10 for AO3). This essay is good enough to be scored at the top of Level 1 but no more than this.

03 Outline **one** research study where social learning was applied to gender. Briefly discuss the findings of this study. *(4 marks)*

Maisie's answer

A study by Perry and Bussey showed film clips to children aged eight and nine. In the film boys and girls were seen selecting an apple or pear, both gender-neutral items. Later the children were given a choice of fruit. Boys selected the fruit they had seen another boy selecting, and the same for girls. This shows that children model gender behaviours they have observed in gender-appropriate models.

Examiner's comments

Maisie offers an effective outline of her chosen study. It is relevant, and described in a way that is concise yet demonstrates what happened and what was found out. She earns both of the AO1 marks on offer. However, there is no discussion of the findings beyond the conclusion and therefore she only earns 1 of the remaining 2 AO3 marks. Maisie could have earned another AO3 mark through evaluation – for example, considering a limitation of the findings.

Ciaran's answer

Bandura did a study with a Bobo doll showing how children learn through observation. In this study some children watched a model hit and punch a Bobo doll and later these children were more likely to repeat the same behaviour than children who didn't see a model behave like this. This shows how any behaviours can be acquired through imitation so the same is true for learning about gender-related behaviours. Children see how male and female models behave and imitate this.

Examiner's comments

This is a study into social learning theory but not one that applies specifically to gender, so Ciaran gets no credit for it. It is important to distinguish between studies that may relate to one field of research but not another, even if the theory behind each is the same.

---

04 Read the item below and then answer the question that follows.

> Martin has a five-year-old son called Freddie. Martin says Freddie has turned into his 'little shadow' – following him everywhere, trying to copy what his dad is doing. The other day, Freddie tried to mow the lawn alongside Martin but using a toy shopping trolley! Freddie also says he really wants to learn to head a football like Martin does, as he thinks it's really cool.

Discuss social learning as an explanation of gender development. Refer to the case of Freddie as part of your answer. *(16 marks)*

Ciaran's answer

The social learning theory of gender development is illustrated by the example of Freddie, who is learning about what men do by observing what his father does and then imitating it. According to SLT behaviour is learned through direct and indirect reinforcement. Our example is about indirect reinforcement. We observe what other people do and especially if we identify with them are likely to copy the behaviour we observe. In Freddie's case he would identify with his father because they are the same and because he likes his father. Both of these factors make his father a good role model.

In SLT vicarious reinforcement is important too – this means seeing someone else rewarded for doing something and then internalising the expectation of getting rewards yourself. This increases the likelihood of repeating a behaviour. But then, when you do repeat a behaviour you may not be rewarded and this prevents future reoccurrence. For example if Freddie started playing with dolls (because he saw his mother praise his sister for this) he might get discouraged by his father who might say 'boys don't do that' and therefore Freddie learns not to do things that girls do. So gender behaviour is maintained through direct reinforcement.

A further element of SLT is that children also learn through direct tuition. This is when someone tells them explicitly what they should do. For example Freddie's father might tell Freddie what boys do such as saying to Freddie that men like football.

The classic evidence used to support SLT was Bandura's study of learning aggressive behaviour where those children who watched a model behaving aggressively to a Bobo doll later behaved more aggressively. This can be generalised to learning any behaviour because the fundamental concept is the same – people imitate behaviours they observe, especially those where they are rewarded and/or identify with the role model – as in Freddie's case.

There is also research specifically related to gender such as a study by Perry and Bussey where children were shown a film of a boy or girl and later watched to see if they would model their behaviour on what they saw. The children modelled the behaviours seen by same-sex children. One important issue in this study was that the children only modelled same-sex behaviour as long as it was not counter to gender stereotypes (e.g. a man wearing a dress).

One criticism of SLT is that it ignores biological influences. Bandura did acknowledge that there are such influences but they were not adequately incorporated into the theory. The theory also ignores the fact that culture does not explain all gender behaviours because there are some universals.

Examiner's comments

Ciaran shows impressive knowledge of social learning theory – not only through accurate use of a range of key terms but by the way they are linked through coherent description. Ciaran also clearly understands these terms as he applies them effectively to the item when he considers each one. Ciaran includes relevant evidence as part of his answer, although could have made more obvious links between it and Freddie's experiences. The weaker part of the answer is the evaluation of the actual theory. This amounts to two brief criticisms at the end of the essay – both of these could have been developed to demonstrate a deeper understanding of the issues. Indeed, Ciaran should have broadened the discussion by bringing in more challenges to the theory as an explanation of gender and/or Freddie's case. This essay just qualifies for a Level 3 response, but this relies primarily on Ciaran's ability to demonstrate skills relating to AO1 and AO2.

Cognition and development

CONTENTS OF CHAPTER

SPECIFICATION CHECKLIST

- Piaget's theory of cognitive development: schemas, assimilation, accommodation, equilibration, stages of intellectual development. Characteristics of these stages, including object permanence, conservation, egocentrism and class inclusion.

- Vygotsky's theory of cognitive development, including the zone of proximal development and scaffolding.

- Baillargeon's explanation of early infant abilities, including knowledge of the physical world; violation of expectation research.

- The development of social cognition: Selman's levels of perspective-taking; theory of mind, including theory of mind as an explanation for autism; the Sally–Anne study. The role of the mirror neuron system in social cognition.

TRY THIS

Do we think logically?

Developmental theories are often described as 'stage theories' – they describe how children change as they age (in terms of how both thinking and behaviour change). Each stage has unique characteristics and all children are expected to go in the same sequence through the stages.

One of the stage theories in this chapter is Jean Piaget's theory of cognitive development, and the final stage of his theory is abstract thinking – being able, for example, to solve maths problems using counters and blocks, and think about abstract logical problems. Piaget claimed that children from the age of 11 onwards can solve abstract problems using deductive reasoning, i.e. a kind of top-down logic where you reach a conclusion based on reason. You think like a scientist – for example, developing hypotheses and testing them.

Peter Wason developed what is called the Wason four-card selection task to test deductive reasoning. Participants are shown four cards with the following symbols visible: E, K, 4 and 7. They are also told that the rule is:

If a card has a vowel on one face, then that card has an even number on the opposite face.

What card or cards would you turn over to test this rule?

Wason and Shapiro (1971) conducted research and found that only 2 out of 16 participants got this right (the answer is below) but 10 out of 16 solved the same deductive problem if it was given in a concrete form: the cards are labelled Manchester, Leeds, car and train. The rule is:

Every time I go to Manchester I travel by car.

What card or cards would you turn over to test this rule?

TRY THIS

Try a bit of research yourself and see whether people of different ages do have difficulties with the problems above.

Explanation

Piaget's stages of cognitive development suggest, as noted above, that the abstract stage of reasoning comes after the concrete stage. However, it appears from the research above that he vastly overestimated development, as many people don't reach the final stage until later in adulthood.

Leda Cosmides (1989) offers an evolutionary explanation. She argues that the evolution of human intellect was primarily driven by selection for social expertise within groups where the most challenging problem faced by early humans was dealing with the other members of their social group. An example of such an adaptation can be seen in the fact that people are most adept at solving the Wason problem when it involves social relations. The four cards are: beer, coke, 19 and 16, and the statement is:

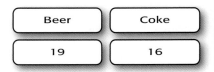

If a person is drinking alcohol, then they must be over 18 years of age.

Which of the cards above must you turn over to test this statement?

Did your participants find this task easier than the abstract Wason task?

The solutions for all the problems are: E and 7; Manchester and train; drinking beer; and 16 years.

Piaget's theory of cognitive development

Piaget's theory of **cognitive development** changed our understanding of how thinking develops in a child. Before Piaget, people believed that the difference in thinking between children and adults was that adults knew more – as you get older, you simply learn more information. In the first part of the 20th century Piaget (1926, 1954) proposed something radically different. He claimed that adults don't just know more – they think in quite a different way.

Piaget believed that cognitive development was a result of two influences: *maturation* and the environment. Maturation refers to the effects of the biological process of ageing. As children get older, certain mental operations become possible. At the same time, through interactions with the *environment*, their understanding of the world becomes more complex.

On this spread we begin with the mechanisms of cognitive development – what causes development to happen. On the next spread we look at Piaget's stages of development.

Insider tip...

If you are asked to describe and evaluate Piaget's theory then you can use the information on this spread and the next spread – but don't sacrifice depth for breadth. List-like answers don't score top marks.

MEET THE RESEARCHER

Jean Piaget (1896–1980) is probably the best-known psychologist after Sigmund Freud. He was born in Switzerland and initially trained as a zoologist – the first thing he published (at the age of 10) was on molluscs.

His interest in cognitive development started when, in the early 1920s, he worked on some of the first intelligence tests. Piaget noticed that children of the same age tended to make similar kinds of errors. He thought that younger children might be following rather different logical rules to older children. Their errors were quite predictable. In other words, the errors made at certain ages formed a kind of stage of development, and these stages formed a sequence. Piaget suggested that children's thinking changes *qualitatively* as they pass through the stages.

KEY TERMS

Accommodation In Piaget's theory of cognitive development, the process of adjusting or changing existing schemas because new, conflicting information creates disequilibrium.

Assimilation In Piaget's theory of cognitive development, the process of fitting new experiences into existing schemas without making any change.

Cognitive development The process by which our mental processes change as we age.

Equilibration Experiencing a balance between existing schemas and new experiences.

Schema A cluster of related facts usually based on previous experiences, and used to generate future expectations.

MECHANISMS OF COGNITIVE DEVELOPMENT

Schemas

Schemas are mental structures that represent a group of related concepts, such as your schema for a dog (fur, four legs, wet nose). Schemas can be *behavioural* (such as grasping an object) or *cognitive* (such as classifying objects). Rather like individual computer programs, schemas are 'programs' that people construct for dealing with the world.

When a child is born it already has a few schemas. An example of such a schema is the grasping reflex. Another example is a mental representation of a human face. It seems that, from birth, infants can distinguish a human face from all the other objects they see.

From birth onwards the infant's schemas develop as a result of interactions with the environment. New experiences lead to new schemas being developed. For example, the infant learns separate schemas for the different faces of people he/she knows, and learns to distinguish between dogs and cats.

Assimilation and accommodation

What is the exact process by which schemas become more complex? Piaget proposed two ways this might happen: **assimilation** and **accommodation**.

Assimilation

A child initially tries to understand any new information in terms of their existing knowledge about the world. For example, a baby who is given a new toy car to play with may grasp or suck that toy in the same way that they grasped or sucked a rattle. Assimilation occurs when an existing schema (such as sucking) is used on a new object (such as a toy car). Assimilation, therefore, involves the incorporation of new information into an existing schema.

Accommodation

Accommodation occurs when a child adapts existing schema in order to understand new information that doesn't appear to fit. Learning to drive a manual car involves developing a convenient schema for working the three pedals. What would happen if you drove an automatic car (no clutch pedal)? Assimilation into your existing schema would not work, so accommodation must (quickly!) occur.

Assimilation is the process of fitting new information and experiences into existing schemas, while accommodation is the process of changing the existing schemas when new information cannot be assimilated. For example, a child may have the schema 'four legs and fur = dog'. Every new instance of a creature with the same characteristics is assimilated into this schema. However, one day someone uses the word 'cat' for an animal with four legs and fur and this challenges the current schema. The child recognises that this animal has four legs and fur and its tail doesn't wag, which doesn't fit the dog schema. This new information cannot be assimilated into the existing schema; instead the child's schemas must alter to accommodate the new information – a new schema is formed. Remember, a schema is a packet of information about a thing or action.

Equilibration

The driving force beyond these changes or 'adaptation' is the principle of equilibrium. The intellect strives to maintain a sense of balance, i.e. equilibrium. If an experience cannot be assimilated into existing schemas, then there is a state of imbalance which is experienced as an unpleasant state and the individual seeks to restore balance through a process called **equilibration**. Cognitive development is the result of adaptation between the individual's existing schemas and environmental 'demands' for change, such as new experiences which don't fit existing schemas.

Lifespan learning

The processes outlined above take place throughout life as our experiences (the 'environment') present us with knowledge. Such knowledge can either be assimilated or we must accommodate by creating new schemas.

However, there are some limitations on what can be learned at different ages. A young child cannot always accommodate new experiences to new schemas because his or her mind is simply not mature enough, as you will learn about on the next spread concerning the stages of cognitive development.

Research shows that face schemas are innate

There is evidence to support the existence of innate schemas. Fantz (1961) showed that infants as young as four days old show a preference for a schematic face rather than the same features all jumbled up (see illustrations on right). This shows that it is the unique configuration of a face rather than a complex pattern that is preferred.

This 'facial preference' finding has been replicated in a number of studies, such as Goren *et al.* (1975), although none of the studies make it clear whether this is just due to a liking for things that are symmetrical. In general an innate face preference makes sense because such a preference would have adaptive significance – a newborn who can recognise and respond to its own species will better elicit attachment and caring.

Equilibration is difficult to demonstrate

There is actually little research to support Piaget's ideas about the effects of disequilibrium. Some of Piaget's co-workers, Bärbel Inhelder *et al.* (1974), did show that children's learning was helped when there was a mild conflict between what they expected to happen and what did happen, but Bryant (1995) argues that this wasn't really the sort of conflict that Piaget was talking about – Piaget's conflict was a more major dissonance between two things. This is a general issue with Piaget's theory – some aspects of the theory are not really testable because concepts (such as assimilation) are difficult to operationalise.

Important applications

Piaget's insights have had important applications in education. Piaget's view was that knowledge develops through equilibration, and this means self-discovery is an important part of learning – true understanding only occurs through the process of making one's own accommodations. As Piaget said: 'Each time one prematurely teaches a child something he could have discovered for himself, that child is kept from inventing it and consequently from understanding it completely' (Piaget, 1970).

There has been some criticism of this 'discovery learning' approach. For example, Bennett (1976) found that, in general, children taught via formal methods did better on reading, maths and English. The general lack of success for discovery learning may be due to the fact that teachers in formal classrooms spend more time on the core topics, and that is why children do better when assessed on core topics. A further reason may be that discovery learning requires much more sensitivity and experience from teachers in knowing how and when to guide pupils. Therefore, it is not the method, but the application of it, that is the problem.

The role of language

Piaget did not feel that language influenced cognitive, whereas Vygotsky (his theory is discussed on page 120) argued it was fundamental to cognitive development. Piaget's views were supported in an experiment by another of his co-workers, Hermina Sinclair-de-Zwart (1969). She first demonstrated that children who were 'non-conservers' differed in terms of their language from 'conservers' ('conservation' is a concept explained on the next spread). The non-conservers tended to use absolute rather than comparative terms such as 'big' rather than 'larger'. They also used a single term for different dimensions such as 'small' to mean 'short', 'thin' or 'few'. These findings suggest that cognitive and linguistic development are tied together, but which comes first? In a further experiment Sinclair-de-Zwart taught appropriate verbal skills to the non-conservers. However, 90% of these children were still unable to conserve. This supports Piaget's view that cognitive maturity is a prerequisite for linguistic development, not the other way round.

A comprehensive theory

Piaget produced the first comprehensive theory of children's cognitive development. The theory has been more extensively developed than any other. It has changed our ideas about children and has had a general influence on educational practice. One strength of any theory is its ability to generate research, and Piaget's theory has certainly done so, as you will see on the next spread.

His theory also is valued for its combination of nature (biological maturation) with nurture (experience) to explain cognitive development. Piaget's conception of 'nurture' is more focused on the *physical* environment, whereas Vygotsky emphasised the *social* environment, as you will see when learning about Vygotsky.

▲ Stimuli used by Fantz to test innate face schemas in newborn infants. Infants preferred the picture that looks like a face – the second face acted as a control because it was the same complexity and brightness.

Infant preference was assessed in terms of the amount of time they spent looking at each face – which may indicate interest rather than recognition.

🔼 UPGRADE

Extended writing questions (okay, let's call them essays…) such as question 4 in the 'Can you?' box below are typically worth 16 marks each. Although AQA do not award separate marks for AO1 (description) and AO3 (evaluation), they do nominally assign a certain number of marks for each in their marking schemes. Of the 16 marks available for an essay question, 6 are assigned to AO1 and 10 to AO3, so it pays to be aware of this when structuring your essays. Assuming most students would write about 480 words in response to the time available for a 16-mark question, that would mean writing about 180 words of AO1, or 30 words each for the 6 points.

To gain a mark in the top mark level for an essay question, the descriptive (AO1, remember…) content should be 'accurate and generally well detailed'. But how do you achieve this? First of all, don't waste time with pointless introductions and definitions – they won't get you any marks. Then pick six things you want to say that cover the AO1 part of the question. To make your answer more 'detailed', try to include technical terms or specific words that fine tune what it is you are trying to say. This means you are going a bit deeper. Perhaps add an example to demonstrate your understanding and push each point up to the 30-word target. Of course, the content also has to be accurate – but that's down to you!

CAN YOU? No. 5.1

1. Explain what is meant by the term *schema*. Refer to Piaget's theory of cognitive development in your answer. (3 marks)

2. Outline how the process of equilibration can be used to explain cognitive development. (4 marks)

3. Piaget used the terms assimilation and accommodation to explain cognitive development. Distinguish between assimilation and accommodation. (4 marks)

4. Discuss Piaget's theory of cognitive development. Refer to the process of equilibration in your answer. (16 marks)

Piaget's stages of intellectual development

Piaget proposed that cognitive (intellectual) development was a result of two influences: maturation and the environment. On the previous spread we discussed the role of the environment: experience leads to the development of new schemas. A child develops both more complex schema (assimilation) and new schemas (accommodation) – and intellectual development takes place.

In addition to the role of experience, biological changes in the brain occur through maturation. This means that a child gradually becomes capable of different kinds of thinking – passing through stages of development.

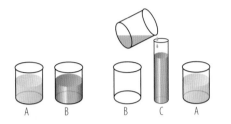

▲ **Conservation of volume** Children are shown the two glasses with water, A and B, and asked whether they contain the same amount of water. The researcher then pours the contents of B into C and again asks whether the quantity is the same. Pre-operational children are dominated by what they see and therefore say 'No'.

▲ **Three mountains task** A child (on the left) is asked to select a picture which shows the view of the mountain that the doll would have. Each mountain has a distinctive top to help the child work out which perspective the doll would see. Young children select the picture with their own view because they have difficulty taking someone else's perspective.

KEY TERMS

Class inclusion The relation between two classes where all members of one class are included in the other.
Conservation The ability to distinguish between reality and appearance, for example to understand that quantity is not changed even when a display is transformed.
Egocentrism Seeing things from your own viewpoint and being unaware of other possible viewpoints.
Object permanence A child's understanding that objects that are no longer visible nevertheless continue to exist.

STAGES OF INTELLECTUAL DEVELOPMENT

The specification refers to Piaget's theory of cognitive development and his stages of intellectual development – cognitive and intellectual are essentially the same. This aspect of Piaget's theory is sometimes referred to as an 'ages and stages' theory because Piaget specified the age at which each stage should occur. Perhaps more important than the age is the *sequence* of development.

Stage 1: Sensorimotor stage (0–2 years)

The task for the infant is first to learn to co-ordinate sensory input (i.e. what they see and feel) with motor actions (i.e. their hand movements and sensations). Piaget used the term 'circular reactions' to describe how an infant repeats actions over and over again to test sensorimotor relationships.

The key development of this stage is **object permanence** – very young infants lose interest in an object when it is hidden behind a pillow because they assume it has ceased to exist. Around eight months they realise that objects that are out of sight still exist.

Stage 2: Pre-operational stage (2–7 years)

Piaget used the term 'operations' to describe internally consistent logical mental rules, such as the rules of arithmetic. At the pre-operational stage children have a kind of logic, but it can't be used as a basis for understanding how the world really works. For example, a very young child believes most things are alive (the table, the moon, etc.).

This lack of logic-based reasoning means that children rely on what they see – they rely on appearance rather than reality. Piaget demonstrated this in his **conservation** tasks (see 'Conservation of volume' on left). A pre-operational child fails to see the logic that volume cannot change, i.e. they fail to be able to 'conserve' volume. Piaget didn't just test this with volume – he also tested number (two rows of six counters and then one row was spread out so it looked like more counters) and mass (two cylinders of plasticine and then one was rolled flat so looked bigger).

Children at this stage are **egocentric** in their thinking. They only see the world from their position and are not aware of other perspectives. Piaget illustrated egocentric thinking using the *three mountains task* (see illustration on left). Children were shown a set of pictures and asked to choose the one which showed the doll's perspective. Four-year-old children tended to choose their own perspective, rather than the perspective of the doll.

A final important quality of thinking in this stage relates to **class inclusion**. Young children can classify objects into categories such as type of animal but they have difficulty with the following kind of categorisation task: when categories include smaller sub-groups which are all part of the bigger category. For example, the category 'animal' includes all cats and dogs, and the category 'dogs' includes spaniels, Doberman, etc. Dobermanns and dogs are included in the category animal – a logical line of reasoning that young children haven't got. The task that Piaget used was to show children four toy cows, three black and one white, and ask: 'Are there more black cows or more cows?' Pre-operational children couldn't answer this correctly and said more black cows.

Stage 3: Concrete operational stage (7–11 years)

At this stage children acquire the rudiments of logical reasoning. Piaget believed that conservation was the single most important achievement of the concrete operational stage because it provides evidence of the child's command of logical operations.

What children are lacking is the ability to think in the abstract. A nice example of abstract versus concrete thinking is the four card selection task described on page 115.

Stage 4: Formal operational stage (11+ years)

Children can now solve abstract problems. They can solve problems using hypothetico-deductive reasoning, thinking like a scientist – for example, developing hypotheses and testing them to determine causal relationships. Children also display idealistic thinking – they are no longer tied to how things are but are able to imagine how things might be if certain changes are made (e.g. thinking about an ideal world).

Piaget's methodology was flawed

Piaget invented a most impressive range of tasks to test the abilities of young children. Bryant (1995) describes them as simple yet ingenious investigations of quite complex topics. However, a number of researchers have criticised these methods – the design of many of the experiments may have confused younger children in particular, which may explain why they appeared to be less capable.

For example, McGarrigle and Donaldson (1974) argued that the deliberate transformation in the conservation task acted as a demand characteristic, demanding an alternative response to the second question ('Are they the same?'). When the researchers arranged for a 'naughty teddy' toy to accidentally mess up the counters, making one row longer, younger children coped better because the change was 'explained' by naughty teddy's behaviour, eliminating the previous demand characteristics (i.e. that the apparent change needed an explanation).

In the three mountains task, Hughes (1975) showed that young children could cope with the task if it was more realistic, for example using a naughty boy doll who was hiding from a toy policeman. This means that children can take another's perspective under more 'real' conditions. In other words, Piaget's method was not actually testing everyday egocentricity.

Further examples of methodological criticisms can be seen in Samuel and Bryant's study (see right) and the research of nativists such as Renee Baillargeon (see pages 122–123).

The idea of biologically driven stages is correct

The research described above demonstrated that Piaget had underestimated children's abilities at younger ages. He also may have overestimated the ability to use abstract logic in the formal operational stage. For example, Dasen (1994) claims that only a third of adults ever reach this stage and even then not during adolescence.

However, the evidence still supports the view that there are qualitative changes in cognitive development as a child matures. Critics tend to take the idea of fixed stages too rigidly, and supporters suggest it should be viewed as a useful model for understanding behaviour and generating research.

Cultural bias

Piaget placed a considerable value on the role of logical operations in the development of thinking. This may be because he came from a middle-class European background and his studies involved children from European academic families who valued academic abilities. In other cultures and social classes, greater value may be placed on, for example, a more basic level of concrete operations (i.e. making things rather than thinking about abstract ideas). Therefore his theory may not be universally applicable.

Important applications

Piaget's stage theory implies that children are not biologically 'ready' to be taught certain concepts until they have reached a certain age. For example, according to Piaget, it would be difficult to teach a pre-operational child to perform abstract mathematical calculations. For real learning to take place (as opposed to rote learning with little understanding), Piaget proposed that activities should be at the appropriate level for a child's age. If a child is not mature enough, they may acquire skills superficially, but in order to truly understand and become competent it is important to wait until they are ready. The Plowden Report (1967) drew extensively on Piaget's theory and led to major changes in primary school education in the UK.

However, if the development of cognitive structures is related to maturity, then practice should not improve performance. In other words, if a person is not biologically ready to move on to the next stage, then no amount of practice should get them there. The evidence is equivocal. For example, Bryant and Trabasso (1971) found that training could improve performance, whereas Danner and Day (1977) found it didn't.

Alternative explanations and conclusions

On the next spread you will learn about Vygotsky's theory of cognitive development. This provides a useful counterpoint to Piaget's theory, suggesting that development can be explained in terms of social rather than individual factors. You will see that both theories may be correct.

Despite the wealth of criticisms, Piaget remains one of the most influential psychologists of the twentieth century. His theory has had an enormous influence on education and on psychological research. Bryant (1995) reminds us that Piaget's key contribution was to highlight the radical differences in the way young children and adults think.

Research methods

A criticism of Piaget's conservation task was that asking two questions may have confused younger children. In the pre-transformation phase Piaget asked the children whether the quantity was the same. After the transformation took place he asked the same question a second time. Younger children may have felt that this form of questioning meant that a different answer was required.

To test this, Samuel and Bryant (1984) tried to see what would happen if they only asked the question once, after the transformation. In this study there were four groups of children (see below). In each age group some children were asked the question once and some were asked the question twice. The children took part in 12 trials in total – four trials with each of the different kinds of task (volume, number and mass).

The table below shows the mean number of errors for each child.

Mean age in years	One question	Standard two questions
5 ¼	7	8
6 ¼	4	6
7 ¼	3	3
8 ¼	1	2

1. What conclusions can you draw from the data in the table? (4 marks)
2. Describe how the children might have been selected for this study and how they would have been allocated to conditions. (4 marks)
3. Identify the experimental design used in this study and explain your answer. (2 marks)
4. Identify a suitable inferential test that could be used with this data and justify your choice. (3 marks)

Extra: Use the test identified in question 4 to find out if the findings show a significant relationship.

LINK TO RESEARCH METHODS

See inferential tests on pages 24–32. The topics in these questions are covered in the research methods chapter of our Year 1 book.

CAN YOU? No. 5.2

1. Explain Piaget's concept of *class inclusion*. Use examples in your answer. (3 marks)
2. Outline **one** study where Piaget investigated conservation. Include details of what he did and what he found. (4 marks)
3. Give **one** criticism of the study you outlined in question 2. (4 marks)
4. Discuss Piaget's stages of intellectual development. (16 marks)

Vygotsky's theory of cognitive development

Russian psychologist Lev Vygotsky agreed with Piaget that a child's thinking is qualitatively different from an adult's. However, he placed much greater emphasis on the importance of the social context of children's learning. Vygotsky (1934) believed that *culture* is the prime determinant of individual development. Cognitive development is driven by a child's biological maturation, but is also, most importantly, a product of a child's interactions with others.

KEY TERMS

Scaffolding An approach to instruction that aims to support a learner only when absolutely necessary, i.e. to provide a support framework (scaffold) to assist the learning process.

Zone of proximal development In Vygotsky's theory of cognitive development, the 'region' between a person's current abilities, which they can perform with no assistance, and their potential capabilities, which they can be helped to achieve with the assistance of 'experts'.

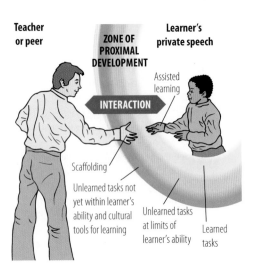

Teacher or peer — **ZONE OF PROXIMAL DEVELOPMENT** — **Learner's private speech**

Assisted learning

INTERACTION

Scaffolding

Unlearned tasks not yet within learner's ability and cultural tools for learning

Unlearned tasks at limits of learner's ability

Learned tasks

MEET THE RESEARCHER

Lev Vygotsky (1896–1934). Piaget and Vygotsky were born in the same year but worlds apart – Vygotsky was Russian, whereas Piaget was Swiss. They never met, although Vygotsky read about Piaget's theory. Piaget was only able to read Vygotsky's works in 1958 when they were first translated into English.

We might know a lot more about Vygotsky and his ideas if he had lived longer – he was in the middle of a major revision of his theory when he died aged 37 from tuberculosis.

VYGOTSKY'S THEORY

Vygotsky believed that cultural influences were the key driving force in cognitive development. Such cultural influences come through interactions with others and through language.

Elementary and higher mental functions

Vygotsky proposed that children are born with *elementary* mental functions, such as perception and memory. These are transformed into *higher* mental functions (such as use of mathematical systems) by the influence of culture. Elementary mental functions are biological and a form of natural development. Higher mental functions are exclusively human. The role of culture is to transform elementary mental functions into higher mental functions.

The role of others: Experts

A child learns through problem-solving experiences shared with someone else, usually a parent or teacher but also more competent peers. All people with greater knowledge than the child are called *experts*. Initially, the person interacting with the child assumes most of the responsibility for guiding the problem-solving activity, but gradually this responsibility transfers to the child.

The role of language

Vygotsky believed that culture is transmitted by experts using *semiotics*, i.e. the signs and symbols developed within a particular culture. Language is the semiotic system of foremost importance, but mathematical symbols are valuable too. Thus both language and mathematics are the means by which culture is transmitted from expert to child. To begin with, language takes the form of shared dialogues between the adult and child (*pre-intellectual speech*), but as the child develops the skill of mental representation, he/she begins to communicate with themselves. In this way language (semiotics) enables intellectual development.

The social and individual level

According to Vygotsky, every function in the child's cognitive development appears twice: first, on the *social* level (between people), and later on the *individual* level (inside the child). The social experiences enable the development of higher mental functions (such as writing and the use of mathematical symbols). The social experiences depend on the use of semiotics such as language.

The zone of proximal development (ZPD)

A child's **zone of proximal development** is the region where cognitive development takes place (see left). Unlike Piaget, Vygotsky believed that learning *precedes* development. According to Vygotsky, learning or cognitive development does not take place in the area of current development (i.e. where the child already is), nor does it take place too far ahead of what the child can already do independently. In the former instance, nothing new would be learned, and in the latter, the new challenges would be too far from the child's current knowledge to be useful.

Scaffolding

Jerome Bruner and his colleagues (Wood *et al.*, 1976) were the first to introduce the term **scaffolding** to describe the process of assisting a learner through the ZPD. Scaffolding is a 'process that enables a ... novice to solve a problem, carry out a task, or achieve a goal which would be beyond his unassisted efforts' (Wood *et al.*, 1976). The expert or tutor creates a 'scaffold' (i.e. temporary support), which is gradually withdrawn when the child is more able to work independently.

Wood and Middleton (1975) found that successful scaffolding depends on something they called 'contingent regulations'. They watched mothers and their 3–4-year-old children assembling a three-dimensional pyramid puzzle, a task that was beyond the children's current abilities. They found that task mastery was related to contingent regulations – when a mother responded to her child's failure by providing more explicit instructions (e.g. identifying what particular piece needs to be moved) and responded to success by providing less explicit instructions (e.g. just praising the strategy that has just been used). This shows that the teaching needs to respond differentially to a learner's responses in order to enhance learning success.

Evidence for the role of culture

Vygotsky's claims about the role of culture in cognitive development have been supported in cross-cultural research. For example, Gredler (1992) pointed to the primitive counting system used in Papua New Guinea as an example of how culture can limit cognitive development. Counting is done by starting on the thumb of one hand and going up the arm and down to the other fingers, ending at 29. This system makes it very difficult to add and subtract large numbers, a limiting factor for cognitive development in this culture.

Research with non-human animals has provided further evidence of the role of culture in cognitive development. Some psychologists believe that non-human animals possess elementary mental functions which may be transformed into higher mental functions by immersing an animal in human culture. For example, Savage-Rumbaugh (1991) has exposed Bonobo apes (such as Kanzi) to a language-rich culture – the apes are 'spoken' to all the time through the use of a lexigram. It is debatable as to whether Kanzi could be said to have acquired human language but he is able to communicate using a symbol system. This suggests that higher mental functions (a symbol system) can be transmitted through culture.

Evidence for the role of language

A cornerstone of Vygotsky's theory is the role of language in cognitive development. Vygotsky believed that language and thought are at first independent, but become interdependent. He suggested that the acquisition of a new word was the *beginning* of the development of a concept. This is supported in a classic study by Carmichael *et al.* (1932) who gave participants one of two labels for certain drawings. For example, they were shown a kidney shape and told either that their drawing was a kidney bean or that it was a canoe. When participants were subsequently asked to draw the shape, it differed according to which label they had been given. This shows that words can affect the way we think about and remember things.

On the other hand, as we noted on page 117, Sinclair-de-Zwart (1969) tried to teach children who could not conserve to use comparative terms, such as bigger and shorter – terms they didn't have in their vocabulary. She found very little improvement in their ability to conserve, a finding that does not support Vygotsky because his theory suggests that cultural tools (such as language) should lead to cognitive development.

Evidence for the role of the ZPD

Evidence for the ZPD was produced in a study by McNaughton and Leyland (1990). They observed young children working with their mothers on jigsaw puzzles of increasing difficulty. The mothers offered help in line with Vygotsky's predictions – if the puzzle was too easy (below the child's ZPD), the mothers did little. If the puzzle was moderately challenging (within the child's ZPD), the mothers focused on helping the children solve the puzzle for themselves. If the puzzle was too difficult for the child (beyond the child's ZPD), the mothers intervened a lot. This shows that experts adjust their input according to where a learner is in the ZPD, supporting Vygotsky's ideas.

Relatively little research support

Despite the number of studies discussed here, there has been relatively little research related to Vygotsky's theory compared with the abundance of research on Piaget's theory. This is partly because Vygotsky's theory doesn't lend itself as readily to experimentation, as the concepts are more difficult to operationalise.

The limitations of the social approach

Whereas Piaget underplayed social influences, Vygotsky may have overplayed the importance of the social environment – if social input was all that was needed to advance cognitive development, then learning would be a lot faster than it is.

Also, the emphasis on social factors meant that biological factors were largely ignored in Vygotsky's theory.

Finally, his theory has been criticised for lacking detail, although this is in part due to the fact that he died at such a young age and did not have time to fully develop his theory (Lindblom and Ziemke, 2003).

UPGRADE

A particular feature of AQA psychology examinations is the 'Application' question. You should be familiar with these questions, but it's worth revisiting the general rules about answering them. Let's illustrate these in the context of the following question:

> Emma is a bright six-year-old who gets bored at school because she finds the work they do a bit 'babyish'. At home her parents constantly stretch her by giving her puzzles to solve that are meant for much older children. They find that, if they help her initially, she soon gets the hang of it and then can solve similar puzzles on her own.

Using your knowledge of Vygotsky's theory, explain why Emma initially needs her parents' help and then is able to solve the puzzles on her own. (4 marks)

For a 4-mark question there would be two mark levels. For the top level you would need to display a 'clear and accurate' knowledge of the specific psychology related to the scenario (in this case it would be the concept of scaffolding). However, having a good understanding of the psychology is not enough on its own – it must be used 'appropriately' to explain the scenario (here it is why Emma is able to solve problems on her own after parental help). The marks awarded reflect how effectively you have used the former to explain the latter. Ignore either of these and you will get half marks at best.

Piaget versus Vygotsky

The differences between Piaget's and Vygotsky's approaches reflect differences between the two men. Vygotsky was a Communist who believed in the power of community, and thus valued the role of society in the development of the individual; Piaget was a product of individualist European society.

Apart from their different cultural backgrounds, the two men may also represent rather different kinds of learner: Piaget's child is an introvert, whereas Vygotsky's child is an extrovert, and this may be a reflection of the men themselves (Miller, 1994).

Thus the two views can be reconciled because they are talking about different styles of learning and different kinds of learner. It is also possible to reconcile the theories by taking the view that they are not that different at their central core (Glassman, 1999). If one contrasts these theories with others in psychology, such as those by Freud, Pavlov or Skinner, we can see that there are similarities. They both place cognition at the centre of the theory; both emphasise the complex interactionist nature of development; both see abstract, scientific thought as the final stage of development; and both see the learner as active rather than passive.

CAN YOU? No. 5.3

1. Explain what is meant by the *zone of proximal development*. (3 marks)
2. Describe **one** study that investigates the process of scaffolding. (6 marks)
3. Discuss **one or more** ways in which Piaget's and Vygotsky's theories differed. (4 marks)
4. Describe and evaluate Vygotsky's theory of cognitive development. Refer to an alternative explanation for cognitive development in your answer. (16 marks)

Baillargeon's explanation of early infant abilities

Piaget was the first researcher to systematically investigate the development of an infant's knowledge of how objects in the physical world behave, for example their knowledge of *object permanence* (see page 118). Psychologists now believe that infants are capable of far more than Piaget suggested – they are more rational, and evidence suggests that these abilities are innately driven. This is a **nativist approach**.

One of the most important researchers in this field has been Renee Baillargeon (pronounced By-ar-jon), who relied on some inventive research methods to investigate what infants can and can't do.

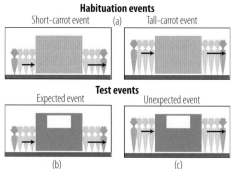

Habituation events

Short-carrot event (a) Tall-carrot event

Test events

Expected event Unexpected event

(b) (c)

▲ **An example of a violation of expectation task.** The infant is first shown the carrots moving along the track in the habituation events (first row labelled (a)) to get used to the activity.

In the test events (second row), the infant sees a small or large carrot going past a window (b) and (c). If the child understands object permanence, he/she should be surprised when the large carrot does not appear in the window in picture (c).

MEET THE RESEARCHER

Renee Baillargeon

(1954–) is Canadian by birth but is now a Professor of Psychology at Illinois University, USA, where she runs the Infant Cognition Lab. This is where most of her research has been conducted. Undergraduate students often help with the research and are often the ones performing the experiments, recording the infants' behaviour and coding the data.

BAILLARGEON'S RESEARCH

Baillargeon's research aims to discover the unsuspected abilities of newborns and young children. Conducting such research is very difficult because infants can't easily indicate what they are thinking. Furthermore, an apparent lack of ability may be due to motor difficulties rather than a lack of mental ability. For example, in the case of object permanence, Baillargeon suggested that the reason infants did not search for objects that were out of sight was because young infants can't plan and execute the necessary actions (motor ability) rather than a failure to understand object permanence (mental ability). In order to overcome this, Baillargeon developed a technique called **violation of expectation research**.

Key study: Violation of expectation (VOE)

This technique is based on the idea that an infant will show surprise when witnessing an impossible event. Consider a study by Baillargeon and DeVos (1991) that used the rolling carrot task.

Procedure In this task (see illustration on the left) there was a large or small carrot sliding along a track and hidden at one point by a screen with a large window. The track is arranged so that the large carrot should be visible as it passes behind the window (but in fact doesn't appear), whereas the small carrot (not as tall) should remain hidden. The impossible event is the large carrot not appearing. If an infant does have object permanence, they show surprise (increased looking) when shown this.

Findings Baillargeon and DeVos found that children as young as three months demonstrated object permanence when tested in this way (whereas Piaget only found this ability to develop at around eight months). The infants looked longer at the large carrot, presumably expecting the top half to be visible behind the window, i.e. they had object permanence and also understood the principle of occlusion (what happens when an object is obstructed behind another).

Explaining an infant's knowledge of the physical world

Baillargeon *et al.* (2009) suggest that infants are primarily equipped with mechanisms to interpret and learn from experience, calling this a **physical reasoning system** (PRS). This differs from Piaget's view because it suggests that infants are born with innate mechanisms that give infants a head start . In contrast Piaget suggested that everything is learned through interaction – there are no innate mechanisms to assist with this.

Baillargeon proposed that, when infants learn to reason about novel physical phenomenon, they first form an all-or-none concept. Later they add to this in terms of the other variables that may affect the concept. Consider an example from Baillargeon's research related to the unveiling phenomenon (the covering principle) – infants are shown a cover with a protuberance, suggesting there is an object hidden under the cover. Infants aged 9.5 months show surprise when a cover is removed with nothing under it. However, they don't show surprise if the object revealed is smaller than the protuberance suggested. By 12.5 months they do show surprise at the size mismatch.

Baillargeon (1994) says this suggests the following developmental sequence: (1) infants first form the concept that a protuberance indicates an object; (2) later they identify a variable that affects this concept (such as size). The same process occurs for all other physical relations – first the concept is understood and then the variations are incorporated. Baillargeon argues that this demonstrates the application of innate learning mechanisms to available data.

An infant's knowledge of the psychological world

Baillargeon has extended her work on an infant's understanding of the physical world to their understanding of the psychological world, such as understanding **false beliefs** in others and having a sense of fairness. In both cases infants are again seen to be born with mechanisms that guide the development of reasoning.

False beliefs

Song and Baillargeon (2008) used VOE to test false beliefs in very young children. The infant watches as a woman is shown two toys: a skunk and a doll with blue pigtails. In a variety of tasks the woman is seen to always reach for the doll, indicating a preference for this toy. (This is similar to the Sally-Anne task described on page 126, reading about that task may help you understand this one.)

On the test trial the two toys are placed in boxes (out of the woman's sight) – the skunk is placed in a box that has blue hair protruding from it and the doll is placed in a plain box. So the infant knows where the preferred doll actually is, but does the infant know where the woman thinks the doll is?

The infant then watches the woman going to open one of the boxes. Infants as young as 14.5 months old showed more surprise if the woman opened the box *without* the blue hair protruding – even though the infant 'knows' the preferred doll is in the plain box, they expect the woman to hold a false belief.

Carefully controlled research

One of the criticisms of Piaget's research is that the participants were all middle-class children. Baillargeon and DeVos used a less biased sample by using birth announcements in the local paper, thus having higher population validity.

Another factor to control is the potential effect of the parent on their infant's behaviour. For each of Baillargeon's studies the infant is sat on the parent's lap, and so the parent could unconsciously communicate cues about how the baby should react. To avoid this, parents were asked to keep their eyes shut and were asked not to interact with the infant.

A final important variable that was controlled was the observers' knowledge of conditions. For each trial there were two observers noting the amount of interest shown by the infant. They did not know whether the event was possible or impossible (i.e. a double blind design), which otherwise might have biased their observations.

Internal validity of the VOE method may be low

A number of researchers (e.g. Smith, 1999) have asked whether the VOE method is actually measuring what it intends to measure (internal validity), i.e. whether it is actually measuring surprise at the violation of expectations. Infants may look longer at an impossible event not because it violates their understanding of the physical world but because one or more features of the impossible event are more interesting than the possible event.

One way to test this criticism is to study infants' gaze during a VOE study – where are they actually looking when shown a VOE task? Schlesinger and Casey (2003) found evidence that suggested the infants' gaze was different for the possible and impossible tasks. However, on impossible tasks, interest was better explained as due to greater perceptual interest. This challenges the conclusions from VOE research.

Alternative explanations of an infant's knowledge of the physical world

Baillargeon has proposed an innate *mechanisms* explanation for how infants develop their understanding of the physical world, i.e. they are born with the ability to acquire certain kinds of knowledge very rapidly. This is a nativist account, which contrasts with Piaget's view.

Elizabeth Spelke, another nativist, offers a contrasting explanation. She believes that infants are born with substantial knowledge regarding objects, an innate *principles* approach. For example, Spelke *et al.* (1992) argue that infants are born with what they call a core knowledge, which includes a basic understanding of the physical world.

Baillargeon argues that the innate principles approach would predict that infants should demonstrate expectations about all events related to one core principle (i.e. the principle of occlusion or of covering) at the same time, but the evidence does not support this.

Was Piaget right after all?

The question involves how we interpret the infant participant's behaviour. The infant may be showing surprise and interest but that does not mean he/she actually *understood* the principle of object permanence (Bremner, 2013). Piaget's conception of cognitive development was that the child should not simply be acting in accordance with a principle but rather they should be able to *understand* the principle.

In addition it could be argued that Baillargeon's research has merely demonstrated that Piaget underestimated what infants can do, but the basic idea that certain mental abilities appear with maturation may not be challenged.

The effect of different experiences

Baillargeon's approach is based on the notion of innate mechanisms driving development, yet she has not specifically researched the capabilities of very young children who have had different experiences (such as those from different cultures). If such research showed that there were differences related to experience, it would challenge Baillargeon's approach. It would mean that experience has a greater role on the development of mechanisms than Baillargeon has claimed. Even so, her inventive methods for studying what young infants can or can't do has enabled researchers to gain many interesting insights.

▲ Babies are tested sitting on their parent's lap watching objects being moved around on a stage. The parent has their eyes shut and is asked not to interact with the infant. Watch videos of Baillargeon's research with babies on YouTube.

Research methods

Another phenomenon studied by Baillargeon is the collision phenomenon. Kotovsky and Baillargeon (1995) showed infants a cylinder rolling down a ramp. At the bottom of the ramp was a wheeled toy bug. In the possible task the cylinder didn't hit the bug and the bug remained stationary. In the impossible event the cylinder hit the bug, which still remained stationary. Infants of 2½ months looked longer at the impossible event.

1. Identify the independent and dependent variables in this experiment. (2 marks)
2. Explain why it might be preferable to use an independent groups design in this study. (3 marks)
3. Identify **two** ethical issues that might be important in this study and explain how each of them could be dealt with. (3 marks + 3 marks)
4. Baillargeon typically recruited participants by getting names from a list of recent births in a newspaper. What kind of sampling method is this? Explain your answer. (2 marks)
5. Give **one** strength of using this method of obtaining participants.

LINK TO RESEARCH METHODS

The topics in these questions are covered in the research methods chapter of our Year 1 book.

CAN YOU? No. 5.4

1. Outline **one** study by Baillargeon that has investigated violation of expectation. (4 marks)
2. Explain Baillargeon's view of how a child gains knowledge of the physical world. (3 marks)
3. Explain how Baillargeon's view of object permanence differs from Piaget's view. (4 marks)
4. Describe and evaluate Baillargeon's explanation of early infant abilities. (16 marks)

The development of social cognition: Selman's theory

The topic of social cognition begins with this spread. 'Social cognition' refers to the role of thinking (cognition) in our behaviour with others of our species (social), i.e. about how our thinking affects our social behaviour. So we are moving on from the more general study of how thinking develops to the more specific area of the relationship between thinking and social behaviour.

There isn't a sharp divide between this and what we have studied so far. For example, Piaget's theory is often applied to understanding how a child's social thinking is related to stages of development.

An example of Selman's perspective-taking dilemma

Holly is an eight-year-old girl who likes to climb trees. She is the best tree climber in the neighbourhood. One day while climbing a tree, she falls off the bottom branch but does not hurt herself. Her father sees her fall, and is upset. He asks her to promise not to climb trees any more, and Holly promises.

Later that day, Holly and her friends meet Sean. Sean's kitten is caught up a tree and cannot get down. Something has to be done right away or the kitten may fall. Holly is the only one who climbs trees well enough to reach the kitten and get it down, but she remembers her promise to her father.

(Selman, 1976)

SELMAN'S LEVELS OF PERSPECTIVE-TAKING

Robert Selman developed a theory of social development based on **perspective-taking**. He argued that perspective-taking (sometimes called role-taking) was the central dynamic of social development. When a child takes someone else's perspective, this enables the child to have insight into what other people think and feel, and these insights become progressively deeper. It is the more mature insights that are a pre-requisite for social relations.

Selman's perspective-taking dilemmas

Selman (1971) conducted research on children's perspective-taking abilities by using a series of dilemmas which explore the child's reasoning when faced with conflicting feelings. The dilemmas require the child to have to take someone else's perspective (or several different people's perspectives).

An example of a dilemma is given on the left. Selman asked children a series of perspective-taking questions; for example: If Holly climbs the tree, should she be punished? Will her father understand if she climbs the tree? Will Sean understand if Holly refuses?

When Selman analysed the responses the children of different ages made, he realised that there was a definite pattern related to reasoning at different ages.

Selman's stage theory

Selman (1977) constructed a five-stage model of the development of perspective-taking by using the children's answers to his questions about the dilemmas.

A key feature of this stage theory is the progression from being egocentric and unaware of any perspective but their own to being quite mature and considering a number of perspectives, and drawing conclusions in line with social norms.

Stage 0 Undifferentiated perspective-taking Approx age 3–6 years	Children can distinguish between self and others but are largely governed by their own perspective. Holly's father will not be mad because whatever is right for Holly is right for others; her father will feel as she does.
Stage 1 Social-informational perspective-taking Approx age 6–8 years	Children are aware of perspectives that are different to their own but assume that this is because others have different information. Holly's father would not be mad if Holly shows him the kitten and he would then change his mind.
Stage 2 Self-reflective perspective-taking Approx age 8–10 years	Child can now view their own thoughts and feelings from someone else's perspective and recognise that others do the same. Holly's father will not be mad because he will understand why Holly saved the kitten.
Stage 3 Mutual perspective-taking Approx age 10–12 years	Can step outside a two-person situation and imagine how the self and other are viewed from the point of view of a third, impartial party. Child can also consider two viewpoints simultaneously. Holly's father will not be mad because he can understand both their points of view.
Stage 4 Societal perspective-taking Approx age 12–15+ years	Personal decisions are now made with reference to social conventions. Holly's father will not be mad because the humane treatment of animals is important.

Relation to deception

An interesting outcome of perspective-taking is the ability to deceive. Deception entails a child being able to plant a *false belief* in someone else's mind. They can usually do this around the age of three. For example, Cole (1986) found that children of this age were able to hide their disappointment when they received the worst present (rather than the best one) if they were being watched by others, but they did show disappointment when filmed secretly on their own.

UPGRADE

On page 117 we explained that, for essays such as question 4 on the facing page, 10 of the 16 marks are assigned to AO3 (evaluation). There is no specific requirement as to the *number* of AO3 points that you would use in your answer (i.e. three well-elaborated points *could* be enough to get you in the top mark, but we have worked on the assumption that five AO3 points (each of approximately 60 words) would be ideal in an essay question.

The absolutely essential quality of any AO3 point is that you make it *effective*. Most teachers have their own technique for this (the 'four-point rule', the 'hamburger technique', SEEL, PEEL and so on). They all involve more or less the same thing in that a critical point is identified, evidence is given to support the point, further elaboration, and then some sort of conclusion is offered. If we take the evaluative point on the facing page regarding real-world applications of Selman's theory, this could be made into an effective AO3 as follows:

'Selman's theory has a number of applications… For example, Selman argues that helping children develop perspective-taking should be one of the main priorities of primary schools… This can be achieved through play as this is the natural way in which perspective-taking skills are learned… This shows that Selman's theory has real-world validity.

Research support for the stage theory

Selman's original research (1971) involved a cross-sectional sample of 225 participants of various ages ranging from 4½ to 32 years. In the first analysis conducted two years later (published in 1978 by Cooney and Selman), 48 boys were re-interviewed. It was found that 40 of the boys had made gains in their level of perspective-taking and none had regressed, supporting the notion that the stages identified by Selman are a progressive age-related developmental sequence.

A further analysis was conducted three years later (published in 1982 by Gurucharri and Selman) involved 41 boys. This again confirmed the progressive developmental sequence in the stages of perspective-taking – no boys regressed and none skipped any stages. Keating and Clark (1980) suggested that the reason for this sequence may be due to the fact that these stages are closely related to Piaget's stages of development (see page 118).

Research support for the role of experience

Even if the stages in the development of perspective-taking are biologically driven, there is much evidence that supports the role of experience in the development of such skills. For example, FitzGerald and White (2003) looked at the development of perspective-taking skills in relation to parental style. They found that children showed more growth when parents encouraged them to take the perspective of the victim during instances when the child may have caused harm (psychological or physical) to someone else.

This shows one of the ways that experience leads to changes in perspective-taking skills. It also shows that the development of perspective-taking is not just cognitive – it is also related to social experience.

The importance of perspective-taking skills

Perspective-taking skills are fundamentally important in all social behaviour. For example, FitzGerald and White (above) also found, as we would expect, that maturity of perspective-taking skills was negatively related to aggression and positively related to prosocial behaviour.

Selman *et al.* (1977) found that children who were poor in their perspective-taking skills had more difficulty in forming and maintaining social relationships and were less popular.

Such research suggests that perspective-taking skills lead to important social developments or can be used to explain the lack of social development.

Correlation, not cause

Much of the research is correlational. Such correlations do not mean that perspective-taking skills *cause* higher levels of social competence. In fact it might be the other way round. For example, more popular children interact with more people, and that may lead to advances in the development of perspective-taking skills. If this is generally the case then perspective-taking skills are simply a marker of how socially developed a child is – it is the social experiences which are the cause.

Real-world applications

Whether or not perspective-taking skills cause social behaviour, evidence suggests that development of perspective-taking skills can be fostered by experience, and this has a number of important implications for schools, therapy and the treatment of criminals. Selman (2003) argues that facilitation of perspective-taking is one of the fundamental missions of primary schools today, and that it should be woven into much of the daily activities. One way to do this with younger children is through play, as this is the natural way in which perspective-taking skills are learned (Smith and Pellegrini, 2008).

Social skills training (SST) programmes are used with older children. SST is also used in therapeutic settings with people with mental disorders or emotional problems.

One explanation offered for anti-social, criminal behaviour is that some criminals lack empathy and perspective-taking skills, and this may explain their 'willingness' to harm others directly or indirectly. Therefore SST programmes have been developed where prisoners are taught perspective-taking skills to increase their empathetic concern for others and their prosocial behaviour on release from prison.

egocentrism

▲ Both Piaget and Selman wrote about the role of egocentrism in the development of thinking and saw egocentrism as a style of thinking characteristic of a pre-school child. Selman's emphasis is on *psychological* perspective-taking, whereas Piaget was focused on *physical* perspective-taking.

KEY TERMS

Perspective-taking involves being able to view a situation or emotions from another person's viewpoint.

MEET THE RESEARCHER

Robert Selman (1942–) trained as a psychoanalyst. He is currently Professor of Psychology in the Department of Psychiatry at Harvard University. His current research is focused on applying our understanding of how positive social relationships are formed and maintained to the prevention of negative psychological, social and health outcomes for youth.

Insider tip…
Don't just focus on learning the stages of Selman's theory – make sure you have a well-rounded understanding of the whole concept.

CAN YOU? No. 5.5

1. Briefly outline **one** level of perspective-taking. Use examples in your answer. (3 marks)
2. Describe **one** study that has investigated levels of perspective-taking. (6 marks)
3. Evaluate Selman's levels of perspective-taking. (10 marks)
4. Discuss Selman's levels of perspective-taking. (16 marks)

The development of social cognition: Theory of mind

The first key point to understand is that **theory of mind** (ToM) is not an actual theory like Piaget's theory of cognitive development. It is an intuitive set of beliefs (or 'theory') developed by each of us. It is our understanding that someone else has a separate mind to our own and therefore does not see or experience the world as we do.

You no doubt can see the relationship between this and the previous spread on perspective-taking. Perspective-taking is about empathising with someone else's thoughts and feelings, and ToM is a component of this.

The Sally-Anne test

Children are shown the story below, often using puppets. The final question is: 'Where will Sally look for her marble/ball?'

A child with ToM would respond that Sally would look in the basket despite the fact that the child knows the ball is in the box. A child without ToM cannot separate their own knowledge from Sally's, and would therefore say that Sally will look in the box because that is where the child would look.

Sally puts her ball in her basket and leaves the room.

Anne moves the ball to her box.

Sally returns. Where will she look for the ball.

SELMAN'S LEVELS OF PERSPECTIVE-TAKING

Early development

The first evidence of children's understanding of others is shown in their ability to imitate other people's expressions. Meltzoff and Moore (1977, 1983) found that even newborns who are less than 72 hours old are able to imitate facial gestures (you may remember this from your Year 1 studies).

The next step is to understand the intentions of another person. Infants as young as three months will follow a person's gaze to nearby objects, which indicates an understanding of communicative intent (D'Entremont et al., 1997). However, a distinction is made between knowing about someone else's internal state and knowing about how they experience the world. The latter is a true theory of mind (Wellman and Woolley, 1990). Infants are capable of social interaction, but social relationships require ToM. ToM first appears around the age of three or four years. At this time children also start using terms like 'think' and 'know' when referring to others.

Key study: Assessing theory of mind

The classic way to test ToM is using a **false belief** task. The first attempt to do this was by Heinz Wimmer and Josef Perner (1983), who devised a story about a boy called Maxi.

Procedure   The story goes: Maxi's mother had brought home some chocolate to make a cake. Maxi sees her put the chocolate into the blue cupboard. Then Maxi goes out to play. His mother uses the chocolate for the cake and puts it back in the green cupboard. When Maxi comes back he wants some chocolate. The researchers acted the story out with dolls and matchboxes to make it more understandable. The final question, which was put to children aged between three and nine years old, is: Which cupboard will Maxi look in?'

Findings   They found that nearly all three-year-olds say the chocolate is in the green cupboard – it is in the green cupboard, but Maxi should think it is in the blue cupboard (a false belief). From four years onwards some children give the correct answer; by the age of six all children can do this.

Theory of mind as an explanation for autism

Simon Baron-Cohen has taken a particular interest in the concept of ToM as an explanation for the childhood disorder of **autism**. One of the typical characteristics of individuals with autism is that they find social interaction difficult, which might be explained by an inability to understand the mental states of other people and be able to predict, and adjust to, the behaviour of others.

Baron-Cohen et al. (1985) adapted the Maxi task (above) to a test involving two dolls, Sally and Anne. The **Sally–Anne test** is illustrated on the left.

Procedure   The study involved three groups of participants: 20 children with autism (mean age of about 12 years), 14 children with Down's syndrome of a similar chronological age but much lower mental age, and 27 'normal' children with a mean age of about 4½ years. The children were all asked some control questions such as 'Where is the marble really?' just to check that they had seen what happened. They were finally asked the 'belief' question about where Sally thought the marble was.

Findings   Most (85%) of the 'normal' children answered the false belief question correctly. The same was true for the Down's syndrome children, demonstrating that ToM is not linked to low intelligence. Only 20% of the children with autism answered correctly.

Later research   Baron-Cohen et al. (1997) considered the question of whether high-functioning individuals on the autistic spectrum might have ToM. To test this they created a new task, the *Eyes Task*, where individuals were shown pictures of people's eyes and asked to select one of two emotions that might be represented, such as attraction versus repulsion, or interested versus disinterested. The reason for using this test was that adults with autism can pass the Sally–Anne task.

The study found that adults on the autistic spectrum had a mean score of 16.3 compared to normal participants with a mean score of 20.3 out of a maximum of 25. The ranges of scores were fairly similar: autism range 13–23; normal range 16–25. This suggests that, in general, there is an impairment in individuals with autism.

Biological basis

The fact that ToM appears to develop at a particular age and the fact that it is likely to be absent in many people with autism suggests a biological basis. Baron-Cohen (1995) has proposed a ToM module (ToMM), which is a specific mechanism that matures in the brain around the age of four and explains an individual's ability to understand the mental states of other people.

Relationship between understanding intentions and ToM

It does not appear that intention is a precursor of ToM. Carpenter *et al.* (2001) tested children with autism for their understanding of intention. This was done by seeing if they followed someone's gaze and also looked where someone was pointing. Children with autism aged two-and-a-half to five years behaved much the same as 'normal' children, which suggests that understanding intentions is a separate ability to ToM.

Evidence for the role of experience and biology

There is considerable evidence that ToM is not solely determined by biology. Research shows that it appears earlier in children from large families (Perner *et al.*, 1994). Having a large family and especially older siblings means that a child is challenged to think about the feelings of others when resolving conflicts. Research has also shown that discussion about motives and other mental states promotes the development of ToM (Sabbagh and Callanan, 1998).

Liu *et al.* (2004) compared over 300 Chinese and North American children in terms of ToM. They found a similar sequence of development in both groups, but the timing differed by as much as two years in different communities, supporting the role of both biological and experiential factors – biological because ToM did appear in both cultures, and experiential because the timing appears to differ related to social environment.

Criticisms of Baron-Cohen's research

Baron-Cohen *et al.* used the *Eyes Task* to assess adults and high-functioning people with autism (see facing page). This may not test what it aims to test, i.e. it may not have been measuring ToM (low internal validity). Baron-Cohen *et al.* claimed that the test measures mindreading, which is essentially the same as ToM. However, such mindreading may not be the same as ToM in everyday life.

Wellman and Woolley (1990) argue that there is a distinction to be made between knowing about someone else's internal state and knowing about how they experience the world. The latter is a true ToM and is something that the Sally–Anne task may assess, but it is not something assessed by the *Eyes Task*.

ToM as an explanation for autism

There are two issues. First is whether children with autism actually do lack a ToM. The research only shows that *some* individuals with autism lack ToM. If a lack of ToM was a central aspect of the condition, we would expect that all of the participants with autism would be impaired.

Second is whether ToM is cause or effect. Children with autism may not acquire a fully developed ToM because their condition prevents them communicating and engaging with others – their abnormal language development, lack of social skills and so on may mean they do not have the appropriate experiences that lead to ToM rather than an inherent lack of ToM causing their poor social interaction.

(Note that the research studies described on the facing page are quasi-experiments because autism (the independent variable) is not something that the researcher can vary, and this means that causal conclusions are not justified.)

Culture bias

Baron-Cohen's sample was entirely British, and this approach to understanding autism has a very Western perspective. Maguire (2013) has suggested that the higher rates of autism diagnosed in the West than elsewhere might be explained in terms of the fact that the symptoms associated with autism may actually not be considered abnormal in some cultures. Therefore our view that the lack of social interaction is a problem to be solved may be a Western but not universal perspective.

🐾 APPLY YOUR KNOWLEDGE

Ewelina helps out at her local preschool nursery one day a week. As Ewelina is studying psychology at a local college, she is keen to explore some of the things she is studying on her psychology course with the children at the nursery. After getting permission from the parents of the children and the management at the nursery, she decides she would like to test the children for theory of mind. She is given the opportunity to test 16 children aged between 3 and 4 and a further 14 children aged between 4 and 5.

(a) Explain how Ewelina might test for theory of mind with the children in the nursery. What questions would she ask the children to test whether they possessed theory of mind?

(b) Ewelina found differences in the way that the 4–5-year-olds responded in the theory of mind test compared to the 3–4-year-olds. What do you think these differences were likely to be?

MEET THE RESEARCHER

Simon Baron-Cohen (1958–) is co-director of the Autism Research Centre (ARC) in Cambridge, where he is Professor of Developmental Psychopathology. His first cousin is the comedian Sacha Baron-Cohen, aka Ali G and Borat.

In an interview for *Psychology Today* (Kunzig, 2004), he describes his motivation for studying people with mental disabilities. He grew up with an older sister who is severely disabled, both mentally and physically. Today she lives in an institution, is confined to a wheelchair and has a very low IQ.

CAN YOU? No. 5.6

1. Explain what is meant by *theory of mind*. (3 marks)
2. Outline the Sally–Anne study used to assess theory of mind. (4 marks)
3. Describe and evaluate research on theory of mind. (16 marks)
4. Discuss theory of mind as an explanation for autism. (16 marks)

End-of-chapter review / CHAPTER SUMMARY

We have identified here the key points of the topics on the AQA A level specification, i.e. the bare minimum that you need to know. You may want to fill in further details to elaborate and personalise this material.

PIAGET'S THEORY OF COGNITIVE DEVELOPMENT

MECHANISMS OF COGNITIVE DEVELOPMENT

DESCRIPTION

- Maturation of the brain enables qualitatively different thinking, interactions with the environment create the stimulus for learning.
- Schema – mental structures represent group of related concepts, some innate (e.g. face schema) but mainly learned.
- Assimilation – incorporation of new information into existing schema.
- Accommodation – new schema developed by adapting existing schema.
- Equilibration – a sense of balance; imbalance created by experiences that don't fit existing schema.
- Lifespan learning – we continue to learn by accommodation and assimilation throughout life.

EVALUATION

- Research shows that face schemas are innate – infants 4 days old prefer faces to jumbled features (Fantz), helps attachment.
- It is difficult to demonstrate equilibration (and other Piagetian concepts); Inhelder et al. showed learning helped by mild conflict.
- Application to discovery learning – teacher creates an environment of disequilibrium to push learning, though Bennett found pupils do better in traditional classroom.
- Language less important – Sinclair-de-Zwart showed that cognitive development preceded language development; contrasts with Vygotsky's approach.
- Comprehensive theory of children's cognitive development, changed the way we think about children's thinking, generated considerable research, but too focused on physical environment.

STAGES OF INTELLECTUAL DEVELOPMENT

DESCRIPTION

- Stage 1: Sensorimotor (0–2 years) – co-ordination of sensations with muscle movements through circular reactions.
  - Object permanence develops around 8 months, understanding that objects continue to exist when can't be seen.
- Stage 2: Pre-operational stage (2–7 years) – lack internally consistent mental rules.
  - Conservation not understood – volume/number/mass cannot change despite the appearance that it has, tested with beakers, row of counters, balls of plasticine.
  - Egocentric – can only see the world from their perspective, tested with three mountains task.
  - Class inclusion not understood – sub-groups which are part of a bigger category.
- Stage 3: Concrete operational stage (7–11 years) – logical thinking, e.g. conservation.
- Stage 4: Formal operational stage (11+ years) – hypothetico-deductive reasoning, thinking like a scientist.

EVALUATION

- Methodology was flawed – younger children can do better, e.g. McGarrigle and Donaldson's naughty teddy, Hughes' naughty boy hiding from policeman and Samuel and Bryant asking one question.
- Idea of biologically driven stages is correct – timing of stages may be wrong but there are qualitative differences.
- Cultural bias – Piaget's ideas and research based on middle-class, academic European values; logical abstract thinking may not be universally important.
- Important applications – school activities should be age-appropriate, otherwise understanding is superficial.
- Alternative explanation – Vygotsky's emphasis on social influences.

VYGOTSKY'S THEORY OF COGNITIVE DEVELOPMENT

DESCRIPTION

- Cultural influences are the key driving force in cognitive development.
- Elementary mental functions (e.g. perception, memory) are innate; transformed into higher mental functions (exclusive to humans) through social interactions.
- Role of others – learning occurs through problem-solving experiences shared with experts (parent, teacher, older child).
- Role of language – using semiotics (signs and symbols developed within a particular culture), experts pass on knowledge.
- Social and individual level – child converts social relations into individual higher mental functions through semiotic mediation.
- Zone of proximal development (ZPD) – learning takes place in the zone just beyond what can currently be done.
- Scaffolding – assisting learner through ZPD with temporary support, contingent relations are important for success.

EVALUATION

- Role of culture – primitive counting system limits maths development in New Guinea (Gredler); exposure to language system raises chimps to higher mental functioning (Savage-Rumbaugh).
- Role of language – a new word is the beginning of a concept; Carmichael et al. showed that words affect memory.
- Role of ZPD – McNaughton and Leyland observed children working with mothers on jigsaw puzzles; greatest input was at the point of the ZPD.
- Lack of research – concepts more difficult to operationalise.
- Limitations of the social approach – overlooks biological influences and on own not sufficient.
- Piaget represents individualist introvert, Vygotsky represents collectivist extrovert. Many similarities: emphasis on cognition and logical thinking and active role of the learner.

BAILLARGEON'S EXPLANATION OF EARLY INFANT ABILITIES

DESCRIPTION

- Infants may fail on Piaget's object permanence because they lack the motor abilities (to plan and execute action), not because they lack the mental ability.
- Violation of expectation (VOE) research – infant will show surprise when witnessing an impossible event.
- Physical reasoning system (PRS) – innate mechanisms which enable learning: such mechanisms enable concepts to be understood (e.g. covering principle) and then variations incorporated.
- Psychological understanding also develops through innate mechanisms, e.g. false beliefs.
- Tested using VOE by Song and Baillargeon with skunk and doll with blue pigtails. Children of 14.5 months show false beliefs.

KEY STUDY: BAILLARGEON AND DEVOS (1991)

- Procedure: Large or small carrot sliding on track and passing a window.
- Findings: Infants aged three months looked longer, much before Piaget's estimate of eight months; demonstrates understanding of occlusion.

EVALUATION

- Carefully controlled research – good population validity (using birth announcements), control of parental behaviour during testing, and observers recording infant interest were blind to condition.
- Internal validity of VOE method – may be assessing perceptual interest, supported by study of infant gaze (Schlesinger and Casey).
- Alternative explanations – Piaget argued that the mechanisms were learned through experience; Spelke argues that infants are born with innate principles, not just mechanisms to acquire the knowledge (Baillargeon's view).
- Was Piaget right? Infants may show surprise but don't actually understand. Piaget may have just underestimated the age.
- Effect of different experiences – lack of research on the effect of culture or different early experiences.

THE DEVELOPMENT OF SOCIAL COGNITION

SELMAN'S LEVELS OF PERSPECTIVE-TAKING

DESCRIPTION

- Perspective-taking is the central dynamic of social relations.
- Levels of perspective-taking based on dilemmas which explore the child's reasoning when faced with conflicting feelings.
- Stage 0 Undifferentiated perspective-taking (3–6 years): largely governed by own perspective.
- Stage 1 Social-informational perspective-taking (6–8 years): children assume that others' perspectives only different if they know something different.
- Stage 2 Self-reflective perspective-taking (8–10 years): can view their own feelings from someone else's perspective.
- Stage 3 Mutual perspective-taking (10–12 years): can view from the point of view of a third, impartial party.
- Stage 4 Societal perspective-taking (12–15+ years): reference to social conventions.
- Related to deception - children can hide disappointment by 3 years (Cole), requires perspective-taking.

EVALUATION

- Support for stage theory – longitudinal studies after 2 years (Cooney and Selman) and a further 3 years (Gurucharri and Selman) showed progressive development.
- Support for role of experience – FitzGerald and White found link between parental style and growth of perspective-taking skills.
- Perspective-taking skills negatively related to aggression (FitzGerald and White) and positively to forming good relationships (Selman et al.).
- Correlation, not cause – social experiences may cause developmental changes in perspective-taking rather than vice versa.
- Real-world applications (SST programmes) to schools, mental health and prisons.

THEORY OF MIND

DESCRIPTION

- 'True' ToM is more than imitation and more than understanding intentions, ToM appears age 3 or 4, means knowing how another person experiences the world (Wellman and Woolley).
- People with autism may lack ToM – would explain difficulties with social interaction.
- Baron-Cohen et al. tested older autistics using the Eyes Task and found general impairment, though range of scores fairly similar to normal participants.
- Biological basis – development at a key age and absence in autistics suggests an innate ToMM (Baron-Cohen).

KEY STUDY: WIMMER AND PERNER (1983)

- Procedure: Wimmer and Perner false belief task about boy called Maxi and where the chocolate was (it was in the green cupboard but Maxi should wrongly believe it is in the blue cupboard).
- Findings: By age 6 all children understand false beliefs and say Maxi would look in the blue cupboard.

KEY STUDY: THE SALLY–ANNE TASK

- Procedure: Baron-Cohen et al. tested autistic children with Sally–Anne test and compared performance with Down's children (low IQ) and 'normal' children.
- Sally puts her marble in basket but Anne moves the marble to her box; where will Sally look?
- Findings: 20% of children with autism answered correctly, 85% of other participants answered correctly.

EVALUATION

- Ability to understand intentions appears to be separate to ToM, as shown in research with autistics (Carpenter et al.).
- Role of experience – being in a large family facilitates development of ToM (Perner et al.) and so does discussion of motives (Sabbagh and Callanan).
- Role of biology – ToM appeared in Chinese and North American children at different times (experience) but similar sequence (biology) (Liu et al.).
- Eyes Task may assess mindreading but not ToM; test lacks internal validity.
- Research does not show that all autistics lack ToM, just most lack it – but then can't be a core symptom.
- Research demonstrates an association between autism and ToM but does not demonstrate a cause; lack of social experience may result in poorly developed ToM.
- Culture bias – higher levels of autism in the West possibly because symptoms not abnormal elsewhere.

THE ROLE OF THE MIRROR NEURON SYSTEM

DESCRIPTION

- Mirror neurons (MNs) – certain neurons active in premotor cortex of monkeys when watching another's actions and when repeating theory (Rizzolatti et al.).
- Explains imitation – important for learning skilled behaviours and requires behavioural regulation (MN response generally off-line).
- Also record intentions – Iacoboni et al. found most activity in inferior frontal cortex when understanding why a person performed actions.
- MNs may be part of ToM (Gallese and Goldman) and empathy, which underlies prosocial behaviour (Eisenberg).
- MNs related to language as imitation is part of learning language; MNs found in Broca's area (Binkofski et al.).
- MNs may be key to human uniqueness because they enable us to excel in social relationships (Ramachandran).

EVALUATION

- Mukamel et al. recorded activity in single neurons, showing that it was not just generalised activity; also anti-mirror neurons found (behavioural regulation).
- Tranel et al. showed link between damage to a MN area and ability to retrieve words, demonstrating link between MNs and action deficits.
- Gender differences shown by Cheung et al. for watching a moving hand (MNs involved) but no difference for moving dot (no MN involvement).
- Explaining autism – brain activity recorded when watching emotional expressions, inferior frontal gyrus showed reduced activity in autistics (Dapretto et al.).
- Critics argue that MNs are not special. Churchland says they are just neurons, and the work of establishing intention etc. is performed by higher-level circuitry.
- Heyes argues that two neurons are paired because they fire at same time (associative learning); they develop through experience and are not innate and thus not the basis of innate human uniqueness.

0 1 Which one of the following statements describes what Piaget meant by 'object permanence'? Write the letter of your chosen answer in your answer booklet. **[1 mark]**

    A. Understanding that something exists even when it's not physically present.

    B. Understanding that something has the same properties even when it appears to change form.

    C. Understanding that something in a sub-group must also belong to the larger grouping.

    D. Understanding what other people can see when they look at something.

0 2 Using an example, outline what is meant by a schema. **[3 marks]**

0 3 Explain how both assimilation and accommodation relate to cognitive development. **[4 marks]**

0 4 Read the item below and answer the questions that follow.

> Jonathan is able to describe what his fellow pupils can see from another side of the classroom.
>
> Malik knows to look for his toy car when it ends up rolling under the chair.
>
> Sadie understands that her sister has the same amount of milk as her even though it is in a taller glass.

    (i) Name the child who demonstrates conservation. **[1 mark]**

    (ii) Name the child who demonstrates object permanence. **[1 mark]**

0 5 **(i)** Name **one** of Piaget's stages of intellectual development. **[1 mark]**

    (ii) Outline the characteristics of the stage you have named. **[4 marks]**

0 6 Outline **one** way in which egocentrism has been investigated. **[3 marks]**

0 7 Discuss Piaget's stages of intellectual development. Refer to research evidence as part of your answer. **[16 marks]**

0 8 Outline and briefly discuss the concept of the zone of proximal development in relation to cognition. **[4 marks]**

0 9 Read the item below and then answer the question that follows.

> Andre has just started school. He is finding it difficult to understand how to work out the sum of two numbers. However, his teacher is convinced that he is ready to learn about addition.

    Explain how the process of scaffolding could be used to support Andre's cognitive development in the example above. **[4 marks]**

1 0 'Although both Vygotsky and Piaget have had a huge impact on education, there were some fundamental differences in their approach.'

    Discuss Vygotsky's theory of cognitive development. Refer to the above statement as part of your answer. **[16 marks]**

1 1 Which **two** of the following statements form part of Baillargeon's explanation of how infants develop knowledge of the physical world? Write the letters of your chosen answer in your answer booklet. **[2 marks]**

    A. Infants are born with an innate physical reasoning system.

    B. Infants' experience of the physical world is irrelevant.

    C. Infants incorporate variations of a physical object after the concept is understood.

    D. Infants must begin by understanding their physical being.

1 2 **(i)** Outline the findings of **one** research study into violation of expectation. **[2 marks]**

    (ii) Explain **one** limitation of the findings you have outlined in (i). **[3 marks]**

1 3 Describe and evaluate research into Baillargeon's explanation of early infant abilities. **[16 marks]**

1 4 Read the item below and answer the questions that follow.

> Helen tells her two daughters that she does not want them playing by the river because she thinks that it is too dangerous. Neither of her daughters agree with her and think she is being over-protective.
>
> The younger daughter, Lily, decides she will play by the river to show it is safe. She thinks her mother will change her mind when she returns safely.
>
> The elder daughter, Ruby, considers playing by the river. She reasons that other people may think her mother should give her more freedom even though they will understand that Helen is right to show concern.

(i) Using Selman's theory, explain which stage of perspective taking Lily is at. [2 marks]

(ii) Using Selman's theory, explain which stage of perspective taking Ruby is at. [2 marks]

1 5 Briefly discuss **one** limitation of Selman's approach to social cognition. [4 marks]

1 6 Outline **two** criticisms of the theory of mind as an explanation of autism. [4 marks]

1 7 Which one of the following is the independent variable in the Sally–Anne study? Write the letter of your chosen answer in your answer booklet. [1 mark]

A. Whether the marble is in the basket or the box.

B. Whether the participant has high or low levels of intelligence.

C. Whether the participant is autistic or not.

D. Whether the puppet is Sally or Anne.

1 8 Explain how the Sally–Anne study can be used to support the theory of mind. [4 marks]

1 9 Explain the role of the mirror neuron system in social cognition. [3 marks]

2 0 Discuss **two** explanations of the development of social cognition. [16 marks]

2 1 Read the item below and answer the questions that follow.

> A psychology student tested children's ability to conserve by asking them to compare the lengths of two identical pieces of string, where one was laid straight and the other moved to form a circle. He used children in the pre-operational stage and children in the concrete operational stage of development.

Below are the results from his investigation.

Stage	Did not show conservation	Did show conservation
Pre-Operational	14	4
Concrete Operational	6	9

(i) The student used the Chi-Squared test to analyse his data.

With reference to the investigation, explain **two** reasons for selecting the Chi-Squared test. [4 marks]

(ii) The student's results were significant for $p \leq 0.05$. Explain what this means with reference to this investigation. [2 marks]

2 2 Read the item below and answer the questions that follow.

> The theory of mind has been investigated using a study sometimes known as the Smartie Tube test. In this experiment, child participants observe another child opening up a Smartie tube, but instead of sweets falling out, a pencil drops out instead. The child then returns the pencil to the tube and exits, leaving the tube on a table. The participants are then told that another child is about to enter and she will also pick up the tube. The experimenter asks the participants what this next child will think is in the Smartie tube. Some of the child participants have autism, others do not.

(i) Write a suitable directional hypothesis for this experiment. [2 marks]

(ii) Explain why this experiment uses an independent groups design. [3 marks]

(iii) Outline **one** ethical issue which is relevant to this experiment. [2 marks]

The exam questions on cognition and development will be varied but are likely to involve some short answer questions (AO1), some application of knowledge questions (AO2), research methods questions and possibly an extended writing question (AO1 + AO3). We've provided answers to some additional questions together with comments from an examiner about how well they've each done.

---

01 Read the item below and then answer the question that follows.

> Andre has just started school. He is finding it difficult to understand how to work out the sum of two numbers. However, his teacher is convinced that he is ready to learn about addition.

Explain how the process of scaffolding could be used to support Andre's cognitive development in the example above. *(4 marks)*

Maisie's answer

The process of scaffolding refers to when a teacher (or other person) teaches a child how to do something by giving hints and assistance, like holding something up using scaffolding. Gradually you withdraw the help when the learner is ready. In the case of Andre the teacher might first do the sums with Andre while he watched, then she might give him another sum and ask him questions about what to do and gradually he would be able to do it for himself.

Examiner's comments

Maisie's response is just good enough to earn full marks. The answer starts with a reasonably detailed outline of what scaffolding is, although the phrase 'holding something up' is ambiguous and could suggest modelling just as much as support. However, Maisie's application to the item does help to clarify the process and there is enough expansion to earn both AO2 marks as well as the 2 AO1 marks.

Ciaran's answer

Andre is in the zone of proximal development where what he is capable of (he can learn about addition) is more than he is currently doing (he can't add two numbers). In order to get him through the ZPD it is important for his teacher to provide some assistance and this is what scaffolding is. The teacher can do this by giving him clues about what to do and always asking if he understands and encouraging him to try himself.

Examiner's comments

Ciaran's answer is limited to 2 marks. Although the zone of proximal development (ZPD) is related to the scaffolding process, he uses more of his time outlining this than what is being asked for. Ciaran also applies the concept of ZPD to the item more explicitly than he does scaffolding. Towards the end of the answer, Ciaran begins to show his understanding of scaffolding and earns the AO1 marks here.

---

02 (i) Outline the findings of **one** research study into violation of expectation. *(2 marks)*

(ii) Explain **one** limitation of the findings you have outlined in (i). *(3 marks)*

Maisie's answer

(i) One study by Baillargeon involved a carrot on a train being driven past a window. If it was a big carrot a child would expect to see it as it went past the window. If the child can't see it then they should show surprise because their expectation is violated. Young children can do this at a younger age than Piaget predicted.

Examiner's comments

This earns 1 mark, as Maisie focuses on how the study was set up more than the findings. Although knowing about the procedure is important for making sense of what was found out, Maisie should have considered how she could have described this in the context of the findings.

Maisie's answer

(ii) One limitation with this study is that it assumes that showing surprise means the child was really expecting to see the carrot. It could be something else that is causing surprise. We are inferring what is actually going on in the child's mind.

Examiner's comments

This earns 2 marks in total. The final sentence clearly states the limitation of the findings and then the information before this makes it directly relevant to the study (using the answer to part (i) to provide some of the context).

Ciaran's answer

(i) Baillargeon and DeVos found that children as young as three months demonstrated object permanence when tested using a violation of expectation test (carrot passing behind window). This was much younger than Piaget suggested.

Examiner's comments

This answer earns 1 mark. The general findings are clear, but Ciaran needs to give some context by explaining the statement in the bracket – otherwise the findings are not specific to Baillargeon and DeVos.

Ciaran's answer

(ii) Critics have suggested that internal validity is low. The researchers interpreted the fact that babies looked longer as surprise at a violation of expectation. The infants may look longer because it is more interesting. This means the researchers didn't measure what they intended to measure.

Examiner's comments

A 3-mark response. Ciaran starts with the broad limitation which is expressed using appropriate terminology. He later explains what 'low internal validity' means, earning a second mark. The third mark comes from linking the point specifically to the study, which he does in the middle of the answer.

03 'Although both Vygotsky and Piaget have had a huge impact on education, there were some fundamental differences in their approach.' Discuss Vygotsky's theory of cognitive development. Refer to the above statement as part of your answer. *(16 marks)*

Maisie's answer

There were definitely fundamental differences in their approaches. Jean Piaget believed that cognitive development was largely driven by maturation (biology), whereas Lev Vygotsky emphasised social processes and influences. I will look at each of these theories and compare their differences.

In Piaget's theory each stage occurs because, as the child gets old, their brain matures and this enables a different kind of thinking moving from more concrete to more abstract. Piaget believed that you could change the ages at which this happens. For example the ability to conserve happens around the age of 7 no matter what experiences a child has.

In Vygotsky's theory there are no stages of development and he saw changes happening through dialogues between child and expert. The expert is communicating cultural knowledge and it is this that transforms elementary to higher mental functions like writing and arithmetic.

Another difference in their approaches is that Piaget's approach was a more individualist, European approach whereas Vygotsky reflected the communism that he grew up in where the community is a fundamental part of society. So, for Piaget, what was important was each individual creating their own knowledge and he thought this led to a deeper understanding. Vygotsky thought that it was through peer and expert tutoring that the biggest progress could be made.

A further issue is in terms of research support. Piaget conducted a lot of empirical research himself to test his ideas, such as his famous conservation experiments. Vygotsky did very little research which makes his theory less scientific. A scientific theory needs to have testable ideas and Vygotsky's theory is harder to test. That said, there were problems with Piaget's research methods so people subsequently have challenged Piaget's findings. For example Baillargeon showed that children of a much younger age were capable of object permanence than Piaget had claimed. Despite such challenges the conclusions tend not to challenge Piaget's idea of distinct stages where thinking changes qualitatively.

There were also some similarities between the approaches in that they both suggested that they both focused on the role of thinking – they were both cognitive theories in contrast to the behaviourist approach which suggests learning happens because of rewards. And both theories saw the learner as active rather than passive. In addition Piaget did see a role for social influence because he suggested that teachers should pose challenging questions to make cognitive development take place.

It could be that both approaches are correct and can be combined, i.e. there are biologically driven stages, but within these stages social interactions help a child achieve their potential.

04 Discuss **two** explanations of the development of social cognition. *(16 marks)*

Ciaran's answer

One example of the development of social cognition is Selman's theory of perspective-taking. He gave children a scenario about a dilemma where the child had to decide what to do – whether to be concerned about their own feelings or someone else's. As children got older their decisions shifted from a self-focus to being able to take the perspective of someone else. The five stages are undifferentiated, social-information, self-reflective, mutual and societal. The final stage may happen over the age of 15. These stages were based on research that Selman did, including a longitudinal study which showed that as children aged their perspective did change, so it was a matter of maturation, otherwise it wouldn't change.

This theory is related to social cognition because the way that children think affects their social behaviour. Research by Fitzgerald and White showed that the stage a child was at was related to their prosocial and anti-social behaviour. Therefore this shows that the stage affects social behaviour. However, the data are correlational so we don't know if the stage actually caused the behaviour or is just an association.

The research has had real-world applications, for example it can be used with criminals to help them understand the feelings of other people. It might be that the reason for their criminal behaviour is that they really didn't think what the victim would feel like. Social skills training (SST) might help them achieve that and this would reduce the chance of reoffending.

Theory of mind is another example of social cognition which is similar to perspective-taking. With theory of mind it is a bit more because it isn't just thinking about someone's feelings but really getting an idea of what the world looks like from their perspective. Theory of mind has been used to explain why autistic children think and behave differently – they are different socially because they can't understand what others are thinking and this makes communication difficult. The classic way to test this is the Sally-Anne test where there are two dolls, Sally and Anne. Sally puts her ball in her basket and leaves the room. Anne moves the ball to her box. When Sally comes back where does she look? A person with a theory of mind says she would look in her basket because Sally doesn't know it has moved. But an autistic child can't separate what is in their mind from another person's mind and since the child knows where it is (in the box) thinks that's where Sally will look.

Like perspective-taking this can explain social behaviour. In terms of autism there is a real-world application because autistics might benefit from training to develop their theory of mind.

6 Schizophrenia

CONTENTS OF CHAPTER

SPECIFICATION CHECKLIST

- Classification of schizophrenia. Positive symptoms of schizophrenia, including hallucinations and delusions. Negative symptoms of schizophrenia, including speech poverty and avolition. Reliability and validity in diagnosis and classification of schizophrenia, including reference to co-morbidity, culture and gender bias and symptom overlap.

- Biological explanations for schizophrenia: genetics, the dopamine hypothesis and neural correlates.

- Psychological explanations for schizophrenia: family dysfunction and cognitive explanations, including dysfunctional thought processing.

- Drug therapy: typical and atypical antipsychotics.

- Cognitive behaviour therapy and family therapy as used in the treatment of schizophrenia.

- Token economies as used in the management of schizophrenia.

- The importance of an interactionist approach in explaining and treating schizophrenia; the diathesis-stress model.

Schizophrenia in the movies

If you watch a movie about schizophrenia, do you find yourself thinking that this is what someone with schizophrenia is really like? Probably not – you are too engrossed in the plot, the characters or that huge carton of popcorn that you bought on the way in to the cinema. However, for most people, their opinion on mental disorders such as schizophrenia is shaped largely by what they see in the media. After all, in the absence of other information about schizophrenia, why wouldn't we believe what we see on the screen?

A problem with the way that mental disorders are portrayed in the movies is that they often perpetuate negative stereotypes. A review of 41 movies released between 1990 and 2010 that featured at least one main character with schizophrenia found that 83% of these characters engaged in dangerous or violent behaviours toward themselves or others, and nearly a third engaged in some kind of homicidal behaviour (Owen, 2012). Compare this to statistics that reveal that, globally, just 6 in every 100,000 people will commit a murder at some point in their lives. As well as the media portrayal of people with schizophrenia being violent, other common myths include people with schizophrenia being unpredictable, untreatable

and, well…just plain evil! The horrific twist that filmmakers put on portrayals of schizophrenia may well be entertaining, but is it accurate? After reading this chapter you should be better able to make your own mind up on this thorny issue, but in the meantime, you could try the following.

TRY THIS

Patricia Owen's study (described above) used two researchers who watched all 41 movies, armed with a checklist that assessed demographic characteristics (gender, ethnicity, socioeconomic status, etc.), symptoms (positive or negative), behavioural characteristics (e.g. violence, unpredictability), causation and treatment. They found that 80% of the characters portrayed as having schizophrenia were male (despite males only being marginally more likely than females to have schizophrenia in real life). Most were of relatively low socioeconomic status (as in real life) and, where treatment was mentioned, it was antipsychotic medication. Psychological treatments were rarely mentioned.

There are lots of Internet databases of films that feature a character with schizophrenia (for example, films such as *Shutter Island*, *Misery* and *Orphan*). If you can get hold of a couple of these films to watch with a friend, you can create your own checklist and then you can tick off some of the categories identified by Owen as they appear in the film. After reading this chapter you might take another look at your findings and consider whether the films you watched showed an accurate portrayal of schizophrenia or simply perpetuated some of the more common myths about this disorder that have filled our screens for the last 60 or so years.

Classification of schizophrenia

The opening voice-over of the 1976 horror film *Schizo* (right) demonstrates two of the most common misconceptions that many people have about schizophrenia. **Schizophrenia** is neither a 'split personality' nor a case of 'multiple personalities'. People with schizophrenia are not perpetually incoherent, nor do they constantly display psychotic (loss of contact with reality) behaviour. Schizophrenia is, however, a severe mental disorder characterised by a profound disruption of cognition and emotion. This affects a person's language, thought, perception, emotions and even their sense of self. The schizophrenic believes things that cannot possibly be true (delusions) or hears voices or sees visions when there are no sensory stimuli to create them (hallucinations). Schizophrenia ranks among the top ten cases of disability worldwide and affects about four in 1,000 people at some time in their lives (Saha *et al.*, 2005).

▶ **Misleading media**
Schizophrenia is often misrepresented in the media. The voice-over in the 1970s film *Schizo* erroneously refers to it as 'a mental disorder, sometimes known as multiple or split personality, characterised by loss of touch with the environment and alternation between violent and contrasting behaviour patterns'.

THE NATURE OF SCHIZOPHRENIA

Schizophrenia is a type of psychosis, a severe mental disorder in which thoughts and emotions are so impaired that contact is lost with external reality. Schizophrenia is the most common psychotic disorder, affecting about 1% of the population at some point in their lifetime, although many continue to lead normal lives after diagnosis and subsequent treatment. Schizophrenia is most often diagnosed between the ages of 15 and 35, with men and women affected equally. Someone diagnosed with schizophrenia would characteristically experience delusions (a belief in something that is not, nor could be, true) and hallucinations (experiencing stimuli that are not present). There are many symptoms of the disorder, although not every patient displays all the symptoms.

Diagnosing schizophrenia

In order to make a diagnosis of schizophrenia, a clinician would use a diagnostic manual such as DSM-V. DSM (*The Diagnostic and Statistical Manual of Psychiatric Disorders*) is a classification and description of over 200 mental disorders, grouped in terms of their common features. Version 5 (DSM-V) is the most recent update. DSM is mostly used in the US, whereas in Europe ICD (*International Classification of Diseases*) is more commonly used. The most recent update of ICD is ICD-10, with ICD-11 due to be published in 2017. The characteristics necessary for a diagnosis of schizophrenia using DSM-V can be seen in the table on the right.

Positive symptoms

The symptoms of schizophrenia are typically divided into **positive symptoms** and **negative symptoms**. Positive symptoms are those that appear to reflect an excess or distortion of normal functions. They include the following:

- **Hallucinations** – bizarre, unreal perceptions of the environment that are usually *auditory* (hearing voices that other people can't hear) but may also be *visual* (seeing lights, objects or faces that other people can't see), *olfactory* (smelling things that other people cannot smell) or *tactile* (e.g. feeling that bugs are crawling on or under the skin or something touching the skin). Many schizophrenics report hearing a voice or several voices, telling them to do something (such as harm themselves or someone else) or commenting on their behaviour.
- **Delusions** – bizarre beliefs that seem real to the person with schizophrenia, but they are not real. Sometimes these delusions can be *paranoid* (i.e. persecutory) in nature. This often involves a belief that the person is being followed or spied upon by someone. They may believe that their phone is tapped or that there are video cameras hidden in their home. Delusions may also involve inflated beliefs about the person's power and importance (*delusions of grandeur*). For example, the individual may believe they are famous or have special powers or abilities. An individual may also experience *delusions of reference*, when events in the environment appear to be directly related to them – for example, special personal messages are being communicated through the TV or radio.
- **Disorganised speech** – is the result of abnormal thought processes, where the individual has problems organising his or her thoughts and this shows up in their speech. They may slip from one topic to another (derailment), even in mid-sentence, and in extreme cases their speech may be so incoherent that it sounds like complete gibberish – something that is often referred to as 'word salad'.
- **Grossly disorganised or catatonic behaviour** – includes the inability or motivation to initiate a task, or to complete it once it is started, which leads to difficulties in daily living and can result in decreased interest in personal hygiene. The individual may dress or act in ways that appear bizarre to other people, such as wearing heavy clothes on a hot summer's day. Catatonic behaviours are characterised by a reduced reaction to the immediate environment, rigid postures or aimless motor activity.

▲ Schizophrenia is most often diagnosed between the ages of 15 and 35.

DSM-V (2013)
SCHIZOPHRENIA
Criterion A.

Two (or more) of the following symptoms:

- a) Delusions
- b) Hallucinations
- c) Disorganised speech (e.g. frequent derailment or incoherence)
- d) Grossly disorganised or catatonic behaviour
- e) Negative symptoms, i.e. affective flattening, alogia or avolition

Note:

Only one Criterion A symptom is required if delusions are bizarre or hallucinations consist of a voice keeping up a running commentary on the person's behaviour or thoughts, or two or more voices conversing with each other.

Criterion B. Social/occupational dysfunction: For a significant portion of the time since the onset, one or more major areas of functioning such as work, interpersonal relations or self-care are markedly below the level achieved prior to the onset.

Criterion C. Duration: Continuous signs of the disturbance persist for at least 6 months. This 6-month period must include at least 1 month of symptoms (or less if successfully treated) that meet Criterion A.

During non-active periods, disturbance may be limited to negative symptoms or two or more symptoms in Criterion A in attenuated form (e.g. odd beliefs, unusual perceptual experiences).

Avolition The reduction, difficulty, or inability to initiate and persist in goal-directed behaviour, often mistaken for apparent disinterest.

Delusions Firmly held erroneous beliefs that are caused by distortions of reasoning or misinterpretations of perceptions or experiences.

Hallucinations Distortions or exaggerations of perception in any of the senses, most notably auditory hallucinations.

Negative symptoms Appear to reflect a diminution or loss of normal functioning.

Positive symptoms Appear to reflect an excess or distortion of normal functioning.

Schizophrenia A type of psychosis characterised by a profound disruption of cognition and emotion.

Speech poverty The lessening of speech fluency and productivity, which reflects slowing or blocked thoughts.

Negative symptoms

The negative symptoms of schizophrenia are those that appear to reflect a reduction or loss of normal functions, which often persist even during periods of low (or absent) positive symptoms. About one in three schizophrenia patients suffer from significant negative symptoms (Mäkinen *et al.*, 2008). Negative symptoms weaken the person's ability to cope with everyday activities, affecting their quality of life and their ability to manage without significant outside help. Individuals with schizophrenia are often unaware of the extent of their negative symptoms, and are typically less concerned about them than their relatives may be.

Enduring negative symptoms are sometimes referred to as the 'deficit syndrome', characterised by the presence of at least two negative symptoms for 12 months or longer. Individuals with the deficit syndrome have been found to have more pronounced cognitive deficits and poorer outcomes than patients who do not have this syndrome, with several studies (e.g. Milev *et al.*, 2005) reporting worse functional outcomes in individuals with more prominent negative symptoms. Negative symptoms respond poorly to antipsychotic treatment, although the newer, 'atypical' antipsychotics (see page 146) are claimed to be superior in this respect than the older, 'typical' antipsychotics.

Negative symptoms include:

- **Speech poverty** (alogia) – characterised by the lessening of speech fluency and productivity, this is thought to reflect slowing or blocked thoughts. Patients who display speech poverty display a number of characteristic signs. They may produce fewer words in a given time on a task of verbal fluency (e.g. name as many animals as you can in one minute). This is not a matter of not knowing as many words as non-schizophrenics, but more a difficulty of spontaneously producing them. Speech poverty may also be reflected in less complex syntax, e.g. fewer clauses, shorter utterances, etc. This type of speech appears to be associated with long illness and earlier onset of the illness.

- **Avolition** – a reduction of interests and desires as well as an inability to initiate and persist in goal-directed behaviour (e.g. sitting in the house for hours every day, doing nothing). Avolition is distinct from poor social function or disinterest, which can be the result of other circumstances. For example, an individual may have no social contact with family or friends because they have none, or communication with them is difficult. This would not, however, be considered avolition, which is specified as a reduction in self-initiated involvement in activities that *are* available to the patient.

- **Affective flattening** – a reduction in the range and intensity of emotional expression, including facial expression, voice tone, eye contact and body language. Compared to controls without this symptom, individuals show fewer body and facial movements and smiles, and less co-verbal behaviour, i.e. those movements of the hands, head and face that usually accompany speech. When speaking, patients may also show a deficit in prosody, i.e. paralinguistic features (such as intonation, tempo, loudness and pausing) that provide extra information that is not explicitly contained in a sentence, and which gives cues to the listener as to emotional or attitudinal content and turn-taking.

- **Anhedonia** – a loss of interest or pleasure in all or almost all activities, or a lack of reactivity to normally pleasurable stimuli. It may be pervasive (i.e. all-embracing) or it may be confined to a certain aspect of experience. Physical anhedonia is the inability to experience physical pleasures such as pleasure from food, bodily contact and so on. Social anhedonia is the inability to experience pleasure from interpersonal situations such as interacting with other people. Because social anhedonia overlaps with other disorders (such as depression), whereas physical anhedonia does not, the latter is considered a more reliable symptom of schizophrenia (Sarkar *et al.*, 2010).

Insider tip…

Examination questions on this material tend to require only a brief overview, but we have included extra detail so you can really understand what you are writing about in response.

APPLY YOUR KNOWLEDGE

Joel is a 20-year-old chemistry student at a university in the North of England. For the last month or so, his family and friends have noticed his behaviour becoming increasingly bizarre. His friends have caught him talking to himself in whispers even though there was nobody there. Lately, he has refused to answer or make calls on his mobile phone, claiming that, if he does, it will activate a chip in his brain that was implanted by the security forces. Soon he stops attending university altogether and becomes a complete recluse.

When a friend from university calls to see him, he finds Joel dressed as Batman, claiming to be a superhero on whom the people of the city depend to keep them safe. His speech is rapid and unfocused, flitting from topic to topic and often completely nonsensical. Joel claims he has to stay in his flat because the people will send him messages through the television when they need his help. His friend alerts Joel's parents, who try to get him to go with them to a psychiatrist for an evaluation, but he refuses, accusing them of conspiring with the security forces to have him locked up. If that happens, he says, who will keep the people of the city safe?

Using your knowledge of the classification of schizophrenia, explain why Joel would be likely to be given a diagnosis of schizophrenia.

CAN YOU?   No. 6.1

1. Explain what is meant by the positive symptoms of schizophrenia. (2 marks)
2. Outline the nature of hallucinations and delusions. (3 marks each)
3. Explain what is meant by the negative symptoms of schizophrenia. (2 marks)
4. Outline the nature of speech poverty and avolition. (3 marks each)

Reliability and validity in diagnosis and classification

Classification systems such as DSM-V are worthless unless they are reliable. **Reliability** refers to the *consistency* of a classificatory system such as DSM, or a measuring instrument, e.g. to assess particular symptoms of schizophrenia. Reliability alone counts for nothing unless these systems and scales are also valid. **Validity** refers to the extent that a diagnosis represents something that is real and distinct from other disorders and the extent that a classification system such as DSM measures what it claims to measure. Reliability and validity are inextricably linked because a diagnosis cannot be valid if it is not reliable.

Insider tip…
Although there are subtle differences in the use of the terms 'diagnosis' and 'classification', exam questions tend not to distinguish between them and make use of the term 'diagnosis/classification' (i.e. and/or) instead.

RELIABILITY

Diagnostic reliability means that a diagnosis of schizophrenia must be *repeatable*, i.e. clinicians must be able to reach the same conclusions at two different points in time (test–retest reliability), or different clinicians must reach the same conclusions (inter-rater reliability). Inter-rater reliability is measured by a statistic called a kappa score. A score of 1 indicates perfect inter-rater agreement; a score of 0 indicates zero agreement. A kappa score of 0.7 or above is generally considered good. In the DSM-V field trials (Regier *et al.*, 2013), the diagnosis of schizophrenia had a kappa score of only 0.46.

Cultural differences in diagnosis

Research suggests there is a significant variation between countries when it comes to diagnosing schizophrenia, i.e. **culture** has an influence on the diagnostic process. Copeland (1971) gave 134 US and 194 British psychiatrists a description of a patient. Sixty-nine per cent of the US psychiatrists diagnosed schizophrenia, but only 2 per cent of the British ones gave the same diagnosis. One of the main characteristics of schizophrenia, 'hearing voices', also appears to be influenced by cultural environment. Luhrmann *et al.* (2015) interviewed 60 adults diagnosed with schizophrenia – 20 each in Ghana, India and the US. Each was asked about the voices they heard. Strikingly, while many of the African and Indian subjects reported positive experiences with their voices, describing them as playful or as offering advice, not one American did. Rather, the US subjects were more likely to report the voices they heard as violent and hateful – and indicative of being 'sick'. Luhrmann suggests that the 'harsh, violent voices so common in the West may not be an inevitable feature of schizophrenia'.

🎧 Research methods

Rosenhan's classic study of the unreliability of the diagnosis of mental disorder is described on the facing page.

Within the study Rosenhan ran a small field experiment in four of the hospitals. Either a pseudopatient or a young lady approached a staff member and asked questions such as: 'Pardon me, Mr/Mrs/Dr X, could you tell me when I will be eligible for grounds privileges?' The pseudopatient did this as normally as possible and avoided asking any particular person more than once in a day. Only 4% of the psychiatrists and 0.5% of the nurses stopped; 2% in each group paused and chatted.

When the young lady approached staff members and asked them the same questions, they all stopped and answered her questions, maintaining eye contact.

1. Identify the independent and dependent variables in this study. (2 marks + 2 marks)
2. Explain why this study is classed as a field experiment. (2 marks)
3. What kind of sampling method was used in this study? (1 mark)
4. Give **one** limitation of this sampling method in the context of this study. (2 marks)
5. What conclusions would you draw from the results of the study? (2 marks)
6. In the first study described on the facing page, Rosenhan found that psychiatrists over-diagnosed schizophrenia. Is this a Type I or a Type II error?

LINK TO RESEARCH METHODS

Type I and Type II errors on page 23.
The other topics in these questions are covered in the research methods chapter of our Year 1 book.

VALIDITY

Gender bias in diagnosis

Gender bias in the diagnosis of schizophrenia is said to occur when accuracy of diagnosis is dependent on the gender of an individual. The accuracy of diagnostic judgements can vary for a number of reasons, including gender-biased diagnostic criteria or clinicians basing their judgements on stereotypical beliefs held about gender. For example, critics of the DSM diagnostic criteria argue that some diagnostic categories are biased toward pathologising one gender rather than the other. Broverman *et al.* (1970) found that clinicians in the US equated mentally healthy 'adult' behaviour with mentally healthy 'male' behaviour. As a result, there was a tendency for women to be perceived as less mentally healthy.

▲ Parents tend to be less tolerant of schizophrenic sons than they are schizophrenic daughters, which may account for their earlier diagnosis.

Symptom overlap

Despite the claim that the classification of positive and negative symptoms would make for more valid diagnoses of schizophrenia, many of these symptoms are also found in many other disorders, such as depression and bipolar disorder. This problem is referred to as **symptom overlap**. For example, Ellason and Ross (1995) point out that people with dissociative identity disorder (DID) actually have *more* schizophrenic symptoms than people diagnosed as being schizophrenic! Most people who are diagnosed with schizophrenia have sufficient symptoms of other disorders that they could also receive at least one other diagnosis (Read, 2004).

Co-morbidity

Co-morbidity is an important issue for the validity of the diagnosis of mental illness. It refers to the extent that two (or more) conditions co-occur. Psychiatric co-morbidities are common among patients with schizophrenia. These include substance abuse, anxiety and symptoms of depression. For example, Buckley *et al.* (2009) estimate that co-morbid depression occurs in 50% of patients, and 47% of patients also have a lifetime diagnosis of co-morbid substance abuse.

Schizophrenia and obsessive-compulsive disorder (OCD) are two distinct psychiatric conditions. Roughly 1% of the population develop schizophrenia, and roughly 2–3% develop OCD. Since both are fairly uncommon, we would expect that only a few people with schizophrenia would develop OCD and vice versa. However, evidence suggests that the two conditions appear together more often than chance would suggest. A meta-analysis by Swets *et al.* (2014) found that at least 12% of patients with schizophrenia also fulfilled the diagnostic criteria for OCD and about 25% displayed significant obsessive-compulsive symptoms.

EVALUATION OF VALIDITY

Research support for gender bias in diagnosis

Loring and Powell (1988) randomly selected 290 male and female psychiatrists to read two case vignettes of patients' behaviour. They were then asked to offer their judgement on these individuals using standard diagnostic criteria. When the patients were described as 'males' or no information given about their gender, 56% of the psychiatrists gave a diagnosis of schizophrenia. However, when the patients were described as 'female', only 20% were given a diagnosis of schizophrenia. Interestingly, this gender bias was not as evident among the female psychiatrists, suggesting that diagnosis is influenced not only by the gender of the patient but also the gender of the clinician.

The consequences of co-morbidity

A number of studies have examined single co-morbidities with schizophrenia, but these studies have usually involved only relatively small sample sizes. By contrast, a US study (Weber *et al.*, 2009) looked at nearly 6 million hospital discharge records to calculate co-morbidity rates. Psychiatric and behaviour-related diagnoses accounted for 45% of co-morbidity. However, the study also found evidence of many co-morbid non-psychiatric diagnoses. Many patients with a primary diagnosis of schizophrenia were also diagnosed with medical problems including hypothyroidism, asthma, hypertension and type 2 diabetes. The authors concluded that the very nature of a diagnosis of a psychiatric disorder is that patients tend to receive a lower standard of medical care, which in turn adversely affects the prognosis for patients with schizophrenia.

Differences in prognosis

In the same way that people diagnosed as schizophrenic rarely share the same symptoms, likewise there is no evidence that they share the same *outcomes*. The prognosis for patients diagnosed with schizophrenia varies with about 20% recovering their previous level of functioning, 10% achieving significant and lasting improvement, and about 30% showing some improvement with intermittent relapses. A diagnosis of schizophrenia, therefore, has little predictive validity – some people never appear to recover from the disorder, but many do. What *does* appear to influence outcome is more to do with gender (Malmberg *et al.*, 1998) and psycho-social factors such as social skills, academic achievement and family tolerance of schizophrenic behaviour (Harrison *et al.*, 2001).

EVALUATION OF RELIABILITY

Lack of inter-rater reliability

Despite the claims for increased reliability in DSM-III (and later revisions), over 30 years later there is still little evidence that DSM is routinely used with high reliability by mental health clinicians. Whaley (2001) found inter-rater reliability correlations in the diagnosis of schizophrenia as low as 0.11. Further problems with the inter-rater reliability of the diagnosis of schizophrenia are illustrated in the Rosenhan study (see right).

Unreliable symptoms

For a diagnosis of 'schizophrenia', only one of the characteristic symptoms is required 'if delusions are bizarre'. However, this creates problems for reliability of diagnosis. When 50 senior psychiatrists in the US were asked to differentiate between 'bizarre' and 'non-bizarre' delusions, they produced inter-rater reliability correlations of only around 0.40, forcing the researchers to conclude that even this central diagnostic requirement lacks sufficient reliability for it to be a reliable method of distinguishing between schizophrenic and non-schizophrenic patients (Mojtabi and Nicholson, 1995).

A comment on cultural differences in the diagnosis of schizophrenia

Research (e.g. Barnes, 2004) has established cultural, and particularly racial, differences in the diagnosis of schizophrenia. However, the prognosis for members of ethnic minority groups may actually be more positive than for majority group members. The ethnic culture hypothesis predicts that ethnic minority groups experience less distress associated with mental disorders because of the protective characteristics and social structures that exist in most ethnic minority cultures. Brekke and Barrio (1997) found evidence to support this hypothesis in a study of 184 individuals diagnosed with schizophrenia or a schizophrenia-spectrum disorder. This sample was drawn from two non-white minority groups (African-Americans and Latinos) and a majority group (white Americans). They found that non-minority group members were consistently more symptomatic than members of the two ethnic minority groups, findings which supported the ethnic culture hypothesis.

On being sane in insane places

Something which highlighted the unreliability of diagnosis was Rosenhan's famous study in which 'normal' people presented themselves to psychiatric hospitals in the US claiming they heard an unfamiliar voice in their head saying the words 'empty', 'hollow' and 'thud' (Rosenhan, 1973). They were all diagnosed as having schizophrenia and admitted. Throughout their stay, none of the staff recognised that they were actually normal. In a follow-up study, Rosenhan warned hospitals of his intention to send out more 'pseudopatients'. This resulted in a 21% detection rate, although none actually presented themselves!

KEY TERMS

Co-morbidity refers to the extent that two (or more) conditions or diseases occur simultaneously in a patient, for example schizophrenia and depression.

Culture The rules, customs, morals, childrearing practices, etc. that bind a group of people together and define how they are likely to behave.

Gender bias refers to the tendency to describe the behaviour of men and women in psychological theory and research in such a way that might not be seen to represent accurately the characteristics of either one of these genders.

Reliability is consistency – the consistency of measurements. We would expect any measurement to produce the same data if taken on successive occasions.

Symptom overlap refers to the fact that symptoms of a disorder may not be unique to that disorder but may also be found in other disorders, making accurate diagnosis difficult.

Validity refers to whether an observed effect is a genuine one.

CAN YOU? | No. 6.2

1. Explain what is meant by the terms *reliability* and *validity* in the context of the classification and/or diagnosis of schizophrenia. (2 marks each)
2. Outline the role of culture and gender bias in the classification and/or diagnosis of schizophrenia. (3 marks each)
3. Outline the role of co-morbidity and symptom overlap in the classification and/or diagnosis of schizophrenia. (3 marks each)
4. Discuss issues of reliability and validity associated with the classification and/or diagnosis of schizophrenia. (16 marks)

Biological explanations for schizophrenia

There are many different explanations for the disorder that we call schizophrenia, but it is the **biological explanations** that have received the most research support to date (Comer, 2013), in particular the role of **genetics** and **neural correlates** such as dopamine. The importance of biological explanations for schizophrenia does not, however, deny the important role that psychological factors play in the onset of this disorder. Current thinking is that a 'diathesis-stress' relationship may be at work, with a biological predisposition (the diathesis) for schizophrenia only developing into the disorder if other significant psychological stressors are present in the person's life. We will be looking further into the diathesis-stress relationship on page 154.

GENETIC FACTORS

One possible cause of schizophrenia may be heredity, i.e. genetics. Schizophrenia tends to run in families, but only among individuals who are genetically related rather than related by marriage. The risk of developing the disorder among individuals who have family members with schizophrenia is higher than it is for those who do not. No one gene is thought to be responsible for this disorder – it is more likely that different combinations of genes make individuals more vulnerable to schizophrenia. Having these genes does not necessarily mean an individual *will* develop schizophrenia, as we will see on later spreads.

Family studies

Family studies (e.g. Gottesman, 1991) find individuals who have schizophrenia and determine whether their biological relatives are similarly affected more often than non-biological relatives. Family studies have established that schizophrenia is more common among biological relatives of a person with schizophrenia, and that the closer the degree of genetic relatedness, the greater the risk. For example, in Gottesman's study, children with two schizophrenic parents had a concordance rate of 46%, children with one schizophrenic parent a rate of 13%, and siblings (where a brother or sister had schizophrenia) a concordance rate of 9%.

Twin studies

Twin studies offer a unique opportunity for researchers to investigate the relative contribution of genetic and environmental influences. If monozygotic (MZ – genetically identical) twins are more concordant (similar) than dizygotic (DZ – who share only 50% of their genes), then this suggests that the greater similarity is due to genetic factors. Joseph (2004) calculated that the pooled data for all schizophrenia twin studies carried out prior to 2001 showed a concordance rate for MZ twins of 40.4% and 7.4% for DZ twins. More recent, methodologically sound studies (e.g. those using 'blind' diagnoses where researchers do not know whether the twin they are assessing is MZ or DZ) have tended to report a lower concordance rate for MZ twins than in earlier studies. Despite this, however, such studies still support the genetic position because they show a concordance rate for MZ twins that is many times higher than that for DZ twins.

Adoption studies

Because of the difficulties of disentangling genetic and environmental influences for individuals who share genes *and* environment, studies of genetically related individuals who have been reared *apart* are used. Probably the most methodologically sound study of this type was carried out by Tienari *et al.* (2000) in Finland. Of the 164 adoptees whose biological mothers had been diagnosed with schizophrenia, 11 (6.7%) also received a diagnosis of schizophrenia, compared to just 4 (2%) of the 197 control adoptees (those born to non-schizophrenic mothers). The investigators concluded that these findings showed that the genetic liability to schizophrenia had been 'decisively confirmed'.

NEURAL CORRELATES: THE DOPAMINE HYPOTHESIS

The **dopamine hypothesis** claims that an excess of the neurotransmitter dopamine in certain regions of the brain is associated with the positive symptoms of schizophrenia. Messages from neurons that transmit dopamine fire too easily or too often, leading to hallucinations and delusions that are the characteristic positive symptoms of schizophrenia. Schizophrenics are thought to have abnormally high numbers of D_2 receptors on receiving neurons, resulting in more dopamine binding and therefore more neurons firing. The key role played by dopamine was highlighted in two sources of evidence:

Drugs that increase dopaminergic activity

Amphetamine is a dopamine agonist, i.e. it stimulates nerve cells containing dopamine, causing the synapse to be flooded with this neurotransmitter. 'Normal' individuals who are exposed to large doses of dopamine-releasing drugs such as amphetamines can develop the characteristic hallucinations and delusions of a schizophrenic episode. This generally disappears with abstinence from the drug. Likewise, some people who suffer from Parkinson's disease, a neurodegenerative disease characterised by low dopamine levels, who take the drug *L-dopa* to raise their levels of dopamine, have been found to develop schizophrenic-type symptoms (Grilly, 2002).

Drugs that decrease dopaminergic activity

Although there are many different types of antipsychotic drug, they all have one thing in common, i.e. they block the activity of dopamine in the brain. By reducing activity in the neural pathways of the brain that use dopamine as the neurotransmitter, these drugs eliminate symptoms such as hallucinations and delusions. The fact that these drugs (known as dopamine antagonists because they block its action) alleviated many of the symptoms of schizophrenia strengthened the case for the important role of dopamine in this disorder.

The revised dopamine hypothesis

Davis and Kahn (1991) proposed that the positive symptoms of schizophrenia are caused by an *excess* of dopamine in subcortical areas of the brain, particularly in the mesolimbic pathway. The negative and cognitive symptoms of schizophrenia are thought to arise from a *deficit* of dopamine in areas of the prefrontal cortex (the mesocortical pathway). Evidence for this revised hypothesis comes from various sources.

Neural imaging e.g. Patel *et al.* (2010), using PET scans to assess dopamine levels in schizophrenic and normal individuals, found lower levels of dopamine in the dorsolateral prefrontal cortex of schizophrenic patients compared to their normal controls.

Animal studies e.g. Wang and Deutch (2008) induced dopamine depletion in the prefrontal cortex in rats. This resulted in cognitive impairment (e.g. memory deficits) that the researchers were able to reverse using olanzapine, an atypical antipsychotic drug thought to have beneficial effects on negative symptoms in humans.

KEY TERMS

Biological explanations emphasise the role of inherited factors and dysfunction of brain activity in the development of a behaviour or mental disorder.

Dopamine hypothesis claims that an excess of the neurotransmitter dopamine in certain regions of the brain is associated with the positive symptoms of schizophrenia.

Genetics Inherited factors make certain individuals more likely to develop a behaviour or mental disorder.

Neural correlates Changes in neuronal events and mechanisms that result in the characteristic symptoms of a behaviour or mental disorder.

EVALUATION OF GENETIC FACTORS

Common rearing patterns may explain family similarities

Research has shown that schizophrenia appears to run in families, supporting the argument for a genetic basis for the disorder. However, many researchers now accept that the fact that schizophrenia appears to run in families may be more to do with common rearing patterns or other factors that have nothing to do with heredity. For example, research on expressed emotion (see page 144) has shown that the negative emotional climate in some families may lead to stress beyond an individual's coping mechanisms, thus triggering a schizophrenic episode.

MZ twins encounter more similar environments

A crucial assumption underlying all twin studies is that the environments of monozygotic (MZ) twins and dizygotic (DZ) twins are equivalent. It is assumed, therefore, that the greater concordance for schizophrenia between MZ twins is a product of greater *genetic* similarity rather than greater environmental similarity. However, as Joseph (2004) points out, it is widely accepted that MZ twins are treated more similarly, encounter more similar environments (i.e. are more likely to do things together) and experience more 'identity confusion' (i.e. frequently being treated as 'the twins' rather than as two distinct individuals) than DZ twins. As a result, argues Joseph, there is reason to believe that the differences in concordance rates between MZ and DZ twins reflect nothing more than the environmental differences that distinguish the two types of twin.

Adoptees may be selectively placed

A central assumption of adoption studies is that adoptees are not 'selectively placed', i.e. adoptive parents who adopt children with a schizophrenic biological parent are no different to adoptive parents who adopt children whose background is normal. Joseph (2004) claims that this is unlikely to have been the case, particularly in the early studies. In countries like Denmark and the US, potential adoptive parents would have been informed of the genetic background of children *prior* to selection for adoption. As Kringlen (1987; cited in Joseph, 2004) points out, 'Because the adoptive parents evidently received information about the child's biological parents, one might wonder who would adopt such a child.'

EVALUATION OF THE DOPAMINE HYPOTHESIS

Evidence from treatment

Much of the evidence supporting the dopamine hypothesis comes from the success of drug treatments that attempt to change levels of dopamine activity in the brain. The basic mechanism of antipsychotic drugs is to reduce the effects of dopamine and so reduce the symptoms of schizophrenia. For example, Leucht *et al.* (2013) carried out a meta-analysis of 212 studies that had analysed the effectiveness of different antipsychotic drugs compared with a placebo. They found that all the drugs tested were significantly more effective than placebo in the treatment of positive and negative symptoms, achieved through the normalisation of dopamine.

Inconclusive supporting evidence

Moncrieff (2009) claims that evidence for the dopamine hypothesis of schizophrenia is far from conclusive. For example, although stimulant drugs such as cocaine and amphetamine have been shown to induce schizophrenic episodes, such stimulants are known to affect many neurotransmitters other than dopamine. Likewise, evidence for dopamine concentrations in post-mortem brain tissue has either been negative or inconclusive. Moncrieff also points out that other confounding sources of dopamine release, such as stress and smoking, have rarely been considered. Therefore, she suggests, the idea that the symptoms of schizophrenia are caused by the overactivity of the dopaminergic system is not supported by current evidence.

Challenges to the dopamine hypothesis

Noll (2009) claims there is strong evidence against both the original dopamine hypothesis *and* the revised dopamine hypothesis. He argues that antipsychotic drugs do not alleviate hallucinations and delusions in about one-third of people experiencing these symptoms. Noll also points out that, in some people, hallucinations and delusions are present *despite* levels of dopamine being normal. Blocking the D_2 receptors of these individuals has little or no effect on their symptoms. This suggests that, rather than dopamine being the sole cause of positive symptoms, other neurotransmitter systems, acting independently of the dopaminergic system, may also produce the positive symptoms associated with schizophrenia.

UPGRADE

Maximising your marks

The biggest mark earners are, of course, the 16-mark essay questions. In previous sections of this book we have looked at how to plan for these questions and how to answer them effectively, but what *specifically* is an examiner looking for if he (or she) is going to give you a mark in the top mark band of 13–16 marks? Let's look at a typical essay question for this section of the specification:

Discuss the biological explanations of schizophrenia. (16 marks)

Although you aren't told this in the question, 10 of the marks are assigned for AO3 (evaluation) and the remaining 6 marks for AO1 (description). It is worth bearing this in mind when planning your response.

Now let's look at the mark descriptor for the top level for this question:

Knowledge of biological explanations for schizophrenia is accurate and generally well detailed. Discussion is thorough and effective. The answer is clear, coherent and focused. Specialist terminology is used effectively. Minor detail and/or expansion of argument sometimes lacking.

Obviously your material has to be accurate, but examiners are pretty forgiving folk and will generally ignore relatively minor inaccuracies. To make sure your description is 'generally well detailed', you should aim to make each point about 30 words. Choose six things you want to say and expand each to 30 words, adding the necessary detail and specialist terminology to give each point descriptive impact. The use of specialist terminology can be quite intimidating in a biological section, but needn't be – it simply means using proper psychological terminology rather than lay expressions, e.g. the 'prefrontal cortex' is preferable to the 'front of the brain'. To make your discussion 'thorough and effective', you should aim for five evaluative points 'distilled' from the 'Evaluation' information on this page to about 60 words. Being able to reduce material down to make it really effective is a skill that we cover in more detail on page 155.

CAN YOU? No. 6.3

1. Outline the genetic explanations of schizophrenia. (4 marks)
2. Evaluate the genetic explanations of schizophrenia. (4 marks)
3. Briefly outline the dopamine hypothesis of schizophrenia and give **one** limitation of this explanation. (6 marks)
4. Discuss the biological explanations of schizophrenia. (16 marks)

Psychological explanations for schizophrenia

Although biological explanations of schizophrenia have attracted the most research support in recent years, psychological explanations of this disorder abound. Explanations based on **family dysfunction** claim that schizophrenia is caused by abnormal patterns of communication within the family. By locating the causes of schizophrenia within the family, proponents of this view advocate family therapy (see page 150) as treatment, during which these abnormal communication patterns can be pointed out and changed. Clinicians have long recognised that abnormalities in cognitive function are also a key component of schizophrenia and can bias an individual towards developing cognitive schemas that see the world in a more threatening way.

FAMILY DYSFUNCTION

Double bind theory

Gregory Bateson *et al.* (1956) suggest that children who frequently receive contradictory messages from their parents are more likely to develop schizophrenia. For example, if a mother tells her son that she loves him, yet at the same time turns her head away in disgust, the child receives two conflicting messages about their relationship on different communicative levels, one of affection on the verbal level, and one of animosity on the non-verbal level. The

▲ A child may receive two conflicting messages about their relationship – one of affection on the verbal level, and one of animosity on the non-verbal level, or vice versa.

child's ability to respond to the mother is incapacitated by such contradictions because one message invalidates the other. These interactions prevent the development of an internally coherent construction of reality, and in the long run this manifests itself as schizophrenic symptoms (e.g. flattened affect and withdrawal). These ideas were echoed in the work of psychiatrist R.D. Laing, who argued that what we call schizophrenia is actually a reasonable response to an insane world.

Expressed emotion

Another family variable associated with schizophrenia is a negative emotional climate or, more generally, a high degree of expressed emotions. Expressed emotion (EE) is a family communication style in which members of the family of a psychiatric patient talk about that patient in a critical or hostile manner or in a way that indicates emotional over-involvement or over-concern with the patient or their behaviour. For example, research by Kuipers *et al.* (1983) found that high EE relatives talk more and listen less. High levels of EE are most likely to influence relapse rates (i.e. an increase in symptoms). A patient returning to a family with high EE is about four times more likely to relapse than a patient whose family is low in EE (Linszen *et al.*, 1997).

This suggests that people with schizophrenia have a lower tolerance for intense environmental stimuli, particularly intense emotional comments and interactions with family members. It appears that the negative emotional climate in these families arouses the patient and leads to stress beyond his or her already impaired coping mechanisms, thus triggering a schizophrenic episode. In contrast, a family environment that is relatively supportive and emotionally undemanding may help the person with schizophrenia to reduce their dependence on antipsychotic medication and help reduce the likelihood of relapse (Noll, 2009).

COGNITIVE EXPLANATIONS

Compared to normal controls, research has found evidence of **dysfunctional thought processing** in people with schizophrenia, i.e. they process information differently to those without the disorder. **Cognitive explanations** of schizophrenia emphasise the role of dysfunctional thought processing particularly evident in those who display the characteristic positive symptoms of schizophrenia such as delusions and hallucinations.

Cognitive explanations of delusions

During the formation of delusions, the patient's interpretations of their experiences are controlled by inadequate information processing. A critical characteristic of delusional thinking is the degree to which the individual perceives him or herself as the central component in events (egocentric bias) and so jumps to conclusions about external events. This is manifested in the patient's tendency to relate irrelevant events to themselves and consequently arrive at false conclusions. Muffled voices are interpreted as people criticising them, and flashes of light are a signal from God. Delusions in schizophrenia are relatively impervious to reality testing, in that patients are unwilling or unable to consider that they may be wrong (Beck and Rector, 2005). They are considered to have 'impaired insight', an inability to recognise cognitive distortions and substitute more realistic explanations for events.

Cognitive explanations of hallucinations

Why are patients with schizophrenia predisposed to experience some thoughts as external 'voices'? Hallucinating individuals focus excessive attention on auditory stimuli (hypervigilance) and so have a higher *expectancy* for the occurrence of a voice than normal individuals. Aleman (2001) suggests that hallucination-prone individuals find it difficult to distinguish between imagery and sensory-based perception. For these individuals, the inner representation of an idea (e.g. 'What other people think of me') can override the actual sensory stimulus and produce an auditory image ('He is not a good person') that is every bit as real as the transmission of actual sound. Hallucinating patients with schizophrenia are significantly more likely to misattribute the source of a self-generated auditory experience to an external source than are non-hallucinating patients with schizophrenia (Baker and Morrison, 1998). These errors are not corrected by disconfirming evidence because patients with schizophrenia do not go through the same processes of reality testing (such as checking external sources) that others would do.

KEY TERMS

Cognitive explanations of mental disorders propose that abnormalities in cognitive function are a key component of schizophrenia.

Dysfunctional thought processing Cognitive habits or beliefs that cause the individual to evaluate information inappropriately.

Family dysfunction The presence of problems within a family that contribute to relapse rates in recovering schizophrenics, including lack of warmth between parents and child, dysfunctional communication patterns and parental overprotection.

EVALUATION OF FAMILY DYSFUNCTION

Family relationships

The importance of family relationships in the development of schizophrenia can be seen in an adoption study by Tienari *et al.* (1994). In this study those adopted children who had schizophrenic biological parents were more likely to become ill themselves than those children with non-schizophrenic biological parents. However, this difference only emerged in situations where the adopted family was rated as disturbed. In other words, the illness only manifested itself under appropriate environmental conditions. Genetic vulnerability alone was not sufficient.

Double bind theory

There is some evidence to support this particular account of how family relationships may lead to schizophrenia. Berger (1965) found that schizophrenics reported a higher recall of double bind statements by their mothers than non-schizophrenics. However, this evidence may not be reliable as patients' recall may be affected by their schizophrenia. Other studies are less supportive. Liem (1974) measured patterns of parental communication in families with a schizophrenic child and found no difference when compared to normal families. Hall and Levin (1980) analysed data from various previous studies and found no difference between families with and without a schizophrenic member in the degree to which verbal and non-verbal communication were in agreement.

Individual differences in vulnerability to EE

Not all patients who live in high EE families relapse, and not all patients who live in low EE homes avoid relapse. Research has found individual differences in stress response to high EE-like behaviours. Altorfer *et al.* (1998) found that one-quarter of the patients they studied showed no physiological responses to stressful comments from their relatives. Vulnerability to the influences of high EE may also be psychologically based. For example, research by Lebell *et al.* (1993) suggests that how patients appraise the behaviour of their relatives is important. In cases where high EE behaviours are not perceived as being negative or stressful, they can do well regardless of how the family environment is objectively rated. This shows that not all patients are equally vulnerable to high levels of expressed emotion within the family environment.

 UPGRADE

As you will be aware from other chapters, AQA psychology examinations often feature an 'Application' question, and this section of the specification is as likely to have one as any other section. Let's look again at the rules of answering these questions, this time in the context of family therapy.

Kyle is 18 and was diagnosed with schizophrenia about six months ago. His family find it very stressful and worry that they are doing the wrong thing and that nothing they do helps Kyle. As a result, Kyle's psychiatrist has recommended that family therapy might be provided to help Kyle and his family deal effectively with Kyle's illness. His parents are very apprehensive about this and don't really understand what it is or why they need it, so they ask you to explain because you study psychology.

Using your knowledge of family therapy, explain what you could tell Kyle's parents about why family therapy will help them all deal with Kyle's schizophrenia. (4 marks)

Advice for answering this question: For a 4-mark question there would be two mark levels. For the top level you would need to display 'clear and accurate' knowledge of the specific psychology related to the scenario (in this case family therapy). However, having a good understanding of the psychology is not enough on its own – it must be used 'appropriately' to explain the scenario (here it is why family therapy would be suitable for Kyle and his family). The marks awarded reflect how effectively you have used the former to explain the latter. Ignore either of these and you would get few, if any, marks.

EVALUATION OF COGNITIVE EXPLANATIONS

Supporting evidence for the cognitive model of schizophrenia

Sarin and Wallin (2014) reviewed recent research evidence relating to the cognitive model of schizophrenia. They found supporting evidence for the claim that the positive symptoms of schizophrenia have their origins in faulty cognition. For example, delusional patients were found to show various biases in their information processing, such as jumping to conclusions and lack of reality testing. Likewise, schizophrenic individuals with hallucinations were found to have impaired self-monitoring and also tended to experience their own thoughts as voices. In addition, they found that patients with negative symptoms also displayed dysfunctional thought processes such as having low expectations regarding pleasure and success.

Support from the success of cognitive therapies

The claim that the symptoms of schizophrenia have their origin in faulty cognition is reinforced by the success of cognitive-based therapies for schizophrenia. In cognitive behavioural therapy for psychosis (CBTp), patients are encouraged to evaluate the content of their delusions or of any voices, and to consider ways in which they might test the validity of their faulty beliefs. The effectiveness of this approach was demonstrated in the NICE review of treatments for schizophrenia (NICE, 2014). This review found consistent evidence that, when compared with treatment by antipsychotic medication, cognitive behavioural therapy was more effective in reducing symptom severity and improving levels of social functioning.

An integrated model of schizophrenia

A problem with any psychological model of schizophrenia is that it deals adequately with one aspect of the disorder (e.g. cognitive impairment) but fails to explain, or ignores, another aspect (e.g. neurochemical changes). Howes and Murray (2014) addressed this problem with an integrated model of schizophrenia. They argue that early vulnerability factors (e.g. genes, birth complications, etc.), together with exposure to significant social stressors (e.g. social adversity), sensitises the dopamine system, causing it to increase the release of dopamine. Biased cognitive processing of this increased dopamine activity results in paranoia and hallucinations, and eventually the development of a psychosis. This contributes to the stress experienced by the individual, leading to more dopamine release, more symptoms and so on.

CAN YOU? No. 6.4

1. Outline family dysfunction explanations of schizophrenia. (4 marks)
2. Evaluate the family dysfunction of schizophrenia. (4 marks)
3. Briefly outline one or more cognitive explanations of schizophrenia and give one limitation of these explanations. (6 marks)
4. Discuss psychological explanations of schizophrenia. (16 marks)

Drug therapy

Prior to the introduction of antipsychotic drugs in the 1950s, there was no effective treatment for schizophrenia. Until this time the standard treatment for schizophrenia consisted of providing patients with a safe and supportive environment in the form of a long-stay psychiatric hospital and hoping for some improvement in symptoms. Following the discovery of dopamine in 1952, drugs were developed that had a direct effect on the action of this neurotransmitter. Some drugs, such as amphetamines, were found to create the symptoms of schizophrenia in healthy people, while others markedly reduced these symptoms in people who were severely ill. Drugs that had the latter effect consequently became known as antipsychotics and were used in **drug therapy**.

Insider tip…

You would not be expected to include all the detailed biology on this page in an answer to question 2, but you would be expected to include some biology because of the need for specialist terms in order to get the highest marks.

ANTIPSYCHOTICS

Drugs that are effective in treating the most disturbing forms of psychotic illness, such as schizophrenia and manic depression (bipolar disorder), are called *antipsychotics*. Antipsychotic medication helps the person with the disorder function as well as possible in their life, while at the same time increasing their feelings of subjective well-being. Antipsychotics are usually recommended as the initial treatment for the symptoms of schizophrenia, after which clinicians tend to use a combination of medication and psychological therapy to manage the disorder. All antipsychotics work by reducing dopaminergic transmission, i.e. reducing the action of the neurotransmitter dopamine in areas of the brain associated with the symptoms of schizophrenia (see 'dopamine hypothesis' on page 142).

Typical antipsychotics (such as *chlorpromazine*) are used primarily to combat the positive symptoms of schizophrenia such as hallucinations and thought disturbances – products of an overactive dopamine system. The **atypical antipsychotic** drugs (such as *clozapine*) also combat these positive symptoms, but in addition there are claims that they have some beneficial effects on negative symptoms as well.

Typical antipsychotics

Typical antipsychotics (also known as 'conventional' or 'first-generation' antipsychotics) were developed in the 1950s. The basic mechanism of typical antipsychotic drugs is to reduce the effects of dopamine and so reduce the symptoms of schizophrenia. Typical antipsychotics are dopamine *antagonists* in that they bind to but do not stimulate dopamine receptors (particularly the D_2 receptors in the mesolimbic dopamine pathway), thus blocking their action (see diagram on right). By reducing stimulation of the dopamine system in the mesolimbic pathway, antipsychotic drugs such as *chlorpromazine* eliminate the hallucinations and delusions experienced by people with schizophrenia.

Hallucinations and delusions usually diminish within a few days of beginning medication, although other symptoms may take several weeks before a significant improvement is noted. The effectiveness of the dopamine antagonists in reducing these symptoms led to the development of the dopamine hypothesis of schizophrenia. Kapur *et al.* (2000) estimate that between 60% and 75% of D_2 receptors in the mesolimbic dopamine pathway must be blocked for these drugs to be effective. Unfortunately, in order to do this, a similar number of D_2 receptors in other areas of the brain must also be blocked, leading to undesirable side effects (see next page). This represents the 'high cost' of using typical antipsychotics to treat schizophrenia. There are several dopamine pathways in the brain, and it appears that blocking dopamine receptors in only one of them is useful, whereas blocking dopamine receptors in the remaining pathways may be harmful for the person. This problem has been addressed by development of the *atypical* antipsychotic drugs described in the next section.

Atypical antipsychotics

Atypical antipsychotic (also known as 'second-generation' antipsychotics) were so called because of three main differences to the first-generation typical antipsychotics. They carry a lower risk of extrapyramidal side effects (see next page), have a beneficial effect on negative symptoms and cognitive impairment, and are suitable for treatment-resistant patients. As with the typical antipsychotics, these drugs also act on the dopamine system by blocking D_2 receptors. However, they only temporarily occupy the D_2 receptors and then rapidly dissociate to allow normal dopamine transmission. It is this characteristic (i.e. 'rapid dissociation') of atypical antipsychotics that is thought to be responsible for the lower levels of extrapyramidal side effects found with these drugs compared to conventional antipsychotics. Because atypical antipsychotics such as *clozapine* have very little effect on the dopamine systems that control movement, they tend not to cause the movement problems found with the typical antipsychotics.

Rapid dissociation is one feature of atypical antipsychotics that distinguish them from typical antipsychotics, but there are others. Typical antipsychotics block only D_2 (dopamine) receptors. However, atypical antipsychotics have a stronger affinity for serotonin receptors (particularly the $5-HT_{2A}$ receptors) and a lower affinity for D_2 receptors. It is this characteristic that explains the different effects of atypical compared to typical antipsychotics.

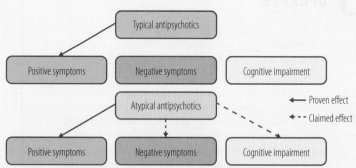

▲ Both typical and atypical antipsychotics have proven efficacy in the treatment of the positive symptoms of schizophrenia. Claims for the efficacy of atypical antipsychotics in the treatment of negative symptoms and cognitive impairment is less well established.

Antipsychotics versus placebo

Support for the effectiveness of antipsychotics comes from studies that have compared relapse rates for antipsychotics and placebos. Leucht *et al.* (2012) carried out a meta-analysis of 65 studies, published between 1959 and 2011, and involving nearly 6,000 patients. All patients had been stabilised on either typical or atypical antipsychotics. Some of these patients were taken off their antipsychotic medication and given a placebo instead. The remaining patients remained on their regular antipsychotic. Within 12 months, 64% of those patients who had been given the placebo had relapsed, compared to 27% of those who stayed on the antipsychotic drug.

Extrapyramidal side effects

Typical antipsychotic drugs can sometimes produce movement problems for the patient. These are called extrapyramidal effects because antipsychotic drugs appear to impact on the extrapyramidal area of the brain, which helps control motor activity. The most common are the Parkinsonian and related symptoms, so called because they resemble the features of the neurological disorder Parkinson's disease (PD). More than half of the patients taking typical antipsychotics experience these symptoms. When people take antipsychotic drugs for an extended period, a second type of extrapyramidal effect can occur – tardive dyskinesia, i.e. involuntary movements of the tongue, face and jaw. These side effects can be so distressing for the patient that other drugs have to be given to control them, or the patient may stop taking their antipsychotic medication completely.

Ethical problems with typical antipsychotics

The problems associated with the use of antipsychotic medication raise significant ethical issues. Critics argue that if side effects, deaths and psychosocial consequences were taken into account, a cost–benefit analysis of its advantages would most probably be negative. In the US recently, a large out-of-court settlement was awarded to a tardive dyskinesia sufferer on the basis of Article 3 of the Human Rights Act 1988, which states that 'no one shall be subjected to inhuman or degrading treatment or punishment' (Chari *et al.*, 2002, cited in Ross and Read, 2004).

Advantages of atypical over typical antipsychotics

Atypical antipsychotics are claimed to have a number of advantages when compared to typical antipsychotics. A key advantage of atypical antipsychotics is that patients experience fewer side effects. Atypical antipsychotics, particularly the more recent newly developed atypical antipsychotics, such as *olanzapine* and *quetiapine*, are less likely to produce the extrapyramidal effects typically found with typical antipsychotics (see above) – therefore patients are more likely to continue with their medication, which in turn means they are more likely to see a reduction in their symptoms.

Are atypical antipsychotics better?

The introduction of atypical antipsychotics led to claims of the superiority of these drugs over the older 'typical' antipsychotics. Crossley *et al.* (2010) carried out a meta-analysis of 15 studies to examine the efficacy (i.e. capacity to reduce symptoms) and side effects of atypical versus typical antipsychotics in the early-phase treatment of schizophrenia. They found no significant differences between atypical and typical drugs in terms of their effect on symptoms but did note differences in the type of side effects experienced. Patients on atypical antipsychotics gained more weight than those on typicals, whereas those on typicals experienced more extrapyramidal side effects. They concluded there was no evidence for differences in efficacy between atypical and typical antipsychotics, but there was a clear difference in the side-effect profile.

Motivational deficits

Ross and Read (2004) argue that when people are prescribed antipsychotic medication, it reinforces the view that there is 'something wrong with *them*'. This prevents the individual from thinking about possible stressors (such as life history or current circumstances) that might be possible for their condition. In turn this reduces their motivation to look for possible solutions that might alleviate these stressors and reduce their suffering. In fact, a number of international surveys have shown that the public, when asked what causes schizophrenia, cite social factors, such as poverty and traumatic childhoods, far more often than biological factors (Read and Haslam, 2004).

Research methods

1. Several studies on this spread are meta-analyses. Explain what is involved in a *meta-analysis*. (2 marks)
2. Select **one** of the meta-analyses on this spread and explain **one** advantage and **one** limitation of using a meta-analysis in this research area. (2 marks + 2 marks)
3. Another method commonly used in research on drugs is a placebo condition. Explain in what way a placebo condition is acting as a control condition in such studies. (2 marks)
4. The study by Leucht *et al.* (2012) involved nearly 6,000 patients; 64% of patients who had been given the placebo had relapsed, compared to 27% of those who stayed on the antipsychotic drug. Work out how many patients had relapsed in both conditions. (1 mark)
5. Place the data for this study in a 2 x 1 contingency table. (2 marks)
6. Identify which statistical test would be suitable to use with this data and explain your choice. (3 marks)
7. Write a suitable hypothesis for this study. (2 marks)

LINK TO RESEARCH METHODS

Inferential tests on pages 24–32. The other topics in these questions are covered in the research methods chapter of our Year 1 book.

KEY TERMS

Atypical antipsychotics carry a lower risk of extrapyramidal side effects, have a beneficial effect on negative symptoms and cognitive impairment, and are suitable for treatment-resistant patients.

Drug therapy involves treatment of mental disorders such as schizophrenia through the use of antipsychotics to reduce the symptoms of the disorder.

Typical antipsychotics are dopamine *antagonists* in that they bind to but do not stimulate dopamine receptors and so reduce the symptoms of schizophrenia.

CAN YOU?   No. 6.5

1. Explain what is meant by *typical* and *atypical* antipsychotics. (3 marks each)
2. Outline the nature of typical and atypical antipsychotics in the treatment of schizophrenia. (4 marks each)
3. Briefly evaluate typical and atypical antipsychotics in the treatment of schizophrenia. (6 marks)
4. Outline and evaluate drug therapies in the treatment of schizophrenia. (16 marks)

Cognitive behavioural therapy

NICE (The National Institute for Health and Care Excellence) recommend that all people with schizophrenia should be offered **cognitive behavioural therapy**. This form of therapy is referred to as CBTp (cognitive behavioural therapy for psychosis) when used in the treatment of schizophrenia. CBTp in schizophrenia was originally developed to provide treatment for residual symptoms that persist despite the use of antipsychotic medication. Treatment with antipsychotic drugs still leaves many psychotic patients with persistent positive and negative symptoms – hence the introduction of CBTp to deal with these symptoms and to improve patients' functioning generally.

Insider tip…
In a six-mark exam answer, not every stage outlined here is required in a description of how CBTp works – just enough to give a flavour of what goes on in this form of therapy.

How does it work?

CBTp usually proceeds through the following phases:

Assessment – the patient expresses his or her thoughts about their experiences to the therapist. Realistic goals for therapy are discussed, using the patient's current distress as motivation for change.

Engagement – the therapist empathises with the patient's perspective and their feelings of distress, and stresses that explanations for their distress can be developed together.

The ABC model – the patient gives their explanation of the activating events (A) that appear to cause their emotional and behavioural (B) consequences (C). The patient's own beliefs, which are actually the cause of C, can then be rationalised, disputed and changed. For example, the belief that 'People won't like me if I tell them about my voices' might be changed to a more healthy belief e.g. 'Some may, some may not. Friends may find it interesting.'

Normalisation – information that many people have unusual experiences such as hallucinations and delusions under many different circumstances (e.g. in situations of extreme stress) reduces anxiety and the sense of isolation. By placing psychotic experiences on a continuum with normal experiences, the patient feels less alienated and stigmatised, and the possibility of recovery seems more likely.

Critical collaborative analysis – the therapist uses gentle questioning to help the patient understand illogical deductions and conclusions. For example, 'If your voices are real, why can't other people hear them?' Questioning can be carried out without causing distress, provided there is an atmosphere of trust between the patient and the therapist, who remains empathetic and non-judgemental.

Developing alternative explanations – the patient develops their own alternative explanations for their previously unhealthy assumptions. These healthier explanations might have been temporarily weakened by their dysfunctional thinking patterns. If the patient is not forthcoming with alternative explanations, new ideas can be constructed in cooperation with the therapist.

COGNITIVE BEHAVIOURAL THERAPY FOR PSYCHOSIS (CBTp)

The basic assumption of CBTp is that people often have distorted beliefs, which influence their feelings and behaviours in maladaptive ways. For example, someone with schizophrenia may believe that their behaviour is being controlled by someone or something else. Delusions are thought to result from faulty interpretations of events, and CBTp is used to help the patient identify and correct these faulty interpretations. CBTp can be delivered in groups, but it is more usual that it is delivered on a one-to-one basis. NICE recommend at least 16 sessions when used in the treatment of schizophrenia. The aim of CBTp when used in this context is to help people establish links between their thoughts, feelings or actions and their symptoms and general level of functioning. By monitoring their thoughts, feelings or behaviours with respect to their symptoms, patients are better able to consider alternative ways of explaining why they feel and behave in the way that they do. This reduces distress and so improves functioning.

The nature of CBTp

In CBTp, patients are encouraged to trace back the origins of their symptoms in order to get a better idea of how they might have developed. They are also encouraged to evaluate the content of their delusions or of any voices, and to consider ways in which they might test the validity of their faulty beliefs. Patients might also be set behavioural assignments so that they might improve their general level of functioning. The learning of maladaptive responses to life's problems is often the result of distorted thinking by the schizophrenic or mistakes in assessing cause and effect (for example, assuming that something terrible has happened because they wished it). During CBTp, the therapist lets the patient develop their own alternatives to these previous maladaptive beliefs, ideally by looking for alternative explanations and coping strategies that are already present in the patient's mind.

▲ CBTp proceeds through a series of phases, culminating with the development of alternative explanations to replace previously unhealthy assumptions.

EVALUATION

Advantages of CBTp over standard care

The NICE review of treatments for schizophrenia (NICE, 2014) found consistent evidence that, when compared with standard care (antipsychotic medication alone), CBTp was effective in reducing rehospitalisation rates up to 18 months following the end of treatment. CBTp was also shown to be effective in reducing symptom severity and, when compared with patients receiving standard care, there was some evidence for improvements in social functioning. However, most studies of the effectiveness of CBTp have been conducted with patients treated at the same time with antipsychotic medication. It is difficult, therefore, to assess the effectiveness of CBTp independent of antipsychotic medication.

Effectiveness of CBTp is dependent on stage of the disorder

CBTp appears to be more effective when it is made available at specific stages of the disorder and when the delivery of the treatment is adjusted to the stage the individual is currently at. For example, Addington and Addington (2005) claim that, in the initial acute phase of schizophrenia, self-reflection is not particularly appropriate. Following stabilisation of the psychotic symptoms with antipsychotic medication, however, individuals can benefit more from group-based CBTp. This can help normalise their experience by meeting other individuals with similar issues. Research has consistently shown that it is individuals with more experience of their schizophrenia and a greater realisation of their problems that benefit more from individual CBTp.

Lack of availability of CBTp

Despite being recommended by NICE as a treatment for people with schizophrenia, it is estimated that in the UK only 1 in 10 of those who could benefit get access to this form of therapy. This figure is even lower in some areas of the country. A survey carried out by Haddock et al. (2013) in the North West of England found that of 187 randomly selected patients diagnosed with schizophrenia, only 13 (6.9%) had been offered CBTp. Of those who are offered CBTp as a treatment for schizophrenia, a significant number either refuse or fail to attend the therapy sessions (Freeman et al., 2013), thus limiting its effectiveness even more.

Problems with meta-analyses of CBTp as a treatment for schizophrenia

One reason why meta-analyses in this area can reach unreliable conclusions about CBTp effectiveness is failure to take into account study quality. Some studies fail to randomly allocate participants to either a CBTp or control condition; others fail to mask the treatment condition for interviewers carrying out subsequent assessments of symptoms and general functioning. Nevertheless, despite such differences and failing, all such studies are grouped together for a meta-analysis. Jüni et al. (2001) concluded that there was clear evidence that the problems associated with methodologically weak trials translated into biased findings about the effectiveness of CBTp. In fact, Wykes et al. (2008) actually found that the more rigorous the study, the weaker the effect of CBTp.

The benefits of CBTp may have been overstated

More recent and methodologically sound meta-analyses of the effectiveness of CBTp as a sole treatment for schizophrenia suggest that its effectiveness may actually be lower than originally thought. One recent large-scale meta-analysis (Jauhar et al., 2014) revealed only a 'small' therapeutic effect on the key symptoms of schizophrenia, such as hallucinations and delusions. However, even these small effects disappeared when symptoms were assessed 'blind' (i.e. when assessors were unaware of whether the patient was in the therapy or control condition). Many studies of the effectiveness of CBTp appear to have similar design problems and, in their meta-analysis, this uncertainty over whether non-drug therapies such as CBTp really do offer superior outcomes to antipsychotic medication has led to conflicting recommendations even within the UK (Taylor and Perera, 2015). In England and Wales, NICE (2014) emphasise non-drug therapies such as CBTp, whereas in Scotland, SIGN (2013) places more emphasis on antipsychotic medications.

▲ Guideline writers in the UK give conflicting advice regarding the care of people with schizophrenia.

UPGRADE

Outline how cognitive behavioural therapy is used in the treatment of schizophrenia. (6 marks)

It is wise to read all questions very carefully. For example, there are several ways in which an examiner might probe your understanding of CBT as a treatment of schizophrenia. One way is simply to ask you to 'outline' CBT as a treatment of schizophrenia. This rather general question invites a general answer, so content about the nature of CBT as well as how it works in practice would be perfectly appropriate *provided* it was focused specifically on the treatment of schizophrenia. However, questions such as the one above make a subtle but quite specific requirement, as shown by the use of the word 'how' in the question. Here you are required to describe, in practical terms, how the technique of CBT is put into practice, i.e. what typically goes on during therapy. There is no need to include all the different phases of CBT treatment given on the opposite page – just give an overview of this technique. For a 6-mark question this would mean about 150 words. So, be prepared and have your 150-word account ready for this question and also for other therapies used in the treatment of schizophrenia. Be flexible though, and also have a 100-word version ready for a possible 4-mark question.

KEY TERMS

Cognitive behavioural therapy A combination of cognitive therapy (a way of changing maladaptive thoughts and beliefs) and behavioural therapy (a way of changing behaviour in response to these thoughts and beliefs).

CAN YOU? No. 6.6

1. Outline how cognitive behavioural therapy is used in the treatment of schizophrenia. (6 marks)
2. Give **two** criticisms of cognitive behavioural therapy as used in the treatment of schizophrenia. (3 marks each)
3. Evaluate the use of cognitive behavioural therapy as used in the treatment of schizophrenia, making reference to one other method of treatment. (6 marks)
4. Outline and evaluate cognitive behavioural therapy as used in the treatment of schizophrenia. (16 marks)

Family therapy

Families can play an important role in helping a person with schizophrenia to recover and stay well. Family intervention in the treatment of schizophrenia has developed as a result of studies of the family environment and its possible role in affecting the course of schizophrenia. Research has consistently shown that the long-term outcome for an individual with schizophrenia has much to do with the relationship between the individual and those who care for them. Poor relationships tend to result in poor outcomes, i.e. a greater chance of relapse (i.e. increased symptoms). The main aim of family therapy, therefore, is to provide support for carers in an attempt to make family life less stressful and so reduce re-hospitalisation.

Family 'therapy' and family 'intervention' are the same thing when used in this context. NICE (The National Institute for Health and Care Excellence) refer to 'family intervention' in their guidelines, whereas AQA use the term 'family therapy'. We have used the latter term so to be consistent with AQA terminology.

How does it work?

By reducing levels of expressed emotion and stress, and by increasing the capacity of relatives to solve related problems, family therapy attempts to reduce the incidence of relapse for the person with schizophrenia.

Family therapy makes use of a number of strategies, including:

- Psychoeducation – helping the person and their carers to understand and be better able to deal with the illness.
- Forming an alliance with relatives who care for the person with schizophrenia.
- Reducing the emotional climate within the family and the burden of care for family members.
- Enhancing relatives' ability to anticipate and solve problems.
- Reducing expressions of anger and guilt by family members.
- Maintaining reasonable expectations among family members for patient performance.
- Encouraging relatives to set appropriate limits whilst maintaining some degree of separation when needed.

Family therapy forms part of an overall treatment package and is commonly used in conjunction with routine drug treatment and outpatient clinical care. During family therapy sessions, the individual with schizophrenia is encouraged to talk to their family and explain what sort of support they find helpful – and what makes things worse for them.

A randomised controlled trial (RCT) is a study in which people are randomly allocated to two (or more) groups to test a specific drug or treatment. One group receives the treatment being tested; the other receives an alternative treatment, a dummy treatment (placebo) or no treatment at all.

FAMILY THERAPY

Family therapy is the name given to a range of interventions aimed at the family (e.g. parents, siblings, partners) of someone with schizophrenia. In their guidance on the treatment and management of schizophrenia, NICE recommend that family therapy should be offered to 'all individuals diagnosed with schizophrenia who are in contact with or live with family members'. They also stress that such interventions should be considered a priority where there are persistent symptoms or a high risk of relapse. Research has shown that schizophrenics in families that expressed high levels of criticism, hostility or over-involvement had more frequent relapses than people with the same problems who lived in families that were less expressive in their emotions.

▲ NICE recommend that family therapy should be offered to 'all individuals diagnosed with schizophrenia who are in contact with or live with family members'.

The nature of family therapy

Family therapy is typically offered for a period of between 3 and 12 months and at least ten sessions. Family-based interventions are aimed at reducing the level of expressed emotion (see page 144) within the family, as expressed emotion has been demonstrated to increase the likelihood of relapse. Garety *et al.* (2008) estimate the relapse rate for individuals who receive family therapy as 25% compared to 50% for those who receive standard care alone.

Family therapy typically involves providing family members with information about schizophrenia, finding ways of supporting an individual with schizophrenia and resolving any practical problems. It should also involve the person with psychosis or schizophrenia if practical. A characteristic of psychoses such as schizophrenia is that individuals are often suspicious about their treatment. Involving the individual more actively in their treatment overcomes this problem. Family therapy improves relationships within the household because the therapist encourages family members to listen to each other and openly discuss problems and negotiate potential solutions together.

Key study: Pharoah *et al.* (2010)

Procedure Pharoah *et al.* (2010) reviewed 53 studies published between 2002 and 2010 to investigate the effectiveness of family intervention. Studies chosen were conducted in Europe, Asia and North America. The studies compared outcomes from family therapy to 'standard' care (i.e. antipsychotic medication) alone. The researchers concentrated on studies that were randomised controlled trials (RCTs).

Findings The main results (individuals receiving family therapy compared to those receiving standard care) were:

- **Mental state** – The overall impression was mixed. Some studies reported an improvement in the overall mental state of patients compared to those receiving standard care, whereas others did not.
- **Compliance with medication** – The use of family intervention increased patients' compliance with medication.
- **Social functioning** – Although appearing to show some improvement on general functioning, family intervention did not appear to have much of an effect on more concrete outcomes such as living independently or employment.
- **Reduction in relapse and readmission** – There was a reduction in the risk of relapse and a reduction in hospital admission during treatment and in the 24 months after.

Why is family therapy effective?

The Pharoah *et al.* (2010) meta-analysis (see previous page) established that family therapy can be effective in improving clinical outcomes such as mental state and social functioning. However, the authors suggest that the main reason for its effectiveness may have less to do with any improvements in these clinical markers and more to do with the fact that it increases medication compliance. Patients are more likely to reap the benefits of medication because they are more likely to comply with their medication regime.

Methodological limitations of family therapy studies

The Pharoah *et al.* meta-analysis described on the previous page also identified a number of methodological issues in the studies reviewed.

- **The problem of random allocation** – Although all 53 studies claimed to have randomly allocated participants to treatment conditions, the researchers note that a large number of studies used in this review were from the People's Republic of China. Evidence has emerged that, in many Chinese studies, random allocation had been stated as having been used, yet was not (Wu *et al.*, 2006).
- **Lack of blinding** – There was the possibility of observer bias where raters were not 'blinded' to the condition (i.e. family intervention or standard care) to which people were allocated. Ten studies reported that no form of blinding was used. A further 16 did not mention whether blinding had been used.

Economic benefits of family therapy

An additional advantage of family therapy is that it has considerable economic benefits associated with the treatment of schizophrenia. The NICE review of family therapy studies (NCCMH, 2009) demonstrated that family therapy is associated with significant cost savings when offered to people with schizophrenia in addition to standard care. The extra cost of family therapy is offset by a reduction in costs of hospitalisation because of the lower relapse rates associated with this form of intervention. There is also evidence that family therapy reduces relapse rates for a significant period after completion of the intervention. This means that the cost savings associated with family therapy would be even higher.

Impact on family members

Family therapy has been shown to improve outcomes for the individual with schizophrenia, but there may be an additional advantage in that they can have a positive impact on family members as well. Lobban *et al.* (2013) analysed the results of 50 family therapy studies that had included an intervention to support relatives. Sixty per cent of these studies reported a significant positive impact of the intervention on at least one outcome category for relatives, e.g. coping and problem-solving skills, family functioning and relationship quality (including expressed emotion). However, the researchers also concluded that the methodological quality of the studies was generally poor, making it difficult to distinguish effective from ineffective interventions.

▲ Family interventions have the additional advantage of having a positive impact on family functioning and the coping skills of family members.

Is family therapy worthwhile?

A study by Garety *et al.* (2008) failed to show any better outcomes for patients given sessions of family therapy compared to those who simply had carers but no family therapy. Individuals in both groups were found to have unexpectedly low rates of relapse, contrasting markedly with the rates found in the 'no carer' group. The researchers found that most of the carers in this study displayed relatively low rates of expressed emotion, which may reflect widespread cultural changes in carers' knowledge and attitudes of schizophrenia. Garety *et al.* suggest that, for many people, family intervention may not improve outcomes further than a good standard of treatment as usual.

Insider tip…

Remember, in order to make your evaluation maximally effective, you need to shape how you use your material, e.g. using the three-point rule or the PEEL technique (see page 75).

Research methods

A meta-analysis by Pharoah *et al.* is described on this spread. One of the studies in this meta-analysis (Bradley *et al.*, 2006) compared relapse rates for patients receiving family therapy with a control group who did not receive family therapy (all groups had a family member with schizophrenia).

1. Explain why this study would be described as a natural experiment. (2 marks)
2. Explain how participants might be randomly allocated to the experimental and control groups. (2 marks)
3. Explain why random allocation is used. (2 marks)
4. Discuss ethical issues related to assigning patients to a family therapy group or a control group. (4 marks)
5. Relapse rates in this study were assessed using the *Scale for the Assessment of Negative Symptoms* (SANS). Explain how both the reliability and the validity of this scale might be assessed. (2 marks + 2 marks)
6. The relapse rates after 18 months were 25% for the family therapy group and 63% for the control group. In total the study involved 59 family groups. Estimate how many individuals relapsed in the therapy group after 18 months. (2 marks)

LINK TO RESEARCH METHODS

See reliability on page 16.
See validity on page 18.
The other topics in these questions are covered in the research methods chapter of our Year 1 book.

KEY TERMS

Family therapy is the name given to a range of interventions aimed at the family (e.g. parents, siblings, partners) of someone with a mental disorder.

CAN YOU? No. 6.7

1. Outline family therapy as used in the treatment of schizophrenia. (4 marks)
2. Give **two** criticisms of family therapy as used in the treatment of schizophrenia. (3 marks each)
3. Evaluate the use of family therapy as used in the treatment of schizophrenia, making reference to one other method of treatment. (6 marks)
4. Outline and evaluate family therapy as used in the treatment of schizophrenia. (16 marks)

Token economy and the management of schizophrenia

As we saw on page 139, some people with schizophrenia suffer from negative symptoms, including apathy and social withdrawal. As a result of experiencing these symptoms, these individuals lack interest in those aspects of a normal healthy life such as washing, eating and maintaining their physical appearance. Research has looked at ways of decreasing these negative symptoms and encouraging such individuals to take part in more positive and adaptive behaviours. The use of a **token economy** system, based on the principles of operant conditioning, was developed as a way of dealing with these negative symptoms and encouraging more positive behaviours.

The token economy was widely used in the management of schizophrenia in the 1960s and 1970s, although nowadays this form of treatment has been replaced by other forms of intervention such as social and life skills training.

How does it work?

The behavioural principles employed in token systems are based mainly on the theory of operant conditioning. The principles of operant conditioning describe the relationship between a behaviour and environmental events. Key within this relationship is the idea of positive reinforcement, i.e. an increase in the frequency of a particular behaviour when it is followed by a desirable event.

There are two types of positive reinforcer:
- Primary reinforcers are anything that give pleasure (e.g. food or comfort) or remove unpleasant states (e.g. that alleviate boredom). Primary reinforcers do not depend on learning in order to acquire their reinforcing value.
- Secondary reinforcers initially have no value to the individual, but acquire their reinforcing properties as a result of being paired with primary reinforcers. In a token economy, the tokens given out when a patient engages in a target behaviour (e.g. taking care over their personal appearance or helping tidy up after a meal) are secondary reinforcers.

To be maximally effective, a reinforcer needs to be delivered immediately after the performance of the target behaviour. If the token does not follow immediately, then another behaviour (e.g. arguing with a fellow patient) may have been performed in the intervening period. It would then be this behaviour that is reinforced, not the target behaviour.

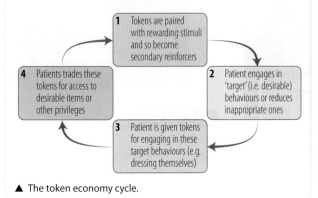

1 Tokens are paired with rewarding stimuli and so become secondary reinforcers

2 Patient engages in 'target' (i.e. desirable) behaviours or reduces inappropriate ones

3 Patient is given tokens for engaging in these target behaviours (e.g. dressing themselves)

4 Patients trades these tokens for access to desirable items or other privileges

▲ The token economy cycle.

The term 'positive reinforcer' is used instead of 'reward' because of a subtle difference between the two terms. A positive reinforcer is defined in terms of its effect on behaviour. Anything that increases the behaviour that it follows is referred to as a positive reinforcer. Rewards, on the other hand, although they may be highly desirable, do not necessarily increase the probability of the behaviour they follow.

THE TOKEN ECONOMY

A token economy is a form of behavioural therapy where clinicians set target behaviours that they believe will improve the patient's engagement in daily activities. These target behaviours might be something as simple as the patient brushing their hair or dressing themselves, or a more socially oriented behaviour such as persevering at a task or helping another patient. Tokens are awarded whenever the patient engages in one of the target behaviours, and these tokens can later be exchanged for various rewards and privileges. The idea behind the token economy is that the patient will engage more often with desirable behaviours because the behaviours become associated with these rewards and privileges.

For example, Ayllon and Azrin (1968) used a token economy on a ward of female schizophrenic patients, many of whom had been hospitalised for many years. They were given plastic tokens, each embossed with the words 'one gift' for behaviours such as making their bed or carrying out domestic chores. These tokens were then exchanged for privileges such as being able to watch a movie. The researchers found that the use of a token economy with these patients increased dramatically the number of desirable behaviours that the patients performed each day.

Assigning value to the tokens

To give the neutral token some 'value', it needs to first be repeatedly presented alongside or immediately before the reinforcing stimulus (e.g. watching a movie). The reinforcing stimulus may take the form of food, privileges or other incentives. By pairing the neutral tokens with the reinforcing stimulus, the neutral token eventually acquires the same reinforcing properties. As a result of this process of classical conditioning, these neutral tokens become secondary reinforcers, and so can be used to modify behaviour.

Reinforcing target behaviours

When patients perform the desirable target behaviours, the clinician awards them tokens. When a token can be exchanged for a variety of different privileges and rewards, it is referred to as a *generalised* reinforcer. The more items or rewards that the token can be exchanged for, the more powerful that token becomes. Sran and Borrero (2010) compared behaviours reinforced by tokens that could be exchanged for one single highly preferred edible item with tokens which could be exchanged for a *variety* of preferred edible items. They found that all participants had higher rates of responding in those sessions where tokens could be exchanged for a variety of items.

The 'trade'

An important part of the token economy is the exchange of tokens for backup rewards chosen by the clinician. These rewards may include food, sweets or other privileges such as being able to watch a movie. During the early stages of the token economy, frequent exchange periods mean that patients can be quickly reinforced and target behaviours can then increase in frequency. The effectiveness of the token economy may decrease if more time passes between presentation of the token and exchange for the backup reinforcers (Kazdin, 1977).

Research support

Dickerson *et al.* (2005) have provided research support for the effectiveness of token economies in a psychiatric setting. They reviewed 13 studies of the use of token economy systems in the treatment of schizophrenia. Eleven of these studies had reported beneficial effects that were directly attributable to the use of token economies. Dickerson *et al.* concluded that, overall, these studies provide evidence of the token economy's effectiveness in increasing the adaptive behaviours of patients with schizophrenia. However, they did caution that many of the studies reviewed had significant methodological shortcomings that limited their impact in the overall assessment of token economies in this context.

Difficulties assessing the success of a token economy

Comer (2013) suggests that a major problem in assessing the effectiveness of token economies is that studies of their use tend to be uncontrolled. When a token economy system is introduced into a psychiatric ward, typically all patients are brought into the programme rather than having an experimental group that goes through the token economy programme and a control group that does not. As a result, patients' improvements can only be compared with their past behaviours rather than a control group. This comparison, claims Comer, may be misleading, as other factors (e.g. an increase in staff attention) could be causing patients' improvement rather than the token economy

Less useful for patients living in the community

Although the token economy has shown to be effective in reducing negative symptoms for people with schizophrenia, it has only really been shown to work when in a hospital setting. Corrigan (1991) argues that there are problems administrating the token economy method with outpatients who live in the community. Within a psychiatric ward setting, inpatients receive 24-hour care and so there is better control for staff to monitor and reward patients appropriately. However, outpatients living in the community only receive day treatment for a few hours a day, so therefore the token method could only be used for part of the day. As a result, even if the token economy did produce positive results within the ward setting, these results may not be maintained beyond that environment.

Ethical concerns

There are a number of ethical concerns concerning the use of token economy programmes in psychiatric settings. For example, in order to make reinforcement effective, clinicians may exercise control over important primary reinforcers such as food, privacy or access to activities that alleviate boredom. Patients may then exchange tokens if they display the target behaviours (e.g. domestic duties or better personal hygiene). However, it is generally accepted that all human beings have certain basic rights (to food, privacy, etc.) that cannot be violated regardless of the positive consequences that might be achieved by manipulating them within a token economy programme.

▲ The token economy is more difficult to administrate when patients are living in the community.

Does it actually work?

Surprisingly, perhaps, researchers are yet to conclusively provide an answer to this question. Very few randomised trials have been carried out to support the claims made for the effectiveness of token economies in the management of schizophrenia. In an era of evidence-based medicine, this lack of support is considered unacceptable and so token economy programmes have fallen out of use in much of the developed world. McMonagle and Sultana (2000) suggest, however, that the token economy may still be a potentially important treatment if such randomised trials could be carried out. They suggest that this is only likely to be possible in those developing countries where some form of token economy is still practised. This would provide an opportunity to finally answer questions about the effects of the token economy in the management of people with schizophrenia.

MEET THE RESEARCHER

Nathan Azrin (1930–2013)
In 1968 Dr Nathan (Nate) Azrin and his colleague Teodoro (Ted) Ayllon introduced a new system of managing female schizophrenics at Anna State Hospital, Illinois. Patients could earn tokens for dressing themselves, doing chores and so on. Before they introduced the new system, some patients wore their undergarments over their clothing, but by awarding tokens for dressing properly, these patients soon corrected their mistakes. Despite all the complicated rationales for the technique, Azrin believed behaviour modification was actually quite easy to achieve. In fact, Azrin received far more attention for a book he wrote in 1974 with Richard Foxx, applying token economics to toilet training. Their book, *Toilet Training in Less Than a Day* sold more than three million copies.

KEY TERMS

Token economy A form of therapy where desirable behaviours are encouraged by the use of selective reinforcements. Rewards (tokens) are given as secondary reinforcers when individuals engage in correct/socially desirable behaviours. The tokens can then be exchanged for primary reinforcers – food or privileges

🐾 **APPLY YOUR KNOWLEDGE**

Annie is a clinical psychologist who is asked to talk to staff at a local psychiatric unit about setting up a token economy in one of the wards. It is a ward of eight female patients between the ages of 30 and 45. These women have been on antipsychotic medication for an average of 12 years and display a variety of negative symptoms including speech poverty and avolition.

Outline what advice Annie might give to staff in the unit about setting up a token economy to address these two particular symptoms.

CAN YOU? No. 6.8

1. Explain what is meant by the term *token economy*. (2 marks)
2. Briefly outline how token economies are used in the management of schizophrenia and explain **one** limitation of using token economies to manage schizophrenia. (4 marks)
3. Discuss token economies as used in the management of schizophrenia. (16 marks)

An interactionist approach

As we have seen on previous spreads, there are a number of different theories about the onset and course of schizophrenia. The **diathesis-stress model** is a slightly different type of explanation in that it proposes that schizophrenia is the result of a *combination* of psychological/environmental and biological/genetic influences. According to this model, the symptoms of schizophrenia are triggered or made worse when significant stressors (the 'stress') in the person's life are combined with a biological vulnerability (the 'diathesis') to the disorder. This model might, therefore, explain why not all people who have a genetic vulnerability to schizophrenia go on to develop the disorder.

▲ In adoptees with high genetic risk of schizophrenia, adoptive-family stress was a significant predictor of the development of schizophrenia.

THE DIATHESIS-STRESS MODEL

The diathesis-stress model sees schizophrenia as the result of an *interaction* between biological (the diathesis) and environmental (stress) influences. Family studies suggest that people have varying levels of inherited genetic vulnerability to schizophrenia, from very low to very high. However, whether or not the person develops schizophrenia is partly determined by this vulnerability and also partly by the amount and level of stresses they experience over their lifetime.

Diathesis

We have seen (on page 142) that schizophrenia has a genetic component in terms of vulnerability. What supports the idea of a genetic role for schizophrenia are the findings that the identical twin of a person with schizophrenia is at greater risk of developing schizophrenia than a sibling or fraternal twin, and that adoptive relatives do not share the increased risk of biological relatives (Tienari *et al.*, 2004). However, in about 50% of identical twins in which one twin is diagnosed with schizophrenia, the other never meets the diagnostic criteria for the disorder. This discordance among identical twins indicates that environmental factors must also play a role in determining whether a biological vulnerability for schizophrenia actually develops into the disorder.

Stress

The sort of stressful life events that can trigger schizophrenia take a variety of forms such as childhood trauma or the stresses associated with living in a highly urbanised environment. For example, Varese *et al.* (2012) found that children who experienced severe trauma before the age of 16 were three times as likely to develop schizophrenia in later life compared to the general population. There was a relationship between the level of trauma and the likelihood of developing schizophrenia, with those severely traumatised as children being at greater risk.

Research has also suggested that a high level of urbanisation is associated with increased risk of developing a range of different psychoses, including schizophrenia. A meta-analysis by Vassos *et al.* (2012) found that the risk for schizophrenia in the most urban environments was estimated to be 2.37 times higher than in the most rural environments. The reason why urbanisation and schizophrenia are linked is not clear, although it is possible that the more adverse living conditions of densely populated urban environments may be a contributory factor. Many people live in densely populated urban areas, but only a tiny minority of these will develop schizophrenia. The relationship between urban stress and schizophrenia is conditional on some other factor, i.e. a pre-existing genetic risk for the disorder or some other biological vulnerability for schizophrenia.

The additive nature of diathesis and stress

There are several ways in which a combination of diathesis and stress can lead to the onset of schizophrenia. For example, relatively minor stressors may lead to the onset of the disorder for an individual who is highly vulnerable, or a major stressful event might cause a similar reaction in a person low in vulnerability. Whatever the combination, this idea pre-supposes additivity, i.e. that diathesis and stress add together in some way to produce the disorder.

Key study: Tienari *et al.* (2004)

This study tested the hypothesis that genetic factors moderate susceptibility to environmental risks associated with adoptive family functioning.

Procedure Hospital records were reviewed for nearly 20,000 women admitted to Finnish psychiatric hospitals between 1960 and 1979, identifying those who had been diagnosed at least once with schizophrenic or paranoid psychoses. The list was checked to find those mothers who had one or more of their offspring adopted away. The resulting sample of 145 adopted-away offspring (the high-risk group) was then matched with a sample of 158 adoptees without this genetic risk (the low-risk group).

Both groups of adoptees were independently assessed after a median interval of 12 years, with a follow-up after 21 years. Psychiatrists also assessed family functioning in the adoptive families using the OPAS (in English this translates to the 'Oulu Family Rating Scale'). This scale measures families on various aspects of functioning such as parent-offspring conflict, lack of empathy and insecurity. The interviewing psychiatrists were kept blind as to the status of the biological mother (i.e. schizophrenia or no schizophrenia).

Findings Of the 303 adoptees, 14 had developed schizophrenia over the course of the study. Of these 14, 11 were from the high-risk group (i.e. those with mothers previously diagnosed with schizophrenia or paranoid psychoses) and 3 were from the low-risk group (i.e. the control group adoptees). However, being reared in a 'healthy' adoptive family (low OPAS ratings) appeared to have a protective effect even for those at high genetic risk for schizophrenia. High-genetic-risk adoptees reared in families with low OPAS ratings were significantly *less* likely to have developed schizophrenia than high-genetic-risk adoptees reared in families with high OPAS ratings. In adoptees at high genetic risk of schizophrenia, but not in those at low genetic risk, adoptive-family stress was a significant predictor of the development of schizophrenia.

Diatheses may not be exclusively genetic

Most diathesis-stress models emphasise 'vulnerability' in terms of genetic influences alone, which are assumed to cause neurochemical abnormalities that, in turn, result in an increased risk for schizophrenia. However, this increased risk can also result from brain damage caused by *environmental* factors. For example, individuals may also develop a vulnerability to schizophrenia if they experience birth complications. Verdoux *et al.* (1998) estimated that the risk of developing schizophrenia later in life for individuals who have experienced obstetric complications at birth (e.g. prolonged labour which can cause oxygen deprivation) is four times greater than those who experience no such complications.

Urban environments are not necessarily more stressful

The Vassos *et al.* study on the previous page suggested that living in densely populated urban environments was a significant stress factor for schizophrenia. However, not all research has agreed with this finding. For example, Romans-Clarkson *et al.* (1990) found no urban–rural differences in mental health among women in New Zealand. Other studies (e.g. Paykel *et al.*, 2000), although finding evidence of urban–rural differences, also noted that these differences disappeared after adjusting for the socioeconomic differences for the two groups. This suggests that, although social adversity may well be a significant trigger for the onset of schizophrenia, claims that social adversity and urbanisation are synonymous is likely to be an over-simplification.

▲ Research is inconclusive about whether living in an urban environment is a significant stressor in the onset of schizophrenia.

Difficulties in determining causal stress

Typically, diathesis-stress models make reference to stressful events that occur close to the onset of schizophrenia. However, it is possible that stressors *earlier* in life can also influence how people respond to later stressful events and increase their future susceptibility to the disorder. For example, Hammen (1992) argues that maladaptive methods of coping with stress in childhood and throughout development means that the individual fails to develop effective coping skills, which in turn compromises their resilience and increases vulnerability. Ineffective coping skills may, therefore, make life generally more stressful for the individual and so trigger mental illness.

Limitations of the Tienari *et al.* study

Researchers in the Tienari *et al.* study identified a number of limitations of their study, particularly in the assessment of adoptive family functioning. For example, when psychiatrists assessed stress in the adoptive family using the OPAS scale, they were assessing family functioning only at one given point in time. Tienari *et al.* acknowledged that this fails to reflect developmental changes in family functioning over time. They also acknowledge that observing *reciprocal* interactions between the adoptive family and the adoptees makes it impossible to determine how much of the stress observed is assigned to the family and how much is actually caused by the adoptee him or herself.

Implications for treatment

If the onset of schizophrenia is a result of the additive effect of genetic vulnerability and environmental stress, then this has implications for the treatment of the disorder. Although genetic vulnerability is, as yet, difficult to control, certain other important factors known to interact with genetic vulnerability can be addressed with current knowledge. For example, Børglum *et al.* (2014) found that women infected with cytomegalovirus during pregnancy were more likely to have a child who developed schizophrenia, but only if both mother *and* child carried a particular gene defect. This suggests that anti-viral medicine during pregnancy may prevent the onset of schizophrenia in the offspring of women known to have this gene defect.

⬆ UPGRADE

In a previous Upgrade feature, we made reference to the fact that, for evaluation to be 'thorough and effective', each AO3 point should be in the region of 60 words. The word 'effective' when used in this context assesses how well you have *used* the material. There is a knack to this, which we have mentioned elsewhere in this book (e.g. page 6). However, this is a point worth repeating here, as getting this right could earn you quite a few extra marks.

Each of the AO3 paragraphs on the right hand side of this spread raises a point of evaluation. Sometimes these are strengths, sometimes limitations and sometimes some other critical point relating to the material. However, there is still work for *you* to do here. If we take the third point as an example ('Difficulties in determining causal stress'), this could be introduced with the phrase '*There are problems in determining the causal diathesis in this model*'. This is then expanded to '*Hammen (1992) suggests stressors earlier in life set up maladaptive coping methods so the person is less able to cope with later stressors*'. This is followed by a final link back to the initial claim '*This suggests that it may not be genetic vulnerability that triggers schizophrenia, but lack of resilience to stress*'.

Diathesis-stress model explains mental disorders as the result of an interaction between biological (the diathesis) and environmental (stress) influences.

Insider tip…
In the specification, 'diathesis-stress' is given as the definitive model representing the 'interactionist approach'. Therefore exam questions may refer to either of these, but the content of your answer would be the same.

CAN YOU? | No. 6.9

1. Explain what is meant by the terms *diathesis* and *stress* as they apply to schizophrenia. (2 marks each)
2. Outline the diathesis-stress model of schizophrenia and give **one** criticism of this model. (6 marks)
3. Outline and evaluate the diathesis-stress model of schizophrenia. (16 marks)

We have identified here the key points of the topics on the AQA A level specification, i.e. the bare minimum that you need to know. You may want to fill in further details to elaborate and personalise this material.

CLASSIFICATION OF SCHIZOPHRENIA

THE NATURE OF SCHIZOPHRENIA
- A severe mental disorder in which thought and emotions are so impaired that contact is lost with external reality.
- Diagnosis made on basis of criteria on DSM-V – requires two or more active symptoms for at least one month.
- Positive symptoms reflect an excess or distortion of normal functions.
- Include hallucinations, delusions, disorganised speech and grossly disorganised or catatonic behaviour.
- Negative symptoms reflect a reduction or loss of normal functions.
- Include speech poverty (alogia), avolition, affective flattening and anhedonia.

BIOLOGICAL EXPLANATIONS FOR SCHIZOPHRENIA

GENETIC FACTORS
- Genetic explanations emphasise the importance of inherited factors in schizophrenia.
- Family studies – schizophrenia more common among biological relatives of a person with the disorder.
- Twin studies – show higher concordance rate for MZ twins than for DZ twins.
- Adoption studies – Tienari et al. found greater link with biological parents than adoptive parents.

NEURAL CORRELATES: THE DOPAMINE HYPOTHESIS
- Dopamine hypothesis claims excess of dopamine causes positive symptoms of schizophrenia.
- Evidence from drugs that increase dopamine (e.g. amphetamines) producing schizophrenic symptoms and drugs that decrease dopamine (antipsychotics) reducing schizophrenic symptoms.
- Revised dopamine hypothesis – includes dopamine underactivity in prefrontal cortex.
- Evidence from neural imaging and animal studies.

EVALUATION
- Genetics – common rearing patterns (e.g. high EE) may explain family similarities rather than genetic factors.
- MZ twins encounter more similar environments which explains higher concordance rates.
- Adoptees may be selectively placed, suggesting that adoptive parents of children at risk of schizophrenia not typical.
- Dopamine hypothesis – evidence from success of antipsychotic treatments that reduce dopamine activity in the brain.
- Inconclusive supporting evidence – e.g. dopamine concentrations in post-mortem tissue have been negative or inconclusive.
- Challenges to the dopamine hypothesis – antipsychotics don't decrease symptoms in everyone and some schizophrenics have normal dopamine levels.

RELIABILITY AND VALIDITY IN DIAGNOSIS AND CLASSIFICATION

RELIABILITY
- Diagnostic reliability means diagnosis must be repeatable (test–retest reliability).
- Different clinicians should reach the same diagnosis.
- Cultural differences in diagnosis (Copeland), experience of voices (Luhrmann et al.) and ethnic differences (Barnes).

VALIDITY
- The extent that a diagnosis represents something that is real and distinct from other disorders.
- Gender bias in diagnosis – tendency to pathologies of one gender rather than another.
- Goldstein and Kreisman – schizophrenic sons more readily seen as 'ill' than schizophrenic daughters, accounting for earlier diagnosis of schizophrenia.
- Symptom overlap – different disorders can share symptoms, making diagnosis difficult.
- Co-morbidity – two or more conditions may co-exist, e.g. 'schizo-OCD' (Swets et al.).

EVALUATION
- Reliability – lack of inter-rater reliability as low as 0.11 (Whaley) and mis-diagnosis of 'pseudopatients' (Rosenhan).
- Unreliable symptoms – psychiatrists found it difficult to agree on what was bizarre and non-bizarre delusion (Mojtabi and Nicholson).
- Culture can have a protective function – ethnic culture hypothesis tested by Brekke and Barrio.
- Validity – research support for gender bias in diagnosis (Loring and Powell) found males more likely to be diagnosed with schizophrenia.
- Consequences of co-morbidity – co-morbid non-psychiatric diagnoses may compromise treatment and prognosis (Weber et al.).
- Differences in prognosis – patients rarely share the same symptoms nor the same prognosis.

PSYCHOLOGICAL EXPLANATIONS FOR SCHIZOPHRENIA

FAMILY DYSFUNCTION
- Double bind theory – conflicting messages within the family prevents coherent construction of reality, giving rise to schizophrenic symptoms.
- Expressed emotion – family communication style likely to influence relapse rates. Suggests lower tolerance for intense environmental stimuli.

COGNITIVE EXPLANATIONS
- Cognitive explanations of delusions – egocentric bias leads person to relate irrelevant events to themselves and arrive at false conclusions.
- Cognitive explanations of hallucinations – hypervigilance leads to greater expectation for stimuli; person likely to attribute these to external sources.

EVALUATION
- Family dysfunction – Tienari et al. found 'disturbed' adoptive families more likely to trigger schizophrenia in children with genetic vulnerability.
- Double bind theory – schizophrenics reported higher recall of double bind statements than non-schizophrenics (Berger), although other studies less conclusive.
- Individual differences in vulnerability to EE – not all schizophrenics respond negatively to high EE. How patients appraise behaviour important.
- Cognitive explanations – supporting evidence for cognitive model: Sarin and Wallin found evidence that positive symptoms arise from faulty processing.
- Support from cognitive therapies – CBT more effective at reducing symptom severity than antipsychotics.
- Integrated model – early vulnerabilities sensitise dopamine system, more dopamine released, biased processing results in paranoia/hallucinations.

DRUG THERAPY

ANTIPSYCHOTICS

- Work by reducing dopaminergic transmission in areas of brain associated with schizophrenia.
- Typical antipsychotics – use to combat positive symptoms. Atypical antipsychotics also claimed to treat negative symptoms.
- Typical antipsychotics are dopamine antagonists – block action of dopamine and so reduce hallucinations and delusions.
- Between 60% and 75% of D_2 receptors must be blocked for drugs to be effective.
- Atypical antipsychotics show rapid dissociation from D_2 receptors, also strong affinity for serotonin receptors.
- Also act as serotonin agonists, leading to increased dopamine release in prefrontal cortex to reduce negative symptoms and cognitive impairment.

EVALUATION

- Typical antipsychotics – antipsychotics more effective than placebo at reducing relapse rates (Leucht et al.).
- Extrapyramidal side effects – typical antipsychotics impact on areas of the brain that control motor activity. Include Parkinsonian symptoms and tardive dyskinesia.
- Ethical problems – cost–benefit analysis may be negative. Also human rights abuse because of side effects.
- Atypical antipsychotics – fewer side effects than typical antipsychotics so more likely to continue with medication.
- Are atypical antipsychotics better than typical? Crossley et al. conclude no difference in efficacy but different side effects.
- Motivational deficits – antipsychotic treatment reinforces 'something wrong' view and reduces motivation to look for other possible causes.

COGNITIVE BEHAVIOURAL THERAPY

COGNITIVE BEHAVIOURAL THERAPY FOR PSYCHOSIS (CBTP)

- Basic assumption is that people have distorted beliefs which need to be changed through therapy.
- CBTp techniques – client encouraged to test validity of their faulty beliefs and set behavioural assignments to improve functioning.
- Therapist helps patient develop alternative explanations to replace maladaptive beliefs.
- How does it work? Through: Assessment; Engagement; ABC model; Normalisation; Critical collaborative analysis; Developing alternative explanations.

EVALUATION

- Advantages of CBTp over standard care – consistent evidence that it reduces hospitalisation rates and symptom severity
- Effectiveness of CBTp is dependent on stage of the disorder – more effective after stabilisation of symptoms with antipsychotic medication
- Lack of availability of CBTp – research (e.g. Haddock et al.) suggests only small proportion of people are offered CBTp
- Problems with meta-analyses of CBTp – they fail to control for study quality, leading to biased findings.
- Benefits of CBTp may have been overstated – as sole treatment may produce only a small beneficial effect (Jauhar et al.)

FAMILY THERAPY

FAMILY THERAPY

- Interventions aimed at the family of someone with schizophrenia.
- Aims to reduce rates of EE within families as EE increases likelihood of relapse.
- Garety et al. estimated relapse rate of 25% for family intervention, 50% for standard care alone.
- Involves providing family members with information about schizophrenia, finding ways to support and resolving practical problems.
- How does it work? Through: Psychoeducation; Forming an alliance with relatives; Reducing emotional climate; Enhancing relatives' problem-solving skills; Reducing expressions of anger and guilt; Maintaining reasonable expectations; Encouraging relatives to set appropriate limits.

KEY STUDY: PHAROAH ET AL. (2010)

- Procedure: 53 studies that had compared family intervention with standard care (antipsychotic medication alone).
- Findings: Strongest effect was on increased compliance with medication. Also reduced relapse and readmission rates, social functioning but mixed results on mental state changes.

EVALUATION

- Why is it effective? May be effective only because it improves compliance with antipsychotic medication.
- Methodological limitations of family therapy studies – not all studies in Pharoah et al. meta-analysis had used randomisation or blinding.
- Economic benefits – extra cost of family intervention is offset by reduction of costs of hospitalisation associated with relapse.
- Impact on family members – Lobban et al. analysed 50 studies and found 60% reported positive impact on relatives.
- Is family intervention worthwhile? Garety et al. found it did not improve outcomes further than that possible with relatives providing a good standard of care.

TOKEN ECONOMY AND THE MANAGEMENT OF SCHIZOPHRENIA

THE TOKEN ECONOMY

- Form of behavioural therapy used in the management of schizophrenia.
- Uses tokens and exchange for rewards to increase target behaviours.
- Ayllon and Azrin increased desirable behaviours on ward of female schizophrenics.
- Tokens are secondary reinforcers exchanged for primary reinforcers.
- Tokens acquire reinforcing abilities through association.
- Generalised secondary reinforcers more powerful.
- Patient trades tokens – timing of reinforcement important.

EVALUATION

- Research support (Dickerson et al.) – 11 of 13 studies reported beneficial effects but some methodological difficulties.
- Limitations of token economies – tend not to involve control group, making it difficult to assess effectiveness.
- Less useful for patients living in the community as difficult to administrate.
- Ethical concerns including infringement of basic human rights.
- Difficult to assess whether it actually works as few randomised trials and no longer front-line treatment in UK.

AN INTERACTIONIST APPROACH

THE DIATHESIS-STRESS MODEL

- Diatheses typically seen as genetic vulnerability to schizophrenia.
- Tienari et al. study showed genetic influence for vulnerable children even when adopted.
- Stressors have additive effect with genetic vulnerability and trigger schizophrenia.
- Example of stressor is living in urban environment (Vassos et al.).
- Whether person develops schizophrenia partly determined by genetic vulnerability, partly by the stressors experienced.

KEY STUDY: TIENARI ET AL. (2004)

- Procedure: Adopted children of mothers with schizophrenia compared with adopted children without this vulnerability.
- Assessed over 21-year period; adoptive family also assessed using OPAS.
- Findings: 14 adoptees developed schizophrenia, 11 from schizophrenic group.
- Healthy adoptive family had protective effect, disturbed family likely to trigger schizophrenia.

EVALUATION

- Diatheses not exclusively genetic, e.g. birth complications also significant (Verdoux et al.).
- Urban environments not necessarily more stressful (e.g. Romans-Clarkson et al. found no difference between urban and rural).
- Difficulties in determining causal stress – Hammen claims stressors earlier in life lead to maladaptive coping methods.
- Limitations of Tienari et al. study – e.g. assessment of adoptive family failed to reflect development changes and to tease out stress caused by family or adoptee.
- Børglum et al. study of cytomegalovirus interacting with defective gene suggests use of anti-viral medicine during pregnancy.

0 1   Which one of the following is a definition of delusions as a symptom of schizophrenia? Write the letter of your chosen answer in your answer booklet.   **[1 mark]**

   A. Blocked thoughts

   B. False beliefs

   C. Lack of interest in surroundings

   D. Perceptions in the absence of sensations

0 2   Distinguish between positive and negative symptoms of schizophrenia.   **[3 marks]**

0 3   Read the item below and then answer the question that follows.

> Veronica has suffered from schizophrenia for many years. She often believes that her family members are plotting against her even though evidence suggests that they are very supportive. She reports that she hears voices that keep telling her that she must escape from home as they are in severe danger. Consequently, Veronica has tried to run away on a number of occasions. However, more recently, she has started to shut herself in her room and has become very withdrawn.

   Outline how schizophrenia is classified. Refer to Veronica's symptoms as part of your answer.   **[4 marks]**

0 4   Outline what is meant by reliability in relation to the diagnosis of schizophrenia.   **[3 marks]**

0 5   Explain how symptom overlap can influence the diagnosis of schizophrenia.   **[3 marks]**

0 6   Briefly discuss how gender **and/or** culture bias affects validity in the diagnosis and classification of schizophrenia.   **[5 marks]**

0 7   *'Schizophrenia is notoriously difficult to diagnose and classify, with some psychologists suggesting that it is not a single disorder at all.'*

   Discuss reliability and validity in the diagnosis and classification of schizophrenia. Refer to the above statement as part of your answer.   **[16 marks]**

0 8   Outline **one** research study that has investigated the role of genetics in schizophrenia.   **[4 marks]**

0 9   Explain **one** limitation of the dopamine hypothesis as an explanation of schizophrenia.   **[3 marks]**

1 0   Briefly discuss the neural correlates explanation of schizophrenia.   **[4 marks]**

1 1   Describe and evaluate **both** genetics **and** the dopamine hypothesis as explanations of schizophrenia.   **[16 marks]**

1 2   Outline the role of dysfunctional thought processing in schizophrenia.   **[2 marks]**

1 3   Outline the findings from **one** research study into the role of family dysfunction in schizophrenia.   **[3 marks]**

1 4   Describe and evaluate cognitive explanations of schizophrenia.   **[16 marks]**

1 5   Discuss psychological explanations of schizophrenia. Refer to **at least one** biological explanation as part of your discussion.   **[16 marks]**

1 7   Explain how typical antipsychotics are different from atypical antipsychotics.   **[3 marks]**

1 8   Outline how **one** research study investigated the use of drug therapy for schizophrenia.   **[3 marks]**

1 9   Discuss the use of **both** drug therapy **and** cognitive behavioural therapy as treatments for schizophrenia.   **[16 marks]**

| 2 | 0 | | Explain **one** limitation of family therapy as a treatment for schizophrenia. | **[3 marks]** |

| 2 | 1 | | Read the item below and answer the question that follows. |

> Stephen has suffered from schizophrenia for many years and currently lives in a psychiatric hospital. He is very withdrawn, and refuses to do simple things such as shower or get himself dressed. When he joins other patients to eat, he often uses his hands rather than using the cutlery because he believes the knives and forks are contaminated.

Using your knowledge of token economies, explain how Stephen's schizophrenia could be managed. **[4 marks]**

| 2 | 2 | | Read the item below and answer the question that follows. |

> Research has shown that when one MZ (identical) twin is diagnosed with schizophrenia, the other twin is later diagnosed with the same disorder in approximately 50% of cases. The remaining 50% may experience other disorders but not schizophrenia.

Using your knowledge of the diathesis-stress model, explain the research findings above. **[4 marks]**

| 2 | 3 | | Discuss the importance of an interactionist approach in explaining and treating schizophrenia. | **[16 marks]** |

| 2 | 4 | | Read the item below and answer the questions that follow. |

> A psychologist wrote a brief case study of an individual who had been diagnosed with schizophrenia. She called the individual Patient X and purposely did not refer to the sex of the patient in her writing. The psychologist then used opportunity sampling to survey people on the streets of her local town. Her participants read the case study at first and then she asked them why they thought Patient X may have developed schizophrenia. When they answered, she noted whether they referred to the patient as a female or male. Her results are detailed below.
>
> | Sex referred to | Female | Male | Neither/both |
> |---|---|---|---|
> | Number of participants | 5 | 34 | 1 |

(i) What percentage of participants referred to the patient as being male? Show your calculations. **[3 marks]**

(ii) Outline **one** limitation of using an opportunity sample in this research study. **[2 marks]**

(iii) Outline **one** ethical issue arising from this research study and explain how it could be dealt with. **[4 marks]**

| 2 | 5 | | Read the item below and answer the questions that follow. |

> A group of psychologists wanted to test the effectiveness of token economies in managing schizophrenia. They selected ten patients, who had recently been admitted to a psychiatric institution, to be their participants. This was done with the consent of the patients' families. The participants were assessed before being on the token economy programme, then after four weeks and finally after ten weeks. The psychologists rated progress in five behaviours that had been identified for each participant.

(i) The psychologists used a repeated measures design.

Explain **one** advantage of using this experimental design in this study. **[3 marks]**

(ii) Briefly explain why patients' families needed to give consent in this study. **[2 marks]**

(iii) Identify the level of data collected in this study. Explain your answer. **[3 marks]**

The exam questions on schizophrenia will be varied but are likely to involve some short answer questions (AO1), some application of knowledge questions (AO2), research methods questions and possibly an extended writing question (AO1 + AO3). We've provided answers to some additional questions together with comments from an examiner about how well they've each done.

---

01 Briefly discuss how gender **and/or** culture bias affects validity in the diagnosis and classification of schizophrenia. (5 marks)

Maisie's answer

Gender bias in the diagnosis of schizophrenia means that many of the behaviours that are considered symptoms of schizophrenia are biased towards males rather than females. As a result, women are often diagnosed as being less psychologically healthy than men. Cultural bias in the diagnosis of schizophrenia is evident in the fact that people are more likely to be diagnosed with schizophrenia in the US than in the UK. This suggests a cultural bias between psychiatrists in the US and the UK, with psychiatrists in the US interpreting the diagnostic criteria differently to psychiatrists in the UK.

Examiner's comments

Maisie's answer shows an understanding of cultural and gender bias in diagnosis of schizophrenia. Cultural bias is dealt with better, with a clear example that supports its occurrence. The description of gender bias is muddled – suggesting a bias in diagnosis against males but then suggesting a bias against females. There is no discussion of the extent or consequence of these biases. Maisie would earn 2 marks for this response.

Ciaran's answer

Broverman et al. (1970) claimed that classification systems like DSM are biased because they are based on one gender more than another. Supporting this claim they showed that psychiatrists in the US equated 'healthy' behaviour with 'male' behaviour so that women were more likely to be diagnosed as being mentally 'unhealthy'. Other research suggests that the diagnosis of schizophrenia is biased against males as their symptoms are less likely to be tolerated by their families and so they are more likely to be referred for diagnosis. Support for this claim comes from Loring and Powell (1988) who found that descriptions of an imaginary patient's symptoms were more likely to lead to a description of 'schizophrenia' if they were labelled as 'male' than if they were labelled as 'female'.

Examiner's comments

Ciaran has decided to just focus on gender bias which can still earn full marks but would require some detail to do so. The answer starts by considering classification in general rather than classification of schizophrenia – meaning the response is not as precise as it could be. However, when Ciaran addresses schizophrenia, he provides two good examples of how bias can occur. Apart from use of evidence, there is no real discussion of the extent or consequence of gender bias. Ciaran's response would earn 3 marks.

---

02 Outline the findings from **one** research study into the role of family dysfunction in schizophrenia. (3 marks)

Maisie's answer

Kuipers et al. (1983) studied expressed emotion. This refers to a way of communicating within a family where family members are very critical and hostile toward the person who has schizophrenia. They found that high levels of expressed emotion made it more likely that the person would relapse.

Examiner's comments

Maisie chooses a relevant study here. The answer earns 2 marks – one for the statement of findings at the end of the response, and one for the explanation of expressed emotion (which helps to make sense of the findings).

Ciaran's answer

In an adoption study by Tienari et al. (1994), they found that adopted children who had schizophrenic biological parents were more likely to develop schizophrenia than those who had non-schizophrenic biological parents. This happened only in specific environmental conditions, i.e. where the adoptive family was dysfunctional.

Examiner's comments

Ciaran's chosen study is not typically associated with family dysfunction but Tienari *et al.* do consider the concept as part of their findings into the diathesis-stress model. Although Ciaran's focus appears to be on genetic factors at first, these are then considered in the context of a dysfunctional adoptive family so meet the demands of the question. Ciaran earns 2 marks – one for each statement of findings. A third mark could have come from a general conclusion.

---

03 Read the item below and answer the question that follows.

> Lester is a 23 year old man who has recently been diagnosed with schizophrenia. His older brother, Wesley, was also diagnosed with the disorder three years ago. Their mother was diagnosed with schizophrenia just a year after Lester was born. Although Wesley and Lester's mother was able to raise her children, their father had to give up work to be home with them too.

Discuss **both** biological **and** psychological explanations of schizophrenia. Refer to Lester and Wesley as part of your answer. (16 marks)

Maisie's answer

Because Lester and Wesley are brothers, they share 50% of their genes with each other. Research has shown that people are more likely to develop schizophrenia if a close genetic relative also has the disorder. For example, if one identical (i.e. MZ) twin develops schizophrenia, there is about a 50% chance that the other twin will also be diagnosed with the disorder. Identical twins share 100% of their genes, whereas siblings share only 50% of their genes, therefore the degree of inheritance (called the concordance rate) is less. Lester and Wesley's mother was also diagnosed with schizophrenia. The two brothers also share 50% of their genes with her.

A problem for genetic explanations of schizophrenia is that genetics alone cannot be enough. For example, if schizophrenia was entirely inherited, then the heritability concordance? for identical twins should be 100%, but it isn't, it is only 50%. This means that environmental factors must also be important. However, despite this problem, it is still the case that people who are more closely related are more likely to develop schizophrenia if their relative has schizophrenia, which supports the genetic explanation. However, another problem with the genetic explanation is that identical twins may be treated as more similar than are non-identical twins. This may explain the higher concordance rates for identical twins than for non-identical twins.

The cognitive explanation of schizophrenia claims that people have dysfunctional thoughts, that they experience as positive symptoms of schizophrenia such as delusions or hallucinations. Delusions are bizarre beliefs that the persons believes are real. For example, they may believe they are being followed by the authorities or that they are being persecuted. Hallucinations are experienced when the person hears voices and believes that they are real. There is some support for the cognitive explanation from the success of cognitive therapies in the treatment of schizophrenia. For example, a review of the use of cognitive therapy in the treatment of schizophrenia by NICE found that it was successful in reducing the experience of delusions and hallucinations. This review found that the use of cognitive therapies combined with antipsychotic medication was more effective than just using antipsychotic drugs on their own. Because cognitive therapies change the way that people think and the way they interpret their delusions and hallucinations, this supports the claim that schizophrenia has a cognitive basis.

388 words

Examiner's comments

Maisie has covered one biological explanation (genetics) and one psychological explanation (cognitive) as required by the essay title. Description of the genetic explanation is clear and accurate with good use of terminology. Maisie has also applied it effectively to the item by identifying the relationships between the characters. The description of the cognitive explanation lacks explanation and, more importantly, has not been applied to the item. This is partly because there is little in the item to support as there is no reference to the characters' symptoms. It would have been more appropriate to consider family dysfunction in this case. The evaluation makes up only a small part of the response despite a number of marks being available for it. Both explanations are evaluated very briefly. There is little breadth to the discussion although some of the points are reasonably developed. It would have been useful to end with a conclusion that considered both explanations alongside each other, especially in the context of the item. Overall, Maisie's response is worth a level 2 response.

---

04 Discuss the use of **both** drug therapy **and** cognitive behaviour therapy as treatments for schizophrenia. (16 marks)

Ciaran's answer

Drug therapies for schizophrenia include the use of typical and atypical antipsychotics. Typical antipsychotics reduce the action of dopamine and so reduce the positive symptoms associated with schizophrenia. The action of typical antipsychotics is that they bind to but do not stimulate the D2 dopamine receptors. This blocks the action of these receptors and so eliminates the hallucinations and delusions that are typically experienced by people with schizophrenia. Atypical antipsychotics also target the positive symptoms of schizophrenia and are believed to reduce the negative symptoms and cognitive impairment associated with the disorder.

Typical antipsychotics have been shown to be more effective in the treatment of schizophrenia than placebos. Leucht et al. (2012) found that far fewer patients treated with typical antipsychotics relapsed within 12 months compared to those treated with placebo, thus demonstrating that it was the action of the drugs that was having the beneficial effect. A problem for typical antipsychotics is that they have been found to cause extrapyramidal side effects such as tardive dyskinesia. These can be distressing for the patient and may cause them to stop taking their medication with the result that any potential benefits are lost. This is an advantage of the atypical antipsychotics, in that they are less likely to produce extrapyramidal side effects, which means that patients are more likely to continue with their medication and so see a reduction in their symptoms.

The use of cognitive behaviour therapy (CBTP) in the treatment of schizophrenia is to help the patient identify and correct the faulty interpretations of events that lead to their symptoms. Patients are encouraged to trace back the origins of their symptoms so they get a better idea of how they might have developed. They are encouraged to evaluate the content of their delusions or of any voices they might be hearing. In this way they can test the validity of these thoughts. Patients are also set behavioural assignments so that they can improve their general level of functioning.

A review of treatments for schizophrenia (NICE, 2014) found that the use of CBTP was more effective at reducing relapse rates than using antipsychotics alone. This review also found that CBTP was effective in reducing the severity of schizophrenia symptoms. However, most of the studies used in the NICE review had looked at patients who were receiving antipsychotic medication at the same time as CBTP, therefore it is difficult to assess the effectiveness of CBTP on its own. There are claims that the effectiveness of CBTP in the treatment of schizophrenia has been overstated. A meta-analysis by Jauhar et al. (2014) found that the therapeutic effects of CBTP were relatively small compared to a control group, but disappeared when raters were unaware of whether patients were in the CBTP condition or the control condition.

462 words

Examiner's comments

Ciaran demonstrates sound knowledge of the two forms of therapies specified in the question, and does so through clear and accurate description. Specialist terminology is used effectively as part of this description, and evidence is relevant too. Ciaran is also able to use the evidence to support his discussion which earns AO3 marks. Although evaluation points are well developed, a limited number are covered. Drug therapy is only discussed in the context of side effects and compliance. As well as other practical issues (e.g. durability of effects), Ciaran could have considered some of the theory behind drug therapy (e.g. reductionism, determinism). Similarly, Ciaran could have gone beyond the effectiveness of CBTP looking at broader issues. It is good that Ciaran considered the two therapies in conjunction as this gives the essay greater coherency. However it would have been even better if he had ended with an overall conclusion. As a whole response, the essay would earn a level 3 mark.

7 Eating Behaviour

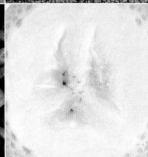

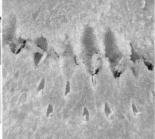

CONTENTS OF CHAPTER

SPECIFICATION CHECKLIST

- Explanations for food preferences: the evolutionary explanation, including reference to neophobia and taste aversion; the role of learning in food preference, including social and cultural influences.

- Neural and hormonal mechanisms involved in the control of eating behaviour, including the role of the hypothalamus, ghrelin and leptin.

- Biological explanations for anorexia nervosa, including genetic and neural explanations.

- Psychological explanations for anorexia nervosa: family systems theory, including enmeshment, autonomy and control; social learning theory, including modelling, reinforcement and media; cognitive theory, including distortions and irrational beliefs.

- Biological explanations for obesity, including genetic and neural explanations.

- Psychological explanations for obesity, including restraint theory, disinhibition and the boundary model. Explanations for the success and failure of dieting.

Neophobia

If you turn your nose up at food you aren't familiar with and panic when there isn't a KFC or a McDonald's on the horizon, then you may be experiencing 'neophobia', the dislike of things that are new or unfamiliar . This goes beyond fussiness or picky eating, as food neophobia (wariness of new foods) is actually 'sensible' from an evolutionary perspective. To our ancestors this was a survival strategy when they were faced with a world of potential foods, some of which might be harmful to them. Food neophobia may have given them a selective advantage by protecting them from harmful foods, but also a disadvantage by narrowing the variety of their diet.

Nowadays, food safety is generally guaranteed in Western societies, and the protective function of food neophobia may no longer be advantageous. However, evolutionary change connected to food preferences is a lot slower than cultural change, so we may still expect to find strong traces of neophobia among modern human beings. In humans, food neophobia is measured by the 'Food Neophobia Scale 'FNS'. High scores on the FNS indicate a low anticipated liking of unfamiliar foods and foreign cuisine, as well as a low willingness to try unfamiliar foods.

Food Neophobia Scale (Pilner, 1994)

Select the response that best describes how much you agree or disagree with the statement for each question. Tick the relevant box and record your total at the end of the questionnaire.

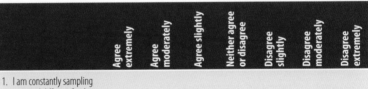

	Agree extremely	Agree moderately	Agree slightly	Neither agree or disagree	Disagree slightly	Disagree moderately	Disagree extremely
1. I am constantly sampling new and different foods							
2. I don't trust new foods							
3. If I don't know what is in a food, I won't try it							
4. I like foods from different countries							
5. I find ethnic food too weird to eat							
6. At dinner parties, I will try a new food							
7. I am afraid to eat things I have never had before							
8. I am very particular about the foods I will eat							
9. I will eat almost anything							
10. I like to try new ethnic restaurants							

Scoring:

Items 1, 4, 6, 9, 10 are scored 1–7 (i.e. agree extremely = 1, disagree extremely = 7)
Items 2, 3, 5, 7, 8 are scored 7–1 (i.e. agree extremely = 7, disagree extremely = 1)
A total score of 35 or above is considered high, suggesting food neophobia.

The evolutionary explanation for food preferences

The goal of any evolutionary explanation is to discover the adaptive function of a particular behaviour. Since the mechanisms that make up human nature were designed by natural selection millions of years ago, we need to consider the problems faced by our distant ancestors to discover why preferences for particular types of food evolved in the first place. **Evolutionary explanations**, therefore, ignore more contemporary explanations for **food preferences** (such as health benefits) and focus instead on the adaptive benefits certain foods would have offered our ancestors living in a very different environment to the one we are familiar with today.

The environment of evolutionary adaptation (EEA)

To understand the adaptive problems faced by our distant ancestors, we must understand the environment in which they lived. The environment of evolutionary adaptation (EEA) refers to the environment in which our species first evolved. Human beings first emerged as a separate species some two million years ago on the African savannah, and natural selection favoured adaptations geared toward survival in that particular environment.

KEY TERMS

Evolutionary explanations focus on the adaptive nature of behaviour, i.e. modern behaviours are believed to have evolved because they solved challenges faced by our distant ancestors and so became more widespread in the gene pool.

Food preference refers to the way in which people choose from among available foods on the basis of biological and learned perceptions such as taste, health characteristics, value, habit, etc.

Neophobia is an extreme dislike and avoidance of anything that is new or unfamiliar.

Taste aversion is a learned response to eating toxic, spoiled or poisonous food, which results in the animal avoiding eating the food that made it ill in the future.

THE EVOLUTION OF FOOD PREFERENCES

Early diets

Early humans were hunter-gatherers whose diet included the animals and plants that were part of their natural environment. Preferences for fatty food would have been adaptive for early humans, because conditions in the EEA meant that energy resources were vital in order to stay alive and also to find the next meal.

Preference for meat

Fossil evidence from groups of hunter-gatherers suggests that the daily diet of early humans was derived primarily from animal-based foods. A meat diet, full of densely packed nutrients, provided the catalyst for the growth of the brain. Without animals, claims Milton (2008), it is unlikely that early humans could have secured enough nutrition from a vegetarian diet to evolve into the active and intelligent creatures they became.

Preference for sweet foods

The taste of sweetness is associated with a high concentration of quickly available sugar and readily available calories. In the EEA, one source of sugar and therefore calories was ripe fruit, which is characterised by a sweet taste. Fruit also provides vitamins and minerals that are necessary for bodily functions and growth and so would have been particularly valuable to our ancestors in the EEA. Therefore, it would have been adaptive for early humans to have evolved an innate preference for sweet-tasting foods. Mennella (2014) found that the children who preferred sweet solutions over salty ones tended to be tall for their age. This makes sense from an evolutionary perspective as, back in the EEA, children who sought out more calories were more likely to grow and also likely to survive.

Taste aversion

Taste aversion is a learned response to eating toxic, spoiled or poisonous food. When taste aversion takes place, the animal avoids eating the food that made it ill or that they associate with the illness. Taste aversion was first discovered by farmers trying to rid themselves of rats. They found that it was difficult to kill the rats by using poisoned bait because rats would only take a small amount of any new food and, if they became ill, would rapidly learn to avoid it. Garcia *et al.* (1955) were the first to study taste aversion in the laboratory. Rats who had been made ill through radiation shortly after eating saccharin developed an aversion to it and very quickly associated their illness with the saccharin.

The adaptive advantages of taste aversion

Despite the name 'taste aversion', subsequent research has found that not only taste but also the *odour* of food can be linked to illness and consequently to the development of a food aversion. The development of taste aversions would have helped our ancestors to survive because, if they were lucky enough to survive eating poisoned food, they would not make the same mistake again. Once learned, such aversions are very hard to shift – an adaptive quality designed to keep our ancestors alive.

Neophobia

Food **neophobia**, a reluctance to consume new or unusual foods, is a naturally occurring reaction that protects animals from the risk of being poisoned by consuming something that is potentially harmful. This response is important as a survival strategy when animals are faced with 'a world of potential foods whose safety is uncertain' (Prescott, 2013). Species that have specialised diets that are restricted to just a few specific food sources (e.g. koala bears eat mostly eucalyptus leaves) tend not to exhibit food neophobia, whereas species that have broad and varied diets do display food neophobia (Ratcliffe *et al.*, 2003). Rats, for example, are extremely neophobic and, if they become ill after eating both a familiar and an unfamiliar food, will avoid the unfamiliar food in the future (Rozin, 1976).

In humans, neophobia accounts for an individual's reluctance to consume new or unusual foods, based on their culture and current diet (Rozin, 1997). Individuals have expectations of how an acceptable food should look and smell, and so unfamiliar foods that do not fall into what is considered 'acceptable' based on these criteria will be rejected (Dovey *et al.*, 2008). For humans, food neophobia is particularly strong in response to animal products rather than non-animal products (Martins *et al.*, 1997). This is most likely to have evolved because of the greater illness threat posed by, for example, rotting meat and other animal products relative to non-animal products (Fessler, 2002).

Are all food preferences a product of evolution?

Many food preferences can be traced back to the adaptive pressures of the EEA, but this is not always the case. A trait that is beneficial today (e.g. consumption of low cholesterol foods) would not have evolved because of its beneficial effects for our ancestors. Many things that were important to our ancestors (such as saturated animal fats) are nowadays harmful to our health, so we are more likely to avoid them in order to survive and lead a healthy life. Krebs (2009) also points out the 'mismatch' between evolved preferences (e.g. for fatty and sweet foods) and modern environments. He suggests that many of the major global health epidemics that have emerged in recent years (e.g. obesity and type 2 diabetes) are a result of this mismatch.

Support for evolved preferences for sweet foods

Support for evolved preferences comes from studies that have shown that early exposure to a sweet taste is not necessary for children to develop a preference for sweet-tasting foods. For example, there are several documented cases where a culture, such as the Iñupiat people of Northern Alaska, that has no experience of sweet foods and drinks, has come into contact with cultures that regularly consume these. In none of these cases has the culture without sugar rejected the sugar-containing foods and drinks of the other culture (Bell *et al.*, 1973). In addition, newborn infants show an acceptance response the first time that they taste something sweet. This response, involving a slight smile, licking of the upper lip and sucking, is an innate response, so that whatever substance elicits the response will tend to be ingested (Grill and Norgren, 1978). These studies provide support for the claimed evolutionary preference for sweet foodstuffs that would have been necessary for bodily functions and growth in our distant ancestors in the EEA.

Real-world application: Taste aversion and chemotherapy

Research on the adaptive origins of taste aversion has been helpful in understanding the food avoidance that can sometimes occur during the treatment of cancer. Some cancer treatments, such as radiation and chemotherapy, can cause gastrointestinal illness. When this illness is paired with food consumption, taste aversions can result. For example, Bernstein and Webster (1980) gave patients a novel-tasting ice cream prior to their chemotherapy and the patients acquired an aversion to that ice cream. These findings have resulted in the development of the 'scapegoat technique', which involves giving cancer patients a novel food along with some familiar food just prior to their chemotherapy. The patient forms an aversion to the novel food and not to the familiar, usual food. This is consistent with an adaptive avoidance of novel (i.e. unfamiliar) foods known as neophobia.

Support for the heritability of neophobia

If food neophobia has evolved because it has adaptive advantages, then we might expect that there is a strong genetic component for this characteristic. This possibility was investigated by Knaapila *et al.* (2007), who measured food neophobia (using the Food Neophobia Scale questionnaire) in a sample of 468 adult female twin pairs (211 MZ and 257 DZ). The heritability estimate for food neophobia in this sample was found to be 67%, suggesting that about two thirds of the variation in food neophobia is genetically determined. This lends support to the view that neophobia evolved among human beings because it protected them from potentially harmful foods.

Neophobia can also be maladaptive

Although neophobia has significant adaptive advantages for humans, it also poses problems for those individuals who may restrict their diet to foods with inadequate nutritional quality, or lose the potential health and advantages of new foods. For example, an Australian study (Perry *et al.*, 2015) found that neophobia is associated with poorer dietary quality among children. However, the consequences of food neophobia can be minimised in situations where it may prove maladaptive. Research has shown that repeated taste exposure *without* visual and olfactory cues increases the preference for initially unfamiliar foods (Birch *et al.*, 1987). Although the neophobic response can be modified using such strategies, this tends only to be temporary, as the underlying neophobic tendency is likely to persist.

⬆ UPGRADE

Maximising your marks
The biggest mark earners are, of course, the 16-mark essay questions. In previous sections of this book we have looked at how to plan for these questions and how to answer them effectively, but what *specifically* is an examiner looking for if he (or she) is going to give you a mark in the top mark band of 13–16 marks? Let's look at a typical essay question for this section of the specification:

Discuss the evolutionary explanation for food preferences. (16 marks)

Although you aren't told this in the question, 10 of the marks are assigned for AO3 (evaluation) and the remaining 6 marks for AO1 (description). It is worth bearing this in mind when planning your response.

Now let's look at the mark descriptor for the top level for this question:

'Knowledge of the evolutionary explanation is accurate and generally well detailed. Discussion is thorough and effective. The answer is clear, coherent and focused. Specialist terminology is used effectively. Minor detail and/or expansion of argument sometimes lacking.'

Obviously your material has to be accurate but examiners are pretty forgiving folk and will generally ignore relatively minor inaccuracies. To make sure your description is 'generally well detailed', you should aim to make each point about 30 words. Choose six things you want to say and expand each to 30 words, adding the necessary detail and specialist terminology to give each point descriptive impact. To make your discussion 'thorough and effective' you should aim for five evaluative points from the information in the 'Evaluation' section on this page. Each of these should be 'distilled' down to about 60 words. Being able to reduce material down to make it really effective is a skill that we cover in more detail on page 75.

CAN YOU?   No. 7.1

1. Explain what is meant by the terms *neophobia* and *taste aversion*. (2 marks each)
2. Briefly outline the role of neophobia in food preferences. (3 marks)
3. Briefly outline and evaluate the role of taste aversion in food preferences. (8 marks)
4. Discuss the evolutionary explanation for food preferences. (16 marks)

The role of learning in food preference

Evolution is not the only influence on human **food preferences**. We **learn** what might be good to eat (or should be avoided) from significant others in our life, most notably our same-age peers and our parents. Parents in particular influence our food preferences as they control the foods bought and served in the home. As we get older, however, our food preferences are increasingly shaped by media influences, particularly in Western cultures where we are constantly bombarded by food advertising and the easy availability of palatable and often unhealthy food choices. In contrast to evolutionary explanations, learning explanations focus on cultural and environmental influences on food preferences.

Insider tip...

The specification mentions 'Social influences' and 'Cultural influences'. Questions might ask for either of these separately, or be phrased more generally, e.g. 'The role of learning in food preferences'. In this latter type of question you could include either or both of these different types of influence.

▲ Jamie Oliver set out to change our dietary habits away from the dangers of too much sugar.

SOCIAL INFLUENCES

Parental influences

One way in which children acquire their eating behaviour and attitudes to food is by observing the behaviour of their parents. Research suggests an association between parents' and children's attitudes to food generally. For example, Brown and Ogden (2004) reported consistent correlations between parents and their children in terms of snack food intake, eating motivations and body dissatisfaction.

Parents may also manipulate the availability of certain foods, either as a reward (e.g. special treats such as takeaways or sweets) or because of a perceived health gain (e.g. foods with reduced fat or with lower levels of sugar or salt). They may also offer one food as a reward for the eating of another: 'You can't have any ice cream unless you eat some fruit'. This approach is not particularly successful, as research (e.g. Birch *et al.*, 1984) has generally shown that, although the preference for the food used as the reward *increases*, there tends to be a *decrease* in the preference for the distasteful food.

Peers

Social learning theory (see page 174) emphasises the impact that observing other people (i.e. models) has on our own attitudes and behaviour. The behaviour of same-age peers in particular has been found to have a powerful influence on the food preferences of children. For example, Greenhalgh *et al.* (2009) found that the observation of peers had both positive and negative effects on food preferences. Children who were exposed to positive modelling (i.e. peers eating novel foods) were more likely to try these foods themselves. However, negative modelling (i.e. peers refusing to eat novel foods) also had an effect on children as it inhibited novel food consumption. Birch (1980) showed how exposure to another child could change food preferences. In this study, for four consecutive lunchtimes, children were seated next to other children who preferred a different vegetable to the one they preferred (i.e. peas or carrots). At the end of the four days, these children showed a change in their vegetable preference that was still evident at a follow-up several weeks later.

CULTURAL INFLUENCES

Media effects

The role of social learning is also evident in the impact of television and other media (such as magazines) on food preferences. MacIntyre *et al.* (1998) found that the media have a major impact both on what people eat, and also their attitudes to certain foods. However, the researchers also state that many eating behaviours are limited by personal circumstances, such as age, income and family circumstances. Thus, people appear to learn from the media about healthy eating, but must place this information within the broader context of their lives (i.e. what they can afford and what is freely available). It was precisely this problem that led chef Jamie Oliver to set up his BBC 'Sugar Rush' campaign in 2015 to inform the British public of the dangers of too much sugar in our diet.

The context of meals

In societies like the US and the UK, 'grazing' rather than eating meals and the desire for convenience foods are increasingly common. As a result, people learn to rely on takeaway meals as a way of feeding themselves. A recent study (Maguire *et al.*, 2015) found that, in the UK, the number of takeaway restaurants has risen by 45 per cent in the last 18 years, with areas of the highest deprivation seeing the highest rise. Gillman *et al.* (2000) commented on the decline of the family meal in Western cultures, with more young people choosing to eat while watching television. Eating meals in front of the TV was associated with a greater consumption of pizza and salty snacks and less consumption of fruit and vegetables. The researchers suggest that eating more 'informally' leads to a learned preference for quickly prepared snack-foods rather than more elaborate meals. Parents whose children watched more television tended to choose foods that were easy to prepare because children usually ate them without complaint.

EVALUATION OF SOCIAL INFLUENCES

Limitations of the parental influence view

A problem for our understanding of the role of parental influences on food preferences is that research in this area is quite limited. Typically studies have been small-scale and carried out on a highly selective sample of white Americans. This means that we are unclear as to whether the findings of these studies generalise to other populations. For example, Robinson *et al.* (2001) studied nearly 800 8–9-year-old children from a number of different backgrounds. Their research revealed a complex association between the behaviour of parents and the food preferences of children, with girls being more influenced by parental modelling and control than were boys.

Not all parental influences are effective

Russell *et al.* (2015) interviewed parents of children aged 2–5 years about the methods they used to influence the foods their children liked and disliked. The researchers discovered that not all the methods used were effective in influencing food preferences in these children. Some of the methods used (e.g. parental modelling and food exposure) were found to be effective in promoting healthy eating, whilst others (e.g. forcing consumption or restricting food access) were ineffective. Parents of children with healthy food preferences were more likely to use the effective feeding than were parents of children with unhealthy food preferences. This supports the claim that children do learn food preferences from their parents, but that some approaches regarding influence are more effective than others.

Research support for the role of peers

Non-experimental studies have shown that the foods that parents consume and make available to their children predict the foods that their children consume. For example, Wardle *et al.* (2005) found that parental fruit and vegetable consumption was a strong predictor of children's fruit and vegetable consumption. Similarly, an experimental study in the Netherlands (Jansen and Tenney, 2001) found that seeing significant others modelling the eating and drinking of 'light' (i.e. sugar free) yoghurts and drinks led to a preference for the taste of light products in primary-age children. This increase in a behaviour in the presence of others displaying the same behaviour (known as social facilitation) most probably serves as a way of ensuring they are consuming foods that have been demonstrated by others to be safe.

EVALUATION OF CULTURAL INFLUENCES

Research support for media influences on food preferences

Boyland and Halford (2013) provided supporting evidence that exposure to food advertising on television influences food preferences *and* actual food intake in children. However, they also found that it influences children of different weight statuses in different ways, with adverts for food high in fat, salt and sugar having a particularly strong influence on overweight and obese children. The relationship between media exposure and food preferences was further supported by the fact that children who had the greatest preference for high carbohydrate and high fat foods were also the ones that watched the most television.

Real-world application: Implications of media influences on food preferences

Research has shown that television appears to be the dominant medium for children's exposure to food marketing, with the majority of such marketing being for unhealthy foods (Cairns *et al.*, 2013). This has led to a number of countries developing regulations concerning unhealthy food advertising on television. These typically focus on limiting the quantity of advertising of unhealthy food to children or on reducing the effect of such advertising on children. For example, the use of promotional characters and offers or making nutritional health claims to promote food to children on TV is already restricted by governments in some countries.

Food preferences and the food environment

Research by Chen and Yang (2014) provides some support for the role of cultural influences on food preferences, particularly the local food environment available to people. They studied Twitter 'tweets' made over five weekdays in Columbus, Ohio. These were analysed for evidence of food activities such as shopping in high-quality grocery stores or dining at fast food outlets, as well as the quality of food choices made. These showed a significant association between healthy food choices and the number of grocery stores around them but, contrary to expectations, no association between the number of fast food outlets and healthy or unhealthy food choices. This study shows that cultural influences do have an effect on learned food habits, but people are able to resist the development of unhealthy habits if a healthy alternative is available.

"They watch television all the time now that junk food adverts have been banned."

▲ Many countries now have regulations to limit the marketing of unhealthy foods to children.

🐾 APPLY YOUR KNOWLEDGE

Layla is a 14-year-old girl living in Bristol. Both her parents work, so when she gets home from school she plonks herself down in front of the TV with biscuits and crisps, which she munches through until tea-time. This is usually a ready meal or chips from the local takeaway, all eaten in front of the TV, washed down with copious amounts of cola.

Layla's teacher has expressed concern that Layla is listless and lacking in energy during the day, and is appalled when she hears of her eating habits. She mentions it to Layla's parents at an open evening and they admit they don't know what to do to make her eat more healthily.

Using your knowledge of the role of learning in food preference, explain two ways in which Layla might be helped to change her eating habits.

CAN YOU?   No. 7.2

1. Outline the role of social influences in food preference. (4 marks)
2. Outline the role of cultural influences in food preference. (4 marks)
3. Outline research findings relating to social and/or cultural influences in food preference. (6 marks)
4. Outline and evaluate the role of learning in food preference. (16 marks)

Neural and hormonal mechanisms

We are so dependent on food that hunger is one of the most compelling of human motives. The need to eat shapes our daily lives and many of our activities. Our television screens and newspapers are crammed with food-related products, and a walk down any high street will leave you in no doubt about the importance of food in our everyday experience. It comes as no surprise then to discover that we have developed a sophisticated physiology for dealing with the related states of hunger (signalling a need for nutrients and the energy they provide) and satiation (signalling the satisfaction of these needs).

NEURAL MECHANISMS IN THE CONTROL OF EATING

Homeostasis

Homeostasis is the mechanism by which an organism maintains a steady internal environment. Part of the homeostatic mechanism is detecting whether the body has enough nutrients and correcting the situation if this is not the case. The body has evolved two separate systems for achieving this, one for turning eating 'on' and one for turning it 'off'. Among humans, glucose levels probably play the most important role in producing feelings of hunger. Hunger increases as glucose levels decrease. A decline in glucose levels in the blood activates a part of the brain called the lateral hypothalamus, resulting in feelings of hunger. This causes the individual to search for and consume food, which causes glucose levels to rise again. This rise in glucose levels activates the ventromedial hypothalamus, which leads to feelings of satiation, which in turn inhibits further feeding. In some animals, however, this does not happen, as can be seen from studies of the protein leptin (see right).

The lateral hypothalamus

Investigation into the role of the **hypothalamus** in eating behaviour began in the 1950s, when researchers discovered that damage to the lateral hypothalamus (LH) in rats caused a condition called aphagia (from the Greek, meaning 'absence of eating'). Researchers also found that stimulation of the LH elicits feeding behaviour. These opposing effects of injury and stimulation led researchers to conclude that they had discovered the 'on switch' for eating behaviour. A neurotransmitter found in the hypothalamus, called neuropeptide Y (NPY), is particularly important in turning on eating. When injected into the lateral hypothalamus of rats, NPY causes them to immediately begin feeding, even when satiated (Reynolds and Wickens, 2000). Repeated injections of NPY into the hypothalamus of rats produces obesity in just a few days (Stanley et al., 1986).

The ventromedial hypothalamus

In contrast to the effect of damage to the lateral hypothalamus, researchers also discovered that damage to the ventromedial hypothalamus (VMH) caused rats to overeat, leading to a condition called hyperphagia (from the Greek, meaning 'overeating'). Similarly, stimulation of this area inhibited feeding. This led researchers to conclude that the VMH signals 'stop eating' as a result of the many glucose receptors in this area. However, damage to the nerve fibres passing through the VMH tends to also damage another area of the hypothalamus, the paraventricular nucleus (PVN), and it is now believed that damage to the PVN alone causes hyperphagia (Gold, 1973). The PVN also detects the specific foods our body needs, and consequently seems to be responsible for many of our 'cravings'.

HORMONAL MECHANISMS IN THE CONTROL OF EATING

The two main hormones involved in the control of eating are **ghrelin** and **leptin**. Ghrelin increases appetite when we are hungry, and leptin decreases appetite when the body has enough stored energy, so working together these two hormones should maintain our body weight at an optimal level. Both ghrelin and leptin are peripheral signals that have central effects, i.e. they are secreted in other parts of the body (peripheral) but affect the brain (central).

Ghrelin

Ghrelin is released in the stomach and stimulates the hypothalamus to increase appetite. If a person's bodily resources are low or if they are undereating, then ghrelin levels increase.

Ghrelin levels also have a role in determining how quickly we feel hungry again after we have eaten. Ghrelin levels go up dramatically before we eat (when we are most hungry) and then go down again for about three hours after a meal.

Ghrelin is thought to be important in the development of obesity because, on stimulating the appetite, it leads to an increase in body weight. Ghrelin's role in appetite control

▲ The human face of a scientific breakthrough – the team that discovered ghrelin in 1999. From left to right, Masayasu Kojima, Kenji Kangawa and Hiroshi Hosoda.

was first noted when it was discovered that when ghrelin was injected into the bloodstream of rats it stimulated food intake. Other evidence came from the observation that mice lacking either ghrelin or its receptor in the hypothalamus are protected from diet-induced obesity.

Leptin

In 1994, researchers noticed that when they administered a new substance to genetically altered obese laboratory mice, the mice lost weight. Leptin, as this new substance became known (from the Greek leptos, meaning 'thin'), is a hormone that plays a crucial role in appetite and weight control. It is normally produced by fat tissue and secreted into the bloodstream, where it travels to the brain and decreases appetite. Circulating leptin levels act as a long-term signal of the amount of fat stored in adipose tissue, whilst short-term fluctuations in leptin levels provide information regarding changes in calorific intake.

Leptin is thought to have two major functions. By binding to receptors in the hypothalamus, it counteracts the effects of neuropeptide Y, a feeding stimulant secreted in the gut and the hypothalamus. Second, leptin increases sympathetic nervous system activity, which stimulates fatty tissue to burn energy.

Limitations of a homeostatic explanation

For a hunger mechanism to be adaptive, it must both anticipate and prevent energy deficits, not just react to them. As a result, the theory that hunger and eating are triggered only when energy resources fall below their desired level is incompatible with the harsh reality in which such systems would have evolved. For such a mechanism to be truly adaptive, it must promote levels of consumption that maintain bodily resources well above the optimal level to act as a buffer against future lack of food availability. Explanations of food intake based solely on homeostatic mechanisms offer a limited perspective on eating behaviour.

Problems with the role of the lateral hypothalamus

The view that the LH served as an 'on switch' for eating turned out to have a few problems. For example, damage to the LH caused deficits in other aspects of behaviour (e.g. thirst and sex) rather than just hunger. Also, more recent research has shown that eating behaviour is controlled by neural circuits that run throughout the brain, and not just by the hypothalamus. Although the LH undoubtedly plays an important role in controlling eating behaviour, it is not, as previously thought, the brain's 'eating centre' (Sakurai *et al.*, 1998).

Support for the role of the ventromedial hypothalamus

Early researchers found that lesions or damage to the VMH resulted in hyperphagia and obesity in a number of different species, including humans. This led them to designate the VMH as the 'satiety centre' in eating behaviour, with the PVN having a particularly important role in this process (Gold, 1973). Most studies showed that, compared to lesions in other brain areas, animals with VMH lesions ate substantially more and gained substantially more weight, supporting the important role played by this region in the control of eating.

Research support for the role of ghrelin in appetite control

Wren *et al.* (2001) provided research support for the role of ghrelin in appetite control in a randomised double-blind study of nine healthy volunteers. These participants either received intravenous ghrelin or a saline infusion and one week later the same participants received the other condition. Appetite was measured in terms of the amount of food taken and consumed at a free-choice buffet under each condition. The results showed a significant increase in food consumption in the ghrelin condition compared to the saline infusion condition, with a mean difference of 28% between the two conditions. In addition to studies that have shown the important role played by ghrelin in non-human species, this study demonstrates that ghrelin is also an important signal which stimulates food intake in human beings.

▲ Participants who received intravenous ghrelin ate more food at a free-choice buffet than participants who received a saline infusion.

Leptin resistance

Although leptin plays an important role in appetite and weight control, some people develop resistance to the hormone and so it fails to control appetite and weight gain. One possible reason is that leptin receptors stop functioning properly and so cells fail to respond to the hormone. Leptin resistance is often found in overweight and obese people, making it even harder for them to lose weight. This problem cannot simply be linked to leptin deficiency, as a study with obese adults found that doses of leptin 20 to 30 times normal concentrations of the hormone were necessary to produce significant weight reduction (Heymsfield *et al.*, 1999).

Research methods

The study by Wren *et al.* (2001) is described on this page. The description says 'These participants either received intravenous ghrelin or a saline infusion and one week later the same participants received the other condition.'

1. This is an example of counterbalancing. Explain why counterbalancing was necessary. (3 marks)
2. This was a randomised double-blind study. This means that participants were randomly allocated to one of the two conditions in the study. Identify the **two** conditions (independent variables) in the study. (2 marks)
3. Explain what 'random allocation' means and how it might be done. (3 marks)
4. Describe the operationalised dependent variable in this study. (2 marks)
5. The term 'double-blind' means that neither the researcher nor the participants knew which condition they were in. Explain why this would improve the validity of this study. (2 marks).
6. Identify the level of measurement in this study. (1 mark)
7. What statistical test could be used with the data collected in this study? Justify your choice. (3 marks)

LINK TO RESEARCH METHODS

Statistical tests on pages 24–32. The other topics in these questions are covered in the research methods chapter of our Year 1 book.

KEY TERMS

Ghrelin is a hormone that is released in the stomach and which stimulates the hypothalamus to increase appetite. Ghrelin levels increase when a person's bodily resources are low.

Hypothalamus is an area of the brain which has a number of important functions, including the regulation of body temperature, hunger and thirst.

Leptin is a hormone that plays a crucial role in appetite and weight control. It is normally produced by fat tissue and secreted into the bloodstream, where it travels to the brain and decreases appetite.

CAN YOU? No. 7.3

1. Outline the role of the hypothalamus, ghrelin and leptin in the control of eating behaviour. (3 marks each)
2. Briefly outline the neural mechanisms involved in the control of eating behaviour and give **one** criticism of their role. (4 marks)
3. Briefly outline the hormonal mechanisms involved in the control of eating behaviour. (6 marks)
4. Discuss the neural and hormonal mechanisms involved in the control of eating behaviour. (16 marks)

Biological explanations for anorexia nervosa

Many of the early explanations of **anorexia nervosa** (AN) concentrated on the influence of psychological factors, but more recent work has highlighted the importance of biological factors in this disorder. These include **genetic explanations** (i.e. those that focus on the possible heritability of these disorders) and **neural explanations** (i.e. relating to changes or dysfunction in the nervous system). The prominence of recent **biological explanations** of AN is a direct result of more sophisticated methodologies that were not available to researchers 20 years ago. Many of the studies on this spread reflect this new-found sophistication.

KEY TERMS

Anorexia nervosa A type of eating disorder in which an individual, despite being seriously underweight, fears that she or he might become obese and therefore engages in self-starvation to prevent this happening.

Biological explanations A belief that a full understanding of thoughts, emotions and behaviour must include an understanding of their biological basis, i.e. the role of genetics, neural correlates and hormones.

Genetic explanations The likelihood of behaving in a particular way is determined by a person's genetic makeup, i.e. it is inherited from parents.

Neural explanations involve areas of the brain and nervous system and the action of chemical messengers in the brain known as neurotransmitters in controlling behaviour.

Clinical characteristics of anorexia nervosa

According to DSM-V criteria, to be diagnosed as having anorexia nervosa a person must display the following:

- Persistent restriction of energy intake leading to significantly low body weight (in context of what is minimally expected for age, sex, developmental trajectory and physical health).
- Either an intense fear of gaining weight or of becoming fat, or persistent behaviour that interferes with weight gain (even though significantly low weight).
- Disturbance in the way one's body weight or shape is experienced, undue influence of body shape and weight on self-evaluation, or persistent lack of recognition of the seriousness of the current low body weight.

There are two main sub-types of AN:

Restricting type: the most common type of AN whereby a person severely restricts their food intake (e.g. by maintaining a very low calorie count or restricting types of food eaten).

Binge-eating or purging type: less common; a person restricts their food intake as above, but may regularly engage in binge-eating or purging behaviour (e.g. self-induced vomiting or misuse of laxatives).

GENETIC EXPLANATIONS

Family studies

Research has shown that eating disorders such as AN run in families. First-degree relatives (i.e. parent, sibling or child) of individuals with AN have approximately a ten-times greater lifetime risk of having AN than relatives of unaffected individuals (Strober et al., 2000). Research also suggests that there is an increased risk of developing other eating disorders (such as bulimia nervosa) in relatives of individuals diagnosed with AN, suggesting that people may inherit a more general vulnerability to eating disorders rather than AN specifically (Tozzi et al., 2005).

Twin studies

Comparing the similarity of MZ twins (who share 100% of their genes) to DZ twins (who share only 50% of their genes) provides a measure of the relative contributions of genetic and environmental factors in the development of AN. Twin studies generally suggest moderate-to-high heritability of AN, with heritability estimates varying between 28% and 74% (Thornton et al., 2010). For example, Wade et al. (2000) interviewed over 2,000 female MZ and DZ twins, evaluating them using the DSM criteria for AN. From this, the researchers claimed a heritability rate for AN of 58%. Twin studies such as this therefore suggest that some people are more genetically predisposed to develop AN than are others.

Adoption studies

Twin studies suffer from the problem that MZ twins not only share the same genes but also share similar environments, which can make it difficult to disentangle the relative influence of genetics and environment. Adoption studies avoid this problem because they study biological relatives that do not share the same environment. Klump et al. (2009) studied 123 adopted sibling pairs (i.e. adopted females and 'sisters' from their adoptive family) and 56 biological sibling pairs (i.e. adopted females and their biological sisters reared in a different family). Because of the relatively low prevalence of AN, disordered eating symptoms (e.g. body dissatisfaction, weight preoccupation) were assessed instead. The heritability estimates ranged from 59% to 82% for the different aspects of disordered eating, with non-shared environmental factors (i.e. experiences that are different for members of each sibling pair) accounting for the remaining variance.

NEURAL EXPLANATIONS

Serotonin

Disturbances in levels of the neurotransmitter serotonin appear to be a characteristic of individuals with eating disorders. Bailer et al. (2007) measured serotonin activity in women recovering from either restricting-type anorexia (restricted food intake) or binge-eating/purging type (periods of restrictive eating and binge-eating/purging). These women were compared with healthy controls. They found significantly higher serotonin activity in the women recovering from the binge-eating/purging type compared to the other two groups. In addition they found the highest levels of serotonin activity in women who showed the most anxiety, suggesting that persistent disruption of serotonin levels may lead to increased anxiety, which may trigger AN.

Dopamine

Studies suggest a role for dopamine in AN. Kaye et al. (2005) used a PET scan to compare dopamine activity in the brains of 10 women recovering from AN, and 12 healthy women. In the AN women, they found overactivity in dopamine receptors in a part of the brain known as the basal ganglia, where dopamine plays a part in the interpretation of harm and pleasure. Increased dopamine activity in this area appears to alter the way people interpret rewards. This matches with the fact that individuals with AN find it difficult to associate good feelings with the things that most people find pleasurable (such as food).

Limbic system dysfunction

Recent research (Lipsman et al., 2015) suggests that the neural roots of AN appear to be related to a dysfunction in the limbic system in the brain, particularly the subcallosal cingulate and the insular cortex. The researchers claim that dysfunction in these areas, whose normal functioning is to regulate emotion, can lead to deficits in emotional processing. These deficits may then lead to the pathological thoughts and behaviours that are typical of AN.

EVALUATION OF GENETIC EXPLANATIONS

Problems with genetic explanations

Fairburn et al. (1999) concluded that despite a number of studies finding evidence for a genetic component in AN, the actual heritability of this disorder is still unknown. They point out that studies in this area have been inconsistent in their estimates of the heritability of AN, giving widely contrasting heritability ranges. Many of these studies also violate the 'equal environments assumption'. Twin researchers assume that MZ and DZ twins raised in the same homes experience equally similar environments. However, research suggests that this is not the case, as MZ twins tend to be treated more similarly than DZ twins. This, claim Fairburn et al., invalidates the claim that the greater concordance for AN in MZ compared to DZ twins must be due to greater *genetic* similarity.

Genetic explanations ignore the role of the media in AN

A criticism of genetic explanations of AN is the assumption that environmental factors such as the media do not matter. The media's idealisation of an ultra-thin female body type has long been viewed as an important risk factor for eating disorders. However, as Bulik (2004) suggests, genetically vulnerable individuals might seek out images of thin role models in the media as a way of reinforcing their body image. This suggestion is supported by a longitudinal study which found that adolescent girls whose AN symptom severity increased over a 16-month period also reported significantly greater fashion magazine reading over the same period (Vaughn and Fouts, 2003).

Real-world application: Is AN *really* biological in nature?

An unlikely application of research in this area has been its implication for insurance payouts for psychiatric conditions. In many states in the US, for example, treatment for AN is restricted under many insurance plans because AN is not considered to be 'biologically based'. This had led to claims that 'denial of benefits is denial of care'. In 2014, the Eating Disorders Coalition in the US tried unsuccessfully to get eating disorders included in the 'essential health benefits' that US law requires insurers to provide, beginning in 2014. However, research such as that described on this spread creates a case for insurance companies to consider AN in the same way as other psychiatric conditions (such as schizophrenia) that are considered to be biologically based.

EVALUATION OF NEURAL EXPLANATIONS

Problems with the serotonin explanation

A problem for explanations of AN based on serotonin imbalance is that SSRIs, drugs which alter levels of available brain serotonin, are ineffective when used with AN patients. For example, Ferguson et al. (1999) found no difference in symptom outcomes between patients taking a SSRI and patients of similar age, body weight and symptoms who were not taking an SSRI. However, Kaye et al. (2001) found that, when used with recovering AN patients, these drugs *were* effective in preventing relapse. This suggests that malnutrition-related changes in serotonin function might negate the action of SSRIs, which only become effective when weight returns to a more normal level.

Research support for the dopamine–AN relationship

Research has provided support for the role of dopamine in AN symptoms. For example, food aversion, weight loss, menstrual dysfunction and distorted body image cognitions have been found to be related to increased activity in dopamine pathways (Kaye, 2008). Other evidence comes from the discovery of increased eye-blink in AN individuals compared to controls (Barbato et al., 2006). Increased -blink is indicative of higher levels of dopamine activity in the brain. Barbato et al.'s research also found a significant correlation between blink rate and the duration of AN, suggesting that the relationship between dopamine activity and AN symptoms develops over time.

Advantages of biological explanations of AN

Explanations of AN that are based on underlying biology have the advantage of reducing the stigma that patients experience because they challenge the belief that the AN individual's challenging behaviour is somehow 'their fault'. They also offer the possibility of treating AN by regulating the brain areas involved in the behaviours that are characteristic of the disorder. For example, Lipsman et al. (2013) used deep brain stimulation (DBS) to change activity in the subcallosal cingulate in patients with chronic, severe and treatment-resistant AN. Treatment led to improvements in mood, emotional regulation and quality of life in most of the patients treated using DBS.

🐾 APPLY YOUR KNOWLEDGE

A pair of identical twins, separated at birth in 1941, were reunited after over 70 years apart. The two women, now in their 70s, were separated when their mother was sent to a forced labour camp in Poland. One of the women was looked after by relatives in Poland, while the other was adopted by a couple in the US. They were reunited after a national television programme in the US tracked down the twin living in Poland and reunited her with her long-lost sister in the US. Although there were many similarities in their life experiences, Flora, the US-raised twin, was amazed to discover that Anya, the Polish-raised twin, had experienced decades of anorexia nervosa, which had started in her teens. Flora had no such experience of anorexia in *her* life-time.

Using your knowledge of biological explanations of anorexia nervosa, explain why these identical twins could have been so different in their experience of this disorder.

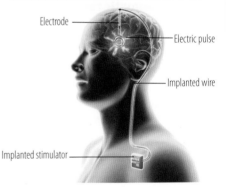

Electrode — Electric pulse — Implanted wire — Implanted stimulator

▲ In deep brain stimulation, electrodes are implanted within specific areas of the brain. These produce electrical impulses that regulate abnormal impulses within those areas. The amount of stimulation is controlled by a pacemaker-like device placed under the skin.

CAN YOU? No. 7.2

1. Outline genetic explanations for anorexia nervosa. (4 marks)
2. Outline neural explanations for anorexia nervosa. (4 marks)
3. Briefly outline **one or more** biological explanations of anorexia nervosa and give **one** limitation of these explanations. (6 marks)
4. Discuss biological explanations for anorexia nervosa. (16 marks)

Family systems theory and anorexia nervosa

The term **family systems theory** was introduced by Murray Bowen in the 1950s and suggests that individuals cannot be understood in isolation from one another, but rather as a part of their family, as the family is an emotional unit. A family systems approach argues that in order to understand a family system we must look at the family as a whole, not just at its individual members. By studying people individually rather than as a part of this whole, the way they interact and communicate within the family unit is lost or clouded. When applied to illnesses such as anorexia nervosa, the family systems approach is exemplified by the work of Salvador Minuchin.

Insider tip…

You may, on occasion, be asked to 'describe research' into family systems theory. The studies on the facing page have been used to provide support for or challenge this approach to AN, and so would count as AO3 evaluation. However, if you simply describe the findings without any critical commentary, they could be used as AO1 research, and therefore suitable for a description question.

▲ Adolescents who grow up in an enmeshed family may rebel against its constraints by refusing to eat.

The child's involvement in the psychosomatic family

Within the psychosomatic family, the child with AN is involved in parental conflict in particular ways. In their therapeutic work with psychosomatic families, Minuchin *et al.* (2009) identified three characteristic patterns of conflict-related behaviour that involved the child.

Triangulation

Triangulation can occur in a variety of ways, but always involves a pair of family members either incorporating or rejecting a third family member. For example, the child may be pressed to ally himself or herself with one parent whilst rejecting the other parent. Because of this, they are put in a position where they feel unable to express themselves without appearing to side with one parent against the other.

Parent–child coalition

The child now moves into a more stable coalition with one parent against the other. The coalition parent may respond to the child's needs with excessive concern (*enmeshment*), while the other parent withdraws and becomes less responsive.

Detouring

When parents are unable to resolve problems between them, they may direct their focus of concern away from themselves and onto the child, perhaps reinforcing behaviour in the child. The child may then become identified as the problematic member of the family. This is sometimes referred to as *scapegoating*, as the child's well-being is sacrificed in order that the marital conflict might be avoided.

THE 'PSYCHOSOMATIC FAMILY'

The term 'psychosomatic' in psychology refers to conditions where no physical basis can be found, so the illness is attributed to psychological factors. Minuchin *et al.* (1978) developed the psychosomatic family model, which states that the prerequisite for the development of AN was a dysfunctional family occurring alongside a physiological vulnerability in the child. Minuchin *et al.* maintained that the psychosomatic family process is a necessary context for the development of AN and, as a result, the aim of treatment must be to change the way the family functions.

Enmeshment, autonomy and control

Enmeshment

Enmeshment refers to an extreme form of proximity and intensity in family interaction (Minuchin *et al.*, 1978). Enmeshed family members are over-involved with each other and, with a lack of boundaries within the family, the individual 'gets lost in the system'. Barber and Buehler (1996) contended that enmeshment stifles the development of children's skills to deal adequately with common social stressors and makes the development of disorders such as AN more likely.

Autonomy

Enmeshed families place great constraints on its members, because they are not allowed to become independent and develop **autonomy**. In non-enmeshed families, when an individual reaches adolescence their family is able to change its transactional patterns in such a way that allows increased age-appropriate autonomy. Enmeshed families, on the other hand, insist on retaining the accustomed patterns of transaction, denying any need for change in the family.

Control

The psychosomatic family is also characterised by overprotective **control** over its members. Overprotectiveness, defined as having a high degree of concern for each other's welfare, can retard individuals' beliefs regarding the extent to which they are able to control or influence outcomes in their lives. An adolescent may rebel against this control by refusing to eat.

Other characteristics of the psychosomatic family

Rigidity

Rigid families show a lack of flexibility in their adaptation to new situations. Minuchin believed that rigidity was a characteristic of pathological families who, in the face of stress, increase the rigidity of their patterns of behaviour and resist any exploration of alternatives.

Lack of conflict resolution

The lack of conflict resolution in AN families refers to low tolerance for conflict and a difficulty in acknowledging and resolving problems. Minuchin believed that AN families were in a state of constant but unresolved conflict, with conflicts being abandoned at their most intense level without resolution of the issues that caused the conflict. This is evident in that families of AN patients typically present a strong façade of togetherness and a tendency to avoid overt conflict (Latzer and Gaber, 1998).

Salvador Minuchin was born in 1921 and raised in a small Jewish community in San Salvador, Argentina. At age 18 he entered university as a medical student, where he became active in the political movement opposing the dictator Juan Peron and was jailed for three months. After graduation he took up psychiatry and, in 1948, moved to the new state of Israel and joined its army, treating young Jewish soldiers who had survived the Holocaust. In the 1960s, he began working therapeutically with children with psychosomatic illnesses. Research with these children and their families indicated that family therapy could help these patients improve and suggested that maladaptive family patterns were partly to blame for these illnesses. He retired in 1996 and currently lives in Florida.

EVALUATION

Support for the concept of enmeshment

Manzi et al. (2006) demonstrated a distinction between family factors that promote positive emotional development and those that stifle it. Family cohesion, for example, was indicative of supportive family interactions, whereas enmeshment was rooted in manipulation and control. Manzi et al. found that cohesion among family members was linked to positive outcomes and psychological well-being among adolescents, whereas enmeshment had the opposite effect, i.e. there was an *inverse* relationship between enmeshment and the same positive outcomes. These findings, which are in line with Minuchin et al.'s predictions, applied across different cultural groups.

Problems with the psychosomatic family model

Research has tried to establish the characteristics that are specific to families in which a family member has AN and test the predictions of the psychosomatic family model. However, this has produced generally disappointing and inconsistent findings. For example, Kog and Vandereycken (1989) failed to find the characteristics predicted by the psychosomatic family model in families of individuals with AN. There is growing evidence that families in which someone has an eating disorder are a diverse group in terms of the nature of family relationships, the emotional climate and patterns of family interaction.

Inconclusive support from family-based therapy

Although family dysfunction is only one potential cause of AN, the success of family-focused therapies has shown that families are a key part of the recovery process. For example, Carr (2009) concluded that there is compelling evidence for the effectiveness of family interventions for adolescent AN. However, le Grange and Eisler (2009) point out that while there is some evidence that family therapy is accompanied by changes in family functioning, these changes are not necessarily those predicted by the psychosomatic family model and may not happen in all families.

Gender bias in family systems theory

Gremillion (2003) claims there is a gender bias in family systems theory because this approach focuses almost exclusively on the mother–daughter relationship. She argues that although any family member can engage in enmeshed interactions with the patient, enmeshment is nearly always seen as maternal in origin. As a result, therapy to reduce enmeshment in families tends to focus on reforming 'dysfunctional' mothers rather than acknowledging the role played by fathers. However, fathers also contribute to the enmeshment process within the family. Gremillion argues that fathers' tendency to be overly controlling, by demanding action and change from the individual, is often overlooked in the development of AN symptoms.

Research support for lack of conflict resolution

Latzer and Gaber (1998) carried out an observational study comparing patterns of conflict resolution in 40 families of adolescent daughters with AN and 40 matched families without an AN family member. Parents and daughters were asked to choose two areas of disagreement between them and were asked to keep off the topic of food and eating as far as possible. There were substantial differences between the two groups. The families with daughters with AN had more difficulties choosing topics, remaining focused on them and moving toward resolution. These findings add support to Minuchin et al.'s claim of the pathological avoidance of conflict in families where one family member has AN.

Insider tip...
Remember, to make these evaluative points truly evaluative, *you need to build them into a critical commentary. The upgrade feature on this page tells you how to do this.*

KEY TERMS

Autonomy The freedom to make decisions and determine actions without the constraints imposed by others.

Control is to direct or to exercise authoritative influence over events or behaviours.

Enmeshment describes a family where parents are over-emotionally involved with their children but may be dismissive of their emotional needs. This can make it difficult for the child to develop an independent self-concept. The concept is used in family systems explanations of disorders such as anorexia.

Family systems theory claims that individuals cannot be understood in isolation from one another, but rather as a part of their family.

⬆ UPGRADE

Effective evaluation

In a previous Upgrade feature, we made reference to the fact that, for evaluation to be 'thorough and effective', each AO3 point should be in the region of 60 words. The word 'effective' when used in this context assesses how well you have *used* the material. There is a knack to this, which we have mentioned elsewhere in this book (e.g. page 75). However, this is a point worth repeating here, as getting this right could earn you quite a few extra marks.

Each of the AO3 paragraphs on the right-hand side of each spread raises a point of evaluation. Sometimes these are strengths, sometimes limitations and sometimes some other critical point relating to the material, such as a real-world application.

However, there is still work for *you* to do here. If we take the evaluation point about gender bias on this spread as an example, this could be introduced with the phrase '*Gremillion (2003) claims there is a gender bias in family systems theory…*' This is then elaborated: '*e.g. because it focuses almost exclusively on the mother–daughter relationship*'. The point can be explored a little more: '*Despite the fact that fathers also contribute to the enmeshment process, enmeshment is mostly seen as maternal in origin…*' followed by a final link back to the initial claim: '*…which means that the father's role in the development of AN is often overlooked.*'

CAN YOU? No. 7.4

1. Explain what is meant by *enmeshment*, *autonomy* and *control* in the context of family systems theory. (2 marks each)

2. Briefly outline family systems theory as an explanation for anorexia nervosa and give **one** criticism of this explanation. (6 marks)

3. Outline and evaluate family systems theory as an explanation for anorexia nervosa. (16 marks)

Social learning theory and anorexia nervosa

Humans learn by observing others, something referred to as **social learning**. Social learning is the most common way that people learn and, therefore, it is likely that many aspects of disordered eating have their roots in social learning. On this spread we examine the role of social learning in anorexia nervosa, particularly the role of the media and the role of significant others in an individual's life.

▲ Studies have found similarities between mothers' and daughters' dieting behaviours among children as young as 10 years old.

THE INFLUENCE OF SOCIAL LEARNING ON ANOREXIA NERVOSA

Bandura (1977) believed that people learn by observing the behaviours of others, as well as by observing the outcomes of those behaviours. Social learning theory suggests that children pay particular attention to significant role models in their life. They observe their attitudes and behaviour, and then, if they also perceive that these are likely to produce a positive response from others, will imitate them in the belief that they will receive the same positive feedback from those around them.

Modelling and reinforcement

Modelling – In order for social learning to take place, someone must carry out or 'model' a particular attitude or behaviour. Models may be parents or peers, or 'symbolic' models, such as someone portrayed in the media. These models provide examples of attitudes to food or dieting behaviour that can be observed by the individual and imitated by them.

Reinforcement – When an individual imitates a model's behaviour, others respond to the imitated behaviour. If the response is positive ('Wow, you've lost so much weight, you look great'), this positive reinforcement makes the individual feel better about themselves and makes them want to continue losing weight. They may also witness others being reinforced for their thinness (vicarious reinforcement) and so, with the expectation that they would also receive the same response from others if they were thin, they attempt to lose weight.

Maternal role models

Research has suggested that problematic eating behaviour is common in families of individuals with eating disorders. In particular, this research has spotlighted the mother–daughter relationship, with some researchers suggesting that mothers 'model' weight concerns for their daughters. For example, studies have found similarities between mothers' and daughters' restraint and dieting behaviours among children as young as 10 years old (Hill *et al.*, 1990). Other research has shown that mothers who complain about their own weight are more likely to have children who have their own weight concerns (Smolak *et al.*, 1999). These influences tend to be greater for daughters than they are for sons, and mothers are more influential than fathers in this form of social learning.

Peer influences

Peer reinforcement is particularly important during adolescence, so adolescents may be particularly susceptible to peer influence on patterns of disordered eating. A US study found that dieting among friends was significantly related to unhealthy weight control behaviours, such as the use of diet pills or purging (Eisenberg *et al.*, 2005). A specific mechanism of peer influence is teasing. Jones and Crawford (2006) found that overweight girls and underweight boys were most likely to be teased by their peers, suggesting that, through teasing, peers serve to enforce gender-based ideals. A study by Gravener *et al.* (2008) examined the association between peer dieting and drive for thinness in over 2,000 men and women of three age groups. They found significant associations between perceived peer dieting and a drive for thinness in both women and men. For women, this association was strongest in late adolescence and for same-sex peers, whereas for men the strength of the association did not differ by age group or the sex of dieting peers.

Media influences

The **media** are a major source of influence for the body image attitudes maintained by Western adolescents. For example, the portrayal of thin models on television and in magazines is a significant contributory factor in body image concerns and the drive for thinness among Western adolescent girls. The media do not influence everyone in the same way; for example, individuals with low self-esteem are more likely to compare themselves to idealised images portrayed in the media (Jones and Buckingham, 2005). Low self-esteem plays a part in the development of eating disorders such as AN, and the portrayal of abnormally thin women in the media can contribute to this. Button *et al.* (1996) found that girls with low self-esteem at age 11–12 were at significantly greater risk of developing an eating disorder at age 15–17.

A report published by the British Medical Association (BMA, 2000) expressed concern about the use of very thin models to advertise products and model clothes for the fashion industry. The report found that images of slim models in the media were in stark contrast to the body size and shape of most children and young women who are becoming increasingly heavier. The report concluded that the degree of thinness exhibited by these models is both unachievable and also biologically inappropriate and provides 'unhelpful role models for young women'. Indeed, a study conducted by *Health* magazine in 2002 concluded that, in the USA, 32% of female characters on TV are underweight, compared to just 5% of the female audience.

Maternal influence is more complex than social learning

Research on the role of mothers as models for eating disorders for their daughters has not always produced consistent results. For example, Pike and Rodin (1991) found that there was no evidence for daughters imitating the weight concern of their parents. Ogden and Steward (2000) found that although mothers and daughters were similar in their weight and BMI, there were no associations for their restrained eating or body dissatisfaction. These findings, therefore, do not support the modelling hypothesis of transmission of eating disorders between mother and daughter. Ogden and Steward suggest that the contribution of the mother to the development of disordered eating in the daughter may be more than simply providing a role model. They suggest that it may instead be the very nature of the mother–daughter relationship itself that is important, particularly the degree to which they are enmeshed.

Research support for peer influences

The social learning approach proposes that adolescent girls are influenced by the perceived weight of their peers. Costa-Font and Jofre-Bonet (2013) investigated the effect of peer weight on the likelihood of an individual developing anorexia. They found that individuals who had peers with a larger BMI (body mass index) had a lower likelihood of subsequently developing an eating disorder such as AN. This association between BMI and the likelihood of becoming anorexic was even more marked in younger women. This suggests that having peers with an average or higher than average BMI 'protects' individuals from eating disorders, whereas having peers with a lower than average BMI makes the development of AN more likely.

Another look at peer influences

Research does not always show a significant relationship between peer influence and development of AN. Shroff and Thompson (2006) found no correlation among friends on measures of disordered eating in an adolescent sample. Although Jones and Crawford (see facing page) found that overweight girls and underweight boys were more likely to be teased, these gender differences did not emerge until adolescence. Other research has highlighted that not all forms of teasing lead to body dissatisfaction. Cash (1995) interviewed young adult women about their experience of teasing during their adolescent years. He found that it was the perceived severity of the teasing that was linked to future body-image rather than just the presence or absence of teasing.

▲ Research has shown that early teasing about weight can be a risk factor for the later development of anorexia.

Research support for media influences

Evidence for the role of the media in shaping perceptions of body image comes from studies of societies where television has been introduced. Eating attitudes and behaviours were studied among adolescent Fijian girls following the introduction of television to Fiji in 1995 (Becker *et al.*, 2002). After exposure to TV the girls stated a desire to lose weight in order to become more like Western television characters. However, other research has shown that instructional intervention prior to media exposure to idealised female images prevents the adverse effects of exposure (Yamamiya *et al.*, 2005). This suggests that the media can be a powerful influence in the development of eating disorders, but that this can be prevented through education.

Not all forms of media have the same effects

Some studies have found that reading magazines is a more consistent predictor of the development of eating disorders than television viewing. Harrison and Cantor (1997) found no association between television exposure and eating disorders, but *did* find a significant association between reading fitness magazines and attitudes to food and dieting. Studies of undergraduate women have also found an association between reading fashion magazines and having a preference for lower weight and having lower confidence about body image, and feeling frustrated because of this (Turner *et al.* 1997).

🎧 Research methods

The study by Becker *et al.* (see left) collected data about eating attitudes using an established questionnaire (EAT-26). The questionnaire was given to the girls in the study on two occasions – at the beginning of the study (1995) and again three years later (1998), after television had been on the island for three years.

1. EAT-26 was constructed from a longer version with 40 questions (EAT-40). Comparisons between EAT-26 and EAT-40 showed a .98 correlation between the two. What does this mean? Refer to the concept of concurrent validity in your answer. (2 marks)
2. One of the questions asked was 'How do you feel about your weight?' Explain why this is an open question and discuss the value of such questions. (3 marks)
3. Data was also collected from respondents using an unstructured interview. Explain what is meant by an 'unstructured interview'. (2 marks)
4. In 1995 the mean BMI was 3.4 (standard deviation 3.4) and in 1998 the mean BMI was 24.9 (standard deviation 2.5). Explain why data on both mean and standard deviation are given. (2 marks)
5. What can you conclude from the data on standard deviation? (2 marks)

> **LINK TO RESEARCH METHODS**
>
> Validity on page 16.
> The other topics in these questions are covered in the research methods chapter of our Year 1 book.

Insider tip...
In order to make these evaluative points truly evaluative, you need to first identify what the critical point is and then elaborate it in the way we suggest on page 173. We have tried to help you with this by using informative titles to each point, but you still need to make this read like a critical point.

CAN YOU? No. 7.5

1. Briefly explain the role of modelling, reinforcement and media in the context of anorexia nervosa. (3 marks each)
2. Give **two** criticisms of the social learning theory explanation of anorexia nervosa. (3 marks each)
3. Outline and evaluate the social learning theory explanation of anorexia nervosa. (16 marks)

Cognitive theory and anorexia nervosa

The **cognitive theory** of emotional disorders was first developed by Aaron Beck in the 1970s (Beck, 1976). Beck believed that the way in which a person processes information affects their feelings and their behaviour. These patterns of thinking (schema), which emerge in the early years, organise and process information about the individual and the world in which they live. In some people, these schema distort reality and lead to mental disorders such as anorexia nervosa. Cognitive theories of anorexia nervosa, therefore, focus on how individuals with this disorder think differently about themselves and their social world, compared to individuals without the disorder.

There is no one definitive 'cognitive theory' that applies to AN, but rather there are a number of different theories that constitute a cognitive 'approach'.

COGNITIVE EXPLANATIONS OF ANOREXIA NERVOSA

Distortions and irrational beliefs

Distortions – Cognitive distortions are errors in thinking that cause the individual to develop a negative body image. These may be the result of comparisons with others (e.g. from exposure to thin models in the media) in terms of how they look or the amount that they eat. This leads to a misperception that the individual must be overweight, which leads to feelings of self-disgust and an attempt to lose weight.

Irrational beliefs – Individuals frequently develop self-defeating (i.e. injurious to their own welfare) habits because of faulty beliefs about themselves and the world around them. Whereas rational beliefs are based on fact and logic, irrational beliefs are not based on fact and tend to be unrealistic. A typical irrational belief in an individual suffering from AN is that they must be thin for others to like them or blaming themselves for their social exclusion because of their weight.

A cognitive behavioural model of AN (Garner and Bemis, 1982)

Garner and Bemis recognised that anorexia patients tend to have a number of characteristics in common. For example, they are typically high-achieving perfectionists, introverted and often full of self-doubt. These characteristics, coupled with the individual's exposure to cultural ideals of thinness lead them to form ideas about the importance of body weight and shape. As a result of this exposure, the AN individual develops the irrational belief that losing weight will reduce their distress and make them more attractive to others.

Losing weight becomes self-reinforcing for the individual because of the sense of achievement and the positive comments from others. Once the importance of being thin is established, anxiety about eating increases. This gradually develops into a fear of food and weight gain, and so food avoidance becomes the norm. As the individual becomes more and more socially isolated, this reduces the chances of them viewing their style of thinking as anything other than normal. Their distorted thinking and interpretation of events convinces them that weight and thinness is the sole referent for judging self-worth and that complete control over these is desirable.

The transdiagnostic model (Fairburn *et al.*, 2003)

Fairburn *et al.* suggest that a better way of understanding eating disorders such as AN is to see the various symptoms as manifestations of a more broadly defined eating disorder (hence the term *transdiagnostic*).

According to this model, the underlying cause of all eating disorders is the same set of cognitive distortions, which Fairburn refers to as 'core psychopathology'. This involves the overestimation of body weight, appearance and an emphasis on self-control, which Fairburn believed to be the central factor in AN. Unlike people whose self-esteem (i.e. their sense of self-worth) is determined by their achievements in many different areas of their life, in those with AN a sense of self-esteem is primarily determined by their weight and appearance and their ability to control these. The experience of being able to control eating, compared to the relative failure they may have in controlling other areas of their lives, makes the control of eating particularly important. The restriction of food that is a characteristic of individuals with AN is maintained by three mechanisms:

1. An enhanced sense of self-control leads to increased self-esteem. When an individual with AN decides not to eat or to eat very little, this provides positive reinforcement in the form of enhanced self-esteem.
2. The physiological and psychological changes they experience as a result of their starvation (e.g. intensified feelings of hunger, impaired concentration) are perceived by the individual as being the result of failures in self-control, which in turn leads to more intensified reliance on food restriction.
3. Because of the focus on weight and appearance, the individual engages in increased self-monitoring of their weight. This includes regular weight checking, examining themselves for hours in the mirror and interpreting each discomfort as a 'sense of being fat'. Any weight gain or a weight loss that is perceived as being too slow leads to increased efforts to restrict food even more in order to re-gain self-control and self-esteem.

Research support for the role of cognitive factors in AN

Lang *et al.* (2015) provided research support for the role of cognitive factors in anorexia nervosa. They compared the performance of 41 children and adolescents diagnosed with AN with 43 healthy control participants on a range of neuropsychological measures. There were no differences in IQ between the two groups. However, compared to the controls, the AN individuals displayed a more inflexible and inefficient cognitive processing style. For example, individuals with AN were less able to overcome previously held beliefs or habits in the face of new information. The inefficient cognitive processing in the AN group was independent of any clinical (e.g. length of illness) or demographic factors (e.g. education), suggesting that it represented an underlying characteristic of AN.

Support from Stroop test studies

There is some support for the predictions of cognitive theories of AN from studies that have used the Stroop test (see right). For example, Garner and Bemis and Fairburn *et al.* predict that an AN individual's attention will be biased toward stimuli that are related to body fatness and to fattening food because such stimuli are perceived as more threatening to people with an eating disorder. Ben-Tovim *et al.* (1989) used a version of the Stroop test (the 'food Stroop' test) and discovered that, compared to normal controls, patients with AN found it harder to colour-name words that were relevant to their weight concerns, suggesting a selective preoccupation with those stimuli and words related to them.

YELLOW BLUE ORANGE
BLACK **RED GREEN**
PURPLE YELLOW RED
ORANGE GREEN BLACK
BLUE RED PURPLE
GREEN BLUE ORANGE

▲ The Stroop test. Ignoring the words and just saying the colour they are written in is difficult because processing the words interferes with our ability to name the colours.

CBT-E: Support from the success of therapy

Further support for the role of cognitive factors in anorexia comes from the success of cognitive behavioural therapies used in its treatment. CBT-E (cognitive behavioural therapy for eating disorders) is a form of treatment specifically designed to address the cognitive problems that underlie eating disorders such as AN. A study by Fairburn *et al.* (2015) compared CBT-E with interpersonal psychotherapy (IPT), a leading alternative treatment that has no cognitive element. One hundred and thirty patients with an eating disorder were randomised to either CBT-E or IPT. At the end of 20 weeks of treatment, two-thirds of the CBT-E participants met the criteria for remission compared with just one-third of the IPT participants. The findings indicate that CBT-E is an effective treatment for the majority of individuals with an eating disorder and reinforces the view that cognitive issues are a root cause of AN.

Methodological limitations of cognitive theories of AN

Viken *et al.* (2002) claim that a limitation of cognitive theories of AN such as that proposed by Garner and Bemis is the over-reliance on self-reports of cognitive processing. For example, there is an assumption that a pre-occupation with thoughts of weight and thinness is somehow accessible through verbal self-report measures. Instead, self-reported cognitions tend to be assessed retrospectively with the assumption that individuals can accurately represent cognitions they have experienced at a previous point in time. Most cognitive scientists have rejected this approach in favour of performance-based measures that sample cognitive-processing directly. This suggests that our understanding of the cognitive distortions thought to occur in AN are limited because of the problems associated with the methods used to access them.

Limitations of the cognitive approach

Cooper (1997) claims that cognitive models of anorexia nervosa are largely the result of clinical observation rather than being based on empirical research. She points out that there has been comparatively little research carried out that tests the hypotheses derived from cognitive models of anorexia, and that many of these studies suffer from methodological problems, such as the over-reliance on self-report questionnaires. As a result, claims Cooper, the development of a cognitive approach to anorexia nervosa has lagged behind the development of cognitive theory in other disorders, such as depression and anxiety disorders.

⬆ UPGRADE

Coping with specific demands in questions

It is wise to read all questions very carefully, as questions may have quite subtle and specific requirements, as shown in Q1 in the 'Can You…?' feature on this page. Here you are required to explain one specific aspect of the cognitive theory explanation – i.e. irrational beliefs. However, the question is quite specific in that it states 'in the context of anorexia nervosa'. You have met the idea of irrational beliefs in your first year, but there it was in the context of depression, so your answer to Q1 here must focus clearly on how these apply to anorexia, and not more generally. Probably the easiest way to do this is by using an example of an irrational belief in anorexia. As there are only 2 marks for this question you would only need a maximum of 50 words in total.

So try this (aiming for 50 words in total):
An irrational belief is…
For example, a person with anorexia might believe that…

It also pays to be flexible when preparing your answers for such questions. For a 3-mark question on the role of irrational beliefs in AN, this would mean about 75 words, but you should also have a 100-word version ready for a possible 4-mark question. So… be flexible in your preparation, read questions carefully and concentrate on the specific requirements to maximise your marks.

CAN YOU? No. 7.6

1. Explain what is meant by the term *irrational beliefs* in the context of the cognitive theory of anorexia nervosa. (2 marks)
2. Explain what is meant by the term *distortions* in the context of the cognitive theory of anorexia nervosa and give **one** example of such a distortion. (2 marks each)
3. Outline and evaluate the cognitive theory explanation of anorexia nervosa. (16 marks)

Biological explanations for obesity

The World Health Organization has identified obesity as one of the major chronic diseases that increases the risk of a number of other diseases, such as Type 2 diabetes and high blood pressure, and so reduces life expectancy. A 2015 government report compared obesity rates for the 20-year period 1993–2013. It reported that, in 1993, 13% of men in the UK and 16% of women were classified as obese, but in 2013 these figures had risen to a staggering 26% and 24% respectively. Over these next two spreads we examine the possible reasons for this 'obesity epidemic', starting with **biological explanations**.

'Heritability' is the proportion of any differences between individuals in a population with regards to a particular trait that is due to genetic variation. Numerical values of heritability range from 0.0 (genes do not contribute at all to individual differences in obesity) to 1.0 (genes are the only reason for individual differences). These figures can also be expressed as percentages (i.e. 0–100%), as on this page.

KEY TERMS

Biological explanations A belief that a full understanding of thoughts, emotions and behaviour must include an understanding of their biological basis, i.e. the role of genetics, neural correlates and hormones.

Genetic explanations The likelihood of behaving in a particular way is determined by a person's genetic makeup, i.e. it is inherited from parents.

Neural explanations involve areas of the brain and nervous system and the action of chemical messengers in the brain known as neurotransmitters in controlling behaviour.

What is obesity?

'Overweight' and 'obese' are terms that refer to an excess of body fat and they are usually defined in terms of a person's body mass index (BMI) and their waist circumference.

BMI is calculated by dividing a person's weight measurement (in kilograms) by the square of their height (in metres). In adults, a BMI of 20–24.9 is considered normal, 25–29.9 overweight, 30–39.9 clinically obese and 40 and above severely obese.

Although the most widely used definition of obesity, it does not allow for differences in weight between muscle and fat or the location of the fat. An analysis of the location of fat is important because abdominal fat is more likely to predict health problems (such as diabetes) than lower body fat. 'Waist circumference' is therefore a second measurement of obesity, with weight reduction recommended when waist circumference is above 40 inches (men) or 35 inches (women).

BIOLOGICAL EXPLANATIONS FOR OBESITY

Genetics

Explanations that emphasise the **genetic** inheritance of obesity risk have used twin studies (a comparison of genetically identical (MZ) and non-identical (DZ) twins) and adoption studies (where adopted individuals are compared with their adopted and biological parents).

Twin studies

There have been many twin studies in obesity, and the average heritability reported in these studies varies between approximately 40% and 75%. For example, a meta-analysis of studies involving 75,000 individuals (Maes *et al.*, 1997) found heritability estimates for BMI of 74% in MZ twins and 32% in DZ twins. Even when MZ twins are reared apart (and therefore experience dissimilar environmental influences), MZ twins are more alike in terms of their BMI than are DZ twins reared together and who experience similar environments (Stunkard *et al.*, 1990).

Adoption studies

Researchers have also studied individuals who have been adopted as infants and raised by biologically unrelated families. Adoption studies allow researchers to look separately at the influence of biological parents (genetics) and adoptive parents (environment). In a Danish study, Stunkard *et al.* (1986) gathered information from 540 adult adoptees, their adoptive parents and their biological parents. This showed a strong relationship between the weight category (i.e. underweight, overweight or obese) of adopted individuals and their biological parents' weight category but no significant relationship with their adoptive parents' weight category.

Neural explanations

Neural explanations include the following:

The hypothalamus

The hypothalamus plays a key role in regulating metabolism and energy expenditure (see page 168). Research has identified one particular part of the hypothalamus, the arcuate nucleus, as playing a key role in appetite and obesity. The arcuate nucleus is a collection of neurons in the hypothalamus, which monitors circulating sugar levels in the blood, and acts when energy levels are low. The arcuate nucleus, when activated, sends messages to other parts of the body, producing the desire to eat and coordinating this with energy utilisation. It is, therefore, responsible for the maintenance of body weight, carefully adjusting food intake to physical activity. Any malfunction with this area can lead to overeating and obesity.

Leptin

Leptin, a hormone secreted by fat cells (see page 168), is a crucial signal of stored bodily energy and acts to decrease feeding behaviour and promote energy expenditure through a number of different neural and endocrine mechanisms. Leptin inhibits food intake by acting on leptin receptors in the appetite control centres in the brain. For example, leptin inhibits the appetite-stimulating hormone neuropeptide Y in the arcuate nucleus. Bates and Myers (2003) showed that disruption of leptin signalling in the hypothalamus results in obesity and confirms the central role of leptin in feeding regulation.

An evolutionary model of obesity: The 'thrifty gene' hypothesis

Geneticist James Neel (Neel, 1962) proposed a theory to explain the prevalence of obesity in modern society. He referred to this as the 'thrifty gene hypothesis'. Neel argued that for most of the history of the human species it was often 'food or famine', i.e. food was available sporadically and there were other periods where early humans would go hungry. As a result, those who gorged themselves when food was abundant and then held reserves of body fat for when food was scarce again were better able to survive.

Neel suggested that these so-called 'thrifty' genes would have been positively selected for in this feast–famine environment because during the feast periods people with these genes were particularly efficient in the intake and utilisation of food. This would make such people fat, which in turn provided the energy necessary for them to survive during famines. During subsequent famines, those individuals with the 'thrifty' genotype would have a survival advantage because they relied on larger amounts of previously stored energy, whereas those without 'thrifty' genotypes would be at a disadvantage and less likely to survive. Nowadays, such genes are disadvantageous because they promote fat deposition in preparation for a famine that never comes, and the result is widespread obesity and diabetes.

The expression of genetic influences varies with age

Research suggests that the genetic contribution to BMI is not stable across a person's lifetime. For example, a meta-analysis of 88 studies by Elks *et al.* (2012) found that heritability estimates varied according to the age group of individuals studied. They found the heritability figure was highest during childhood and then decreased during adulthood. This is most probably due to the greater gene expression during childhood, compared to adulthood, where individuals have adopted individual dietary and exercise habits, decreasing the genetic contribution to their BMI and increasing the environmental (cognitive) contribution.

The problem of time and geography

A 2015 government report described a sharp increase in obesity rates in the UK over the last 20 years. For example, in 1993, 13% of UK males were classified as obese, but this figure had risen to 26% by 2013. However, the nature of the gene pool has remained constant over the same period. An explanation based on genetics alone, therefore, could not explain this sudden increase in obesity rates. Likewise, obesity rates vary within the same culture because of geographical differences. In China, for example, the overall rates of obesity are below 5% in the countryside, but higher than 20% in some cities. Such differences are likely to be due to psychological factors (such as the availability of fast food in urban areas) rather than genetic factors.

▲ The rapid increase in obesity rates, particularly in urban areas, poses problems for genetic explanations, as the gene pool changes at a much slower rate.

Research support for the leptin–obesity relationship

Although most research on this relationship has been carried out on non-humans, there is some evidence that suggests that some humans do not produce leptin, which predisposes them to obesity. Montague *et al.* (1997) reported on two severely obese cousins of Pakistani origin but living in the UK. Both children were found to have very low leptin levels despite their elevated fat levels. Gibson *et al.* (2004) also reported on a child from the same region of Pakistan and who also suffered from severe obesity. After four years of treatment with leptin injections, the child had dramatically beneficial effects on appetite, metabolism and weight. These studies support the role of leptin in regulating appetite and its deficiency as a risk factor in obesity.

Advantages of biological explanations

An advantage of biological explanations of obesity is that they offer explanations of obesity that are perceived as being out of the individual's personal control and therefore less stigmatising. This is in sharp contrast to many psychological explanations of obesity that highlight the personal failing of the individual (e.g. overeating or lack of exercise). The simplicity of biological explanations makes them more 'attractive' than complex psychological explanations, which focus on a number of contributory factors. Because of the 'scientific' nature of biological explanations, treatments based on remedial leptin injections, for example, offer individuals some hope of dealing with their disorder.

Problems with the thrifty gene hypothesis

Speakman (2008) argues that if the thrifty gene explanation is correct, then the majority of human beings should have inherited these 'thrifty genes'. If these mutations cause obesity, as the explanation suggests, then the majority of people should be obese. Despite recent concerns about the 'obesity epidemic' in Western cultures, this is both fairly recent and restricted to only a few cultures where cultural habits lead people to consume high quantities of fatty and sugary food. For example, a study by Ng *et al.* (2014) found that more than half of the world's 671 million obese people live in 10 countries. This suggests that the relatively high levels of obesity found in these cultures can be more easily explained by cultural factors rather than evolved adaptations.

Insider tip…

Remember that to make your evaluation truly 'evaluative', you need to introduce it as such. For example, you might begin the first point with the statement that 'A problem for genetic explanations of obesity is that the expression of genetic influences varies with age'.

🐾 APPLY YOUR KNOWLEDGE

Santa Claus has a bit of a weight problem. He has always been a bit 'well-rounded', even as a child. He claims it is nothing to do with all the mince pies that are left for him (which he mostly ignores), and Mrs Claus has him on a strict diet the whole year round leading up to Christmas. Most of his biological family at the North Pole have the same problem, i.e. they are carrying more than a few extra pounds. His brother Bob Claus and his sister Holly Claus are also clinically obese, which leads Santa into thinking that maybe his problem is 'something biological'.

Using your knowledge of biological explanations of obesity, explain why Santa might struggle to keep the weight off.

CAN YOU?   No. 7.7

1. Briefly explain and give **one** criticism of genetic explanations of obesity. (6 marks)
2. Briefly explain and give **one** criticism of neural explanations of obesity. (6 marks)
3. Discuss biological explanations for obesity. (16 marks)

Psychological explanations for obesity

Obesity is as much a psychological as a biological problem. Biological explanations cannot explain why obesity rates have increased so rapidly in recent years. To address this problem, researchers have turned their attention to the role of psychological factors and what Hill and Peters (1998) refer to as the 'obesogenic environment', for example the easy availability of fast food and persuasive food advertising. This obesogenic environment makes it easy to gain weight and hard to lose it. On this spread we examine some of the reasons why attempts to *lose* weight can often result in overeating and obesity.

Insider tip…

The explanations offered on this page are based on theories related to overeating because that has been the approach psychologists take in understanding obesity. However, when answering an exam question on psychological explanations of obesity you should make sure your answer is shaped to address obesity specifically.

Herman and Mack (1975)

In this study, participants who had eaten nothing for several hours were randomly assigned to one of three groups, i.e. no milkshake, one milkshake or two milkshakes. They were then given three flavours of ice cream to taste, being told that this was to determine whether the flavour of the milkshake affected their sensory experience of the ice cream.

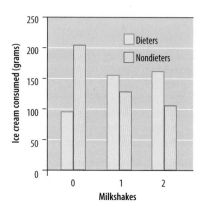

As we might expect, participants who weren't on a diet (the unrestrained eaters) ate less of the ice cream if they had already had the milkshake (the preload) prior to the the ice cream tasting. However, participants who were on a diet (i.e. restrained eaters) reacted differently. Those who had not had the milkshake were very restrained when tasting the ice cream. However, those who had already had the milkshake ate *more* ice cream. In fact, the bigger the preload, the more ice cream they ate!

PSYCHOLOGICAL EXPLANATIONS FOR OBESITY

Restraint theory

Restrained eating has become synonymous with dieting, and lack of restraint with obesity. Peter Herman and Deborah Mack (1975) developed the **restraint theory**, suggesting that attempting not to eat actually increases the probability of overeating. They claim that in the majority of cases, rather than restraint leading to weight loss, it leads to overeating and weight gain and therefore increases the risk of becoming obese.

Different types of restraint have been identified. 'Rigid' restraint represents an all-or-nothing approach to dieting and, 'flexible' restraint represents a less strict approach to dieting where fattening foods can be eaten in limited quantities without guilt. Provencher *et al.* (2003) reported that rigid restraint tends to be positively associated with amount of body fat, waist circumference and BMI, and flexible restraint tends to be negatively associated with these three measures of obesity. For example, women who scored higher on flexible restraint reduced their subsequent ice cream intake following a preload of milkshake, whereas women who scored higher on rigid restraint did not reduce their ice cream intake following the preload (Westenhoefer *et al.*, 1994).

The boundary model

In an attempt to explain why dieting might lead to overeating, Herman and Polivy (1984) developed the boundary model. According to this model, food intake is regulated along a continuum, with hunger at one end and fullness at the other. At either end of this continuum, food intake is driven by biological processes. When the body's energy levels are low, we experience hunger, which gives rise to eating. At the other extreme, when we have taken in sufficient energy, we experience unpleasant feelings of fullness, and we stop eating. In between these two points is what Herman and Polivy refer to as the 'zone of biological indifference', where the individual is neither hungry nor full and food intake is determined more by cultural and social factors.

Restrained eaters (dieters) have a larger zone of biological indifference, in that they have a lower threshold for hunger and a higher threshold for satiation (feelings of fullness). This means they are less sensitive to feelings of hunger but are also less sensitive to feelings of fullness.

Herman and Polivy also claimed that dieters have a self-imposed 'diet boundary' that is set lower than the satiation threshold. This boundary is cognitively determined and represents what the dieter believes he or she *should* eat. However, if the dieter goes over this limit, they experience what Herman and Polivy refer to as the 'what the hell' effect. Because the diet boundary has already been surpassed, the person continues to eat until they reach satiation or even beyond.

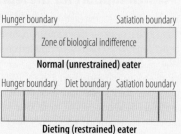

Disinhibition

Disinhibition is the tendency to overeat in response to different stimuli, and can occur in a variety of circumstances such as when an individual is presented with lots of palatable foods or is under emotional distress (Hays and Roberts, 2008). In these situations, the normal inhibitions that prevent us from eating too much are removed, and so people respond less to feelings of satiation and are more susceptible to overeating. Studies have shown that disinhibition is strongly associated with adult weight gain and BMI (e.g. Bellisle *et al.*, 2004).

Bond *et al.* (2001) have identified three different types of disinhibition, each with their own impact on overeating:

- Habitual disinhibition – the tendency to overeat in response to daily life circumstances.
- Emotional disinhibition – the tendency to overeat in response to emotional states such as anxiety or depression.
- Situational disinhibition – the tendency to overeat in response to specific environmental cues (e.g. social occasions such as wedding buffets or parties).

Of these, habitual disinhibition has been shown to be the most important correlate of weight gain and obesity because of the high number of daily overeating opportunities people face in the typical Western food environment (Hays and Roberts, 2008). Bryant *et al.* (2008) suggest that this form of eating is better described as 'opportunistic eating'. Situational and emotional disinhibition, on the other hand, occur less frequently, so have less potential for contributing to obesity.

Support for restraint theory

Support for the claim that dietary restraint can lead to overeating comes from Wardle and Beales (1988). They randomly assigned 27 obese women to either a diet group (focusing on restrained eating patterns), an exercise group or a non-treatment group for seven weeks. At weeks four and six, all participants were assessed under laboratory conditions. At week four, food intake and appetite were assessed before and after a 'preload' (i.e. a small snack, such as a milkshake or chocolate bar). At week six, food intake was assessed under stressful conditions. Results showed that, at both assessment sessions, women in the diet condition ate more than women in the exercise and non-treatment groups, as predicted by restraint theory.

A challenge to restraint theory

Tomiyama et al. (2009) argued that most research relating to restraint theory (such as the Herman and Mack study described on the facing page) have been restricted to the laboratory. Such research typically shows that restrained eaters overeat after they violate their diet. Tomiyama et al. challenged this view of restraint, arguing that, outside of this artificial setting, restrained eaters would be able to control their eating. In two studies they showed that dieters who tracked their food intake over a period of days did not overeat following violations of their diet (a milkshake that was part of an ostensibly unrelated study). Tomiyama et al.'s findings appear to dispel the belief that diet violations lead to overeating in everyday life.

The 'what the hell' effect: Motivational collapse or rebellious reaction?

Herman and Polivy's 'what the hell' effect, experienced when dieters go past their self-imposed diet boundary, is described as a breakdown in the dieter's self-control, as the person simply gives in to overpowering urges to eat. Ogden and Wardle (1991) argue, however, that rather than passively giving in to a desire to eat, the individual may actively decide to overeat as a form of rebellion against their self-imposed food restrictions. This idea of overeating as an expression of rebelliousness is supported in a study by Loro and Orleans (1981). They found that obese binge eaters frequently reported bingeing as a way of 'unleashing resentment' against their diet.

Disinhibition may not be important in all groups

Most research on disinhibition has been restricted to women, particularly white women, which means that conclusions about men or other racial groups cannot be made. Atlas et al. (2002) reported that both restraint and disinhibition scores were significantly lower in African American students compared to white college students. This suggests that disinhibited eating behaviours may be less prevalent among African American women. Similarly, several studies (e.g. Bellisle et al., 2004) have reported that restraint and disinhibition scores are lower in men compared to women, suggesting that disinhibition might be a more important influence in adult weight gain in women compared to men.

Disinhibited eating may be related to attachment style

Research suggests that disinhibited eating may be linked to an insecure avoidant attachment style in adulthood. Wilkinson et al. (2010) recruited 200 adults whose BMIs ranged from 17 to 41. Measures of disinhibition and attachment style showed that 'attachment anxiety' was significantly linked to disinhibited eating and to BMI. The researchers suggest that a tendency to deal with anxiety through overeating leads, over time, to an increase in BMI. This is consistent with other research that has identified that significant life events such as leaving home or entering prison can lead to shifts in BMI. This suggests that anxiously attached individuals may be more sensitive to these events and so more likely to engage in disinhibited eating as a way of coping.

KEY TERMS

Disinhibition In relation to eating behaviour, this is the removal of the normal inhibitions to overeating (e.g. satiation), resulting in the tendency to overeat in response to a range of different stimuli.

Restraint theory Restraint is the conscious restriction of food intake to prevent weight gain or promote weight loss. This theory proposes that attempting to restrain eating actually increases the probability of overeating.

Research methods

A researcher used content analysis to look at the reasons why young women diet. Data was collected using open-ended questions asking people to describe their attitudes about dieting and the methods that they used.

1. Explain why the data collected could be classed as qualitative. (2 marks)
2. Explain the strength of collecting qualitative data for this study. (3 marks)
3. Once the data was collected, the researcher performed a thematic analysis of the data. Explain how this would be performed. (6 marks)
4. Once the themes were identified, the data was coded for each participant. This was done by two coders for each set of data. Why was it necessary to have two coders? (2 marks)

LINK TO RESEARCH METHODS

Thematic analysis on page 13.
The other topics in these questions are covered in the research methods chapter of our Year 1 book.

CAN YOU? No. 7.8

1. Briefly outline the restraint theory of obesity and give **one** criticism of this explanation. (6 marks)
2. Briefly outline the disinhibition explanation of obesity and give **one** criticism of this explanation. (6 marks)
3. Briefly outline the boundary model of obesity and give **one** criticism of this explanation. (6 marks)
4. Outline research into psychological explanations of obesity. (6 marks)
5. Discuss psychological explanations for obesity. (16 marks)

Explanations for the success and failure of dieting

A consequence of body dissatisfaction is the need to diet as an attempt to modify body size and shape to fit in with perceived cultural ideals. Three basic forms of dieting have been identified: (1) restricting the total amount of food eaten; (2) refraining from eating certain types of food; and (3) avoiding eating for long periods of time. The potential to influence weight change then becomes the primary (in many cases the exclusive) criterion for food selection. Dieting may also be associated with a particular mentality or mindset, characterised by a pervasive concern with body size, shape and weight (Higgins and Gray, 1999). On this spread we examine the psychological reasons why **dieting** sometimes succeeds but often fails.

▲ Attempts to suppress thoughts of 'forbidden' foods only serve to increase the dieters' preoccupation with them.

KEY TERM

Dieting A deliberate reduction of food intake in an attempt to lose weight.

▲ Redden's jelly bean experiment suggests that people are more likely to stick to a diet if they focus on the detail, i.e. the different components (flavours, colours, etc.) of each meal.

EXPLANATIONS FOR THE SUCCESS AND FAILURE OF DIETING

A theory of hedonic eating

Stroebe (2008) suggests that restrained (i.e. dieting) eaters' problems in maintaining their diets might begin with the fact that they are more sensitive to the hedonic (i.e. pleasurable) properties of food. Due to this increased sensitivity, the perception of attractive food triggers in restrained eaters a desire to eat food because of its perceived pleasurable qualities. As a result, restrained eaters' cognitive processes will be geared towards pursuing this goal, and any conflicting goals (i.e. maintaining their diet) will be inhibited. Stroebe argues that, because eating enjoyment and eating control are incompatible goals, increasing thoughts of eating enjoyment should inhibit access to thoughts of eating control.

Attention allocation

Mischel and Ayduk (2004) describe a second process that makes it difficult for dieters to resist the temptation of attractive food – attention allocation. The difficulty of these individuals in resisting the temptation of attractive food might be aggravated by the fact that, once this food has triggered pleasurable thoughts, restrained eaters find it difficult to withdraw their attention from the attractive food item. Thus, according to this theory, the failure of dieting in restrained eaters is due to a sequential process. Exposure to attractive food triggers hedonic thoughts, which result in selective attention to these food items and the inhibition of thoughts of dieting. Unless these individuals are reminded of their dieting goal, they find it difficult to withdraw their attention from the food and to resist the temptation to eat.

The role of denial

Research in cognitive psychology has shown that attempting to suppress or deny a thought frequently has the opposite effect, making it even more prominent. For example, Wegner *et al.* (1987) asked some participants not to think about a white bear, but to ring a bell if they did, and others to think about the bear. Results showed that those told not to think about the bear rang their bells far more often than participants instructed to think about the bear. Wegner (1994) refers to this phenomenon as the 'theory of ironic processes of mental control' because it represents a paradoxical effect of thought control, i.e. denial often backfires.

The theory of ironic processes of mental control

Central to any dieting strategy is the decision not to eat certain foods, or to eat less of them. This results in a similar state of denial to the example above, as dieters try to suppress thoughts about foods deemed to be 'forbidden' as part of their diet. According to this theory, therefore, attempts to suppress thoughts of foods such as pizza and chocolate only serve to increase the dieters' preoccupation with the very foods they are trying to deny themselves. As soon as a food is denied, therefore, it simultaneously becomes more attractive.

Detail – the key to a successful diet

So far on this spread we have concentrated on the reasons why diets fail, but research by Redden (2008) suggests that the secret of successful dieting lies in the attention we pay to what is being eaten. He claims that people usually like experiences less as they repeat them. When it comes to dieting, this makes it harder to stick to a particular regime. To overcome this, suggests Redden, instead of thinking 'not another salad', we should focus on the details of the meal (e.g. rocket, tomato, apple, etc.). By focusing on the specific details of each meal, people get bored less easily and so are better able to maintain their diet.

The jelly beans experiment

To test this idea, Redden gave 135 people 22 jelly beans each, one at a time. As each bean was dispensed, information about it was flashed onto a computer screen. One group saw general information (e.g. 'bean number 7'), whereas the other group saw specific flavour details (e.g. 'cherry flavour number 7'). Participants got bored with eating beans faster if they only saw the general information, and enjoyed the task more if they saw the specific flavour details. This shows that details of the food consumed cuts down on any repetitive feeling and boosts enjoyment, which in turn would make sticking to a diet more likely.

EVALUATION

Research support for ironic processes of mental control

Soetens *et al.* (2006) provided experimental support for this theory. Participants were divided into restrained and unrestrained eaters, and the restrained group was then subdivided into those who were either high or low on disinhibition. The disinhibited restrained group (i.e. those who tried to eat less but who would often overeat) used more thought suppression than the other groups, and also showed a rebound effect (i.e. thought more about food) afterwards. This study shows that restrained eaters who tend to overeat try to suppress thoughts about food more often but, when they do, think more about food afterwards. However, Wegner (1994) admits that the 'ironic effects' observed in research are not particularly huge. As experimental effects go, they are detectable but far from overwhelming. However, as such effects may underlie more serious pathological forms of eating behaviour, their influence could be considered overwhelming in terms of everyday human cost.

Support for the hedonic theory

Support for the claim that restrained eaters are more likely than unrestrained eaters to focus on the pleasurable aspects of food come from studies of physiological and affective reactions to the perception of food. The presence or even the smell of palatable food induces more salivation in restrained than in unrestrained eaters. For example, Brunstrom *et al.* (2004) tested salivary reactivity in 40 female participants when they were in close proximity to hot pizza. Participants who were dieting (i.e. restrained eaters) showed a greater salivary response to the pizza than did

▲ Restrained eaters show a greater salivary response in the presence of attractive food than do unrestrained eaters.

participants who were not dieting (i.e. unrestrained eaters). This suggests a difference between the reaction of restrained and unrestrained eaters in their perception of food.

Real-world application: Anti-dieting programmes

Concerns about the ineffectiveness and potentially damaging effects of many diet programmes has led to the development of programmes aimed at replacing dieting with conventional healthy eating. These programmes emphasise regulation by body hunger and satiety signals and the prevention of inappropriate attitudes to food (e.g. comfort-eating or food avoidance). A meta-analysis of the effectiveness of anti-dieting programmes (Higgins and Gray, 1999) found that participation in these programmes was associated with improvements in both eating behaviour and psychological well-being and with weight stability rather than weight change. This suggests that eating only when hungry and stopping when satiated is more likely to be successful than trying to restrict or restrain food intake.

Limitations of anecdotal evidence

Many studies of dieting success or failure rely on the personal accounts of individuals, i.e. anecdotal evidence. Such evidence is often used to justify claims concerning particular dieting strategies. However, anecdotal evidence has a number of problems that properly controlled scientific studies do not have. The main limitation is that memory is not 100% accurate, nor is assessment of the success or failure of dieting entirely objective, which creates problems for the reliability of the evidence provided by personal accounts and anecdotes. An additional problem is that causal connections between a particular approach to dieting and weight loss are made too easily without the control over extraneous variables that is possible with randomised controlled trials.

Free will or determinism – Born to be fat?

It is likely that a number of genetic mechanisms exert an influence on weight, suggesting that the success or failure of dieting may be determined by factors other than an individual's choice of lifestyle. One such gene codes for lipoprotein lipase (LPL), an enzyme produced by fat cells to help store calories as fat. If too much LPL is produced, the body will be especially efficient at storing calories. LPL also makes it easier to regain lost weight. In one study, nine people who lost an average of 90 pounds had their LPL levels measured before dieting and again three months later. Levels of LPL rose after weight loss, and the fatter the person was to start with, the higher the LPL levels were, as though the body was fighting to regain the weight (Kern *et al.*, 1990). The researchers believe that weight loss activated the gene producing the enzyme, which might explain why it is easier for a dieter to regain lost weight than for someone who has never been obese to put weight on. This suggests that some people will struggle to lose weight because of their genetics regardless of their intentions to do so.

🐾 APPLY YOUR KNOWLEDGE

Estrella is studying psychology at her local sixth-form college. Her mum, Carla, is fascinated when she finds the topic of dieting in Estrella's textbook, because Carla runs a 'health and well-being' scheme at a large company in the area. Carla is always being asked about how employees might lose weight, and she hits upon the idea of Estrella writing a short 150-word piece for their weekly newsletter from a psychological perspective. This would be an accessible and informed piece on why diets tend to fail and how psychologists have suggested that they might succeed if they are approached in the right way.

Using your knowledge of why diets succeed or fail, suggest which 150 words Estrella should use in her piece to accurately represent this area of psychological research.

▲ Research suggests that, for some people, dieting will always be difficult because of a genetic predisposition to obesity.

CAN YOU? No. 7.9

1. Outline research into the success and/or failure of dieting. (6 marks)
2. Briefly outline **one** explanation for the success and/or failure of dieting and give **one** criticism of this explanation. (6 marks)
3. Outline and evaluate **one or more** explanations for the success and/or failure of dieting. (16 marks)

We have identified here the key points of the topics on the AQA A level specification, i.e. the bare minimum that you need to know. You may want to fill in further details to elaborate and personalise this material.

THE EVOLUTIONARY EXPLANATION FOR FOOD PREFERENCES

THE EVOLUTION OF FOOD PREFERENCES

- Preference for fatty food in EEA important for energy resources.
- Meat important for early humans because densely nutritious, so led to growth of the brain.
- Preference for sweet foods – available sugar and calories. Tall children had sweet preference (Mennella et al.).
- Taste aversion – learned response to eating poisonous food, adaptive and hard to shift once acquired.
- Neophobia – a reluctance to consume new or unusual foods. In humans, stronger to animal than non-animal products (Martins et al.).
- Environment of evolutionary adaptation (EEA) refers to the environment in which our species first evolved.

EVALUATION

- Not all food preferences are a product of evolution – mismatch between evolved preferences and modern environments (Krebs).
- Support for evolved preferences for sweet foods – cultures without experience of sweet foods show preference on first exposure (Bell et al.).
- Real-world application: taste aversion and chemotherapy – Bernstein and Webster, development of 'scapegoat technique'.
- Support for the heritability of neophobia – neophobia may be genetically determined (Knaapila et al.).
- Neophobia can also be maladaptive – e.g. it is associated with poorer dietary quality in children (Perry et al.).

THE ROLE OF LEARNING IN FOOD PREFERENCE

SOCIAL INFLUENCES

- Brown and Ogden – correlation between parents and their children in terms of snack food intake, eating motivations and body dissatisfaction.
- Parents may manipulate the availability of certain foods, either as a reward or because of perceived health gain.
- Behaviour of same-age peers influences food preferences of children through positive and negative modelling (Greenhalgh et al.).

CULTURAL INFLUENCES

- Media have major impact on what people eat, and attitudes to certain foods (MacIntyre et al.).
- Many eating behaviours limited by personal circumstances, such as age, income and family circumstances.
- Higher availability of takeaway food has led to more consumption of unhealthy food, higher BMI and greater odds of obesity (Burgoine et al.).
- Eating more 'informally' leads to a preference for snack-foods rather than more elaborate meals (Gillman et al.).

EVALUATION

- Limitations of parental influence view – highly selective samples. Study with wider sample found relationship far more complex (Robinson et al.).
- Not all parental influences are effective – parental modelling and food exposure effective; forcing consumption and restricting food access ineffective.
- Research support for the role of peers – e.g. Wardle et al., parental fruit and veg consumption; Jansen and Tenney, modelling of 'light' products.
- Research support for media influences on food preferences – exposure to food advertising on TV influences food preferences and food intake in children but differently for different weight statuses.
- Implications of media influences on food preferences – TV the dominant medium for children's exposure to food marketing, majority being for unhealthy foods (Cairns et al.). Has led to increased regulation on food advertising.
- Food preferences and the food environment – 'Twitter' study found relationship between healthy food outlets and quality of food choices but not between fast food outlets and unhealthy choices (Chen and Yang).

NEURAL AND HORMONAL MECHANISMS

NEURAL MECHANISMS IN THE CONTROL OF EATING

- Homeostasis involves mechanisms that detect whether the body has enough nutrients and correct the situation to restore the body to its optimal state.
- Stimulation of lateral hypothalamus (LH) initiates eating behaviour after stimulation by neuropeptide Y.
- Ventromedial hypothalamus (VMH) signals 'stop eating' with damage to paraventricular nucleus, leading to overeating.

HORMONAL MECHANISMS IN THE CONTROL OF EATING

- Ghrelin increases appetite when hungry, and leptin decreases appetite when body has enough stored energy.
- Ghrelin stimulates hypothalamus to increase appetite. If bodily resources are low then ghrelin levels increase.
- Leptin is secreted into the bloodstream where it travels to the brain and decreases appetite.
- Leptin counteracts the effects of neuropeptide Y and increases SNS activity to burn energy.

EVALUATION

- Limitations of a homeostatic explanation – does not anticipate and prevent energy deficits, so not truly adaptive.
- Problems with the role of LH – damage causes deficits in other circuits and eating controlled by other areas of the brain.
- Problems with the role of VMH – inconclusive evidence over the importance of VMH as satiety centre in the brain.
- Research support for the role of ghrelin in appetite control – ghrelin is an important signal which stimulates food intake (Wren et al.).
- Leptin resistance – some people develop resistance to leptin, which can lead to obesity (Heymsfield et al.).

BIOLOGICAL EXPLANATIONS FOR ANOREXIA NERVOSA

GENETIC EXPLANATIONS

- Family studies – first-degree relatives of individuals with AN have ten times greater risk of having AN than relatives of unaffected individuals (Strober et al.).
- Twin studies – suggest moderate-to-high heritability for AN, varying between 28% and 74% (Thornton et al.).
- Adoption studies – Klump et al. found heritability estimates ranging from 59–82% for disordered eating.

NEURAL EXPLANATIONS

- Serotonin – disturbances in serotonin levels a characteristic of individuals with AN (Bailer et al.).
- Dopamine – Kaye et al. (2005) found overactivity in dopamine receptors in basal ganglia among AN individuals.
- Limbic system dysfunction – neural roots of AN related to dysfunctional limbic circuits driving pathological thoughts and behaviours (Lipsman et al.).

EVALUATION

- Problems with genetic explanations – many studies violate 'equal environments assumption'.
- Genetic explanations ignore role of the media in AN – genetically vulnerable individuals might seek out images of thin role models as a way of reinforcing their body image (Bulik).
- Real-world application: is AN really biological in nature? Implications for insurance payouts if 'biologically based'.
- Problems with the serotonin explanation – SSRIs are ineffective when used with AN patients (Ferguson et al.) but can prevent relapse (Kaye et al.).
- Research support for dopamine–AN relationship – food aversion and weight loss related to increased activity in dopamine pathways (Kaye). Increased blink rate in AN suggests increased dopamine activity (Berbato et al.).
- Advantages of limbic system dysfunction explanations – reduce stigma and offer treatment possibilities (e.g. DBS, Lipsman et al.).

FAMILY SYSTEMS THEORY AND ANOREXIA NERVOSA

- Psychosomatic family model – prerequisite for development of AN was dysfunctional family occurring alongside physiological vulnerability in the child.
- Enmeshment – enmeshed family members are over-involved with each other.
- Autonomy – enmeshed families place constraints on its members, who are not allowed to become independent and develop autonomy.
- Control – enmeshed families exert overprotective control over members. Adolescent reacts by refusal to eat.
- Characteristics of AN families include rigidity and lack of conflict resolution.
- The child with AN is involved in parental conflict through triangulation, parent–child coalitions and detouring.

EVALUATION

- Support for the concept of enmeshment – cohesion among family members linked to positive outcomes, enmeshment had opposite effect (Manzi et al.).
- Problems with psychosomatic family model – Kog and Vandereycken failed to find characteristics predicted by model in families of individuals with AN.
- Inconclusive support from family-based therapy – changes following therapy not necessarily those predicted by psychosomatic model (le Grange and Eisler).
- Gender bias in family systems theory – focuses almost exclusively on mother–daughter relationship and ignores father's role.
- Research support for lack of conflict resolution – AN group showed significantly more conflict avoidance behaviour than non-AN families (Latzer and Gaber).

SOCIAL LEARNING THEORY AND ANOREXIA NERVOSA

- Modelling – models provide examples of attitudes to food or dieting behaviour that can be observed by the individual and imitated by them.
- Reinforcement – positive reinforcement, either directly or vicariously, can increase social learning.
- Maternal role models may model weight concerns for their daughters (Hill et al.).
- Peer influences through reinforcement and modelling, e.g. teasing (Jones and Crawford) and perceived peer dieting (Gravener et al.).
- BMA report – media provides unhelpful role models for young women.

EVALUATION

- Maternal influence more complex than social learning, e.g. Ogden and Steward – the nature of the relationship important.
- Research support for peer influences – having peers with a lower than average BMI makes the development of AN more likely (Costa-Font and Jofre-Bonet).
- Another look at peer influences – research casts doubt that eating disorders are consequence of social learning from peers (Shroff and Thompson).
- Research support for media influences – Fijian girls stated a desire to lose weight in order to become more like Western television characters (Becker et al.).
- Not all forms of media have same effects – Harrison and Cantor found significant association between reading fitness magazines and attitudes to dieting.

PSYCHOLOGICAL EXPLANATIONS FOR OBESITY

- Restraint theory attempting not to eat increases probability of overeating.
- Rigid dieting more likely to lead to overeating than flexible (Provencher et al.).
- Boundary model – food intake regulated from hunger to satiety boundaries.
- Dieters have lower hunger and higher satiety boundaries with self-imposed diet boundary which, when exceeded, can lead to overeating.
- Disinhibition – tendency to overeat in a variety of circumstances.
- Bond et al. identified habitual, emotional and situational disinhibition.

EVALUATION

- Support for restraint theory – Wardle and Beales: women in diet condition ate more than women in exercise and non-treatment groups.
- Challenge to restraint theory – research restricted to laboratory; restrained eaters able to control their eating in natural settings (Tomiyama et al.).
- The 'what the hell' effect – dieters more active than passive in their desire to overeat after breaking diet boundary.
- Disinhibition may not be important in all groups – restraint and disinhibition scores lower in men and in African Americans (Bellisle et al.).
- Disinhibited eating may be related to attachment style – Wilkinson et al. found 'attachment anxiety' significantly linked to disinhibited eating and to BMI.

COGNITIVE THEORY AND ANOREXIA NERVOSA

- Cognitive distortions are inaccurate ways of thinking that cause the individual to develop a negative body image.
- Irrational beliefs are beliefs that are illogical and inconsistent with social reality.
- Cognitive behavioural model – losing weight self-reinforcing, leads to increased anxiety about eating and a fear of food and weight gain.
- Transdiagnostic model sees the underlying cause of all eating disorders as the same set of cognitive distortions ('core psychopathology').
- AN is maintained by enhanced self-esteem as a result of self-control; starvation changes seen as failure of self-control, leading to more food restriction and increased self-monitoring.

EVALUATION

- Research support for role of cognitive factors in AN – AN individuals displayed a more inflexible and inefficient cognitive processing style (Lang et al.).
- Support from Stroop test studies – Ben-Tovim et al. found preoccupation with stimuli related to weight concerns in AN patients.
- CBT-E: support from success of therapy reinforces view that cognitive issues are a root cause of AN.
- Methodological limitations of cognitive theories – reliance on self-reports of cognitive processing makes it difficult to accurately assess distortions.
- Limitations of the cognitive approach – comparatively little research carried out to test the hypotheses derived from cognitive models of anorexia (Cooper).

BIOLOGICAL EXPLANATIONS FOR OBESITY

- Twin studies (e.g. Maes et al.) heritability for obesity of 40% and 75%.
- Adoption studies show strong relationship between weight category of adopted individuals and biological parents but not with adoptive parents'.
- Arcuate nucleus in hypothalamus produces the desire to eat and coordinates this with energy utilisation.
- Bates and Myers – disruption of leptin in the hypothalamus results in obesity.
- Thrifty gene hypothesis – those who gorged themselves when food was abundant were better able to survive when food was scarce again.
- Such genes are disadvantageous today because they promote diabetes.

EVALUATION

- Expression of genetic influences varies with age. Elks et al. found heritability of BMI highest during childhood and decreased during adulthood.
- The problem of time and geography – historical and geographical differences in obesity cannot be explained by genetics alone.
- Research support for leptin–obesity relationship show some humans do not produce leptin, which predisposes them to obesity.
- Advantages of biological explanations – removes stigma of obesity.
- Difficult to assess whether it actually works as few randomised trials.
- Problems with thrifty gene hypothesis – to be adaptive, it would be more widespread, suggesting greater role for cultural factors (Speakman).

EXPLANATIONS FOR THE SUCCESS AND FAILURE OF DIETING

- Theory of hedonic eating (Stroebe) – restrained eaters are more sensitive to the pleasurable properties of food.
- Increasing thoughts of eating enjoyment inhibit thoughts of control.
- Attractive food triggers hedonic thoughts → selective attention to food → inhibition of thoughts of dieting (Mischel and Ayduk).
- Attempting to suppress or deny a thought makes it even more prominent.
- The theory of ironic processes of mental control – denying thoughts of food makes it become more attractive.
- Paying attention to what is being eaten (detail) makes people less bored.
- Jelly beans experiment (Redden) – enjoyed more with specific flavour details.

EVALUATION

- Support for theory of ironic processes of mental control – restrained eaters suppress thoughts about food, but think more about it later (Soetens et al.).
- Support for hedonic theory – Brunstrom et al. found greater salivary response to pizza among dieters compared to non-dieters.
- Real-world application – meta-analysis of anti-dieting programmes (Higgins and Gray) found improvements in weight stability rather than weight change.
- Limitations of anecdotal evidence – memory not 100% accurate, nor objective.
- Free will or determinism – failure of dieting may be due to gene code for LPL to store fat (Kern et al.).

01 Read the item below and then answer the questions that follow.

> Anya does not eat cream as she does not like the look or smell of it.
> Roland does not eat cream any more as once it made him very ill.
> Tamsin does not eat cream because she is anxious that it will make her gain weight.

(i) Name the person who demonstrates neophobia. **[1 mark]**

(ii) Name the person who demonstrates taste aversion. **[1 mark]**

02 Outline **one** example of social **and/or** cultural influences on food preferences. **[2 marks]**

03 Outline **one** criticism of the evolutionary explanation of food preferences. **[2 marks]**

04 'Food preferences are a product of both nature and nurture.'

With reference to the above statement, discuss both the role of evolution and the role of learning when explaining food preferences. **[16 marks]**

05 Read the item below and then answer the question that follows.

> Gordon has suffered from obesity for most of his life. He knows that he overeats when he has a meal. He also knows he shouldn't snack in between meals. However, he feels he cannot control either of these behaviours.

Using your knowledge of the hormonal mechanisms, explain why Gordon suffers from obesity. **[4 marks]**

06 Briefly discuss the findings from **one** research study into the role of ghrelin **or** leptin in the control of eating behaviour. **[4 marks]**

07 Which one of the following is the part of the brain that signals when an individual is hungry and full? Write the letter of your chosen answer in your answer booklet. **[1 mark]**

A. amygdala

B. cerebellum

C. hippocampus

D. hypothalamus

08 Describe how **one** research study investigated the role of genetics in anorexia nervosa. **[3 marks]**

09 Outline the findings from **one** research study into neural explanations of anorexia nervosa. **[3 marks]**

10 Describe and evaluate biological explanations of anorexia nervosa. Refer to **at least one** psychological explanation as part of your evaluation. **[16 marks]**

11 Which one of the following describes the extreme intensity seen in families of people with anorexia nervosa? Write the letter of your chosen answer in your answer booklet. **[1 mark]**

A. autonomy

B. control

C. enmeshment

D. reinforcement

12 Explain **one** limitation of the family systems theory of anorexia nervosa. **[3 marks]**

13 Read the item below and answer the questions that follow.

> Rory is a teenage boy with anorexia nervosa. His mother blames this on the media as she believes there is currently too much emphasis on males keeping fit, with too many famous men who are below their expected weight. She says it does not help when Rory's friends say that he looks better now that he is not as chubby as he used to be.

(i) Using the case of Rory, explain the role of modelling in the development of anorexia nervosa. **[3 marks]**

(ii) Using the case of Rory, explain the role of reinforcement in the development of anorexia nervosa. **[3 marks]**

1 4   Describe **one** research study which investigated the role of the media in the development of anorexia nervosa.   **[4 marks]**

1 5   Evaluate social learning theory as an explanation of anorexia nervosa.   **[4 marks]**

1 6   Discuss **both** family systems theory **and** social learning theory as explanations of anorexia nervosa.   **[16 marks]**

1 7   Read the item below and answer the question that follows.

> Niamh has anorexia nervosa. Even though she is clearly underweight, when she looks in the mirror she perceives that she is overweight. This really upsets her, as she thinks that nobody is going to want to socialise with someone who is so unattractive.

Distinguish between distortions and irrational beliefs. Use the case of Niamh as part of your response.   **[4 marks]**

1 8   Outline **one** cognitive explanation of anorexia nervosa.   **[4 marks]**

1 9   Discuss **two** psychological explanations of anorexia nervosa. Refer to research evidence as part of your answer.   **[16 marks]**

2 0   Outline the genetic explanation of obesity.   **[4 marks]**

2 1   Describe and evaluate biological explanations of **both** obesity and anorexia.   **[16 marks]**

2 2   Outline how the boundary model can be used to explain obesity.   **[3 marks]**

2 3   Explain **one** criticism of restraint theory as an explanation of obesity.   **[3 marks]**

2 4   Read the item below and then answer the question that follows.

> Vikesh is obese. He attended a family celebration even though he was feeling very low that day. Consequently he ended up over-eating. Vikesh knows it didn't help that there was so much food on the buffet table, and it felt like everyone was just sat around eating.

Using your knowledge of the concept of disinhibition, explain why Vikesh may have over-eaten.   **[4 marks]**

2 5   Read the item below and then answer the question that follows.

> Patricia and Marilyn were both obese when they joined a slimming club six months ago. Patricia followed her diet and has now met her target weight. Marilyn kept over-eating at weekends and now weighs more than she did when she started the club.

Discuss explanations of obesity **and** dieting. Refer to both Patricia and Marilyn as part of your answer.   **[16 marks]**

2 6   Read the item below and then answer the questions that follow.

> A psychologist did a content analysis of a TV drama targeted at adolescents. She was interested in the ways that the media influences eating behaviour and whether it was different for males and females.

(i)   The psychologist found that female characters' weight was referred to 24 times and male characters' weight was referred to 8 times.
What is the ratio of the number of times female characters' weight was referred to compared to male characters' weight? Show your calculations. The main female and male characters were categorised in terms of whether they were average weight or below or above. The findings are shown below.   **[3 marks]**

	Above average weight	Average weight	Below average weight
Female	1	3	5
Male	1	5	2

(ii)   What percentage of female characters were categorised as below average weight? Show your calculations.   **[3 marks]**

(iii)   What was the modal category for the characters' weight?   **[1 mark]**

The exam questions on eating behaviour will be varied but are likely to involve some short answer questions (AO1), some application of knowledge questions (AO2), research methods questions and possibly an extended writing question (AO1 + AO3). We've provided answers to some additional questions together with comments from an examiner about how well they've each done.

---

01 Read the item below and answer the questions that follow.

> Ruby is 15 years old and the youngest member of her family of five. She has just been diagnosed with anorexia nervosa. Ruby feels her parents and older sisters give her no privacy and no independence, and this makes her disorder more difficult to cope with. Since she has been diagnosed, she thinks her parents are making decisions for her – even more so than they did in the past.

Using your knowledge of family systems theory, explain why Ruby may have been diagnosed with anorexia nervosa. **(6 marks)**

Maisie's answer

Family systems theory suggests that psychosomatic families have characteristics that make its members more vulnerable to the development of anorexia nervosa. Some of these characteristics are evident in Ruth's family. Psychosomatic families are characterised by enmeshment, where family members are over-involved with each other and there are a lack of personal boundaries, which makes it difficult for the individual to develop their independence. This is evident in Ruth's family, where her parents and older sisters give her no privacy and no independence.

Psychosomatic families also display overprotective control over its members, which influences the degree to which individuals believe they can control events in their life. This is also evident in Ruth's family as her parents have started making decisions for her, and so she deals with this lack of control by refusing to eat.

Examiner's comments

Maisie's response is worth all 6 marks. She demonstrates knowledge of the key features of families associated with anorexia nervosa. She is also able to explain these features and begin to relate them to the eating disorder. Maisie is able to make the correct links between the features and the details in the item, and earns the two AO2 marks on offer.

Ciaran's answer

Family systems theory claims that the families of adolescents with anorexia nervosa, such as Ruth's, are enmeshed. This means that there aren't sufficient boundaries within the family, with each family member over-involved in the behaviour of all the other members. The result of this is that adolescents within the family are never given the chance to develop their own independence and autonomy and are instead controlled by the other family members. As a result, they lose their ability to deal with the stressors in their life, and rely on family members to do this instead.

One way that adolescents (such as Ruth) can deal with this is by refusing to eat. This gives them some control over events in their life, and is why they are diagnosed with anorexia nervosa, which is what has happened to Ruth.

Examiner's comments

Ciaran earns 4 marks here. He understands the family systems theory well and describes it in accurate detail. However, he earns neither of the AO2 marks as his attempt to apply to the item is too weak. He only really uses Ruth's name in his answer. He should have explained which aspects of her situation relate to the theory that he has described.

---

02 'Food preferences are a product of both nature and nurture.'

With reference to the above statement, discuss both the role of evolution and the role of learning when explaining food preferences. **(16 marks)**

Maisie's answer

Early humans evolved a preference for sweet-tasting foods. Fruit, which is a source of sugar, provided the necessary vitamins and minerals for bodily functions and growth. Taste aversion is a learned response to eating poisoned food and would have helped our ancestors to survive because having eaten poisoned food, they would not make the same mistake again. Food neophobia is an evolved tendency to avoid new or unusual foods. This protects individuals from the risk of being poisoned by something that is potentially harmful. This is particularly strong in response to animal products because of the greater illness threat associated with rotting meat.

Although many food preferences can be explained in terms of evolved adaptations, this is not true for all food preferences. Many foods that were important to our ancestors are nowadays harmful to our health, so we are more likely to avoid them in order to remain healthy.

If food neophobia has adaptive advantages, then it should have a strong genetic component. Knaapila et al. (2007) studied adult twin pairs and found that about two thirds of the variation in food neophobia was genetically determined, lending support to the view that neophobia evolved because it protected early humans from potentially harmful foods.

Maisie's answer continues on the next page…

Research on taste aversion has helped understand the food avoidance that can occur during cancer treatments, such as radiation and chemotherapy, which can cause gastrointestinal illness. This has led to cancer patients being given a novel food along with familiar food just prior to their chemotherapy. The patient forms then an aversion to the novel food (neophobia) and not to the familiar, usual food.

Children also acquire their food preferences by observing the behaviour of their parents. Brown and Ogden (2004) found similarities between parents and their children in terms of their intake of snack foods and their motivation for eating. Parents can also control the availability of certain foods because of some perceived health gain (e.g. low sugar foods). The behaviour of same-age peers has also been shown to have an influence on the food preferences of children. For example, Greenhalgh et al. (2009) found that children who were exposed to peers eating new foods were then more likely to try these foods themselves.

A problem for the role of parental influences on food preferences is that most of the research is carried out on a selective sample of white Americans. The findings may not, therefore, generalise to other populations. For example, a study by Robinson et al. (2001) looked at children from a number of different backgrounds and found a complex association between the behaviour of parents and the food preferences of children.

The role of peers in the development of food preferences is supported by research (Jansen and Tenney, 2001) that showed that seeing significant others modelling the consumption of sugar free foods and drinks led to children developing a preference for the taste of these products.   *484 words*

Examiner's comments

Maisie shows a sound understanding of the role of evolution and learning in this well balanced essay. Lots of evidence is included and generally used to good effect which does begin to earn AO3 marks. Although the content of Maisie's answer is all relevant, the structure could be improved to give the essay more coherency. In this essay, Maisie tends to juxtapose paragraphs so it is not clear how they follow on from each other. It would have helped if Maisie had made reference to the statement, and used the nature/nurture debate as a template for her essay. Her evaluation is quite implicit, and mainly comes from offering different perspectives on food preferences. It would have been better if Maisie had included more direct criticisms of the evolutionary and learning theories as part of her evaluation. If Maisie is going to evaluate evidence, as she does part way through this essay, then she needs to be careful to relate this back to the focus of the essay to ensure it is credited as AO3. This is a level 3 response but needs to include more evaluation relative to the description.

---

03 Read the item below and then answer the question that follows.

> Patricia and Marilyn were both obese when they joined a slimming club six months ago. Patricia followed her diet and has now met her target weight. Marilyn kept over-eating at weekends and now weighs more than she did when she started the club.

Discuss explanations of obesity **and** dieting. Refer to both Patricia and Marilyn as part of your answer. (16 marks)

Ciaran's answer

Biological explanations of obesity see it as being caused by genetics. For example, studies such as Maes et al. found that heritability of obesity was higher in MZ (genetically identical) twins than in DZ (non-identical) twins. Other research has emphasised the importance of leptin in obesity. Disruption of leptin has been shown to lead to obesity. It is possible that Marilyn has inherited genes that make her more vulnerable to obesity, or has a dysfunction in the action of leptin that causes he to overeat and so become obese.

A problem for explanations based on genetics is that heritability of a tendency toward obesity has been shown to be at its peak during childhood (Elks et al., 2012). As Marilyn is most probably an adult if she is going to a slimming club, then the genetic contribution becomes less important than other factors. Advantages of biological explanations of obesity, such as those emphasising the role of genetics and the role of leptin is that they are less stigmatising and there is also the possibility of treatment. This means that Marilyn could seek treatment, perhaps the use of leptin injections to help her lose weight.

An explanation based on dieting failure is the theory of hedonic eating. This claims that some people are more sensitive than others to the pleasurable features of food, such as its taste, smell or visual appeal. This means once they see or smell or taste a particular food, it becomes difficult for them to stop thinking about it, and so they are more likely to want to eat it again. This could explain why Patricia and Marilyn are different in how successful they are at keeping to their diets. Patricia may not have the same sensitivity to attractive foods, so is more successful at restraining her eating than is Marilyn, who gets more pleasure out of food, so eats more of it.

A problem for explanations of why diets seem to fail is that the evidence is often anecdotal, i.e. it relies on what people choose to report rather than on scientific evidence. There are also many other factors than might influence the likelihood of a diet failing. For example, it is possible that Marilyn is facing significant stressors that cause her to comfort eat. Patricia may not be experiencing the same stressors in her life so can stick to her diet. There is also the possibility that Marilyn had a period where she overate simply because of some social event, for example she may have been on a two week all inclusive cruise, whereas Patricia went on a walking holiday.   *435 words*

Examiner's comments

Ciaran has produced a level 3 response here demonstrating sound knowledge and understanding of different explanations of obesity and dieting. Application is really effective in this response and Ciaran has thought carefully about how he can use the item to illustrate his points. Evidence has been included and adds weight to the response. There are some good examples of evaluation where Ciaran tries to give a balanced perspective on different explanations. He also manages to continue to use application when evaluating which is quite impressive. Overall, Ciaran needs to do more of the same to broaden the essay – possibly offering more detail on the different explanations, and trying to include more advantages and disadvantages of the different explanations. It would also be useful to end the essay with a clear conclusion.

Stress isn't all negative – the term *eustress* describes positive stress.

Some people enjoy the adrenaline rush of a bungee jump.

CONTENTS OF CHAPTER

SPECIFICATION CHECKLIST

- The physiology of stress, including general adaptation syndrome, the hypothalamic pituitary-adrenal system, the sympathomedullary pathway and the role of cortisol.

- The role of stress in illness, including reference to immunosuppression and cardiovascular disorders.

- Sources of stress: life changes and daily hassles. Workplace stress, including the effects of workload and control.

- Measuring stress: self-report scales (Social Readjustment Ratings Scale and Hassles and Uplifts Scale) and physiological measures, including skin conductance response.

- Individual differences in stress: personality types A, B and C and associated behaviours; hardiness, including commitment, challenge and control.

- Managing and coping with stress: drug therapy (benzodiazepines, beta blockers), stress inoculation therapy and biofeedback. Gender differences in coping with stress. The role of social support in coping with stress; types of social support, including instrumental, emotional and esteem support.

TRY THIS

HOW STRESSED ARE YOU?

One of the problems facing psychologists who study stress is to find a way of measuring how stressed a person is. Once they have a number that represents a person's stress level, this can be used to see if stress is, for example, associated with being ill more often.

Of course you could simply ask someone to rate their stress level, but that would be a rather crude measure. One of the common ways to measure stress is to use a questionnaire, and many of them have been developed, such as the *Hassles and Uplifts Scale* (Kanner *et al.*, 1981). Hassles are negative events that annoy or bother you. The negative effects of daily hassles can in turn be offset to some degree by the more positive experiences that you have every day that make you feel happy.

Jointly, hassles and uplifts indicate how much stress a person may be experiencing. The actual scale has 117 Hassles and 135 Uplifts; a selection of items are shown below.

DIRECTIONS: Please think about how much of a hassle and how much of an uplift each item was for you over the previous week. Hassles are rated in terms of severity and uplifts rated in terms of frequency:

1 = somewhat severe   2 = moderately severe   3 = extremely severe
1 = somewhat often   2 = moderately often   3 = extremely often

Hassles	Rating	Uplifts	Rating
Misplacing or losing things.	1 2 3	Getting enough sleep.	1 2 3
Social obligations.	1 2 3	Practising your hobby.	1 2 3
Troubling thoughts about your future.	1 2 3	Being lucky.	1 2 3
Health of a family member.	1 2 3	Saving money.	1 2 3
Not enough money for clothing.	1 2 3	Liking fellow workers.	1 2 3
Concerns about owing money.	1 2 3	Feeling healthy.	1 2 3
Smoking too much.	1 2 3	Finding something presumed lost.	1 2 3
Too many responsibilities.	1 2 3	Recovering from illness.	1 2 3
Care for pet.	1 2 3	Staying or getting in good physical shape.	1 2 3
Trouble relaxing.	1 2 3	Visiting, phoning or writing to someone.	1 2 3
Trouble making decisions.	1 2 3	Relating well with your spouse or lover.	1 2 3
Too much time on hands.	1 2 3	Relating well with friends.	1 2 3
Being lonely.	1 2 3	Meeting your responsibilities.	1 2 3
Fear of confrontation.	1 2 3	Quitting or cutting down on drugs.	1 2 3
Silly practical mistakes.	1 2 3	Solving an ongoing practical problem.	1 2 3
Physical appearance.	1 2 3	Daydreaming.	1 2 3
Fear of rejection.	1 2 3	Weight.	1 2 3
Concerns about health in general.	1 2 3	Having enough time to do what you want.	1 2 3
Being exploited.	1 2 3	Eating out.	1 2 3
Concerns about bodily functions.	1 2 3	Having enough (personal) energy.	1 2 3
Not getting enough sleep.	1 2 3	Cooking.	1 2 3
Problems with your lover.	1 2 3	Capitalising on an unexpected opportunity.	1 2 3
Too many things to do.	1 2 3	Life being meaningful.	1 2 3
Unchallenging work.	1 2 3	Being well prepared.	1 2 3
Regrets over past decisions.	1 2 3	Relaxing.	1 2 3
Nightmares.	1 2 3	The weather.	1 2 3
Transportation problems.	1 2 3	Reading.	1 2 3
Shopping.	1 2 3	Shopping.	1 2 3
Prejudice and discrimination from others.	1 2 3	Giving a present.	1 2 3
Concerns about news events.	1 2 3	Getting a present.	1 2 3
Noise.	1 2 3	Doing volunteer work.	1 2 3
Traffic.	1 2 3	Hugging and/or kissing.	1 2 3

- Add up your hassles score and subtract your uplifts score.
- Calculate how many times you have been ill during the last six months.
- Collect the same data from other people and plot it on a scattergram.

The physiology of stress

We start with the biological elements of stress – but don't feel challenged, as you know these well. Imagine you are in the exam room and just about to look at the exam paper. Do you feel a tightening in your chest? That isn't because you are scared – it is because a massive dose of **adrenaline** just rushed through your body.

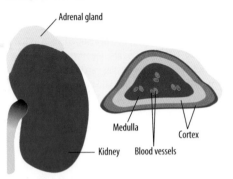

Adrenal gland
Medulla
Cortex
Kidney
Blood vessels

KEY TERMS

Adrenaline and **noradrenaline** Hormones associated with arousal of the sympathetic nervous system, causing the physiological sensations related to the stress response (raised heart rate, sweating, etc.). Also neurotransmitters.

Cortisol A hormone produced as a result of chronic stress, with both positive and negative effects (e.g. burst of energy and reduced immune response).

General adaptation syndrome describes how all animals cope with stress in an initially adaptive way, but ultimately leading to illness. The three stages are alarm, resistance and exhaustion.

Hypothalamic pituitary-adrenal system Parts of the brain and body that are involved in the long-term (chronic) stress response, involving cortisol.

Sympathomedullary pathway The parts of the body involved in the immediate response to stress (fight-or-flight) involving adrenaline.

MEET THE RESEARCHER

Hans Selye
(pronounced sell-yeh) was born in Hungary but spent most of his working life in Canada. He came from a family of physicians, and trained as a medical doctor in Prague. His work as a doctor led him to observe that people who were sick all shared certain signs and symptoms, the first step in his recognition of the concept of 'stress' – in fact he coined the term.

He was a very hardworking researcher – typically he would rise at 5.00am, take a dip in his pool, and then cycle some 10 km to his lab, where he would then work for up to 14 hours. He rarely had days off, and went in to work at weekends and on holidays.

SHORT- AND LONG-TERM STRESS RESPONSES

Stress is an emotional response to situations of threat. Such threats may be physical (a lion is attacking) or psychological (you are worried about your exams). In both cases your body produces a short-term (immediate) response and, should the stressor continue, a long-term (ongoing) response.

Response to short-term (immediate) stressors

When faced with a stressful situation, an animal responds with an immediate fight-or-flight response. We described this in detail in the Year 1 book, so this is a recap of what was there.

The short-term response is called the **sympathomedullary pathway** or the SAM system.
- 'S' – *sympathetic nervous system* (SNS). This branch of the autonomic nervous system is alerted as soon as a stressor is perceived.
- 'M' – *adrenal medulla*. A signal is sent via the central nervous system to two endocrine glands located just above the kidneys. The middle part of the adrenal gland (the medulla) responds by releasing adrenaline and smaller amounts of **noradrenaline** into the bloodstream.
- 'A' – *adrenaline* and noradrenaline circulate through the body and affect key target organs such as the heart and the muscles, causing the heart to beat faster and blood pressure to rise. Thus the animal is prepared to deal with the stressor.

When the threat has passed, the parasympathetic branch of the autonomic nervous system (ANS) dampens down the stress response, returning the body to its normal resting state.

Response to long-term (ongoing) stressors

At the same time as the initial SNS response is triggered, a second system also starts, but this is a slower response. It is called the **hypothalamic pituitary-adrenal system** (HPA axis).
- 'H' – *hypothalamus*, which releases corticotrophin-releasing hormone (CRH) into the bloodstream.
- 'P' – *pituitary gland*. CRH causes the pituitary to produce and release adrenocorticotrophic hormone (ACTH) into the bloodstream.
- 'A' – *adrenal cortex*. The hormone ACTH stimulates the adrenal cortex to release various stress-related hormones, including **cortisol**. Cortisol has some positive effects (e.g. a lower sensitivity to pain and a quick burst of energy through the release of glucose), whereas others are negative (e.g. impaired cognitive performance and a lowered immune response).

GENERAL ADAPTATION SYNDROME (GAS)

Much of our understanding of the nature of stress can be traced back to the pioneering work of Hans Selye in the 1930s. His research (see facing page) led him to conclude that when animals are exposed to unpleasant stimuli, they display a universal response to all stressors. He called this the **general adaptation syndrome** (GAS). It is 'general' because it is the same response to all agents. The term 'adaptation' is used because it is adaptive – it is the best way for the body to cope with extreme stress. It is a 'syndrome' because there are several symptoms in the stress response.

Selye proposed three stages to the GAS response:
- *Stage 1: Alarm reaction*. The threat or stressor is recognised and a response is made. The hypothalamus in the brain triggers the production of adrenaline/noradrenaline from the adrenal glands. These hormones lead to readiness for 'fight-or-flight'.
- *Stage 2: Resistance*. If the stress continues, then it is necessary for the body to find some means of coping. The body is adapting to the demands of the environment, but at the same time resources are gradually being depleted – the term 'resources' refers to the biochemical substances constantly manufactured in the body (sugars, neurotransmitters, hormones, proteins, etc.). The body appears to be coping, whereas in reality, physiologically speaking, things are deteriorating, e.g. the immune system becomes less effective.
- *Stage 3: Exhaustion*. Eventually the body's systems can no longer maintain normal functioning. At this point, the initial symptoms of the adrenaline response may reappear (sweating, raised heart rate, etc.). The adrenal glands may be damaged from previous over-activity, and the immune system may not be able to cope because production of necessary proteins has been slowed in favour of other needs. The result may be seen in stress-related illnesses such as ulcers, depression, cardiovascular problems and other mental and physical illnesses.

EVALUATION OF SHORT- AND LONG-TERM STRESS

Gender differences

Biological research generally relies on male animals because female hormones fluctuate with ovulation and this complicates matters. The conclusions drawn from earlier research into the stress response may reflect a male bias. Shelley Taylor and colleagues (2000) suggest that, for females, behavioural responses to stress are more characterised by a pattern of tend and befriend than fight-or-flight. During our evolutionary past (the environment of evolutionary adaptiveness – the EEA), this would have involved protecting themselves and their young through nurturing behaviours (tending) and forming protective alliances with other women (befriending). Women may have a completely different system for coping with stress because their responses evolved in the context of being the primary caregiver of their children. Fleeing too readily at any sign of danger would put a female's offspring at risk. Studies using rats suggest there may be a physiological response to stress in females that inhibits fight/flight – the release of the hormone oxytocin. This increases relaxation, reduces fearfulness and decreases the stress responses characteristic of the fight-or-flight response.

Such differences mean that the standard description of the SAM and HPA systems is a gender-biased account.

Negative consequences of the fight-or-flight response

The physiological responses associated with fight-or-flight may be adaptive for a stress response that requires energetic behaviour (such as fleeing from a lion or moving out of the path of an oncoming car). However, the stressors of modern life rarely require such levels of physical activity (e.g. worrying about exams). The problem for modern humans arises when the stress response is repeatedly activated. For example, the increased blood pressure that is characteristic of SNS activation can lead to physical damage in blood vessels and eventually to heart disease. Similarly, although cortisol may assist the body in fighting a viral infection or healing damaged tissue, too much cortisol suppresses the immune response, shutting down the very process that fights infection.

The transactional model of stress

Richard Lazarus (1999) argued that the physiological stress response was not inevitable – it depends on how the stressor is perceived, which determines how the body responds. Therefore a physiological account is not sufficient on its own. Lazarus and Folkman (1984) developed the transactional model, realising that *cognitive appraisal* was the key – *perceived* demands and *perceived* ability to cope. The emphasis is on what the individual *thinks* (i.e. cognitive), which moderates the way an individual responds to a stressor.

Lazarus demonstrated this in a study where participants watched a film of gruesome initiation rites (Speisman *et al.*, 1964). Those participants who had been told beforehand that the initiation rites were exciting (because it signalled arrival into manhood) showed less arousal of the autonomic nervous system than those who had the pain of the experience emphasised beforehand.

EVALUATION OF GAS

Research support for GAS

Selye's model was based on his observations working with human patients – he noticed that they all shared a common set of symptoms (aches and pains, loss of appetite) no matter what was actually wrong with them. He investigated this with research with rats (Selye, 1936). No matter what noxious substance the rats were injected with, they always produced a similar response. This included the common cold, surgical injury, production of spinal shock (cutting the spinal cord), excessive muscular exercise, or intoxications with sublethal doses of diverse drugs.

The results of his research support his 'doctrine of non-specificity' – that there is a non-specific response of the body to any demand made upon it, i.e. the body responds in the same way to any stressor.

Stress-related illness may not be due to depletion of resources

The GAS model proposes that resources become depleted so that the body can no longer fight infections. However, more recent research has shown that many 'resources' (sugars, neurotransmitters, hormones, proteins, etc.) do not become depleted even under extreme stress. The current view is that the exhaustion phase is associated with *increased* hormone activity, such as cortisol, and it is this rather than depletion of resources that leads to stress-related illness (Sheridan and Radmacher, 1992). On the next spread we look at more recent explanations for the role of stress in illness.

▲ What did men and women do in the EEA? The argument is that it would have been adaptive for men to respond to stress with a 'fight-or-flight' response, but for women 'tend and befriend' was more adaptive.

The role of stress in illness

The relationship between stress and illness is fairly well known – people generally believe that stress is bad for their health. What is not well known is why there should be a link between the two. Why do people who are stressed become ill?

On this spread we will look at two explanations – one related to immediate stress (and adrenaline) and the other to ongoing stress (and cortisol).

KEY TERMS

Cardiovascular disorder Refers to any disorder of the heart (such as coronary heart disease, CHD) and circulatory system (such as hypertension, commonly known as high blood pressure) as well as strokes (restricted blood flow to parts of the brain).

Immunosuppression literally means the suppression of the body's immune system – a system of cells within the body that is concerned with fighting intruders such as viruses and bacteria so they cannot infect the body. For example, white blood cells (leucocytes) identify and eliminate foreign bodies (antigens).

MEET THE RESEARCHER

Janice Kiecolt-Glaser's research has led her to a position of international prominence in the study of the impact of stress on the immune system. She and her colleagues at Ohio State University have helped bring this area of research from infancy to its current status as a thriving area of study.

As well as her research into stress, she has published two mystery novels: *Detecting Lies* and *Unconscious Truths*.

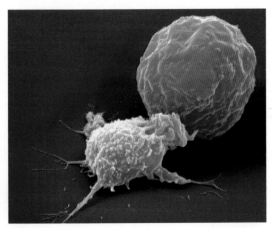

▲ Cancer cell (pink) attacked by human natural killer (NK) cell (yellow), in a picture taken by a scanning electron micrograph. The NK cell's numerous long projections are beginning to flow around the large cancer cell. NK cells are a type of white blood cell known as T-lymphocytes. These have the ability to destroy virus-infected cells and tumour cells. On contact with the surface of a tumour cell, the NK cell recognises certain proteins called antigens, which activate its cell-killing mechanism. The NK cell then binds to and destroys the cancer cell using toxic chemicals.

THE ROLE OF STRESS IN ILLNESS

On the previous spread you learned that immediate (short-term) stressors lead to the production of adrenaline and that ongoing (long-term) stressors result in the production of cortisol. Each of these hormones can, in turn, be linked to **cardiovascular disorder** and **immunosuppression**.

Immediate stress: Adrenaline and cardiovascular disorders

Stress activates the sympathetic branch (SNS) of the autonomic nervous system, leading to the production of adrenaline (and noradrenaline). High levels of adrenaline will have the following effects:

- Increased heart rate causes the heart to work harder and takes a toll over time.
- Constriction of the blood vessels increases blood pressure, which puts tension on blood vessels, causing them to wear away.
- Increased pressure can also dislodge plaques on the walls of blood vessels, and this leads to blocked arteries (*atherosclerosis*). This may cause a heart attack or a stroke.

Key study: Cardiovascular disorders

Williams *et al.* (2000) conducted a study to see whether anger was linked to heart disease (anger, like stress, also activates the SNS).

Procedure About 13,000 people completed a 10-question anger scale, including questions on whether they were hot-headed, if they felt like hitting someone when they got angry, or whether they got annoyed when not given recognition for doing good work. None of the participants suffered from heart disease at the outset of the study.

Findings Six years later, the health of participants was checked; 256 had experienced heart attacks. Those who had scored highest on the anger scale were over two-and-a-half times more likely to have had a heart attack than those with the lowest anger ratings. People who scored 'moderate' in the anger ratings were 35% more likely to experience a coronary event than those with lower ratings. This suggests that SNS arousal is closely associated with cardiovascular disorders.

Ongoing stress: Cortisol and immunosuppression

Ongoing stress activates the HPA system, which results in the production of various hormones including cortisol. One effect of cortisol is to reduce the body's immune response, making it more likely that a person will become ill because invading viruses and bacteria are not attacked.

Key study: Immunosuppression

Janice Kiecolt-Glaser has been one of the key researchers in this area. In one study with colleagues (Kiecolt-Glaser *et al.*, 1984), she conducted a natural experiment investigating whether the stress of important examinations had an effect on immune system functioning.

Procedure There were 75 medical students who took part in the study. Blood samples were taken one month before their exams (low stress) and during the exam period itself (high ongoing stress). Immune system functioning was assessed by measuring natural killer (NK) cell activity in the blood samples. Participants also completed a questionnaire (the *Social Readjustment Rating Scale*, SRRS, described on page 202) to measure other life stressors they were experiencing, and also the students completed a 'loneliness scale' that assessed how many interpersonal contacts they had, i.e. their social support network.

Findings NK cell activity was significantly reduced in the second blood sample compared to the sample taken one month before. This suggests that ongoing stressors reduce immune system functioning. This is further supported by the fact that those students whose life stressors were generally high (as measured by the SRRS) had the lowest NK cell levels. Furthermore, loneliness contributed to the effect – the students with fewest friends had the lowest NK cell activity.

Self-report

Exposure to stress and cardiovascular outcomes are often based on self-report (e.g. questionnaires). If an individual has a general tendency toward negative perceptions (i.e. remembering more unpleasant events than pleasant ones), this may lead to an exaggerated score on both measures. This in turn would lead to a significant correlation being more likely, resulting in an unjustified association between higher perceived stress and cardiovascular symptoms.

Supporting research for the effect of stress on cardiovascular disorders

There is a large body of research that has linked stress with cardiovascular disease. For example, Sheps *et al.* (2002) focused their research on volunteers with ischaemia (reduced blood flow to the heart). They gave 173 men and women a variety of psychological tests, including a public speaking test. Their blood pressure typically soared dramatically, and in half of them, sections of the muscle of the left ventricle began to beat erratically. Of all the participants, 44% of those who had shown the erratic heartbeats died within four years, compared to just 18% who had not. This shows that psychological stress can dramatically increase the risk of death in people with poor coronary artery circulation.

Individual differences in cardiovascular effects

People react differently to stress. Research has shown consistent gender differences in the stress/immune system relationship. Women show more adverse hormonal and immunological changes in the way they react to marital conflict (Kiecolt-Glaser *et al.*, 2005). There are also age differences; as people age, stress has a greater effect on immune system functioning, making it harder for the body to regulate itself (Segerstrom and Miller, 2004).

Furthermore, research suggests that the sympathetic branch of the ANS in some individuals is more reactive than in others (Rozanski *et al.*, 1999). This would mean that some people (described as '*hyperresponsive*') respond to stress with greater increases in blood pressure and heart rate than others, and this would lead to more damage to the cardiovascular system in hyperresponsive individuals.

Later in this chapter we will look further at research into the relationship between individual differences, cardiovascular disorders and stress when we look at Type A behaviour.

Stress does not always have a negative effect on the immune system

There is research that shows that, in some situations, stress may *enhance* the activity of the immune system. For example, Evans *et al.* (1994) looked at the activity of an antibody – sIgA – which helps protect against infection. Evans *et al.* arranged for students to give talks to other students (immediate stress). These students showed an increase in sIgA, whereas levels of sIgA decreased during examination periods which stretched over several weeks.

Therefore Evans *et al.* (1997) propose that stress may have two effects on the immune system: up-regulation (i.e. increased efficiency) for short-term acute stress, and down-regulation (i.e. decreased efficiency) for chronic stress. This was supported by a meta-analysis by Segerstrom and Miller (2004) which reviewed almost 300 studies of stress and the immune system, finding that short-term stressors promote the body's ability to fight infection. However, the longer the stress, the more the immune system shifted from potentially adaptive changes to potentially detrimental changes.

Stress and illness is not a simple relationship

Richard Lazarus (1992) suggests there are various reasons why a relationship between stress and illness is difficult to establish.

1. Health is affected by many different factors (including genetic influences, lifestyle, etc.). As a result, there may be little variance left that can be accounted for by stress.
2. Health is generally fairly stable and slow to change. As a result, it makes it difficult to demonstrate that exposure to particular stressors have caused a change in health.
3. To demonstrate how stress affects long-term health would involve continuous measurement over time. This would be expensive and impractical – therefore most research has concentrated on relatively short periods of time.

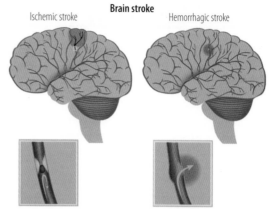

Brain stroke
Ischemic stroke · Hemorrhagic stroke

Blockage of blood vessels; lack of blood flow to affected area

Rupture of blood vessels; leakage of blood

▲ Cardiovascular disorders are not simply heart attacks. They include anything related to the heart and blood vessels. The pictures above show that stroke may be due to a lack of oxygen to a part of the brain (blocked blood vessel) or blood leaking into the brain causing pressure and damaging the brain. Both are cardiovascular events.

⌗ Research methods

A group of students conducted their own study on the role of stress in illness. They did this by keeping a record over a period of two months of stress and illness. Every Monday they asked each participant to rate how stressed they felt on a scale of 1 to 7 where 7 was very stressed. They also asked each participant to note whether they had been ill in the previous week.

They calculated a stress score for each participant by adding up their ratings for the two-month period, and they calculated an illness score by adding up the number of times a person said they had been ill in the previous week. For each participant they therefore had two scores.

1. Write a suitable directional hypothesis for this study. (2 marks)
2. Write a null hypothesis for this study. (1 mark)
3. Explain **one** difficulty with the way that stress was measured. (2 marks)
4. Identify a suitable sampling method for this study and explain why you chose this method. (3 marks)
5. Invent a set of data for this study and display it in a table. (4 marks)
6. Identify a suitable statistical test to use with this data and explain your choice. (3 marks)

LINK TO RESEARCH METHODS

Null hypothesis on page 23.
Statistical tests on pages 24–32.

CAN YOU? | No. 8.2

1. Explain what is meant by *immunosuppression*. (2 marks)
2. Describe **one** study of the role of stress in cardiovascular disorders. In your answer, explain what the researcher(s) did and what was found. (4 marks)
3. Evaluate research on the role of stress on immunosuppression. (8 marks)
4. Discuss the role of stress in illness. (16 marks)

Sources of stress: Life changes

What sort of things actually cause the ongoing stress reactions we have been describing? In the 1950s Dr Thomas Holmes became interested in investigating the link between stress and physical illness, following Selye's GAS model. His early research with TB (tuberculosis) patients showed that people who became ill had experienced an increase in 'disturbing occurrences' in the two years prior to admission to hospital (Hawkins *et al.*, 1957). This led Holmes, together with Dr Richard Rahe, to develop the idea of **life changes**.

▲ The participants in Rahe *et al.*'s study were serving aboard US Navy cruisers. The researchers argued that a ship presents a natural unit in which to conduct a study of the distribution of diseases because all the crew are exposed as a whole to common work stresses, climatic change and infectious agents. Differences in illness rates among crew members are therefore likely to be due to constitutional vulnerabilities rather than environmental factors.

KEY TERMS

Life changes Events in a person's life (such as divorce or bereavement) that require a significant adjustment in various aspects of a person's life. As such, they are significant sources of stress.

Life change units (LCUs) A number assigned to each life event to represent how much stress is created. The higher the number, the more stressful.

MEET THE RESEARCHER

As a medical student, **Richard Rahe** came to work with Dr Holmes. His subsequent career has focused on research into stress and coping, working largely for the US Navy. He currently consults with military and National Guard medical commands to improve recovery from stress for services personnel who have returned from Afghanistan and Iraq. In 1997, Rahe received the *Hans Selye Award* for making a significant contribution to our understanding of stress.

LIFE CHANGES

Explaining the effect of life changes

Life changes are those events (such as getting married or dealing with bereavement) that necessitate a major transition in some aspects of our life. These changes may be from either positive or negative events – and both have one thing in common: they involve change. Change requires psychic energy to be expended, i.e. it is stressful. Holmes and Rahe suggested that this psychic energy affects health.

Measuring life change

In order to conduct research on the effect of life changes on health, Holmes and Rahe (1967) recognised that they needed a standard measurement tool. They developed the *Social Readjustment Rating Scale* (SRRS) to do this, consisting of 43 life events (see examples below left). An individual identifies which items occurred within a set time period (this could be 3 months, 6 months or a year). Each event has a score in terms of **life change units (LCUs)**. Death of a spouse is 100 LUCs, whereas pregnancy is 40. A score can be calculated for each individual. The SRRS is discussed in more detail on page 202.

Key study: Rahe *et al.* (1970)

Rahe *et al.* used a slightly adapted version of the SRRS to investigate the relationship between stress and illness. The version they used is called the *Schedule of Recent Experiences* (SRE). The study focused on a 'normal' population, as distinct from the populations previously studied of individuals who were already ill in hospital.

Procedure The sample consisted of 2,664 men who were naval and marine personnel serving aboard three US Navy cruisers. The men were asked to fill in the SRE for events experienced in the previous two years. The SRE was adapted to be specifically relevant to military experiences, such as including a life event for being selected for a promotion. This produced a total LCU score.

During the 6–8-month tour of duty, a record was kept of any time one of the men visited sick bay on board the ship, as well as the type and severity of the illness. Thus an illness score could be calculated.

Findings Rahe *et al.* found a significant positive correlation between LCU score and illness score of +.118. Those men who scored low in terms of their SRE scores also had low levels of illness while at sea. As both positive and negative events are included in the SRRS (even Christmas is stressful), it appears that it is change rather than the negativity of change that is important in creating stress. It is the overall amount of 'psychic energy' (mental and emotional effort) required to deal with a life event that creates the stress.

Other research on life changes

Cohen *et al.* (1993) gave nasal drops to participants that contained the common cold virus and also assessed life changes using the *Schedule of Recent Experiences* (a measure of life changes). The researchers further assessed psychological stress using a perceived stress scale. Participants were quarantined to see if they did develop a cold.

The results of this study showed that participants with higher LCUs were more likely to get infected with the cold virus, supporting the link between life changes and illness. There was no link between perceived stress and likelihood of becoming ill, suggesting that what matters is the actual stress rather than how a person perceives it that matters.

(This research by Cohen *et al.* also suggests that life changes result in immunosuppression – because participants were more likely to become infected.)

The Social Readjustment Rating Scale (SRRS)	
Example items	
Rank	**Life event (number in brackets represents LCU)**
1	Death of a spouse (100)
2	Divorce (73)
4	Jail term (63)
6	Personal injury or illness (53)
7	Marriage (50)
8	Fired at work (47)
10	Retirement (45)
12	Pregnancy (40)
17	Death of a close friend (37)
22	Change in responsibilities at work (29)
23	Son or daughter leaving home (29)
25	Outstanding personal achievement (28)
27	Begin or end school (26)
28	Change living conditions (25)
30	Trouble with boss (23)
33	Change in schools (20)
36	Change in social activities (18)
41	Holiday (13)
42	Christmas (12)
43	Minor violations of the law (11)

A valuable approach

The life changes approach generated a large amount of research, with many adaptations of the SRRS turning up in self-help publications and magazines.

It has provided insights into many types of psychological problem. For example, Heikkinen and Lönnqvist (1995) used it to explain the causes of suicide. They found that, in the three-month period preceding suicide among 219 suicide victims in Finland, the main causal factor seemed to be changes in life events such as family discord, loss (through separation or death), financial troubles and unemployment.

Despite the apparent success of the approach, however, it is not without its problems (Jones and Bright, 2001), as discussed below.

Reliability of recall

The life changes approach generally is based on people's memory for events over months or years. Such recall for events that occurred so long ago may not be reliable. Rahe (1974) investigated the test–retest reliability of the SRRS and found that it varies depending on the time interval between testing.

However, most researchers have reported acceptable levels of reliability for retrospective reports of life events. Hardt et al. (2006) interviewed 100 patients with a history of childhood abuse with a time lag of 2.2 years between interviews. Reliability of reports of family situation (e.g. separation of parents) were assessed as well as physical and sexual abuse. The results show moderate-to-good reliability of recall for most childhood experiences.

Individual differences

The life change approach ignores the fact that life events will inevitably have different significance for different people. For example, the untimely death of a much-loved spouse will undoubtedly have a devastating effect on the surviving partner, but the death of an elderly spouse after a long and painful illness may not be quite so stressful for the survivor. Similarly, what are relatively minor stressors for some people, such as a son or daughter leaving home or even a particularly busy Christmas, would be major stressors for other people.

Daily hassles may be a more significant measure of stress

Another criticism of the life changes approach, made by Richard Lazarus (1990), is that major life changes are relatively rare in the lives of most people. It is the minor daily stressors (i.e. hassles) of life that are the more significant source of stress for most people. For example, Anita DeLongis et al. (1988) studied stress in 75 married couples (see next spread). They gave the participants a life events questionnaire and a Hassles and Uplifts Scale. They found no relationship between life events and health, but did find a significant positive correlation of +.59 between hassles and next-day health problems such as flu, sore throats, headaches and backaches.

Spurious relationship

Most studies of the relationship between life changes and illness have produced correlational data, i.e. they do not tell us about any possible *causal* relationship between the two. It is possible that an observed relationship may result from a third variable. Anxiety is one possible intervening variable. Brown (1974) suggests that people with high levels of anxiety would be more likely to report negative life events and would also be more prone to illness.

Brown also suggests that people who are unwell may feel the need to provide an explanation for their illness, and therefore are more likely to report stressful events than those who are not ill. He cites the fact that, in the past, mothers of children with Down's syndrome reported far more traumatic events in their pregnancy than did mothers of non-Down's children – at that time they didn't know that Down's was a chromosomal abnormality. There were no real differences in the experiences of the two groups of mothers during pregnancy but the Down's mothers perceived more trauma as an explanation for the child's problems.

UPGRADE

Maximising your marks

In previous sections of this book we have looked at how to plan for essay questions and how to answer them effectively, but what *specifically* is an examiner looking for if he (or she) is going to give you a mark in the top mark band of 13–16 marks? Let's look at a typical essay question for this section of the specification:

> *Describe and evaluate research on life changes as a source of stress.* (16 marks)

In this question, 10 of the marks are assigned for AO3 (evaluation) and the remaining 6 marks for AO1 (description). It is worth bearing this in mind when planning your response.

Let's look at the mark descriptor for the top level for this question:

> *'Knowledge of research on life changes as a source of stress is accurate and generally well detailed. Discussion is thorough and effective. The answer is clear, coherent and focused. Specialist terminology is used effectively. Minor detail and/or expansion of argument sometimes lacking.'*

Obviously your material has to be accurate, but examiners are pretty forgiving folk and will generally ignore relatively minor inaccuracies. To make sure your description is 'generally well detailed', you should aim to make each point about 25 words. Choose six things you want to say and expand each to 25 words (remembering to cover the three areas mentioned in the question), adding the necessary detail and specialist terminology to give each point descriptive impact. To make your discussion 'thorough and effective', you should aim for five evaluative points from the information in the 'Evaluation' section on this page. Each of these should be 'distilled' down to about 50 words. Being able to reduce material down to make it really effective is a skill that we cover in more detail on page 203.

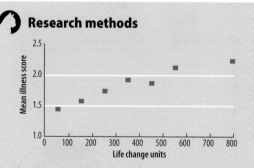

Research methods

1. Above is a graph illustrating the results from Rahe *et al.*; what kind of graph is it? (1 mark)
2. A correlation of .118 might seem not to be significant – can you explain why it is significant? (1 mark)

LINK TO RESEARCH METHODS

Correlation on page 30.

CAN YOU? No. 8.3

1. Explain why life changes may be a source of stress. (2 marks)
2. Describe **one** study of the role of life changes as a source of stress. In your answer, explain what the researcher(s) did and what was found. (4 marks)
3. Give **one** criticism of the role of life changes in stress. (3 marks)
4. Describe and evaluate research on life changes as a source of stress. (16 marks)

Sources of stress: Daily hassles

Although major life changes undoubtedly have a significant impact on our well-being, we noted on the previous spread that they are relatively rare in our day-to-day lives. Richard Lazarus and colleagues (1980) suggested that it might make better sense to focus on more everyday stressors, such as a broken computer, a missed bus or arguments with our families. These **daily hassles** may have a more significant part to play as a source of stress and in our psychological well-being.

▲ Are family arguments a source of stress? Just looking at this picture makes me feel stressed. This is a hassle, not a life event.

The five most common hassles and uplifts (Kanner *et al.*, 1981)			
Hassles		**Uplifts**	
Concerns about weight	52.4%	Relating well with spouse/lover	76.3%
Health of a family	48.1%	Relating well with friends	74.4%
Rising prices of common goods	43.7%	Completing a task	73.3%
Home maintenance	42.8%	Feeling healthy	72.7%
Too many things to do	38.6%	Getting enough sleep	69.7%

*The percentage shown indicates how many people selected each item as a hassle/uplift.

MEET THE RESEARCHER

Richard Lazarus (1922–2002) is considered to be one of the most influential psychologists of the last century. He began work at a time when behaviourism was the main force in psychology; he supported the alternative view – that emotion and cognition needed to be considered as well in order to truly understand behaviour. He was especially interested in the role of appraisal as part of emotional (and stress) responses and focused attention on coping mechanisms.

Lazarus defined stress as arising 'when individuals perceive that they cannot adequately cope with the demands being made on them or with threats to their well being' (1966).

DAILY HASSLES

Daily hassles are relatively minor events that arise in the course of a normal day. They may involve the everyday concerns of work, such as a disagreement with a colleague, or issues arising from family life.

The negative effects of daily hassles can in turn be offset to some degree by the more positive experiences that we have every day. **Daily uplifts**, such as a smile from someone in the street or an e-mail from a long-lost friend, are thought to counteract the damaging effects of stress.

Explaining the effect of daily hassles

Accumulation

One explanation for this is that an *accumulation* of minor daily stressors creates persistent irritations, frustrations and overloads which then result in more serious stress reactions such as anxiety and depression (Lazarus, 1999).

Amplification

An alternative explanation is that chronic stress due to major life changes may make people more vulnerable to daily hassles. For example, a husband trying to come to terms with a recent divorce may find the relatively minor squabbling of his children to be a major irritation. As a result, he may experience higher-than-expected levels of distress given the relatively trivial nature of the irritation. As the person is already in a state of distress, the presence of associated minor stressors may *amplify* the experience of stress. The presence of a major life change may also deplete a person's resources so that they are less able to cope with minor stressors than they would be under normal circumstances.

Key study: Kanner *et al*. (1981)

Allen Kanner, along with Richard Lazarus and other researchers, tested the view that daily hassles might be a better predictor of illness than the life changes approach.

Procedure The study involved 100 participants (48 men and 52 women) aged 45–67. Each participant completed the *Hassles and Uplifts Scale* (HSUP), for events over the previous month, and continued to do this once a month for nine months. Details of the HSUP scale are described on page 202.

Participants also completed a life events scale for the six months preceding the beginning of the study and also for the two-yearly periods prior to that. Finally they completed it again at the end of the study.

Two measures were used to assess psychological well-being: the *Hopkins Symptom Checklist*, which assesses symptoms such as anxiety and depression, and the *Bradburn Morale Scale*, which assesses positive and negative emotion. Participants filled these out every month.

Findings The five most common hassles and uplifts identified in this study are displayed on the left. In general the hassles and uplifts differed to those selected by another group of participants who were students; for example, they identified more problems related to having too much to do and not being able to relax.

There was a significant negative correlation between frequency of hassles and psychological well-being; in other words, those participants with fewest hassles showed the highest levels of well-being. Most importantly Kanner *et al.* found that hassles were a better predictor of well-being than life events. Hassles were also a better predictor of well-being than uplifts.

Other research on daily hassles

Bouteyre *et al.* (2007) investigated the relationship between daily hassles and the mental health of French psychology students during the initial transition period from school to university. The students completed the hassles part of the HSUP and the Beck Depression Inventory as a measure of symptoms of depression. There was a positive correlation between scores on the hassles scale and the incidence of depressive symptoms. This study shows that the transition to university is frequently fraught with daily hassles, and that these can be considered a significant risk factor for depression.

Support for importance of daily hassles

Research has continued to support the view that daily hassles are a much more significant source of stress than life events/life changes. For example, in an Australian study (Ruffin, 1993), daily hassles were linked to greater psychological and physical dysfunction than were major negative life events.

Flett *et al.* (1995) considered why this might be. They asked 320 students (160 men, 160 women) to read a scenario describing a male or female individual who had experienced either a major life event or daily hassles. The participants then rated the amount of support (both emotional and practical) that the person would receive and would seek from others. Flett *et al.* found that individuals who had suffered major life events were rated higher in both seeking and receiving support from significant others. This suggests that the reason daily hassles may be a greater source of stress is because there is less social and emotional support received from others than for life events.

Reliability of recall

As with life events, participants are usually asked to rate the hassles experienced over the previous month. The same problems with retrospective reporting that were discussed on the previous spread therefore apply.

Some researchers have overcome this problem by using a diary method, where participants rate minor stressors and feelings of well-being on a daily basis. For example, Charles *et al.* (2013) studied 700 participants for eight consecutive days. On each day they reported daily hassles and also how negative they were feeling. This shows that alternative methods can be used which avoid the problems of retrospective recall.

Problems with self-report

A further issue for the validity of data collected is that people may not always report their experiences honestly. Social desirability bias might explain why some people do not indicate all of their hassles because it puts them in a 'bad light', for example not wanting to admit that you have problems with your children or have an inability to express yourself. In fact most of the hassles are obviously quite negative, and therefore some people may play down their severity.

Individual differences

There are gender differences in what constitutes a 'hassle', for example when it comes to pets. Miller *et al.* (1992) found that pets appear to serve different roles for female and male pet owners. For females, pets were commonly associated with uplifts (e.g. leisure and lack of psychological pressure), but for males, pets were more likely to be associated with hassles (e.g. time and money necessary to care for them).

What does the research tell us?

Most of the data from research on daily hassles is correlational (as with the data from research on life events). This means we cannot draw causal conclusions about the relationship between daily hassles and well-being.

It is not necessarily clear which direction the cause might be. It could be argued that someone who is depressed is more likely to be thinking negatively and would record higher severity of hassles – so the depression is causing the hassles rather than vice versa.

However, the study by Charles *et al.* (above) found that the hassles score predicted depression ten years later. This suggests that hassles (or something that co-varies with hassles) *causes* depression. As a result, we would be unwise to ignore the message in such research.

🐾 **APPLY YOUR KNOWLEDGE**

Research on commuting has found that people who reported a difficult day at work subsequently tended to report higher levels of stress on their commute home. Among those who commuted by car, many reported that they experienced more road rage after a stressful day at work, and admitted shouting at other road users or displaying other violent outbursts when they were faced with heavy traffic, diversions or inconsiderate drivers.

Using your knowledge of daily hassles and stress, explain the relationship between stress during the day and increased road rage on the commute home.

KEY TERMS

Daily hassles are the 'irritating, frustrating, distressing demands that to some degree characterise everyday transactions with the environment' (Kanner *et al.*, 1981).

Daily uplifts are the opposite – they are the minor positive experiences of everyday life, for example receiving a compliment at work or feeling good about one's appearance.

CAN YOU? No. 8.4

1. Explain why daily hassles may be a source of stress. (2 marks)
2. Describe **one** study of the role of daily hassles as a source of stress. In your answer, explain what the researcher(s) did and what was found. (4 marks)
3. Give **one** criticism of the role of daily hassles in stress. (3 marks)
4. Discuss sources of stress. Include both life changes and daily hassles in your answer. (16 marks)

Sources of stress: Workplace stress

Stress at work might be regarded as both a life event and a daily hassle (e.g. 'trouble with boss' is a life event, and 'too many responsibilities' or 'don't like fellow workers' are daily hassles). You may be thinking of lots of other features of the workplace that cause people to feel stressed at work – do they match up to the two key issues that psychologists have identified for workplace stress: **workload** and **job control**?

It's a serious issue

Stress and illness in the workplace is of major economic importance. A report in the *Huffington Post* (Shearer, 2013) claimed the cost in the UK reached £6.5 billion in 2012 because 10.4 million days were lost due to staff absenteeism related to stress. Compare this with the estimated £22.5 billion spent for health and social issues – it's a significant sum of money.

Shearer also says that 'presenteeism' is on the rise – employees coming to work disengaged, tired, unmotivated and too stressed to work. It is hard to measure the cost of time lost, but it adds to the total bill.

And furthermore, too little work or unchallenging work (work underload) can lead to 'rust out', a problem similar to 'burn out'. People enjoy a moderate challenge. Positive psychologists have found that work satisfaction is a key element of happiness – Csikszentmihalyi and LeFevre (1989) found that people enjoy a sense of flow (being caught up in the moment) three times as much at work than at leisure.

KEY TERMS

Job control The extent to which a person feels they can manage aspects of their work, such as deadlines and work environment.

Workload The amount of effort and/or activity involved in a job. It is quite often discussed as 'job demand', i.e. the amount required for a person to do during their working day.

Workplace stress Aspects of our working environment (such as work overload or impending deadlines) that we experience as stressful, and which cause a stress reaction in our body.

▲ Who would have thought that working hard is good for you – positive psychologists say it is.

WORKPLACE STRESS

The job-strain model

The issues of workload and control have jointly been combined in the *job-strain model* of **workplace stress**. This model proposes that the workplace creates stress and illness in two ways: (1) high workload (creating greater job demands) and (2) low job control (e.g. over deadlines, procedures, etc.). Two classic studies have looked at these issues of workload and control.

The Whitehall study (Marmot *et al.*, 1997)

Procedure This study, led by Sir Michael Marmot, has followed over 10,000 UK civil servants (men and women) who have worked in Whitehall, London, since 1985. Some participants, who work in higher grades (e.g. professional staff such as accountants), have high levels of workload and control, whereas those at lower grades (e.g. administrative staff) have less workload and control. Therefore both grades are likely to experience stress but for different reasons.

At the beginning of the study participants completed a range of questionnaires assessing their job workload, subjective sense of job control and the social support they had. Eleven years later coronary heart disease (CHD) risk was assessed as a measure of the effects of stress.

Findings The researchers found that the highest-grade workers tended to have the highest workload and also the highest sense of job control. High workload was not associated with CHD whereas low job control was. The combined effect of low job control/high workload (the job-strain model) was strongest among the younger workers and was not reduced by high levels of social support.

Swedish sawmill (Johansson *et al.*, 1978)

Procedure Gunn Johansson and colleagues studied 28 manual labourers in a sawmill. The high-risk group (high workload and low control) were 14 sawyers, edgers and graders, who were compared to a low-risk group of stickers, repair men and maintenance workers, matched in terms of factors such as education and job experience.

The researchers measured levels of adrenaline daily (to assess stress) and obtained self-reports of job satisfaction and illness.

Findings The high-risk group were found to have higher illness rates and also higher levels of adrenaline in their urine than the low-risk group, and more reports of illness.

The self-report data confirmed that the sawyers, edgers and graders had a greater workload and a lowered sense of control – their jobs were repetitive and constrained, and since the tasks were pre-planned there was little possibility of individual design of work routines and self-control of work pace. This group also reported more sense of social isolation.

Is workload more important in creating stress than job control?

Kivimäki *et al.* (2002) looked at stress in about 800 Finnish workers from a range of occupations. They found, as with the studies above, that stress had a greater toll in those with high workload and low control – those workers with 'job strain' were 2.2 times more likely to die from CHD than those with low workload and high control.

However, interestingly they found that, when either workload or job control were considered separately, there was no effect. This suggests that workload or job control may not always be experienced as stressful. It is the combination that is significant.

They also found that the influence of job control disappeared if occupational group was taken into account. This means that other factors related to occupational group may be significant rather than just the issue of control. For example, people in lower occupational groups may have lower socioeconomic status, which is a major determinant of health status.

EVALUATION

Individual differences

Lazarus (1995) claims that the study of stressful factors in the workplace misses the point that there are wide individual differences in the way people react to and cope with individual stressors. Lazarus's *transactional approach* (discussed earlier in this chapter) emphasises that the degree to which a workplace stressor is perceived as stressful depends largely on the person's perceived ability to cope.

For example, Schaubroeck *et al.* (2001) found that some workers are *less* stressed by having no control or responsibility. In this study Schaubroeck *et al.* measured saliva and therefore assessed immune system functioning directly. They found that some people had *better* immune responses in low-control situations. Some people view negative work outcomes as being their fault and, for these employees, high control can actually exacerbate the unhealthy effects of stress.

Work underload

Most research on work-related stress has focused on work overload, or having too many job demands, as opposed to work *underload*. Work underload refers to situations where people are employed in jobs that are beneath their capacities or where they are given tasks that are lacking in any creativity or stimulation. Work underload was overlooked in the studies on the facing page. Shultz *et al.* (2010) gathered data from 16,000 adult employees across 15 European countries. They discovered that employees reporting work overload had the highest levels of stress-related illness. However, those who reported work underload also reported low job satisfaction and significant levels of absence due to stress-related illness.

The research on underload and individual differences suggests that the job-strain model may be an oversimplification.

Validity

Most of the studies of workplace stress that we have covered here have made use of questionnaires. There are many criticisms that can be made about data collected in this way, for example the issue of social desirability bias.

A specific issue related to this research was raised by Dewe (1989), who suggests that traditional questionnaires may distort the importance of some items that may no longer be important while ignoring others that are. Keenan and Newton (1989) found that, in a study of engineers, the use of *interviews* instead of questionnaires revealed stressors not usually covered by traditional methods (e.g. time-wasting job demands and interpersonal conflicts). Similarly, role conflict and ambiguity which *are* usually included in questionnaires were seldom mentioned as significant stressors. Interviews, therefore, may offer a more valid way of assessing the impact of workplace stressors than traditional questionnaires.

Workplace stress and mental health

Workplace stress may have wider implications. Work is generally seen as good for our mental health, but there are times when it can be harmful. Although workplace stress may not cause depressive illness directly, high levels of stress at work, combined with other problems (such as difficulties at home or daily hassles), can make depression more likely to occur. Warr (1987) used the analogy of 'vitamins' to explain how certain features of the workplace might contribute to the mental health of the worker. Low levels of vitamins lead to poor physical health, so low levels of these work-related features may lead to poor *mental* health. This shows the wider implications of workplace stress.

The evolution of work and workplace stressors

The changing nature of the work environment, with the advent of new technology, virtual offices and the blurring of home/work environments, means that our current knowledge of workplace stressors rapidly becomes out of date. As the ultimate purpose of research in this area is to help people manage the stresses of their working day, psychological research may inevitably lag behind actual work practices.

Research methods

Three studies are explained on the facing page; each of them would be described as a natural experiment.

1. Explain why they would be considered to be natural experiments. (2 marks)
2. Outline **one** strength and **one** limitation of natural experiments. (2 marks)
3. Identify the experimental design used in these studies and explain **one** limitation with using this design in such studies. (3 marks)
4. A further issue in these studies is that questionnaires were used to collect information, for example on workload, sense of control and social support. Discuss **two** problems with collecting this data using a questionnaire. (3 marks + 3 marks)
5. Identify **one** ethical issue that might be important in these studies and suggest how the researchers might have dealt with it. (4 marks)
6. One of the features of science is replication. Explain how the studies on the facing page demonstrate replication and how this contributes to the scientific nature of this research. (3 marks)
7. Identify **one** other feature of science and give an example from the research on this spread.

LINK TO RESEARCH METHODS

Features of science on page 20.
The other topics in these questions are covered in the research methods chapter of our Year 1 book.

▲ Some people find that work underload is stressful.

CAN YOU?   No. 8.5

1. Explain what is meant by *workplace stress*. (3 marks)
2. Explain what research has shown about the role of workload and control as sources of stress. (6 marks)
3. Give **one** limitation of research on workplace stress. (4 marks)
4. Describe and evaluate research related to workplace stress. Include the effects of workload and control in your answer. (16 marks)

Measuring stress: Self-report scales and physiological measures

An obvious requirement for any research in this area is having a method to measure stress. So far in this chapter we have seen how stress has often been measured using self-report scales – invariably questionnaires where a person provides their own assessment of the experiences they have had. On this spread we look more deeply at these questionnaires which are often called 'scales'.

Other research has used **physiological measures of stress**, such as blood pressure or levels of adrenaline. Such responses are signs of arousal of the sympathetic nervous system (SNS). There is another physiological measure that is used – the **skin conductance response** – which is also due to SNS activity. This is more commonly referred to as the lie detector test (which involves some other physiological measures).

You can see example items for the SRRS on page 196 and HSUP on pages 196 and 198.

KEY TERMS

Hassles and Uplifts Scale (HSUP) A self-report scale devised to assess both daily hassles and daily uplifts. Hassles and uplifts are scored on a 3-point scale for severity and frequency respectively. The two scores are reported separately.

Physiological measures of stress Any method that is based on the body's physical response to stress and thus related to effects of the sympathomedullary pathway or hypothalamic pituitary-adrenal system.

Skin conductance response A measurement of the electrical conductivity of the skin, because this is increased when sweat is produced, and sweat is related to arousal of the sympathetic nervous system.

Social Readjustment Ratings Scale (SRRS) A self-report scale devised to assess life events over a set period of time. There are 43 events on the scale, each of which is related to a certain number of life change units (LCUs).

▼ Skin conductance response is measured by placing two electrodes, usually on the index and middle fingers, and measuring the current that flows between them.

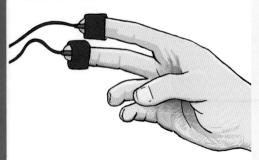

SELF-REPORT SCALES

There are many scales used to measure stress, but the two best known are the ones below, both of which should be familiar to you by now.

Social Readjustment Ratings Scale (SRRS)

Thomas Holmes and Richard Rahe (1967) developed the **Social Readjustment Ratings Scale (SRRS)** in order to test their hypothesis about the relationship between life changes and physical illness. They analysed 5,000 patient records and identified 43 common life events reported by patients as issues in their lives.

In order to establish the stressfulness of each event, they enlisted the help of about 400 participants. The participants were asked to score each event in terms of how much readjustment they felt would be required by the average person. The participants were asked to provide a numerical figure for this readjustment, taking marriage as an arbitrary baseline value of 50. If an event would take longer to readjust to than marriage, then they were told to give the event a larger score. Scores for all participants were totalled and averaged to produce life change units (LCUs) for each life event (see example scores on page 196).

The scale is completed by selecting the life events that have occurred within a particular time period and then the life change units for those events are added up.

Hassles and Uplifts Scale (HSUP)

The **Hassles and Uplifts Scale (HSUP)** was also developed in order to test a hypothesis, this time that hassles and uplifts are a significant factor in illness.

Allen Kanner *et al.* (1980) asked research staff to generate a list of hassles and uplifts related to work, health, family, friends, the environment, practical considerations and chance occurrences, creating a list of 117 hassles and 135 uplifts.

Initially participants were asked to rate each hassle on a 3-point scale in terms of both severity and persistence. Kanner *et al.* found that the two scales elicited very similar responses, and therefore only severity is now used (somewhat severe, moderately severe or extremely severe).

The uplift items were rated for severity and frequency on a 3-point scale, but again both scores were very similar, and therefore only frequency is now used (somewhat often, moderately often, extremely often).

The scale is completed with reference to a specific time period such as the last month or week.

PHYSIOLOGICAL MEASURES

Skin conductance response

You already know that immediate stress is related to sympathetic arousal of the autonomic nervous system, resulting in the production of the hormones adrenaline and noradrenaline. Adrenaline and noradrenaline cause a variety of physiological responses, such as increases in heart and breathing rates, blood pressure and sweating. Scientists in the nineteenth century realised that skin is electrically active and that this electrical activity is conducted when the skin is wet. This is called the skin conductance response.

As sweat is produced, the amount of electricity that is conducted increases. This effect is strongest in the palms of the hands and soles of the feet because of the high density of eccrine sweat glands at these points – glands which are partly responsive to emotional stimuli.

To measure the skin conductance response, two electrodes are placed on a person's index and middle finger. A very small voltage (0.5V) is applied across these electrodes. By measuring the current that flows, conductance can be reported. The preferred unit of conductance is microSiemens.

Other physiological measures

A simple way to assess stress is by measuring blood pressure. Kamarck *et al.* (1990) looked at the effect of social support on stress by measuring a person's blood pressure and heart rate before doing a set of mental tasks and again afterwards. Those participants who had a close same-sex friend touching their wrist throughout the task were less stressed.

Cortisol is the hormone produced as a response to ongoing stressors and can be measured in saliva or urine. For example, Gunnar *et al.* (2010) assessed stress in children (3–4½ years) by measuring salivary cortisol. Children in day care showed higher stress levels, and these were highest in situations of intrusive, over-controlling care.

EVALUATION OF SELF-REPORT SCALES

Criticisms of the SRRS

One of the major criticisms of the SRRS is that events have different meanings for different people, a point raised on page 197. For example, a divorce may be experienced as less stressful if the marriage was unhappy. This means that giving a fixed LCU rating for each life event may be unrepresentative of the actual stress. On the other hand Holmes and Rahe argued that events are stressful whether they are positive or negative – both have a cost in terms of psychic energy.

A second criticism is that the events on the scale only apply to adults. Itula-Abumere (2013) has produced a modified version for young people which places unwed pregnancy at the top of the list followed by death of a parent, getting married and divorce of parents.

A further criticism is that the scale ignores factors that may moderate the negative effects of stress. Moos and Swindle (1990) addressed this in the *Life Stressors and Social Resources Inventory* (LISRES), which includes an assessment of social resources available to the individual.

Criticisms of the HSUP scale

The original scale contained some items related to physical well-being (physical illness, side effects of medication, not enough energy). Such items would increase the likelihood of a correlation with illness and therefore were removed to improve the validity of the scale.

A further issue with the scale is the sheer length of it – a total of over 250 items. It is likely that respondents don't maintain thoughtful, focused attention throughout completing the scale. Test–retest correlations support this, as the figure is only .48 for scores on severity ratings of hassles and a higher .60 for frequency ratings of uplifts.

Anita DeLongis, together with Lazarus and Folkman, produced a shorter and simpler version with 53 items. For each item the respondent has to indicate, on a scale of 1 to 3, whether it was a hassle or an uplift (somewhat, quite a bit, a great deal) (DeLongis *et al.*, 1988).

Continuing influence

Despite the limitations mentioned, both scales have remained popular in psychological research. Both the SRRS and HSUP scale are used in many current studies and, if not those scales, adaptations of the scales are used. So this approach to measuring stress has been a success and has contributed to the opportunity to research the causes of stress in people.

EVALUATION OF PHYSIOLOGICAL MEASURES

More appropriate in some situations

Using a physiological measure avoids some of the problems associated with self-report measures (e.g. social desirability bias and response set). It is also the only way to measure stress with certain groups of participants, such as young children or non-human animals.

On the other hand, as Lazarus has pointed out, stress is not just a physiological response – the way it is perceived may be very much part of the experience. Thus, physiological measurements only tell us part of the story.

Non-specific response

What is actually being measured is sympathetic arousal, which occurs as a response to any emotion, so it may not just be stress that has caused the activity of the sympathetic nervous system. It could be that the participant is experiencing fear, anger, surprise or sexual arousal, which would all lead to increased sweat and increased skin conductance. There are also changes in skin conductance in relation to whether a person feels they are being treated fairly or unfairly – an example of how cognitive perception can change the physiological response (Oshumi and Ohira, 2010). Finally, temperature and humidity also affect the response, as do any medications someone is taking.

Other applications

The skin conductance response has been used as a way of determining whether someone (particularly a criminal) is lying – the polygraph or lie detector test. This is a very appealing idea because it would make it so easy to determine dishonesty. However, for all the reasons outlined above, this is not a very dependable measure of deceitfulness – especially because Oshumi and Ohira (above) found that psychopaths are much less affected by whether they were treated fairly or unfairly (and generally lack emotional responsiveness), which means they can lie without any associated physiological response.

▲ People like to seem appealing, even when answering a questionnaire. There are many other criticisms of self-report measures, for example response set where a person prefers to answer yes or no, or prefers to select items on the right rather than the left..

⬆ UPGRADE

Effective evaluation

In a previous Upgrade feature, we made reference to the fact that for evaluation to be 'thorough and effective', each AO3 point should be in the region of 60 words. The word 'effective' when used in this context assesses how well you have *used* the material. There is a knack to this, which we have mentioned elsewhere in this book (e.g. page 75). However, this is a point worth repeating here, as getting this right could earn you quite a few extra marks.

The AO3 paragraphs on the right-hand side of each spread raises a point of evaluation. Sometimes these are strengths, sometimes limitations and sometimes some other critical point relating to the material, such as a real-world application.

However, there is still work for *you* to do here. If we take the final point on this spread as an example ('Other applications'), this could be introduced with the phrase '*An advantage of physiological measures is that they can be used to detect if someone is lying . . . '*. This is then elaborated: '*. . . e.g. the polygraph is used in the investigation of crime*'. The point can be explored a little more: *. . . 'However, some criminals lack emotional responsiveness and so can lie without any associated physiological response . . . '*. This is followed by a final link back to the initial claim: '*. . . which suggests that physiological measures are not effective in detecting stress in all people*'.

CAN YOU? No. 8.6

1. Outline **one** self-report scale used to measure stress. (6 marks)
2. Explain how the skin conductance response is used to measure stress. (6 marks)
3. Distinguish between the Social Readjustment Ratings Scale and the Hassles and Uplifts Scale. (3 marks)
4. Describe and evaluate ways that stress can be measured. In your answer make reference to self-report scales and physiological measures. (16 marks)

Individual differences in stress: Personality

There are important differences in how people react to stress in the same way as there are differences in how they react to many other influences in their lives. These are referred to as 'individual differences'. One of psychology's favourite individual differences is 'personality'. In its broadest terms, personality can be thought of as a set of characteristic behaviours, attitudes and general temperament that remain relatively stable over the course of a person's life and distinguish one individual from another. Research has established that some personality characteristics make us more vulnerable to the negative effects of stress (such as illness), while other personality characteristics make us more resistant to these effects.

KEY TERMS

Type A personality is characterised as someone who experiences constant time pressure, competitiveness in work and social situations, and anger, i.e. being easily frustrated by other people.

Type B personality is characterised by an easygoing, relaxed and patient approach to life.

Type C personality is characterised by extreme emotional suppression and a desire to please others.

▲ Type A meets Type C.

MEET THE RESEARCHERS

Meyer Friedman and **Ray Rosenman** shared a cardiology practice in San Francisco. Friedman recognised himself as a Type A personality and, after two heart attacks aged 55, took his own advice and tried to reduce his Type A tendencies. It must have worked, because he died in 2001, aged 90. Ray Rosenman, a recipient of the Hans Selye Award for stress research, died in 2013, aged 93. He must have followed the advice too.

PERSONALITY TYPES A, B AND C

Type A and B personality

Two medical doctors, Meyer Friedman and Ray Rosenman, asked people to identify what they thought were the major causes of coronary heart disease (CHD). The answer was that CHD is due to exposure to chronic emotional trauma as a consequence of excessive drive and competitiveness, having to meet deadlines, and economic frustration. This led Friedman and Rosenman to propose two key personality types: **Type A** and **Type B**.

The Type A individual, according to Friedman and Rosenman, possesses three major characteristics: competitiveness and achievement striving, patience and time urgency, and hostility and aggressiveness. These characteristics would, they believed, lead to raised blood pressure and raised levels of stress hormones, both of which are linked to ill health, particularly CHD.

In contrast, Type B was proposed as a personality relatively lacking in these characteristics, being patient, relaxed and easygoing. These behaviours are believed to *decrease* an individual's risk of stress-related illness.

Key study: Friedman and Rosenman (1959, 1974)

Friedman and Rosenman set up the Western Collaborative Group (WCG) to study the link between Type A behaviour and CHD.

Procedure At the beginning of the longitudinal study, approximately 3,000 men aged 39 to 59, living in California, were examined for signs of CHD (to exclude any individuals who were already showing signs of CHD) and their personalities were assessed by interview. The interview consisted of 25 questions about how they responded to everyday pressures. For example, respondents were asked how they would cope with having to wait in a long queue. The interview was conducted in a provocative manner to try to elicit Type A behaviour. For example, the interviewer might speak slowly and hesitantly, so that a Type A person would want to interrupt. On the basis of the interview, participants were classed as Type A or B.

Findings After 8½ years, 257 of the original participants had developed CHD. As can be seen from the table on the right, over 12% of the Type A participants had experienced a heart attack, compared to just 6% of the Type Bs. Type As also had higher blood pressure and higher cholesterol. Perhaps most dramatically, twice as many Type A participants had died of cardiovascular problems.

It is worth noting that they were also more likely to smoke and have a family history of CHD, both of which would increase their risk.

Western collaborative group study	Type A	Type B
Heart attacks	12.8%	6.0%
Recurring heart attacks	2.6%	0.8%
Fatal heart attacks	2.7%	1.1%

Type C personality

Type C individuals strongly suppress their emotions, particularly negative ones, and are unassertive, likeable people who rarely get into arguments and are generally helpful to others. They cope with stress in a way that ignores their own needs, even physical ones, in order to please others, and this has negative physiological consequences.

Type C behaviour has been linked to cancer. Lydia Temoshok (1987) suggests that this is because some stressors activate the autonomic nervous system (ANS), and this is related to CHD. More chronic stressors affect the immune system and increase the risk for cancer.

Key study: Morris *et al.* (1981)

Tina Morris and colleagues investigated the link between Type C behaviour and cancer.

Procedure Over a period of two years, women attending a cancer clinic in London were asked to participate in a study. In total ,75 women were interviewed and asked about how often they expressed affection, unhappiness by crying or losing control when angry in order to assess typical patterns of emotional behaviour. The interviewer was not aware of the initial diagnosis of cancer.

Findings Those women whose breast lumps were found to be cancerous were also found to have reported that they both experienced and expressed far less anger (Type C) than those women whose lumps were found to be non-cancerous. This supports the idea of a link between cancer and the suppression of anger.

Further evidence from the WCG study

Ragland and Brand (1988) carried out a follow-up study of the Western Collaborative Group participants, 22 years after the start of the study. They found that 214 (approximately 15%) of the men had died of CHD. This study confirmed the importance of the usual CHD risk factors (age, smoking and high blood pressure), but found little evidence of a relationship between Type A behaviours and mortality, thus challenging the earlier conclusion that Type A behaviour was a significant risk factor for CHD mortality.

However, one suggestion is that, after the widely publicised results from the first phase of the study, many Type A men may have changed their behaviours, reducing their stress levels and thus their exposure to adrenaline.

The key component of Type A

More recent research has isolated hostility as the key factor in the negative effects of Type A personality; in other words, it is hostility alone that is creating the effect rather than a particular cluster of characteristics (a 'personality').

For example, Myrtek (2001) carried out a meta-analysis of 35 studies on Type A personality, and found an association between CHD and hostility alone. Other than this, there was no evidence of an association between Type A personality and CHD.

Gender bias

The original sample consisted of men only. In fact Riska (2002) claimed that psychology's preoccupation with Type A behaviour was a reflection of the importance of traditional masculinity in the 1950s and 1960s. The behaviours and attributes of Type A are very masculine – competitiveness and assertiveness.

Friedman *et al.* (1986) conducted another study, this time with over 800 men *and* women who had experienced CHD. Participants were randomly allocated to a treatment group (who received cardiac counselling and Type A counselling) or a control group (who received cardiac counselling only). The treatment group were less likely to have further problems with CHD (13% compared to 28%), suggesting that both men and women experience Type A behaviours and benefit from strategies to reduce them.

Are the effects of personality direct or indirect?

There appears to be evidence that some aspects of personality are linked to CHD and other illnesses. But is this because some aspect of personality actually *causes* the immune system to underperform and/or *causes* blood pressure to increase (i.e. it is a direct effect)? Or is it that personality has an indirect effect, for example making it more likely that an individual would smoke and this would increase the likelihood of CHD?

Nemeroff and Musselman (2000) found evidence of a direct link between personality and illness. This study found that depressed people had 41% more sticky platelets in their blood than normal participants. Sticky platelets block arteries and increase the risk of heart attack. Nemeroff and Musselman found that giving these patients Prozac, an antidepressant, almost got rid of these platelets. You might think that it was the Prozac that reduced the platelets, but if some patients were given a placebo (told they were taking Prozac but actually given a substance with no pharmacological effects), the number of blood platelets dropped! This suggests that mood itself is influencing the body's physical systems, i.e. a direct effect.

Challenges to the concept of Type C

Greer *et al.* (1979) found that women with a 'fighting spirit' were more likely to recover from cancer. This suggests that, as with Type A, it is possible to counter the negative emotional type and reduce illness.

However, subsequent research has not supported this. For example, a six-year follow-up study in Italy by Giraldi *et al.* (1997) found no association between psychosocial variables (such as either emotional suppression or a 'fighting spirit') and cancer progression – they did find more stressful life events in the months before a cancer diagnosis.

"TYPICAL 'TYPE A' BEHAVIOR."

▲ Since the early research in the 1960s, Type A rapidly became a popular concept that everyone, not just psychologists, became familiar with.

Research methods

The study by Myrtek (left) was a meta-analysis.

1. Explain what is involved in a meta-analysis. (2 marks)
2. Explain **one** advantage and **one** limitation of using a meta-analysis in this research area. (2 marks + 2 marks)

The study by Friedman and Rosenman (facing page) was a longitudinal study.

3. Give **one** limitation of such longitudinal studies and explain how this may have affected the results of this particular study. (2 marks + 2 marks)
4. In the follow-up study, after 8½ years, there were 257 participants who had experienced problems with CHD. Seventy per cent of that 257 were Type A. Estimate how many men in this sample were Type A. (1 mark)
5. The original sample in this study consisted of volunteers. Explain **one** limitation of this kind of sample in the context of this study. (2 marks)

LINK TO RESEARCH METHODS

The topics in these questions are covered in the research methods chapter of our Year 1 book.

CAN YOU? No. 8.7

1. Explain what is meant by *Type A behaviour* in relation to stress. (2 marks)
2. Outline **one** study that has investigated Type A and B behaviour. (4 marks)
3. Explain why Type C behaviour could be linked to stress. (3 marks)
4. Describe and evaluate the relationship between personality and stress. Refer to personality Types A, B and C in your answer. (16 marks)

Individual differences in stress: Hardiness

The concept of **hardiness** is also a style of personality. It is a pattern of traits that are possessed by some people which make them more able to resist the negative effects of stress. In the same way that a hardy plant is physically more resilient to bad weather conditions, a hardy person can cope better with difficult circumstances than someone who isn't hardy. In this way it is an individual difference.

KEY TERM

Hardiness A style of personality which provides defences against the negative effects of stress. The characteristics are: having control over one's life, commitment (i.e. a sense of involvement in the world) and challenge (i.e. life changes are opportunities rather than threats).

Insider tip...
The topics in this chapter are quite interconnected. For example, on earlier spreads we have used examples of individual differences as a way to evaluate explanations. On this spread and the previous spread we are looking at examples of individual differences. You can use these examples in your evaluative arguments in other parts of this chapter.

🐾 APPLY YOUR KNOWLEDGE

Lydia and Silas are being interviewed for the same job in a very successful marketing company. The company are concerned that they get the right sort of person, as the high pressure of the work has taken its toll on recruits in the past. The company has relatively high levels of staff absence, and a large proportion of their graduates leave in the first year after finding themselves unable to cope with the pressure of the job.

The firm is keen that the person they appoint should be 'hardy' enough to cope, so in the interview they ask questions that will give them information about each candidate's 'hardiness'. First they ask about their work preferences. Lydia says she has always worked better on her own because *'if you don't do well, you don't eat'*. Silas emphasises the importance of working in a team, as his previous colleagues *'would always be there to bail me out if things went wrong'*. When asked about attitude to work, Lydia answers that, *'after my family, my job is the most important thing in my life'*. Silas sees work as a means to an end, as after all *'there are more important things in life than work'*. Finally, when asked about the stresses of high-pressure work, Lydia claims she *'relishes'* the challenge, whereas Silas asks whether there was *'private health insurance'*.

Using your knowledge of the hardy personality, and the desire of this company to appoint someone who is suitably 'hardy', which candidate should be appointed and why?

HARDINESS

The hardy personality

Suzanne Kobasa and Salvatore Maddi (1977) suggested that some people are psychologically more 'hardy' than others. The hardy personality includes a range of characteristics which, if present, provide defences against the negative effects of stress.

The characteristics are the three Cs:
- *Control* – Hardy people see themselves as being in control of their lives, rather than being controlled by external factors beyond their control.
- *Commitment* – Hardy people are involved with the world around them, and have a strong sense of purpose.
- *Challenge* – Hardy people see life challenges as problems to be overcome rather than as threats or stressors. They enjoy change as an opportunity for development.

All three characteristics should help in coping with stressful situations.

Key study: Kobasa (1979)

Kobasa aimed to investigate why some people who were highly stressed managed not to become ill whereas, in contrast, others with similar levels of stress did get ill.

Procedure About 800 American middle- and upper-level executives from a large utility company in the US were contacted and asked to identify the life events they had experienced in the previous three years (using a slightly adapted version of Holmes and Rahe's *Social Readjustment Rating Scale*). They were also asked to list any illness episodes they had experienced in this time.

This enabled Kobasa to draw up a list of participants who were either high stress/low illness (there were 86 participants in this group) or high stress/high illness (there were 75 participants in this group). The participants were all men.

Three months later the final participants were asked to complete several personality tests, which included assessments of control, commitment and challenge.

Findings The individuals in the high-stress/low-illness group scored high on all three characteristics of the hardy personality, whereas the high-stress/high-illness group scored lower on these variables.

This supports the view that some people who have high stress do not experience illness because they have a hardy personality.

Other research

Both Kobasa and Maddi have conducted other studies, continuing to demonstrate this relationship. For example, Maddi (1987) studied employees of a US company (Illinois Bell Telephone) that was, over a period of a year, dramatically reducing the size of its workforce. Two-thirds of employees suffered stress-related health problems over this period, but the remaining third thrived. This 'thriving' group showed more evidence of hardiness attributes, i.e. commitment, control and challenge.

Lifton *et al.* (2006) measured hardiness in students at five US universities to see if hardiness was related to the likelihood of their completing their degree. The results showed that students scoring low in hardiness were disproportionately represented among the drop-outs, and students with a high score were most likely to complete their degree.

Problems of measurement

Most of the research support for the link between hardiness and health has relied upon data obtained through self-report questionnaires. Early research relied on the use of a number of quite lengthy scales measuring control, commitment and challenge. More recently, specific scales were developed, such as the *Personal Views Survey* (Maddi, 1997). This questionnaire addresses many of the criticisms raised with respect to the original measure, such as long and awkward wording and negatively worded items.

However, not all of the problems have been resolved. For example, some studies show low internal reliability for the challenge component of hardiness.

Direct effects

Research has indicated a physiological basis for the concept of hardiness. For example, Maddi (1999) found that hardy individuals had lower blood pressure than individuals who measured low in hardiness. In addition, Contrada (1989) found that people who were both hardy and Type B had the lowest blood pressure.

This suggests that the components of hardiness may have a direct effect on the autonomic nervous system and reduce the physiological responses that lead to coronary heart disease.

Real-world application

A benefit of any research is being able to apply it to real-world situations. Maddi has developed hardiness training (see right). His own research (Maddi *et al.*, 1998) assessed the effectiveness of this training for 54 managers as part of a hardiness training programme, comparing this with a relaxation/meditation condition and a placebo/social support control. The hardiness training condition was more effective than the other two conditions in increasing self-reported hardiness and job satisfaction while decreasing self-reported strain and illness severity.

The appeal of hardiness training has been widespread, not being just restricted to business but also used in education and in the military. For example, elite military units, such as the US Navy Seals, are now screened for hardiness and use the concepts in their training.

Hardiness and negative affectivity

Some critics argue that the characteristics of the hardy personality (i.e. commitment, control and challenge) can be more simply explained by the concept of negative affectivity (NA) (Watson and Clark, 1984). High-NA individuals are more likely to report distress and dissatisfaction, dwell more on their failures, and focus on negative aspects of themselves and their world. NA and hardiness correlate reasonably well, suggesting that 'hardy individuals' are simply those who are low on NA.

Funk (1992) also argues that low hardiness is the same as being negative, and it is negativity rather than lack of hardiness that leads to the ill effects of stress.

Is hardiness a personality type?

It is possible that all three elements of hardiness are not equally important.

Sandvik *et al.* (2013) assessed 21 Navy candidates and found that all were hardy personalities but some were low in the challenge component, and that these individuals also showed a weaker immune response – suggesting that they were more affected by stress. This suggests that challenge may be the key component.

On the other hand, some people argue that control is likely to be the key factor. The work by Julian Rotter (1966) on locus of control (a concept you studied as part of the Year 1 course) shows that individuals who have a high internal locus of control feel stress less and are less disrupted by it. For example, Kim *et al.* (1997) found that children with an internal locus of control showed fewer signs of stress when their parents divorced. Cohen *et al.* (1993) found that participants who felt their lives were unpredictable and uncontrollable were twice as likely to develop colds as those who felt in control.

If it boils down to one characteristic rather than a cluster of traits, then this is not really a personality type.

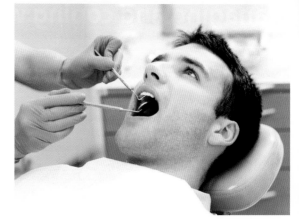

The understanding of the role of control in stress can be applied to situations where individuals receive painful treatments, such as at the dentist. Some dentists offer you the opportunity to give a signal if and when the pain gets too much (like raising your hand or pressing a button). Patients in such situations do tolerate more pain, showing the benefits of a greater sense of control (Brown, 1986).

The Hardiness Institute

Salvatore Maddi founded the Hardiness Institute in California. The aim of the training programme is to increase self-confidence and sense of control so that individuals can deal more successfully with change. Both Maddi and Kobasa suggested the following ways to train hardiness:

- *Focusing*. The client is taught how to recognise signs of stress, such as muscle tension and increased heart rate, and also to identify the sources of this stress.
- *Reliving stress encounters*. The client relives stress encounters and is helped to analyse his or her stress situations. This helps the client to an understanding of *current* stressors and *current* coping strategies.
- *Self-improvement*. The insights gained can now be used to move forwards and learn new techniques. In particular the client is taught to focus on seeing stressors as challenges and thus learn to take control. Control, commitment and challenge are the bases of hardiness training.

MEET THE RESEARCHER

Suzanne Kobasa gained her PhD from the University of Chicago and is currently Professor Emerita at the City University of New York. As well as her academic life, she is also trained in fine art. You can see her artwork at www.souellette.com.

CAN YOU? No. 8.8

1. Explain the terms *commitment*, *challenge* and *control* in relation to hardiness. (3 marks)
2. Outline **one** study of hardiness in relation to stress. (6 marks)
3. Describe and evaluate research related to the role of hardiness in stress. (16 marks)
4. Discuss individual differences in stress. (16 marks)

Managing and coping with stress: Drug therapies

Note that the title of this spread includes 'managing and coping'. Drug therapies are not a cure for stress – they aim to reduce the anxiety associated with stress, i.e. help with managing and coping with stress. Because they aim to reduce anxiety, the drugs are referred to as anti-anxiety drugs. There are links between drug therapies and the physiology of the stress response. **Benzodiazepines** target the central nervous system and assist the body's natural anti-anxiety mechanism. **Beta blockers** target the sympathetic nervous system and block the effect of adrenaline on the heart. The use of anti-anxiety drugs is regarded as a *biological* approach to stress management.

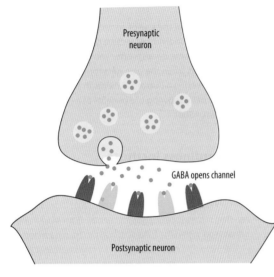

▲ GABA is released from one neuron across the synaptic gap. It then opens a channel in the GABA receptors, letting chloride ions into the postsynaptic neuron and making it harder for the neuron to be stimulated by other neurotransmitters.

▲ Beta blockers have been shown to significantly reduce the symptoms of anxiety that can hinder individuals who are performing, such as musicians or singers.

DRUG THERAPIES

Benzodiazepines (BZs)

The group of drugs most commonly used to treat anxiety and stress are benzodiazepines (e.g. *Librium*, *Diazepam*). These drugs aim to slow down the activity of the central nervous system.

BZs and GABA

One of the ways that BZs reduce anxiety is by enhancing the action of the neurotransmitter GABA (gamma-aminobutyric acid).

GABA is a neurotransmitter that is the body's natural form of anxiety relief. About 40% of the neurons in the brain respond to GABA, which has a general quietening effect on many of the neurons in the brain. The neurotransmitter GABA does this by reacting with GABA receptors on the outside of postsynaptic neurons (see diagram on left). When GABA locks into these receptors it opens a channel that increases the flow of chloride ions into the postsynaptic neuron. Chloride ions make it harder for the postsynaptic neuron to be stimulated by other neurotransmitters, thus slowing down its activity and making the person feel more relaxed and less anxious.

BZs enhance the action of GABA by binding to special sites on the GABA receptor and boosting the actions of GABA. This allows more chloride ions to enter the neuron, making it even more resistant to excitation. As a result, the person feels calmer.

BZs and serotonin

Serotonin is another neurotransmitter that has an arousing effect in the brain. BZs reduce any increased serotonin activity, which then reduces anxiety.

Beta blockers (BBs)

Beta blockers are also called *beta-adrenoceptor blocking agents*. In other words, they block sites which normally are activated by the hormones adrenaline and noradrenaline. As you will remember from the beginning of this chapter, adrenaline and noradrenaline are produced as a result of the sympathomedullary response to immediate stressors.

Sympathetic arousal

Stress leads to the arousal of the sympathetic nervous system, which triggers the production of adrenaline and noradrenaline from the adrenal medulla. Adrenaline and noradrenaline have an immediate effect on target organs, most especially the heart muscle, leading to raised blood pressure and increased heart rate as well as other effects such as increased breathing and sweating.

Beta blockers bind to beta-receptors in the cells of the heart and other parts of the body that are usually stimulated during sympathetic arousal. Therefore they prevent adrenaline and noradrenaline having such a strong effect. As a result, heart rate and blood pressure, breathing rate and sweating do not increase, and the person feels calmer and less anxious.

Other uses

The drug can be taken to prevent the physiological effects of anxiety, but is also taken by people with coronary heart disease to generally dampen the effect of everyday sympathetic arousal and thus reduce the wear and tear on the cardiovascular system.

The drug is ideal for stage performance because it doesn't affect the brain or alertness. It is also useful for sports people where accuracy is more important than physical stamina (e.g. snooker and golf) because it benefits hand–eye co-ordination. However, because of this, it is banned by the International Olympic Committee because it would give users a significant advantage.

Effectiveness

Effectiveness of drug therapies is best tested with randomised controlled trials, where one group of participants are given a placebo and another group the drug being tested. For example, Kahn *et al.* (1986) followed nearly 250 patients over eight weeks and found that BZs were significantly superior to a placebo for the treatment of anxiety and stress.

Lockwood (1989) studied over 2,000 musicians in major US symphony orchestras and found that 27% reported taking beta blockers. The musicians in this study said they felt better about their performance after taking beta blockers, and music critics consistently judged their performances to be better. However, Schweizer *et al.* (1991) looked at the effects of beta blocker use on stress associated with taking an arithmetic test. They found that the beta blockers reduced heart rate compared to a placebo condition but not all kinds of beta blocker reduced participants' subjective sense of stress.

Ease of use

One of the great benefits of using drug therapies for stress (or any psychological disorder) is that the therapy requires little effort from the user. You just have to remember to take the pills. This is much easier than the time and effort needed to use psychological methods. For example, stress inoculation therapy (discussed on the next spread) requires a lot of time, effort and motivation on the part of the client if it is to be effective. Therefore patients are likely to take the option of a quick drug therapy rather than months of psychological training.

Problems with addiction

BZs were first introduced over 40 years ago and replaced barbiturates, which tended to be addictive, i.e. patients exhibited withdrawal symptoms when they stopped taking the drug, indicating a biological dependence. However, similar problems surfaced with BZs, especially the problems of low-dose dependence on BZs. Patients taking even low doses of BZs show marked withdrawal symptoms when they stop taking them. Because of such addiction problems there is a recommendation that use of BZs should be limited to a maximum of four weeks (Ashton, 1997).

As a result of such problems with addiction (and also because of the side effects, described below), BZs are not appropriate as a treatment for everyday stress – they are prescribed for people experiencing psychological disorders with an anxiety component, such as OCD or phobias. Despite all these attendant dangers, Donoghue and Lader (2010) report that they continue to be used as long-term treatments.

Side effects

Side effects of BZs include 'paradoxical' symptoms (so called because they are the opposite of what might be expected) such as increased agitation or panic as well as aggressiveness and cognitive side effects. These cognitive side effects include impairment of memory, especially the ability to store acquired knowledge in long-term memory.

Most people who take beta blockers do not experience any side effects, although some studies have linked them with an increased risk of developmental diabetes.

Treating the symptoms rather than the problem

Drugs may be very effective at treating symptoms, but the effect only lasts while a person takes the drugs. As soon as they stop taking the drugs the effectiveness ceases. It may be that the problem has passed, but in cases of continuing stress it may not be appropriate to simply put a temporary 'bandage' on the problem, especially if the treatment produces further problems of its own (such as addiction). This means that it may be preferable to seek a treatment that addresses the problem itself (i.e. a psychological method) rather than one that deals only with the symptoms.

⬆ UPGRADE

Coping with specific demands in questions

It is wise to read all questions very carefully. For example, there are several ways in which an examiner might probe your understanding of drug therapies as a way of dealing with stress. One way is simply ask you to 'Outline drug therapies…'. This rather general question invites a general answer, so content about the nature of drug therapies as well as how these work in practice would be perfectly appropriate *provided* they were focused specifically on managing and coping with stress.

However, questions may also have quite subtle and specific requirements, as shown by the use of the word 'how' in questions 1 and 2 in the 'Can You?…' feature on this page. Here you are required to describe, in practical terms, *how* a specified drug (benzodiazepines in Q1 and beta blockers in Q2) helps people deal with stress, i.e. what physiological changes they produce that relieve anxiety associated with stress.

It also pays to be flexible when preparing your answers for such questions. For a 3-mark question this would mean about 75 words, but you should also have a 100-word version ready for a possible 4-mark question, and even a 150-word version for a 6-mark question. So…be flexible in your preparation, read questions carefully and concentrate on the specific requirements to maximise your marks.

▲ Drug therapies may offer a quick fix, but unpleasant side effects may stop people using them – which means they aren't very effective after all.

KEY TERMS

Benzodiazepines A class of drug used to treat stress and anxiety. They facilitate the action of the neurotransmitter GABA in quietening down neurons in the brain.

Beta blockers Decrease stress and anxiety by blocking the effects of adrenaline and noradrenaline, which are part of the sympathomedullary response to stress.

CAN YOU? No. 8.9

1. Explain how benzodiazepines help people cope with stress. (3 marks)
2. Explain how beta blockers help people cope with stress. (3 marks)
3. Discuss the use of drug therapy in managing and coping with stress. (16 marks)

Managing and coping with stress: Stress inoculation therapy

On the previous spread we looked at one biological approach to managing stress – drug therapy. This kind of approach treats the symptoms but not the underlying problem. In contrast, **stress inoculation therapy**, a psychological therapy, does the opposite – targeting the underlying problem with the assumption that the biological symptoms will then go away. However, stress inoculation therapy (or SIT) isn't for everyone because it involves a substantial commitment of time and effort. This also means it is really only suitable for people with long-term stress issues where it is worth the investment of time.

KEY TERM

Stress inoculation therapy A type of CBT which trains people to cope with anxiety and stressful situations more effectively by learning skills to 'inoculate' themselves against the damaging effects of future stressors.

🐾 APPLY YOUR KNOWLEDGE

David and Rosemary's son, Joe, is taking his gap year working at an animal rescue reserve in a war-torn area of central Africa. Although he really wants to go, he is worried about how he will cope with all the stressors that go with the job. These include the constant threat of disease, worry about kidnapping and poachers and his ability to deal with the everyday death and destruction that are a fundamental part of the region where he will be working.

Rosemary works as a psychological therapist and decides that Joe would profit from some stress inoculation therapy to prepare him to deal with the extreme stresses he will face while away.

Using your knowledge of stress inoculation therapy, explain why Rosemary believes this would be suitable for Joe and *how* she would use it with him.

STRESS INOCULATION THERAPY (SIT)

The principles behind SIT

SIT is a form of Cognitive Behavioural Therapy (CBT) that was developed specifically to deal with stress. It is different from other stress treatments because Donald Meichenbaum (1985) suggested that an individual should develop a form of coping *before* the problem arises. He suggested that a person could inoculate themselves against the 'disease' of stress in the same way that they would receive inoculations against infectious illnesses such as measles.

Meichenbaum believed that although a person cannot (usually) change the *causes* of stress in their life (e.g. a stressful job is still a stressful job), they can change the way that they *think* about these stressors. Thus this is a cognitive approach to dealing with stress because it is the way that a person thinks that is being targeted.

As negative thinking (e.g. 'I failed to hit a deadline – people must think I'm hopeless') may lead to negative outcomes such as anxiety and depression, positive thinking (e.g. 'My boss will still be delighted by what I've achieved') leads to more positive attitudes and feelings. These reduce the stress response and help us to cope better in the future.

How it works

Meichenbaum proposed three main phases to this process:

1. Conceptualisation phase

This first phase is a collaborative process between therapist and client. The therapist investigates the client's sources of stress through interviews with the client and significant others. It is important that the client is allowed to 'tell their story'. The client should be helped to see what current strategies are maladaptive and identify the things that can be changed. The client is taught to view perceived threats as problems to be solved, and to break down global stressors into specific components that can be coped with. This enables the client to think differently about (i.e. reconceptualise) their problem.

2. Skills acquisition, rehearsal and consolidation

Coping skills are taught and practised primarily in the clinic and then gradually rehearsed in real life. The therapist selects skills that match the client's preferred mode of coping and that are tailored to the individual's own specific problems.

Such skills include positive thinking, relaxation, social skills, methods of attention diversion, using social support systems and time management. Clients may be taught to use coping self-statements (see right).

The skills taught are both cognitive and behavioural: cognitive because they encourage the client to think in a different way, and behavioural because they involve learning new, more adaptive behaviours.

Skills are rehearsed using imagery (imagining how to deal with stressful situations), modelling (watching someone else cope with stressors and then imitating this behaviour) and role playing (acting out scenes involving stressors).

3. Application and follow-through

Clients are given opportunities to apply the newly learned coping skills in different situations, which become increasingly stressful. It is particularly important for clients to be taught to anticipate situations where it may be difficult to apply the skills and rehearse coping responses. Clients may even be asked to help train others. Booster sessions (follow-through) are offered later on.

Examples of coping self-statements

Preparing for a stressful situation
- You can develop a plan to deal with it.
- Don't worry; worry won't help anything.

Confronting and handling a stressful situation
- One step at a time – you can handle it.
- Relax – you're in control. Take a slow breath.

Coping with the feeling of being overwhelmed
- Keep the focus on the present.
- Label your fear 0 to 10 and watch it change.

Reinforcing self-statements
- It worked – you did it.
- It wasn't as bad as you expected.

Effectiveness

Meichenbaum (1977) compared SIT with another form of psychological treatment for phobias (systematic desensitisation, which was part of your Year 1 course). Patients used SIT or desensitisation to deal with their snake phobia. Meichenbaum found that both forms of therapy reduced the phobia, but that SIT was better because it helped clients deal with a second, non-treated phobia. This shows that SIT can inoculate against future stressful situations as well as offering help in coping with current problems.

Many other studies have demonstrated the effectiveness of SIT in a large variety of different situations, for example for parents who are stressed because their children are undergoing medical procedures (Jay and Elliott, 1990), for law students dealing with academic stress (Sheehy and Horan, 2004) and to reduce stress in public speaking (Jaremko, 1980).

The hello–goodbye effect

It is difficult to assess the effectiveness of a therapy such as SIT because we depend on subjective reports from clients. Clients often exaggerate their problems when they first consult a therapist because they wish to convince the therapist that they really do need help. When discussing their initial problem during the conceptualisation phase, the client may make it look like their problem is worse than it actually is.

At the end of treatment, patients are grateful for the help they were given and therefore may minimise any remaining issues.

Preparation for future stressors

A major advantage of SIT as a method of stress management is that it doesn't just deal with current stressors, but also gives the client the skills and confidence to cope with future problems. It isn't just a one-off treatment for a current problem. The focus on skills acquisition provides long-lasting effectiveness so that the individual is less adversely affected by stressors in the future. This particularly contrasts with drug therapy which only addresses current symptoms rather than the underlying problem. And SIT goes even further than just addressing the underlying problem – it offers a way of approaching any difficulties which may occur at a future time.

A challenging therapy

The key criticism of SIT is that it is time-consuming and requires high motivation. In the study by Sheehy and Horan (above), students had to attend four weekly sessions, each lasting 20 minutes. In fact Meichenbaum (2007) suggests that it takes much longer than that when dealing with clinical disorders – 8–15 sessions plus follow-up sessions over as much as a year. On the other hand it may take as little as 20 minutes when preparing someone for surgery.

Therefore, for some kinds of stress, the time investment may be more than some people wish to invest. In addition, some people do not like to discuss their feelings and do not like to work at changing the way they think. For this reason they may not complete the therapy, and thus its effectiveness is considerably reduced.

Unnecessarily complex

It may be that the effectiveness of SIT is due to certain elements of the training rather than all of it. It is hard to know whether, for example, the cognitive element is more important than the skills which are practised. This means that the range of activities (and time) could be reduced without losing much of the effectiveness.

One suggestion is that the key ingredient in the success of SIT is just learning to talk more positively and relax more. Relaxation reduces activity in the sympathetic nervous system so that a person feels less stressed.

▲ Would that it were so easy. An inoculation against stress means the client has to work – the individual has to work hard to build up skills that will prevent future negative stress responses.

Insider tip…
Questions on therapies, such as stress inoculation therapy, may ask you to outline the therapy – i.e. describe the therapy. However, sometimes such questions say: 'How would stress inoculation therapy be used?' In this case your focus must be on describing how the therapist would actually conduct the therapy rather than a more straightforward description of the stages. You use the same content but need to present it from a slightly different perspective.

MEET THE RESEARCHER

As well as being named the most cited psychology researcher within Canadian universities, **Donald Meichenbaum** was voted 'one of the ten most influential psychotherapists of the century' by American clinicians. He worked with victims of Hurricane Katrina in 2005 and the Oklahoma bombing in 1993, as well as with Canadian soldiers serving in Afghanistan.

1. Outline what is involved with stress inoculation therapy. (3 marks)
2. Explain how a psychologist might use stress inoculation therapy to treat a person with stress. (4 marks)
3. Describe and evaluate the use of stress inoculation therapy in managing and coping with stress. (16 marks)

Managing and coping with stress: Biofeedback

We now turn to the final method of stress management. **Biofeedback** combines both of the previous approaches we have looked at – it is both biological and psychological.

It is in part biological, as the name *bio*feedback suggests, because it involves paying attention to physical information from your body about heartbeat or blood pressure.

It is in part psychological as it involves conditioning; successful behaviour is rewarded and therefore continued.

Another aspect of biological and psychological methods of stress management is to consider whether the method helps to cope with the symptoms (a biological approach) or the situation itself (a psychological approach). You will see that biofeedback claims to do both.

▲ One study found that doctors, who have quite stressful jobs, reported less stress after using biofeedback three times daily for a period of one month (Lemaire *et al.*, 2011).

▲ Woman undergoing biofeedback testing, showing electrodes connected to her forehead and sensors attached to her fingers. The electrodes are connected to monitoring equipment in the background. Biofeedback is a type of relaxation technique which uses visual and auditory stimuli with monitoring devices to bring about a reduction in, for example, blood pressure.

BIOFEEDBACK

Biofeedback, like drug therapy, also deals with the body's physiological response to stress – the arousal of the sympathetic nervous system which leads to, for example, increased heart rate and blood pressure. Heart rate and blood pressure are not under our voluntary control as they are part of the autonomic nervous system (ANS) for good reason. If these systems were controlled consciously, we would spend our time thinking about nothing else!

Biofeedback is a method by which an individual learns to exert voluntary control over involuntary (autonomic) behaviours by being made aware of what is happening in the ANS.

How it works

Biofeedback involves four processes, discussed below.

Relaxation

The client is taught techniques of relaxation. These have the effect of reducing the activity of the sympathetic nervous system and activating the parasympathetic nervous system. This means that adrenaline and noradrenaline are no longer produced, and the result should be reduced heart rate, blood pressure and all the other symptoms associated with stress.

Feedback

The client is attached to various machines which provide information (feedback) about the activity of the ANS. For example, the client can hear his/her heartbeat or is given a signal (using light or sound) to show any increases or decreases in blood pressure or changes in muscle tension. Other ANS activities that can be monitored include heart rate, breathing patterns and sweat gland activity. The machines that are used include EMG (electromyograph), which responds to changes in muscles; skin conductance response, which measures sweat activity; and EEG (electroencephalograph), which measures electrical activity in the brain.

The client then practises relaxation while seeing/listening to the feedback. The aim is to hear/see a change in the feedback and respond by relaxing (and activating a parasympathetic response). For example, heart rate should decrease because of the relaxation techniques.

Operant conditioning

When relaxation leads to a reduction in heart rate, this is experienced as rewarding because the person has achieved their goal and this reinforces the behaviour. This increases the likelihood of the same behaviour being repeated. Such learning (conditioning) takes place without any conscious thought. The reward leads to an unconscious 'stamping in' of the behaviour.

Transfer

The client finally needs to learn to transfer the skills learned to the real world, using their relaxation techniques in response to stressful situations that they encounter.

Demonstration of biofeedback

The biofeedback technique was based on a classic study by Neal Miller and Leo DiCara (1967). They used curare to paralyse 24 rats, keeping the rats alive using artificial respiration. Half of the rats were rewarded whenever their heart rates slowed down, and the other half were rewarded when their heart rates speeded up. The reward was 'a sense of pleasure' – this was achieved by electrically stimulating a part of the brain known as the pleasure centre.

The outcome was that the heart rates of the rats in the 'fast' group speeded up, and the heart rates of the rats in the 'slow' group slowed down. Two things are important. First, the learning that took place was entirely involuntary, as the rats were paralysed. It was the automatic ANS responses (heart rate) that were conditioned. Second, the learning was the result of operant conditioning – behaviour stamped in because it was rewarded.

EVALUATION

Research support

Gruber and Taub (1998) successfully trained four monkeys to raise and lower body temperature and reduce muscle tension using biofeedback. This demonstrates that biofeedback learning does not depend on conscious thought because non-human animals cannot be using the power of thought.

Many studies have been conducted with human participants, including studies that specifically link biofeedback to activity in the sympathetic nervous system. For example, Lewis *et al.* (2015) showed that biofeedback training with military personnel led to a decreased heart rate.

The operant conditioning component may be irrelevant

The origins of biofeedback lie with the work of Miller and DiCara. Leo DiCara continued conducting research on biofeedback after the original study. However, subsequent attempts to replicate his research failed. When DiCara was pressed to share his data with other researchers, he claimed it had been lost and, following further pressure, he tragically committed suicide. Miller had designed the studies but DiCara had collected all the data, and it is now believed that he invented it (Klintworth, 2014).

That leaves us to conclude that the successes reported for biofeedback may actually be more to do with relaxation than any unconscious operant conditioning. The success of biofeedback may simply be due to the fact that relaxation reduces sympathetic activity. Or it may be that the method offers clients a sense of increased control and this makes people feel better.

Continued popularity

Despite the lack of evidence that feedback is required, the biofeedback method has remained popular for a whole range of disorders: curvature of the spine, migraine headaches, asthma and Reynaud's disease (where there is restricted blood flow to the fingers and toes).

There is even research to show that biofeedback is superior to relaxation only. Bradley (1995) compared the effectiveness of using biofeedback versus relaxation to control muscle-tension headaches. The biofeedback group was given seven 50-minute sessions with feedback about muscle activity (using EMG). After treatment, the biofeedback group had significantly fewer headaches than the relaxation group. This may be explained in terms of a placebo effect – the presence of sophisticated machines may make people believe that the method is more effective and therefore they improve more.

Strengths

The method offers a number of advantages over other methods. For example biofeedback is not an invasive technique. In other words, it does not alter the body in any permanent way as drugs do. The method is useful for treating children who cannot be treated with drugs and cannot cope with the more mentally demanding stress inoculation therapy.

Furthermore, it is a method that does tackle the problem as well as the symptoms. It provides a long-lasting way of reducing stress through relaxation, and this has a positive effect on lowering the activity of the sympathetic nervous system.

Limitations

On the negative side biofeedback requires specialist equipment, which means that it is expensive and can only be undertaken with supervision. It is also a relatively lengthy treatment, lasting more than a month, and sometimes takes considerably longer.

Furthermore, like stress inoculation therapy, biofeedback requires some effort from the client. If the success of biofeedback is mainly due to relaxation rather than feedback and conditioning, there is no need for these expensive and time-consuming procedures.

▲ Post-traumatic stress disorder (PTSD) is just one of the many conditions that have been successfully treated with biofeedback. PTSD is a disorder that sometimes develops when a person experiences a traumatic event. The individual remains in a state of stress.

Research methods

This is the abstract for a research study similar to the one by Lewis *et al.* (see left):

Research has shown that post-traumatic stress disorder (PTSD) is associated with high levels of activity in the sympathetic nervous system and that biofeedback can be used to improve the symptoms of the disorder. The aim of this study was to see if stress responses could be reduced using biofeedback training. A large sample of military personnel were randomly assigned to either a biofeedback training programme or to a control group who received no training. After biofeedback training, participants in the biofeedback group showed reduced arousal during a combat simulation compared to participants in the control group. A future training programme could be designed to teach self-help skills to enable individuals to learn how to reduce their autonomic stress responses.

1. Explain the key features of an abstract. (3 marks)
2. Distinguish between stating the aims of a research study and stating the hypothesis. (3 marks)
3. Identify the independent and dependent variables in this study. (2 marks)
4. Identify a possible confounding variable in this study and explain why it might be confounding. (3 marks)
5. Explain the purpose of randomly assigning participants to conditions. (2 marks)
6. Explain the purpose of the control group. (2 marks)

> **LINK TO RESEARCH METHODS**
>
> The topics in these questions are covered in the research methods chapter of our Year 1 book.

CAN YOU?   No. 8.11

1. Explain how a psychologist might use biofeedback to treat a person with stress. (4 marks)
2. Explain **one** criticism that has been made relating to biofeedback as a method of managing and coping with stress. (4 marks)
3. Describe and evaluate the use of biofeedback in managing and coping with stress. (16 marks)

Gender differences in coping with stress

At the beginning of this chapter we looked at the physiology of stress and described both the sympathomedullary pathway (SAM) and the hypothalamic pituitary-adrenal system (HPA). One of the criticisms of the research on the SAM pathway is that it was derived from studies using male participants only. Males are preferred because their hormone levels do not alter due to an ovulation cycle. Subsequent research with female participants has shown that there are significant gender differences in coping with stress.

On this spread we revisit these physiological differences, and look at psychological differences as well in coping with stress.

▼ Seems a bit harsh to suggest men don't do any tending and befriending.

Key study: Peterson *et al.* (2006)

Various studies have found that men tend to have a problem focus and women tend to have a preference for emotional focus, for example a study by Peterson *et al.* (2006).

Procedure Just over 1,000 men and women seeking fertility treatment at a hospital were recruited for a study on coping styles and asked to complete several questionnaires, including the *Ways of Coping Questionnaire* designed by Lazarus and Folkman.

Findings They found clear gender differences. Women used confrontive coping, i.e. a style where they try to alter the situation to reduce the emotional impact (emotion-focused). They were also more likely to seek social support and avoidance when compared to men. In contrast, men engaged in problem-solving and also distanced themselves from the problem (a kind of problem focus). There was some emotion-focused coping in men, indicating that the gender difference is not clear cut.

GENDER DIFFERENCES IN COPING WITH STRESS

Physiological explanations for gender difference

Shelley Taylor and colleagues (2000) first proposed the notion of the **tend-and-befriend response** to stress, suggesting that this would have evolved as a typical response in females to situations of threat. She argued that the fight-or-flight response would be displayed by both genders but, for females, there would be a greater adaptive advantage to produce a tend-and-befriend response, and thus this is the more common stress response for females.

The reason this tend-and-befriend response is a more adaptive response for females is due to differential parental investment – females invest more in each single reproduction than males. Therefore, female stress responses have evolved to maximise the survival of self and offspring.

At a physiological level the question is, how does this happen? Both males and females experience the same physiological response to stress – producing adrenaline, noradrenaline and cortisol. Alongside the production of these stress hormones, another hormone is produced in both males and females – oxytocin, sometimes called the 'love hormone' because it promotes feelings of bonding and general social-ness. In males, testosterone levels also rise, and testosterone has a dampening effect on oxytocin. Therefore males become more aggressive (due to testosterone) and females seek closeness to others (because of the unrepressed oxytocin). This response would be at its strongest in women who are breastfeeding because oxytocin is also released at this time.

Psychological explanations for gender differences

Richard Lazarus and Susan Folkman (1984) distinguished between two different coping styles for dealing with stress: **problem-focused** and **emotion-focused coping** styles. Stress can be managed by tackling the problem itself (problem-focused), but often this is not possible, and so an alternative approach is to reduce the stress response (emotion-focused). The gender differences in these two styles is illustrated in the key study on the left.

Stress experienced and coping

Some research suggests men may experience different kinds of stress, and this may explain differences in coping. For example, Matud (2004), in a study of almost 3,000 Spanish men and women aged between 18 and 65 years, found that men listed relationship, finance and work-related events as most stressful (and these would require more problem focus), whereas women listed family and health-related events (which would require more emotion focus). It is worth noting that, in this study, women showed a more emotion-focused style of coping and men were more problem-focused.

So it may be that it *appears* that men and women are coping differently, but that is because they are coping with different stressors. This is called role constraint theory, i.e. their roles dictate their way of coping.

Not simply a tend-and-befriend response by females

It would also be adaptive for women to be aggressive, in order to protect their offspring. Taylor *et al.* do note that, while females are less aggressive in general than males, they are aggressive towards an intruder who threatens their offspring. In other words, they are aggressive in situations requiring defence rather than the more generalised 'fight response' in males. The same is true of the flight response in females. In situations of threat, animals whose offspring are mobile fairly soon after birth will flee rather than stay huddled together.

Thus the female response is not simply tend and befriend but it encompasses a whole range of strategies that are adapted to parental investment by females.

Lack of research support for coping focus

The finding that men are more problem-focused when coping with stress and women more emotion-focused is not upheld by most research studies. For example, Hamilton and Fagot (1988) assessed male and female first-year undergraduates over an eight-week period and found no gender differences and, in fact, the study by Peterson *et al.*, described on the facing page, found some emotion-focused coping in men.

Some of the issue may lie in the rather simplistic division of coping styles into problem focus versus emotion focus. Subsequent research has shown that there are more than just two coping styles. For example, Endler and Parker (1990) devised the *Multidimensional Coping Inventory*, which identified a third strategy – avoidance-oriented.

Confounding variables

Coping varies as a function of a number of factors which act as confounding variables. As we saw on the facing page, coping style varies with the type of stressor. In addition, degree of social support may act as a confounding factor. Women are more likely to receive social support than men and, as you will see on the next spread, social support reduces the amount of stress experienced. This means that women may be experiencing less stress and as a consequence select different coping styles.

Other methodological issues

All of the research on coping strategies relies on the use of self-report scales where people describe how they have dealt with specific situations. Women may be more willing to reveal the emotional side of coping, whereas men play down their emotional difficulties. This means that there may be no differences in coping style – it is a difference in willingness to reveal a softer side (social desirability bias).

In addition, research typically involves retrospective recall of events in the past and how a person responded to them. Such recall is notoriously unreliable and may well be biased by how stressed the person is feeling – the more stressed, the more likely that recall will be negative.

Changing roles and lives of men and women

Where research has identified gender differences in coping, these may be explained in terms of lifestyle difference rather than some inherent coping tendency in men and women. For example, it has been argued that men experience more job-related stress, but as women enter the workforce they experience more stress from this source. Frankenhauser (1986) found that females in non-traditional gender roles (e.g. lawyers, bus drivers, engineers) had higher levels of stress hormones than women in traditional roles. This suggests that male stress may be a consequence of the activities they engage in.

🐾 APPLY YOUR KNOWLEDGE

Rachel and Jack work together in the same office, where they process appeals against parking tickets. It is a stressful job, as they have to deal with a large number of difficult, and often abusive, telephone calls from people who are clearly unhappy about having received a parking ticket. They deal with this stress in different ways, sometimes successfully, and sometimes not.

Using your knowledge of gender differences in coping with stress, explain how Rachel and Jack are likely to cope with the specific stressors associated with their work role.

1. Explain **one** gender difference in coping with stress. (2 marks)
2. Describe **one** study of gender differences in coping with stress. (4 marks)
3. Describe and evaluate gender differences in coping with stress. (16 marks)

The role of social support in coping with stress

Social support refers to the help you may receive from other people at times of stress. Perhaps this doesn't seem so very surprising, as many of us turn to friends when feeling distressed. You may also remember the study by Janice Kiecolt-Glaser on page 194 which found that having friends was a buffer to stress. It may simply be the affection that other people offer us that makes us feel better, or there may be other factors that are important such as physical comfort or actual offers of help.

see page 194

KEY TERMS

Emotional support is focused on what a person is feeling – the anxiety associated with stress and trying to find ways to reduce those feelings.

Esteem support Increasing a person's sense of self-worth so they can feel more confident about coping with both instrumental and emotional issues.

Instrumental support is when direct aid and actual material services are offered. Is sometimes called *tangible support*.

▲ 'You've got a Friend'

A classic hit in the 1970s for Carole King (at least for us oldies). Friendship appears to be a key factor in protecting people against the negative effects of stress. For example, Brown and Harris (1978) interviewed 400 women living in Camberwell, London. Some of them had experienced a stressful event in the preceding year, yet not all had developed any serious psychological problems such as depression. Those who did develop such problems shared one important factor – the absence of a close, supportive relationship.

THE ROLE OF SOCIAL SUPPORT

Sources of social support

Both friends and family may be important sources of stress, though this is clearly related to the quality of those relationships.

People are also supported by having a general safety net of relationships. For example, Nabi *et al.* (2013) surveyed 400 undergraduate Facebook users and found that number of friends was associated with stronger perceptions of social support and lower levels of stress and less physical illness. They concluded that 'the more friends, the better' was the best predictor of reduced stress.

If a general increase in social opportunities is beneficial, then the opposite is likely to be true as well. Dickinson *et al.* (2011) suggest that this may be a major consideration for older people. Their reduced social contact may be an important factor in their ill health.

Different kinds of support

In trying to understand social support, it is useful to distinguish between the different kinds of support that may be given.

Instrumental support refers to offers of tangible assistance such as providing money or driving you to the doctor. This is a problem-solving kind of approach to coping with stress where the focus is on doing something. Some psychologists (e.g. Schaefer *et al.*, 1981) identify information support as a separate category to instrumental support, which involves giving advice or feedback. This kind of support may be offered by anyone, not just known friends and family.

Emotional support, which is obviously the more emotional side of coping (emotion-focused coping), as distinct from a problem focus. This is where another person is aware of the associated emotions that a stressed person is presenting and will address those needs. This might just mean listening to a friend or giving them advice about how to reduce the emotions. This kind of support is less likely to be offered by strangers – but it is possible; for example, in an emergency situation a stranger may offer comfort.

Esteem support means that someone else makes you feel better about yourself and this would reduce a sense of being stressed. Self-esteem refers to the way that you value yourself, so esteem support aims to improve your feelings of self-worth, giving you more confidence and greater self-efficacy about being able to cope. This kind of support is most likely to be unique to close relationships.

Explaining the effects of social support

The buffering hypothesis suggests that social support is especially important at times of stress but not necessarily at other times. At times of stress, friends protect an individual from the negative effects of stress; they help friends think about stress differently. This kind of support is seen as the instrumental type because it is problem-focused.

Direct physiological effects A number of studies have demonstrated the direct effect of social support on the activity of the autonomic nervous system, possibly to increase relaxation.

Key study: Kamarck *et al.* (1990)

Procedure The study involved 39 female psychology student volunteers who were recruited to perform a difficult mental task (stressful) while their physiological reactions were monitored. Each participant attended the lab session alone or they were asked to bring a close same-sex friend with them. During the mental task the friend was told to simply touch the participant on the wrist. In order to avoid the participant feeling evaluated by the friend, the partner was given a task to complete at the same time and therefore was not monitoring what the participant was doing.

All participants filled in questionnaires related to mood and personality.

Findings In general the participants who were with a friend showed lower physiological reactions (e.g. lower heart rate) than those who were alone, supporting the direct physiological effect of social support.

For some of the tasks, only Type A participants showed reduced physiological responses. This also supports the buffering hypothesis, which suggests that buffering is only experienced by those who show a high level of response to a stressful situation.

Gender differences

Men and women differ in the extent to which they benefit from social support in coping with stress. One review by Lucknow *et al.* (1998) found that in 25 out of 26 studies there was a gender difference – women were more likely to use social support than men. However, such findings depend quite a bit on what *type* of social support was being investigated. For example, as we might expect, when looking at instrumental social support (more problem-focused), men would actually use social support more. The fact that most studies look at emotional types of social support may explain why women appear to use social support more.

The fact that there are gender differences questions the validity of studies of coping that have used all-female or all-male participants.

Cultural differences

One of the dimensions that is used to compare cultures is the individualistic-collectivist one. Bailey and Dua (1999) compared Asian students (belonging to a collectivist culture) and Anglo-Australian students (belonging to an individualist one) and found that Asian students tend to employ collectivist coping strategies, whereas Anglo-Australians tended towards the use of individualist coping styles. The longer the Asian student remains in Australian culture, the more they use individualist coping styles. An individualist coping style is one of more explicit support (instrumental) and individual support, whereas collectivist support is implicit because it exists anyway due to the interconnected nature of the society.

Distinguishing types of social support

The value of identifying all the different types of social support is questionable as there doesn't appear to be universal agreement about where to draw the boundaries. For example, House (1981) suggested that esteem support is part of emotional support, which also includes group belonging (a collectivist concept). Schaefer *et al.* (1981) list emotional, tangible (i.e. instrumental) and informational support as the three main categories of social support.

This lack of consistency in types of social support suggests that this kind of categorisation is not a very useful approach. A number of researchers are happy just to make the distinction between tangible and social/emotional support.

Pets can provide support

The term 'social' refers to one's own species; however, there is research that shows that the presence of pets can reduce stress as well. Allen (2003) reviewed research findings on pets and reported that, for example, the presence of pets reduced blood pressure in children reading aloud, buffered the elderly against life event stresses and reduced cardiovascular risk. One study even found that talking to pets was more effective than talking to people in the reduction of stress responses.

In the Kamarck *et al.* study on the facing page the experience of someone else's touch was enough to reduce the stress response. Therefore the explanation for the emotional benefits of social support might be more to do with not feeling alone (which may create anxiety).

Relative importance of social support

Kobasa *et al.* (1985) conducted a study on the effects of hardiness on stress – but also included assessments of social support and physical exercise in this study of 70 business executives. They found that social support was the least important factor in reducing stress levels, and hardiness the most important. Anecdotally, people feel that social support is important in coping with stress, but the evidence above suggests this may just not be true.

In addition, social support is not always beneficial. Sometimes the presence of other people can lead to increased physiological activity, for example if a friendship is strained or a romantic relationship is in turmoil. Kiecolt-Glaser and Newton (2001) reviewed 64 studies of marital relations and found that social support didn't always result in benefits in terms of physical and psychological health. The benefits were related to the quality of the relationship.

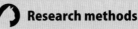

Research methods

On the facing page a study is described by Nabi *et al.* (2013) where Facebook users were questioned about their friendships. You could conduct a study by looking at different people's Facebook accounts to observe whether people with higher numbers of friends reported less stress and less physical illness than those with lower number of friends.

1. How would you decide on a sample of Facebook accounts to use? Explain your decision. (2 marks)
2. What ethical issues arise in using such accounts? For example, do you think you need to ask the owner's permission to use their data? Explain your decisions. (4 marks)
3. In order to 'observe' whether the person has reported physical illness and stress, what behavioural categories would you use? (3 marks)
4. Explain how you could insure that your observations were reliable? (4 marks)
5. There are many different kinds of observation: naturalistic and controlled observation; covert and overt observation; participant and non-participant observation – which of these would terms would describe this study? (3 marks)

LINK TO RESEARCH METHODS

Reliability page 16.

▲ Pets reduce stress – but what type of social support is that? Certainly not instrumental.

CAN YOU?   No. 8.13

1. Explain the following kinds of social support that may be offered at times of stress: instrumental, emotional and esteem support. (2 marks each)
2. Describe **one** study of the role of social support in coping with stress. (4 marks)
3. Discuss research related to the role of social support in coping with stress. (16 marks)

We have identified here the key points of the topics on the AQA A level specification, i.e. the bare minimum that you need to know. You may want to fill in further details to elaborate and personalise this material.

THE PHYSIOLOGY OF STRESS

SHORT- AND LONG-TERM STRESS RESPONSES

- Short-term (immediate) stress response – sympathomedullary pathway (SAM):
  - **S**ympathetic nervous system.
  - **M**edulla (adenal medulla).
  - **A**drenaline and noradrenaline cause increased heart rate, etc.
- Long-term (ongoing) stress – hypothalamic pituitary-adrenal system (HPA):
  - **H**ypothalamus produces corticotrophin-releasing hormone (CRH).
  - **P**ituitary produces adrenocorticotrophic hormone (ACTH).
  - **A**drenal cortex produces cortisol.

EVALUATION

- Gender differences – tend-and-befriend response adaptive for females to promote survival of offspring (Taylor *et al.*).
- Negative consequences of fight-or-flight – valuable in an environment where physical response required but not in modern world; adrenaline and cortisol have damaging effects.
- Transactional model – Lazarus argued that physiological explanation not sufficient on own; cognitive appraisal of stressor is relevant.

GENERAL ADAPTATION SYNDROME

- Stage 1: Alarm reaction – adrenaline released ready for 'fight-or-flight'.
- Stage 2: Resistance – body adapts to demands but resources being depleted.
- Stage 3: Exhaustion – stress-related illness due to depletion of resources.

EVALUATION

- Research support – Selye subjected rats to many noxious substances and all produced the same non-specific response.
- Stress-related illness not due to depletion of resources – damaging effects due to adrenaline and cortisol.

THE ROLE OF STRESS IN ILLNESS

THE ROLE OF STRESS IN ILLNESS

- Immediate stress – adrenaline leads to cardiovascular disorders because of increased heart rate; constriction of blood vessels increases pressure; pressure dislodges plaques blocking arteries.
- Ongoing stress – cortisol reduces the immune response.

KEY STUDY: KIECOLT-GLASER *ET AL.*

Immunosuppression – effect of exams

- Procedure: 75 medical students, NK cell activity measured before and during exams, plus life events (SRRS) and loneliness assessed.
- Findings: NK cell activity significantly reduced during exams, especially in those with many life events and high loneliness scores.

KEY STUDY: WILLIAMS *ET AL.*

Cardiovascular disorders – effect of anger

- Procedure: 13,000 completed anger scale.
- Findings: 6 years later, those who scored highest were 2½ times more likely to have had a heart attack.

EVALUATION

- Self-report – negative perceptions may produce spurious correlation between stress and illness.
- Supporting research for the effect on cardiovascular disorders – Sheps *et al.* found that 44% of participants with ischaemia died within 4 years compared to 18% without.
- Individual differences in cardiovascular effects – gender (Kiecolt-Glaser *et al.*), age (Segerstrom and Miller), responsiveness (Rozanski *et al.*) and personality (Friedman and Rosenman).
- Stress does not always have a negative effect on the immune system – Evans *et al.* found increased sigA activity for immediate stress (public speaking), enhancing the immune response (upregulation).
- Stress and illness is not a simple relationship – Lazarus explains this is due to multiple factors being involved, health is slow to change and research tends to be short term.

MEASURING STRESS: SELF-REPORT SCALES AND PHYSIOLOGICAL MEASURES

SELF-REPORT SCALES

- Social Readjustment Ratings Scale (SRRS) – 43 common life events identified by Holmes and Rahe.
- Life change units (LCUs) decided by asking 400 people to assign a value for the change required, relative to baseline of 50 for marriage.
- Hassles and Uplifts Scale (HSUP) – Kanner *et al.* asked for lists of hassles/uplifts related to work, family, friends, chance, etc.
- 117 hassles assessed for severity and 135 uplifts assessed for frequency on 3-point scales.

EVALUATION

- Criticisms of the SRRS – doesn't take into account individual perceptions; the scale applies mainly to adults and ignores factors that moderate stress.
- Criticisms of the HSUP – original scale had physical illnesses (a confounding variable when correlating with illness); also scale is very long, which may explain low reliability ratings.
- Continuing influence – the scales or their adaptations have continued to be popular.

PHYSIOLOGICAL MEASURES

- Skin conductance response – electrical activity in the skin is conducted when skin is wet, e.g. when sweating, part of physiological stress response.
- Electrodes placed on two fingers and small voltage applied (0.5V); conductance measured in microSiemens.
- Adrenaline can be assessed for immediate stress (e.g. Kamarck *et al.*, social support).
- Cortisol can be measured for ongoing stressors (e.g. Gunnar *et al.*, day care).

EVALUATION

- More appropriate in some situations – e.g. with children or non-human animals, and avoids issues such as social desirability bias.
- Non-specific response – measures any emotional arousal, not just stress, and affected by medications.
- Other applications – e.g. lie detector test. May not be valid way of assessing honesty, especially because psychopaths have less emotional response.

SOURCES OF STRESS

LIFE CHANGES

LIFE CHANGES

- Holmes and Rahe – events (e.g. marriage, divorce) require change which expends psychic energy.
- SRRS developed to measure LCUs, based on 43 life events identified over a set period of time.
- Cohen et al. – participants with higher LCUs more likely to be infected with cold virus than control group; shows poor immunosuppression.

KEY STUDY: RAHE ET AL.

- Procedure: 2,664 naval men completed SRE and record kept of illnesses during 6-month tour of duty.
- Findings: Significant positive correlation of +.118 between LCU and illness score.

EVALUATION

- A valuable approach – insights into psychological problems, e.g. suicide linked to life event-related stress (Heikkinen and Lönnqvist).
- Reliability of recall – Hardt et al. found moderate-to-good reliability over mean 2.2 years.
- Individual differences – the psychic cost of an event varies, e.g. death of elderly versus young spouse.
- Daily hassles may be better measure of stress because life events are rare; DeLongis et al. found no correlation between life events and illness but did for daily hassles and uplifts.
- Spurious relationship – anxiety may be an intervening variable, or people who are unwell are more negative.

DAILY HASSLES

DAILY HASSLES

- Daily hassles are relatively minor events in day-to-day life, offset by daily uplifts.
- Explanations – may be accumulation or amplification (life changes make a person more vulnerable).
- Bouteyre et al. – transition to university fraught with daily hassles which were a risk factor for depression.

KEY STUDY: KANNER ET AL.

- Procedure: 100 participants aged 45–67 completed HSUP for 10 months, plus life events scale and measure of well-being.
- Findings: Significant negative correlation with psychological well-being; daily hassles were better predictor than life events.

EVALUATION

- Support for importance of daily hassles compared to life events (e.g. Ruffin), may be because of less emotional support for hassles than life events (Flett et al.).
- Reliability of recall – can be overcome using diary studies, e.g. Charles et al.
- Problems with self-report – social desirability bias; people play down the severity of hassles.
- Individual differences – gender differences, e.g. related to pets (Miller et al.).
- What does the research tell us? Hassles appear to predict later psychological well-being, not just a correlation.

WORKPLACE STRESS

WORKPLACE STRESS

- Job-strain model – high workload and low job control create highest levels of stress.
- Workload versus job control – Kivimäki et al. found neither had much effect on their own, and that occupational group may be a contributing factor.

KEY STUDIES

WHITEHALL STUDY (MARMOT ET AL.)

- Procedure: 10,000 UK civil servants assessed on workload and job control, and then 11 years later CHD risk assessed.
- Findings: Findings: high workload associated with greatest CHD risk; next most important was low control.

SWEDISH SAWMILL (JOHANSSON ET AL.)

- Procedure: high-risk group (e.g. sawyers) matched to low-risk group (e.g. repairmen), adrenaline measured daily and self-report of satisfaction.
- Findings: high-risk group (high workload, low job control) had higher levels of adrenaline, more reports of illness and more social isolation.

EVALUATION

- Individual differences – transactional approach emphasises perceived ability to cope; Schaubroeck et al. found some people prefer low-control situations.
- Work underload – Shultz et al. found overload was a key factor, but underload also related to dissatisfaction and illness.
- Validity – using questionnaires may mean that non-standard responses are overlooked (Dewe); interviews may be better.
- Workplace stress and mental health – Warr's vitamin model suggests that accumulated factors lead to poor mental as well as physical health problems.
- The evolution of work and workplace stressors – the changing work environment means research may lag behind current practice.

Summary continued on following spread ...

MANAGING AND COPING WITH STRESS

DRUG THERAPIES

DRUG THERAPIES

- Benzodiazepines (BZs) enhance activity of body's natural anxiety relief – neurotransmitter GABA.
  - GABA reacts with GABA receptors on postsynaptic neuron, opening a channel to let chloride ions in. Makes it harder for other neurotransmitters to excite the neuron.
  - BZs also open the GABA receptors, enhancing their action.
  - BZs also reduce serotonin activity, which is otherwise stimulating.
- Beta blockers (BBs) block beta-receptors so adrenaline can't stimulate them.
  - Sympathetic arousal releases adrenaline/noradrenaline which stimulates the heart muscle and other sites.
  - Blocked beta-receptors don't respond, reducing the symptoms of anxiety (e.g. increased heart rate).
  - BBs used for CHD sufferers to reduce negative effects of adrenaline, and by sportsmen and musicians.

EVALUATION

- Effective – BZs tested in placebo trials (Kahn *et al.*); BBs led musicians to perform better (Lockwood) but Schweizer reports BBs don't always reduce sense of stress.
- Ease of use – avoids time and effort needed for psychological therapies.
- Problems with addiction – BZs recommended for four weeks only, and for mental illness only; nevertheless they are still in common use (Donoghue and Lader).
- Side effects – BZs have paradoxical effects (e.g. agitation), BBs may be linked to diabetes.
- Treating the symptoms rather than the problem – not suitable for ongoing stresses.

STRESS INOCULATION THERAPY

STRESS INOCULATION THERAPY (SIT)

- Meichenbaum developed a cognitive therapy to deal with stressors before they happen.
- Better to deal with the way we think about stress because causes can't be changed.
- Step 1: Conceptualisation phase – collaboration between therapist and client to reconceptualise the problem.
- Step 2: Skills acquisition, rehearsal and consolidation, e.g. social skills, attention diversion and coping self-statements, all rehearsed through imagery, modelling and role play.
- Step 3: Application and follow-through – practise in increasingly stressful situations and anticipate problems.

EVALUATION

- Effectiveness – Meichenbaum used it to treat snake phobia but also effective for a second, non-treated phobia; also used for surgery, academic stress and public speaking.
- The hello–goodbye effect – patients exaggerate problem before therapy and minimise problem afterwards.
- Preparation for future stressors – goes beyond the current problem in providing new skills and anticipating future challenges.
- A challenging therapy – may take as long as a year, though sometimes very quick; also requires discussing feelings.
- Unnecessarily complex – learning to think more positively and relax may be all that is needed.

BIOFEEDBACK

BIOFEEDBACK

- Biological and psychological – targets the sympathetic response to stress and conditions involuntary responses.
- Relaxation – activates parasympathetic nervous system and relaxed state.
- Feedback – machines produce information (light or sound) so patient can monitor e.g. heart rate. Using relaxation, aims to reduce this.
- Operant conditioning – any reduction in e.g. heart rate is rewarding and therefore the behaviour is reinforced.
- Transfer – newly acquired behaviours transferred to everyday life.
- Demonstration of biofeedback – Miller and DiCara paralysed rats (no control over muscles) and rewarded some of them when heart rate increased; led to learned response.

EVALUATION

- Research support – monkeys could be trained without conscious thought (Gruber and Taub), military personnel decreased heart rate (Lewis *et al.*).
- Operant conditioning component may be irrelevant – DiCara's original work appears invented (Klintworth), so results may simply be due to relaxation or sense of control.
- Continued popularity despite lack of support for operant conditioning; Bradley showed biofeedback superior to relaxation only – may be placebo effect due to use of sophisticated machines.
- Strengths – can be used with children (who can't use other methods) and does tackle the problem.
- Limitations – expensive machinery and time-consuming (more than a month); requires input from client.

INDIVIDUAL DIFFERENCES IN STRESS

PERSONALITY

PERSONALITY TYPES A, B AND C
- Type A personality – time pressured, competitive, angry; prone to CHD because of active stress response (Friedman and Rosenman).
- Type B personality – easygoing, relaxed and patient.
- Type C personality – suppress emotion and wish to please, deny own needs at a physiological cost.

KEY STUDY: FRIEDMAN AND ROSENMAN (WCG)
- Procedure: 3,000 men aggressively interviewed to determine personality type.
- Findings: After 8½ years, Type A individuals twice as likely to have had a heart attack as Type B.

KEY STUDY: MORRIS *ET AL.*
- Procedure: 75 women at cancer clinic interviewed about emotional responses.
- Findings: Those whose cancer turned out to be malignant were more Type C.

EVALUATION
- Further evidence for the WCG study – a 22-year follow-up found no link between Type A and CHD (Ragland and Brand), but possibly Type A men had altered their behaviour.
- Key component of Type A may be hostility; Myrtek found correlation between CHD and hostility only, not Type A.
- Gender bias – Type A personality is masculine and original sample was just men; however, a treatment programme to reduce Type A behaviours was successful with men and women (Friedman *et al.*).
- Are the effects of personality direct or indirect? Nemeroff and Musselman found placebo as effective as Prozac in reducing platelets; shows that psychological state can have direct physical effects.
- Challenges to the concept of Type C – 'fighting spirit' doesn't have an effect on cancer recovery (Giraldi *et al.*).

HARDINESS

HARDINESS
- Hardy personality resists the negative effects of stress (Kobasa and Maddi).
- Based on high levels of control (internal, not external), commitment (sense of purpose) and challenge (problems are opportunities).
- Maddi studied Bell telephone employees; 1/3 thrived in a difficult period for the company – they had 'hardiness'.
- Lifton *et al.* studied students; those with high hardiness were most likely to complete their degree.

KEY STUDY: KOBASA
- Procedure: Two groups of men selected from 800 US executives using SRRS to assess stress over last three years. Final participants all had high stress levels.
- Findings: Those with low illness record had more control, commitment and challenge than those with high illness.

EVALUATION
- Problems with measurement – original scales were long and wordy; more recent scales still have low internal reliability.
- Direct effects – link between hardiness and low blood pressure (Maddi), especially for Type B (Contrada).
- Real-world application – Maddi showed hardiness training was more effective than relaxation or social support for decreasing strain and illness.
- Hardiness and negative affectivity – low hardiness may simply be negative affectivity (Watson and Clark) and negativity lowers ability to cope with stress.
- Is hardiness a personality type? It may simply be challenge (Sandvik *et al.*) or control that is the key factor (Rotter) – not really a type of personality.

GENDER DIFFERENCES IN COPING WITH STRESS

GENDER DIFFERENCES IN COPING WITH STRESS
- Biological explanation – tend and befriend adaptive for females because of greater parental investment (Taylor *et al.*).
- Oxytocin (promotes social-ness) released at times of stress but effect dampened by testosterone in males.
- Psychological explanation – males tend to use problem focus, females use emotion focus coping style.
- Stress experienced – Matud found men had finance and work-related stress which would require more problem focus, whereas women had more family and health-related stress which would require more emotion focus.

KEY STUDY: PETERSON *ET AL.*
- Procedure: 1,000 men and women seeking fertility treatment, used *Ways of Coping* scale.
- Findings: Women tried to reduce emotional impact and men engaged in problem-solving.

EVALUATION
- Not simply a tend-and-befriend response by females who will fight an intruder or flee with mobile children; stress response involves a range of strategies.
- Lack of research support for coping focus – most studies don't find a difference (e.g. Hamilton and Fagot), may be more than two styles, e.g. avoidance-orientation.
- Confounding variables – type of stress and social support affect the experience of stress.
- Other methodological issues – self-report (men may be less willing to reveal emotional approach) and retrospective recall.
- Changing roles and lives of men and women – as women enter workplace their coping styles are changing (Frankenhauser).

THE ROLE OF SOCIAL SUPPORT IN COPING WITH STRESS

THE ROLE OF SOCIAL SUPPORT
- Sources of support – the more friends the better (Nabi *et al.*); reduced social contact may be a problem for older people (Dickinson *et al.*).
- Instrumental support – tangible assistance; may include information which can be given by anyone.
- Emotional support – usually from friends but may be from strangers in an emergency.
- Esteem support – increasing another person's value of themselves will improve confidence.
- Can be explained in terms of buffering or direct physiological effects from e.g. relaxation.

KEY STUDY: KAMARCK *ET AL.*
- Procedure: 39 female students doing stressful task with or without friend touching their wrist.
- Findings: Lower physiological response with friend. Type A participants showed reduced responses on some tasks, supporting buffering hypothesis.

EVALUATION
- Gender differences – Lucknow *et al.* found most studies showed women use social support more than men, but opposite true if looking at instrumental support.
- Cultural differences – collectivist coping styles (more implicit) used by Asian students but changed to individualist (more instrumental and individual support) the longer in Australia (Bailey and Dua).
- Distinguishing types of support – not much agreement, may be just two categories: tangible and emotional.
- Pets can provide support for stressful situations (Allen); support may be reducing anxiety from loneliness.
- Relative importance of social support – Kobasa *et al.* found social support less important than hardiness; some social support can create more anxiety (Kiecolt-Glaser and Newton).

0 1 Which one of the following is the final stage of the general adaption syndrome? Write the
letter of your chosen answer in your answer booklet. **[1 mark]**

A. Alarm Reaction

B. Exhaustion

C. Fight-or-flight

D. Resistance

0 2 Which one of the following statements best describes the role of the hypothalamic
pituitary-adrenal system? Write the letter of your chosen answer in your answer booklet. **[1 mark]**

A. a physiological system that balances the effects of stress

B. a physiological system that is activated by immediate stress

C. a physiological system that responds to long-term stress

D. a physiological system that signals potential stress

0 3 Read the item below and then answer the questions that follow.

> Harjit and Hamara lost their son in a tragic accident last year. They have both since
> suffered a lot of stress because of this. Harjit was recently rushed to hospital after
> he had a heart attack. Hamara has been suffering from various illnesses over the
> last few months and has been particularly vulnerable to flu viruses.

(i) With reference to the cardiovascular disorders, explain Harjit's response to his stress. **[3 marks]**

(ii) With reference to immunosuppression, explain Hamara's response to her stress. **[3 marks]**

0 4 Identify **two** life changes that may be seen as a source of stress. **[2 marks]**

0 5 Choose **one** research study which investigated life changes as a source of stress.
Describe **two** limitations of the way that this study was carried out. **[4 marks]**

0 6 Choose **one** research study which investigated daily hassles. Evaluate the findings of this study. **[4 marks]**

0 7 Read the item below and answer the questions that follow.

> Jason is finding his job very stressful. His colleague has been absent for a number
> of weeks and he has had to take on some of her cases as well as his own. This
> means he has to meet many more deadlines than usual. Jason cannot negotiate
> new deadlines as they are all decided by very important clients.

Using your knowledge of research into workplace stress, explain why Jason is finding his job very stressful. **[6 marks]**

0 8 Discuss the view that both life changes and daily hassles are a source of stress. **[16 marks]**

0 9 Outline how the Hassles and Uplifts Scale measures stress. **[4 marks]**

1 0 Explain **two** physiological measures of stress. **[6 marks]**

1 1 Discuss the use of self-report scales for measuring stress. Refer to physiological
measures of stress as part of your discussion. **[16 marks]**

1 2 Read the following item and answer the questions that follow.

> Louise has a calm approach to life and very few people bother her.
> Nathan is very competitive and finds it difficult to give control over to others.
> Priya likes to keep her feelings hidden especially if it keeps others happy
> Stefan is a very open individual who likes to socialise with others.

(i) Name the person who demonstrates features of a Type A personality. [1 mark]

(ii) Name the person who demonstrates features of a Type B personality. [1 mark]

(iii) Name the person who demonstrates features of a Type C personality. [1 mark]

1 3 Hardiness has three key characteristics: control, commitment and challenge.
Choose **one** of these characteristics and explain its role in reducing stress. [3 marks]

1 4 Discuss the extent to which individual differences have an effect on stress responses.
Refer to research evidence as part of your discussion. [16 marks]

1 5 Briefly discuss the effectiveness of using drug therapy to manage stress. [4 marks]

1 6 Read the item below and answer the question that follows.

> Natalie is off work as she is suffering with stress brought on by the
> demands of her job. If she does not return to work soon, she will lose
> out on pay. Natalie has decided that she needs to get treatment to
> help her cope with her job.

Outline **two** different techniques that could be used to help Natalie to cope with her stress. [6 marks]

1 7 Discuss **at least two** ways of managing and coping with stress. [16 marks]

1 8 (i) Briefly outline the findings from **one** research study into gender differences in coping with stress. [2 marks]

(ii) Briefly discuss **one** limitation of this research study. [4 marks]

1 9 Describe how instrumental social support is different from emotional social support in
relation to coping with stress. [3 marks]

2 0 Outline the role of esteem support in helping an individual cope with stress. [2 marks]

2 1 Discuss the role of social support in helping people to cope with stress. [16 marks]

2 2 Read the item below and answer the questions that follow.

> A psychologist compared the stress levels of three different types
> of personality using a questionnaire. The higher the score on the
> questionnaire, the higher the stress level. The results from the study
> are shown below:

Personality type	Type A	Type B	Type C
Median score	55	23	49
Range	12	11	23

(i) Outline **one** limitation of using a questionnaire in this study. [2 marks]

(ii) Outline **one** reason why the psychologist used a median to summarise the results from the study. [2 marks]

(iii) What could the psychologist conclude from this study? Use both the median and the
range to justify your answer. [4 marks]

2 3 Read the item below and answer the questions that follow.

> A psychologist wanted to compare the success rates of biofeedback
> and stress inoculation therapy as treatments for stress. She used 30
> volunteers, who were randomly allocated to receive one of the two
> treatments. She took a baseline measure of their stress levels using
> two physiological measures: blood pressure and the level of cortisol
> in the participants' urine.

(i) Identify the independent variable in this study. [1 mark]

(ii) Explain why the psychologist randomly allocated the participants to the two treatments. [2 marks]

(iii) Explain the level of data that is collected when level of cortisol is measured. [2 marks]

(iv) Explain how taking two measures of stress improves the reliability of this study. [3 marks]

9 Aggression

CONTENTS OF CHAPTER

SPECIFICATION CHECKLIST

- Neural and hormonal mechanisms in aggression, including the roles of the limbic system, serotonin and testosterone. Genetic factors in aggression, including the MAOA gene.

- The ethological explanation of aggression, including reference to innate releasing mechanisms and fixed action patterns. Evolutionary explanations of human aggression.

- Social psychological explanations of human aggression, including the frustration–aggression hypothesis, social learning theory as applied to human aggression, and de-individuation.

- Institutional aggression in the context of prisons: dispositional and situational explanations.

- Media influences on aggression, including the effects of computer games. The role of desensitisation, disinhibition and cognitive priming.

Finger-length ratio and aggression

Take a look at your index finger (the one next to your thumb) and your ring finger (the one next to your little finger). Which one is longer? Men typically have relatively longer ring fingers than index fingers. The bigger the difference, the more 'masculine' such individuals are considered to be, possibly the result of exposure to higher prenatal testosterone levels.

Strange as this might seem, several studies have found a relationship between finger-length ratio and aggressive behaviour. For example, Bailey and Hurd (2005), in a sample of Canadian college students, found that men with lower finger-length ratios (i.e. index finger length divided by ring finger length) scored higher for the trait of physical aggression. This relationship between finger-length ratio and physical aggression did not hold true for women. Coyne *et al.* (2007) found that, although this finger-length ratio was not associated with direct physical aggression in women, it *was* positively correlated with their levels of indirect aggression (e.g. spreading rumours or generally 'being bitchy').

This is probably best done as a class study, perhaps using separate calculations for boys and girls in the class.

First, measure your finger-length ratio. To do this, straighten your fingers and look at the palm of your right hand. At the base of your ring and index fingers there are creases where the fingers join the palm. Choose a point on each of these creases midway across the base of the finger and mark it with a pen. Measure from the mark to the tip of the finger. Calculate the ratio between the ring and index finger lengths by dividing the length of your index finger by the length of your ring finger. For example, if your ring finger is 82mm and your index finger 80mm, this gives a ratio of 82:80 or 1.03. For example, if your index finger is 78mm and your ring finger 82mm, this gives a ratio of 78:82 or 0.95 (the average for a man). If your index finger is 70mm and your ring finger 72mm, that would give a ratio of 70:72 or 0.97 (the average for a woman).

Ring finger   Index finger

Next, we need a convenient measure of aggression. An online measure is the Buss-Perry Aggression Questionnaire, available at:

https://psychology-tools.com/buss-perry-aggression-questionnaire

This questionnaire gives scores for various aspects of aggression, including physical and verbal aggression. You can either add all the different scores together or just use the physical and verbal scores separately.

Finally, using the class (boys only) data, calculate a Spearman's *Rho* (see page 30) on physical aggression scores and finger-length ratio. Do the same for verbal aggression scores. Now carry out two further correlation tests using class (girls only) data.

What did you find? Did *your* results agree with the published studies described above?

Neural and hormonal influences

Biological explanations of aggression assume that aggression is located within the biological make-up of the individual rather than in the environment around them. Many research studies in the last 30 years have shown that violent criminals were high in the hormone testosterone, encouraging some people to conclude that castration (which reduces levels of testosterone) of highly aggressive males would stop them from killing or injuring innocent people. However, the relationship between biological mechanisms and aggressive behaviour is not that simple.

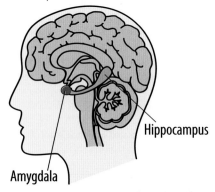

Hippocampus

Amygdala

KEY TERMS

Limbic system A system of structures lying beneath the cortex (i.e. subcortical), including the amygdala, hippocampus and hypothalamus. The region is associated with emotional behaviour.

Serotonin A neurotransmitter implicated in many different behaviours and physiological processes, including aggression, eating behaviour, sleep and depression.

Testosterone A hormone produced mainly by the testes in males, but also occurring in females. It is associated with the development of secondary sexual characteristics in males (e.g. body hair), but has also been implicated in aggression and dominance behaviours.

NEURAL INFLUENCES

The limbic system

The **limbic system** is an area of the brain that helps to coordinate behaviours that satisfy motivational and emotional urges, such as aggression and fear. Two key structures in the limbic system that are associated with aggression are the amygdala and the hippocampus.

The amygdala

This is responsible for quickly evaluating the emotional importance of sensory information and prompting an appropriate response. If certain areas of the amygdala are stimulated electrically, an animal responds with aggression, for example snarling and adopting an aggressive posture. If the same areas are surgically removed, the animal no longer responds to stimuli that would have previously led to rage. For example, Kluver and Bucy (1937) discovered that the destruction of the amygdala in a monkey who was dominant in a social group caused it to lose its dominant place in the group.

The hippocampus

This is involved with the formation of long-term memories, and so allows an animal to compare the conditions of a current threat with similar past experiences. For example, if an animal had previously been attacked by another animal, the next time they encounter that animal they are likely to respond either with aggression or fear, whichever is more appropriate. Impaired hippocampal function prevents the nervous system from putting things into a relevant and meaningful context, and so may cause the amygdala to respond inappropriately to sensory stimuli, resulting in aggressive behaviour. For example, Boccardi *et al.* (2010) found that habitually violent offenders exhibited abnormalities of hippocampal functioning.

Serotonin

Serotonin, in normal levels, exerts a calming, inhibitory effect on neuronal firing in the brain. Serotonin typically inhibits the firing of the amygdala, the part of the brain that controls fear, anger and other emotional responses. Low levels of serotonin remove this inhibitory effect, with the consequence that individuals are less able to control impulsive and aggressive behaviour (the 'serotonin deficiency hypothesis'). As a result, when the amygdala is stimulated by external events, it becomes more active, causing the person to act on their impulses, and making aggression more likely.

Serotonin is also thought to reduce aggression by inhibiting responses to emotional stimuli that might otherwise lead to an aggressive response. Low levels of serotonin in the brain have been associated with an increased susceptibility to impulsive behaviour, aggression and even violent suicide. Some drugs are thought to alter serotonin levels and thus increase aggressive behaviour. Mann *et al.* (1990) gave 35 healthy participants *dexfenfluramine*, which is known to deplete serotonin. Using a questionnaire to assess hostility and aggression levels, they found that *dexfenfluramine* treatment in males (but not females) was associated with an increase in hostility and aggression scores.

HORMONAL INFLUENCES

Testosterone

Testosterone produces male characteristics, one of which is thought to be aggressive behaviour. Levels reach a peak in young males, then decline. The male sex hormone testosterone is thought to influence aggression from young adulthood onwards due to its action on brain areas involved in controlling aggression. Sapolsky (1998) summarised research evidence in this area by describing how removing the source of testosterone in different species typically resulted in much lower levels of aggression. Subsequently reinstating normal testosterone levels with injections of synthetic testosterone led to a return of aggressive behaviour.

The idea that testosterone is related to human aggression comes from various sources. For example, men are generally more aggressive than women (Archer, 2009), and have much higher concentrations of testosterone than women (Dabbs, 1990). In addition, at an age when testosterone concentrations are at their highest (21–35), there is an increase in male-on-male aggressive behaviour (Daly and Wilson, 1998). Dabbs *et al.* (1987) measured salivary testosterone in violent and non-violent criminals. Those with the highest testosterone levels had a history of primarily violent crimes, whereas those with the lowest levels had committed only non-violent crimes. Carré and Olmstead (2015) claim that testosterone concentrations are not static, but fluctuate rapidly in the context of changes to the social environment. Changes in testosterone levels appear to influence aggressive behaviour by increasing amygdala reactivity during the processing of social threat (e.g. angry facial expressions).

Evidence for the role of the amygdala in aggression

Pardini *et al.* (2014) found that reduced amygdala volume can predict the development of severe and persistent aggression. They carried out a longitudinal study of male participants from childhood to adulthood. Some 56 of the participants with varying histories of violence were subjected to a brain MRI at age 26. The results showed that participants with lower amygdala volumes exhibited higher levels of aggression and violence. The relationship between amygdala volume and aggressive behaviour remained even after other confounding variables were controlled. This suggests that the amygdala plays an important role in evaluating the emotional importance of sensory information and that lower amygdala volume compromises this ability and makes a violent response more likely.

Evidence for the role of the hippocampus in aggression

Raine *et al.* (2004) provided support for the role of the hippocampus in aggressive behaviour in their study of violent offenders. They studied two groups of violent criminals: some who had faced conviction ('unsuccessful psychopaths', as they had been caught) and some who had evaded the law ('successful psychopaths'). The latter group were considered to be 'cold, calculating' criminals, whereas the former group had acted more impulsively, which is why they were caught. MRI scans revealed asymmetries in the hippocampus (part of the limbic system) in the 'unsuccessful' group. The hippocampus in either hemisphere of the brain in these individuals differed in size, an imbalance presumed to have arisen early in brain development. The researchers suggested this asymmetry might impair the ability of the hippocampus and the amygdala to work together, so that emotional information is not processed correctly, leading to inappropriate verbal and physical responses as a result.

Inconsistent evidence

Despite many studies showing a positive relationship between testosterone and aggression, other studies find no such relationship, particularly those that have compared testosterone levels of aggressive and less aggressive individuals. For example, positive correlations have been reported between levels of testosterone and self-reported levels of aggression among prison inmates (Albert *et al.*, 1994), and between testosterone levels and the likelihood of responding aggressively to provocation (Olweus *et al.*, 1988). On the other hand, no correlation was found between testosterone levels and *actual* violent behaviour among male inmates in prison. This suggests that the relationship between testosterone and aggression in humans remains unclear.

Aggression or dominance?

Mazur (1985) suggests we should distinguish aggression from *dominance*. Individuals act aggressively when their intent is to inflict injury, whereas they act dominantly if their wish is to achieve or maintain status over another individual. Mazur claims that aggression is just one form of dominance behaviour. In non-human animals the influence of testosterone on dominance behaviour might be shown through aggressive behaviour. In humans, however, the influence of testosterone on dominance is likely to be expressed in more varied and subtle ways (e.g. through status-striving behaviour). For example, Eisenegger *et al.* (2011) found that testosterone could make women act 'nicer' rather than more aggressively depending on the situation. This lends support to the idea that, rather than directly increasing aggression, testosterone promotes status-seeking behaviour, of which aggression is one type.

Research support for the serotonin deficiency hypothesis

Duke *et al.* (2013) provided some support for the serotonin deficiency hypothesis as an explanation for aggressive behaviour in human beings. They carried out a meta-analysis of 175 studies, involving 6,500 participants. This analysis found a small inverse relationship between serotonin levels and aggression, anger and hostility. They also found that the magnitude of the relationship varied with the methods used to assess serotonin functioning, with year of publication (effect sizes tended to diminish with time) and with self-reported versus other-reported aggression. Only other-reported aggression was positively correlated to *serotonin* functioning. This suggests that the relationship between serotonin and aggression is more complex than originally thought.

Evidence from studies of non-human species

Raleigh *et al.* (1991) found that vervet monkeys fed on experimental diets high in tryptophan (which increases serotonin levels in the brain) exhibited decreased levels of aggression. Individuals fed on diets that were low in tryptophan exhibited increased aggressive behaviour, suggesting that the difference in aggression could be attributed to their serotonin levels. Other evidence for the importance of serotonin in aggression comes from studies of aggressive dogs. Rosado *et al.* (2010) compared a sample of 80 dogs of various breeds that had been referred to Spanish veterinary hospitals for their aggressive behaviour toward humans with a control sample of 19 dogs of various breeds that did not show such aggressive behaviour. The aggressive dogs averaged 278 units of serotonin, while the non-aggressive dogs averaged 387 units.

▲ Indirectly lowering serotonin levels increases aggression in vervet monkeys.

CAN YOU?   No. 9.1

1. Explain the role of the limbic system in aggression. (3 marks)
2. Explain the role of serotonin in aggression. (3 marks)
3. Explain the role of testosterone in aggression. (3 marks)
4. Outline and evaluate the role of neural and/or hormonal mechanisms in aggression. (16 marks)

Insider tip...
Exam questions may be general (e.g. 'neural mechanisms') or specific ('limbic system', 'serotonin', testosterone). Make sure you know what material goes with what, i.e. the limbic system and serotonin are neural *mechanisms, and testosterone is a* hormonal *mechanism.*

Genetic factors in aggression

The biological approach to aggression includes the belief that the propensity for aggressive behaviour lies in an individual's genetic make-up. Researchers must try to establish whether genetically related individuals are more similar in their aggressive tendencies than non-related individuals. This also has important implications for understanding the origins of violent crime. Although the question of genetic influences for aggression and violent crime has perhaps not interested researchers quite as much as the general public, research suggests that aggressive tendencies may, at least in part, be inherited.

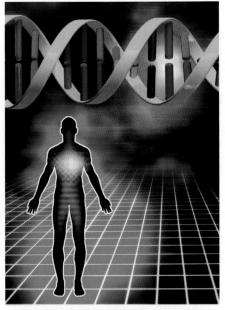

▲ All in the genes? Research suggests that aggressive tendencies may be inherited.

KEY TERMS

Genetic factors The likelihood of behaving in a particular way is determined by a person's genetic make-up, i.e. it is inherited from parents.

MAOA Monoamine oxidase A (MAOA) is an enzyme that, among other things, regulates the metabolism of serotonin in the brain.

▲ The 'warrior gene': according to research, people with a low-activity version of the MAOA gene are more likely to respond aggressively when provoked.

GENETICS AND AGGRESSION

Trying to determine the role of **genetic factors** in aggression is essentially a question of *nature* and *nurture*. To disentangle the relative contributions of nature (genetic inheritance) and nurture (environmental influences), researchers have employed a variety of methodological techniques, including twin and adoption studies, studies of individual genes and studies of violent populations.

Twin studies

Monozygotic (identical) twins share all of their genes, while *dizygotic* (non-identical) twins share only 50%. In twin studies, researchers compare the degree of similarity for a particular trait (such as aggression) between sets of monozygotic (MZ) twins and compare this to the similarity between sets of dizygotic (DZ) twins. If the MZ twins are more alike in terms of their aggressive behaviour, then this should be due to genes rather than environment (both types of twin share the same environment as each other, but monozygotic twins are more genetically alike). Most twin studies have focused on criminal behaviour generally, but one of the few studies to specifically study aggressive behaviour using adult twin pairs found that nearly 50% of the variance in direct aggressive behaviour (i.e. aggression toward others) could be attributed to genetic factors (Coccaro *et al.*, 1997).

Adoption studies

Adoption studies can help to untangle the relative contributions of environment and heredity in aggression. If a positive correlation is found between aggressive behaviour in adopted children and aggressive behaviour in their biological parents, a genetic effect is implied. If a positive correlation is found between the adoptee's aggressive behaviour and the rearing family, then an environmental effect is implied. A study of over 14,000 adoptions in Denmark found that a significant number of adopted boys with criminal convictions had biological parents (particularly fathers) with convictions for criminal violence (Hutchings and Mednick, 1975), providing evidence for a genetic effect.

Research on genetic factors in aggression

Miles and Carey (1997) carried out a meta-analysis of 24 twin and adoption studies that demonstrated the genetic basis of aggression. The results suggested a strong genetic influence that could account for as much as 50% of the variance in aggression. Age differences were notably important, with both genes and family environment being influential in determining aggression in youth, but at later ages the influence of rearing environment decreased and the influence of genes increased.

A later meta-analysis by Rhee and Waldman (2002) combined the results of 51 twin and adoption studies and also concluded that aggressive anti-social behaviour was largely a product of genetic contributions. However, in this study, as with the Miles and Carey study above, several variables, including age of participant and assessment method for aggression, moderated the genetic influence on aggression, suggesting that, although genetic factors play a significant part in the development of aggressive behaviours, the influence of other factors affects their expression.

MAOA: A gene for aggression?

The role of MAOA Although no individual gene for aggression has been identified in humans, a gene responsible for producing an enzyme called monoamine oxidase A (**MAOA**) has been associated with aggressive behaviour. MAOA regulates the metabolism of serotonin in the brain, and low levels of serotonin are associated with impulsive and aggressive behaviour (see page 228). In the 1980s, a study of a Dutch family found that many of its male members behaved in a particularly violent and aggressive manner, and a large proportion had been involved in serious crimes of violence, including rape and arson. These men were found to have abnormally low levels of MAOA in their bodies, and a defect in this gene was later identified (Brunner *et al.*, 1993).

MAOA-H and MAOA-L A second study (Caspi *et al.*, 2002), linking MAOA to aggressive behaviour, involved 500 male children. Researchers discovered a variant of the gene associated with high levels of MAOA (MAOA-H) and a variant associated with low levels (MAOA-L). Those with the MAOA-L variant were significantly more likely to grow up to exhibit anti-social behaviour but *only* if they had been maltreated as children. Children with the MAOA-H variant who were maltreated, and those with the MAOA-L variant who were not maltreated, did not display anti-social behaviour.

The 'warrior gene' MAOA-L is much more frequent in populations with a history of warfare, with about two-thirds of people in these populations having this version of the gene. By way of contrast, only about one-third of people in Western populations have this low-activity version of the gene. This has led to it being referred to as the 'warrior gene'. McDermott *et al.* (2009) found that MAOA-L participants displayed higher levels of aggression (forcing a fictional participant to eat unpleasantly hot and spicy sauce), when provoked, than did MAOA-H subjects.

Problems of sampling

Many studies in this area have focused exclusively on individuals convicted of violent crime. Two particular difficulties arise when trying to draw meaningful conclusions from these studies. The first problem lies with the participants themselves. Convictions for violent crime are relatively few compared to the vast number of violent attacks by individuals that never result in a conviction. They therefore represent just a small minority of those regularly involved in aggressive behaviour. Second, contrary to popular belief, offenders designated as 'violent' on the basis of a court conviction are not necessarily the most serious, persistent offenders. For example, a convicted murderer would be designated as violent for one offence despite, perhaps, having otherwise had a lifetime free from crime. This might explain why so many studies have found little or no evidence of heritability for violence.

Difficulties of determining the role of genetic factors

We have discussed the role of genetic factors in aggression, but what does this really mean? The connection between genetic factors and aggression is far from straightforward because of problems determining what is, and what is not, a product of genetic inheritance. It is difficult to establish genetic contributions to aggressive behaviour for the following reasons:

- More than one gene usually contributes to a given behaviour.
- As well as genetic factors, there are many non-genetic (i.e. environmental) influences on the manifestation of aggressive behaviour.
- These influences may interact with each other. Genetic factors may affect which environmental factors have an influence, and vice versa (gene–environment interaction).

This last point is clearly demonstrated in the study by Caspi *et al.* (2002) described on the facing page.

Problems of assessing aggression

Many of the reported studies of aggression have relied on either parental or self-reports of aggressive behaviour, whereas other studies have made use of observational techniques. In the Miles and Carey meta-analysis reported on the facing page, mode of assessment was found to be a significant moderator of aggressive behaviour in the 24 studies that made up their analysis. They found that genetic factors explained a large proportion of the variance in aggressive behaviour in studies that had used parental or self-reports. However, those that had made use of observational ratings showed significantly *less* genetic contribution and a greater influence of environmental factors. These inconsistencies in findings make it difficult to accurately assess the relative contributions of genetic and environmental factors in aggression.

▲ Once dubbed 'the most dangerous men in Britain', here are Reggie and Ronnie Kray in 1965. Their violent tendencies may have had less to do with their genetic similarity and more to do with similarities in upbringing.

Evidence for the influence of the MAOA gene

In many countries, the majority of all violent crime is committed by a small group of persistent offenders. A recent study in Finland has added research support that the MAOA gene is implicated in severe violent behaviours such as murder. Tiihonen *et al.* (2015) studied Finnish prisoners, revealing that the MAOA low-activity genotype (MAOA-L) in combination with another gene (the CDH13 gene) was associated with extremely violent behaviour. There was no substantial evidence for either of these genes among non-violent offenders, indicating that this combination of genes was specific for violent offending only. However, critics argue that although these genes may make it harder for some people to control violent urges, they do not predetermine violent behaviour.

The MAOA gene might explain gender differences in aggressive behaviour

An advantage of MAOA gene research is that it offers an explanation for the uneven rates of violence for males and females. Niehoff (2014) suggests this may be a consequence of the differential genetic vulnerability that males and females have to the MAOA gene. The MAOA gene is linked to the X chromosome. Women have two X chromosomes, whereas men have only one. When men inherit an X-linked gene from their mothers, they are more likely to be affected by it, whereas women inheriting the same gene are generally unaffected (as they also have a second X chromosome with a 'normal' gene for MAOA that prevents expression of the abnormal version of the MAOA gene). This could explain why males typically show more aggressive behaviour than females.

Insider tip…

When making an evaluative point about the type of participants used (e.g. students, males, or as here violent criminals), it is important to stress why this limits the validity of the conclusions we might draw from the research.

⏻ Research methods

Brunner *et al.* (1993) studied five generations of one Dutch family. One sister of the family requested an evaluation of the men in the family, many of whom were affected by borderline mental retardation and displayed impulsive aggression. No female members of the family displayed these traits. Assessment in this study involved making comparisons between eight male members of the family and three female (unaffected) members in terms of their DNA. Participants were assessed mentally (e.g. IQ tests) and physically (for physical abnormalities). In addition, other family members were interviewed about the behavioural characteristics and life histories of the eight target participants.

1. Identify the sample in this study. (1 mark)
2. Suggest a suitable directional hypothesis for this study. (2 marks)
3. Explain why this study might be considered to be a quasi-experiment. (3 marks)
4. Explain why this study might be considered to be a case study. (3 marks)
5. Explain **one** strength and **one** limitation of a case study in relation to this topic. (2 marks + 2 marks)
6. Typically the eight males studied had an IQ score of 85, which is one standard deviation below the mean IQ score of 100 based on a normal distribution. What percentage of people have an IQ below 85? (1 mark)

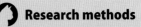

LINK TO RESEARCH METHODS

Case studies on page 14.
The other topics in these questions are covered in the research methods chapter of our Year 1 book.

CAN YOU? No. 9.2

1. Outline the role of genetic factors in aggression. (4 marks)
2. Explain the role of the MAOA gene in aggression. (3 marks)
3. Outline research findings into the role of genetic factors in aggression. (4 marks)
4. Give **one** limitation of genetic explanations of aggression. (3 marks)
5. Outline and evaluate the role of genetic factors in aggression. (16 marks)

The ethological explanation of aggression

Ethologists study the behaviour patterns shown by animals in natural environments. Ethologists such as Konrad Lorenz recognised that, while the potential for aggression may be innate, actual aggressive behaviour is elicited by specific stimuli in the environment, known as releasers. Lorenz believed that aggression has survival value to animals. For example, intraspecies aggression serves to distribute individuals within a group in a way that makes the most efficient use of available resources, such as food, access to mates and territory.

Characteristics of FAPs (Lea, 1984)

1. *Stereotyped* – the behaviour always occurs in the same way.
2. *Universal* – the behaviour is the same in all conspecifics.
3. *Independent of individual experience* – the behaviour is innate, with no learning involved.
4. *Ballistic* – once triggered, the FAP cannot be changed or stopped.
5. *Specific triggers* – each FAP has a specific trigger (sign stimulus).

The 'hydraulic model'

Each FAP has a reservoir of 'action-specific energy' (ASE) that builds up over time. The appropriate sign stimulus causes the IRM to release this energy and the animal then performs the FAP. After performing the FAP, the reservoir of ASE is empty and the behaviour cannot be repeated until the ASE has built up again. This is sometimes called the hydraulic model of instinctive behaviour (Lorenz, 1950).

Lorenz's model provides a way of visualising how these various hypothetical systems might work together to organise an animal's response to its internal and external environment. In the model, ASE is represented by fluid in a reservoir that, as it builds up, places pressure on a spring (the IRM), which is also being pulled by weights (the sign stimulus). Together these lead to the release of the FAP when ASE is high enough and the appropriate sign stimulus is present. However, the FAP may also be produced in the absence of the sign stimulus if the level of ASE is sufficiently high, i.e. a behaviour can occur spontaneously.

KEY TERMS

Ethological explanation stresses the adaptive value of animal behaviours. Ethologists study the behaviour patterns of animals in their natural environments.

Fixed action pattern A repertoire of stereotyped behaviours which occur in specific conditions (i.e. in response to specific triggers) and which do not require learning.

Innate releasing mechanism A neural network that, when stimulated by the presence of a sign stimulus, communicates with motor control circuits to activate the fixed action pattern associated with that sign stimulus.

ETHOLOGICAL EXPLANATIONS OF AGGRESSION

Fixed action patterns and innate releasing mechanisms

The **ethological explanation** states that all members of the same species (i.e. conspecifics) have a repertoire of stereotyped behaviours which occur in specific conditions and which do not require learning, i.e. are innate. Ethologist Niko Tinbergen called these innate behaviours **fixed action patterns** (FAPs) (see left for other characteristics of FAPs). FAPs are produced by a neural mechanism known as an **innate releasing mechanism** (IRM) and are triggered by a very specific stimulus known as a sign stimulus. The IRM receives its input from sensory recognition circuits that are stimulated by the presence of the sign stimulus. The IRM then communicates with motor control circuits to activate (i.e. *release*) the FAP associated with that sign stimulus. Tinbergen's research with sticklebacks showed that a male stickleback fish will produce a fixed sequence of aggressive actions when another male enters its territory. The sign stimulus in this case is not the presence of the other male, but the sight of its distinctive red underbelly that acts as the sign stimulus. If this is covered up, the intruder is not attacked (Tinbergen, 1951).

Ritualistic aggression

Ethologists have shown that not all aggressive behaviour involves fighting but may be ritualised in the form of threat displays. These threat displays are important for contestants because they help individuals to assess their relative strength before deciding to escalate a conflict. As a result, they make costly and dangerous physical aggression less likely to occur. For example, male gorillas use a variety of different vocalisations (such as hooting) and gestures (such as chest pounding) to intimidate an opponent without the need for physical contact. Threat displays are intended to make an opponent back down and are the last step before an animal either fights or submits and leaves.

Anthropologists have found evidence of the use of ritualised aggression in tribal warfare in human cultures. Gardner and Heider (1968) described how the Dani of New Guinea engaged in highly ritualised patterns of intergroup hostility. Fox (1978) also found evidence of highly ritualised 'fighting' among males of the Gaelic-speaking Tory Island off the coast of Ireland, where threat displays appear to take the place of actual aggression.

▲ A male silverback gorilla shows his strength in order to intimidate potential opponents.

Wolves and doves

Some species have evolved fearsome weapons that make them effective hunters – wolves, for example, have powerful jaws and strong teeth. Lorenz (1952) claimed that such species must also have instinctive inhibitions that prevent them using these weapons against members of their own species. When two wolves fight, if the individual who is losing submissively exposes its neck to its adversary, then instinctive inhibitions prevent the dominant animal from continuing the fight. Non-hunting species, argued Lorenz, have no such powerful natural weapons, and therefore have not developed the same inhibitions against hurting their own kind. For example, when two birds (such as doves) fight, the loser can simply fly away.

Lorenz believed this comparison had implications for the human species. Humans, he argued, are more like the dove than the wolf when it comes to dealing with other human beings. We do not have powerful natural weapons, like wolves do, and thus have had no need to develop strong instinctive inhibitions against killing one another. Unfortunately, science and technology has far outpaced our biological evolution, as humans have developed weapons of tremendous destructive power without also developing instinctive inhibitions against using them.

Criticisms of an 'instinctive' view of aggression

Lehrman (1953) criticised Lorenz's instinctual explanation of aggressive behaviour. Lehrman believed that Lorenz had underestimated the role of environmental factors in the development of species-typical aggressive behaviour patterns. These environmental factors, largely the result of learning and experience, interact with innate factors in complex ways. Nowadays the term 'fixed action pattern' tends not to be used within ethology and has been replaced by the term 'behaviour pattern' to reflect the fact that these are not simply innate and can be modified by experience. Nor is behaviour as 'fixed' as implied by the term fixed action pattern. There are subtle variations between members of the same species in the production of aggressive behaviours, showing that patterns of aggressive behaviour are not as fixed as Lorenz claimed.

Do humans have fixed action patterns for aggression?

Eibl-Eibesfeldt (1972) identified a number of human FAPs or human 'universals', e.g. smiling and the 'eyebrow-flash' as a sign of greeting. However, because the environment in which humans exist changes so rapidly, Eibl-Eibesfeldt suggests FAPs such as aggression are no longer adaptive in modern times. The flexibility of human behaviour and the ability to respond to an ever-changing environment has proved more effective than the production of stereotypical, fixed patterns of behaviour. This suggests that, although non-human species may respond aggressively to specific sign stimuli, human behaviour is far more varied and less predictable.

A problem for the hydraulic model

A problem, however, for Lorenz's hydraulic model was the issue of feedback. Lorenz argued that when levels of ASE reached a critical point, this would lead to performance of a fixed action pattern (the aggressive action). This would then lead to a reduction in biological energy and a corresponding reduction in the likelihood of aggressive behaviour. However, this argument was challenged by the work of von Holst (1954). Von Holst showed that the performance of an aggressive behaviour could itself provide a further stimulus which, rather than reducing the likelihood of further aggressive behaviour, made it more likely.

The benefits of ritualised aggression

In non-human species, the main advantage of ritualised aggression is that it prevents conflicts escalating into potentially dangerous physical aggression. Anthropological evidence suggests that this advantage is also evident in human cultures. For example, Chagnon (1992) describes how, among the Yanomamö people of South America, chest pounding and club fighting contests can settle a conflict short of more extreme violence. Similarly, Hoebel (1967) found that, among Inuit Eskimos, song duels are used to settle grudges and disputes. This shows that, even in moderately to highly violent cultures such as the Yanomamö, rituals have the

▲ The scars of club fighting. Among the Yanomamö, conflicts can be settled through ritualised club fighting, where each contestant must bear a blow to their head from an opponent's club before delivering their own blow in return.

effect of reducing actual aggression and preventing injury or death of the combatants.

Killing conspecifics is not that rare

A problem for the ethological explanation of aggression concerns the claim that predator species must also have instinctive inhibitions that prevent them using their natural weapons against members of their own species. The argument that among such species the killing of members of the same species would occur only by accident is not borne out by evidence on animal behaviour. In some predator species, the killing of conspecifics is more systematic than accidental. For example, male lions will kill off the cubs of other males, and male chimpanzees will routinely kill members of another group. These findings pose a challenge for the ethological explanation of aggression as they cast doubt on the claim that much of animal aggression is ritualistic rather than real.

MEET THE RESEARCHER

Konrad Lorenz was born in 1903 in Austria. From a young age his interest in animal behaviour was obvious, and his collection of animals included fish, monkeys, insects, ducks and geese. Although he wanted to be a palaeontologist, he reluctantly followed his father's wishes, and studied medicine at the University of Vienna. He was awarded a doctorate in zoology from the University of Munich in 1936. Later that year he was introduced to Niko Tinbergen and the two became the founding fathers of the new science of ethology. In his 1966 book, *On Aggression*, Lorenz claimed that human aggressive impulses are largely innate, and drew analogies between human and animal behaviour, a view that aroused a great deal of controversy.

🏠 UPGRADE

The first 'Can You' question below asks you to explain two concepts, i.e. innate releasing mechanisms and fixed action patterns. There is a temptation to approach questions like this by just offering a brief description of the term without the necessary elaboration to justify the full 3 marks.

For example, for the concept of 'innate releasing mechanism', a basic answer (that would be worth just 1 mark) might look something like this:

An innate releasing mechanism activates a fixed action pattern.

A better answer (worth 2 marks) would include a little more detail:

An innate releasing mechanism is a neural network that, when stimulated by the presence of a sign stimulus, activates the fixed action pattern associated with that sign stimulus.

Because you are asked to 'explain' the concept, an example would serve that purpose and guarantee the full 3 marks.

For example, Tinbergen found that the presence of another male stickleback, particularly the sign stimulus of its red underbelly, activated an IRM, which then caused a male to release the fixed action pattern of aggression toward the other male.

CAN YOU? No. 9.3

1. Explain what is meant by *innate releasing mechanisms* and *fixed action patterns* in the context of aggression. (3 marks each)
2. Outline the ethological explanation of aggression. (4 marks)
3. Outline and evaluate the ethological explanation of aggression. (16 marks)

Evolutionary explanations of human aggression

Humans have evolved adaptations designed to harm other individuals in relatively minor ways (e.g. competing in order to achieve status) and in more serious ways (e.g. by maiming or murdering others). Evolutionary theorists believe these adaptations are fundamental and universal components of human nature and cannot be explained in terms of learning or cultural influences. Unlike the ethological explanation discussed on the previous spread, this does not imply that human beings have an 'aggression instinct', but rather that humans, particularly human males, have inherited from their ancestors psychological mechanisms that improve their odds of passing on their genes to future generations.

KEY TERM

Evolutionary explanations focus on the adaptive nature of behaviour, i.e. modern behaviours are believed to have evolved because they solved challenges faced by our distant ancestors and so became more widespread in the gene pool.

Ultimate and proximate causes

In searching for the causes of human aggression we should make a distinction between proximate and ultimate causes. Social scientists may be interested in why one individual decides to attack another, or the link between frustration and aggressive behaviour. These are *proximate* causes, i.e. things that are immediately responsible for a particular behaviour. Evolutionary explanations, on the other hand, concentrate on the *ultimate* causes of behaviour, i.e. why was that aggressive behaviour so effective for early humans so that a tendency to solve problems in this way became established in the gene pool?

▲ Male-on-male aggression is often caused by sexual jealousy.

An **evolutionary explanation** of aggression is based on the premise that the human brain is a product of evolution by natural selection. In particular, evolutionary psychologists believe that the human brain comprises a number of adaptations to cope with the various challenges associated with group living. These adaptations, including those that function to inflict costs on other humans, comprise our human nature (Duntley and Buss, 2004).

Aggression is a strategy that would have been effective for solving a number of adaptive problems among early humans (e.g. gaining resources, intimidating or eliminating male rivals for females, and deterring mates from sexual infidelity). Solving these problems enhanced the survival and reproductive success of the individual, and as a result this mental module would have spread through the gene pool. Mental modules have evolved in response to particular selection pressures faced by ancestral humans. They 'tell us what to do' in order to deal with situations similar to those faced by ancestral humans. For example, aggressive thoughts and behaviours are found to increase among males when resources such as territory, mates and food are scarce.

Sexual competition

Ancestral males seeking access to females would have had to compete with other males (i.e. sexual competition). One way of eliminating the competition would have been through aggression, perhaps in the form of physical competition. Those individuals who used aggression successfully against competitors would have been more successful in acquiring mates and so would be more successful in passing on their genes to offspring. This would then have led to the development of a genetically transmitted tendency for males to be aggressive towards other males.

Puts (2010) argues that various male traits seem to imply that competition with other males did take place among ancestral males. For example, men have 75% more muscle mass than women (Lassek and Gaulin, 2009), are far more aggressive than women, and are far more likely to die violently (Buss, 2005). Anthropological evidence shows that, universally, males have thicker jawbones, which Puts believes may have come from men hitting each other, with the thickest-boned men surviving and passing on their genes to subsequent generations. Competition with other males may also explain why males have more robust skulls and brow ridges than women.

Sexual jealousy

Male aggression can also occur as a result of sexual jealousy, which arises as a result of paternal uncertainty (Archer, 2013). Unlike women, men can never be entirely certain that they are the fathers of their children, as fertilisation is hidden from them, inside the woman. As a result, men are always at risk of *cuckoldry*, the reproductive cost that might be inflicted on a man as a result of his partner's infidelity. The consequence of cuckoldry is that the man might unwittingly invest his resources in offspring that are not his own. The adaptive functions of sexual jealousy, therefore, would have been to deter a mate from sexual infidelity, thereby minimising the risk of cuckoldry.

Buss (1988) suggests that males have a number of strategies that have evolved specifically for the purpose of keeping a mate. These include the use of violence or threats of violence to prevent her from straying, as well as violence toward a perceived love rival. Because sexual jealousy is a primary cause of violence against women, those who are perceived by their partner to be threatening infidelity (e.g. by looking at another man) are more at risk of violence than those who are not. Studies of battered women, for example, have shown that, in the majority of cases, women cite extreme jealousy on the part of their husbands or boyfriends as the key cause of the violence directed toward them (Dobash and Dobash, 1984). Dell (1984) concluded that sexual jealousy accounted for 17% of all cases of murder in the UK. Men are predominantly the perpetrators and the victims.

Aggression in warfare

War is undoubtedly dangerous and costly – therefore it is difficult to see why any organism, selected to survive, should engage in behaviours associated with such extremes of personal cost and danger. An evolutionary explanation, therefore, would lead us to expect that any behaviour associated with warfare would have evolved because of the adaptive benefits for the individual and their offspring. Livingstone Smith (2007) claims that human warfare originated not only to obtain valuable resources but also to attract mates and forge intragroup bonds.

Displays of aggressiveness and bravery are attractive to females, and the absence of such displays reduces the attractiveness of individual males. For example, male warriors in traditional societies tend to have more sexual partners and more children, suggesting a direct reproductive benefit (Chagnon, 1988). Aggression in combat can also increase status for individual warriors. This would lead peers to respect them more and so strengthen the bond between them and other males in the group. Displays of aggressiveness and bravery in battle means that individuals are more likely to share the benefits associated with status.

Gender differences in aggression may be better explained by socialisation

Prinz (2012) argues that differences in the aggressive behaviour of males and females may also be the product of different socialisation experiences. For example, Smetana (1989) found that parents are more likely to physically punish boys for bad conduct, whereas when girls misbehave, parents tend to explain to them why their actions were wrong. This, suggests Prinz, could increase male physical violence. As girls learn that they are less powerful than boys, this may lead them to adopt other more social forms of aggression (i.e. behaviours designed to harm another person's social status or self-esteem) rather than physical aggression. This casts doubt on the claim that males alone have evolved aggression as a way of dealing with rivals, as females have simply developed a *different* form of aggressive behaviour.

Aggressive behaviour may not always be adaptive

One problem with seeing aggressive behaviour as being an effective way to meet the challenges of social living is that violent or aggressive behaviour can result in social ostracism, injury or even death in extreme cases. For example, violent males might be rejected as mates, and warriors might die in battle. In other words, it might be considered more *mal*adaptive than adaptive in some cases. However, Duntley and Buss (2004) point out that the benefits of aggression must only have outweighed the costs *on average* relative to other strategies in the evolutionary past. If this is the case, then natural selection will favour the evolution of aggressive behaviours, eventually making them fundamental components of human nature.

Support for the link between aggression and status

The claim that increased aggression confers greater status is supported by anthropological evidence that many tribal societies bestow increased status and honour to men who have committed murder (Daly and Wilson, 1988). This phenomenon is also evident in industrialised societies such as the United States, where the most violent gang members often have the highest status among their peers (Campbell, 1993). Males also display a heightened sensitivity to perceived affronts to their status and reputation, such that many acts of male-on-male violence result from one male perceiving a slight to his status from another male (Buss, 2005). This suggests that not only is aggression an important way of gaining status among males, but it is also a consequence of threats to that status.

Gender bias in evolutionary explanations of aggression

Evolutionary explanations for physical aggression in warfare demonstrate a gender bias as they do not adequately reflect the behaviour of women in this process. Adams (1983) claimed that the idea of the woman warrior is almost unheard of within most societies. Even within those societies that allow women to participate in war, they are always the rare exception. Women would have considerably less to gain from fighting in near certain-death situations and considerably more to lose (in terms of loss of their reproductive capacity). This is fundamental to women's exclusion from warfare, as women simply do not increase their fitness as much as men do. Our understanding of the physical aggressive displays typically found in warfare, therefore, is limited to the behaviour of males rather than females.

Limitations of evolutionary explanations of aggression

Explanations of aggression that are based on mating success, sexual jealousy or the acquisition of status in warfare fail to explain the astonishing levels of cruelty that are often found in human conflicts yet are not evident among non-human species. For example, they do not explain the wide-scale slaughter of whole groups, as was evident in the Rwandan genocide in 1994. Nor do they tell us why humans torture or mutilate their opponents when they have already been defeated and no longer pose a threat. Anthropological evidence (e.g. Watson, 1973; see page 241) suggests this may be more a consequence of de-individuation effects than of evolutionary adaptations.

▲ In many situations, aggressive behaviour may appear to be more maladaptive than adaptive.

🎧 Research methods

Judith Smetana's study (described on the left) involved a content analysis of interviews with parents and their children. In total 102 children and their parents were interviewed. The children ranged in age from 10 to 18 years and mainly came from white, middle-class to upper-middle-class homes. The interviewers asked family members to recall arguments and then asked pre-determined questions such as 'Why do you think it is OK [wrong] for you to do [not to do] X?' or 'Why do you think your parents [child] think[s] it is wrong [OK] for you to do [not to do] X'.

1. Discuss the sample that was used in this study. (4 marks)
2. Would you call this a structured or unstructured interview? Explain your answer. (2 marks)
3. Explain **one** advantage of using this kind of interview. (2 marks)
4. What kind of data would be produced by questions such as the ones above? Explain your answer. (1 mark)
5. Describe how a content analysis might be performed using the data generated by such questions. (4 marks)
6. How could the reliability of the content analysis be checked? (2 marks)

LINK TO RESEARCH METHODS

Content analysis on page 12. The other topics in these questions are covered in the research methods chapter of our Year 1 book.

CAN YOU?　　No. 9.4

1. Explain what is meant by an *evolutionary* explanation of human aggression. (2 marks)
2. Outline evolutionary explanations of human aggression and give **one** limitation of this explanation(s). (6 marks)
3. Outline and evaluate evolutionary explanations of human aggression. (16 marks)

The frustration–aggression hypothesis

In 1939 a group of researchers from Yale University, led by John Dollard, published a book called *Frustration and Aggression*. In this book they laid out their explanation of the causes of violence, which emphasised the link between frustration and aggression. Dollard *et al.*'s explanation, which came to be known as the '**frustration–aggression hypothesis**', was summarised in the opening pages of the book by two bold sentences: (a) 'the occurrence of aggressive behaviour always presupposes the existence of frustration' and (b) 'the existence of frustration always leads to some form of aggression'.

▲ A bus that doesn't stop may create frustration and anger, but less so if the reason for not stopping is seen as justified (i.e. the bus is out of service) than if it is seen as unjustified (i.e. the driver chooses not to stop).

🐾 APPLY YOUR KNOWLEDGE

Homer had worked hard all day at the power plant. He was hot and he was thirsty. On the way home he noticed a vending machine selling Buzz Cola, his favourite. He just about had enough money for one bottle. Carefully inserting all his loose change into the machine, he inched his way to the £1.60 it was going to cost him. £1.00…£1.20…£1.40…£1.50…£1.55…£1.60! The final coin trickled down into the machine's innards…he looked forward to the ice-cold cola quenching his thirst. The bottle started to move, then before it could fall into the waiting dispenser, it stopped. Homer blinked in bewilderment. 'Insert coins' said the machine's display – rather smugly, thought Homer. He pressed the coin return button but nothing happened. His bewilderment gave way to anger, then to blind rage as he shook and then kicked the machine violently. Of course none of this dislodged the bottle, so he trudged off, stopping only to aim a kick at a passing dog (he missed of course…).

Using your knowledge of the frustration–aggression hypothesis, explain Homer's behaviour.

THE FRUSTRATION–AGGRESSION HYPOTHESIS

The basic claim of Dollard *et al.*'s frustration–aggression hypothesis was that all aggression was the result of frustration, which they defined as 'any event or stimulus that prevents an individual from attaining some goal and its accompanying reinforcing quality' (Dollard *et al.*, 1939). In other words, frustration is caused when people are prevented from getting something they want. Although Dollard *et al.* claimed that frustration was a necessary condition for aggression, they also believed that contextual factors, such as threat of punishment, could inhibit aggressive behaviour in some situations.

The frustration–aggression hypothesis predicts a cause–effect relationship between frustration, aggression and *catharsis*, a form of emotional release that is achieved by the person engaging in aggressive behaviour or having aggressive thoughts about the target. Frustration, according to the hypothesis, leads to the arousal of an aggressive drive, which then leads to aggressive behaviour. Aggressive urges can be relieved through the production of an aggressive behaviour, which therefore has a cathartic effect on the individual.

Frustration increases when our motivation to achieve a goal is very strong, when we expect gratification, and when there is nothing we can do about it. For example, Brown *et al.* (2001) surveyed British holidaymakers who were prevented from travelling by ferry to France because French fishing boats blocked the French port of Calais. Brown *et al.* found an increase in hostile attitudes toward the French as a result of the passengers' frustration.

Justified and unjustified frustration

In early research designed to investigate the conditions under which frustration would lead to aggression, Doob and Sears (1939) asked participants to imagine how they would feel in a number of different frustrating situations, such as waiting for a bus which went by without stopping. Most participants reported that they would feel angry in all of the frustrating situations. However, Pastore (1952) distinguished between justified and unjustified frustration, arguing that it was mainly the latter that produces anger and aggression. Pastore produced different versions of the situations used by Doob and Sears but this time using situations involving justified as well as unjustified frustration. For example, the situation involving a bus that did not stop was changed to indicate that the bus was clearly displaying an 'out of service' message. Under this condition (i.e. *justified* frustration) participants expressed much lower levels of anger.

Displaced aggression

The frustration–aggression hypothesis states that, when people are frustrated, they experience a drive to be aggressive towards the object of their frustration. However, because it is often impossible or inappropriate to behave aggressively towards the source of frustration, and as a result any attempt to be aggressive is inhibited, Dollard *et al.* assumed that aggression is sometimes displaced from the source of the frustration on to someone or something else. This is sometimes referred to as the 'kicking the dog' effect, because a person may have an impulse to attack the source of their frustration (e.g. their boss, the bank, the government, etc.), but because this is impossible they respond by kicking the dog instead. In other words, in order to experience catharsis, a scapegoat needs to be found.

A revised frustration–aggression hypothesis (Berkowitz, 1989)

A major problem for the original frustration–aggression hypothesis is that frustration is neither necessary nor sufficient for aggression. Aggression can also occur in the absence of frustration, and frustration does not necessarily result in aggression. Berkowitz's revised frustration–aggression hypothesis argued that frustration is only one of many different types of unpleasant experience that can lead to aggression. These unpleasant experiences create 'negative affect' in the individual, i.e. negative, uncomfortable feelings. It is these negative feelings, argues Berkowitz, and not the frustration, that triggers the aggression.

For example, anything that interferes with our ability to reach an anticipated goal is experienced as an aversive (i.e. unpleasant) experience. This frustration produces negative affect (such as anger), and it is the anger that creates the tendency to engage in aggressive behaviour. Berkowitz argued that an *unanticipated* interference is more likely to provoke an aggressive reaction than an *anticipated* interference because the former is experienced as more unpleasant. Under this reformulation of the frustration–aggression hypothesis, the nature of the frustrating event is less important than how negative is the resulting affect.

Aggression is not an automatic consequence of frustration

Social learning theorists (e.g. Bandura, 1973) have argued that aggressive behaviour is only one possible response to frustration. They claim that frustration produces only generalised arousal in the individual, and that social learning determines how that arousal will influence an individual's behaviour. An individual *may* respond to frustration by engaging in aggressive behaviour if it has been effective for them before (i.e. direct conditioning) or if they have observed it being effective in others (i.e. social learning). This alternative view states that rather than frustration always leading to some form of aggression, as claimed by the frustration–aggression hypothesis, an individual *learns* to produce aggressive actions and also learns the circumstances under which they are likely to be successful.

Lack of research support for the central claims

Early critics of the frustration–aggression hypothesis claimed that many of the claims made by Dollard *et al.* simply had no support, either in research or in real life. The concept of catharsis, for example, that aggression reduces arousal so that people are less likely to be aggressive, has not been supported by research. Some researchers (e.g. Bushman, 2002) have found that behaving aggressively is likely to lead to *more* rather than less aggression in the future. Bushman found that aggressive behaviour kept aggressive thoughts and angry feelings active in memory and made people more angry and more aggressive, directly contradicting the claims that catharsis reduces aggression.

Not all aggression arises from frustration

A problem for the frustration–aggression hypothesis is that not all aggression arises from frustration. Frustration is only one of a large number of aversive events (others include pain, extreme temperatures and other noxious stimuli) that can lead to aggression. For example, in a study of baseball games in the US, Reifman *et al.* (1991) found that, as temperatures increased, so did the likelihood that pitchers would display aggressive behaviour toward the batters, with balls often thrown at 90mph direct at the batter's head. This does, however, offer some support for the *revised* frustration–aggression hypothesis in that extreme temperatures, as with frustration, are aversive stimuli that tend to make people angry, which in turn increases the likelihood of aggression.

Real-world application: Frustration and mass killings

The frustration–aggression hypothesis has been used as an explanation of mass killings. Staub (1996) suggests that mass killings are often rooted in the frustration caused by social and economic difficulties within a society. These frustrations typically lead to scapegoating (i.e. finding someone to blame) and then discrimination and aggression against this group. Following the First World War, many Germans blamed Jews both for the loss of the war and the severe economic problems that followed. Although ordinary Germans were not directly responsible for the subsequent murders, some historians (e.g. Goldhagen, 1996) have argued that they condoned the violence meted out on Jews during this period, seeing them as being responsible for Germany's plight. This shows that widespread frustration, particularly when skilfully manipulated by a propaganda machine, can have violent consequences for a scapegoated group.

Real-world application: Sports violence

Priks (2010) found supporting evidence for the frustration–aggression hypothesis in a study of violent behaviour among Swedish football fans. He used teams' changed position in the league as a measure of frustration and the number of objects (missiles, fireworks, etc.) thrown as a measure of aggression. The study showed that, when a team performed worse than their fans expected, its supporters threw more things onto the pitch. A one-position drop in the league led to a 5% increase in such unruly behaviour. Priks also found that supporters were more likely to fight with opposition supporters when the team performed worse than expected. These findings suggest that supporters become more aggressive when expectations of good performance are frustrated, thus supporting the frustration–aggression hypothesis.

▲ When a football team plays badly it can cause an increase in violent behaviour from fans.

MEET THE RESEARCHER

John Dollard was a social scientist best known for his studies on race relations in America. His classic study *Caste and Class in a Southern Town* described the social system that kept African-Americans in a lower caste and economic class in 1930s USA. His frustration–aggression hypothesis was a consequence of this research. During the Second World War he was a consultant in the US 'Morale Services Division', during which time he and fellow psychologists at Yale University produced a study titled *Fear and Courage under Battle Conditions*, investigating the fear and morale of soldiers in combat conditions. He died in 1980.

▲ Hot days can lead to hot tempers in baseball.

KEY TERM

Frustration–aggression hypothesis This sees aggression being the consequence of frustration, defined as 'any event or stimulus that prevents an individual from attaining some goal and its accompanying reinforcing quality'.

CAN YOU?   No. 9.5

1. Explain what is meant by the *frustration–aggression hypothesis*. (3 marks each)
2. Outline research into the frustration–aggression hypothesis. (4 marks)
3. Briefly evaluate the frustration–aggression hypothesis. (4 marks)
4. Outline and evaluate the frustration–aggression hypothesis. (16 marks)

Social learning theory

Social learning theory is a social psychological approach to aggressive behaviour generally associated with Albert Bandura. Bandura argued that children learn to be aggressive because either they are directly rewarded for their aggressive behaviour or they observe someone else appearing to be rewarded for *their* aggression. Despite the apparent simplicity of this approach, it has been effective in explaining many aspects of human behaviour. In fact, some commentators believe that social learning theory has been better able to explain the most facts with the fewest principles than any other theory in the history of social psychology.

EVERY TIME YOU SCREAM AT A DRIVER, SHE LEARNS A LESSON.

You're always teaching. *Teach carefully.*

www.ACTAgainstViolence.org

Ad Council   MetLife Foundation   act

▲ Sponsored by the American Psychological Association, ACT Against Violence seeks to prevent violence by providing children with positive role models.

Insider tip…
Beware of exam questions that ask for theories of aggression. Bandura et al.'s Bobo doll study can illustrate some of the claims of the theory, but it is the material elsewhere on this spread that explains the theory of social learning.

SOCIAL LEARNING THEORY

Bandura and Walters (1963) believed that aggression could not be explained using traditional learning theory where only *direct* experience was seen as responsible for the acquisition of new behaviours. Social learning theory (SLT) suggests that we also learn by observing others. We learn the specifics of aggressive behaviour (e.g. the forms it takes, how often it is enacted, the situations that produce it and the targets towards which it is directed).

Observation

Children primarily learn their aggressive responses through *observation* – watching the behaviour of role models and then *imitating* that behaviour. Whereas Skinner's operant conditioning theory claimed that learning takes place through direct reinforcement, Bandura suggested that children also learn by observing role models with whom they identify.

Vicarious reinforcement

Children observe and learn about the consequences of aggressive behaviour by watching others being reinforced or punished. This is called indirect or vicarious reinforcement. Children witness many examples of aggressive behaviour at home and at school, as well as on television and in films. By observing the *consequences* of aggressive behaviour for those who use it, a child gradually learns something about what is considered appropriate (and effective) conduct in the world around them. Thus they learn the behaviours (through observation) and they also learn whether and when such behaviours are worth repeating (through vicarious reinforcement).

Mental representation

Bandura (1986) claimed that, in order for social learning to take place, the child must form mental representations of events in their social environment. The child must also represent possible rewards and punishments for their aggressive behaviour in terms of *expectancies* of future outcomes. When appropriate opportunities arise in the future, the child will display the learned behaviour *as long as* the expectation of reward is greater than the expectation of punishment. To accommodate this focus on mental representation, social learning theory has been extended to include the idea of a particular kind of cognitive schema – the script. Children learn rules of conduct from those around them, such as when and how to be aggressive. These rules (the script) then become internalised. Once established in childhood, this pattern of aggression can become a way of life.

Production of behaviour

Maintenance through direct experience

If a child is rewarded (i.e. gets what he or she wants or is praised by others) for a behaviour, he or she is likely to repeat the same action in similar situations in the future. A child who has a history of successfully bullying other children will therefore come to attach considerable value to aggression.

Self-efficacy expectancies

In addition to forming expectancies of the likely outcomes of their aggression, children also develop confidence in their ability to carry out the necessary aggressive actions. Children for whom this form of behaviour has been particularly disastrous in the past (e.g. they weren't very good at it) have less confidence (lower sense of self-efficacy) in their ability to use aggression successfully to resolve conflicts, and therefore may turn to other means.

Key study: Bandura *et al.* (1961)

Procedure   The participants were male and female children ranging from three to five years. Half were exposed to adult models interacting aggressively with a life-sized inflatable Bobo doll and half exposed to models that were non-aggressive towards the doll. The model displayed distinctive physically aggressive acts toward the doll, e.g. striking it on the head with the mallet and kicking it about the room, accompanied by verbal aggression, such as saying 'POW'. Following exposure to the model, children were frustrated by being shown attractive toys which they were not allowed to play with. They were then taken to a room where, among other toys, there was a Bobo doll.

Findings   Children in the aggression condition reproduced a good deal of physically and verbally aggressive behaviour resembling that of the model. Children in the non-aggressive group exhibited virtually no aggression toward the doll. Approximately one-third of the children in the aggressive condition repeated the model's verbal responses, while none of the children in the non-aggressive group made such remarks. Boys reproduced more imitative physical aggression than girls, but they did not differ in their imitation of verbal aggression.

Lack of realism in research

Early research on social learning relied heavily on the sort of experimental study carried out by Bandura and colleagues described opposite. However, there are significant methodological problems with the Bobo doll studies. A doll is not a living person, and does not retaliate when hit. This raises questions about whether these studies tell us much about the imitation of aggression toward other human beings (who of course may well retaliate). However, Bandura responded to this criticism by having children watch a film of an adult model hitting a live clown. When the children were subsequently let into the room with the clown, they proceeded to imitate the same aggressive behaviours they had seen in the film.

Research support for social learning theory

Gee and Leith (2007) carried out a study of ice hockey players that supports the social learning theory explanation of aggression. They analysed penalty records from 200 games of the National Hockey League (NHL) in North America. The NHL is the main professional ice hockey league in North America, and includes top players from many different countries. Gee and Leith believed that,when they were young, players born in North America were more likely to have been exposed to aggressive models of aggression and less likely to have been punished for their aggressive play compared to players born in Europe. In line with these beliefs, and the predictions of social learning theory, Gee and Leith found that the players born in North America were much more likely to be penalised for aggressive play and fighting than players born in other countries.

▲ American ice hockey players who had been exposed to aggressive models during their childhood were found to behave more aggressively when playing than players from outside the US.

Explaining inconsistencies in aggressive behaviour

A strength of this theory is that it can explain inconsistencies in an individual's use of aggressive behaviour. For example, a young male may behave aggressively when out with friends, but does not respond in the same way when at school or work. Social learning theory would explain this difference in terms of the consequences of acting aggressively in the two situations. When out with friends, acts of aggression may be more likely to receive positive consequences (e.g. status, encouragement), whereas positive consequences are less likely at school or work. Therefore, the expectation of consequences in each situation determines the likelihood of aggression being used. As a result, this means that we can predict whether or not aggression is likely in a particular situation by knowing its likely consequences.

Cultural differences in aggression

Social learning theory can be used to explain cultural differences in aggression. Among the !Kung San of the Kalahari Desert, aggression is comparatively rare, so why is this the case? The answer lies in the child-rearing practices of the !Kung San. First, when two children argue or fight, parents neither reward nor punish them, but physically separate them and try to distract their attention on to other things. Second, parents do not use physical punishment, and aggressive postures are avoided by adults and devalued by the society as a whole. The absence of direct reinforcement of aggressive behaviour as well as the absence of aggressive models means there is little opportunity or motivation for !Kung San children to acquire aggressive behaviours.

The consequences of social learning

The belief that aggressive behaviour can be learned through social learning, and can remain persistent throughout life, has raised concerns about the widespread availability of aggressive models in young people's lives. The American Psychological Association (APA) believes that if aggression can be learned in this way, then it can also be modified. ACT Against Violence is an intervention programme sponsored by the APA that aims to educate parents and others about the dangers of providing aggressive role models and to encourage parents to provide more positive role models instead. For example, Weymouth and Howe (2011) found that, after completing the programme, parents demonstrated increases in positive parenting and discontinuation of physical punishment, thus showing that the power of social learning can be used to decrease aggressive behaviour.

⬆ UPGRADE

Q2 above asks you to give two *criticisms* of the social learning theory of aggression. There are a number of things to bear in mind when answering questions like this.

1. The term 'criticism' does not imply something negative about the theory – it can also be something positive about it. For example, the theory can explain inconsistencies in aggressive behaviour or cultural differences in aggressive behaviour (see fourth and fifth evaluation points above).

2. If the term 'limitation' had been used instead, then this would have prompted you to look at the negative aspects of the theory, for example the lack of realism in some of the research studies used to test the theory.

3. To maximise your marks in these questions, you need to *elaborate* your answer. As we have said elsewhere in this book (e.g. page 75), there are lots of ways to do this. A straightforward one is to *identify* the criticism, *justify* the criticism by providing evidence that this is the case, and then *explain* why this is good or bad for the theory.

Using the evaluation on this spread, here's one that we've done – then you can have a go at the second one (aiming for about 75 words)!

A strength of this theory is that it can explain inconsistencies in individuals' use of aggressive behaviour. For example, people may behave aggressively in one situation but not in another because there may be positive consequences (e.g. increased status or encouragement) associated with aggression in one situation but not in the other. This supports the predictions of social learning theory because the expectation of consequences in each situation determines the likelihood of aggression being used.

CAN YOU?   No. 9.6

1. Outline social learning theory as it applies to human aggression. (4 marks)
2. Give **two** criticisms of social learning theory as it applies to human aggression. (3 marks each)
3. Outline **one** research study of social learning theory as it applies to human aggression. (4 marks)
4. Outline and evaluate social learning theory as it applies to human aggression. (16 marks)

De-individuation

Not all aggressive behaviour is between individuals. Psychologists have explored the idea that membership of large, anonymous groups leads people to behave in a more anti-social manner than they would on their own. To explain this, Philip Zimbardo (1969) introduced the theory of **de-individuation**, whereby people, when part of a relatively anonymous group, lose their personal identity and hence their inhibitions about violence. De-individuation theory has been used as an explanation of the collective behaviour of violent crowds, mindless hooligans and social atrocities, such as genocide. In some countries, de-individuation has even been accepted as grounds for extenuating circumstances in murder trials (Colman, 1991).

▲ The psychological state of de-individuation is aroused when individuals join crowds or large groups.

DE-INDIVIDUATION THEORY

De-individuation theory is based, to a large extent, on the classic crowd theory of Gustave Le Bon (1895). Le Bon described how an individual was transformed when part of a crowd. In a crowd, the combination of anonymity, suggestibility and contagion mean that a 'collective mind' takes possession of the individual. As a consequence, the individual loses self-control and becomes capable of acting in a way that goes against personal or social norms.

The nature of de-individuation

Festinger *et al.* (1952) described de-individuation as a psychological state in which inner restraints are lost when 'individuals are not seen or paid attention to as people'. However, it was Zimbardo who developed the concept of de-individuation more fully. The psychological state of de-individuation is aroused when individuals join crowds or large groups. Zimbardo believed that being in a large group gave people a 'cloak of anonymity' that diminished any personal consequences for their actions. Factors that contribute to this state of de-individuation include anonymity (e.g. wearing a uniform) and altered consciousness due to drugs or alcohol.

The process of de-individuation

People normally refrain from acting in an aggressive manner partly because there are social norms inhibiting such 'uncivilised' behaviour and partly because they are easily identifiable. Being anonymous (and therefore effectively unaccountable) in a crowd has the psychological consequence of reducing inner restraints and increasing behaviours that are usually inhibited. Although Zimbardo has stressed that these same conditions may also lead to an increase in *prosocial* behaviours (for example, crowds at music festivals and large religious gatherings), the focus of de-individuation theory has been almost exclusively on *anti-social* behaviour.

According to Zimbardo, being part of a crowd can diminish awareness of our own individuality. In a large crowd, each person is faceless and anonymous – the larger the group, the greater the anonymity. There is a diminished fear of the negative evaluation of actions and a reduced sense of guilt. Conditions that increase anonymity also minimise concerns about evaluation by others, and so weaken the normal barriers to anti-social behaviour that are based on guilt or shame. Research has demonstrated that individuals who believe their identities are unknown are more likely to behave in an aggressive manner.

Research on de-individuation

Zimbardo's classic study on de-individuation is described below, but you will already be familiar with another study that demonstrated the effects of de-individuation from your first year. Zimbardo *et al.*'s Stanford prison study (1972) found that participants who played the role of guards (and therefore in a de-individuated state) acted aggressively towards other participants who were in the role of prisoners. In addition the guards wore mirrored sunglasses to accentuate their de-individuated state. Other researchers have found that wearing mirrored sunglasses makes people feel greater anonymity, which in turn increases the experience of de-individuation (Zhong, 2010).

'Sure this robe of mine doth change my disposition.'

William Shakespeare – The Winter's Tale

Key study: Zimbardo (1969)

Zimbardo's classic study on de-individuation led to the suggestion that anonymity, a key component of the de-individuation process, increased aggressiveness.

Procedure Groups of four female undergraduates were required to deliver electric shocks to another student to 'aid learning'. Half of the participants wore bulky lab coats and hoods that hid their faces, sat in separate cubicles and were never referred to by name. The other participants wore their normal clothes, were given large name tags to wear and were introduced to each other by name. They were also able to see each other when seated at the shock machines.

Findings Participants in the de-individuation condition (i.e. hooded and no name tags) were more likely to press a button that they believed would give shocks to a 'victim' in another room. They held the shock button down for twice as long as did identifiable participants.

Gender differences

Cannavale *et al.* (1970) found that male and female groups responded differently under de-individuation conditions. An increase in aggression was obtained only in the all-male groups and not in all-female groups. This was also the finding of Diener *et al.* (1973), who found greater disinhibition of aggression (i.e. removal of the normal inhibitions that prevent aggression) in de-individuated males than de-individuated females. One possible reason for these gender differences is that males tend to respond to provocation in more extreme ways than do females and that these tendencies are magnified under de-individuation conditions (Eagly, 2013).

Anonymity and de-individuation

Rehm *et al.* (1987) found support for Zimbardo's de-individuation concept through an investigation of the effect of increased anonymity on aggressive behaviour in sport. They observed 30 games of handball in three German schools. One team in each game wore the same bright orange shirts, while the other team wore their own different-coloured shirts. The researchers found that the uniformed teams showed significantly more aggressive acts during the game than did the teams without uniforms. The results support the claim that de-individuation through increased anonymity leads to more aggressive acts.

Inconclusive support for de-individuation

Evidence for de-individuation theory is mixed. A meta-analysis of 60 studies of de-individuation (Postmes and Spears, 1998) concludes that there is insufficient support for the major claims of de-individuation theory. For example, Postmes and Spears found that disinhibition and anti-social behaviour are not more common in large groups and anonymous settings. Rather, they found that de-individuation increases people's responsiveness to situational norms, i.e. what most people regard as appropriate behaviour in a given situation. This may lead to aggressive, anti-normative behaviour, but it could also lead to increased *pro*social behaviour. For example, Spivey and Prentice-Dunn (1990) found that de-individuation could lead to either prosocial or anti-social behaviour depending on situational factors. When prosocial environmental cues were present (such as a prosocial model), de-individuated participants performed significantly more altruistic acts (giving money) and significantly fewer anti-social acts (giving electric shocks) compared to a control group.

Real-world application – The baiting crowd

Mann (1981) used the concept of de-individuation to explain a bizarre aspect of collective behaviour – the 'baiting crowd' and suicide jumpers. The baiting crowd lends support to the notion of the crowd as a de-individuated 'mob'. Mann analysed 21 suicide leaps reported in US newspapers in the 1960s and 1970s. He found that, in 10 of the 21 cases where a crowd had gathered to watch, baiting had occurred (i.e. the crowd had urged the potential suicide jumper to jump). These incidents tended to occur at night, when the crowd was large and some distance from the person being taunted (particularly when the 'jumper' was high above them). All these features were likely to produce a state of de-individuation in the members of the crowd.

The power of the baiting mob was also evident in Mullen's analysis of newspaper cuttings of 60 lynchings in the United States between 1899 and 1946 (Mullen, 1986). He found that the more people there were in the mob, the greater the savagery with which the perpetrators killed their victims.

Cultural differences

Dramatic support for the deadly influence of de-individuation comes from a study by anthropologist Robert Watson (1973). He collected data on the extent to which warriors in 23 societies changed their appearance prior to going to war and the extent to which they killed, tortured or mutilated their victims. As can be seen from the figures in the table to the right, those societies where warriors changed their appearance (e.g. through war paint, tribal costumes, etc.) were more destructive toward their victims compared to those who did not change their appearance.

KEY TERM

De-individuation A psychological state in which individuals have lowered levels of self-evaluation (e.g. when in a crowd or under the influence of alcohol) and decreased concerns about evaluation by others.

🐾 APPLY YOUR KNOWLEDGE

Hannah is very much against fox hunting and has been to many demonstrations against this sport, which still appears to take place despite the ban. The demonstrations are usually relatively peaceful, but on one particular occasion she arrives home, saying that there were many more protestors than usual, many of them wearing masks and hoods. Things had quickly got out of hand and there was lots of violence. She is visibly shaken and doesn't understand why this protest had been so violent compared to all the others.

Using your knowledge of de-individuation, explain why this particular protest had become so violent.

'When darkness fell,
Excitement kissed the crowd
And made them wild,
In an atmosphere of freaky holiday
When the spotlight hit the boy,
The crowd began to cheer
He flew away'.

(Simon and Garfunkel – 'Save the Life of My Child')

▼ Comparative levels of killing, torture and mutilation in warriors who significantly change their appearance when going to war and those who don't.

	No change	Changed
Low	7	3
High	1	12

Source: Watson, 1973.

CAN YOU? No. 9.7

1. Outline the de-individuation explanation of human aggression. (4 marks)
2. Give **two** criticisms of the de-individuation explanation of human aggression. (3 marks each)
3. Outline **one** research study of de-individuation in the context of human aggression. (4 marks)
4. Outline and evaluate the de-individuation explanation of human aggression. (16 marks)

Institutional aggression in prisons

Prisons are violent and dangerous places. In July 2015, the Chief Inspector of Prisons, Nick Hardwick, gave a damning indictment of prisons in England and Wales in his annual report. This suggested that the most alarming feature was the 'accelerating increase in serious assaults', with more prisoners murdered or the victims of serious assaults than five years ago. Why are prisons so violent? One theory (the importation model – a **dispositional explanation**) is that, because prisons are full of dangerous people, these violent characteristics must be 'imported' into the prison when prisoners are sentenced. A second theory (the deprivation model – a **situational explanation**) focuses on the stressful nature of the prison itself and how that influences the inmates that are subject to this form of stress.

SITUATIONAL EXPLANATION: THE DEPRIVATION MODEL

Institutional aggression, according to the deprivation model, is the product of the stressful and oppressive conditions of the prison itself (Paterline and Peterson, 1999). The deprivation model argues that, in response to these oppressive conditions, inmates may act more aggressively.

Sykes (1958) described the specific deprivations that inmates experience within prison and which might be linked to an increase in violence. These included the loss of liberty, the loss of autonomy and the loss of security. Inmates may cope with the pains of imprisonment in several ways. Some choose to withdraw through seclusion in their cell or living space, whereas others choose to rebel in the form of violence against other prisoners or against staff.

From this perspective, institutional aggression is influenced and determined solely by prison-specific variables, rather than inmate characteristics (as in the importation model). A study of over 200 prison inmates (Kimmet and Martin, 2002) discovered that violence in prison is frequently a way of surviving the risk of exploitation (i.e. by appearing weak), an ever-present threat within prison culture. They found that most violent situations in prisons were more to do with non-material interests such as the need for respect and fairness or as a way of expressing loyalty and honour.

The role of prison characteristics

Cooke *et al.* (2008) claim that, in order to understand institutional aggression, we need to consider the situational context where violence takes place. They argue that 'violent prisoners are only violent in certain circumstances'.

These circumstances include the following:
- *Overcrowding* – A government report in 2014 (Ministry of Justice, 2014) attributed the record rates of murder, suicide and assaults to the increased overcrowding in British prisons. A Japanese study (Yuma, 2010) found that prison population density had a significant effect on inmate–inmate violence rates, even after controlling for other possible contributing factors.
- *Heat and noise* – Prisons tend to be hot and noisy places. High temperatures and noise exacerbate the effects of overcrowding and may predispose inmates to aggressive behaviour. For example, Griffitt and Veitch (1971), in a study of students, found that a combination of high temperature and high population density produced more negative emotions than was the case with more comfortable temperatures and lower population density.
- *Job burnout* – Job burnout among prison staff refers to the experience of being psychologically worn out and exhausted from a job and a gradual loss of caring about the people with whom they work. This has been linked to the development of violence in prison settings because of a deterioration in relationships with inmates (Maslach *et al.*, 2001) and the overall functioning of the prison.

DISPOSITIONAL EXPLANATION: THE IMPORTATION MODEL

Irwin and Cressey (1962) claim that inmates bring with them to prison their violent pasts and draw on their experiences in an environment where toughness and physical exploitation are important survival skills. Prisoners are not 'blank slates' when they enter prison, and many of the normative systems developed on the outside would be 'imported' into the prison. In many cities, street culture has evolved what may be called a 'code of the streets', a set of informal rules governing interpersonal public behaviour, including violence. At the heart of this code is the issue of respect, i.e. being granted the deference one deserves. Cultural belief systems such as 'the code of the street' define how some individuals behave once in prison, particularly when this code relates to gang membership.

Gang membership

Within prison environments, gang membership is consistently related to violence and other forms of anti-social behaviour. Pre-prison gang membership appears to be an important determinant of prison misconduct. Several studies (e.g. Allender and Marcell, 2003) have found that gang members disproportionately engage in acts of prison violence. Members of street gangs offend at higher levels while in prison than their non-gang counterparts and account for a disproportionate amount of serious and violent crime. A study of over 1,000 inmates in prisons in the south-west of the USA (Drury and DeLisi, 2011) found that individuals who had been members of gangs prior to imprisonment were significantly more likely to commit various types of misconduct in prison, including murder, hostage taking and assault with a deadly weapon.

▲ Gang membership has been consistently related to violent behaviour in prison.

The role of dispositional characteristics

Other dispositional characteristics that have been found to relate to aggressive behaviour in prison include the following:
- *Anger, anti-social personality style and impulsivity* – Wang and Diamond (1999) found that these three individual characteristics were stronger predictors of institutional aggression than ethnicity and type of offence committed. Of these, anger was the best predictor of violent behaviour while in prison.
- *Low self-control* – DeLisi *et al.* (2003) found that low self-control, particularly the tendency to lose one's temper easily, was a significant predictor of aggressive behaviour both before and during incarceration.

EVALUATION OF THE DISPOSITIONAL EXPLANATION

Research support for the importation model

This model has received some research support. Mears *et al.* (2013) tested the view that inmate behaviour stems in part from the cultural belief systems that they import with them into prison. They measured the street code belief system and the prison experiences of inmates. Their results supported the argument that a 'code of the street' belief system affects inmate violence. This effect is particularly pronounced among those inmates who lack family support and are involved in gangs prior to incarceration. Other research support for the importation model comes from Poole and Regoli (1983). They found that the best indicator of violence among juvenile offenders was pre-institutional violence regardless of any situational factors in the institution.

Challenges to the importation model

Evidence from DeLisi *et al.* (2004) challenges the claim that pre-prison gang membership predicts violence whilst in prison. They found that inmates with prior street gang involvement were no more likely than other inmates to engage in prison violence. The lack of an association found in this study, however, can be explained by the fact that violent gang members tend to be isolated from the general inmate population, therefore greatly restricting their opportunities for violence. For example, Fischer (2001) found that isolating known gang members in a special management unit reduced the rates of serious assault by 50%.

EVALUATION OF THE SITUATIONAL EXPLANATION

Research support for the deprivation model

There is substantial research evidence to support the claim that peer violence is used to relieve the deprivation experienced in institutional cultures, such as prisons. McCorkle *et al.* (1995), in a major study of 371 US prisons, found that situational factors such as overcrowding, lack of privacy and the lack of meaningful activity all significantly influenced inmate-on-inmate assaults and inmate-on-staff assaults. Franklin *et al.* (2006) also found a relationship between age of inmates and crowding. Their meta-analysis found that crowded prison conditions increased aggressive behaviour in younger inmates (aged 18 to 25) more so than in other age groups.

Challenges to the deprivation model

The link between situational factors and institutional aggression is challenged by the findings of one of the most exhaustive studies of prison violence (Harer and Steffensmeier, 1996). They collected data from more than 24,000 inmates from 58 prisons across the US. They included importation variables (e.g. race and criminal history) and deprivation variables (e.g. staff-to-prisoner ratio and security level) and tested which of these variables predicted the individual likelihood of aggressive behaviour while in prison. Harer and Steffensmeier concluded that race, age and criminal history were the only significant predictors of prison violence, whereas none of the deprivation variables were significant in this respect.

Real-world application: HMP Woodhill and the deprivation model

A real-world application of the deprivation model happened at HMP Woodhill in the early 1990s. Prison Governor David Wilson reasoned that if most violence occurs in environments that are hot, noisy and overcrowded, then this could be avoided by reducing these three factors. Wilson set up two units for violent prisoners that were less claustrophobic and 'prison-like' and gave a view to outside. The typical noise associated with prison life was reduced and masked by music from a local radio station. Temperature was lowered so that it was no longer stiflingly hot. These changes virtually eradicated assaults on prison staff and other inmates, providing powerful support for the claim that situational variables are the main cause of prison violence (Wilson, 2010).

UPGRADE

In other upgrades in this book (e.g. pages 65 and 75) we have offered advice about how to answer essay questions such as Q3 below. It is always worth spending a bit of time planning your response to such questions as there are so many marks up for grabs.

The specific issue in Q3 here is that there are a number of distinct requirements, and all must be covered in appropriate detail to ensure you get a good mark. Let's look at some of these issues here:

- The question says 'Discuss'. This is not another term for 'Chat about', but is an alternative to the term 'Outline and evaluate'. That means there is a requirement for both description *and* evaluation in your answer.
- You are required to cover both dispositional (i.e. the importation model) *and* situational (i.e. the deprivation model) explanations in your answer. It is easier to plan an answer if you allocate more or less the same amount of time to each.
- Finally, your answer *must* be in the context of institutional aggression 'in prisons'. That means not talking about these explanations out of context, or in some other context rather than prisons.

To plan a response, consider a good answer to be around 480 words (that's 30 words a mark). That would be 240 words for each explanation. Given that the marking allocation for this question nominally allocates 6 marks for AO1 (description) and 10 for AO3 (evaluation), that could mean the following plan:

Dispositional explanation – 90 words AO1 (e.g. three points @ 30 words each) and 120 words AO3 (e.g. two points @ 60 words each)

Situational explanation – 90 words AO1 (e.g. three points @ 30 words each) and 180 words AO3 (e.g. two points @ 90 words each or three points @ 60 words each)

CAN YOU?   No. 9.8

1. Outline **one or more** dispositional explanations of institutional aggression. (4 marks)
2. Outline **one or more** situational explanations of institutional aggression and give **one** limitation of this explanation. (6 marks)
3. Discuss dispositional and situational explanations of institutional aggression in the context of prisons. (16 marks)

Media influences on aggression

The question of how media violence might influence aggression has been the subject of intense research for at least the last 50 years. Edgar (1977) notes, for example, that, in every country where television exists, it has generated social concern, and that public opinion, in spite of the uncertain nature of any research findings, tends to unequivocally blame the media for any rise in levels of aggressive behaviour in young people. More recently, the focus of attention in **media influence** research has been on the dangers of playing violent computer games, raising concerns in the media and among regulatory bodies about the possible link between excessive game play and violent behaviour in real life.

KEY TERM

Media influences are changes in behaviour that are attributed to exposure to media such as TV or computer games.

▲ Longitudinal studies have shown that habitual exposure to violent TV in childhood predicts higher levels of adult aggression.

Key study: Greitemeyer and Mügge (2014)

Procedure Greitemeyer and Mügge carried out a meta-analysis of 98 studies carried out since 2009. This involved a total of nearly 37,000 participants. They were testing the effects of violent video games in which the goal is to harm another game character and also pro-social games in which the goal is to benefit another character. The researchers were interested in how playing these games influenced aggressive and prosocial behaviour (e.g. aggression and helping) as well as aggressive and prosocial cognitions and emotions (e.g. anger and empathy).

Findings The researchers found a small average effect size (i.e. the difference between groups exposed to violent media and control groups who were not) in these studies, i.e. violent video game use was linked to an increase in aggressive outcomes *and* a decrease in prosocial outcomes. Prosocial games showed the opposite effect – they were linked to a *reduction* in aggressive behaviour and an increase in prosocial, cooperative behaviour. These effects were evident regardless of the type of study (i.e. experimental, correlational or longitudinal).

VIOLENT FILMS AND TV

Laboratory and field experiments

In a typical experimental study, researchers randomly assign participants to either an experimental condition, where they view violent film scenes, or a control condition where they watch non-violent scenes. They are then observed to see how they interact with other people after viewing the film. A consistent finding from both laboratory and field experiments is that those who watch violent scenes subsequently display more aggressive behaviour and have more aggressive thoughts or aggressive emotions than those who do not. For example, Bjorkqvist (1985) exposed 5 to 6-year-old Finnish children to either violent or non-violent films. Compared with the children who had viewed the non-violent film, those who had watched the violent film were subsequently rated much higher on measures of physical aggression (e.g. hitting other children).

Longitudinal studies

Longitudinal studies allow researchers to track individuals over time in order to assess the impact of early experiences on behaviour later in life. For example, Huesmann *et al.* (2003) studied 557 children between the ages of 6 and 10, growing up in Chicago in 1977, and then 329 of these 15 years later in 1992. They found that habitual early exposure to TV violence was predictive of adult aggression later in life and that this applied to both boys and girls. This relationship persisted even when the possible effects of socioeconomic status, intelligence and any differences in parenting styles were controlled.

Meta-analyses

Meta-analyses allow researchers to aggregate the findings of many different individual studies of the effects of media violence. For example, Bushman and Huesmann (2006) carried out a meta-analysis of 431 studies, involving over 68,000 participants. Of these, 264 studies involved children and 167 involved adults. Most of the studies had looked at the impact of violent TV, but others had also looked at the effect of video games, music and comic books. Overall, they found modest but significant effect sizes for exposure to media violence on aggressive behaviours, aggressive thoughts, angry feelings and arousal levels. The short-term effects of violent media were greater for adults than for children, whereas the long-term effects were greater for children than for adults.

VIOLENT COMPUTER GAMES

Research on the impact of violent computer games is still in its relative infancy, yet, as Porter and Starcevic (2007) suggest, interactive violence in video games has the potential to exert even more influence than TV violence, where the viewer plays a more passive role. In addition, during violent game play, aggression is rewarded and is portrayed as being both appropriate and effective.

Experimental studies

Lab experiments have found short-term increases in levels of physiological arousal, hostile feelings and aggressive behaviour following violent game play compared to non-violent game play (Gentile and Stone, 2005). Aggressive behaviour cannot be studied directly, as this is not permitted on ethical grounds, so other forms of behaviour must be used instead. For example, Anderson and Dill (2000) found that participants blasted their opponents with white noise (a random, multi-frequency sound) for longer and rated themselves higher on the *State Hostility Scale* after playing *Wolfenstein 3D* (a violent 'first person shooter' game) compared to those who played *Myst* (a slow-paced puzzle game).

Longitudinal studies

Anderson *et al.* (2007) surveyed 430 children aged between seven and nine at two points during the school year. Children who had high exposure to violent video games became more verbally and physically aggressive and less prosocial (as rated by themselves, their peers and their teachers). Adachi and Willoughby (2013) suggest that the longitudinal link found between violent video games and aggression may be due to the competitive nature of the games, rather than the violence, as violent video games tend to be more competitive than non-violent games.

Media violence research: Overstating the case

Some critics point out that, although many studies claim a 'statistically significant' relationship between media violence and violent behaviour, this is an overstatement of the case. Studies that *have* found an effect attributable to exposure to violent media have typically reported only small-to-medium effect sizes. However, very few of these have actually measured aggression against another person. Ferguson and Kilburn (2009) note that, when aggression towards another person or violent crime is the measure of aggression used in research, the relationship between exposure to media violence and aggressive behaviour is actually close to zero.

Simple questions but complex answers

Livingstone (1996) claims that asking questions such as 'Does violent media increase aggressive behaviour in viewers?' may *appear* to be a simple question, but answers are much more complex. As most studies are American, the generality of findings to countries with different media and cultural histories is problematic. Effects research has also mostly tended to use unrepresentative samples (e.g. male students) and then made generalisations about all viewers. Livingstone argues that there is a need for better methodologies in more natural viewing conditions. She suggests that field experiments conducted with better experimental controls and a longer follow-up period would provide the most convincing evidence.

Failure to consider other causal variables

Many studies in this area fail to account for other variables that explain why some people display aggressive behaviour and why those same people may choose to play violent computer games. For example, Ferguson *et al.* (2009) claim that much of the research on the effects of computer game violence has failed to control for other variables known to influence aggressive behaviour. Their meta-analysis showed that the effects of violent media content on aggressive behaviour disappears when other potential influences such as trait aggression, family violence and mental health are taken into consideration. The researchers suggest that these other risk factors, as opposed to exposure to media violence, are the primary cause of aggressive and violent behaviour.

Problems with research on the effects of computer games

A major weakness of lab experiments in this area is that researchers cannot measure 'real-life' aggression. They therefore must use measures of aggressive behaviour that have no relationship to real-life aggression, and can only measure short-term effects. These alternative 'measures' of aggressive behaviour include administering noise blasts or even hot chilli sauce to another participant, neither of which have much to do with actual aggressive behaviour. Longitudinal studies are able to observe real-life patterns of behaviour and document both short-term and long-term effects. However, a problem for most longitudinal studies in this area is that participants may be exposed to other forms of media violence (e.g. on television) during the course of the study, meaning that the effect from violent video game exposure alone is uncertain.

Game difficulty rather than content may lead to aggression

It is frequently claimed that the violent content of games creates feelings of aggression in players, which then spills over into aggressive behaviour in their own life. However, a study by Przybylski *et al.* (2014) suggests that aggressive behaviour may be linked to a player's experiences of failure and frustration during a game rather than the game's violent storyline. They found that it was not the storyline or imagery, but the lack of mastery and difficulty players had in completing the game, that led to frustration and aggression. This was evident across both violent and non-violent games. The researchers suggest that we tend to have fairly simplistic views when it comes to the link between video games and aggression, as even non-violent games can leave players feeling aggressive if they are poorly designed or too difficult.

▲ Recent research suggests that failure and frustration during game play is more likely to produce aggressive behaviour than any violent content.

APPLY YOUR KNOWLEDGE

Your mother has been reading the *Daily Mail* again and is now convinced that playing violent computer games will turn you into a raging psychopath. Being a reasonable woman, she agrees that she will let you continue to play these games if you can convince her why the *Daily Mail*'s scaremongering is wrong. Your mum is an intelligent woman, so won't be swayed by claims that aren't backed up with evidence or reasoned argument.

She has asked for your 'side' of the debate in just 100 words. What would you write in those 100 words to convince her?

We might expect that there would be larger effects with newer studies, as violent video games have become more violent over time. This is what Gentile and Anderson (2003) found, with earlier studies showing smaller effect sizes than more recent studies.

CAN YOU?   No. 9.9

1. Outline research findings on the effects of computer games on aggression. (4 marks each)
2. Give **two** criticisms of research showing a link between computer game violence and aggressive behaviour. (4 marks)
3. Outline and evaluate media influences on aggression. (16 marks)

We have identified here the key points of the topics on the AQA A level specification, i.e. the bare minimum that you need to know. You may want to fill in further details to elaborate and personalise this material.

NEURAL AND HORMONAL INFLUENCES

NEURAL INFLUENCES
- Limbic system coordinates behaviours that satisfy motivational and emotional urges.
- Stimulation of amygdala produces aggressive response.
- Impaired hippocampal function causes inappropriate amygdala response.
- Serotonin exerts calming effect by inhibiting firing of amygdala.
- Low levels of serotonin associated with increased susceptibility to aggression.

HORMONAL INFLUENCES
- Testosterone influences brain areas (particularly the amygdala) associated with aggression.
- Removing source of testosterone lowers levels of aggression.
- Evidence from gender differences, age differences and high levels in violent criminals.
- Testosterone concentrations are not static, but fluctuate in the context of changes to the social environment.

EVALUATION
- Evidence for role of amygdala – Pardini et al.: lower amygdala volumes predicted aggression.
- Evidence for role of hippocampus – Raine et al.: 'unsuccessful psychopaths' had asymmetrical hippocampi.
- Research support for serotonin deficiency hypothesis – Duke et al. meta-analysis found inverse correlation between serotonin and aggression levels.
- Evidence from non-human species – Raleigh et al. (vervet monkeys); Rosado et al. (dogs): higher levels of aggression with lower serotonin levels.
- Inconsistent evidence for testosterone link – some studies show positive relationship in self-reports of aggression (Albert et al.), but no relationship with actual violence.
- Aggression or dominance – aggression only one way to express dominance (Mazur); could make women act 'nicer' (Eisenegger et al.).

THE ETHOLOGICAL EXPLANATION OF AGGRESSION

ETHOLOGICAL EXPLANATIONS OF AGGRESSION
- All members of the same species have repertoire of stereotyped behaviours that occur in response to specific sign stimuli and do not require learning (FAPs).
- These are activated by neural networks that respond to these sign stimuli (IRMs).
- Lorenz's 'hydraulic model' – FAP released when ASE is high enough and appropriate sign stimulus is present.
- Humans have some FAPs, but aggressive FAPs would be maladaptive in ever-changing environment.
- Ritualistic aggression – threat displays prevent escalation of conflict.
- Evidence of ritualised aggression in New Guinea (Gardner and Heider) and Tory Island (Fox).
- Wolves and doves – predator species have instinctive inhibitions that prevent intraspecies aggression.
- Humans are not a predator species, so have no such inhibitions to prevent aggression against conspecifics.

EVALUATION
- Criticisms of an instinctive view of aggression – underestimates role of environmental factors and variations in expression of behaviour.
- Support for Lorenz's hydraulic model – stimulation of neural networks associated with FAP led to increase in aggressive behaviour (Moyer).
- A problem for the hydraulic model – expression of FAP should lead to decrease in aggression but may increase it (von Holst).
- The benefits of ritualised aggression – anthropological evidence among Yanomamö (Chagnon) and Inuit Eskimos (Hoebel).
- Killing conspecifics is not that rare – e.g. lions and chimpanzees. Better explained by selfish gene theory.

GENETIC FACTORS IN AGGRESSION

GENETICS AND AGGRESSION
- Twin studies suggest nearly 50% of variance in aggression could be attributed to genetics (Coccaro et al.).
- Adoption studies – adopted boys with criminal convictions had biological parents with criminal convictions.
- Miles and Carey meta-analysis – strong evidence for genetic influence in aggression.
- Rhee and Waldman – also found strong evidence but acknowledged role of other factors.
- MAOA regulates metabolism of serotonin in the brain.
- Brunner et al. – low levels of MAOA found in male members of particularly violent family.
- MAOA-L gene variant associated with aggression in people who were also mistreated in childhood (Caspi et al.).
- 'Warrior gene' – MAOA-L more frequent in violent cultures; predicts more aggressive responses to provocation (McDermott et al.).

EVALUATION
- Problems of sampling – most studies restricted to narrow and unrepresentative group of violent criminals.
- Difficulties of determining the role of genetic factors – more than one gene involved; also non-genetic factors that interact with genetic factors.
- Problems of assessing aggression – parental and self-reports not reliable way of measuring aggression.
- Evidence for the influence of MAOA gene: Tiihonen et al. – MAOA-L coupled with CDH13 gene predicted aggression.
- MAOA gene may explain gender differences in aggression – linked to X chromosome, so males more influenced by gene (females have dominant 'normal' version as well).

EVOLUTIONARY EXPLANATIONS OF HUMAN AGGRESSION

EVOLUTIONARY EXPLANATIONS OF HUMAN AGGRESSION
- Aggression would have been effective at solving a number of adaptive problems associated with group living.
- These would include inflicting costs on other humans to enhance survival and reproductive benefits.
- Evolutionary explanations emphasise ultimate rather than proximate causes of aggressive behaviour.
- Sexual competition involves eliminating competition through physical aggression.
- Evidence for physical competition includes physical differences between men and women and anthropological evidence.
- Fear of cuckoldry because of paternal uncertainty drives sexual jealousy, a primary cause of violence against women.
- Sexual jealousy accounts for 17% of all murders in the UK (Dell).
- Livingstone Smith claims human warfare originated in order to obtain resources, attract mates and forge intragroup bonds.
- Displays of aggressiveness in battle means individuals are more likely to share the benefits associated with status, which would increase their reproductive fitness.

EVALUATION
- Gender differences in aggression may be better explained by socialisation – e.g. Smetana found boys and girls treated differently with respect to aggression.
- Aggressive behaviour may not always be adaptive – but benefits of aggression need only outweigh costs on average.
- Support for the link between aggression and status – supported by anthropological evidence (Daly and Wilson) and in US gangs (Campbell).
- Gender bias in evolutionary explanations of aggression – understanding of the aggressive displays typically found in warfare is limited to the behaviour of males rather than females.
- Limitations of evolutionary explanations of aggression – do not explain extreme cruelty found in warfare.

DE-INDIVIDUATION

DE-INDIVIDUATION
- A psychological state in which inner restraints are lost when anonymous.
- Being anonymous reduces inner constraints on aggressive behaviour.
- Increased anonymity minimises concerns about evaluation by others.
- Rehm et al. found de-individuated sports teams played more aggressively.
- SPE (Zimbardo et al.) and Zhong et al.'s mirrored sunglasses study.

KEY STUDY: ZIMBARDO
- Procedure: De-individuated and individuated groups delivered shocks to other participants.
- Findings: De-individuated participants gave longer shocks.

EVALUATION
- Gender differences – aggression only in all-male groups (Cannavale et al.).
- Anonymity and de-individuation – support from (Rehm et al.).
- Inconclusive support for de-individuation – can also lead to prosocial behaviour.
- Real-world application: the baiting crowd – crowds baiting suicide jumpers.
- Cultural differences – warriors who change their appearance when going to war more brutal than those who don't (Watson).

EXPLANATIONS OF MEDIA INFLUENCES

THE ROLE OF DESENSITISATION, DISINHIBITION AND COGNITIVE PRIMING
- Desensitisation: exposure to media violence removes anxiety about violence.
- Desensitised individuals show reduction in physiological arousal when exposed to violence in real life.
- Disinhibition: exposure to violent media changes standards of what is considered acceptable behaviour.
- May have both an immediate effect and a long-term effect.
- Cognitive priming: lowers threshold for activation of other aggressive thoughts.
- The more accessible a thought, the more likely it is used to interpret social information.

EVALUATION
- Desensitisation: research support for desensitisation – Carnagey et al. found physiological desensitisation to violence after playing violent computer game.
- The good and bad of desensitisation – consequences of individuals desensitised to violence after exposure to violent media (Bushman and Anderson).
- Disinhibition: the disinhibition effect depends on other factors – mediated by individual and social characteristics, e.g. age and upbringing.
- Negative consequences make disinhibition more likely – e.g. boxing (Goranson).
- Cognitive priming: research support for cognitive priming – faster reaction times to aggressive words (Bushman).
- Priming less likely with less realistic media – game realism important factor (Atkin).

SOCIAL LEARNING THEORY

SOCIAL LEARNING THEORY
- We learn aggressive behaviours by observing role models with whom we identify.
- Children also learn through vicarious reinforcement.
- Children must also have *expectancies* of future outcomes.
- Aggressive behaviour can be produced if directly rewarded.

KEY STUDY: BANDURA *ET AL.*
- Procedure: Children exposed to model acting aggressively toward Bobo doll.
- Findings: Children in the aggression condition reproduced aggressive behaviour resembling that of the model.

EVALUATION
- Lack of realism in research – Bandura's studies criticised for being too artificial.
- Research support for social learning theory – ice hockey players (Gee and Leith).
- Explaining inconsistencies in aggressive behaviour – e.g. different situations offer different consequences for aggressive behaviour.
- Cultural differences in aggression – e.g. the !Kung San have very little aggression.
- The consequences of social learning – can lead to perpetuation of aggression but being tackled by ACT Against Violence (APA).

INSTITUTIONAL AGGRESSION IN PRISONS

DISPOSITIONAL EXPLANATION: THE IMPORTATION MODEL
- Inmates bring with them to prison their violent pasts.
- Pre-prison gang membership an important determinant of prison misconduct.
- Other dispositional characteristics include inability to cope with adversity, anger.

SITUATIONAL EXPLANATION: THE DEPRIVATION MODEL
- Institutional aggression is the product of stressful conditions of prison.
- Violence is a way of surviving the risk of exploitation (Kimmet and Martin).
- Other situational characteristics include overcrowding, heat and noise.

EVALUATION
- Research support for the importation model – a 'code of the street' belief system is imported into prison and affects inmate violence (Mears et al.).
- Challenges to the importation model – inmates with street gang involvement were no more likely to engage in prison violence (DeLisi et al.).
- Research support for the deprivation model – e.g. overcrowding, lack of privacy and lack of meaningful activity influenced assaults (McCorkle et al.).
- Challenges to the deprivation model – Harer and Steffensmeier found that deprivation variables were not significant predictors of prison violence.
- Real-world application: HMP Woodhill and the deprivation model.

MEDIA INFLUENCES ON AGGRESSION

VIOLENT FILMS AND TV
- Experiments (e.g. Bjorkqvist) found that watching violence = aggression.
- Natural experiments (e.g. Charlton et al.) found little change in aggression
- Longitudinal studies (e.g. Huesmann et al.) found habitual early exposure to TV violence predictive of adult aggression later in life.
- Meta-analyses (e.g. Bushman and Huesmann) found modest relationship.

VIOLENT COMPUTER GAMES
- Interactive nature of game play has greater potential for influence.
- Increase in aggressive behaviour following violent game play (Anderson and Dill).
- Longitudinal studies (e.g. Anderson et al.) have found that high exposure to violent games = more aggression and less prosociality.
- Aggression due to competitive nature of games (Adachi and Willoughby).

KEY STUDY: GREITEMEYER AND MÜGGE (2014)
- Procedure: Meta-analysis of 98 studies involving 37,000 participants.
- Findings: Violent game play = increase in aggression, decrease in prosociality.

EVALUATION
- Overstating the case, little effect if aggression against a person used as DV.
- Simple questions but complex answers – difficult to conclude simple relationship.
- Failure to consider other causal variables – other factors primary cause not media.
- Problems with research evidence on effects of computer games – e.g. cannot use actual aggression as DV and other influences in longitudinal studies.
- Game difficulty rather than content may lead to aggression – failure or frustration more likely to produce aggression than content (Przybylski et al.).

THE FRUSTRATION–AGGRESSION HYPOTHESIS

THE FRUSTRATION–AGGRESSION HYPOTHESIS
- Aggression is the result of frustration.
- Aggressive urges relieved through aggressive behaviour – a cathartic effect.
- Frustration increases when motivation to achieve a goal is very strong.
- Mainly unjustified rather than justified frustration that produces aggression.
- Aggression is displaced from the source of the frustration on to something else.
- Berkowitz – the nature of the frustrating event (e.g. unanticipated rather than anticipated) is less important than how negative is the resulting affect.

EVALUATION
- Aggression is not an automatic consequence of frustration.
- Lack of research support for the central claims may lead to more aggression.
- Not all aggression arises from frustration (e.g. Reifman et al.'s baseball study).
- Frustration and mass killings – rooted in social and economic difficulties (Staub).
- Real-world application: sports violence – supporters become more aggressive when expectations of good performance are frustrated (Priks).

0 1 Which one of the following pair of hormones is associated with aggression? Write the
letter of your chosen answer in your answer booklet. **[1 mark]**

    A. cortisol and dopamine

    B. cortisol and serotonin

    C. dopamine and testosterone

    D. serotonin and testosterone

0 2 Explain the role of neural mechanisms in aggression. **[4 marks]**

0 3 Evaluate the role of hormonal mechanisms in aggression. **[4 marks]**

0 4 Outline and briefly evaluate **one** research study which investigated the role of the limbic
system in aggression. **[4 marks]**

0 5 Outline and briefly evaluate the role of the MAOA gene in aggression. **[4 marks]**

0 6 Read the item below and answer the question that follows.

> Research has shown that aggressive behaviour often runs in families. For example, men convicted of violent crime
> are more likely to have fathers convicted of violent crime than other types of criminals.

Discuss the role of genetic factors in aggression. Refer to the item above as part of your discussion. **[16 marks]**

0 7 Outline **one** example of a fixed action pattern used in aggression. **[2 marks]**

0 8 Which one of the following statements about an innate releasing mechanism is **false**?
Write the letter of your chosen answer in your answer booklet. **[1 mark]**

    A. It activates fixed action patterns.

    B. It is a neural mechanism.

    C. It is strengthened through experience.

    D. It is triggered by a sign stimulus.

0 9 'An ethological approach better explains aggression in other animals besides humans.'

With reference to the above statement, discuss ethological explanations of aggression. **[16 marks]**

1 0 Describe and evaluate evolutionary explanations of aggression. Refer to **at least one**
social-psychological explanation as part of your evaluation. **[16 marks]**

1 1 Read the item below and answer the questions that follow.

> Holly blames her aggression on being exposed to violent role models in the media.
> Stuart blames his aggression on instinctive urges that he believes he cannot control.
> Gabriella blames her aggression on all the barriers that seem to stop her from progressing in life.

    (i) Identify the person whose comment supports the frustration-aggression hypothesis. **[1 mark]**

    (ii) Identify the person whose comment supports the social learning theory. **[1 mark]**

1 2 Describe **two** limitations of the frustration-aggression hypothesis. **[4 marks]**

1 3 Read the item below and answer the question that follows.

> Frank returned from spending an afternoon in town with a gang of mates. He could not believe that he had joined in
> their attack on an innocent youth. Frank wasn't normally so violent, but once he and his mates had pulled up their
> hoods and started to chase the youth, he had felt a real surge of aggression.

Using your knowledge of de-individuation, explain Frank's aggressive behaviour. **[4 marks]**

1 4 Describe and evaluate research into social learning theory as applied to aggression. **[16 marks]**

| 1 5 | Discuss **two** social psychological explanations of human aggression. | [16 marks] |

| 1 6 | Distinguish between dispositional and situational explanations of aggression. | [4 marks] |

| 1 7 | Read the item below and answer the question that follows.

> Vanessa has recently been appointed the warden of a prison with a reputation for violent behaviour. The inmates frequently attack each other, and sometimes the guards too. There have been a number of riots in recent years too. Vanessa wants to understand why the prison is so violent before she introduces any new policies or procedures.

Using your knowledge of institutional aggression, outline **at least two** reasons why Vanessa's prison is so violent. | [6 marks] |

| 1 8 | Describe and evaluate the situational explanation of institutional aggression. Refer to the dispositional explanation as part of your evaluation. | [16 marks] |

| 1 9 | Explain the difference between desensitisation and disinhibition with reference to media influences on aggression. | [4 marks] |

| 2 0 | Read the item below and answer the question that follows.

> Kristian has stopped watching violent films because he was concerned that they were encouraging him to have aggressive thoughts. One night, after watching a particularly violent film, he had a real urge to go to his local bar and start a fight.

Using your knowledge of cognitive priming, explain why Kristian may behave more aggressively after watching violent films. | [4 marks] |

| 2 1 | Briefly discuss the view that computer games can have an influence on aggression. | [6 marks] |

| 2 2 | 'It is important to monitor and regulate media output because of the influence it can have on aggressive behaviour.'

Discuss the extent to which the media influences aggressive behaviour. Refer to the statement above as part of your discussion. | [16 marks] |

| 2 3 | Read the item below and then answer the questions that follow.

> A psychologist investigated the effects of computer games on aggressive behaviour. Using content analysis, he categorised a selection of computer games as aggressive or neutral. He randomly selected three games from each category.
>
> Using 20 volunteers as participants, he used an independent groups design where 10 participants played three aggressive computer games one after the other while the other 10 played three neutral games one after the other.
>
> Immediately after playing the games, the participants completed a questionnaire which scored their current levels of aggression using statements followed by rating scales. The median score for the group who played aggressive computer games was 12.5, whereas the median for the other group was 8.

(i) Outline how content analysis could have been used to categorise the computer games. [3 marks]

(ii) Outline how the psychologist could have randomly selected three games from a category. [2 marks]

(iii) Explain **one** limitation of using an independent groups design in this study. [2 marks]

(iv) Explain **one** strength of using a questionnaire to measure current levels of aggression. [2 marks]

(v) Give **one** reason why the median was an appropriate measure of central tendency in this study. [1 mark]

| 2 4 | Read the item below and then answer the questions that follow.

> A group of psychologists conducted a covert observation to investigate if men displayed more aggressive behaviours in the presence of women rather than if there were no women present. They observed men in a number of contexts including nightclubs, leisure centres, shopping centres and parks. Each time, a different group of males was observed as all situations were naturally occurring.

(i) Outline **one** advantage and **one** disadvantage of using a covert observation in this study. [4 marks]

(ii) Identify an inferential test that could be used to analyse the data from this study. Give **two** reasons for your choice of test. [3 marks]

(iii) State why the study could be said to have 'high ecological validity'. [1 mark]

The exam questions on aggression will be varied but are likely to involve some short answer questions (AO1), some application of knowledge questions (AO2), research methods questions and possibly an extended writing question (AO1 + AO3). We've provided answers to some additional questions together with comments from an examiner about how well they've each done.

---

01 Outline and briefly evaluate the role of the MAOA gene in aggression. *(4 marks)*

Maisie's answer

MAOA is involved in aggression. The MAOA gene was found to be common in a Dutch family who were particularly aggressive. Many of them had been in trouble for their violent behaviour. The link between the MAOA gene and aggression helps to explain gender differences in aggressive behaviour, with males typically showing more aggression than females. This is because the MAOA is carried on the X chromosome.

Examiner's comments

There is little substance to Maisie's answers. The questions already tells us that there is a link between the MAOA gene and aggression and that is essentially what the response tells us too. There is a brief reference to evidence and to the X chromosome but nothing is explained to show understanding. 1 mark overall.

Ciaran's answer

The MAOA gene is responsible for producing MAOA, which regulates metabolism of serotonin in the brain, and low levels of serotonin are associated with impulsive and aggressive behaviour. Defects in this gene have been associated with aggressive behaviour. A study by Tilhonen et al. (2015) provided support that the MAOA gene is involved in extreme aggressive behaviours. They found that a particular variant of this gene (MAOA-L) in combination with the CDH13 gene was associated with extremely violent behaviour in Finnish prisoners, but not with other forms of criminal behaviour, suggesting that this combination of genes was associated only with violent behaviour.

Examiner's comments

Ciaran earns 3 marks for his answer. Two AO1 marks are awarded for the knowledge and understanding of the effect of the gene – which is partly done through evidence. The use of evidence is worth an AO3 mark in itself, but there is not enough evaluation for full marks. Ciaran could possibly have questioned the extent to which a gene can explain aggressive behaviour.

---

02 Outline **one** example of a fixed action pattern used in aggression. *(2 marks)*

Maisie's answer

A fixed action pattern used in aggression is the aggressive behaviour of male fish when they see another male.

Examiner's comments

No marks for this response. Although Maisie knows FAP applies to animals and that aggression can be male on male, this is not much more than common sense.

Ciaran's answer

An example of a fixed action pattern used in aggression is the aggressive attack behaviour of a male stickleback when they see the sign stimulus of the red underbelly of another male.

Examiner's comments

Ciaran earns 2 marks for this response. There is some detail on the type of aggression (males attacking males) and, importantly, the trigger for the FAP is included too.

---

03 Read the item below and answer the question that follows.

> Frank returned from a spending an afternoon in town with a gang of mates. He could not believe that he had joined in their attack on an innocent youth. Frank wasn't normally so violent but once he and his mates had pulled up their hoods and started to chase the youth, he had felt a real surge of aggression.

Using your knowledge of de-individuation, explain Frank's aggressive behaviour. *(4 marks)*

Maisie's answer

Frank is de-individuated because he is with a group of mates rather than being on his own. He isn't normally aggressive when he is in an individuated state, but with his hood up and being surrounded by his mates, he slips into a de-individuated state. In this state he is more likely to act aggressively, which is what happens when he attacks the youth.

Examiner's comments

Maisie just manages to earn 2 marks. Although she shows no explicit knowledge of de-individuation, she understands that it increases the likelihood of aggression and earns one AO1 mark for this. She also earns an AO2 mark for making the link between de-individuation and being in a group with hoods up.

Ciaran's answer

People are in a de-individuated state in conditions that increase feelings of anonymity. There are two things mentioned in the description that suggest de-individuation is the cause of Frank's aggressive behaviour. First, he is with a group of mates and second, he wears his hood up to increase feelings of anonymity. Anonymity decreases any concerns about being evaluated negatively by others and also removes any feelings of guilt that Frank might feel after attacking an innocent youth. Frank's situation is similar to Zimbardo's prison study where the uniforms of mirrored sunglasses made the guards act more aggressively toward the prisoners.

Examiner's comments

Ciaran earns 3 marks for his answer. He is awarded both AO1 marks – one for a definition of de-individuation at the start and then a further mark for an explanation of its effect later in the response. He is awarded one of the AO2 marks for making the link with being in a group with a hood up. However, to be awarded the second AO2 mark, Ciaran would need to explain more fully how each of these leads to anonymity. The inclusion of Zimbardo's research was not necessary here and adds nothing to this particular response.

04 Describe and evaluate the situational explanation of institutional aggression. Refer to the dispositional explanation as part of your evaluation. *(16 marks)*

Maisie's answer

The situational explanation of institutional aggression sees violence as being caused by the specific situation that people find themselves in, e.g. when they are in prisons, which are known to be violent places. This is often called the deprivation model, because people are deprived of things that they would usually have outside the prison. For example, prisoners may be deprived of home comforts and privacy, and so experience frustration. As a result, they become aggressive and so get into fights with other prisoners or get into trouble with the authorities.

There is evidence to support this explanation. A study by McCorkle et al., which took place in American prisons, found that different aspects of the situation were the main causes of aggressive behaviour within the prisons. In particular it was things like overcrowding and the lack of privacy. It was these situational factors that were most responsible for things like attacks on other prisoners and on members of the prison staff. Not all research supports this explanation though. Another study carried out within US prisons found that it was not so much the situation that made prisoners violent but the violent nature of the individuals that made up the prison population.

A second way of explaining institutional aggression is the dispositional model. This claims that prisoners often come from a violent background, for example they may be in violent gangs, and so when they get into prison they bring the violence that they learned from their gangs into the prison. This is often referred to as the importation model of institutional aggression because violent behaviour is thought to be imported into prison rather than being caused by the deprivation experienced within the prison itself.

Although there is some support for this explanation, there are also studies that challenge it. For example, one study found that violent gang members were no more likely to be violent when in prison than the other prisoners who had not been members of violent gangs before coming into prison. However, this might be explained by the fact that in many prisons, the most violent prisoners are kept separate from the rest of the prison population and are more closely supervised, so don't have the same opportunity to commit violent acts against other prisoners.   *378 words*

Examiner's comments

Maisie's essay would be awarded a level 2 mark. She demonstrates knowledge and some understanding of the situational explanation of institutional aggression and does this through describing relevant evidence as well as theory. Evidence is also used effectively to challenge the explanation and this earns AO3 marks. Maisie does consider the dispositional explanation as directed, and this also counts as AO3. Maisie could have developed this part of the essay by drawing out more comparisons between explanations rather than just describing an alternative explanation. In general, the essay needs more AO3 content as there are more marks available for this. Maisie should have considered including more explicit criticisms of the situational explanation to help with this.

---

05 'It is important to monitor and regulate media output because of the influence it can have on aggressive behaviour.'
Discuss the extent to which the media influences aggressive behaviour. Refer to the statement above as part of your discussion. *(16 marks)*

Ciaran's answer

A meta-analysis that looked at the impact of violent TV (Bushman and Huesmann, 2006) showed a significant, but small, relationship between exposure to media violence and aggressive thoughts and behaviours. This suggests that media output may not need be monitored as much as it is. However, violent media had both short-term and long-term effects. The short-term effects tended to be greater for adults than for children and the long-term effects were greater for children than for adults. On this basis, we may need to regulate more of what children are exposed to compared to adults – as seems to happen currently (e.g. age related certification of films).

Porter and Starcevic (2007) claim the interactive nature of violent video games has the potential to have more influence than TV violence, where the viewer is more passive. This would suggest that regulation of video game violence is more important because the potential for negative effects is greater. Anderson et al. (2007) surveyed 7 to 9 year old children at two points in the school year and found that those children who had high exposure to violent video games between these two points became more aggressive. Greitemeyer and Mügge (2014) found that violent video game use was linked both to an increase in aggressive behaviour and a decrease in prosocial behaviour.

A problem for research on the relationship between media violence and aggressive behaviour is that although many studies have shown a relationship between media violence and violent behaviour, very few of these studies have actually measured aggression against another person. Ferguson and Kilburn (2009) claim that when aggression towards another person is used as a measure of aggression, the relationship is close to zero. This is a major weakness of experimental research on violent video games because, for ethical reasons, researchers cannot measure 'real-life' aggression. As a result, they have to use measures of aggressive behaviour that have little relationship to real-life aggression, including giving noise blasts or hot chilli sauce to another person. Therefore, is it right to monitor and regulate on the basis of evidence which potentially lacks validity?

Livingstone (1996) suggests that many studies in this area have tended to use unrepresentative samples (e.g. male students), which makes it difficult to generalise the findings of such research to all viewers. As the quotation suggests regulating media output because of its effect on viewers, it would be inappropriate to introduce regulation based on such a narrow sample of the overall population. Ferguson et al. (2009) claims that many studies of violent video games have failed to control for other variables that influence aggressive behaviour. They argue that these other risk factors (such as family violence), are the primary cause of aggressive and violent behaviour, and are the reason why some people engage in aggressive behaviour and why they play violent video games.

Przybylski et al. (2014) found that it was not the violent storyline or imagery of video games, but the lack of mastery and the difficulty individuals had in completing the game that led to frustration and aggression. Games can leave players feeling aggressive if they are poorly designed or too difficult. Monitoring video games, therefore, focuses too much on the violent content and not enough on the likelihood that they will frustrate players or be too difficult for them to succeed.   *553 words*

Examiner's comments

Ciaran's essay demonstrates very good knowledge of the influence of the media on aggression and this is demonstrated through a series of relevant studies. Ciaran is good at not just evaluating the evidence but then relating this back to the focus of the question. The essay has a good discursive style, and is well structured around the debate. A real strength of Ciaran's response is the way that he refers to the statement throughout his commentary, something he has to do to secure a mark at level 4.

CONTENTS OF CHAPTER

SPECIFICATION CHECKLIST

- Problems in defining crime. Ways of measuring crime, including official statistics, victim surveys and offender surveys.

- Offender profiling: the top-down approach, including organised and disorganised types of offender; the bottom-up approach, including investigative psychology; geographical profiling.

- Biological explanations of offending behaviour: a historical approach (atavistic form); genetics and neural explanations.

- Psychological explanations of offending behaviour: Eysenck's theory of the criminal personality; cognitive explanations; level of moral reasoning and cognitive distortions, including hostile attribution bias and minimalisation; differential association theory; psychodynamic explanations.

- Dealing with offending behaviour: the aims of custodial sentencing and the psychological effects of custodial sentencing. Recidivism. Behaviour modification in custody. Anger management and restorative justice programmes.

TRY THIS

Are criminals born or are they made?

Is it nature or nurture? Much of this chapter is concerned with biological and psychological explanations of offender behaviour. One possibility is that people have an innate personality type which predisposes them to become criminal. Hans Eysenck argued that this was possible (this theory is discussed on pages 266–267). He identified three dimensions of personality – extraversion, neuroticism and psychoticism. According to Eysenck, each of these has a biological basis. For example, he argued that extraverts are biologically under-aroused and therefore seek stimulation to increase their physiological arousal. One way to do this is to engage in risky behaviours – an ingredient of the criminal personality.

Eysenck developed a questionnaire, the *Eysenck Personality Questionnaire* (EPQ) to assess the three personality characteristics. The full EPQ has 100 items, but several shorter versions have been compiled and validated against the original (concurrent validity), including the 24-item version below (Sato, 2005).

Write the numbers 1 to 24 on a piece of paper and record your answer for each question – either yes or no.

Eysenck Personality Questionnaire

1. Are you a talkative person?
2. Does your mood often go up and down?
3. Are you rather lively?
4. Do you ever feel miserable for no reason?
5. Do you enjoy meeting new people?
6. Are you an irritable person?
7. Can you usually let yourself go and enjoy yourself at a lively party?
8. Are your feelings easily hurt?
9. Do you usually take the initiative in making new friends?
10. Do you often feel 'fed-up'?
11. Can you easily get some life into a rather dull party?
12. Would you call yourself a nervous person?
13. Do you tend to keep in the background on social occasions?
14. Are you a worrier?
15. Do you like mixing with people?
16. Would you call yourself tense or 'highly strung'?
17. Do you like plenty of action and excitement around you?
18. Do you worry too long after an embarrassing experience?
19. Are you mostly quiet when you are with other people?
20. Do you suffer from nerves?
21. Do other people think of you as being very lively?
22. Do you often feel lonely?
23. Can you get a party going?
24. Are you often troubled about feelings of guilt?

Scoring

For numbers 3, 5, 7, 10, 15, 16, 17, 19, 20, 22 you score 1 mark for No and 0 for Yes. For all other numbers you score 0 marks for No and 1 for Yes.

    Extraversion score – add scores for questions 1, 9, 11, 14, 18, 21
    Neuroticism score – add scores for questions 2, 4, 13, 15, 20, 23
    Psychoticism score – add scores for questions 3, 6, 8, 12, 16, 22

There is also a lie scale – add your scores for questions 5, 7, 10, 17, 19, 24

This lie scale tells you how truthful you were in your answers. Data from people with a high lie score should be discarded as lacking validity.

Offender profiling: The top-down approach

Offender profiling relates to popular conceptions of how murderers are caught, as portrayed in books, TV and films – the police build up a picture of who they are looking for and this enables them to make an arrest.

In reality it is not possible to identify someone so easily; offender profiling is less concerned with actually catching a suspect and more with narrowing down the number of potential suspects. Two different methods of offender profiling have been developed. The first, the **top-down approach**, starts from a general classification of the crime scene and then a profiler uses this classification to drill down to make judgements about likely offenders who would fit the circumstances (going from classification to data). The alternative, bottom-up approach also collects details of the crime scene, but this data is then analysed using statistical techniques to generate predictions (going from data to classification).

KEY TERMS

Disorganised type of offender The crime scene is left with many clues such as fingerprints, there is little evidence of engagement with the victim, and the offender has lower intelligence and competence.

Offender profiling A method of working out the characteristics of an offender by examining the characteristics of the crime and crime scene.

Organised type of offender This type of offender commits a planned crime and may engage in violent fantasies with the victim and is high in intelligence and socially competent.

Top-down approach (also called crime scene analysis) An analysis of previous crimes creates a profile of a likely offender. A profiler uses this knowledge to narrow the field of possible suspects. Unlike the bottom-up approach, the top-down approach relies on the intuition and beliefs of the profiler.

◀ The FBI wanted poster for Theodore Robert 'Ted' Bundy.

Ted Bundy is often given as an example of an organised type of offender. He was intelligent, having a degree in psychology and studying law. He had several serious relationships and even married during the course of one of his trials. He ultimately confessed to 30 murders of women but it may have been as many as 100. He was handsome and charismatic and often lured women in public places to a more secluded spot where he murdered them violently. He left very little evidence at any crime scene, using his extensive knowledge of the law, and was very deliberate in his planning. He maintained an interest in the victims after their death, revisiting crime scenes as well as the decomposing bodies.

THE TOP-DOWN APPROACH

The top-down approach originates with the FBI (Federal Bureau of Investigation) in the US. This method was first developed as a way of trying to solve some of the most bizarre and extreme murder cases and designed to produce a profile of the most likely offender. In contrast with the bottom-up approach (on the following spread), the top-down approach is regarded as a more intuitive application of a profiler's prior knowledge – the profiler has a 'feel' for the kind of person who committed the crime (i.e. a less explicit line of reasoning). The bottom-up approach is regarded as more scientific and logical.

There are six main stages in the top-down process (Douglas *et al.*, 2006):

1. Profiling inputs

The data collected at this stage includes a description of the crime scene (including photographs and sketches), background information about the victim (employment, habits, relationships) and details of the crime itself (weapon, cause of death autopsy report). All information, even if it appears trivial, should be included. Possible suspects should not be considered, as this may bias the information collected.

2. Decision process models

The profiler starts to make decisions about the data and organises it into meaningful patterns. Some of the following issues are considered:

- Murder type – mass, spree or serial murders (a spree murder is one where a number of people are killed at one time, e.g. in one hour, whereas serial murders are committed over an extended period of time, e.g. several months).
- Time factors – did the crime take a short or long time, and was it at night or during the day?
- Location factors – was the crime scene (e.g. where a person was kidnapped) the same as the murder scene?

3. Crime assessment

Based on data collected, the crime is classified as organised or disorganised. This organised–disorganised distinction presumes that there is a correspondence between offences and offenders.

- **Organised type of offender** – the crime tends to be planned and the victim is specifically targeted, the body is often transported from the scene, the weapon is usually hidden and violent fantasies may be acted out on the victim. Such offenders are generally high in intelligence, socially and sexually competent, they usually live with a partner, have a car in good working order and follow their crimes in the media.
- **Disorganised type of offender** – is the opposite: tends to be an unplanned crime, random selection of victim, offender likely to engage very little with the victim and sexual acts are performed after death on the body. The crime scene is likely to contain many clues such as blood and semen from the offender, fingerprints and the weapon.

4. Criminal profile

A profile is now constructed of the offender which includes hypotheses about their likely background, habits and beliefs of the offender. This description is used to work out a strategy for the investigation to help catch the offender. It is important to anticipate how this person will respond to various investigative efforts, including how the offender might be interviewed if he was caught.

5. Crime assessment

A written report is given to the investigating agency (e.g. the police) and persons matching the profile are evaluated. If new evidence is generated and/or no suspect is identified, then the process goes back to step 2.

6. Apprehension

If a suspect is apprehended, the entire profile-generating process is reviewed to check that at each stage the conclusions made were legitimate, i.e. valid, and consider how the process may be revised for future cases.

Is the method useful?

Police who have used FBI methods believe it is useful. For example, Copson (1995) questioned 184 US police officers, of whom 82% said the technique was operationally useful and over 90% said they would use it again.

The technique may not result in an actual identification of the offender, but Scherer and Jarvis (2014) defend the use of top-down processing by looking at other potential contributions beyond the identification of the offender. For example, the approach offers investigators a different perspective, opens up new avenues for investigation and may prevent wrongful conviction.

The basis of the method flawed

The original data on which the organised/disorganised classification is based came from interviews with 36 of the most dangerous and sexually motivated murderers, including Ted Bundy and Charles Manson. The data was used to identify the key characteristics that would help police 'read' a crime scene. This in itself is dubious, as such individuals (who are highly manipulative) are not likely to be the best source of reliable information. In addition, their approach and rationale may be quite different to more 'typical' offenders.

On the other hand, the six-stage process outlined on the facing page allows improvements to constantly be made.

Potential harm caused by using top-down approaches

Brent Snook et al. (2008) argue that profilers actually do little more than psychics who, it could equally be argued, often have a wealth of experience in 'reading' behaviour. The process of top-down analysis is not based in any science or theory; in fact, courts have been known to regard it as 'junk science'. The believability of profiles based on the top-down approach might be explained in terms of the *Barnum effect* – ambiguous descriptions can be made to fit any situation, such as in the case of horoscopes. We might expect that, in a list of 20 statements about a person, 10 will often be correct or nearly correct, and this explains why profiles often appear to be 'right'.

This might be acceptable if it were not for the fact that profiling has the potential to cause harm because profiles may mislead investigations if they are wrong. In fact, Jackson and Bekerian (1997) suggest that smart offenders can read about how profiles are constructed and deliberately mislead profilers by providing misleading clues. This raises the question about whether information about the techniques used by the police should be generally available.

Measuring the accuracy of the approach

The data on usefulness can also be questioned in terms of how usefulness is measured. One way to measure usefulness is to consider, at the end of the case, how close the profile is to actual offender characteristics. If they are close, this demonstrates the usefulness of the method. However, a study by Alison et al. (2003) shows that such judgements are not reliable. In this study police officers were given a profile along with one of two versions of the offender's actual characteristics (one of these versions was real) – for example, in the 'real' version they were told the offender was 37, knew the victim, etc. and in the fake version participants were told the offender was 19, did not know the victim, etc. Over 50% of the officers rated the profile they were given as generally or very accurate, even though half of them were given a fake version.

Distinguishing between organised and disorganised types of offender

Turvey (1999) suggests that such a dichotomy is false as it is more likely to be a continuum rather than two distinct categories. This is further supported by the fact that the descriptions may, at best, be generalisations as they use phrases such as 'tends to be' and thus have little utility. One solution, proposed by Douglas et al. (1992), was to have a third category called the 'mixed' offender, but this would seem to lessen the usefulness of the classification because there is now a kind of dustbin category.

David Canter et al. (2004) provided evidence that the classification has little basis in reality. They analysed 39 aspects of serial killings in murders committed by 100 US serial killers. Their analysis revealed no clear division between organised and disorganised types of offender. Instead they found a number of subsets of organised-type crimes and little evidence for disorganised types.

▲ Some people suggest that experienced profilers are not actually doing anything more than psychics because the top-down process is not informed by science or theory.

APPLY YOUR KNOWLEDGE

Laura is a forensic psychologist who works with Merseyside Police. She is called in to construct an offender profile following a spate of murders in the region. There have been five similar murders over the previous 18 months, and the police believe they may be the work of one person.

She discovers that there is a pattern to the murders. The bodies are always dumped in remote wooded areas well away from where the murder has taken place. The victims typically live alone and are known drug abusers. Even the way in which the murders are carried out follows a pattern, with strangling being the killing method of choice.

Using your knowledge of the top-down approach, outline a brief offender profile for these crimes.

CAN YOU? No. 10.2

1. Explain what is meant by an *organised type of offender*. (2 marks)
2. Distinguish between an organised and a disorganised type of offender. (4 marks)
3. Briefly explain how the top-down approach is used to create an offender profile. (4 marks)
4. Discuss the top-down approach to offender profiling. (16 marks)

Offender profiling: The bottom-up approach

A distinction is made between the US crime scene analysis approach to offender profiling (discussed on the previous spread) and the British approach called **investigative psychology**. This British approach offers a **bottom-up approach**. Both the US and British approach, rely on an analysis of the crime scene and making inferences from this about possible offenders. However, in the bottom-up approach, the inferences (profiles) are driven from the actual data rather than from 'above' by the judgements of a profiler.

MEET THE RESEARCHER

David Canter began his psychology career with an interest in environmental psychology, exploring how people made sense of the places where they lived, such as buildings and urban environments. This work led to studies of how people react in emergencies and to investigative psychology.

Canter came to public notice through his involvement in the case of the Railway Rapist. During the 1970s and 80s a number of young women were raped and some were murdered at railway stations in the London area. Police sought help from David Canter, who drew up a profile based on interviews with rape survivors and other clues from the crimes. Canter predicted the following details about the murderer:

- Aged 25 to 30 years, about 5'9", fair-haired.
- Probably semi-skilled, not working with public.
- Living in Kilburn/Cricklewood area of London.
- Had a few close friends but more of a loner.
- Had a wife or girlfriend.
- Knew the railway system.
- Martial arts/body builder.
- Probably arrested between October 1982 and January 1984 because there was a pause in the crimes.

The police re-interviewed 2,000 potential suspects and one of them matched many of the aspects of the profile created by Canter. This led to the arrest and subsequent conviction of John Duffy. It later emerged that Duffy had committed the crimes with John Mulcahy.

THE BOTTOM-UP APPROACH

There are two examples of the data-driven approach that we will discuss: investigative psychology and geographic profiling.

Investigative psychology

This approach was developed by David Canter, a psychologist who proposed that profiling can and should be based on psychological theory and research. There are three main features of his approach, as described below:

Interpersonal coherence

People are consistent in their behaviour and therefore there will be links (correlations) with elements of the crime and how people behave in everyday life. At the same time people's behaviour changes over time, and therefore looking at the differences in crimes over a four-year period might offer further clues.

Forensic awareness

Certain behaviours may reveal an awareness of particular police techniques and past experience; for example, Davies *et al.* (1997) found that rapists who conceal fingerprints often had a previous conviction for burglary.

Smallest space analysis

This is a statistical technique developed by Canter (and used in his research described on the previous page). Data about many crime scenes and offender characteristics are correlated so that most common connections can be identified. For example, Gabrielle Salfati and David Canter (1999) analysed the co-occurrence of 48 crime scene and offender characteristics taken from 82 UK murder cases where the victim was a stranger. They were able to identify three underlying themes:

- Instrumental opportunistic – 'instrumental' refers to using murder to obtain something or accomplish a goal; 'opportunistic' means that the offender took the easiest opportunities.
- Instrumental cognitive – a particular concern about being detected and therefore more planned.
- Expressive impulsive – uncontrolled, in the heat of strong emotions, may feel provoked by victim.

Geographical profiling

Canter has also proposed that people do not just reveal themselves through the crimes they commit but also through the locations they choose. Geographical profilers are concerned with where rather than who. It makes sense to assume that offenders are more likely to commit a crime near where they live or where they habitually travel to because it involves least effort. Thus the location of a crime can be a prime clue in an investigation.

Geographical profiling analyses the locations of a connected series of crimes and considers where the crimes were committed, the spatial relationships between different crime scenes and how they might relate to an offender's place of residence.

Circle theory

David Canter and Paul Larkin (1993) proposed that most offenders have a spatial mindset – they commit their crimes within a kind of imagined circle.

- Marauder – the offender's home is within the geographical area in which crimes are committed.
- Commuter – the offender travels to another geographical area and commits crimes within a defined space around which a circle can be drawn.

Criminal geographic targeting (CGT)

This is a computerised system developed by Kim Rossmo and based on Rossmo's formula.

The formula produces a three-dimensional map (see example on right) displaying spatial data related to time, distance and movement to and from crime scenes. The map is called a *jeopardy surface*. The different colours indicate likely closeness to crime scene.

A jeopardy surface: probability of offender residence

Scientific basis of the bottom-up approach

One advantage claimed for bottom-up approaches is that they are considered to be more scientific than top-down approaches because of the use of objective statistical techniques and computer analysis. However, such techniques are only as good as the data that is input and the underlying assumptions used to work out links between data items. One issue is that the data that is used to drive such systems is only related to offenders who have been caught, and therefore this tells us little about patterns of behaviour related to unsolved crimes.

In terms of computer programming, someone has to develop the formula that are used and these may be incorrect. For example, the jeopardy surface shown on the facing page is based on Rossmo's formula, which has been criticised (see below).

This means that bottom-up approaches may have the potential to be objective and systematic (i.e. scientific), but in practice they are inevitably biased.

Is investigative psychology useful?

Canter's very first attempt at profiling (see 'MEET THE RESEARCHER' on the facing page) was very impressive and led to police interest in the method. Some research supports the usefulness of the approach; for example, Gary Copson (1995) surveyed 48 UK police forces using investigative profiling and found that over 75% of the police officers questioned said that profilers' advice had been useful. However, only 3% said that the advice had helped identify the actual offender – nevertheless most said they would use a profiler again. This suggests that the method may not be that useful in actually catching offenders, but the slight benefit that it affords makes it worthwhile.

It should be pointed out that by no means all police use profilers. In Copson's study, in one year, the maximum number of crimes per year where profiling was used was only 75 cases.

Is circle theory successful?

Canter and Larkin (1993) studied 45 sexual assaults and showed support for their model by distinguishing between marauders and commuters. However, 91% of the offenders were identified as marauders – if almost all offenders are marauders, then the classification doesn't seem particularly useful.

Petherick (2006) pointed to a number of flaws with the model. For example, if a person's home base is not actually at the centre of the circle, this means that police may look in the wrong place. Also, representing ranges in terms of circles is oversimplistic, and in cities the patterns may form an ellipse or some other shape.

Is geographic profiling generally successful?

Rossmo (1999) is one of the key supporters of the geographical approach and claims that, while it may not solve crimes specifically, it can be useful in prioritising house-to-house searches or identifying a geographical area where DNA could be collected. However, one issue is that it can't distinguish between multiple offenders in the same area, and also the method is simply limited to spatial behaviour (not any personality characteristics). As such it is questionable as to how much more it offers than the traditional method of police placing pins on a map to see where a group of crimes were committed.

Rossmo worked for many years for the Vancouver Police Department and introduced geographical profiling to the Department. In 2001 he was dismissed, and the Department ceased using his methods as they did not feel it enhanced policing outcomes (Turvey, 2011). Rossmo continues to promote geographic profiling and his software.

Final conclusions

Taken overall, the success rates for offender profiling and the views of police forces who have used the techniques suggest that what profiling can't reliably do is identify an offender. What profiling can do is assist police is narrowing down the field of possibilities. The big danger lies in sticking too closely to any one profile, as was the case in the murder of Rachel Nickell. In 1992 the 21-year-old mother was stabbed to death. The forensic psychologist Paul Britton helped the police to create a profile which led to the identification of Colin Stagg. It later turned out, after having spent a considerable amount of time and money trying to convict Colin Stagg, that the actual murderer was Robert Napper, who had been ruled out because he was taller than the picture given in the profile.

▲ Offender profiling techniques are reminiscent of the methods used by fictional detectives such as Hercule Poirot, Sherlock Holmes and Miss Marple. They too solved crimes all by looking for patterns of behaviour and drawing on their past experience. Top down or bottom up?

⬆ UPGRADE

The second question below asks you to distinguish between two approaches to offender profiling, i.e. the top-down and bottom-up approaches. There is a temptation to just outline each approach without actually saying how they are different. That would certainly not get you the full 4 marks.

These are not difficult questions to answer, but there are a couple of things to remember to make sure you get all the marks available.

First, the really important information... In AQA marking guidelines for this sort of question, the instruction to examiners states that 'The question is about differences, so no credit is given for simply describing the two approaches'. So there you have it – ignore the instruction to 'distinguish between' and you end up with zero marks.

The second thing is to add a bit of detail to your answer. You could outline one difference between the two approaches in detail or perhaps two differences in less detail. For example, if you state that a difference between the two approaches is the degree to which they make use of existing crime scene evidence to build a profile, then you could add detail by describing how the two different approaches are different in this respect.

CAN YOU? No. 10.3

1. Explain what is meant by *geographic profiling*. (2 marks)
2. Distinguish between the top-down and bottom-up approach to offender profiling. (4 marks)
3. Briefly explain how investigative psychology is used to create an offender profile. (4 marks)
4. Discuss the bottom-up approach to offender profiling. (16 marks)

Biological explanations of offending behaviour: A historical approach

Over the coming spreads we are going to consider explanations about why people become criminals. Why do some people commit crimes and others don't? Like any other area of psychology, we will consider whether it is nature or nurture – something in a person's biological make-up or something more related to life experiences.

We begin with two biological explanations. One of the earliest explanations of criminal behaviour, **atavistic form**, may seem bizarre and extreme yet it had a profound influence on the development of the study of criminology.

KEY TERM

Atavistic form An explanation for criminal behaviour, suggesting that certain individuals are born with a criminal personality and this innate personality is a throwback to earlier primate forms.

MEET THE RESEARCHER

Cesare Lombroso (1835–1909) was an Italian physician and psychiatrist working with the insane and also in prisons. Aside from his theories about the criminal mind he also wrote about artistic genius as a form of insanity. Later in life he became interested in spiritualism.

His work on criminal types influenced many writers, for example he is mentioned in books by Joseph Conrad and Leo Tolstoy. Bram Stoker, in his book *Dracula*, based the appearance of Count Dracula on Lombroso's idea of what a criminal type should look like. In the book Dracula is described as having massive eyebrows that meet across the nose, pointed ears and a thin nose with arched nostrils – and Stoker says these are the 'characteristics identified by Lombroso'.

▲ Death masks of criminals in the Cesare Lombroso Museum in Turin, Italy. The Museum of Criminal Anthropology was created by Lombroso in 1876.

CRIMINAL PERSONALITY TYPES

A general approach to explaining behaviour has been to identify different personality types based on physical characteristics. The Greeks were the first to link physical form to personality – they suggested that there were four personality types (sanguine, melancholic, choleric, phlegmatic) each related to a particular body fluid (called 'humours').

Atavistic form

Cesare Lombroso wrote *L'uomo delinquente* (The criminal man) in 1876 setting out his view that offenders possessed similar characteristics to lower primates and this could explain their criminality. He subsequently produced four further editions of this book, revising his views each time. He formulated his ideas at the time when Charles Darwin had recently introduced the theory of evolution. Based on this theory, Lombroso suggested that criminals are essentially throwbacks to an earlier species. 'Atavistic' means a tendency to revert to an ancestral type (*atavus* is the Latin for ancestor). Lombroso wrote:

> There is an 'asymmetry of the face, excessive dimensions of the jaw and cheekbones, eye defects and peculiarities. Ears of unusual size, or occasionally very small, or standing out from the head as do those of the chimpanzee; nose twisted, upturned, or flattened in thieves, or aquiline or beak-like in murderers, or with a tip rising like a peak from swollen nostrils… Chin receding, or excessively long, or short and flat, as in an ape… Excessive length of arms; [more than the usual number of] fingers and toes.'

In total, Turvey (2011) identifies 18 different characteristics that make up the atavistic type. The basic assumption is that the innate physiological make-up of the person causes them to become a criminal.

Lombroso also linked different features to different crimes in the final edition of his book containing an *Atlas of criminal types*.

Empirical evidence

Lombroso based his theory on his own research using post-mortem examinations of criminals and studying the faces of living criminals. He made precise measurements of skulls and other physiological characteristics – called *anthropometry*, the measurement of humans.

Over the course of his career he and his co-workers examined over 50,000 bodies. In one particular study of 383 convicted Italian criminals, he found that 21% had just one atavistic trait and 43% had at least five.

Environmental influences

Lombroso later recognised that it was unlikely that only one factor would be the cause of criminality. He proposed that inherited atavistic form interacted with a person's physical and social environment. This is still a determinist view because it suggests that factors outside a person's control (nature and nurture) determine whether they become criminal.

This led Lombroso, in later editions of his book (1897), to distinguish between three types of criminals, moving away from the atavistic form as the only explanation for criminality:

- *Born criminals* – the atavistic type; 'throwbacks' identifiable from their physical characteristics.
- *Insane criminals* – suffering from mental illness.
- *Criminaloids* – a large general class of offenders whose mental characteristics predisposed them to criminal behaviour under the right circumstances (i.e. certain physical/social environments).

Somatotypes

There were a number of other historical approaches to criminal types, some of them based on body shape or somatotype ('soma' is body). One of them, proposed by the German psychiatrist Ernst Kretschmer (1921), suggested that there were four types. This classification was based on his own studies of over 4,000 criminals:

- *Leptosome or asthenic* – tall and thin; petty thieves.
- *Athletic* – tall and muscular; crimes of violence.
- *Pyknic* – short and fat; commit crimes of deception and sometimes violence.
- *Dysplastic or mixed* – more than one type; crimes against morality (e.g. prostitution).

Contribution to the science of criminology

Many writers (e.g. Carrabine *et al.*, 2014) praise Lombroso's approach as he brought science to the study of crime. He is regarded as the founder of modern criminology. Prior to his work, the 'classical school' studied crime but not the criminal and assumed that crime was a choice (free will) which could be deterred if punished. Lombroso believed in less harsh treatment for criminals and a more humane view that both biology and environment may remove the option of free will. More importantly he felt that an evidence-based approach was required, which is what he tried to do. He based his ideas on empirical observation and detailed measurement. His methods and conclusions may now be criticised, but the key issue is that he raised the possibility of scientific studies of the criminal mind.

Criticisms of Lombroso's methods

The key failure in Lombroso's research was the lack of adequate controls. When he studied prisoners he didn't pay the same kind of attention to non-prisoners. Had he done so, it is likely that he would have found as many non-prisoners with the same characteristics as he found in prisoners.

A key study conducted by Charles Goring (1913) did just this. He compared 3,000 convicts with a group of non-convicts, finding no differences except for the fact that convicts were slightly smaller.

Gender bias

Lombroso (with his daughter Gina Ferrero) also wrote the book *La donna delinquente* (1893), setting out his ideas about female criminality. There is no doubt that he had some outlandish androcentric ideas about women which were even more inexcusable because he actually didn't study women directly. Lombroso believed that women were less evolved than men. They were naturally jealous and insensitive to pain but they were also passive, low in intelligence and had a maternal instinct – all of which neutralised their negative traits and meant they were less likely to be criminals. Those women who did become criminals, according to Lombroso, had masculine characteristics which were beneficial in a man but in a woman created a 'monster'. It is fairly easy to see typical nineteenth-century views about women in this characterisation.

Criticisms of somatotypes

Kretschmer's evidence has been criticised because it has never been presented for scrutiny and therefore it is not clear if it was actually based on fact. However, there has been some evidence to support the link between body type and criminality; for example, Glueck and Glueck (1970) found that 60% of delinquents were mesomorphs, roughly equivalent to the athletic type.

William Sheldon (1949) created a fairly similar set of somatotypes (ectomorphs, mesomorphs and endomorphs). Based on his own study of 200 young adults, he concluded that there were differences between delinquents and non-delinquents in terms of body type – the delinquents tended to be mesomorphs. This supports the notion of innate criminal types identified by their physical features.

Link between personality type and criminality

We may laugh at some of Lombroso's proposals, but the basic notion of criminal types has not gone away – they have just become more sophisticated (Canter, 2010). For instance, we look at Eysenck's theory of the criminal personality later in this chapter (page 266). Eysenck's theory is based on large data sets using rigorous research methods – but it is basically a theory of the relationship between personality types and criminality.

The same can be said about the next spread, which looks at genetics. The implication of research into genetics is that some people are born to be criminals, which is essentially the claim made by Lombroso – he just used language that seems unfamiliar and naïve (such as calling criminals 'throwbacks' to an earlier species).

Finally, it should also be emphasised that Lombroso, in subsequent editions of his book, suggested that the atavistic (or inherited) form was not the only basis of criminality, which is again in line with more modern conceptions.

▲ An aquiline nose is one that looks a little like an eagle's beak being slightly curved.

Research methods

A group of psychology students are interested in studying the idea of somatotypes, to see if there is any relationship between facial features and certain personality traits.

In order to do this they take photographs of people aged 15 to 25, and for each photo count up the number of atavistic traits. The maximum number is 18. They also give a questionnaire to each person they photograph to assess their moral standards. The questionnaire produces a score so that each participant can be classed as having high or low moral standards.

1. Write a suitable hypothesis for this study. (2 marks)
2. Is your hypothesis directional or non-directional? (1 mark)
3. Identify what statistical test would be appropriate to use and explain your choice. (3 marks)
4. In order to decide on the number of atavistic traits present in each photograph, two people examined the photograph. Explain why it was a good idea to have two people rate each photograph. (2 marks)
5. Select **one** atavistic trait and explain why it might be difficult to reliably categorise this feature. (2 marks)
6. Explain in what way the task of rating the photographs was an example of content analysis. (2 marks)
7. What ethical issues should the students have been concerned about? (4 marks)

LINK TO RESEARCH METHODS

Statistical tests on pages 24–32.
Content analysis on page 12.

CAN YOU?　No. 10.4

1. Outline the atavistic form as a biological explanation for offending behaviour. (4 marks)
2. Explain **one** criticism of the historical approach (atavistic form). (4 marks)
3. Discuss the historical approach to explaining offending behaviour. Include research on the atavistic form in your answer. (16 marks)

Biological explanations of offending behaviour: Genetic and neural

The idea that some people are born to be a criminal has origins in the work of Cesare Lombroso in the nineteenth century. Modern research methods have provided more insight into the actual genetic and neural mechanisms that underlie the inheritance of criminal traits – not facial characteristics (as Lombroso suggested), but those related to behaviour.

However, it is worth remembering that biological abnormalities may be the effect of life experience rather than genetic, i.e. not necessarily inherited. For example, a virus or accident may cause a brain injury. So we should not assume that neural explanations are linked to genetics.

▲ Criminal twins.

Identical (MZ) twins are genetically the same whereas DZ twins share about 50% of the same genes. If MZ twins are more likely to both be criminals than DZ twins this supports a genetic explanation. However, there is evidence that the environments for MZ twins are more similar than for DZ twins. For example, the fact that they look the same means they may be treated more similarly than DZ twins. This means that the concordance rates may reflect both greater genetic *and* environmental similarity.

KEY TERMS

Epigenetics refers to the material in each cell of the body that acts like a set of 'switches' to turn genes on or off.

Genetic explanations The likelihood of behaving in a particular way is determined by a person's genetic makeup, i.e. it is inherited from parents.

Neural explanations involve areas of the brain and nervous system and the action of chemical messengers in the brain known as neurotransmitters in controlling behaviour.

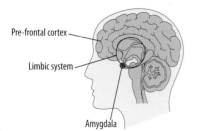

Pre-frontal cortex
Limbic system
Amygdala

GENETIC EXPLANATIONS

Genetic explanations propose that one or more genes predispose individuals to criminal behaviour. The evidence for a genetic component comes, for example, from twin studies where identical and non-identical (MZ and DZ) twins are compared. Adrian Raine (1993) reviewed research on the delinquent behaviour of twins and found 52% concordance for MZ twins compared with 21% for DZ twins.

Searching for candidate genes

Monoamine oxidase A (MAOA) On page 47 we discussed the case of Stephen Mobley who argued that he should escape the death penalty because he was not personally responsible for his behaviour – he was 'born to be a criminal'. This claim was based on research by Han Brunner on 28 male members of a Dutch family who had histories of impulsive and violent criminal behaviours such as rape and attempted murder (see page 231). Brunner *et al.* (1993) analysed the DNA of these men and found they shared a particular gene that led to abnormally low levels of MAOA.

Cadherin 13 (CDH13) A recent Finnish study by Jari Tiihonen *et al.* (2015) with 900 offenders found evidence of low MAOA activity and also low activity from the CDH13 gene. They estimated that 5–10% of all violent crime in Finland is due to abnormalities in one of these two genes.

Diathesis-stress

Modern understanding of genetic influence no longer proposes that one or even a few genes on their own will determine behaviour. Instead, current thinking in terms of **epigenetics** proposes an interplay where genes are 'switched' on or off by epigenomes, which in turn have been affected by environmental factors. One particular possibility is maltreatment in childhood (an environmental factor). Caspi *et al.* (2002) used data from the longitudinal Dunedin study (in New Zealand) that has followed about 1,000 people from when they were babies in the 1970s. Caspi *et al.* assessed anti-social behaviour at age 26 and found that 12% of those men with low MAOA genes had experienced maltreatment when they were babies but were responsible for 44% of violent convictions.

NEURAL EXPLANATIONS

Neural explanations consider how structures of the brain may be different in criminals as well as there being differences in neurotransmitter levels.

Regions of the brain

A common observation is that criminals report having had some head injury – in general 8.5% of the US population have had a brain injury compared with 60% in US prisons (Harmon, 2012). Therefore brain differences may be due to nurture – or they may be inherited (nature).

Prefrontal cortex Raine (2004) cited 71 brain imaging studies showing that murderers, psychopaths and violent individuals have reduced functioning in the prefrontal cortex, the area of the brain that is involved in regulating emotion and controlling moral behaviour in general. Lowered activity in this area is associated with impulsiveness and loss of control.

Limbic system This is a set of subcortical structures, such as the thalamus and the amygdala, that are linked to emotion and motivation. In another study Raine *et al.* (1997) studied murderers who were found not guilty by reason of insanity (NGRI). Compared with matched controls, they found abnormal asymmetries in the limbic system of the murderers, especially the amygdala – there was reduced activity on the left and increased activity on the right.

Neurotransmitters

Serotonin Researchers (e.g. Seo *et al.*, 2008) suggest that low levels of the neurotransmitter serotonin may predispose individuals to impulsive aggression and criminal behaviour, partly because this neurotransmitter normally inhibits the prefrontal cortex. Dopamine hyperactivity may enhance this effect.

Noradrenaline Both very high and very low levels of this neurotransmitter have been associated with aggression, violence and criminality (Wright *et al.*, 2015). High levels of noradrenaline are associated with activation of the sympathetic nervous system and the fight-or-flight response, and thus are linked to aggression. Noradrenaline also helps people react to perceived threats, so low levels would reduce this ability.

EVALUATION OF GENETIC EXPLANATIONS

Research support from adoption studies

Twin studies are not the only kind of genetic research undertaken that indicates there must be some element of inheritance in offending behaviour. Another line of evidence comes from adoption studies. Crowe (1972) found that adopted children who had a biological parent with a criminal record had a 50% greater risk of having a criminal record by the age of 18, whereas adopted children whose mother didn't have a criminal record only had a 5% risk. Mednick *et al.'s* (1987) study of 14,000 adoptees found that 15% of sons adopted by a criminal family went on to be criminals compared to 20% whose biological parents were criminal, suggesting that inherited genes are a marginally more significant factor.

Can genetic (and neural) explanations explain non-violent crimes?

Most of the genetic (and neural) research relates to the association between offending and violent or aggressive behaviour. Offending behaviour includes theft, fraud, drug use and bigamy – all non-violent. At best, biological explanations may just account for certain kinds of crimes such as those involving violence and also psychopathy – a psychopath is a person who lacks empathy with what other people feel and thus is more likely to commit crimes. There is evidence that this personality trait is inherited; for example, Blonigen *et al.* (2005) found support for a genetic basis looking at over 600 male and female twins.

Lynn Findlay (2011) points out that crime is 'neither a natural nor a homogenous category of behaviour; it is a social construction' – in other words, people have created the category of criminal behaviour and it includes many different types of crime. This makes it difficult to argue that such a behaviour can be simply explained in terms of genetics and its interaction with the environment.

Problems with determinist explanations

Genetic explanations are presented as if the genes a person is born with determine later behaviour. Indeed that was the argument put forward by Stephen Mobley's lawyers to excuse his crime (see facing page). The evidence on the facing page shows that criminality cannot be 100% explained in terms of genetics. In the study by Tiihonen *et al.*, those with the defective gene were 13 times more likely to have a history of repeated violent behaviour, but this means that not everyone with the gene had become an offender.

On the other hand, the law asks the question about whether the cause of behaviour is outside a person's control. At the very least it is harder for some men to avoid criminal violence – and this may be due to both their biology and the environment in which they grew up (as shown in the study by Caspi *et al.* on the facing page). Therefore a determinist view of criminal behaviour cannot be totally ruled out.

EVALUATION OF NEURAL EXPLANATIONS

Cause or effect?

Neural explanations also raise concerns about determinism (see above). One issue is about whether abnormalities in regions of the brain or levels of neurotransmitters are the cause of offending behaviour, the result of it or actually just an intervening variable. Research only highlights a correlation between head injuries and later criminality. It is possible that it is a spurious relationship; for example, someone who grew up in a violent household or engages in risky behaviours might be more likely to suffer head injury. In such a case the link between head injury and offending behaviour could be because of a violent childhood or a preference for risk.

Real-world applications

One potential benefit of research on neural abnormalities is that it could lead to possible methods of treatment. For example, if low levels of serotonin cause increased aggressiveness in criminals, then people in prison could be given diets that would enhance their serotonin levels and hopefully decrease their aggression. Artificial sweeteners are high in phenylalanine and low in tryptophan, both of which make the production of serotonin difficult.

Based on research related to aggression rather than offending

Research on neurotransmitters often relies on studies of non-human animals (Curran and Renzetti, 2001). In such cases it is not criminality that is being studied but aggressiveness, as is also the case in many of the human studies. This undermines the potential relevance of such information for understanding offending behaviour.

Furthermore, as with the genetic evidence, there is not 100% correspondence with any area of the brain or neurotransmitter, so the data cannot be used to predict who might become an offender or who might not.

APPLY YOUR KNOWLEDGE

Bart is a bit of a bad boy. He has started getting into low-level crime around the local neighbourhood, shoplifting from the Mini-Mart, spray-painting buildings and so on. His teachers wonder if he is simply 'in with a bad crowd', but his best friend Millhouse shows no such tendencies, and other than hanging out with Millhouse, Bart is a bit of a loner.

School Superintendent Chalmers suggests looking into his family background. He discovers that Bart comes from a long line of delinquents, stretching back to his great-great-grandfather, Jeremiah Simpson.

Using your knowledge of genetic explanations of offending behaviour, explain why Bart behaves in the way that he does.

CAN YOU? No. 10.5

1. Outline neural explanations of offending behaviour. (4 marks)
2. Describe **one** study that has investigated genetic explanations of offending behaviour. (4 marks)
3. Outline and evaluate genetic and neural explanations of offending behaviour. (16 marks)
4. Discuss biological explanations of offending behaviour. (16 marks)

265

Psychological explanations of offending behaviour: Eysenck's theory

We now move from biological insights into offending behaviour to psychological ones. In other words, we will now consider how such factors as life experiences and the way people think can lead to offending behaviour.

In fact, biological and psychological explanations are not that sharply distinguished. The biological diathesis-stress model included life experiences (psychological), and the first psychological explanation we will look at actually combines both psychological and biological elements. Eysenck proposed that there are identifiable personality traits and these have a genetic basis. An individual's adult personality is a mix of biological tendencies combined with learning experiences. This mix can be used to explain why some people commit crimes.

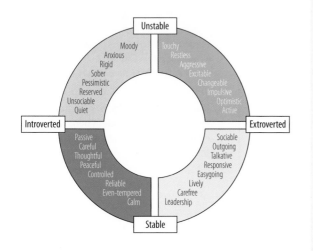

KEY TERMS

Extraversion According to Eysenck, this refers to outgoing people who enjoy risk and danger because their nervous systems are under-aroused.

Neuroticism According to Eysenck, this refers to people with a negative outlook who get upset easily. Their lack of stability is due to an over-reactive response to threat (fight-or-flight).

Psychoticism According to Eysenck, this refers to an aggressive, anti-social person who lacks empathy. This may be related to high levels of testosterone.

▲ Neurotic introvert, not likely to be a criminal type?

EYSENCK'S THEORY OF THE CRIMINAL PERSONALITY

Eysenck's theory of personality

Hans Eysenck (1967, 1978) developed a theory of personality based on the idea that character traits (such as moodiness, talkativeness, etc.) tend to cluster along three dimensions. Two of the dimensions are displayed in the diagram to the left; these are the most important. He added the third dimension (psychoticism) later. The dimensions are:

- **Extraversion–introversion** – extraverts are characterised as outgoing, having positive emotions, but may get bored easily.
- **Neuroticism–stability** – neuroticism is the tendency to experience negative emotional states (such as anger, anxiety and depression) rather than positive emotional states.
- **Psychoticism–normality** – psychotics are egocentric, aggressive, impulsive, impersonal, lacking in empathy and generally not concerned about the welfare of other people.

Each of these dimensions are normally distributed, so we would expect about 68% of any population to fall within one standard deviation from the mean.

The personality test devised by Eysenck to assess an individual's personality is called the *Eysenck Personality Questionnaire* (EPQ), which is discussed at the beginning of this chapter (see page 255).

Biological basis

Eysenck (1982) suggested that each trait has a biological basis which is mainly innate; he claimed that 67% of the variance for the traits is due to genetic factors.

Extraversion is determined by the overall level of arousal in a person's nervous system. A person who is under-aroused requires more stimulation, whereas an over-aroused person doesn't require this. Extraverts seek external stimulation to increase their cortical (brain) arousal. Introverts are innately over-aroused and thus seek to reduce or avoid stimulation.

Neuroticism is determined by the level of stability (i.e. amount of reactivity) in the sympathetic nervous system – how much a person responds in situations of threat (fight-or-flight). A neurotic person is someone who is slightly unstable and reacts/gets easily upset quickly. At the opposite end of this dimension the 'stable' personality has a more unreactive nervous system. They are calm under pressure.

Psychoticism has been related to higher levels of testosterone, which means that men (who have higher levels of testosterone than women) are more likely to be found at this end of the spectrum.

Link to criminal behaviour

The link between personality and criminal behaviour can be explained in terms of arousal – extraverts seek more arousal and thus engage in dangerous activities. Neurotics are unstable and therefore prone to over-react to situations of threat, which would explain some criminal activity. The final trait, psychoticism, can be easily linked to criminality because individuals are aggressive and lacking empathy.

Eysenck also explained criminality in terms of the outcome between innate (biologically determined) personality and socialisation. A person is born with certain personality traits, but interaction with the environment is key in the development of criminality.

This can be seen particularly in conditioning. In a 'normal' person, wrongdoing is avoided because of previous punishment – when a person does something wrong they are punished and this reduces the likelihood that the behaviour is repeated (operant conditioning). Eysenck claimed that people who were high in extraversion and neuroticism were less easily conditioned and therefore they do not learn to avoid anti-social behaviour.

Research on the genetic basis of personality

A key element of Eysenck's theory is that personality types have a biological basis. Support for this comes from twin studies. For example, Zuckerman (1987) found a +.52 correlation for identical (MZ) twins on neuroticism compared with .24 for non-identical (DZ) twins, showing a large genetic component. For extraversion the figures were +.51 and +.12 respectively. Zuckerman (1987) provided similar data for psychoticism.

However, even though this shows there is a considerable genetic component, it is not as high as Eysenck had claimed – a +.50 correlation means that about 40% of the variance in these traits is due to genes. This figure may also be slightly inflated because MZ twins tend to be treated more similarly. (The discrepancy between the correlation and the variance is due to the fact that the correlation is based on observations of current behaviour, which is a combination of genotype and phenotype. Variance is calculated in a way to remove for the theoretical contribution of the environment so it reflects actual genetic contribution.)

Personality may not be consistent

Any theory based on personality assumes that personality is consistent. In other words, a person who is lively or anxious is like that all the time. However, a number of psychologists support a situational perspective, suggesting that people may be consistent in similar situations but not across situations. For example, someone may be relaxed and calm at home but quite neurotic at work. Walter Mischel has supported this situational theory with research. Mischel and Peake (1982) asked family, friends and strangers to rate 63 students in a variety of situations and found almost no correlation between traits displayed. Any regularity of behaviour is likely to be due to the fact we often tend to be in similar situations.

This means that the notion of a criminal personality is flawed as people don't simply have 'one' personality.

Personality tests may not be reliable

A further issue with any theory of personality is that the score or label given to any person depends on the answers they provide on a personality questionnaire, such as the EPQ. When a person answers the EPQ, they are responding to the demands of a questionnaire – they are asked to select traits that apply to them, but their responses may not represent 'reality'. For example, consider the question 'Are you rather lively?'. For most people the answer is probably 'sometimes', but the questionnaire forces them to say yes or no. In addition, people may tend towards a socially desirable answer and thus their answers are not truthful.

This is countered by the use of lie scales in such questionnaires. This is a set of questions such as 'Are all your habits good and desirable?' A person who says 'yes' consistently to lie scale items is probably being 'dishonest' through the questionnaire, tending towards socially desirable answers, and their data is discarded.

Support for link between personality and criminal behaviour

There has been research comparing the personalities of criminals and non-criminals. Dunlop et al. (2012) found that both extraversion and psychoticism, as well as lie scales, were good predictors of delinquency. However, in this study participants were all students and their friends (aged 15–75 years), and delinquency was an assessment of minor offences in the previous 12 months (e.g. theft, traffic offences, though armed robbery was included). Another study by Van Dam et al. (2007) found that only a small group of male offenders in a juvenile detention centre had high scores on all three of Eysenck's variables.

Basis as a theory on offending behaviour

Eysenck's theory of personality was foremost a theory of personality rather than one of offending behaviour. There is some merit in the idea that certain traits, such as psychoticism, would be found in criminals as such people are aggressive and lack empathy. However, it is difficult to know what we can actually do with this information. Even though the three traits are good predictors of delinquency, it is not close enough to use as a means of detecting who is likely to become an offender. On the other hand, it may provide some useful ideas of how to treat offenders, for example by modifying the socialisation experiences of children who may have the potential to become offenders. Another application could be to pay greater attention to conditioning experiences to ensure that people with high extraversion and neuroticism do learn from their experiences.

MEET THE RESEARCHER

Hans Eysenck
(1916–1997) was born in Berlin and came to the UK between the two World Wars. He studied psychology with the infamous psychologist Cyril Burt (accused of inventing IQ data on twins) and went on to have an illustrious career researching and writing about personality and mental illness, writing more than 1,600 journal articles and 80 books. His views on the heritability of intelligence caused much anger to be directed towards him, including once being punched on the nose by a protester. His son, Michael Eysenck, also became a professor of psychology and writes books – including one for A level students.

Research methods

The *Eysenck Personality Questionnaire* (EPQ) is one of the best-known psychological tests. A number of shorter versions have been developed including the EPQ-BV ('BV' stands for brief version). Sato (2005) assessed this new scale in terms of test–retest reliability and concurrent validity.

1. Explain how test–retest reliability is calculated. (3 marks)
2. If the reliability was low, explain how this could be improved. (2 marks)
3. Explain what is meant by concurrent validity. (1 mark)
4. Concurrent validity was calculated by comparing the current scale and the original scale. A figure of .88 was produced. Explain what this value means in the context of concurrent validity. (3 marks)
5. Name **one** other method that could be used to assess the validity of a questionnaire/psychological test and explain how it could be used here. (3 marks)
6. Describe **two** factors that threaten the validity of psychological tests such as the EPQ. (4 marks)

LINK TO RESEARCH METHODS

Reliability on page 16.
Validity on page 18.

CAN YOU? No. 10.6

1. Briefly outline Eysenck's theory of the criminal personality. (4 marks)
2. Give **one** criticism of Eysenck's theory of the criminal personality. (3 marks)
3. Describe and evaluate Eysenck's theory of the criminal personality. (16 marks)

Psychological explanations of offending behaviour: Cognitive

Cognitive explanations are focused on the way that thinking affects behaviour. You will be familiar with the cognitive approach in general from your Year 1 study, looking, for example, at how cognitive explanations are used to explain depression in terms of irrational thinking.

A different kind of cognitive approach is to consider **moral reasoning** – the way that people think about right and wrong. This should influence the decisions they make about committing crimes.

▲ The case of the Columbine murders has been explained in terms of hostile attribution bias. In 1999 Eric Harris and Dylan Kiebold shot and killed a number of their fellow students. They were convinced that some of the students bullied them and so targeted these students in their attack.

▼ Kohlberg's levels of moral reasoning

Pre-conventional level		
Children accept the rules of authority figures and judge actions by their consequences. Actions that result in punishments are bad; those that bring rewards are good.	Stage 1	Punishment and obedience: focuses on rules enforced by punishment.
	Stage 2	Instrumental purpose: what counts as 'right' is defined by one's own needs.

Conventional level		
Individuals continue to believe that conformity to social rules is desirable, but this is not out of self-interest. Maintaining the current social system ensures positive human relationships and social order.	Stage 3	Good boy/girl: what is 'right' is defined by what others expect.
	Stage 4	Social order: reference to duties of each citizen.

Post-conventional level		
Individual moves beyond unquestioning compliance to the norms of the social system. The individual now defines morality in terms of abstract moral principles that apply to all societies and situations.	Stage 5	Social-contract: individual rights may be more important than the law.
	Stage 6	Universal ethical principles.

COGNITIVE DISTORTIONS

Cognitive distortion is a form of irrational thinking. In particular, 'distortions' are ways that reality has become twisted so that what is perceived no longer represents what is actually true. The result is that a person's perception of events is wrong but they think it is accurate. In the context of criminal behaviour, such distortions allow an offender to deny or rationalise their behaviour.

Two examples of cognitive distortions which are particularly relevant to crime are discussed here.

Hostile attribution bias

'Attribution' refers to what we think when we observe someone's actions and draw an inference about what it means. For example, if a person smiles at you, you might infer they are communicating that they like you. A **hostile attribution bias** is when someone has a leaning towards always thinking the worst. For example, someone smiles at you but you think that the person is actually thinking bad thoughts about you. Such negative interpretations then lead to more aggressive behaviour.

In terms of criminal behaviour, hostile attribution bias is most likely to be linked to increased levels of aggression.

Minimalisation

Both magnification and **minimalisation** are cognitive distortions where the consequences of a situation are either over- or under-exaggerated. In the case of criminal behaviour, minimalisation can explain how an offender may reduce any negative interpretation of their behaviour before or after a crime has been committed. This helps the individual accept the consequences of their own behaviour and means that negative emotions can be reduced.

For example, a burglar might think, when planning a crime, that stealing a few things from a wealthy family really has very little effect on their lives. Because of this way of thinking, the burglar doesn't feel as bad about committing the crime.

LEVEL OF MORAL REASONING

Lawrence Kohlberg's (1969) theory of moral reasoning was discussed in Chapter 2 (see page 42). Kohlberg interviewed boys and men about the reasons for their moral decisions and constructed a stage theory of moral development. Each stage represents a more advanced form of moral understanding, resulting in a more logically consistent and morally mature form of understanding. There are three levels of moral reasoning (see left), and each level is divided into two stages. People progress through these stages as a consequence of biological maturity and also as a consequence of having opportunities to discuss and develop their thinking, such as learning to take the perspective of another person.

Link to offending behaviour

In a longitudinal study, Kohlberg found that about 10% of adults reach the post-conventional level (Colby *et al.*, 1983), so the most common level is the conventional level of moral reasoning. Adults at the conventional level of moral development who break the law would feel that their behaviour was justified because it helps maintain relationships or society. So, an offender might accept breaking the law to protect a member of his/her family or protecting other people.

Criminals are likely to be at the pre-conventional level (Hollin *et al.*, 2002). They believe that breaking the law is justified if the rewards outweigh the costs or if punishment can be avoided. Most people reach this stage around the age of 10 – in Kohlberg's longitudinal study, just under 20% of the children at age 10 were at stage 1 and about 60% of children were at stage 2.

In fact, this fits with the idea of an 'age of criminal responsibility'. In England and Wales, children under 10 cannot be charged with a crime because it is believed that they don't understand the idea of moral responsibility, i.e. they are thought to be at the pre-conventional level where they judge right and wrong only in terms of consequences rather than any principles of morality.

EVALUATION OF COGNITIVE DISTORTIONS

Research support for hostile attribution bias

Schönenberg and Aiste (2014) showed emotionally ambiguous faces to 55 violent offenders in prison and compared their responses to matched control 'normal' participants. The faces showed angry, happy or fearful emotions, in varying levels of intensity of the target emotion. The offenders were more likely to interpret any picture that had some expression of anger as an expression of aggression. The researchers concluded that such misinterpretation of non-verbal cues (e.g. facial expressions) may at least partly explain aggressive-impulsive behaviour in susceptible individuals.

Research support for minimalisation

Kennedy and Grubin (1992) found that sex offenders' accounts of their crimes often downplayed their behaviour. For example, the offenders suggested that the victim's behaviour contributed in some way to the crime. Some also simply denied that a crime had been committed.

Maruna and Mann (2006) suggested that this is part of a fairly 'normal' behaviour where all people try to blame events on external sources as a way to protect the self. In this way it is not especially deviant behaviour.

Real-world application

Understanding cognitive distortions probably can't be used in the identification of criminals or potential criminals; however, it can be used in treatment. Heller *et al.* (2013) worked with a group of young men who were mainly from disadvantaged groups in Chicago. They used cognitive behavioural techniques to reduce judgement and decision-making errors (cognitive distortions). Those participants who attended 13 one-hour sessions had a 44% reduction in arrests compared to a control group.

EVALUATION OF LEVEL OF MORAL REASONING

Research support

The notion of a developmental sequence for moral reasoning was demonstrated in the research by Colby *et al.* (facing page). Other research has also been conducted in a range of different countries. Colby and Kohlberg (1987) reported that the sequence of stages appears to be universal, though post-conventional reasoning was less common in rural communities (Snarey, 1985).

In terms of links with offending behaviour, there is also some support. For example Gudjonsson and Sigurdsson (2007) used their *Offending Motivation Questionnaire* to assess 128 male juvenile offenders. They found that 38% did not consider the consequences of what they were doing and 36% were confident they would not be caught. This suggests that they were at Kohlberg's pre-conventional level of moral reasoning, supporting the relationship between moral reasoning and offender behaviour.

Chen and Howitt (2007) used a test based on Kohlberg's stages to assess 330 male adolescent offenders (aged 12–18) in Taiwan. Those offenders who showed more advanced reasoning were less likely to be involved in violent crimes.

Limitations of Kohlberg's theory

One major issue is that Kohlberg's theory concerns moral *thinking* rather than behaviour. Krebs and Denton (2005) suggest that moral principles are only one factor in moral behaviour and may be overridden by more practical factors, such as making personal financial gains. In fact, Krebs and Denton found, when analysing real-life moral decisions, that moral principles were used to justify behaviour *after* it had been performed.

A second issue concerns the fact that Kohlberg's research was based only on male samples, a gender bias. Furthermore, Carol Gilligan (1982) suggested that the theory is focused on a male perspective – one of justice rather than caring (see page 42).

Real-world application

Kohlberg observed that children raised on Israeli kibbutzim were morally more advanced than those not raised on kibbutzim, which led him to suggest that belonging to a democratic group and being involved in making moral judgements facilitated moral development. With Carol Gilligan, he set up a number of *Cluster Schools* (also called 'just' communities) in a number of schools, and even one in a prison. Members had the power to define and resolve disputes within the group, encouraging moral development.

(see page 42)

KEY TERMS

Cognitive distortion Thinking that has a bias, such that what is perceived by a person does not match reality.

Hostile attribution bias When a person automatically attributes malicious intentions to another.

Minimalisation (or minimisation) Underplaying the consequence of an action to reduce negative emotions such as feeling guilty.

Moral reasoning Thinking in a consistent and logical way about right and wrong, with reference to socially agreed principles.

⬆ UPGRADE

Question 3 below asks you to evaluate levels of moral reasoning as an explanation for offending behaviour. There are a number of things to bear in mind when answering questions like this:

1. The term 'evaluate' does not mean that you have to say something negative about this explanation – evaluation also invites you to write something positive about it. For example, there is research support for the moral reasoning explanation (see first evaluation point for level of moral reasoning), plus there are real-world applications (such as the development of Cluster Schools – see third evaluation point).

2. If the term 'limitation' had been used instead, then this would have prompted you to look specifically at some negative aspect of the explanation, for example the claim that Kohlberg's theory deals with moral *thinking* rather than *behaviour* or the claim of gender bias in the theory.

3. To maximise your marks in these questions, you need to *elaborate* your answer. As we have said elsewhere in this book, there are lots of ways to do this. A straightforward one is to *identify* the criticism, *justify* the criticism by providing evidence that this is the case, and then *explain* why this is good or bad for the theory.

CAN YOU?   No. 10.7

1. Explain what is meant by *hostile attribution bias*. (2 marks)
2. Explain how cognitive distortions can be used to explain offending behaviour. (4 marks)
3. Evaluate levels of moral reasoning as an explanation for offending behaviour. (6 marks)
4. Discuss **one or more** cognitive explanations of offending behaviour. (16 marks)

A kibbutz is a special kind of farming community in Israel where a number of families live together and share all of their profits. The children are largely raised in a communal home.

Psychological explanations of offending behaviour: Differential association

Most of the explanations looked at so far have contained elements of nature and nurture – a view that personality is the outcome of both genetic predispositions and experience. We now turn to a theory that focuses entirely on the influence of learning and, in particular, how the people you associate with influence the behaviours you acquire. This is a social approach and can be used to explain why criminal behaviours might be passed from fathers to sons – not because of genetic inheritance but because of observation and reinforcement.

🐾 APPLY YOUR KNOWLEDGE

Lauren's mother and father divorced and Lauren and her mother had to move to the rough part of town to find cheaper accommodation. Initially Lauren found it difficult to make friends but then started hanging out with the 'bad girls' in the neighbourhood, many of whom have been excluded from school.

Lauren's behaviour seems to go from bad to worse, and the visits from the police soon start after she is found to be selling stolen property at school.

How can we explain Lauren's behaviour in terms of differential association theory?

DIFFERENTIAL ASSOCIATION THEORY

Edwin Sutherland (1939) proposed **differential association theory**, suggesting that offending behaviour can be explained entirely in terms of social learning. It is regarded as a sociological theory because it suggests that people are socialised into a life of crime.

The concept of 'differential association' is that people vary in the frequency with which they associate with others who have more or less favourable attitudes towards crime, and these attitudes influence their own attitudes and behaviour. Sutherland believed it might be possible to develop a mathematical formula which would predict whether or not someone would turn to crime based on the frequency, duration and intensity of their social contacts.

What is learned?

A child learns attitudes towards crime, i.e. whether it is desirable or undesirable. Thus a potential criminal is someone who has learned pro-criminal attitudes from those around them. Furthermore, children will learn which particular *types* of crimes are acceptable within their community and also desirable (i.e. worth doing). For example, they may learn that burglary is acceptable but that violent crime isn't.

And finally, a child may also learn about specific methods for committing crimes. Some techniques are quite complicated, whereas others are simple (e.g. robbing a bank rather than a corner shop).

Who is it learned from?

Attitudes and behaviours are learned from intimate personal groups, such as family and/or peer group.

They are also learned from the wider neighbourhood. The degree to which the local community supports or opposes criminal involvement (differential social organisation) determines the differences in crime rates from one area to another.

The individuals or social groups may not be criminals themselves, but they may still hold deviant attitudes or an acceptance of such attitudes.

How is it learned?

Sutherland suggested that the frequency, length and personal meaning of such social associations will determine the degree of influence.

Sutherland did not specify the actual mode of learning, but it is likely to be both direct and indirect operant conditioning. A child may be directly reinforced for deviant behaviours through praise, or may be punished for such behaviour by family and peers. Role models would provide opportunities to model behaviours and, if the role models are successful themselves in criminal activities, this would provide indirect (vicarious) reinforcement. Social groups also establish norms by which we define behaviour.

Sutherland proposed nine key principles

1. Criminal behaviour is learned rather than inherited.
2. It is learned through *association* with others.
3. This association is with intimate personal groups.
4. What is learned are techniques and attitudes/motivations.
5. This learning is directional – either for or against crime.
6. If the number of favourable attitudes outweigh unfavourable ones, then a person becomes an offender.
7. The learning experiences (differential associations) vary in frequency and intensity for each individual.
8. Criminal behaviour is learned through the same processes as any other behaviour.
9. General 'need' (e.g. for money) is not a sufficient explanation for crime because not everyone with those needs turns to crime.

Major contribution

The major strength of this theory is that it changed people's views about the origins of criminal behaviour. The theory marked an important shift from 'blaming' individual factors to pointing to social factors. The theory suggested that crime did not need to be explained in terms of personality (mad or bad) but could be explained in terms of social experiences. Such an approach has important real-world implications because learning environments can be changed, whereas genes cannot be changed.

Sutherland also introduced the new concept of 'white collar crime', highlighting transgressions against the law committed by people otherwise seen as respectable and high in social status (the middle classes). These are non-violent crimes by business and government professionals, such as fraud, bribery, copyright infringements, forgery and so on.

Supporting evidence

One form of evidence that supports differential association theory is that criminality appears to run in families. For example, Osborne and West (1979) found that, where there is a father with a criminal conviction, 40% of the sons had committed a crime by age 18 compared to 13% of sons of non-criminal fathers. Such findings can of course be explained in terms of genetics as well – which is a problem for this kind of evidence.

Other evidence includes a study by Akers *et al.* (1979) surveying 2,500 male and female adolescents in the US to investigate drinking and drug behaviour. Akers *et al.* found the most important influence on this form of deviant behaviour was from peers and that differential association, differential reinforcement and imitation combined to account for 68% of the variance in marijuana use and 55% of alcohol use.

Methodological issues

The data collected is correlational, which does not tell us what is cause and what is effect. In terms of peer influences, it could be that offenders seek out other offenders and this would explain why offenders are likely to have peers who are offenders.

Some critics (e.g. Cox *et al.*, 2014) argue that the theory is not testable because of the difficulty of disentangling learned and inherited influences. The issue is about how one measures the effect of number and strength of associations on subsequent attitudes. It is also not clear what ratio of favourable to unfavourable influences would tip the balance so that a person becomes criminal.

Can't account for all kinds of crime

Social learning influences are probably confined to 'smaller' crimes rather than violent and impulsive offences such as rape and murder. So, in that sense, differential association is only a partial account of offending behaviour. On the other hand, this kind of 'smaller' crime accounts for a bigger percentage of the crimes committed than violent and impulsive offences (which tend to grab newspaper headlines). For example, in England and Wales in 2014, there were about 500 homicides but more than 400,000 burglaries (ONS, 2015).

A related criticism is that differential association can't explain why most offences are committed by younger people – Newburn (2002) found that 40% of offences are committed by people under 21. By contrast, Eysenck's personality theory can offer an explanation in terms of desire for risk taking as an element of criminal behaviour; Gudjonsson and Sigurdsson (2007) found that desire for risk was a key factor in crime.

The role of biological factors

The absence of biological factors from this account is a drawback. As we have seen earlier, the diathesis-stress model may offer a better account by combining social factors with vulnerability factors. Such vulnerability factors may be innate genetic ones, or it might be that early experiences (such as maltreatment) act as a vulnerability. On the next spread we will consider the role of attachment problems in early childhood; such emotional problems may then make a child vulnerable to deviant peer influences in adolescence at a time when young people tend to have a need for riskiness. The social approach, on its own, may be insufficient.

▲ **Illegal downloads.** It is a crime to make films, music or books available without the copyright holder's permission – yet a great number of people take advantage of pirate sites that do this, and thus are breaking the law. Can this be explained in terms of differential association?

MEET THE RESEARCHER

Edwin Hardin Sutherland

(1883–1950), born in the US state of Indiana, was a sociologist and considered to be one of the most influential criminologists of his day. His book *White Collar Crime* (1949) was censored because some of the largest corporations in the US threatened to sue, and therefore their names and suspected crimes were removed from the text. An uncensored version was finally published in 1983.

Insider tip…

The specification identifies biological and psychological explanations of offending behaviour, which means that exam questions may not identify any particular theory – the question may just ask for one biological or one psychological theory and you can choose which one to write about.

In the case of Question 3 below, which asks for 'one or more' explanations, it may be wisest to just focus on one theory in order to provide a detailed account (which attracts high marks). If you try to cover two in the time available, you may end up with lots of quantity but little explanation (which results in low marks).

CAN YOU? No. 10.8

1. Briefly outline differential association theory as an explanation of offending behaviour. (3 marks)
2. Describe and evaluate differential association theory as an explanation of offending behaviour. (16 marks)
3. Discuss **one or more** psychological explanations of offending behaviour. (16 marks)

Psychological explanations of offending behaviour: Psychodynamic

The final explanation for offending behaviour draws on your knowledge from your Year 1 studies of attachment – **maternal deprivation** theory. John Bowlby was a Freudian psychiatrist, and his early theory of maternal deprivation was based on psychodynamic principles.

There are other **psychodynamic explanations**, and we will look at one of these (the role of the **superego** in moral behaviour) in addition to maternal deprivation.

The key elements of the psychodynamic approach are that early experiences coupled with innate drives create the adult personality.

▲ The Joker in Batman typifies the pure 'id' criminal – someone who is ruled by what he wants and aims to create chaos with little reference to reality. In such cases the superego has failed to exert control (weak or underdeveloped superego).

PSYCHODYNAMIC EXPLANATIONS

Maternal deprivation theory

John Bowlby (1951, 1953) proposed that prolonged separations between a mother and child would have long-term emotional consequences. Separation will only have this effect *if* this happens before the age of about two and a half years, and *if* there is no substitute mother-person available. Bowlby also felt there was a continuing risk up until the age of five years.

Bowlby suggested that one potential long-term consequence of separation is **affectionless psychopathy**, a lack of normal affection, shame or sense of responsibility. This is related to the general notion of a psychopath as someone who lacks understanding of the feelings of other people.

Explaining delinquent behaviour

Bowlby's work as a psychiatrist in a Child Guidance Clinic in London meant that he regularly worked with children who had been caught stealing as his patients. He observed that a number of these delinquent thieves had experienced early and frequent separations and they also displayed signs of affectionless psychopathy. Such characteristics enabled them to be 'thieves' because they could steal from others since it didn't matter to them.

To test this hypothesis, Bowlby (1944) compared 44 of the thieves attending his clinic with 44 control patients. He found that none of the control participants experienced early separations, whereas 39% of the thieves had experienced early separations. He also found that those thieves with an affectionless character had almost all experienced frequent separations – 86% of the affectionless thieves (12 out of 14), compared with 17 % (5 out of 30) of the other thieves.

The superego

In Sigmund Freud's theory of psychoanalysis, the personality develops from three components: the id, ego and superego, each of which demands gratification.

The id represents our primitive wants and operates according to the *pleasure principle*. The superego determines which behaviours are permissible and causes feelings of guilt when rules are broken. It functions as a moral compass. The ego mediates between the impulsive demands of the id and the moralistic demands of the superego. The ego is anchored in the reality of the external world (the *reality principle*).

Thus, the superego is likely to be related to offending behaviour because it is concerned with right and wrong. There are three ways this might happen:

Weak or underdeveloped superego

According to Freud, the superego develops around the age of four (during the phallic stage) as an outcome of the Oedipus complex or Electra complex (in boys and girls respectively – see page 100 for a more detailed explanation of these complexes). A child who does not identify with their same-sex parent or whose parent is absent develops a weak superego. The consequence is that the person has little control over anti-social behaviour and is likely to act in ways that gratify their instinctual id impulses.

Harsh or overdeveloped superego

At the other extreme a child may develop a very strong identification with a strict parent. The consequence is excessive feelings of guilt and anxiety much of the time because, any time the person did act on id impulses, they would feel bad. The individual would commit a crime with a wish to be caught and then the punishment would reduce their feelings of guilt.

Deviant superego

Normal identification with the same-sex parent means that the child takes on the same moral attitudes as that parent. In the case of children with a criminal parent, the child would then adopt the same deviant attitudes.

Important consideration of emotion

The psychodynamic approach is the only explanation for offending behaviour that deals with the role of emotional factors. A key criticism often made of explanations in psychology is that certain factors are overlooked; for example, cognitive explanations miss out on how emotion affects behaviour. The psychodynamic approach addresses this issue and includes how anxiety and/or feelings of rejection may contribute to offending behaviour.

The psychodynamic approach also recognises the role of biological influences and the importance of early childhood experiences in moulding adult personality, both of which have been shown to be important in other theories.

Not causal findings

It is tempting to draw the conclusion from Bowlby's study of 44 thieves that prolonged separation caused the emotional problems experienced by many of the thieves. However, separation was not manipulated. All that is demonstrated in the study is an *association* between separation and emotional problems; there may be other variables that caused the emotional problems. For example, it might be that discord in the home 'caused' prolonged separations between mother and child and also caused the affectionless nature of some of the children. It could even be that the affectionless character caused the separations in some cases (e.g. a difficult child might be more likely to be placed in care).

Real-world application

Bowlby drew the conclusion from his research that the findings had implications for prevention of delinquency. Treatment of emotional problems in young delinquents is slow and difficult, so he suggested that it is preferable to try to prevent the problem in the first place by avoiding early separations. In his early research, Bowlby, together with James and Joyce Robertson, demonstrated that the key was emotional separation rather than just physical separation. They showed that children coped reasonably well with separations from parents as long as alternative *emotional* care was provided.

Gender bias in Freud's theory

Freud's explanation of events during the phallic stage proposed that women should develop a weaker superego than men because they don't identify as strongly with their same-sex parent as boys do. This is due partly to the fact that the resolution of the Electra complex is less satisfactory and partly because Freud believed there was little reason for anyone to identify with a woman because of her lower status. Such views represent an alpha bias – exaggerating the difference between men and women and devaluing women.

If Freud's views were correct, we would expect to see more women as criminals than men because of a weaker superego, whereas this is not the case.

Complex set of factors

Bowlby acknowledged that juvenile delinquency is undoubtedly the consequence of many complex factors, such as poverty, bad housing and lack of recreational facilities, none of which actually figure in psychodynamic explanations – but it still does have a contribution to make. Consider the report by David Farrington *et al.* (2009) of a 40-year longitudinal study in the UK, beginning in the 1950s with 400 boys from South London. The study concluded that the most important risk factors at age 8–10 for later offending were:

- Family history of criminality (could be genetics and/or differential association).
- Daring or risk-taking personality (Eysenck's theory).
- Low school attainment.
- Poverty.
- Poor parenting (the psychodynamic approach).

This shows that all the different explanations we have considered (including the psychodynamic approach) can be combined to give a clearer picture of the origins of offending behaviour.

UPGRADE

In other upgrades in this book (e.g. pages 65 and 75), we have offered advice about how to answer essay questions such as question 3 below. It is always worth spending a bit of time planning your response to essay questions as there are so many marks up for grabs.

There are a number of distinct requirements in question 3, so it is a good idea to unpack these before you start writing so you can allocate your time accordingly. Let's look at some of these requirements here:

- The particular explanations of offending behaviour in this question are the psychodynamic explanations. It would be easy to confuse the terms 'psychodynamic' and 'psychological', so make sure you know what is and what is not a 'psychodynamic' explanation.
- The question says 'Describe and evaluate'. This is not an invitation to simply chat about psychodynamic explanations of offending behaviour, but is a clear instruction to present AO1 description *and* AO3 evaluation.
- Finally, the question uses the word 'explanations' (note the plural), so you need to choose at least *two* (no need for more than two), such as maternal deprivation and the role of the superego. Be careful, however, and make sure you don't get carried away and write general answers about these without emphasising their explanation of offending behaviour.

To plan a response, consider a good answer to be around 480 words (that's about 30 words a mark). Given that the marking allocation for this question nominally allocates 6 marks for AO1 (description) and 10 for AO3 (evaluation), that would mean about 180 words of AO1 and 300 of AO2 (five critical points @ 60 words a point).

Serious Freud Squad

CAN YOU? No. 10.9

1. Briefly outline **one** psychodynamic explanation of offending behaviour. (3 marks)
2. Outline **one** study related to the psychodynamic explanations of offending behaviour. In your answer include details of what the researcher(s) did and what was found. (4 marks)
3. Describe and evaluate psychodynamic explanations of offending behaviour. (16 marks)

Dealing with offending behaviour: Custodial sentencing and recidivism

In the UK in 2015 there were about 80,000 men and 4,000 women in prison. This population has almost doubled from 20 years ago. As a percentage of the total population, this figure is somewhere in the middle of countries worldwide, with about 150 per 100,000 members of the population in prison compared to the US with 700 per 100,000 people. However, the figure in the UK is much greater than in the rest of Europe.

A more frightening figure is the current level of **recidivism**. The Prison Reform Trust (2014) reports that 46% of adults are reconvicted within one year of release and over 67% of under-18-year-olds are reconvicted within a year. The cost to the economy of such re-offending is at least £9.5 billion per year.

Such costs means that research on custodial sentencing (prisons) and on recidivism is very important for the economy of the country.

▲ David Wilson (2014), in his book on prisons, says that most people's idea of imprisonment is from television and films. Few people, including government ministers, actually understand the reality of prison and think it might be like a holiday camp.

Therapy in prison

The London Pathways Partnership is one of many initiatives where psychologists work with other professionals in the probation and prison service to offer support to individuals with offending histories. At HMP Swaleside in London, a *Psychologically Informed Planned Environment* (PIPE) has been created for men with personality disorders who are especially seen as a re-offending risk. They live in a special wing of the prison where there is a focus on interpersonal relationships and motivation to engage through individual and group meetings with prisoners and prison staff as well as psychologists.

The emphasis is on progression, and this means different pathways for individual prisoners. Some may move from the PIPE to a more intensive therapeutic setting such as the Therapeutic Community at HMP Grendon, some may engage in prison treatment programmes, and some may be released on parole. The community environment of the PIPE at Swaleside emphasises respect from everyone, and decisions are made jointly (Atwell, 2015). For more and more people, such alternatives are worth exploring as a means to reduce the prison population and reduce recidivism.

CUSTODIAL SENTENCING

A custodial sentence is one where the court requires an offender to be held in a prison or some other closed community like a psychiatric hospital.

Aims of custodial sentencing

To protect the public: incapacitation Putting criminals in prison is necessary in the case of violent offenders or psychopaths who may not be capable of controlling their behaviour, and the public needs to be protected.

To punish an offender and prevent recidivism This is essentially a behaviourist approach to dealing with offending behaviour. The principle is that punishment decreases the likelihood of a behaviour being repeated. Punishment or the threat of punishment may not work, but it is *believed* by many people to be the reason why most people don't commit crimes.

To deter others The fact that people are given prison sentences should discourage the general population from committing crimes. If the punishment was seen as less serious, people may be willing to take the risk and break the law. This is a social learning approach, that we learn indirectly from the consequences of others' behaviour.

To atone from wrongdoing: retribution The victim and their friends/family wish to feel a sense of justice being done. The offender should be seen to pay in some way for the crime they committed. Just paying a fine is often seen as insufficient.

To rehabilitate offenders Many people take the view that the only way to prevent criminal behaviour is through some form of education or therapy, especially in the case of offenders with mental health issues. Having a person in prison may offer the best opportunity for therapy as they have fewer distractions and there may be incentives for participation. On the final three spreads of this chapter we will look at methods of rehabilitation that are used to help offenders avoid future criminal behaviour.

Psychological effects of custodial sentencing

De-individuation The Stanford Prison study (Zimbardo *et al.*, 1973), which was part of your Year 1 studies, illustrates how prison and guard uniforms may lead to a loss of individual identity (called **de-individuation**) which is associated with increased aggression and treating people in inhuman ways (see discussion of de-individuation on page 240).

Depression, self-harm and suicide Depression can be explained in terms of hopelessness. Offenders entering prison may initially feel quite anxious about the whole new and frightening environment, hopeless about their future and lacking in control (helplessness). Abramson *et al.* (1989) suggest that depression is caused by both helplessness and hopelessness.

Depression may be expressed in terms of self-harm. The Howard League for prison reform reported 10,000 incidents of self-harm in 2008, though self-harm may also be explained in terms of conformity – Newton (1980) reported that it was a way of becoming part of inmate culture.

Finally, suicide is also an outcome of depression. The greatest risk group is single young men in first 24 hours of imprisonment.

Overcrowding and lack of privacy The growing prison population in the UK has not been matched by a increase in the number of prisons. Recent data suggests that 25% of prisoners are in overcrowded accommodation, for example two people occupying a cell for one (Ministry of Justice, 2012). This has an inevitable effect on the psychological state of prisoners. A classic study by Calhoun (1962) with rats showed that overcrowding led to increased aggression as well as hypersexuality, stress and increased physical illness.

Effects on the family Children with a mother or father in prison are deeply affected financially and psychologically, and the reverse is true. Parents in prison may feel guilt and also separation anxiety (Glover, 2009).

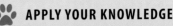

EVALUATION

The effectiveness of punishment

The high rates of recidivism suggest that, for at least 50% of the prison population, punishment doesn't work.

According to behaviourist principles, punishment is most effective when it occurs immediately, which doesn't happen in the case of a custodial sentence. An offender might actually see the sentence as a punishment for being caught rather than for the offending. Thus what is learned is to learn to avoid being caught.

We would also expect the severity of punishment to be a deterrent, yet US statistics show that murder rates are not lower in states where there is the death penalty (Amnesty International, 2015). Another argument is that crime is often committed when a person is in a highly emotional condition, when people do not pause to consider negative consequences.

Other benefits of custodial sentencing

A further proposed benefit of custodial sentencing is incapacitation. However, this is only relevant to a small range of dangerous prisoners and it is not relevant to reducing recidivism. Thus this benefit is a limited one.

Retribution is another potential benefit but one which can be achieved without a custodial sentence. It may be achieved through restorative justice (discussed on page 280), where offenders have to make amends to their victims and may also have to face their own conscience. This offers the potential of changed attitudes towards re-offending.

The final potential benefit is rehabilitation in the context of a custodial sentence. Offenders cannot be forced to take part in such programmes and, if they do, it may only be a kind of superficial involvement with the aim of trying to reduce their sentence rather than a wish to change (research on page 279 considers the importance of the desire to change for the success of such programmes).

Prisons as a training ground for crime

It has been argued that being in prison may increase the likelihood of re-offending rather than decrease it. According to Sutherland's differential association theory (page 270), this would happen because offending behaviour is a consequence of increasing association with people who have pro-criminal attitudes. This both affects an individual's attitudes towards crime (it becomes more 'normal') and provides opportunities for learning about how to be more successful at committing crimes.

There is some research support for this; for example, Latessa and Lowenkamp (2006) concluded that placing low-risk offenders (in terms of recidivism) with high-risk offenders makes it more likely that the low-risk individuals will re-offend.

On the other hand, there are other explanations for why imprisonment may encourage increased criminal behaviour on release. For example, imprisonment may lead to lowered self-esteem, reduced empathy for others and/or anger towards the system (Pritkin, 2009).

Individual differences in recidivism

A custodial sentence may be more effective with some offenders than others. For example, Walker et al. (1981) found that length of sentence made little difference to habitual offenders who were just as likely to re-offend no matter what their sentence was.

Rates of recidivism vary with age and crimes – younger people are more likely to re-offend, and those committing crimes such as theft and burglary are more than twice as likely to re-offend than those committing drug or sexual offences (Home Office, 2005).

Thus, sentencing should be targeted in different ways with different groups of offenders.

The benefits of non-custodial sentencing

The cost of prison care and the problems associated with it means alternatives might be preferred. Alternatives include probation, compensatory penalties, electronic monitoring, fines, community service and anti-social behaviour orders. Evidence suggests, for example, that cautions are more effective deterrents than arrests (Klein et al., 1977) and that offenders sentenced to community rehabilitation were less likely to re-offend (though this may be because less serious offenders are given community sentences) (Home Office, 2005).

A further advantage of non-custodial sentencing is that some of the problems that occur in prison (e.g. inmate culture, de-individuation, suicide) can be avoided by non-custodial sentences. Community sentences may be especially advantageous for new offenders and also offenders who are non-violent.

🐾 APPLY YOUR KNOWLEDGE

Luke is a 20-year-old male who has drifted into a life of crime, mostly stealing cars and crashing them while high on drink and drugs. He is well known to police for his behaviour, and he has received many police cautions and fines from the local magistrates court. After one particular incident, involving a high-speed pursuit by police and thousands of pounds' worth of damage along the way, he finds himself in court yet again. The magistrate can give him a sentence of six months in prison, but must weigh up the pros and cons of a custodial sentence (rather than a fine or community service) in this case.

Using your knowledge of custodial sentencing, explain what sorts of things the magistrate must consider before making his decision about whether to send Luke to prison.

KEY TERMS

De-individuation A psychological state in which individuals have lowered levels of self-evaluation (e.g. when in a crowd or under the influence of alcohol) and decreased concerns about evaluation by others.

Recidivism This is when a person re-offends after receiving some form of punishment for previous offences.

CAN YOU?   No. 10.10

1. Explain what is meant by *recidivism*. (2 marks)
2. Outline the aims of custodial sentencing. (4 marks)
3. Outline the psychological effects of custodial sentencing. (4 marks)
4. Describe and evaluate research on custodial sentencing and its effects on recidivism. (16 marks)

Dealing with offending behaviour: Behaviour modification in custody

On the previous spread we considered custodial sentencing as a form of punishment, which aims to decrease re-offending and deter others. An alternative to punishment is to use rewards – reinforce desirable behaviours instead of punishing undesirable behaviours.

Behaviour modification techniques are based on the behaviourist principles of **operant conditioning**. Both positive and negative reinforcement can be used to encourage people to use certain behaviours, and punishment can be used to discourage them. One such behaviour modification technique is a **token economy**.

▲ Tokens are secondary reinforcers. Their value is learned through association with primary reinforcers such as food.

Research methods

In the study by Hobbs and Holt (see right), data was gathered by recording behaviour on a daily chart. Two supervisors recorded what each boy did in the following categories:

- Following cottage rules (e.g. no smoking during games, not destroying property).
- Following instructions of cottage supervisor (e.g. lowering noise level when told).
- Before dinner: following rules of group games, completing assigned chores (sweeping, taking out rubbish).
- After dinner: interacting with peers 30–50% of the time (defined as being less than 3 feet away, talking and looking at peer, and body facing peer).
- Line behaviour: walking in straight line.
- Inappropriate behaviour was scored if any assaultive behaviour shown (e.g. swearing, threats, hitting).

1. The list above are the behavioural categories used in this study. Give **one** strength and **one** weakness of these behavioural categories. (4 marks)
2. Two supervisors recorded the behaviour for each boy. Why were two supervisors used? (2 marks)
3. In this study the boys' behaviour was compared before and after they were awarded tokens. Identify the independent and dependent variables. (2 marks)
4. Explain why this study might be classed as a natural experiment. (2 marks)

LINK TO RESEARCH METHODS

Reliability on page 16.

TOKEN ECONOMY

A token economy is given that name because it is a system of exchange of goods (economy) based on tokens (something neutral which has no intrinsic value). Such a token economy works well in a closed society such as a prison or other institution because rewards can be very precisely manipulated.

Reinforcement

Operant conditioning involves the reinforcement of new behaviours. In a token economy, prisoners are given tokens when they perform desirable behaviours, such as making their bed or obeying orders.

These tokens can then be used to obtain desirable goods such as tobacco, food or watching TV. The items purchased with the tokens act as reinforcers, increasing the likelihood that a behaviour will be repeated. The items such as food are primary reinforcers and the tokens are secondary reinforcers because they become reinforcers through being repeatedly presented alongside the reinforcing stimulus (this is classical conditioning).

Target behaviours must be clearly specified, and there may be a hierarchy where some behaviours get more tokens than others. Simply giving rewards for good behaviour is not a token economy.

Rewards (primary reinforcers) must also be clearly defined at the outset.

Punishment

A further strategy is to remove tokens because of undesirable behaviour, which would be a punishment.

Shaping

Longer-term objectives or complex behaviours consisting of smaller components can be taught through the process of shaping, whereby tokens are given for behaviours that progressively become more complex. For example, initially tokens would be given for prisoners making their bed daily (something easily achievable) and then later it might be for being polite to prison guards.

Key study: Hobbs and Holt (1976)

Tom Hobbs and Michael Holt observed a token economy in use at Alabama Boys Industrial School, a state training school for adolescent delinquents (aged 12–15 years). The aim was to reduce inappropriate social behaviour before and after dinner and when lining up.

Procedure The staff at the centre were given extensive training: 3 × four hours and then twice weekly over three months. This was to identify and define target behaviours, discuss methods of observing and recording data, and work out logistical problems. After the training phase there were weekly sessions to assess the operation of the programme.

In total 125 delinquent males were observed living in four cottages. One cottage served as a control group where the boys did not receive tokens. Baseline data, before tokens, was collected for all groups.

Data collection methods are described on the left. Boys were told the target criteria and told how many tokens they could earn in each category. Each day the boys were told how many tokens they had earned and were given a piece of paper with this information. They were taken to a token economy store once a week where they could buy drinks, sweets, toys and cigarettes. They could also save tokens and use them for more expensive off-campus activities such as baseball games or a visit home.

Findings The baseline mean percentages for social behaviours before the boys were given tokens were 66%, 47% and 73% for each of the three cottages. These increased post-tokens to 91%, 81% and 94%, an average increase of 27%. The control group showed no increase in the same time period.

Advantages over other methods of rehabilitation

The appeal of a token economy system is that it is clearly defined and thus relatively easy to implement. It means that prison staff can think about what behaviours are desirable and increase such behaviours, improving the prison environment for staff and prisoners. It can be implemented without trained psychologists and provides a means of controlling unmanageable behaviour.

In order to do this successfully, sufficient pre-planning needs to go into setting up a token economy and staff must remain consistent in the way they award tokens. In one study (Bassett and Blanchard, 1977), a failing token economy system was improved by re-establishing consistency.

Success of token economies in custody

In general, the token economy approach has proved very successful for schools and dealing with people with autism (Tarbox *et al.*, 2006). However, it has been less successful with prison populations. In the 1970s it became popular in the US and was being used in nearly all states (Burchard and Lane, 1982). Research showed that socially approved behaviours were enhanced and criminal behaviours diminished (e.g. Milan and McKee, 1976). However, it fell out of favour after this time because good results did not persist. Use in the UK was limited to young offenders' institutions (Cullen and Seddon, 1981).

Short- versus long-term goals

In the short term, a token economy can improve behaviour in the prison environment, and this goal seems achievable (Brewer, 2000). The bigger question is whether such a system can have long-term effects on offenders when they return to their natural environment. Research suggests that such systems have little effect on re-offending rates (e.g. Moyes *et al.*, 1985).

This can be understood within the principles of operant conditioning. Once rewards cease, the stimulus-response link is extinguished. Furthermore, the behaviours learned in prison may not apply in the real world, such as walking in a straight line. It might be possible to implement an intermediate strategy where prisoners live in a half-way house and can then be rewarded for more complex 'natural' behaviours as a way to re-integrate into the community. This was found to be successful with disabled adults (Stocks *et al.*, 1987).

This doesn't mean that all behaviourist therapies lack long-term success – in fact, restorative justice might be included as a form of behaviourist therapy because the discomfort of facing a victim may act as a punishment.

Individual differences

Some people respond better to operant conditioning than others. For example, programmes with young delinquents have been reasonably successful, but there has been much less success with violent offenders. Cohen and Filipcjak (1971) found that juvenile delinquents who had been trained with a token economy system were less likely to re-offend after one year. In contrast, Rice *et al.* (1990) studied 92 men in a Canadian maximum security psychiatric hospital and found that 50% of men treated in this way re-offended.

Ethical issues

Probably the major issue with token economy systems is the violation of human rights because individuals' behaviour is being manipulated, not always with their agreement. This can be overcome, as Hall (1979) suggests, with procedures and goals being agreed upon by prisoners, officers and administrators and periodically reviewed.

Nevertheless, objections still remain about basic needs being conditional on good behaviour (such as food or visiting rights). Some prisoners are not able to earn any tokens because they can't control their behaviour and thus they are denied such privileges or even necessities.

In addition, the use of punishment to earn tokens is unethical and counter to the goals of rehabilitation. Some establishments included punishment as part of the token economy, i.e. offenders lost tokens when they behaved badly (as explained on the facing page). Nietzel (1979) suggests that this practice led to the collapse of using such systems.

▲ Prisoners playing basketball in a US prison. Such privileges may only be allowed for prisoners who have earned a certain number of tokens.

Insider tip. . .

When answering questions on this topic, it is easy to lapse into a general description of operant conditioning and token economy systems without making reference to its use in prison. Marks will be awarded to the extent that your answers are focused on offending behaviour.

CAN YOU? No. 10.11

1. Explain what is meant by behaviour modification in custody. Use examples in your answer. (3 marks)
2. Give **one** limitation of the use of behaviour modification as a means of dealing with offender behaviour. (3 marks)
3. Describe and evaluate the use of behaviour modification in custody as a means of dealing with offender behaviour. (16 marks)

Dealing with offending behaviour: Anger management

The previous spread considered a behaviourist approach to dealing with offending behaviour. We now look at a cognitive approach, i.e. one which focuses on the way a person thinks. In fact, cognitive therapies are usually cognitive behaviourist. **Anger management** is a kind of **cognitive behavioural therapy (CBT)**. The aim is to reduce an emotional response (anger) by reconceptualising the emotion using a range of cognitive behavioural skills. Anger management has become one of the most common rehabilitation programmes.

▲ The aim is to manage anger rather than remove it altogether.

ANGER MANAGEMENT

The use of anger management with prisoners has two aims. First, a short-term aim of reducing anger and aggression in prisons where it is a serious issue. Raymond Novaco (2013) describes prisons as 'efficient anger factories' due to the social climate (violent inmates, overcrowding and a tendency towards a hostile attribution bias or other irrational ways of thinking which can benefit from cognitive therapy).

There is also the longer-term aim of rehabilitation and reduction of recidivism. This is especially the case for violent prisoners.

As this is a cognitive approach the aim is to change the way a person *handles* anger and aggression – cognitive therapy accepts that the situation itself may not be changeable but a person can change the way they think about it and thus change their behaviour. The therapy is one of 'management'.

Key aims

Novaco (2011) has identified three key aims for any anger management programme:
- *Cognitive restructuring* – greater self-awareness and control over cognitive dimensions of anger.
- *Regulation of arousal* – learning to control the physiological state.
- *Behavioural strategies* – such as problem solving skills, strategic withdrawal and assertiveness.

Stress inoculation model

Most anger management programmes used with offenders are based on work by Novaco (1975, 1977). His model drew on the stress inoculation approach (see page 210) – stress inoculation aims to provide a kind of vaccination against future 'infections'. The therapy tends to be conducted with a group of offenders either inside prison or outside, for example during a probation period. The three key steps are:

1. **Cognitive preparation** In the initial phase, clients learn about anger generally, how it can be both adaptive and non-adaptive. They analyse their own patterns of anger and identify situations which provoke anger in them.

2. **Skill acquisition** In the second phase, clients are taught various skills to help manage their anger, such as self-regulation, cognitive flexibility and relaxation. They are also taught better communication skills so they can resolve conflicts assertively without being angry

3. **Application training** Clients apply the skills initially in controlled and non-threatening situations such as role plays of situations that previously made them angry. They receive extensive feedback from the therapist and other group members. Later clients can try out their skills in real world settings.

Examples of anger management programmes with offenders

Jane Ireland (2004) assessed the effectiveness of an anger management therapy with 87 young male offenders. A baseline measure was made assessing pre-intervention anger (using a self-report questionnaire) and also each participant was assessed by prison officers. An experimental group of 50 took part in the treatment programme, while the other 37 were placed on a waiting list. The treatment consisted of 12 one-hour sessions over three days.

Eight weeks after the treatment, all participants were re-assessed using the questionnaire and also assessed by prison officers. The study found significant improvements in the experimental group and no changes in the control group over that time period.

Timothy Trimble *et al.* (2015) reported on an anger management programme with 105 offenders on probation in Northern Ireland. It was a condition of their probation that they attend an anger management programme.

The programme did not include offenders who had a poor history of anger and aggressive behaviour alone. It included those whose anger and poor emotional control predisposed them to offend.

The programme was conducted across a range of centres. There were nine weekly sessions lasting two hours, with a 15-minute break.

It was found that the programme significantly reduced the expression of anger as well as the amount of anger experienced among offenders compared to their pre-treatment scores.

Success of anger management programmes

In general, anger management programmes are successful in reducing anger, for example Taylor and Novaco (2006) report 75% improvement rates (based on six meta-analyses). Using such programmes with offenders also appears, on average, to be successful. Landenberger and Lipsey (2005) analysed 58 studies using CBT with offenders, 20 of which used anger control as part of the therapy. They found that having an anger control element was significantly related to amount of improvement.

Not all studies have been so positive. For example, Howells *et al.* (2005) cite five meta-analytic studies which showed only moderate benefits of anger management programmes. Law (1997) reported a study where only one person improved.

Methodological issues with research

The difficulties with research and making comparisons is the variability in anger programmes. Some are quite brief, lasting just a few days (see Ireland's intervention described on the facing page), whereas others may span years (Jones and Hollin, 2004, assessed a course run over three years). Some courses are run by psychologists, whereas others are run by less experienced prison staff.

Further variability includes different kinds of offender and different anger management programmes (some of which target wider behaviour problems), which makes comparability difficult.

One other important issue is the way that anger is assessed. This is done either using self-report measures or observations by prison staff, both of which are subject to bias. One particular issue related to the assessment of treatments is the 'hello–goodbye effect' where patients may portray themselves in a more positive light after treatment because they want to be helpful in showing that the therapy worked.

Limitations of anger management programmes

CBT in general isn't for everyone; some offenders don't like having to reflect on their styles of thinking and find it difficult to make the effort involved in changing attitudes and behaviours. Such individuals may well drop out of voluntary anger management programmes for offenders. One alternative is the use of drama-based courses which are less reliant on verbal ability and more engaging. A number of such courses with offenders (e.g. Blacker *et al.*, 2008) have proved successful.

Research has also shown that one way to cope with dropout is to assess 'readiness to change' before the start of an anger management programme rather than waste time with individuals who won't benefit (Howells and Day, 2003). There are scales to measure readiness to change such as the *Anger Readiness to Change Questionnaire*.

It is also probably true that anger management programmes are best as part of a wider therapeutic approach.

Short- versus long-term goals

Most assessments of the success of anger management programmes focus on the short-term goal of reducing aggression in prison, and these are the ones reported above.

Fewer studies have looked at long-term effects on recidivism rates, partly because it is more difficult to follow up. McGuire (2008) looked at a number of such studies and found some instances of reduction in re-offending after one year compared with individuals just on probation. It is likely that the success of such programmes is related to more than just anger management but some kind of general therapeutic support.

The relationship between anger and aggression and crime

One final issue to consider is whether anger and aggression are related – ultimately it is aggression (and crime) that we are trying to reduce. If anger doesn't contribute to aggression, then anger management may be irrelevant. Loza and Loza-Fanous (1999) claim that research that has linked anger and crime is based on lab studies using students. In their own study of almost 300 males in prison they found no differences between violent and non-violent offenders in terms of anger. However, this may be because violent individuals mask their anger. Loza and Loza-Fanous further suggest that one danger with anger management programmes is that such programmes can be harmful because offenders attribute their violent behaviour to anger rather than taking personal responsibility.

Howells *et al.* (2005) concluded that 'anger is neither a necessary nor a sufficient condition for aggression and violent crime' (p. 296). Much violence can take place without anger acting as a prominent antecedent.

APPLY YOUR KNOWLEDGE

Brad is a regular in the local magistrates court. He frequently gets into fights when he goes out to town for the evening and has a bit of a reputation in the bars and clubs around town as a 'hard man'. After he is arrested for fighting yet again, the local magistrate finally decides that Brad has 'anger issues' and suggests that he seek anger management treatment.

Suggest an appropriate anger management programme suitable for Brad and explain how this treatment would proceed.

Novaco Anger Inventory, example items
To get a feel for what kind of questions are asked, here are some sample items.
For each item, indicate the degree to which you would feel angry or annoyed (very little, little, moderate amount, much or very much):
- *You unpack an appliance you have just bought, plug it in, and discover it doesn't work.*
- *Being singled out for correction, while the actions of others go unnoticed.*
- *You are talking to someone and they don't answer you.*
- *You have hung up your clothes but someone knocks them to the floor and fails to pick them up.*

CAN YOU? No. 10.12

1. Identify **one** method of dealing with offending behaviour and briefly outline its aims. (3 marks)
2. Explain **one** strength and **one** weakness of using anger management to deal with offending behaviour. (4 marks)
3. Describe and evaluate anger management as a method for dealing with offending behaviour. Refer to evidence in your answer. (16 marks)

Dealing with offending behaviour: Restorative justice programmes

The concept of **restorative justice** is that offenders should in some way restore the situation to what it was before their crime was committed; in other words, they should put right their wrong. As an official policy, restorative justice is a fairly new approach. Carrabine *et al.* (2014) report that in the last 20 years it has moved from the margins of criminology to the centre of the field. The failure of previous systems to reduce offending behaviour has led to the search for alternative approaches.

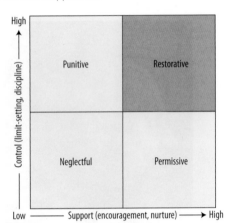

▲ Social discipline window.

Wachtel and McCold (2003) have created this window to represent the choices available for social discipline – one dimension is 'control', which can be high or low; the second dimension is 'support', which again can be high or low. Ignoring a criminal is simply neglectful (low control, low support), high control with low support is just punishment (punitive); and giving support with no control is permissive. Restoration aims to have high control along with high support.

▼ Wachtel and McCold (below) represent the way all the 'stakeholders' (victim, community, offender) can individually or jointly be supported. Full restorative justice requires the involvement of all three stakeholders: victim, offender and community.

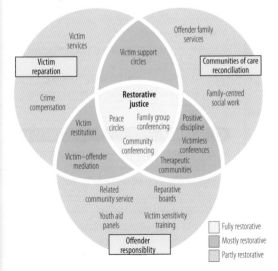

RESTORATIVE JUSTICE PROGRAMMES

Restorative justice seeks to achieve justice by repairing the harm done by an offender rather than punishing them. The process usually (but not always) involves communication with the victim. The offender may simply give payment as reparation (no communication). More often the offender may write a letter to a victim or there may be an interaction between offender and victim, for example video conferencing or a face-to-face meeting between victim and offender in the presence of an impartial facilitator.

Offenders are often offered restorative justice as an option instead of a prison sentence, if the victim has agreed.

Aims of restorative justice

Restorative justice has the potential to address two key aims of custodial sentencing: rehabilitation of offenders so they do not re-offend, and atonement for wrongdoing.

Rehabilitation of offenders

The victim has an opportunity to explain the real impact of the crime and this enables the offender to understand the effects on the victim. Offenders may learn to take the perspective of others, which reduces the possibility of re-offending.

In particular, the offender is encouraged to take responsibility for the crime and this should have an effect on their future behaviour. Being punished is a passive process, but rehabilitative justice requires the criminal's active participation.

Atonement for wrongdoing

Offenders may offer concrete compensation for the crime (money or doing unpaid community work). Most importantly the 'atonement' is psychological by simply showing their feelings of guilt. The offender can also show an understanding of the effects of their action. The victim has the opportunity to express their distress, and this provides the offender with a chance of developing empathy by taking the perspective of the victim.

Victim's perspective

From the victim's perspective this can reduce their sense of victimisation because they are no longer powerless and have a voice. Furthermore, a victim may develop a greater understanding of the offender by listening to their account which, in turn, reduces the victim's sense of being harmed.

A theory of restorative justice

Ted Wachtel and Paul McCold (2003) propose a theoretical framework. Their starting point is that the focus should be on relationships rather than punishment. Crime harms people and their relationships, and justice requires that harm to be healed as much as possible.

Early models of restorative justice focused on the offender and victim only, but more recent ideas recognise the effect on the wider community. The involvement of three 'stakeholders' is necessary – the victim seeks reparation, the offender must take responsibility and the community aims to achieve reconciliation to maintain a healthy society.

If only one stakeholder is involved, the process is only partly restorative, for example if the government pays financial compensation. If two stakeholders are involved then it is mostly restorative, for example if the offender receives therapy. Full restoration involves all three stakeholders, for example in peace circles.

Peace circles have been set up in many communities where violence and crime levels are high. They aim to foster an environment of respect where the community offers support to victims of crime but also welcomes the offender into the circle to enable mutual understanding.

Everyone sits in chairs placed in a circle. A 'talking piece' is passed from one person to another around the circle so that a person can speak uninterrupted. There is a 'keeper' whose task is to maintain an atmosphere of respect and articulate constructive solutions (Pranis *et al.*, 2003).

There are other kinds of 'circles of support' that have developed with the aim of giving community support to offenders to prevent re-offending instead of excluding them (Wilson *et al.*, 2007).

Success from the victim's perspective

There is a good evidence that victims who have taken part in restorative justice schemes feel it was beneficial. The UK Restorative Justice Council (2015) report 85% satisfaction from victims in face-to-face meetings with their offender(s). These reports of victim satisfaction covered a large range of different crimes from theft to violent crime. One police force, Avon and Somerset, reported 92.5% victim satisfaction with restorative justice when the victim had been the subject of a violent crime (www.bbc.co.uk/news/uk-england-bristol-22024927).

Victims also claim a greater sense of satisfaction than when cases go through mainstream courts (Dignan, 2005).

Success in terms of reduced offending

Restorative justice not only seeks to help victims recover from the effects of crime but also to reduce re-offending and thus reduce crime rates. Research indicates this aim has been achieved. For example, Sherman and Strang (2007) reviewed 20 studies of face-to-face meetings between offender and victim in the US, UK and Australia. All studies showed reduced re-offending and none were linked to higher re-offending. In one of the studies (142 males convicted of violence and property offences) there were lower re-offending rates (11%) as compared with a matched control group who served a short prison sentence (37%).

The UK Restorative Justice Council (2015) report an overall figure of 14% reduction in re-offending rates.

Advantages of restorative justice compared with custodial sentencing

The above research indicates that two of the key aims of custodial sentencing can be achieved through restorative justice. A third aim of custodial sentencing is punishment which may also be part of a restorative justice programme, as the process of facing a victim is unpleasant though probably preferable to incarceration. It still may be unpleasant enough to act as a deterrent, especially for those who have experienced it before.

By avoiding custodial sentencing, the influences of a deviant sub-culture can be avoided. On page 275 we considered how being in prison may actually encourage re-offending because of exposure to criminal attitudes.

Finally the issue of expense is important. The Restorative Justice Council claims that reduced re-offending means that £8 is saved for every £1 spent on the restorative process (e.g. reduced custodial costs, court costs, police time, etc.). The cost of restorative justice is sometimes funded by the fines paid by offenders.

Zehr (2002) reminds us that the main reason for restorative justice is that the traditional penal system did not address the needs of victims, nor did it promote offender accountability.

Selecting which offenders and which victims

The system will never be able to apply to all offenders and all victims. First of all, you need to have an offender who has admitted to the crime, though Zehr (2002) claims that restorative justice can take place without an offender's presence. Second, some kinds of crime may not be suitable, though, in fact, the process is used for every crime imaginable (see restorativejustice.org). Finally, some victims may decline the offer. This means that restorative justice can't be a global solution to dealing with offending behaviour.

Ethical issues

From the victim's perspective, one of the major ethical concerns is what happens if the victim actually feels worse afterwards.

From the offender's perspective, making people face up to their wrongdoing can lead to abuses of power. Victims can gang up on an offender especially where the offender is a child. Victims may try to shame the offender, which is not the intention of the process.

Restorative justice programmes need to be carefully balanced and ensure benefit to both victim and offender.

APPLY YOUR KNOWLEDGE

Anwar works as a community support worker in the centre of Bristol. Over the last 12 months, there has been a spate of crimes such as car theft and burglary. This has created considerable tension between residents of the community and the relatively small number of young men who are responsible for most of the crimes. Having studied forensic psychology at university, Anwar would like to implement a restorative justice programme in the community in an attempt to reduce this tension.

What sort of restorative justice programme might Anwar introduce and how would this help to reduce tensions within the community?

Restorative justice A method of reducing and atoning for offending behaviour through reconciliation between offender and victim, as well as the wider community.

YOUR VICTIM IS KEEN TO MEET YOU.

RESTORATIVE JUSTICE

SLANE

CAN YOU? | No. 10.13

1. Explain what is meant by *restorative justice*. (3 marks)
2. Outline what is involved in a restorative justice programme. (4 marks)
3. Briefly evaluate restorative justice programmes. (4 marks)
4. Describe and evaluate restorative justice programmes. (16 marks)

We have identified here the key points of the topics on the AQA A level specification, i.e. the bare minimum that you need to know. You may want to fill in further details to elaborate and personalise this material.

DEFINING AND MEASURING CRIME

DEFINING CRIME

- Crime is a violation of the law as defined by the state.
- Crime is a social construction related to cultural views. It varies across countries and historical periods.

EVALUATION

- Universal concepts, e.g. murder, rape, theft; though there are variations with the law (e.g. crime passionnel).

WAYS OF MEASURING CRIME

- Official statistics – produced in the UK by the Home Office (incidents reported to or by the police) and *National Crime Reporting Standard* (NCRS; reports any incident, even those not 'crimes').
- Victim surveys – *Crime Survey for England and Wales* (CSEW): 50,000 households interviewed, randomly selected from postal addresses.
- Offender surveys – *Offending, Crime and Justice Survey* (OCJS): conducted for four years with same 5,000 people.

EVALUATION

- Official statistics – the 'dark figure' of crime: 58% may go unreported to the police (Walker *et al.*) because people may think the police will ignore them or they may wish to avoid the stigma.
- Victim surveys – do show the 'dark figure', though people may still be reluctant to report everything; sampling may be biased (only 75% respond and sample is just of people with postal addresses); data capped at five incidents and may miss three million incidents a year (Farrell and Pease).
- Offender surveys – offenders may not be honest about criminal behaviours and drug use, though they claim to be (Hales *et al.*).

OFFENDER PROFILING

THE TOP-DOWN APPROACH

THE TOP-DOWN APPROACH

- Originated with the FBI, focused on bizarre murders; intuitive application of profiler's prior experience.
  1. Profiling inputs – all data collected, e.g. details of crime scene, information about victim.
  2. Decision process models – data organised into meaningful patterns, e.g. murder type, time factors.
  3. Crime assessment – organised or disorganised classification based on type of offender. Organised offenders plan their crime, leave few clues, may transport body away from crime scene, intelligent and socially competent.
  4. Criminal profile constructed and used to plan investigation, including where to look and eventually how to interview offender.
  5. Crime assessment – new information may mean return to step 2.
  6. Apprehension – experience used to revise the process.

EVALUATION

- Is the method useful? 82% said it was useful (Copson); may open new avenues of investigation and prevent wrongful conviction (Scherer and Jarvis).
- Flawed basis – based on interviews with 36 dangerous murderers who are not typical and might give dishonest information; however, process allows for self-correction and change.
- Potential harm caused by top-down approaches – Snook *et al.* claim that profiles are not much better than what psychics do (Barnum effect), may mislead investigations and may provide ideas for criminals about how to mislead investigators.
- Measuring the accuracy in terms of closeness of profile to actual offender is not reliable; Alison *et al.* found over 50% of police rated a fake (and wrong) profile as generally or very accurate.
- Distinguishing between organised and disorganised types of offender – a false dichotomy; Canter *et al.* found very few disorganised types in analysis of 100 serial killers.

THE BOTTOM-UP APPROACH

THE BOTTOM-UP APPROACH

- Data driven and based on psychological theory and research.
- Investigative psychology – using characteristics of the person (Canter).
  - Interpersonal coherence – personality is consistent which provides clues, and changes in circumstance may provide other clues.
  - Forensic awareness – an experienced criminal may reveal their knowledge, e.g. wiping fingerprints.
  - Smallest space analysis – data items from crime scenes correlated, leading to three themes: instrumental opportunistic, instrumental cognitive and expressive impulsive.
- Geographical profiling – location of a crime provides clues (Canter).
  - Circle theory (Canter and Larkin) – criminals commit crimes within a circle: marauder (live within the circle) or commuter (travels to the circle).
  - Criminal geographic targeting (CGT) – Rossomo's formula produces a 3D map (jeopardy surface) which will show probability of offender residence.

EVALUATION

- Scientific basis – computer programs based on incomplete data (related to solved rather than unsolved crimes) and algorithms may be incorrect.
- Is investigative psychology useful? Copson found 75% of police thought profiler's advice was useful but not used that much in the UK.
- Is circle theory successful? Canter and Larkin found support but very few 'commuters'; the concept assumes an offender lives in the centre of a shape that is circular.
- Is geographic profiling successful? Can help prioritise house-to-house searches but not much better than traditional pins on a map.
- Final conclusions – can't identify murderer but can narrow field, but has potential to be misleading as in case of Rachel Nickell.

BIOLOGICAL EXPLANATIONS OF OFFENDING BEHAVIOUR

A HISTORICAL APPROACH

CRIMINAL PERSONALITY TYPES

- Atavistic form proposed by Lombroso, a throwback to a more primitive species – innate characteristics predispose a person to criminal behaviour.
- Physical characteristics include facial asymmetry, heavy jaw, eye defects, nose twisted in thieves or aquiline in murderers.
- Turvey identified 18 characteristics in the atavistic type.
- Empirical evidence from precise measurements of skulls (anthropometry) using post-mortem examination and living faces of criminals; in one study 43% had at least five atavistic traits.
- Environmental influences – later Lombroso suggested that atavistic form interacted with social environment so there are born criminals, insane criminals and criminaloids (who only become offenders in certain environments).
- Somatotypes – Kretschmer identified four body types related to different crimes: leptosome (thin thieves), athletic (muscular and violent), pyknic (short and prone to deception), dysplastic (mixed, crimes against morality).

EVALUATION

- Contribution to the science of criminality – sought an evidence-based approach to study of criminality, and raised the possibility that biology and/or environment may cause offending rather than free choice.
- Criticisms of Lombroso's methods – lacked adequate controls; Goring compared criminals and non-criminals and found no differences in atavistic traits.
- Gender bias – Lombroso displayed an androcentric view of why women weren't criminals (more primitive but neutralised by low intelligence); women who were criminals had masculine characteristics, thus creating a monster.
- Criticisms of somatotypes – Kretschmer's evidence never open to examination, but support from Glueck and Glueck's study of delinquents, 60% of whom were mesomorphs.
- Link between personality type and criminality – Lombroso had naïve ideas but there are similarities with modern theories, e.g. Eysenck.

GENETIC AND NEURAL

GENETIC EXPLANATIONS

- Genetic influence demonstrated by twin studies – Raine found 52% concordance for delinquent behaviour in MZ twins compared to 21% for DZ twins.
- Candidate genes – MAOA (Brunner *et al.*, study of Dutch family) and CDH13 (Tiihonen *et al.*) jointly may account for up to 10% of violent crime.
- Diathesis-stress – longitudinal study found 12% of men had low MAOA gene and also had been maltreated in childhood; accounted for 44% of violent convictions (Caspi *et al.*).

EVALUATION

- Research support from adoption studies, e.g. Crowe found 50% greater risk if biological parent had a criminal record compared to 5% without.
- Can genetic (and neural) explanations account for non-violent crime? Can explain psychopathy (Blonigen *et al.*), but crime is a social construction so not likely to be biologically explained.
- Problems with determinist explanations – not everyone with the same genes becomes a criminal, but does show that for some people the cause of their behaviour is outside their control.

NEURAL EXPLANATIONS

- Brain damage may be due to head injury – 8.5% of US population have head injuries; Harmon found 60% in US prisons.
- Prefrontal cortex – reduced functioning in violent individuals (Raine); area regulates emotion and controls behaviour; damage leads to impulsive behaviour.
- Limbic system – asymmetries found in murderers not guilty by reason of insanity (Raine *et al.*); region linked to emotion and motivation.
- Serotonin – low levels predispose individuals to aggression and crime; normally inhibits prefrontal cortex (Seo *et al.*).
- Noradrenaline – low and high levels linked to aggression; low levels reduce ability to react to threats (Wright *et al.*).

EVALUATION

- Cause or effect? It could be that growing up in a violent household increases risk of a head injury and also causes criminality.
- Real-world applications – could make prisoners' diets higher in serotonin, e.g. reduce artificial sweeteners.
- Based on research related to aggression, not offending – studies of non-human animals and studies of aggressiveness may not generalise to offending behaviour.

Summary continued on following spread …

CHAPTER SUMMARY
CONTINUED

PSYCHOLOGICAL EXPLANATIONS OF OFFENDING BEHAVIOUR

EYSENCK'S THEORY

EYSENCK'S THEORY OF THE CRIMINAL PERSONALITY

- Theory of personality identifies three dimensions – extraversion (outgoing, bored easily), neuroticism (negative emotional states), psychoticism (egocentric, lacking in empathy).
- Personality assessed by EPQ.
- Biological basis – each dimension has a mainly innate basis (67% of variance): extraversion (under-arousal, seeks excitement/risk), neuroticism (over-reactive, unstable), psychoticism (higher levels of testosterone).
- Link to criminal behaviour – extraverts seek arousal in dangerous activities, neurotics over-react to threat, psychotics lack empathy.
- People high in extraversion and neuroticism are less easily conditioned and don't learn to avoid wrongdoing when punished.

EVALUATION

- Research on the genetic basis of personality – good correlations between MZ and DZ twins on the three factors (e.g. Zuckerman) but only 40%, not as high as Eysenck claimed.
- Personality may not be consistent – Mischel and Peake showed personality is related to consistent situations rather than consistent traits, therefore no criminal 'personality'.
- Personality tests may not be reliable – because of forced choice answers and social desirability bias, but lie scale items may weed out untruthful respondents.
- Support for link between personality and criminal behaviour – Dunlop et al. found extraversion and psychoticism were predictors of delinquency but Van Dam et al. didn't.
- Basis as a theory of offending behaviour – not a good enough predictor of criminality but could be used to improve conditioning experiences.

DIFFERENTIAL ASSOCIATION

DIFFERENTIAL ASSOCIATION THEORY

- A sociological theory based on social learning (Sutherland).
- The greater the frequency, duration and intensity of criminal contacts, the more likely a person is to become a criminal.
- What is learned – pro-criminal attitudes in general and related to types of crimes, and specifics of how to do it.
- Who it is learned from – intimate personal contacts and wider neighbourhood (may not be criminals but hold deviant attitudes).
- How it is learned – direct reinforcement/punishment and vicarious reinforcement and modelling.
- It is associations rather than need for money that explains crime because not everyone who needs money turns to crime.

EVALUATION

- Major contribution, marking a shift from the idea of a criminal personality to looking at social influences; Sutherland also introduced 'white collar crime' – crimes committed by the middle classes.
- Supporting evidence – 40% of sons with criminal fathers commit crimes compared to 14% with non-criminal fathers (Osborne and West); 68% of marijuana use predicted by differential association and reinforcement (Akers et al.).
- Methodological issues – correlational data; deviant individuals might seek deviant company. Hard to measure differential association (Cox et al.).
- Can't account for all types of crime – explains 'smaller' crimes but not violent and impulsive offences, nor can it explain why most crimes committed by younger people.
- The role of biological factors is absent; a better account combines social factors with vulnerability (biological or psychological, e.g. maltreatment).

COGNITIVE EXPLANATIONS

COGNITIVE DISTORTIONS

- Cognitive distortions occur when a twisted version of reality is believed, a form of irrational thinking.
- Hostile attribution bias – tendency towards negative interpretations of someone else's behaviour; may lead to increased aggression.
- Minimalisation – under-exaggerating importance of what you have done; helps offender avoid considering bad outcomes and feeling responsibility.

EVALUATION

- Research support for hostile attribution bias – violent offenders more likely to interpret angry faces as aggressive than 'normal' controls (Schönenberg and Aiste).
- Research support for minimalisation – sexual offenders downplayed their roles (Kennedy and Grubin), though people do typically do this.
- Real-world application – CBT can reduce judgement and decision-making errors in offenders; in one study led to 44% reduction in arrests (Heller et al.).

LEVEL OF MORAL REASONING

- Kohlberg's theory outlined three levels (pre-conventional, conventional and post-conventional), reflecting progressively more logically consistent and mature forms of moral thinking.
- Colby et al. found that 10% of adults reach post-conventional level; an offender at this level might break the law for a matter of principle.
- Most criminals at pre-conventional level; crime is justified if rewards outweigh costs.

EVALUATION

- Research support – developmental sequence and universal sequence supported (Colby et al., Snarey); juvenile offenders assessed at level 1 (Gudjonsson and Sigurdsson); offenders with more advanced reasoning less likely to commit violent crimes (Chen and Howitt).
- Criticism of Kohlberg's theory – moral principles used to justify behaviour, not cause it (Krebs and Denton); theory based on male perspective of justice, not one of caring (Gilligan).
- Real-world application – Cluster Schools can encourage moral discussions which foster moral development.

PSYCHODYNAMIC EXPLANATIONS

PSYCHODYNAMIC EXPLANATIONS

- Explanation 1: Maternal deprivation theory (Bowlby) – prolonged early separations between mother-substitute and child have long-term emotional consequences.
  - One consequence is affectionless psychopathy – a lack of empathy, normal affection and guilt.
  - Delinquent behaviour (stealing) observed by Bowlby in young patients who had frequent early separations.
  - Study by Bowlby found that none of 44 control children had early separations whereas 39% of the thieves had; 86% of the affectionless thieves had experienced early separations.
- Explanation 2: The superego is the component of personality that acts as a moral compass.
  - Weak or undeveloped superego – occurs because of lack of identification with same-sex parent; results in little control over anti-social id impulses.
  - Harsh or overdeveloped superego – overidentification with same-sex parent means excessive feelings of guilt and a desire to be caught, so punishment can reduce feelings of guilt.
  - Deviant superego – child identifies with a deviant parent and thus adopts deviant attitudes.

EVALUATION

- Important consideration of emotion – omitted from other accounts and here combined with biological and early childhood influences.
- Not causal findings – 44 thieves study demonstrated that separation and emotional problems are associated but some other factor may be causal (e.g. discord in the home).
- Real-world application – reduce early separation and you may reduce delinquency; Bowlby did change practices in hospitals.
- Gender bias in Freud's theory – an alpha bias suggesting that women were deviant because identification with same-sex parent is weaker; we would expect more women to be criminal.
- Complex set of factors – Farrington et al. found that the key risk factors for offending were family history of criminality, risk-taking personality, low school attainment, poverty and poor parenting (the latter from the psychodynamic approach).

DEALING WITH OFFENDING BEHAVIOUR

CUSTODIAL SENTENCING AND RECIDIVISM

CUSTODIAL SENTENCING

- Aims of custodial sentences:
  - Protect the public (incapacitation) from violent offenders and psychopaths.
  - Punish offender and prevent recidivism – operant conditioning.
  - Deter others – learn through seeing others punished (social learning).
  - Atone for wrongdoing (retribution) – criminals should be seen to pay a price.
  - Rehabilitate offenders – education and/or therapy may prevent recidivism; prison makes them a captive audience.
- Psychological effects of custodial sentencing:
  - De-individuation – as in Stanford Prison study, leads to increased aggression and dehumanising individuals.
  - Depression, self-harm and suicide – being in prison creates sense of hopelessness and helplessness, related to depression (Abramson et al.); may lead to self-harm and suicide (greatest risk in young men in first 24 hours).
  - Overcrowding and lack of privacy – 25% overcrowding; leads to aggression, stress and physical illness (Calhoun).
  - Effects on the family – parents in prison may feel guilt and experience separation anxiety.

EVALUATION

- Effectiveness of punishment – high levels of recidivism suggest if punishment doesn't work, people may avoid being caught rather than avoid punishment; severity of punishment has no effect (e.g. death penalty in different US states).
- Other benefits of custodial sentencing – protection only applies to a small range of criminals (e.g. violent ones); retribution can be achieved through restorative justice; and rehabilitation may lack effectiveness because of poor motivation.
- Prisons as a training ground for crime – differential association predicts increased pro-criminal attitudes, supported by research (Latessa and Lowenkamp), but there are other explanations such as anger towards the system (Pritkin).
- Individual differences in recidivism – custodial sentence has little effect on habitual re-offenders (Walker and Farrington); less effect on young people and those committing theft.
- The benefits of non-custodial sentencing – many alternatives, e.g. probation, electronic monitoring – fewer costs, greater deterrents, less re-offending and avoids negative psychological effects.

BEHAVIOUR MODIFICATION IN CUSTODY

TOKEN ECONOMY

- Token economies involve rewards (tokens) for target behaviours which are then exchanged for desirable items (e.g. food, visiting privileges).
- Operant conditioning – behaviours are rewarded with food etc. (primary reinforcers); tokens become secondary reinforcers through association with primary reinforcers.
- Target behaviours and primary reinforcers must be clearly defined at the outset, a highly structured system.
- Punishment – tokens may be removed for undesirable behaviours.
- Shaping – target behaviours gradually increase in complexity from easily achievable to more difficult ones.
- Key study: Hobbs and Holt, token economy with delinquents aged 12–15.
  - Procedure: 125 boys in 4 cottages, one was a control. Staff trained beforehand and developed the system; boys' behaviour recorded on daily charts.
  - Findings: Average increase in social behaviours was 27%.

EVALUATION

- Advantages over other methods of rehabilitation – clearly defined and relatively easy to implement by prison staff; needs consistency.
- Success of token economies in custody – successful in education and with autism (Tarbox et al.) and successful in the 1970s in the US (e.g. Milan and McKee) but fell out of favour.
- Short- versus long-term goals – in the long term less effective because behaviours don't continue to be reinforced and rates of re-offending aren't affected (Moyes et al.).
- Individual differences – successful with juvenile delinquents (Cohen and Filipcjak) but not with violent offenders (Rice et al.).
- Ethical issues – prisoners should agree to involvement; basic privileges withheld from those who can't control their behaviour, use of punishment is counter to the goals of rehabilitation.

ANGER MANAGEMENT

ANGER MANAGEMENT

- CBT approach, conducted inside or outside prison over a few days or weeks often with a group of offenders; may be part of a wider therapy.
- Short-term aim – to reduce anger and make the prison environment less violent (can't change overcrowding etc. but can change the way people think about it).
- Long-term aim of rehabilitation and reduction of recidivism.
- Key aims – cognitive restructuring, regulation of arousal and behavioural strategies.
- Stress inoculation model (Novaco):
  - Cognitive preparation – learn about anger and analyse own responses to situations that provoke anger.
  - Skill acquisition – teach self-regulation, cognitive flexibility, relaxation, etc.
  - Application training – role plays of previous experiences, real-world practice.

EVALUATION

- Success of anger management programmes – in general 75% success (Taylor and Novaco) but only moderate benefits with offenders (Howells et al.).
- Methodological issues with research – different programmes of different duration and different kinds of offender and lack comparability; assessment may be biased (e.g. self-report).
- Limitations of anger management programmes – some people resist the effort to think about change (drama therapy may be better); good to assess 'readiness to change' beforehand.
- Short- versus long-term goals – long-term goals harder to assess; some evidence that re-offending is lower (McGuire et al.).
- The relationship between anger and aggression and crime – evidence derived from lab studies; Loza and Loza-Fanous found no differences between violent and non-violent prisoners in terms of anger.

RESTORATIVE JUSTICE PROGRAMMES

RESTORATIVE JUSTICE PROGRAMMES

- Repairing wrong through some form of payment or through communication with victim by letter or in conversation with a facilitator present.
- Rehabilitation of offenders – understanding impact of crime enables perspective taking to develop; taking responsibility may also affect future behaviour.
- Atonement for wrongdoing – through payment or doing unpaid work, expressing guilt or showing empathy for victim.
- Victim's perspective – may reduce feelings of victimisation and may be helped by having empathy for offender.
- Theory of restorative justice (Wachtel and McCold) – programmes should focus on relationships and on three stakeholders: victim, offender and community.
- Peace circles – offer community support to victims and offenders.

EVALUATION

- Success from the victim's perspective – 85% satisfaction (UK Restorative Justice Council), more than cases in mainstream courts.
- Success in terms of reduced offending – overall 14% reduction in re-offending; one study found re-offending rates were 11% compared to matched controls in prison with 37% re-offending (Sherman and Strang).
- Advantages of restorative justice versus custodial sentencing – no exposure to deviant subculture, saves money, addresses needs of victim and offender accountability.
- Selecting which offenders and which victims – not all offenders and victims agree; has been used with all types of crime.
- Ethical issues – victims may feel worse, offenders may be abused; programmes must seek equal benefit to both victim and offender.

0 1 Outline **two** problems in defining crime. **[4 marks]**

0 2 Explain **one** limitation of using official statistics to measure crime. **[3 marks]**

0 3 Describe and evaluate different ways of measuring crime. **[16 marks]**

0 4 Evaluate the use of geographical profiling in forensic psychology. **[4 marks]**

0 5 Explain how investigative psychology is an example of a bottom-up approach in offender profiling. **[3 marks]**

0 6 Discuss a top-down approach to offender profiling. Refer to bottom-up approaches as part of your discussion. **[16 marks]**

0 7 'At best, offender profiling is an art. It is definitely not a science.'

With reference to the above quote, discuss the usefulness of offender profiling. Include research evidence as part of your discussion. **[16 marks]**

0 8 Outline what is meant by atavistic form in relation to offending behaviour. **[2 marks]**

0 8 Outline and evaluate the findings from **one** research study which has investigated neural explanations of offending behaviour. **[4 marks]**

1 0 Explain **one** limitation of using a genetic explanation for offending behaviour. **[3 marks]**

1 1 'A historic approach to offender behaviour tells us little about crime today.'

Outline and discuss a historic approach to offender behaviour. Refer to the statement above as part of your answer. **[16 marks]**

1 2 Discuss **two** biological explanations of offender behaviour. Refer to **at least one** psychological explanation as part of your discussion. **[16 marks]**

1 3 Which one of the following is *not* a trait used in Eysenck's theory of the criminal personality? Write the letter of your chosen answer in your answer booklet. **[1 mark]**

    A. extraversion

    B. hostility

    C. neuroticism

    D. psychoticism

1 4 Describe and evaluate **one** cognitive explanation of offending behaviour. **[8 marks]**

1 5 (i) Identify and outline the level of moral reasoning associated with offending behaviour. **[2 marks]**

    (ii) Explain why this level of moral reasoning is associated with offending behaviour. **[2 marks]**

1 6 Read the case below and then answer the question that follows.

> Yvette has been arrested for attacking her neighbour. In her mind, the neighbour deserved it because he kept annoying her by constantly coming around to her house. She also does not see what the problem is because he is much bigger than her anyway.

Using your knowledge of cognitive distortions, explain Yvette's offending behaviour. **[4 marks]**

1 7 Describe **one** research study which has investigated differential association theory. **[4 marks]**

1 8 Read the case below and answer the question that follows.

> Jayesh has recently been convicted of rape. He blames this on a difficult childhood where his mother died when he was still a baby. He was then passed around various members of the family but never settled anywhere. Jayesh's father never recovered from his wife's death, emotionally speaking, and has not been there for his son.

Using your knowledge of psychodynamic explanations of crime, explain Jayesh's offending behaviour. **[4 marks]**

1 9 Discuss **one** limitation of psychodynamic explanations of offending behaviour. [4 marks]

2 0 Read the case below and answer the question that follows.

> Aaron has been sent to prison for the second time in his life. He thinks it is really difficult to change his ways as he comes from a family with a long history of committing crimes. His father, brother and a number of his uncles have been convicted of theft and burglary like him. His grandfather was also an infamous fraudster.

Discuss **two** possible explanations for Aaron's offending behaviour. Refer to the case as part of your answer. [16 marks]

2 1 Outline **two** aims of custodial sentencing. [4 marks]

2 2 Briefly discuss the psychological effects of custodial sentencing. [6 marks]

2 3 Which one of the following terms describes reoffending following conviction? Write the letter of your chosen answer in your answer booklet. [1 mark]
  A. deterrence
  B. incapacitation
  C. recidivism
  D. rehabilitation

2 4 Read the case below and answer the questions that follow.

> Jordan was given a custodial sentence after being convicted of assault after a fight between two gangs in his community. He is due to leave prison soon, as the agencies involved in his rehabilitation are pleased with the progress towards being a law-abiding citizen. They are keen that he sets up home in a different locality to the one he came from.

  (i) Outline **one** behaviour modification programme that could have been used while Jordan was in custody. [4 marks]
  (ii) Evaluate the likely effectiveness of this programme in rehabilitating Jordan. [4 marks]

2 5 Outline how **one** research study has been used to investigate the effectiveness of anger management in dealing with offending behaviour. [3 marks]

2 6 Discuss the usefulness of restorative justice programmes in dealing with offending behaviour. Refer to research evidence as part of your discussion. [8 marks]

2 7 Read the case below and answer the questions that follow.

> A psychologist investigated the genetic basis of criminal behaviour by studying a group of criminals convicted of a violent offence. He compared them with a group of people who had not committed a violent offence which he established through self-report. He then questioned both groups to find out whether any of their first degree relatives had ever been arrested for violent offences. The results of his study are shown below.

	Had at least one first degree relative who was arrested for a violent offence	Had no first degree relatives arrested for a violent offence
Participant convicted of a violent offence	5	5
Participant had not committed a violent crime	5	15

  (i) What was the fraction of participants that had been convicted of a violent offence? Show your calculations. [3 marks]
  (ii) What percentage of participants who had not committed a violent crime reported having no first degree relatives arrested for a violent offence? [3 marks]
  (iii) Outline **one** limitation of using self-report to establish whether someone had committed a violent offence or not. [2 marks]
  (iv) Name **one** statistical test that the psychologist could use to analyse his data. Justify your choice of test with reference to the investigation. [6 marks]

The exam questions on forensic psychology will be varied but are likely to involve some short answer questions (AO1), some application of knowledge questions (AO2), research methods questions and possibly an extended writing question (AO1 + AO3). We've provided answers to some additional questions together with comments from an examiner about how well they've each done.

---

01 Distinguish between victim surveys and offender surveys as ways of measuring crime. *(3 marks)*

Maisie's answer

These two methods are methods of finding out how much crime has been committed. The obvious difference is that one is from victims and the other from offenders.

Examiner's comments

As Maisie says herself, the basic difference is obvious but she should know that she would be expected to do more than this in an A-Level exam! She could have outlined the sort of information collected from victims and offenders to make a distinction. Her first statement states what the surveys have in common rather than making a distinction. No marks are available for this kind of answer.

Ciaran's answer

A victim survey can provide information about the 'dark figure' of crime i.e. the crimes that tend to go unreported because people are embarrassed or ashamed or don't think the police will do anything. Whereas offender surveys concern people who have committed an offense and are willing to own up to it through the survey. Although both should give more valid data about crime than official statistics, offender surveys may be even more valid because only the offenders themselves can be sure a crime has been committed whereas victims may sometimes be unaware of a crime.

Examiner's comments

Ciaran earns 3 marks here. He demonstrates some knowledge of how the surveys are different although initially this is implicit. He then suggests that this will impact on validity and in doing so makes a clearer distinction between the two types of survey, earning a third mark.

---

02 Read the item below and then answer the question that follows.

> A forensic psychologist was approached by a police force to provide an offender profile of a murderer who had killed five times. There were clear patterns in the murders: each one was well planned, the victim appeared to be specifically targeted and a murder weapon had never been found at any of the crime scenes.

Using your knowledge of offender profiling, explain how the forensic psychologist would use this information. *(4 marks)*

Maisie's answer

The profiler could use this in a top-down way and decide first of all if this was an organised or disorganised type of offender. From the information it is clearly organised because there are clear patterns and evidence of planning. On this basis the profiler can suggest the likely habits of the murderer and work out a strategy to help catch them.

Examiner's comments

A 3-mark answer. Maisie demonstrates knowledge of organised and disorganised types. However, Maisie's reference to a top-down approach needs explanation for further credit. Maisie does get credit for extracting relevant information from the item and relating it to the right type of offender, and for also saying how this information can be used to help solve the crime.

Ciaran's answer

The knowledge that the murders appear to be carefully planned and the murder weapon was hidden suggests that this is an organised type of crime. The only clue appears to be the fact that the victims were specifically targeted and therefore there might be clues here about the murder which can be used to build up a profile – for example the kind of work they did or where they lived. This information may also be important later when interviewing any suspect because the police know the person is likely to be highly intelligent and manipulative.

Examiner's comments

A 3-mark answer. Ciaran first links relevant information from the item to a type of crime. However, he needs to be a little clearer on the categorisation of different types of offence for further credit. Ciaran does get further credit for knowledge of what a profile may include, and for saying how this information may be used in further investigation of the crime.

03 Explain what Eysenck meant by the 'criminal personality'. *(4 marks)*

Maisie's answer

Eysenck's concept of the criminal personality is based on his general theory of personality where he identified three dimensions – extraversion, neuroticism and psychoticism. Eysenck proposed that criminals are likely to be high in extraversion and therefore seek stimulation, high in neuroticism and therefore unstable and prone to over-react to situations of threat and finally high in psychoticism and thus lacking empathy.

Examiner's comments

This is a three mark answer. Maisie shows knowledge of the criminal personality by identifying the key traits and then goes on to explain how these traits may show themselves in behaviour. For the final mark, Maisie need to make more explicit links to criminal behaviour – for example, explaining why we might associate a lack of empathy with criminality.

Ciaran's answer

Personality refers to consistent traits that a person possesses. According to Eysenck certain personality characteristics could be linked to criminal behaviour. First of all there is psychoticism. Psychotic people are aggressive and impulsive and generally lacking an understanding of the feelings of others. This obviously sounds like a criminal. Second, neuroticism is generally negative thinking which also fits the criminal profile especially the cognitive factors such as hostile attribution bias. Third is extraversion which is an outgoing personality and easily bored, so they might be looking for things to occupy themselves with.

Examiner's comments

Ciaran's answer is worth 3 marks. He firstly defines what a personality is, which is creditworthy, but then he needs to outline the criminal personality more specifically. He does go on to do this by identifying the relevant traits and then explaining how they impact on behaviour. He makes some effort to link these behaviours to criminality but the application is rather implicit which stops him earning full marks.

---

04 Describe and evaluate differential association theory as an explanation of offending behaviour. Refer to **one other** explanation as part of your evaluation. *(16 marks)*

Ciaran's answer

The differential association theory explains criminal behaviour in terms of social factors, specifically it is about the people you mix/associate with. If you grow up in a family who hold positive attitudes towards crime this shapes your own attitudes towards crime and makes it more likely that you will become a criminal. It is not only their attitudes that affect you but they may also teach you how to, for example, rob a bank and they act as role models.

Family are not the only possible associations. A person's peer group also matter and will have a similar effect to the family, and also the community in which you live has attitudes about crime. So if you live in a middle-class neighbourhood it is likely that they wouldn't have positive attitudes about crime whereas an inner city area might certainly view some kinds of crime as acceptable and this would encourage any individual to think such behaviour is OK.

Sutherland, who developed the theory of differential association, also invented the term 'white collar crime' so it would also be the case that people working in certain organisations might learn from their bosses that fraud is OK and this would encourage them to do it.

Sutherland suggested that it might be possible to actually make a calculation about the likelihood of someone's criminal behaviour if you knew their associations.

An interesting aspect of this theory is it offers a different explanation to the biological approach for why people become criminal. According to the biological approach people become criminal because they are born that way. They may have certain genes such as the MAOA genes which predispose them to behave violently. There is evidence of one family (studied by Brunner) where the men had a history of violent behaviour and violent crime and they found that most of the men in the family had a gene for a defective version of MAOA. In contrast, differential association can explain why crime runs in families – and it is because of the norms that are passed from parent to child. In the case of the family studied by Brunner it could be a mixture of nature and nurture because the children may have an inherited predisposition but also the behaviour of family members would have affected their attitudes.

The two accounts can be combined as a kind of diathesis-stress model where people are more likely to become criminal if, in the first place they are biologically predisposed to it. For example, Eysenck's theory proposed that some people are born to seek arousal and born with a lack of empathy. A person like that might then be exposed to pro-criminal attitudes and is more likely to become a criminal, whereas someone who does not have the predisposition would be less likely to be affected by exposure to pro-criminal social norms.

One problem with differential association theory is that it is a less good explanation for violent types of crime such as rape and murder but is a good explanation for smaller types of crime such as fraud and theft, and in fact this type of crime is hugely more common and important. Another strength of Sutherland's theory is that it changed the way people thought about crime because, before his theory, people really thought about crime in terms of personality – that there was something in a person that made them a criminal. Sutherland suggested the social attitudes can shape criminal behaviour and also pointed the finger at a whole other area of criminal behaviour – the 'nice' person in an office who commits anti-social acts such as people do in big financial institutions. An advantage of his approach is that it offers a real-world application in terms of understanding that, in order to reduce crime, we need to change communities that have pro-crime attitudes.

In conclusion I think we can see that Sutherland's theory offers an interesting and different perspective to other explanations for offender's behaviour. It also can be combined with other explanations to offer a more complex insight into why some people commit crimes. Furthermore it did introduce a different kind of crime which is important to consider. It is difficult to establish one overall theory when there are so many different kinds of crime. *710 words*

Examiner's comments

Ciaran demonstrates a good broad knowledge of the differential association theory, and uses examples reasonably effectively to illustrate its ideas. The essay reads better where it is supported by empirical evidence rather than anecdotal evidence. The discussion largely centres on the nature/nurture debate, and this is where the essay has some depth. More importantly, Ciaran refers to another explanation here (genetic) – which is a requirement of the essay. The other evaluative comments are relevant but some could have been developed to show a deeper understanding. The conclusion doesn't add much to the essay. It is simplistic and mainly relies on repeating points already made. In general, the use of language is sound if not sophisticated with the potential to bring in more key terminology. Ciaran's answer does qualify for a level 3 response but the quality of the discussion needs to be more consistent for the level 4 mark.

CONTENTS OF CHAPTER

SPECIFICATION CHECKLIST

- Describing addiction: physical and psychological dependence, tolerance and withdrawal syndrome.

- Risk factors in the development of addiction, including genetic vulnerability, stress, personality, family influences and peers.

- Explanations for nicotine addiction: brain neurochemistry, including the role of dopamine, and learning theory as applied to smoking behaviour, including reference to cue reactivity.

- Explanations for gambling addiction: learning theory as applied to gambling, including reference to partial and variable reinforcement; cognitive theory as applied to gambling, including reference to cognitive bias.

- Reducing addiction: drug therapy; behavioural interventions, including aversion therapy and covert sensitisation; cognitive behavioural therapy.

- The application of the following theories of behaviour change to addictive behaviour: the theory of planned behaviour and Prochaska's six-stage model of behaviour change.

Internet addiction

The Internet is clearly a wonderful invention, and has made life a lot easier for all of us. However, it also means that some of us spend far too much time surfing the Internet on our computer, tablet or phone. Having access to the Internet becomes a central (and crucial) part of our lives. When the Internet becomes so important to us that we panic when deprived of Wi-fi, this may be indicative of an Internet addiction. Indeed, the latest edition of the *Diagnostic and Statistical Manual of Mental Disorders* (DSM-V) actually includes Internet addiction as a disorder 'that needs further study and research'.

How widespread is Internet addiction? A Stanford University study (Aboujaoude *et al.*, 2006) found that one in eight American adults showed signs of Internet addiction. The researchers also found that many people hid their non-essential Internet use or used the Internet to escape a negative mood, much the same way that alcoholics might. A 2015 study carried out by the Pew Research Center discovered that 1 in 4 adolescents in the 13–17 age group admit that they go online 'almost constantly'.

Can we recognise Internet addiction? Research suggests that there are typical emotional (e.g. feelings of guilt, agitation, avoidance of work tasks) and physical (e.g. headaches, sleep disturbance and blurred or strained vision) symptoms. The *Internet Addiction Test* was developed by Kimberley Young to measure whether an individual has mild, moderate or severe Internet addiction.

Internet Addiction Test (IAT) (Young, 1991)

Step 1: Answer the following 20 questions by ticking (or recording on a separate piece of paper) whichever of the choices best fits a description of your Internet behaviour.

Step 2: After all the questions have been answered, add the numbers for each response to obtain a final score (e.g. 'Rarely or never' scores 1 and 'Always' scores 5). The higher the score, the greater is the level of your Internet addiction. The 'severity index' is as follows:

	Rarely or never	Every once in awhile	Sometimes	Often	Always
1 Do you find that you stay online longer than you intended?	☐	☐	☐	☐	☐
2 Do you neglect household chores to spend more time online?	☐	☐	☐	☐	☐
3 Do you prefer the excitment of the internet to intimacy with your partner?	☐	☐	☐	☐	☐
4 Do you form new relationships with fellow online users?	☐	☐	☐	☐	☐
5 Do others in your life complain to you about the amount of time you spend online?	☐	☐	☐	☐	☐
6 Does your work suffer because of the amount of time you spend online?	☐	☐	☐	☐	☐
7 Do you check your email before something else you need to do?	☐	☐	☐	☐	☐
8 Does your job performance or productivity suffer because of the internet?	☐	☐	☐	☐	☐
9 Do you become defensive or secretive when anyone asks you what you do online?	☐	☐	☐	☐	☐
10 Do you block disturbing thoughts about your life with soothing thoughts of the internet?	☐	☐	☐	☐	☐
11 Do you find yourself anticipating when you will go online again?	☐	☐	☐	☐	☐
12 Do you fear that life without the internet would be boring, empty or joyless?	☐	☐	☐	☐	☐
13 Do you snap, yell, or act annoyed if someone bothers you while you are online?	☐	☐	☐	☐	☐
14 Do you lose sleep due to late night internet use?	☐	☐	☐	☐	☐
15 Do you feel preoccupied with the internet when not online, or fantasize about being online?	☐	☐	☐	☐	☐
16 Do you find yourself saying "just a few more minutes" when online?	☐	☐	☐	☐	☐
17 Do you try to cut down on the amount of time you spend online and fail?	☐	☐	☐	☐	☐
18 Do you try and hide how long you've been online?	☐	☐	☐	☐	☐
19 Do you choose to spend more time online over spending time out with others?	☐	☐	☐	☐	☐
20 Do you feel depressed, moody, or nervous when you are not online, and do these feelings go away when you go back online?	☐	☐	☐	☐	☐

NONE (0–30 points)

MILD (31–49 points): You are an average online user. You may surf the Web a bit too long at times, but you have control over your usage.

MODERATE (50–79 points): You are experiencing occasional or frequent problems because of the Internet. You should consider their full impact on your life.

SEVERE (80–100 points): Your Internet usage is causing significant problems in your life. You should evaluate the impact of the Internet on your life and address the problems directly caused by your Internet usage.

Describing addiction

Addiction is the compulsion to use a substance or engage in behaviour despite its harmful consequences. It is characterised by an inability to stop using that substance or engaging in the behaviour to the extent that there is a failure to meet work, social or family obligations. In the case of some drugs, such as heroin and nicotine, the individual needs larger and larger doses to achieve the same effect (tolerance) and experiences unpleasant symptoms if they attempt to stop taking the drug (withdrawal symptoms). At this point they are said to be physically dependent on that drug.

What is the nature of an 'addiction'?

According to Soper and Miller (1983), 'addiction' involves:
(1) a compulsive behavioural involvement
(2) a lack of interest in other activities
(3) association mainly with other addicts
(4) physical and mental symptoms when attempting to stop.

An example of physical dependence: Caffeine

Although we typically associate physical dependence with 'drugs of abuse', there is growing evidence that caffeine, the most commonly used mood-altering drug in the world, can also lead to physical dependence. Meredith *et al.* (2013), in a review of research in the area, argue that caffeine produces behavioural and physiological effects similar to other drugs of dependence. For example, the caffeine withdrawal syndrome has been demonstrated in numerous studies. Caffeine withdrawal symptoms include headaches, fatigue, sleepiness and difficulty in concentrating. Significant caffeine withdrawal has been shown to occur even after stopping a regular one-cup-a-day habit.

Tolerance to caffeine has also been demonstrated, in that among high-dose users of caffeine its effects are no longer different to a placebo. This tends not to be the case for low or 'typical' dose users. Because a number of studies have shown that physical dependence on caffeine can, for some people, meet DSM criteria for substance dependence, the latest version of DSM (DSM-V) characterises caffeine use disorder as a 'condition for further study'.

Although the word 'addiction' is used in the specification, researchers tend to shy away from this term when writing about smoking, gambling, drinking, etc. Words like 'problem' or 'pathological' are often used instead. The important point when considering whether something is 'addictive', however, is whether the behaviour is excessive to the point that it has the characteristics described on this spread, and causes difficulties for the individual when they attempt to stop.

CHARACTERISTICS OF ADDICTION

Physical dependence

Physical dependence can occur with the long-term use of many drugs. Many different types of drug can lead to physical dependence if abused. These include drugs of abuse such as heroin and nicotine, but physical dependence is also possible with many prescription drugs such as sedatives and anti-anxiety drugs. Physical dependence on a drug often follows heavy daily use over several weeks or longer. People who are physically dependent on a particular substance, such as heroin or nicotine, need to take the drug in order to feel 'normal'. Physical dependence does not necessarily mean the individual is 'addicted' to the drug, but such dependence often accompanies addiction.

Physical dependence can be demonstrated by the presence of unpleasant physical symptoms referred to as **withdrawal syndrome** (see facing page) if the person suddenly abstains from the drug. The person depends on the drug to avoid these withdrawal symptoms and to function normally. Physical dependence is often accompanied by increased **tolerance** to the drug, in that the user requires increased doses in order to obtain the desired effect.

Psychological dependence

Psychological dependence occurs when a drug becomes a central part of an individual's thoughts, emotions and activities. It can be demonstrated by a strong urge to use the drug, despite being aware of any possible harmful effects associated with its use.

A characteristic of both types of dependence is the experience of cravings. A craving is experienced as an intense desire to repeat the experience associated with a particular drug or activity. If the individual attempts to abstain from the subject of their addiction, or cut down on their usage, they will experience intense cravings to use the substance or engage in the behaviour. If these cravings are not met, the person begins to feel very anxious, and these feelings make ending the addiction extremely difficult. The individual may feel unable to cope without a particular substance or activity, and the desire to use it again may become so intense that it takes over their thinking completely.

Psychological dependence may also arise for non-physical addictions. For example, for gamblers who are motivated by the thrill of winning money or 'gymaholics' who relieve the tension in their lives by spending many hours in the gym, changing their habits is a very hard thing to do. They may also experience cravings to gamble or to exercise that are every bit as strong as those experienced by drug addicts.

Why does psychological dependence arise?

People commonly experience differences between what they *think* and what they *feel*. What they are experiencing are the outcomes of two different information-processing systems – rational and experiential (Epstein, 1994). The rational system operates according to culturally transmitted rules of reasoning. It is conscious, analytical and relatively emotion-free. Using this system, we are able to work out the right and appropriate way to behave in a clear and rational manner.

The experiential system, on the other hand, is preconscious, automatic and strongly associated with emotion. It drives us to behave in a particular way based largely on how that makes us *feel*. The relative contribution of each varies from none at all to complete dominance by one of the systems. However, under some circumstances, their different priorities become apparent. Acting irrationally (as is frequently the case with psychological dependence) means that the experiential system has taken priority over the rational system.

Tolerance

When drugs such as heroin are used for a long time, tolerance can develop. This means that an individual no longer responds to the drug in the same way, with the result that larger and larger doses are needed in order to feel the same effects as before. There are three ways in which tolerance can occur. First, enzymes responsible for metabolising the drug do this more efficiently over time (*metabolic tolerance*). This results in reduced concentrations in the blood and at the sites of drug action, making the effect weaker. A second way is that prolonged drug use leads to changes in receptor density, reducing the response to the normal dose of the drug. The final way is *learned tolerance*, which means that a user will experience reduced drug effects because they have learned to function normally when under the influence of the drug.

Tolerance: An illustration

A dramatic illustration of tolerance comes from a study of prisoners carried out in the 1950s (Isbell *et al.*, 1955). A group of prisoners volunteered for a study where they were administered the same amount of alcohol daily over a 13-week period to keep them in a constant state of intoxication. However, despite the fact that for the first couple of weeks all the prisoners showed pronounced changes in blood alcohol levels and behavioural signs of intoxication, these dropped in the following weeks, as the men no longer appeared drunk despite receiving the same amount of alcohol.

This was due to increased tolerance for the alcohol. For example, in *metabolic tolerance* there was an increase in the enzymes needed to break down alcohol in the body, with the result that alcohol was metabolised more quickly and so blood-alcohol levels were reduced. In *learned tolerance*, prisoners learned to cope with the daily demands of living while under the influence of alcohol, and so no longer appeared to be drunk.

Withdrawal syndrome

If taking a drug such as heroin or nicotine is discontinued, withdrawal symptoms can occur. As the effect of the drug wears off, the person may experience symptoms such as increased anxiety, shakiness or trembling, insomnia, irritability or loss of appetite and headaches. Withdrawal symptoms are different depending on the drug in question, but what they all share is their negative impact on the individual, who may then take the drug again to relieve these symptoms. The appearance of withdrawal symptoms is an indication of the person's physical dependence on that drug.

Withdrawal symptoms occur because the body is attempting to deal with the absence of a drug's effects. Just as tolerance is a consequence of the body adjusting to chronic drug use, withdrawal symptoms are a consequence of the body reacting to the cessation of the drug.

The two phases of withdrawal

Acute withdrawal begins within hours of drug cessation and gradually resolves after a few weeks. During this stage, the physical cravings that the addict experiences are intense and persistent, as the body has yet to adjust to the loss of the drug it had become used to for so long.

Post-acute withdrawal can last for months or even years after the person has stopped taking the drug. This is characterised by emotional and psychological turmoil as addicts experience alternating periods of dysfunction and near-normality as the brain slowly re-organises and re-balances itself.

Insider tip…

It pays to be flexible in your preparation for exam questions. You will never be asked for more than 6 marks' worth of descriptive material for any one of four terms (physical dependence, psychological dependence, tolerance and withdrawal), but you could also be asked for 2, 3, 4 (or even 5) marks' worth. You could also be asked for an example of each, so be prepared!

KEY TERMS

Addiction A state characterised by compulsively engaging in rewarding stimuli despite the associated adverse consequences.

Physical dependence to a drug is evident when an individual needs to take the drug in order to feel 'normal'. It can be demonstrated by the presence of withdrawal symptoms if the individual abstains from the drug.

Psychological dependence occurs when a drug becomes a central part of an individual's thoughts, emotions and activities, resulting in a strong urge to use the drug.

Tolerance means that an individual no longer responds to a drug in the same way, with the result that larger and larger doses are needed in order to experience the same effects as before.

Withdrawal syndrome can occur when a drug on which an individual is physically dependent is discontinued. In such situations, withdrawal symptoms, such as shaking and anxiety, can occur, as the body attempts to deal with the absence of a drug's effects.

CAN YOU? No. 11.1

1. Explain what is meant by the terms *physical dependence*, *psychological dependence*, *tolerance* and *withdrawal*. (2 marks each)
2. Explain the nature of *physical dependence*, *psychological dependence*, *tolerance* and *withdrawal* as they apply to addiction. (4 marks each)

🐾 APPLY YOUR KNOWLEDGE

Nia injects herself with heroin several times each day, and spends a lot of money on her drug habit. If she goes longer than 12 hours without the drug, she starts to feel nauseous and anxious and has to inject as soon as possible.

Aodhagan loves to gamble. He started by buying lottery scratch cards and a bit of online gambling, and now spends much of his time at a local casino. At the request of his family, he has tried to give up, but if he has to go without gambling for longer than a few days he feels a strong urge to gamble. These urges can be particularly strong when he is feeling down in the dumps or bored.

Using your knowledge of physical and psychological dependence, tolerance and withdrawal syndrome, explain the two examples of addiction described above.

Risk factors: Genetics, stress and personality

What makes some people more vulnerable to addiction than others? On this first of two spreads that address this question, we examine three possible explanations. The first is **genetic** vulnerability – research has shown that addiction frequently runs in families, so therefore it is possible that some individuals are predisposed to addictive behaviour because of genes inherited from their parents. The second explanation is **stress** – people engage in behaviour such as drug abuse, drinking and gambling as a response to the stressors in their life. The third risk factor on this spread is **personality** – the possibility that some people are more 'addiction-prone' because of personality characteristics that make them more likely to engage in potentially addictive behaviours.

People do not necessarily inherit a gene that pushes them into gambling or substance abuse, but may instead inherit a genetic predisposition to other behaviours (such as risk-taking or impulsivity) that makes potentially addictive habits more likely.

▲ In Vietnam, many soldiers developed a drug habit as a way of coping with the severe stress they were under.

KEY TERMS

Genetic refers to inherited characteristics that are passed from parents to their children in the form of information carried on their chromosomes.

Personality refers to the stable traits of a person that underlie consistencies in the way they behave over time and in different situations.

Stress A state of physiological arousal produced by demands from the environment (stressors).

GENETIC VULNERABILITY, STRESS AND PERSONALITY

Genetic vulnerability

Some people appear to be born with a genetic vulnerability to substance abuse and other forms of 'unhealthy' behaviour. For example, an Australian study (Slutske *et al.*, 2010) interviewed 2,889 pairs of twins to investigate the role of genetic and environmental factors in the development of gambling addiction. Monozygotic (MZ) twins had a higher rate of both twins being pathological gamblers (if one twin was a pathological gambler) than did dizygotic (DZ) twins. Male MZ twins had a heritability estimate of 49% compared with 21% for male DZ twins. For female MZ twins, the heritability estimate was 55% compared with 21% for female DZ twins.

Likewise, smoking also appears to have a strong genetic influence. Vink *et al.* (2005) studied 1,572 Dutch twin pairs. They found that, for both males and females, individual differences in smoking initiation were explained by genetic (44%) and environmental (56%) influences. Vink *et al.* also found that the likelihood of becoming addicted to nicotine was influenced primarily (75%) by genetic factors.

The dopamine receptor gene

Blum and Payne (1991) suggest that individuals who are vulnerable to drug addiction suffer from abnormally low levels of the neurotransmitter dopamine and a decreased ability to activate dopamine receptors in the reward centre of the brain. This means that anything that increases the amount of dopamine can produce strong feelings of euphoria. This is consistent with research involving the genetic origins of addictive behaviours. For example, Blum *et al.* (1990) reported that a particular variant of the dopamine receptor gene associated with decreased dopamine receptor availability (the A1 variant) occurred with a much higher frequency in the DNA of samples taken from alcoholics compared to non-alcoholics (Sinha *et al.*).

Stress

Stress as a risk factor for substance abuse is well established. People deal with stressful events in their life by engaging in a variety of behaviours that make them feel better or help them forget the stress. We look at two examples of this below.

Self-medication

The 'self-medication' model (Gelkopf *et al.*, 2002) proposes that some individuals intentionally use different forms of pathological behaviour (e.g. alcohol, drugs and pathological gambling) to 'treat' the psychological symptoms they experience because of everyday stressors in their life. Research on drug abusers, for example, has shown that stress is one of the strongest predictors of relapse (Dawes *et al.*, 2000) and increased drug cravings (Sinha *et al.*, 2000). Although engaging in such behaviour may not actually make things better (i.e. decrease the stress the person is under), the perception that it does is instrumental in that behaviour becoming an addiction.

Traumatic stress

People exposed to severe stress are more vulnerable to addictions. For example, Robins *et al.* (1974) interviewed US soldiers within a year of their return from the Vietnam War. Of these, almost half had used either opium or heroin during their tour of duty, with about 20% reporting that they had developed physical or psychological dependence for heroin at some point during their time in Vietnam.

In a general population study (Kessler *et al.*, 1995), for men with a history of PTSD (post-traumatic stress disorder), 34% reported drug abuse or dependence at some point in their lives, compared to 15% of men without PTSD. For women, 27% of those with a history of PTSD reported drug abuse or dependence, compared to 8% of women without PTSD.

Personality

Research studies have shown that personality characteristics do appear to play an important role in predicting patterns of substance abuse and the development of addiction. Krueger *et al.* (1998) identified a number of personality traits (e.g. sensation seeking and impulsivity) that are commonly associated with addiction. For example, impulsivity ('behaving without thinking and without considering the risk involved in the behaviour') is believed to contribute to a wide range of addictive behaviours such as alcohol abuse, gambling and polysubstance use (i.e. a combination of substances such as alcohol and drugs).

The addiction-prone personality

Barnes *et al.* (2000) developed the addiction-prone personality (APP) scale as a way of assessing the influence of personality factors on addictive behaviour. For example, using the APP, Barnes *et al.* (2005) found that personality was a significant predictor of 'heavy' marijuana use. Studies using the APP scale have shown that this scale is an effective way of discriminating drug addicts from non-addicts, and predicting the severity of addiction and likelihood of remission during recovery.

Addiction and personality disorders

Research suggests a relationship between addiction and personality disorders such as anti-social personality disorder and borderline personality disorder. A review of research in this area (Verhheul *et al.*, 1995) found that the overall prevalence of personality disorders was estimated to be 44% in alcoholics, 70% for cocaine addicts and 79% for opiate addicts. Personality disorders are even more common among polysubstance users. DeJong *et al.* (1993) found evidence of at least one personality disorder in 91% of their sample of polydrug users.

Gender differences in genetic vulnerability to addiction

A limitation of genetic explanations is that although studies of male alcoholics have consistently supported the important role played by genetic factors in the development of alcoholism, research with women has produced inconsistent findings (McGue, 1997). McGue points out that only two of four adoption studies have reported a significant correlation between alcoholism in female adoptees and their biological parents. Likewise, only two of five twin studies found significantly greater concordance for alcoholism among female MZ twins than among female DZ twins. This suggests that genetic factors may be less important in the development of alcoholism in women than in men.

Genetics and the diathesis-stress model

An advantage of genetic explanations of addiction is that they can explain why some people develop addictive behaviour, yet others who have the same environmental experiences and life pressures do not. Some people are more likely to develop an addiction because of their genetic vulnerability (i.e. the diathesis-stress model – see page 154). For example, the A1 variant of the dopamine-receptor gene has been found to be associated with cocaine dependence (Noble et al., 1993), nicotine dependence (Connor et al., 2007) and polydrug abuse (Smith et al., 1992). This suggests that individuals who inherit this gene variant are more vulnerable to develop addictive behaviour because of their low levels of dopamine and the increase in dopamine that is possible with drugs that activate the brain-reward pathway. The exact nature of the addiction, however, appears to be determined by environmental factors, as predicted by the diathesis-stress model.

If stress leads to addiction, does coping lead to abstinence?

It follows that if addiction is a consequence to the experience of stress, then individuals who develop effective coping strategies for stress should have less of a need for addictive behaviour. Research by Matheny and Weatherman (1998) lent some support to this suggestion. They carried out a follow-up study of 263 smokers who had completed a national smoking cessation programme, and found that there was a strong relationship between participants' use of stress coping resources (such as problem solving, tension control and perceived confidence in being able to succeed) and their ability to maintain abstinence from smoking once they had given up.

The role of stress varies by type of addiction

A limitation of stress explanations of addiction is that the relationship between stress and addiction appears to vary according to the type of addiction. The role of stress and drug addiction is fairly well established, for example Dawes et al. (2000) found that stress was a significant predictor of drug relapse. However, support for the role of stress in other forms of addiction is not as convincing. For example, Arévalo et al. (2008) interviewed 393 women from substance abuse programmes in Massachusetts. From these interviews they found evidence of an association between stress and illicit drug use, but no association between stress and alcohol addiction.

Support for the role of impulsivity

Research support for the influence of impulsivity in predicting later substance use and addiction comes from longitudinal studies. For example, Labouvie and McGee (1986) found that adolescents who progressed to heavier levels of alcohol abuse tended to score higher on scores of impulsivity. Blonigen et al. (2011) have gone further in highlighting the impact of impulsivity. They found that alcohol-prone individuals who scored higher on impulsivity had a greater mortality risk than individuals scoring low on impulsivity. For such individuals, impulsivity is linked to a wide range of health-risk behaviours beyond excessive alcohol use, in particular illicit drug abuse.

Personality: Implications of an addiction-prone personality

Empirical evidence supports the claim that there is a relationship between certain personality characteristics and addictive behaviours. For example, research has shown that personality is a key predictor in the initiation of substance use, the development of substance abuse and the maintenance of substance dependence (Barnes et al., 2000). An implication of this research finding is that, by identifying vulnerable individuals in advance (e.g. people most likely to become alcoholics), help could be given to stop their behaviour developing into an addiction. This could potentially prevent the development of substance disorders, reducing the enormous personal costs to those individuals and the costs to society in the treatment of their addictions.

Insider tip…
About 60 words is a good target for an AO3 point. Most of the points on this page are in excess of 100 words, so you need to practise editing these down to about 60 words each to make an effective AO3 point.

⬆ UPGRADE

With questions such as question 1 below, students can get very nervous in deciding how much to write and often end up writing either too much or too little. A rule of thumb is to look at the marks available for this question (4), the total number of marks awarded for the paper (96) and the time allowed for the paper as a whole (2 hours). To save you having to do the maths, if 96 marks = 120 minutes, then 4 marks = 5 minutes.

So, how much would you be expected to write in 5 minutes (given that you also need reading and thinking time)? For these shorter questions (as opposed to the longer essay questions), you should think in terms of about 25 words per mark, giving you a target of 100 words for a question of this type. As well as extent, of course, you also have to think of the amount of detail you include. If you make four distinct points, each of 25 words, that gives you the right amount of extent and an appropriate level of detail for the question.

Let's give it a go – we'll pick the first point, and then you can select the other three and give them the 25-word treatment!

> Slutske et al. (2010) found evidence of genetic vulnerability for gambling addiction with MZ twins having a higher concordance for pathological gambling than DZ twins.

▲ Research suggests that people who develop effective stress coping strategies are more likely to abstain from addictive behaviours.

CAN YOU? No. 11.2

1. Outline the role of genetic vulnerability as a risk factor in the development of addiction. (4 marks)
2. Outline the role of stress as a risk factor in the development of addiction. (4 marks)
3. Briefly outline and evaluate the role of personality as a risk factor in the development of addiction. (6 marks)
4. Outline and evaluate the role of **two or more** risk factors in the development of addiction. (16 marks)

Risk factors: Family influences and peers

The origins of many addictive behaviours can be traced back to childhood and adolescence. Research has consistently shown that early involvement with alcohol, tobacco and drug use increases the risk of dependency and abuse later in life. As a result, researchers have examined the family and peer contexts in an attempt to explain how and why they influence individuals to engage in these risky behaviours.

Sibling influence

Studies have shown that the behaviour of older siblings is strongly associated with adolescent substance use (Griffin *et al.*, 2002). In fact, sibling influence has generally been shown to be stronger than parental influence when it comes to substance use and deviant behaviour in general. In a sample of high school students in the US, sibling alcohol use had a stronger association with adolescent alcohol use than did parental alcohol use (Windle, 2000).

The influence of siblings on the development of substance abuse and other undesirable behaviours appears to be a product of modelling in the sibling relationship (Snyder *et al.*, 2005). The power imbalance between older and younger siblings suggests that older siblings serve as 'role models' for the younger sibling (Whiteman and Christiansen, 2008). Because modelling normalises substance use, it is likely that younger siblings would gravitate toward peers who resemble and validate their older siblings' behaviour.

▲ Older siblings act as role models for their younger siblings.

FAMILY INFLUENCES

Social learning theory (Bandura, 1977) claims that behaviours are learned through the observation of those people with whom a person has the most social contact. For example, Reith and Dobbie (2011) demonstrated the importance of the family in the transmission of gambling behaviour. Drawing on interviews with 50 gamblers, they found that gambling knowledge and behaviour was passed on through the routines of everyday life. Individuals watched and heard family members doing and talking about their gambling and eventually joining in with it.

Parental influences

Parents exert influence on their offspring's addictive behaviour in two main ways. First, they provide social models for their offspring, for example, adolescents with substance abusing parents are more likely to abuse themselves (Biederman *et al.*, 2000). Reith and Dobbie (2011) also found that patterns of gambling were transmitted within families in gendered ways, with males' first experience of gambling being through their fathers, and females' through their mothers. The types of gambling activity that individuals were introduced to in this way were also gendered, with females introduced mainly to machines and bingo and males to sports betting.

A second route of parental influence is via their style of parenting, particularly in terms of the degree of parental control (how much a parent intervenes in their child's life) and parental warmth (how much positive affect a parent shows for their child). *Authoritative* parents show warmth but also exert appropriate control. This form of parenting is associated with the shaping of psychological resilience and emotional well-being in children, and lowered levels of substance abuse (Fletcher *et al.*, 1995).

PEERS

Peer pressure, the direct or indirect encouragement from one's own age group to engage in activities that they may or may not want to engage in, is often cited as a reason for why adolescents engage in potentially risky behaviours such as smoking or substance abuse. **Peers** exert their influence by introducing individuals to these risky behaviours or pressuring them to take part and to continue to do so. Social identity theory (Tajfel and Turner, 1986) explains why individuals are likely to be influenced by peer pressure. This theory suggests that a significant part of an individual's self-concept is formed as a result of the groups of which they are a part (the 'ingroups'). As it is essential to be associated with the ingroup in order to be socially accepted, this makes individuals more likely to adopt their behaviours.

Social networks

Research on the emergence of risky behaviour and the subsequent development of addictive behaviour has focused on the importance of peer networks. For example, among adolescents, smokers tend to befriend smokers, and non-smokers befriend other non-smokers (Eiser *et al.*, 1991) – therefore social networks often comprise of individuals with similar habits. Individual substance use may develop because of the prevalence of substance use within a particular network. Latkin *et al.* (2004) found that the probability of drug abuse was related to the number of members within an individual's social network who used drugs. By modelling behaviours such as alcohol use, members of social networks represent such behaviours as a positive and socially acceptable experience (Kinard and Webster, 2011).

Indirect peer influence

Shakya *et al.* (2012) argue that peer influences may sometimes be expressed through indirect parental influence. For example, positive parenting may discourage substance abuse in adolescents, which can then lead to reduced substance abuse in their friends. Shakya *et al.* claim that an adult who uses positive parenting behaviours with their own adolescent child may also act as an effective mentor for their child's friends. Because the parents of friends are not a part of that individual's adolescent–parent conflict, these adolescents may feel freer to express concerns they may not be able to express with their own parents, and may be more open to influence from their friends' parents as a result.

EVALUATION OF FAMILY INFLUENCES

Support for the role of family influences

There is evidence that supports the importance of family influences on substance abuse and addictive behaviour. For example, Bahr et al. (2005) found that the family characteristics that were most strongly associated with an increased prevalence of binge drinking, smoking and drug use were tolerant parental attitudes and sibling substance use. They also found that adolescents with parents who were tolerant of substance use were more likely to interact with peers who smoked, drank or used illicit drugs. These findings suggest that family influences and peer influences are not independent of each other, in that the tolerant parental attitudes make it more likely that adolescents will seek the company of peers that endorse substance abuse.

Substance abuse may be due to a *lack* of parental influence

Although most explanations of parental influences on substance use focus on the importance of parental modelling and parenting style, it is also possible that alcohol and drug use may result from a *withdrawal* of parental involvement rather than any particular type of parent–adolescent interaction. For example, Stattin and Kerr (2000) suggest that a lack of parental monitoring may result from adolescents disclosing too much information about their substance abuse to their parents. Parents' inability to deal with this information may cause them to stop monitoring offspring whom they perceive as already beyond their control. The consequence of this lack of monitoring and control is that the adolescent continues to abuse and becomes more vulnerable to peer influences.

Intervention studies tend to ignore sibling influences

Most attempts at family intervention relating to substance use in adolescence target only parents rather than siblings. Feinberg et al. (2012) claim that failure to address sibling influences is likely to hinder efforts to reduce early substance use and later substance dependence. Interventions targeted only at the adolescent user or their parents could be undermined by sibling influences, given that older siblings are more likely to be engaged in anti-social and substance use behaviours than their younger siblings, and therefore more likely to be the main source of influence for them.

EVALUATION OF PEER INFLUENCES

Support for peer influences through social media

Research on social media supports the claim that peer influences are an important influence on addictive behaviour. For example, Moreno et al. (2010) studied the MySpace profiles of 400 17–20-year-olds and found that 56% of these profiles contained references to alcohol. Litt and Stock (2011) found that teenagers who viewed peers' Facebook profiles that portrayed alcohol use are more likely to drink themselves. After exposure to these profiles, these teenagers reported a greater willingness to use alcohol, more positive feelings toward it and lower perceptions of its negative consequences. Given that having older friends who drink or use drugs increases the risk of substance use among adolescents, Litt and Stock's research suggests that exposure to social media alters adolescents' normative perceptions and other alcohol-related risk cognitions.

Peer influences may be overstated

Research has generally supported the idea that peers influence adolescent substance abuse through the modelling of risky behaviour (drinking, illicit drug use, etc.), normative beliefs concerning substance use, and offers to participate in the behaviour through social networks. However, the results of a study by De Vries et al. (2006) challenge the claim that peer influence is an important part of this process. They suggest that similarity in smoking behaviour among adolescents is more likely to be a consequence of friendship selection, i.e. smokers befriend other smokers rather than smokers influence non-smokers to take up the habit. Their study found that parental smoking behaviour was a stronger predictor of smoking adoption than peer influence.

Real-world application: Reducing peer influences

Adolescent alcohol abuse has become a major public health concern. For example, a Finnish longitudinal study of 155 women and 176 men (Pitkänen et al., 2005) collected data on alcohol consumption at regular intervals between the ages of 14 and 42. They found that early onset of drinking was a significant risk factor for alcohol dependence in adulthood. Social norm interventions were developed to address this problem. This approach is based on the idea that adolescent behaviour is influenced by misperceptions of how their peers think and act. Overestimations of problem behaviour in peers (e.g. patterns of alcohol or drug use) cause them to increase their own drinking or drug use. Correcting these misperceptions (e.g. through media campaigns) will then result in a decrease in the problem behaviour and lessen the likelihood of later substance dependence.

▲ Exposure to peers' social media posts about alcohol consumption creates the belief that alcohol use is the norm within an individual's social network.

Research methods

The study by Reith and Dobbie (facing page) involved 50 gamblers interviewed three times between 2006 and 2009. Participants were recruited in various ways including visiting gambling venues and displaying posters in local community venues. In the first of these interviews, respondents were encouraged to tell their 'gambling story': retrospective accounts of how they began to gamble and how their playing developed.

1. Identify the **two** sampling methods that were used. (2 marks)
2. Discuss the relative advantages of each method that was used. (3 marks)
3. Identify the kind of interview method that was used and explain your answer. (2 marks)
4. Explain why the data collected would be described as qualitative data. (2 marks)
5. Explain what is meant by *thematic analysis*. (2 marks)
6. Explain how thematic analysis could be used to analyse the data collected in this study. Refer to *coding* in your answer. (4 marks)
7. Give **one** strength and **one** limitation of using qualitative data. (2 marks + 2 marks)

LINK TO RESEARCH METHODS

Thematic analysis page 13.

KEY TERM

Peers refers to individuals of the same age who possess common values and standards of behaviour. Peer groups tend to develop in middle childhood, when belonging to a group becomes more important for a child.

CAN YOU? No. 11.3

1. Outline the role of family influences as a risk factor in addiction. (4 marks)
2. Explain **one** limitation of family influences as a risk factor in addiction. (2 marks)
3. Outline research findings relating to the role of peers as a risk factor in the development of addiction. (6 marks)
4. Discuss risk factors in the development of addiction. (16 marks)

Explanation for nicotine addiction: Brain neurochemistry

A World Health Organization report in 2012 estimated that, globally, 36% of males and 7% of females smoke, although in Europe the percentage of females that smoke is higher, at 19%. But why do people engage in a habit that has such negative health consequences? The answer appears to lie with the **brain neurochemistry** and neurotransmitter **dopamine**. Dopamine is the main neurotransmitter of the reward system in the brain. It plays a role in many different emotions and behaviours, including giving feelings of pleasure when we engage in certain behaviours that activate this reward system. Most recreational drugs act upon the brain's reward system by heightening dopaminergic activity and, as a result, such substances tend to become addictive.

KEY TERMS

Dopamine One of the key neurotransmitters in the brain, with effects on motivation and drive.

Neurochemistry The study of chemical and neural processes associated with the nervous system.

Nicotine is the main active ingredient of tobacco. Nicotine is known to have a number of effects, including stimulant and relaxant effects.

Insider tip…

The sheer weight and complexity of the biology on this page can be daunting, but remember that you are never going to be asked for more than 6 marks worth of description. At most that would be 180 words worth, so bear that in mind when reading this material and when preparing your revision.

Dopamine reward pathway

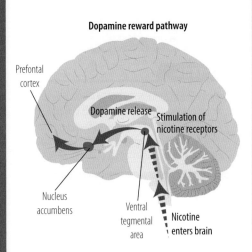

Prefontal cortex

Dopamine release

Stimulation of nicotine receptors

Nucleus accumbens

Ventral tegmental area

Nicotine enters brain

BRAIN NEUROCHEMISTRY AND NICOTINE ADDICTION

Nicotine is the main active ingredient of tobacco. When inhaled through cigarette smoke, nicotine can have a range of different effects, including tranquillisation, decreased irritability, increased alertness and even improved cognitive functioning. However, the performance improvements associated with nicotine inhalation are less evident among regular smokers, who appear to develop tolerance to its effects (Jarvis, 2004).

The finding that nicotine has both stimulant *and* relaxation effects is known as the 'nicotine paradox', i.e. smoking can feel invigorating at some times and calming at others. This paradox can be explained by the fact that smoking only *appears* relaxing because smokers are often in a state of mild nicotine withdrawal, so smoking a cigarette allows the nicotine level in the body to return to normal.

Dopamine and the brain's reward pathways

The typical smoker takes in approximately 1–2 mg of nicotine per cigarette. Nicotine is absorbed through the lining of the mouth and nose and by inhalation in the lungs. After inhalation, nicotine reaches peak levels in the bloodstream and the brain in less than 10 seconds. Nicotine becomes addictive because it activates areas of the brain that regulate feelings of pleasure, i.e. the 'reward pathways' of the brain.

Nicotine attaches to neurons in a region of the brain called the ventral tegmental area (VTA). These neurons trigger release of the neurotransmitter dopamine in a nearby brain region called the nucleus accumbens (NAc). As well as directly influencing the NAc to release dopamine, nicotine also stimulates the release of the neurotransmitter glutamate, which triggers additional release of dopamine. This release of dopamine produces pleasure and a disposition to repeat the behaviours that led to it. It is this pleasure and the drive to repeat the process that leads to addiction.

Glutamate, GABA and MAO

To explain why dopamine levels remain high after the direct nicotine stimulus ends, researchers have investigated the action of two other neurotransmitters in the brain: glutamate and GABA. Glutamate speeds up the activity of neurons, whereas GABA slows down neuron activity. Zickler (2003) discovered that nicotine's effects on glutamate and GABA are responsible for the longer-lasting pleasurable effects of nicotine. Nicotine causes glutamate to speed up dopamine release, but nicotine also prevents GABA from slowing it down after dopamine levels have been raised. This combination of dopamine release and the inhibition of GABA results in an increase in dopamine and an amplification of the rewarding properties of nicotine.

However, this is not the end of the process. Cigarette smoke also contains an as yet unknown substance that blocks the action of an enzyme called monoamineoxidase (MAO). MAO is responsible for breaking down dopamine after it has had its effects. Blocking MAO results in even higher dopamine levels, strengthening the smoking habit by maintaining the feelings of pleasure.

The development of nicotine addiction

Because the effects of nicotine disappear within a few minutes, this creates a need to continue the intake of nicotine throughout the day in order to get the dopamine 'rush'. However, continued activation of the dopamine-enhancing neurons changes their sensitivity to nicotine, resulting in tolerance, dependence and ultimately addiction.

DiFranza (2008) believed that limited exposure to nicotine, even just one cigarette, is enough to cause neuronal changes that stimulate the craving to smoke. For example, a large-scale study in New Zealand found that 25% of the participants had experienced withdrawal symptoms after smoking fewer than five cigarettes (DiFranza, 2008). Although brain activity to the first 'dose' of nicotine is relatively limited, it soon becomes more intense and widespread after just a few more cigarettes. The brain quickly becomes sensitised to nicotine, enabling a nicotine-dependent state to develop. This state is associated with significant withdrawal symptoms when the smoker attempts to abstain from smoking, which can only be overcome by smoking another cigarette.

EVALUATION: BRAIN NEUROCHEMISTRY

Support for the nicotine–dopamine link

Support for the link between nicotine and dopamine comes from the finding (Paterson and Markou, 2002) that an epilepsy drug (gamma-vinyl GABA – GVG) reduces the surge of dopamine in the NAc that occurs after taking nicotine. This reduces the addictive tendencies of nicotine and other drugs that boost the brain levels of dopamine. By counteracting any pleasurable experiences that may be gained by the increase in dopamine, this drug may offer an alternative way of treating nicotine addiction. The researchers claim that GVG would work better than other stop-smoking treatments as it is not addictive, is not based on nicotine and has fewer side effects.

Support for the role of glutamate and GABA

The role of glutamate and GABA in nicotine addiction is supported by a study of nicotine-dependent rats (D'Souza and Markou, 2013). The researchers blocked transmission of the neurotransmitter glutamate, which resulted in a decrease in nicotine intake and nicotine seeking in the animals. Nicotine intake and nicotine seeking also decreased when GABA neurotransmission was facilitated. This is consistent with explanations of the role of these two neurotransmitters, as glutamate enhances the dopamine-releasing effects of nicotine – so blocking it would decrease those effects, making nicotine less rewarding. Likewise, the inhibition of GABA by nicotine keeps the dopamine effect going for longer – therefore facilitation of GABA would overcome this inhibitory effect and also decrease the pleasurable effects of nicotine.

Nicotine and Parkinson's disease

Further support for the link between nicotine and dopamine comes from an unusual source – the treatment of patients with Parkinson's disease (PD). Parkinson's is a progressive neurodegenerative disorder, which is characterised by a gradual loss of dopamine-producing nerve cells, causing the symptoms of PD to appear. Research suggests that smokers are less likely to get PD than those who have never smoked, suggesting that nicotine may have a neuroprotective function against the development of PD and may also be beneficial in its treatment. For example, Fagerstrom et al. (1994) treated two elderly PD patients with nicotine gum and patches. They found significant changes in symptoms that were attributed to the increased levels of dopamine caused by the nicotine administration.

Implications: Nicotine addiction and depression

A Canadian study (Khaled et al., 2009) found that long-term smoking can have an adverse effect on mood because it alters brain neurochemistry. They found that the incidence of depression was highest in long-term smokers and lowest in those who had never smoked. This was also the case in a Chinese study where smoking was associated with a greater risk of depression in both males and females (Luk and Tsoh, 2010). However, in this study, female smokers were particularly at risk of developing depression. The researchers explain that female gender is considered a risk factor for depression in both Western and Chinese cultures, so therefore the greater prevalence of depression in Chinese female smokers could be understood in terms of the additive effects of altered brain chemistry due to smoking and female gender.

▲ Research in China suggests that nicotine addiction was a risk factor for depression, particularly for females.

Nicotine affects men and women differently

Cosgrove et al. (2014) studied the brains of men and women using positron emission tomography (PET) scans in order to measure the changing levels of dopamine when smoking. They observed the dopamine levels of 16 long-term cigarette smokers (8 men and 8 women) while smoking a cigarette. For women, there was a rapid and strong dopamine effect in an area of the brain called the dorsal putamen, whereas men only had moderate to low activation in this area. Men had a rapid and strong activation effect in the ventral striatum, whereas women were only mildly affected. Cosgrove et al. concluded that this finding supports the claim that men and women smoke for different reasons – men for the nicotine effect itself, and women to relieve stress and manage mood.

🐾 APPLY YOUR KNOWLEDGE

Gerry teaches psychology at a university in the south-west. He is a long-term smoker, usually smoking between 15 and 20 cigarettes a day. He finds it difficult to get going in the morning until he has had his first cigarette, and when he is teaching a two-hour seminar he often has to give his students something to do while he nips outside to have a quick cigarette. Smoking gives him a real buzz and energises him for the rest of the seminar. This works quite well for him because he can normally go for about 40 minutes before he needs another nicotine 'fix'.

Using your knowledge of the brain neurochemistry of nicotine addiction, explain Gerry's smoking behaviour.

CAN YOU?   No. 11.4

1. Outline the brain neurochemistry of nicotine addiction. (6 marks)
2. Outline the role of dopamine in nicotine addiction. (4 marks)
3. Explain **one** limitation of the brain neurochemistry explanation of nicotine addiction. (6 marks)
4. Outline and evaluate the brain neurochemistry explanation of nicotine addiction. (16 marks)

Explanation for nicotine addiction: Learning theory

Addiction can be seen as a learned behaviour in that the pleasure or enjoyment from a particular behaviour, such as smoking, is reinforcing, making it more likely the person will repeat the experience. On this spread we look at **learning theory**: how learning operates during the initiation phase of smoking, when people first take up the habit; the maintenance phase, where the habit becomes established; and the relapse phase where learned associations make it difficult to end a habit that has been associated with pleasure for so long. Impulses to smoke can, for some people, become so powerful that they can overwhelm conscious desires to restrain these activities, i.e. they have become addicted to nicotine.

▲ Cigarettes deliver nicotine to the brain extremely efficiently, producing a sudden 'rush' associated with activation of the brain's reward pathways.

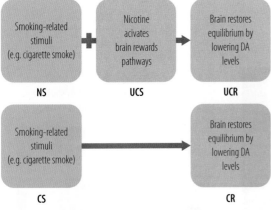

▲ Smokers often relapse because smoking-related cues trigger the same compensatory mechanisms in the brain, motivating them to smoke again in order to feel better.

Nicotine is not the only reinforcing stimulus that leads to smoking

An investigation by the US Food and Drug Administration (FDA, 1995) brought to light tobacco manufacturers' use of additives besides nicotine in cigarettes. These additives (e.g. ingredients to enhance the taste of tobacco smoke) can lead to the increased appeal and addictiveness of tobacco products, i.e. make them even *more* reinforcing for the individual. Research (e.g. Rose, 2006) has shown that the effects of non-nicotine ingredients in tobacco are an important part of maintaining tobacco use. Therefore, although nicotine is the primary drug of addiction, it appears that non-nicotine tobacco ingredients may also contribute to tobacco dependence.

LEARNING THEORY AND NICOTINE ADDICTION

Nicotine addiction is characterised by three phases: initiation, maintenance and relapse (**cue reactivity**).

Initiation

Nicotine addiction begins when people first experiment with smoking. Social learning theory explanations of experimental smoking propose that young people begin smoking as a consequence of the social models they have around them who smoke (Kandel and Wu, 1995). From this perspective, smoking is initially a function of parental and peer role modelling and the vicarious reinforcement that leads young people to expect positive consequences from smoking.

According to the principles of operant conditioning, rewarded behaviours will increase in frequency. Addictive substances and activities are immediately rewarding, which means they are learned quickly, which explains why people get 'hooked' on nicotine very quickly after starting to smoke.

Cigarette smoking is a particularly effective method of nicotine administration. Inhaled nicotine enters the circulation rapidly and enters the brain within seconds. As a result, the individual feels a sudden 'rush', which reinforces the activity that produced it. As we saw on page 298, nicotine activates particular areas of the brain that regulate feelings of pleasure, i.e. the 'reward pathways' of the brain.

Maintenance

The maintenance of the smoking habit is due, in part, to conditioning. When repeated many times, smoking becomes an established behaviour because of the positive consequences for the individual (positive reinforcement). They may, for example, learn that they can manipulate moods by smoking. Not being able to smoke makes them irritable, and smoking provides them with relief (negative reinforcement).

Most people maintain their smoking habit to avoid withdrawal symptoms (see page 293), which can occur if the person does not smoke. As the effect of the nicotine wears off, the person may experience symptoms such as increased anxiety, irritability or low mood. These withdrawal symptoms increase the craving for another cigarette and relief from the withdrawal symptoms. The appearance of withdrawal symptoms when a person abstains from smoking is an indication of the person's physical dependence on nicotine.

Relapse: Cue reactivity

When a person who is addicted to nicotine stops smoking, the urge to smoke again (i.e. relapse) persists long after withdrawal symptoms disappear. With regular smoking, the person comes to associate specific moods, situations or environmental factors (i.e. smoking-related cues) with the rewarding effects of nicotine. These cues often trigger relapse.

Why is this the case? We can explain this in terms of classical conditioning (see left). Nicotine activates brain reward pathways, increasing the release of dopamine. The repetition of the act of smoking thousands of times a year eventually leads to a strong conditioned association between the sensory aspects of smoking (the sight of cigarettes, smell of the smoke, etc.) and the reinforcing effects of nicotine.

This 'nicotine effect' acts as an unconditioned stimulus (UCS). In response to this change in dopamine levels, the brain attempts to restore equilibrium by lowering dopamine levels back to normal. In classical conditioning terms, this is the unconditioned response (UCR). Any stimulus that is associated with the nicotine input into the brain (such as the smell of cigarette smoke) eventually changes from being a neutral stimulus (NS) to become a conditioned stimulus (CS). This CS signals that nicotine is on its way, and with repeated associations it is capable of activating the same conditioned response (CR). This occurs even in the absence of the UCS because, in these situations, the brain's response in the absence of nicotine and its effects means that dopamine levels are lowered *below* the optimum level. This is experienced as withdrawal symptoms, and the person is motivated to smoke again in order to feel better.

Support for social learning explanations of smoking initiation

Many of the claims of social learning influences on the development of addictive behaviours have been supported by research evidence. For example, peer group influences have been found to be the primary influence for adolescents who experiment with smoking (DiBlasio and Benda, 1993). Those adolescents who smoked were more likely to 'hang out' with other adolescents who also smoked. Karcher and Finn (2005) found that youth whose parents smoked were 1.88 times more likely to take up smoking. If their siblings smoked, they were 2.64 times more likely to smoke, and if close friends smoked, they were up to 8 times more likely to smoke than if their parents, siblings and friends did not smoke.

Support for smoking and mood manipulation

Research evidence has supported the claim that negative mood experiences often increase nicotine craving and risk of relapse among those trying to quit smoking. For example, Shiffman and Waters (2004) found that sudden increases in negative mood states, rather than slow changes in stress levels, were associated with relapse. Even among individuals not trying to quit smoking, there is evidence that manipulations of negative affect can increase craving to smoke (Maude-Griffin and Tiffany, 1996). These findings support the negative reinforcement explanation because of the greater likelihood of smoking behaviour during the experience of negative mood.

Support for the role of cue reactivity

Wiers et al. (2013) provided support for the importance of classically conditioned cues in nicotine cravings. They compared a group of current heavy smokers, a group of ex-smokers who had been abstinent for at least five years and a group of individuals who had never smoked. They were asked to respond to pictures of smoking-related and neutral cues with either an 'approach' response or with an 'avoid' response. Craving scores were measured using a questionnaire of smoking urges. Heavy smokers showed a significant approach bias toward smoking-related cues compared to the other two groups. The extent of this bias was positively correlated with their craving scores. This was not the case for ex-smokers or non-smokers, confirming that smoking cues are present in heavy smokers and play a significant role in nicotine addiction.

Gender differences in patterns of nicotine addiction

A limitation of current learning theory explanations of nicotine addiction is that they fail to acknowledge the fact that it follows a different pattern in men and women, according to López et al. (1994). They found that women start smoking later than men, and that there are gender-related differences in relation to both the development and context of smoking behaviour. Other research has shown that women are more likely than men to light up in stressful situations and their nicotine dependence grows more rapidly (Baewert et al., 2014). Women also experience withdrawal effects sooner and have a harder time giving up the habit. Learning theory explanations of nicotine addiction generally fail to address these specific gender differences.

▲ Research has shown that women are more likely than men to light up in stressful situations and their nicotine dependence grows more rapidly.

Implications for treatment

Drummond et al. (1990) propose a treatment approach based on the idea that the cues associated with smoking or other forms of drug taking are an important factor in the maintenance of that habit. The proposed treatment, cue exposure therapy (CET), involves presenting the cues without the opportunity to engage in the smoking behaviour. This leads to a phenomenon known as stimulus discrimination, as without the reinforcement provided by the actual nicotine, the association between the cue and smoking is extinguished, thereby reducing the craving for cigarettes that arises when exposed to that particular cue. Unrod et al. (2014) demonstrated the effectiveness of this approach in a study of 76 moderately dependent smokers, with CET resulting in a progressive decline in cue-provoked craving within six sessions of treatment.

UPGRADE

Question 2 below asks you to give two *criticisms* of the learning theory of nicotine addiction. There are a number of things to bear in mind when answering questions like this:

1. The term 'criticism' does not necessarily imply something negative about the theory – it can also be something positive about it. For example, the theory has implications for the treatment of nicotine addiction, for example cue exposure therapy.
2. If the term 'limitation' had been used instead, then this would have prompted you to look at the negative aspects of the theory, for example that it ignores the different patterns of nicotine addiction in men and women.
3. To maximise your marks in these questions, you need to *elaborate* your answer. As we have said elsewhere in this book (e.g. page 75), there are lots of ways to do this. A straightforward one is to *identify* the criticism, *justify* the criticism by providing evidence that this is the case, and then *explain* why this is good or bad for the theory.

Using the evaluation on this page, have a go at constructing a 60 word critical point following the advice above. We've done one for you, so you can do a second one.

A strength of learning theory is that it has implications for treatment of nicotine addiction. Cue exposure therapy presents cues associated with smoking without the opportunity to smoke. Without the reinforcing effects of nicotine, the association between cue and smoking is extinguished. Unrod et al. demonstrated the effectiveness of CET resulting in a decline in cue-provoked craving within six sessions, supporting the claim that many aspects of nicotine addiction are learned.

KEY TERMS

Cue reactivity Objects and environments associated with a drug or behaviour become conditioned stimuli, so people experience greater craving and physiological arousal when exposed to the objects and environments associated with their addiction.

Learning theory Explanations (such as classical and operant conditioning) which explain behaviour in terms of learning rather than any inborn tendencies, physiological factors or cognitive reasoning.

CAN YOU? No. 11.5

1. Briefly explain the learning theory explanation of nicotine addiction. (4 marks)
2. Give **two** criticisms of the learning theory of nicotine addiction. (3 marks)
3. Outline the role of cue reactivity in nicotine addiction. (3 marks)
4. Outline and evaluate the learning theory explanation of nicotine addiction. (16 marks)

Explanation for gambling addiction: Learning theory

Learning theory explains gambling as a behaviour that is subject to reinforcement, which in turn strengthens gambling tendencies. Skinner (1953) argued that the individual's gambling behaviour is a function of his or her previous reinforcement, i.e. initial success with gambling leads to an increased likelihood that the behaviour will continue. A problem for this explanation is why some people persist with their gambling behaviour even when there is very little reinforcement, i.e. when they lose far more than they win. On this spread we look at this tricky relationship between reinforcement and gambling addiction.

The term 'addiction' is not often used in the literature when talking about gambling. Terms like 'pathological' or 'problem' gambling are preferred. We have used these terms interchangeably with 'gambling addiction' throughout this chapter, so you recognise that they are all describing the same thing.

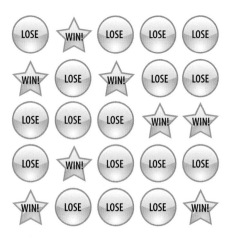

▲ With a variable reinforcement schedule, the uncertainty of when a payout is due keeps a gambler playing for longer.

In the UK, all gaming machines (slot machines, fruit machines) are required by law to clearly display the percentage return-to-player figure or RTP (expressed as a percentage of money staked). Average RTP is generally measured over 10,000 or 100,000 games. For example, if a machine displays an 85% RTP, that means that, over 10,000 games (for example), the machine will pay out 85% of the money staked by players. Although there is no legal minimum for RTP, most machines have at least a 70% RTP.

▼ Casinos have many ways of making gambling appear exciting and rewarding for the gambler.

LEARNING THEORY EXPLANATIONS OF GAMBLING ADDICTION

Operant conditioning proposes that any behaviour that produces a consequence that the individual finds rewarding then becomes more frequent. Griffiths (2009) argues that gamblers playing slot machines may become addicted because of the physiological rewards (e.g. getting a buzz from winning), psychological rewards (e.g. the near miss) and social rewards (e.g. peer praise), as well as the financial rewards if they win. This may seem strange given that the gambler generally loses but, as Delfabbro and Winefield (1999) point out, gamblers are not always rational in their thinking, and greater weight may be given to the experience of winning.

Partial reinforcement

Gamblers are people who are particularly susceptible to conditioning, with winning representing the rewards. For example, the sequence of outcomes in some forms of gambling (e.g. fruit machines) is determined by a **partial reinforcement** schedule. With a partial reinforcement schedule, wins follow some bets, but not all. Partial reinforcement means that any behaviours acquired are much slower to extinguish because of the uncertainty of reinforcement. In gambling terms this means it is more difficult to stop gambling despite losing for much of the time.

Variable reinforcement

Casinos use the draw of a partial reinforcement schedule to attract gamblers, because the uncertainty of when a payout is due keeps players playing for longer. A particular type of partial reinforcement, where only a proportion of a player's responses are rewarded, is known as **variable reinforcement**. Gambling machines use a particular type of variable reinforcement, known as variable-ratio reinforcement, with wins occurring after an unpredictable number of responses. For example, sometimes a win will come after two responses, sometimes after four responses, sometimes after six responses and so on. The average ratio of wins to losses may be one to four, but when they occur is unpredictable. It is the unpredictability of these rewards that keeps people gambling.

Gambling and its rewards

To people who don't gamble, the idea that gambling is 'rewarding' may seem somewhat bizarre, so let's look a little closer at the different ways that gamblers are 'rewarded' for gambling and why it is so hard to give up.

The 'big win' hypothesis

Early experiences with a potentially addictive substance or behaviour are particularly important in shaping long-term addictive behaviour. Many pathological gamblers report having a 'big win' early in their gambling career or an early prolonged winning streak. They continue to gamble because of a desire to repeat that early 'peak experience' (Aasved, 2003).

The 'near miss'

Gambling can provide reinforcement even in the absence of a win. Near misses or losses that are 'close' to being wins create a brief period of excitement and thrill that encourage further gambling (Reid, 1986). Some fruit machines are designed to ensure a higher than chance frequency of near misses, as this form of reinforcement occurs at no expense to the casino.

The gambling environment

The casino itself is experienced as reinforcing. Flashing lights, ringing bells and the sound of coins tumbling out of the fruit machines are all exciting for the gambler. People are often lured into the 'exciting' gambling environment with free bets for a limited period of time, as the casino environment or the Internet betting environment become conditioned stimuli, and exhilaration the conditioned response. These stimuli act as triggers for gambling because they have the ability to increase arousal (classical conditioning).

Learning theory can't explain all forms of gambling

A problem for explanations of gambling based on operant conditioning is that it is difficult to apply the same principles to all different forms of gambling. For example, some forms of gambling have a short time-period between the behaviour and the consequence (e.g. scratch cards), whereas others (such as sports betting) have a much longer period between bet and outcome, and so have less to do with chance and simple conditioning and more to do with the skill of the individual.

Fails to explain why only some people become addicted

A learning explanation of pathological gambling explains addiction in terms of the consequences of the gambling behaviour. However, there are problems with seeing addiction solely as a product of its reinforcing properties. Although many people gamble at some time during their lives and experience the reinforcements associated with this behaviour, relatively few become addicts. This suggests, therefore, that there are other factors involved in the transition from gambling behaviour to gambling addiction.

Support for the influence of partial reinforcement

Horsley *et al.* (2012) tested the assumption that partial reinforcement is fundamentally important to the persistence of gambling in the absence of winning, particularly among high-frequency gamblers. They subjected high- and low-frequency gamblers to either partial or continuous (i.e. full) reinforcement. After partial reinforcement, high-frequency gamblers continued to respond on a gambling simulation for longer compared to low-frequency gamblers despite the lack of further reinforcement. The researchers concluded that the greater persistence of response among this group may be a result of increased dopamine function that is particular to high-frequency gamblers, making them more likely to continue gambling, even in the absence of reinforcement.

Reinforcement schedules may lead to irrational beliefs

There is some support for the claim that an early big win can lead to persistence in gambling behaviour. Sharpe (2002) claimed that the placement of wins early in the gaming experience (i.e. a big win when first gambling) and the patterns of wins and losses within gaming sessions may lead to irrational thoughts generated by beliefs about gaming machine reinforcement schedules. For example, an early big win may give the gambler the illusion that they can control the outcomes and that they possess the skill necessary to win. The resulting overestimation of the chances to win and the underestimation of the possible losses encourage persistent gambling.

Different pathways to gambling addiction

Blaszczynski and Nower (2002) claim there are different pathways for gambling addiction. Gamblers who are 'behaviourally conditioned' may have begun gambling because of exposure to gambling through role models or peer groups. Their gambling addiction may, therefore, be explained largely through the processes of social learning and reinforcement. However, a second subgroup tends to have accompanying anxiety and/or depression, a history of poor coping skills, as well as negative background experiences and life events. These factors produce an 'emotionally vulnerable' gambler, who uses gambling primarily to relieve their aversive emotional states. This suggests that learning theory can only explain some types of gambling addiction, but does not explain all forms of gambling addiction.

▲ Learning theory is better able to explain some types of gambling than others.

🎧 Research methods

A group of psychology students decided to compare the effect of continuous and partial reinforcement schedules on the behaviour of dogs. To do this they collected a sample of 50 dogs and tried to teach them a very simple trick (sitting down on the click of their owner's fingers). There were 100 trials for each dog. Half of the dogs were rewarded using continuous reinforcement and half rewarded using partial reinforcement. At the end, the students measured whether the dogs had learned the trick.

1. Identify the independent variable in this study. (1 mark)
2. Explain how the dogs could be randomly allocated to conditions. (2 marks)
3. Outline how the dogs could be taught using a partial reinforcement schedule. (3 marks)
4. Explain how the dependent variable might be operationalised in this study. (2 marks) HINT: You need some way to measure the success of each dog in learning the trick.
5. In order to analyse the results, a statistical test was used. Identify a suitable test and explain the reasons for your choice. (3 marks)
6. Identify and describe **one or more** potential confounding variables in this study. (3 marks)

LINK TO RESEARCH METHODS

The topics in these questions are covered in the research methods chapter of our Year 1 book.

KEY TERMS

Learning theory Explanations (such as classical and operant conditioning) which explain behaviour in terms of learning rather than any inborn tendencies, physiological factors or cognitive reasoning.

Partial reinforcement Only some responses are reinforced, compared to full reinforcement where every response is reinforced. For example responses may be reinforced every 5th time (regular interval) or at variable intervals.

Variable reinforcement A response is reinforced after an unpredictable number of responses. In variable ratio reinforcement, the delivery of reinforcement is unpredictable but averages out at a specific rate.

CAN YOU? No. 11.6

1. Explain what is meant by the terms *partial reinforcement* and *variable reinforcement* in the context of gambling. (2 marks each)
2. Give **two** criticisms of the learning theory explanation of gambling addiction. (3 marks each)
3. Outline and evaluate the learning theory explanation of gambling addiction. (16 marks)

Explanation for gambling addiction: Cognitive theory

In contrast to the previous spread, a cognitive view of addiction emphasises habitual ways of thinking and of interpreting events that might lead to the development of addictive behaviour. The cognitive approach to behaviour sees many abnormal behaviours resulting from irrational thought processes. From this perspective, the development of a gambling addiction depends, in part, on the individual reasons for a person's gambling behaviour, the way it makes them feel and their expectations of being able to 'beat the system'.

▲ Close…but no win. Research suggests that near misses reinforce gamblers' behaviour so they are more likely to continue playing as a result.

Gambling addiction and deficits in executive cognitive function

Research studies of adult pathological gamblers have found evidence of deficits in executive cognitive functions, such as working memory, reward processing and impulse control. These functions, which are essential for cognitive and emotional self-regulation, are impaired in pathological gamblers. For example, Goudriaan *et al.* (2006) found that pathological gamblers showed relatively poor performance on inhibition, cognitive flexibility and planning tasks compared to control participants.

Executive cognitive functions are localised in an area of the brain called the prefrontal cortex (PFC) and mature gradually during adolescence and into early adulthood. The deficits observed in pathological gamblers are thought to represent a dysfunction in PFC circuitry. For example, Cavedini *et al.* (2002) found that pathological gamblers showed similar decision-making impairments to those found in frontal lobe damaged patients. The role of the PFC in impulse control and the late maturation of some of its functions suggest that the relatively high levels of risky behaviour seen in adolescence may, in part, be a consequence of immature prefrontal executive function (Romer *et al.* 2011).

COGNITIVE THEORY AND GAMBLING ADDICTION

The role of cognitive biases

The cognitive approach to gambling addiction is based on the assumption that irrational beliefs and distorted thinking patterns contribute to the development and maintenance of problem gambling. These are referred to as **cognitive biases**, and include overestimating personal ability to influence the outcome of random events (illusions of control), expectations of imminent wins after losing streaks (gambler's fallacy), selective recall of winning and losing (the recall bias) and seeing 'nearly winning' as encouragement for further play (the 'near miss' bias).

The gambler's fallacy

The gambler's fallacy is the belief that completely random events such as a coin toss are somehow influenced by recent events. For example, a gambler might believe that runs of a particular outcome (two or three heads in a row) will be balanced out by the opposite outcome (i.e. the same number of tails).

Illusions of control

Illusions of control are demonstrated through the performance of superstitious behaviours, which the gambler believes helps them to manipulate the event outcome in their favour. Pathological gamblers may also show an exaggerated self-confidence in their ability to 'beat the system' and influence chance. This is in part due to the different attributions that many gamblers make about their gambling, with success being attributed to their personal ability or skill, and failure attributed to chance factors, such as bad luck.

The 'near miss' bias

Near misses occur when an unsuccessful outcome is *close* to a win; for example, when a horse the gambler has bet on finishes in second place or when two out of three cherries are displayed on the slot machine pay line. As a consequence of these near misses, the gambler may feel that he is 'not constantly losing but constantly nearly winning' (Griffiths, 1991). Near misses appear to have some rewarding value for the gambler despite the lack of any monetary reinforcement associated with winning.

The recall bias

Pathological gamblers often suffer from a recall bias, i.e. the tendency to remember and overestimate wins while forgetting about, underestimating or rationalising losses (Blanco *et al.*, 2000). Consequently, a string of losses does not always act as a disincentive for future gambling. Such individuals believe they will eventually be rewarded for their efforts and could be motivated to return on subsequent occasions because of a belief that they 'deserve' to win, having lost so often on previous occasions (the 'just world' hypothesis).

Key study: Cognitive bias in fruit machine gambling

Mark Griffiths (1994) set out to discover whether regular gamblers thought and behaved differently to non-regular gamblers when playing fruit machines.

Procedure The study took place in an amusement arcade. Griffiths compared 30 regular gamblers (who played fruit machines more than once a week) with 30 non-regular gamblers, who played less than once a month. Each individual was given £3 to spend playing a fruit machine ('*Fruitskill*') in the arcade. Griffiths was interested in the gamblers' verbalisations as they played the machine, assuming that this would give some insight into the particular cognitive biases that were operating at the time.

Findings The regular gamblers believed they were more skilful than they actually were. They were more likely to make irrational statements during play such as 'Putting only a quid in bluffs the machine', an example of the 'illusion of control' bias. Subsequent interviews with the participants revealed that whereas the majority of the non-regular gamblers believed playing the game was 'mostly chance' and none believed it was 'skill', 26 of the 30 regular gamblers believed success was either due to skill or equally chance and skill. Regular gamblers also explained away their losses by seeing 'near misses' as 'near wins', something that justified their continuation. For example, one-third of the regular gamblers continued playing until they had lost all their money, whereas only 2 of the non-regular gamblers did so.

EVALUATION

Research support for the role of cognitive biases

There is a great deal of evidence demonstrating the presence of high rates of cognitive biases in populations of problem gamblers. Studies (e.g. Ladouceur *et al.*, 2002) have found that up to 80% of gambling-related verbalisations made by problem gamblers seeking treatment would be classified as irrational. In contrast, research with recreational gamblers (those who gamble only occasionally and only for pleasure) has not found the same high degree of cognitive biases. This lends support to the claim that irrational beliefs are what sustains the gambling habit and makes people more vulnerable to developing a gambling addiction (Petry, 2005).

Implications for treatment

An implication of the cognitive explanation of gambling addiction is that cognitive behavioural therapy (CBT) might be helpful in reducing that addiction. Interventions such as CBT (see page 310) could be used to correct cognitive biases (such as the gambler's fallacy), which in turn would reduce the motivation to gamble. This type of intervention has been shown to have positive outcomes in reducing gambling behaviour. For example, Echeburúa *et al.* (1996) found that CBT was particularly effective in preventing relapse in gamblers who played slot machines. The researchers did acknowledge, however, that slot-machine pathological gamblers may not be totally representative of the larger population of problem gamblers.

Irrational thinking varies with type of gambling

Lund (2011) argues that some types of gambling are more likely than others to encourage cognitive biases and other irrational beliefs. Lund looked at the association between irrational beliefs and gambling preferences in nearly 5,000 adults. She found that increased frequency of gambling was related to increased cognitive biases, but this effect was stronger for some types of gambling than for others. Cognitive biases were more likely in gamblers who preferred gambling machines and Internet gambling than sports betting and horse racing. The use of gambling machines and Internet gambling games is characterised by the mistaken beliefs that skill is involved when actually it is not. Lund concluded that mistaken ideas of skill and illusions of control are important factors in the development of cognitive biases, which in turn can lead to gambling addiction.

Awareness does not decrease susceptibility to cognitive bias

Despite the logic underlying cognitive explanations of pathological gambling, research suggests that possessing relevant knowledge does not make people less susceptible to cognitive distortions. For example, Benhsain and Ladouceur (2004) administered a gambling-related cognition scale to two groups of university students: one group trained in statistics and the other in a non-statistical field. They found no difference between the two groups in their susceptibility to irrational gambling-related cognitions. Likewise, Delfabbro *et al.* (2006) found that pathological gamblers were more irrational in some forms of gambling-related cognition, but were just as accurate as non-gamblers in estimating the odds of winning.

Cognitive biases may have a biological basis

Research has shown that gambling addicts may have developed a different pattern of brain activity compared to non-gamblers. This particular pattern of brain activity gives them the misguided belief that they are able to beat the odds in games of chance. Clark *et al.* (2014) identified a region of the brain that appears to play a critical role in supporting the distorted thinking that makes people more likely to develop gambling addiction. The researchers discovered that if this region (the insula) is damaged as a result of brain injury, then people become immune to cognitive biases such as the gambler's fallacy. The findings suggest that if the cognitive biases found in gambling addicts have a neurological basis, then they could be treated with drugs that target specific regions of the brain.

⬆ UPGRADE

In other upgrades in this book (e.g. pages 65 and 75), we have offered advice about how to answer essay questions such as question 3 below. It is always worth spending a bit of time planning your response to such questions as there are so many marks up for grabs.

The specific issue in question 3 here is that there are a number of distinct requirements, and all must be covered in appropriate detail to ensure you get a good mark. Let's look at some of these issues here:

- The question says 'Discuss'. This is not another term for 'Chat about', but is an alternative to the term 'Outline and evaluate'. That means there is a requirement for both description *and* evaluation in your answer.
- You are required to cover cognitive biases in your answer. The material on the left side of this spread is all about cognitive biases.
- Finally, the question uses the term 'research'. The term 'research' as opposed to 'research studies' can include reference to theories/explanations and/or studies, so you could write about the Griffiths study on the left side of this spread as well as the different biases and the self-medication explanation of gambling addiction.

To plan a response, consider a good answer to be around 480 words (that's about 30 words a mark). Given that the marking allocation for this question nominally allocates 6 marks for AO1 (description) and 10 for AO3 (evaluation), that would mean about 180 words of AO1 and 300 of AO3 (five critical points @ 60 words a point). This means you have to be selective in your choice of material, particularly for the AO1 content.

🔲 KEY TERMS

Cognitive biases are irrational beliefs that are unhelpful, illogical and inconsistent with our social reality, and which can lead us to behave in inappropriate ways.

CAN YOU?　　　　　No. 11.7

1. Explain what is meant by the term *cognitive biases* in the context of the cognitive theory of gambling addiction. (2 marks)
2. Outline the findings of **one** study relating to the cognitive theory explanation of gambling addiction. (4 marks)
3. Discuss research relating to the cognitive theory explanation of gambling addiction, including the role of cognitive biases. (16 marks)

Reducing addiction: Drug therapy

Because addictive behaviour is costly, both for the individual and for society as a whole, psychologists have developed a number of therapies to help people deal with the misery of their addiction. Of course, this does assume that people *want* to overcome their addiction, and live a life that's free of drugs, alcohol or gambling opportunities. On this and the next spread we look at some of the different therapies that are available to help reduce these problem behaviours. We begin by looking at drug therapies.

▲ NRT gradually releases nicotine into the bloodstream at much lower levels than in a cigarette and so reduces the urge to smoke.

Heroin addiction and methadone

Methadone is a synthetic drug widely used in the treatment of heroin addiction. Methadone mimics the effects of heroin but lasts longer in the body and is less addictive. Like heroin, it produces feelings of euphoria, but to a lesser degree. Initially, a drug abuser is prescribed gradually increasing amounts of methadone to increase tolerance to the drug. The dose is then slowly decreased until the addict no longer needs either methadone or heroin.

▲ A heroin addict takes his prescription methadone.

DRUG THERAPIES FOR THE REDUCTION OF ADDICTION

Drug therapy is a general term for interventions that use medication in order to treat addiction. Drugs interact with receptors or enzymes in the brain to reduce cravings for a drug or the desire to engage in a particular behaviour. Drug therapy for nicotine addiction typically involves either the use of a nicotine replacement – including nicotine patches, spray and gum – or the use of pharmacological interventions.

Drug treatments for nicotine addiction

After a person smokes for a while, the body gets used to getting regular doses of nicotine from cigarettes. When people stop smoking, this nicotine quickly disappears from the body, leading to withdrawal symptoms and a craving for another cigarette.

Nicotine replacement therapy

Nicotine replacement therapy (NRT) works by gradually releasing nicotine into the bloodstream at much lower levels than in a cigarette and also without all the other harmful chemicals found in cigarette smoke. This helps the individual control their cravings for a cigarette, improves their mood and helps to prevent relapse.

Drug treatments – varenicline and bupropion

In addition, two prescription medications have been NHS approved for nicotine addiction – varenicline (trade name *Champix*) and bupropion (trade name *Zyban*). These are nicotine-free pills that reduce a person's craving for tobacco and help with any withdrawal symptoms. They have different mechanisms of action in the brain, but both help prevent relapse in people trying to quit. For example, bupropion, which was originally developed as an antidepressant, works by inhibiting the re-uptake of dopamine and has been shown to be effective as a smoking cessation drug (Hughes *et al.*, 2004).

Drug treatments for gambling addiction

No drug has yet been approved for use in the UK to treat pathological gambling, but research suggests that drug treatments can have beneficial effects. Drug treatments can reduce the urges and cravings to gamble and can also reduce the symptoms of depression or anxiety that may trigger continued gambling. The main types of drug used in the treatments are opiate antagonists, antidepressants and mood stabilisers.

Opioid antagonists

The term opioid antagonist is used to describe a type of drug that acts upon the opioid receptors, an important step in the pathway for processing dopamine, the neurotransmitter that activates the brain's feelings of reward. Opioid antagonists bind to the opioid receptors in the body, which results in the blocking of these receptors. As a result, this prevents the individual experiencing the rewarding response they associate with a particular substance or behaviour, including gambling. By reducing the reinforcing properties of gambling behaviour, this reduces the urge to gamble. For example, Kim *et al.* (2002) conducted a 12-week double-blind placebo-controlled trial, where they gave either naltrexone (an opiate antagonist) or a placebo to 45 pathological gamblers. Naltrexone targets the 'D2' dopamine pathway in the brain, which is associated with rewards. They found that naltrexone was effective in reducing the frequency and intensity of gambling urges, as well as gambling behaviour itself. Naltrexone also appeared more effective in gamblers with severe urges to gamble rather than those who described their urges to gamble as moderate.

Antidepressants

There is evidence to support serotonin dysfunction in pathological gambling (George and Murali, 2005). Research suggests that gamblers treated with SSRIs to increase serotonin levels show significant improvements in their gambling behaviour compared to a control group. There are a number of reasons why pathological gamblers would be helped by receiving SSRIs. First, SSRIs reduce symptoms of depression and anxiety. As many gamblers report gambling as a response to the stressors in their life, reducing the symptoms associated with these stressors lessens the urge to gamble. Second, impulsivity is believed to contribute to a wide range of addictive behaviours, including gambling (see page 294). Low levels of serotonin have been found in individuals with impaired impulse control, including pathological gamblers. Administration of SSRIs, which raise serotonin activity and therefore should reduce impulsivity, should also reduce pathological gambling.

'Blinding' refers to a method used in research design whereby the participant doesn't know what condition they are in (single blind), or neither the participants nor experimenter knows who is in which condition (double blind).

EVALUATION

Support for the effectiveness of nicotine replacement therapy

Stead *et al.* (2012) investigated the effectiveness of nicotine replacement therapy (NRT) compared to placebo in the treatment of nicotine addiction. They identified 150 trials that had compared NRT with either a placebo treatment or a non-NRT control group. They concluded that all the different types of NRT (e.g. patch, gum, inhaler) were effective in helping people kick their nicotine habit, and were 70% more effective than a placebo. The effectiveness of NRT was independent of any additional support provided to the individual, suggesting that quitting was a consequence of the NRT treatment alone.

Lack of blinding in NRT studies

Critics argue that clinical trials of NRT are not truly 'blind', because the patients receiving nicotine recognise the sensation and the ones receiving a placebo feel the withdrawal effects of no nicotine. A study by Mooney *et al.* (2004) found that, of 73 double-blind placebo controlled NRT trials, only 17 had conducted blinding assessments, i.e. asking participants whether they believed they were using a real nicotine delivery device or an empty placebo. The researchers found that, in these 17 studies, almost two-thirds of those in the placebo condition were 'confident' that they had not received the real nicotine patch. This lack of effective blinding in NRT trials means that conclusions about the effectiveness of this form of treatment are more uncertain than has been claimed.

Naltrexone can make fun activities seem 'uninspiring'

A problem with the use of opioid antagonists such as naltrexone concerns its basic mechanism, i.e. it works by blocking the brain's reward system when the person engages in gambling behaviour. Unfortunately, this mechanism is a fairly crude and general one, in that by stopping the brain from releasing dopamine (which makes the activity feel good), it could cause some patients to lose pleasure in other areas of life (e.g. playing sport, having sex, etc.) while they are on the drug. This tendency to make fun activities seem 'uninspiring' is a downside of naltrexone for many addicts, and one reason why some choose not to continue with their treatment.

Methodological issues in drug therapies for gambling addiction

Although there is some evidence to suggest that gambling addiction is amenable to drug treatment, the validity of such conclusions is compromised by methodological limitations of research in this area. Blaszczynski and Nower (2007) claim that research studies are characterised by small sample sizes, high dropout rates and low numbers of females who are problem gamblers. Many studies fail to include control groups or randomly assign gamblers to different treatment conditions. Moreover, they argue, research has generally failed to address the impact of co-morbidity (i.e. the presence of other psychiatric or medical conditions) on treatment response, which makes it difficult to draw conclusions about the influence of drug therapies alone.

Support for the effectiveness of drug treatments for gambling

Research provides support for the claim that SSRIs, which raise serotonin activity in the brain, have beneficial effects on gambling behaviour. Grant and Potenza (2006) gave 13 gambling addicts escitalopram (an SSRI) for three months. At the end of the three months, some of the individuals who had improved (in that they gambled less and had fewer anxiety symptoms) were randomly assigned to either continue with the escitalopram for three months or receive a placebo. Of the three who received escitalopram, improvement continued for the next three months, whereas for the one person who had received the placebo, both gambling symptoms and anxiety had returned within just four weeks. This demonstrates that the improvements noted in the first part of the study were due to the effects of the drug rather than some other factor (e.g. receiving attention, visiting the surgery, etc.).

Research methods

You can read about the study by Grant and Potenza on this spread ('Support for the effectiveness of drug treatments for gambling, below left). The study is an example of a randomised control trial because participants were randomly assigned to conditions.

1. Identify the **two** conditions in the study. (2 marks)
2. How might participants be randomly assigned to one of the conditions? (1 mark)
3. Write a suitable directional hypothesis for the study. (2 marks)
4. Participants' anxiety levels were assessed. Explain how the researchers might have done this. (2 marks)
5. Identify **one** other potential limitation to this study and consider its importance. (3 marks)
6. Select **one** feature of science and use it to explain in what way this study is scientific. (2 marks)
7. The research study was published in a peer-reviewed journal. Explain what is meant by 'peer review'. (2 marks)

LINK TO RESEARCH METHODS

Features of science page 20.

KEY TERM

Drug therapy Interventions that use medication in order to treat addiction. Drugs interact with receptors or enzymes in the brain to reduce cravings for a drug or the desire to engage in a particular behaviour.

CAN YOU?   No. 11.8

1. Briefly explain and give **one** criticism of drug therapy as a way of reducing addiction. (6 marks)
2. Outline and evaluate drug therapy as a way of reducing addiction. (16 marks)

Reducing addiction: Behavioural interventions

Behavioural interventions work on the assumption that addictive behaviours are learned and so can be reduced or eliminated by changing the consequences of these behaviours. Because people usually choose to do things based on the past consequences of these behaviours, therapies based on this approach try to replace pleasant consequences with unpleasant consequences so the individual is no longer motivated to smoke, gamble and so on. On this spread we look at two such interventions: **aversion therapy** (sometimes known as overt sensitisation) and **covert sensitisation**.

KEY TERMS

Aversion therapy aims to decrease or eliminate the undesirable behaviours associated with addiction by associating them with unpleasant or uncomfortable sensations.

Behavioural interventions work on the assumption that addictive behaviours are learned and so can be reduced or eliminated by changing the consequences of these behaviours.

Covert sensitisation involves eliminating an unwanted behaviour by creating an imaginary association between the behaviour and an unpleasant stimulus or consequence.

Insider tip…

The two examples on this page (i.e. the treatment of gambling addiction and problem drinking) serve two main purposes. First they provide extra detail to add depth to your description of aversion therapy and covert sensitisation. Second, they show how these two techniques might be used in practice, should you be asked to apply them to a novel scenario.

Insider tip…

In an exam you might be asked to describe how this technique might be used in practice. The examples on this page should help to deal with such questions.

BEHAVIOURAL THERAPIES FOR THE REDUCTION OF ADDICTION

People often begin engaging in behaviours such as gambling and smoking because they find it pleasurable. This explains why people begin abusing substances or engaging in gambling. Once they associate alcohol or drugs or gambling with reward, they have an increasing desire to engage in the same behaviours in the future. Behavioural therapies try to change a person's motivation to engage in these behaviours. This can be achieved in one of two ways, either by introducing a *real* unpleasant association, as in aversion therapy (also known as 'overt sensitisation'), or by introducing an *imagined* unpleasant association, as in covert sensitisation.

Aversion therapy

The aim of aversion therapy is to decrease or eliminate the undesirable behaviours associated with addiction by associating them with unpleasant or uncomfortable sensations. Aversion therapy is based on the principles of classical conditioning – an individual learns to associate an *aversive* stimulus (the UCS – something that causes a strong feeling of dislike or disgust) with an action they had previously enjoyed (the NS – e.g. taking a drink, smoking a cigarette or playing online poker).

During aversion therapy, the patient is asked to engage in the behaviour while at the same time being exposed to something unpleasant such as a drug that makes them nauseous, a foul smell or even mild electric shocks. Once the behaviour becomes associated with the unpleasant stimulus (i.e. it becomes a CS), it will begin to decrease in frequency or stop entirely. The addictive behaviours that have been treated with aversion therapy include alcohol abuse, drug abuse, smoking and pathological gambling.

An example: Treatment of gambling addiction

The patient is asked to keep a behavioural diary, which is used as a baseline to measure whether change is occurring during the course of treatment. A small, battery-powered electrical device is placed on the patient's wrist, and the patient is asked to preselect a level of shock that is uncomfortable but not too painful. This shock is then briefly and repeatedly paired with stimuli (such as pictures of a betting shop, casino chips, online poker images, etc.) that the patient has chosen for their association with their problem gambling. The duration and intensity of the shock are carefully planned by the therapist to ensure that the patient experiences a discomfort level that is aversive and that the conditioning effect occurs. The discomfort from the electric shock becomes associated with the gambling behaviour and the patient reports loss of desire and stops gambling.

Covert sensitisation

Like aversion therapy, covert sensitisation involves eliminating an unwanted behaviour by creating an association between the behaviour and an unpleasant stimulus or consequence, i.e. classical conditioning. Once this association is firmly established, engaging in the behaviour is no longer appealing for the individual (i.e. gambling, smoking, etc.). Covert sensitisation works very similarly to aversion therapy, but with *one major difference* – the unpleasant stimulus is only *imagined* by the individual.

Rather than experiencing actual physical consequences such as pain from an electric shock, the consequences are instead pictured in the person's mind. This must be vivid enough so that the individual experiences feelings of considerable discomfort or anxiety when they imagine themselves engaging in the addictive behaviour. By associating these unpleasant sensations with the undesirable behaviour, this leads to decreased desire and avoidance of the situation in the future.

An example: Treatment of problem drinking

Individuals using covert sensitisation would imagine themselves engaging in the various behaviours associated with drinking (e.g. opening a bottle, going into a pub, putting a glass to their lips) and then, as vividly as possible, imagine a very unpleasant consequence. This might be the thought of them experiencing intense feelings of nausea followed by the experience of vomiting all over themselves, the bar and the floor, as well as being humiliated because others see them in this state. By consistently associating the behaviour and its unpleasant consequence over and over in their mind, they eventually lose the desire to drink.

Research support for aversion therapy

Smith and Frawley (1993) studied a sample of 600 patients being treated for alcoholism using aversion therapy at three addiction treatment hospitals in the US. Seventy-five of these patients were also being treated for cocaine dependence. Contact was made a minimum of 12 months after completion of treatment. Of the patients contacted, 65% were totally abstinent from alcohol at this point. The 12-month abstinence rate for cocaine was 83.7%. This study provides research support for the claim that aversion therapy eliminates the urges to drink or use drugs.

Ethical problems with aversion therapy

Although aversion therapy has been shown to be effective in reducing addictive behaviour, there are significant ethical concerns surrounding its use as a form of treatment. For example, some forms of aversion therapy used in the treatment of problem drinking use drugs that cause extremely uncomfortable consequences, including nausea and vomiting. These effects might lead to poor compliance with treatment and high dropout rates, which, of course, decreases the potential positive impact of this type of treatment. Its critics consider the use of aversion therapy as a form of treatment to be morally objectionable.

Support for covert sensitisation

Kraft and Kraft (2005) provided support for the effectiveness of covert sensitisation in treating a variety of different addictive behaviours. They used hypnotic suggestion to associate feelings of nausea with problem behaviours such as cigarette smoking, alcoholism and chocolate addiction. For example, they successfully treated a patient with a chocolate addiction using this method, eliminating her cravings for chocolate in just four sessions. Kraft and Kraft concluded that covert sensitisation was a rapid and effective form of treatment for the elimination of the cravings associated with unwanted behaviour. Although not all patients respond to this form of treatment, Kraft and Kraft claim it is effective in 90% of cases.

Covert sensitisation is a more ethical form of treatment

An obvious advantage of covert sensitisation compared to aversion therapy is that covert sensitisation is considered a *more ethical* approach to treatment. Aversion therapy is often criticised because people experience actual physical consequences, whereas in covert sensitisation they do not. As a result, there are no physical risks involved in this form of treatment, such as an adverse reaction to a sickness-inducing drug in the treatment of alcohol addiction or the use of electric shock in the treatment of gambling addiction. Nor are individuals actually required to engage in the problem behaviour, but merely imagine it, thus reducing the possibility of harm even further.

Problems with behaviour modification of addiction

Behaviour modification therapies such as aversion therapy and covert sensitisation share a common problem in that they focus only on the learned aspect of addictive behaviours. As a result, these forms of treatment fail to address other psychological factors that might drive addictive behaviours. Addictions are often highly complex in the reasons for their development – therefore failure to address the underlying issues that led to the addiction in the first place may be doomed to failure. Treating only the symptoms of an addiction (e.g. stopping someone actually engaging in gambling behaviour) may leave individuals at risk of developing another addiction even if the addiction being treated is eliminated.

▲ If you have a chocolate addiction, don't worry, it can be reduced with covert sensitisation!

Insider tip…
Essay questions on the topic of reducing addiction can be specific (asking for one particular specified method, such as drug therapy or covert sensitisation) or more general (such as asking for behavioural interventions or methods of reducing addiction). In this latter example, don't be tempted to cram all of the different methods into your answer!

🐾 APPLY YOUR KNOWLEDGE

Hitesh is studying A Level psychology and learns about behavioural interventions as a way of reducing addiction. He tells his friend Sunil about what he has learned, and Sunil asks him if he can use one of these techniques to help reduce his gambling habit. Sunil spends most of his earnings at a local casino, and when he isn't in the casino he is gambling online. Hitesh offers to try covert sensitisation to help his friend kick his gambling habit.

Using your knowledge of covert sensitisation, explain how this technique could be used to reduce Sunil's gambling addiction.

CAN YOU? No. 11.9

1. Explain what is meant by the terms *aversion therapy* and *covert sensitisation* in the context of addiction reduction. (2 marks each)
2. Briefly explain and give **one** criticism of aversion therapy as a way of reducing addiction. (4 marks)
3. Briefly explain and give **one** criticism of covert sensitisation as a way of reducing addiction. (4 marks)
4. Outline and evaluate the behavioural interventions used to reduce addiction. (16 marks)

Reducing addiction: Cognitive behavioural therapy

Researchers are now beginning to make significant progress in their search for treatments that reduce addictive behaviour. The outcomes of **cognitive behavioural therapy (CBT)**, which you studied in your first year, have been extremely promising in this respect. The 'cognitive' aspect of this therapy alters the way individuals *think* about their gambling (i.e. their cognitive biases) and the 'behavioural' aspect changes what they then do (i.e. reduce their gambling behaviour). For example, research has shown that CBT can not only alter the erroneous cognitions that underlie gambling, but also reduce the frequency of gambling and help a gambler stay away from gambling once they have stopped.

KEY TERMS

Cognitive behavioural therapy (CBT) A combination of cognitive therapy (a way of changing maladaptive thoughts and beliefs) and behavioural therapy (a way of changing behaviour in response to these thoughts and beliefs).

Insider tip…
When describing the use of CBT, you need to describe it explicitly in the context of reducing addictive behaviour.

▲ How much have you won on your lucky machine, and how much have you lost?' In CBT for gambling, a client's cognitive biases are challenged and corrected.

COGNITIVE BEHAVIOURAL THERAPY

Cognitive behavioural therapy (CBT) is based on the idea that addictive behaviours are maintained by the person's thoughts about these behaviours. The main goal of CBT is to help people change the way they think about their addiction, and to learn new ways of coping more effectively with the circumstances that led to these behaviours in the past (e.g. coping with difficult situations or when exposed to peer pressure).

CBT and gambling addiction

CBT can be an effective treatment for problem gambling. It can be used to help gamblers identify the triggers to their problem behaviour, challenge their irrational thinking and find better ways to cope with the feelings and urges that prompt a gambling episode. For example, cognitive errors, such as the belief that the individual can control and predict outcomes, play a key part in the maintenance of gambling. CBT attempts to correct these errors in thinking, thus reducing the urge to gamble. CBT treatment can be delivered either in a group format or as individual sessions, and can even be delivered remotely, by means of telephone or email.

CBT and Internet addiction

Young (2011) used a form of CBT (called CBT-IA) as a way of reducing Internet addiction – the excessive and pathological use of technology and the Internet. The first stage of this treatment aims to modify behaviour by learning to control Internet usage. In the second stage, the therapist concentrates on reducing maladaptive cognitions – the thoughts that trigger excessive online activity. In this stage, patients get rid of the false assumptions about their Internet use. In the third phase, they deal with real problems existing in their lives that led to addiction, problems such as addiction to drugs or alcohol, anxiety or depression.

How CBT works in the reduction of addiction

CBT is typically given in about 10 one-hour sessions. These sessions focus on how the individual thinks or feels whenever they engage in a particular behaviour (e.g. gamble or use the Internet) and help these individuals develop more helpful ways of thinking and behaving. In the months following treatment, follow-up sessions help to stop people relapsing back into the problem behaviour.

Identifying and correcting cognitive biases

CBT involves identifying and changing cognitive distortions about the problem behaviour. For example, clients being treated for gambling addiction are not always aware of the cognitive biases on which they base their decisions. To bring these underlying assumptions to the surface, the therapist asks how the client makes decisions while gambling, and asks them to explain these beliefs in detail. The therapist can then educate clients about the nature of cognitive biases and what randomness means, i.e. that gambling outcomes are determined by chance, which involves an unpredictable event or accidental occurrence (Ladouceur, 2001). The client can also be asked how effective *their* strategy has been over time (i.e. challenging the effectiveness of their beliefs).

Changing behaviour

After this process of 'cognitive restructuring', where the individual begins to think differently about their problem behaviour, they are encouraged to practise these changes in their daily life. For example, gamblers may be asked to visit a casino and refrain from betting. For Internet addiction they may be asked to avoid going online for 6 hours, then 12 hours and so on, or to leave their phone or tablet at home to avoid going online. During this time clients are encouraged to keep a diary to record the triggers related to their problem behaviour and to record their progress in overcoming their addiction.

Relapse prevention

CBT usually incorporates some relapse prevention techniques. Relapse prevention involves learning to identify and avoid those risky situations that can trigger feelings or thoughts that can lead to relapse to the particular problem behaviour. For example, in the treatment of gambling addiction, clients learn to identify places (e.g. casinos, betting shops), feelings (e.g. boredom, stress) and other difficulties (e.g. finances, problems with work or family) that might prompt gambling behaviour.

Supporting evidence for the role of CBT in treating addiction

CBT has been effective in the treatment of a number of different addictions. For example, Magill and Ray (2009), in a meta-analysis of CBT trials, found CBT to be effective in reducing both alcohol and illicit drug addiction. In the treatment of gambling addiction, CBT has been successfully applied in both individual and group settings. Echeburúa *et al.* (1996) found that CBT yielded better outcomes than waiting-list or behavioural interventions. CBT has also been shown to be more effective in reducing gambling than referral to 'Gamblers Anonymous' (Petry *et al.*, 2006) and drug therapy (Ravindran *et al.*, 2006).

Support for CBT in the treatment of Internet addiction

Research has demonstrated the effectiveness of CBT-IA in the treatment of Internet addiction. For example, Kim *et al.* (2012) studied 65 adolescents who showed excessive online game play. During the therapy, various measures such as the severity of Internet use and life satisfaction were taken, both before and after CBT-IA treatment. After therapy, those participants who were subjected to CBT-IA scored higher on life satisfaction and lower on Internet addiction compared to those who did not receive CBT-IA. This provides support for CBT's ability to increase positive outcomes as a result of changing unhealthy thinking patterns associated with Internet addiction.

Advantages of CBT as a treatment for addiction

There are a number of advantages associated with CBT in this context. For example, addicts frequently suffer from negative thought patterns that contribute to their feelings of helplessness. The development of more positive ways of thinking means these individuals no longer feel overwhelmed by everyday circumstances and are less likely to engage in addictive behaviours in order to cope.

A second advantage is the ability to resist peer pressure that develops as a result of CBT. Addicts are particularly vulnerable to peer pressure, so with CBT they are able to learn new behaviours that will make them more confident in their ability to resist pressures to take substances or engage in activities that had created the addiction.

Irrational thinking or irrational environment?

A problem in using CBT alone as a treatment for addiction is that there is an over-emphasis on an individual's irrational thinking rather than acknowledging the stressful environment that may perpetuate their addictive behaviour. These stressful environments (e.g. an unhappy marriage or demanding job) exist beyond the therapeutic setting and so continue to produce and reinforce problem behaviours once the therapy has finished. This suggests that CBT can be effective as a way of reducing addiction but only as part of a wider form of intervention that also addresses the social environment in which addiction occurs.

Making the transition from use to non-use

McHugh *et al.* (2010) suggest that a particular challenge to the success of CBT in the treatment of addictive behaviours is the shift in lifestyle associated with use, relative to non-use. For example, among those who have long histories of substance misuse, there are often significant life consequences, such as unemployment, family difficulties, reduced social networks, etc. For such individuals, their 'fit' to society is within the context of others with similar misuse problems, and this context may vary dramatically from more mainstream culture. Thus, in treatment, as well as being asked to give up their addictive behaviour, the patient is also required to make the transition to a culture in which he or she may have few skills and resources, relinquishing the parts of their life in which there *is* a sense of effectiveness and belonging. The sense of belonging to the substance use culture, claim McHugh *et al.*, can make the individual ambivalent about change, and the reduction of addictive behaviour more difficult.

APPLY YOUR KNOWLEDGE

Jane works as a doctor in a city centre hospital. Her colleagues who run a smoking cessation clinic disapprove of the fact that their friend Jane is a heavy smoker and suggest that she tries to reduce her nicotine dependence. Jane doesn't trust the drug therapies they offer, but agrees to cognitive behavioural therapy. She doesn't really believe this will work, as she has tried to give up before and became anxious and bad-tempered and unable to concentrate on her work. She has a very stressful job and relies on cigarettes to help her cope with it.

Using your knowledge of cognitive behavioural therapy, suggest how this form of therapy might help Jane to reduce her nicotine addiction.

1. Briefly explain and give **one** criticism of cognitive behavioural therapy as a way of reducing addiction. (6 marks)
2. Explain how cognitive behavioural therapy might be used to reduce either nicotine or gambling addiction. (4 marks)
3. Outline and evaluate cognitive behavioural therapy as a way of reducing addiction. (16 marks)

The theory of planned behaviour

Changing or preventing risky or unhealthy behaviour, such as gambling, smoking or excessive alcohol use, has become a major concern of health professionals and governments alike. One way to approach change or prevention is to consider the factors that contribute to a person's intention to change an addictive behaviour. On this spread we look at one such model that was developed in the 1980s by social psychologist Icek Ajzen – the **theory of planned behaviour**.

THE THEORY OF PLANNED BEHAVIOUR (TPB)

Main assumptions

The theory of planned behaviour (TPB) (Ajzen, 1989) was a refinement of an earlier theory (the theory of reasoned action) developed by Ajzen and Martin Fishbein in the 1970s. According to the TPB, an individual's decision to engage in a particular behaviour (e.g. to take drugs, or to give up alcohol) can be directly predicted by their intention to engage in that behaviour. Intention is a function of three factors:

Behavioural attitude

This reflects an individual's personal views toward a behaviour such as gambling or smoking. They are more likely to hold a favourable attitude toward an addictive behaviour if they believe that engaging in that behaviour will lead to mostly positive outcomes. This attitude is formed on the basis of their beliefs about the consequences of performing the behaviour (e.g. I will feel good; I will get my life back together), and an appraisal of the value of these consequences (i.e. whether they will be good or bad for them).

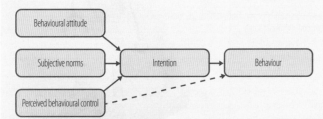

Subjective norms

Subjective norms are a product of social influence. They are a product of an individual's subjective awareness of social norms relating to that particular behaviour, i.e. not simply social norms but the individual's own beliefs about them. They reflect what we believe significant others feel is the right thing to do (the 'injunctive norm'), as well as perceptions of what other people are *actually* doing (the 'descriptive norm'). For example, we may believe that the majority of people frown on heavy drinking (the injunctive norm) but also that heavy drinking is widespread (the descriptive norm).

Perceived behavioural control

Perceived behavioural control refers to the extent to which an individual believes they can actually perform a particular behaviour, such as giving up an addictive behaviour. This belief is assumed to act either on the intention to behave in a particular way, or directly on the behaviour itself. This is because:

(i) The more control people believe themselves to have over the behaviour in question (i.e. their self-efficacy), the stronger their intention to actually perform that behaviour will be.

(ii) An individual with higher perceived behavioural control is likely to try harder and to persevere for longer than someone with low perceived behavioural control.

Using the TPB to reduce addiction

The TPB can be used as a way of understanding the processes that lead to addiction but also as a means to understand prevention and treatment. Thus it can be used to help develop appropriate programmes to bring about long-lasting changes in addiction behaviour.

Changing behavioural attitude

The US *Office of National Drug Control Policy* (ONDCP) launched a campaign in 2005 to lower teenage marijuana use. A review of the effectiveness of this campaign (Slater *et al.*, 2011) attributed its success to its influence on attitudes. The campaign the ONDCP launched ('Above the influence') aimed to create a different attitude toward the effect of marijuana use, namely that it is inconsistent with being autonomous and achieving aspirations.

Changing subjective norms

Anti-drug campaigns often seek to give adolescents actual data about the percentage of people engaging in risky behaviour. This is done in order to change subjective norms. For example, adolescents who smoke are usually part of a peer group who smoke and therefore might believe that smoking is the norm for teenagers. However, generally, most adolescents do not smoke – therefore exposure to accurate statistical information should correct subjective norms and should form part of any effective campaign (Wilson and Kolander, 2003).

Perceived behavioural control

Godin *et al.* (2002) examined the extent to which the TPB could explain smoking intentions and behaviours in adults intending to give up smoking. Data was collected using questionnaires and also at home using trained interviewers. Participants were surveyed at the start of the study and again six months later.

The researchers found that the three elements of the TPB (attitudes, subjective norms and perceived behavioural control) helped to explain intentions, whereas perceived behavioural control was the most important predictor of ultimate behaviour.

The researchers concluded that prevention programmes should help smokers to focus on the willpower required to give up smoking and also alert smokers to the effort that is required to modify smoking behaviour.

Self-efficacy

The TPB proposes, as part of perceived behavioural control, that intentions to change behaviour will be stronger in people who have an increased sense of control. This self-efficacy (i.e. a belief in one's ability to succeed in specific situations or accomplish a task) has been shown to be important in many aspects of addiction prevention, such as relapse prevention programmes. For example, Majer *et al.* (2004) investigated the role of cognitive factors, including self-efficacy, on abstinence. They found that encouraging an addict's belief in their ability to abstain was related to optimism and ultimately a positive outcome. Therefore, they concluded that enhancing self-efficacy should form a primary goal of treatment plans.

EVALUATION

TPB is too rational

A limitation of the TPB is the criticism that it is too rational, failing to take into account emotions, compulsions or other irrational determinants of human behaviour (Armitage *et al.*, 1999). When completing a questionnaire about attitudes and intention, people might find it impossible to anticipate the strong desires and emotions that compel their behaviour in real life. The presence of strong emotions may help to explain why people sometimes act irrationally by failing to carry out an intended behaviour (e.g. stop drinking) even when it is in their best interest to do so (Albarracín *et al.*, 2005).

Ignores other factors

Aside from emotion, there are many other influential factors that are ignored by the TPB. For example, Topa and Moriano (2010) suggest that group variables, such as identification with peers, could play a mediating role in the relation with tobacco addiction or indeed any addictive behaviour. Another element that is missing from the TPB is motivation. Klag (2006) studied 350 substance abusers in Australia and found that recovery was consistently more successful in individuals who had decided themselves to give up rather than people who were coerced (e.g. because of a court sentence). Self-determination theory, according to Klag, is preferable to the TPB because it emphasises the importance of self-motivation (i.e. intrinsic motivation).

▲ Research suggests that people are more successful at giving up addictive behaviour if they are motivated to do so.

Methodological issues with the TPB

In studies of the TPB, attitudes and intentions that are assessed by questionnaires may, according to Albarracin *et al.* (2005), turn out to be poor representations of the attitudes and intentions that eventually exist in the behavioural situation, and thus poor predictors of actual behaviour. For example, a smoker may develop a negative attitude toward cigarettes based on their threat to his or her health, and intend to give them up. This is what they express when answering a questionnaire. However, their actual intention and behaviour may differ greatly when they find themselves in a group of heavy smokers with all the associated sights and smells of smoking.

Predicts intention rather than behaviour change

Armitage and Conner's (2001) meta-analysis of studies using the TPB found that this model was successful in predicting intention to change rather than actual behavioural change. This pattern of results is typically found in the prediction of health behaviours that involve the adoption of difficult behavioural change, such as stopping using drugs of abuse, eating a healthy diet and so on. This suggests that the TPB is primarily an account of intention formation rather than specifying the processes involved in translating the intention into action (Ajzen and Fishbein, 2005). In the context of changing risky behaviours such as drug taking or gambling, therefore, we can make a distinction between a motivational phase that results in the formation of a behavioural intention, and a post-decisional phase which involves behavioural initiation and maintenance (Abraham *et al.*, 1998).

The influence of alcohol and drugs

A limitation of the model is that it fails to take into account the influence of alcohol or drugs, which can produce a discrepancy between measured intention and actual behaviour. Attitudes and intentions tend to be measured when sober, whereas risky behaviours such as gambling or unprotected sex may be performed when under the influence of alcohol or drugs. This is consistent with the idea of alcohol myopia (Steele and Josephs, 1990), the tendency for alcohol to decrease cognitive capacity so that only the most obvious characteristics of a situation are attended to. Indeed, MacDonald *et al.* (1996) found that alcohol intoxication actually increased measured intention to engage in unprotected sex and other risky behaviours.

MEET THE RESEARCHER

Icek Ajzen was born in 1942 in Poland. He is Professor of Psychology at the University of Massachusetts. He has published numerous empirical papers and books and has won many awards for his work. His research deals primarily with the relationship between verbal attitudes and overt behaviour.

Research methods

Ajzen (2013) has proposed a design for a *Theory of Planned Behavior Questionnaire* (TPB Questionnaire) which assesses each of the theory's major constructs: attitude, perceived norm, perceived behavioral control and intention. Seven-point bipolar adjective scales are typically employed; for example, the following is a statement to assess perceived norms related to exercising:

> Most people who are important to me approve of my exercising for at least 20 minutes, three times per week for the next three months.
>
> Agree 1   2   3   4   5   6   7 Disagree

In total, such a questionnaire might have 20 items.

1. What level of measurement is the data produced by this statement? Explain your answer. (2 marks)
2. Reliability is an important aspect of questionnaire design. Explain how the reliability of this questionnaire might be assessed using test–retest. (4 marks)
3. Once test–retest has been performed, a correlation coefficient is produced. Explain what is meant by a *correlation coefficient*. (1 mark)
4. In one case the correlation coefficient was calculated as .6435. Give this answer to two decimal places. (1 mark)
5. Before using a questionnaire, a researcher might conduct a pilot study. What is the reason for doing this? (2 marks)

LINK TO RESEARCH METHODS

The topics in these questions are covered in the research methods chapter of our Year 1 book.

CAN YOU? No. 11.11

1. Briefly explain the theory of planned behaviour. (3 marks)
2. Outline **one** limitation of the theory of planned behaviour. (2 marks)
3. Outline the findings of research into the theory of planned behaviour as it relates to the reduction of addiction. (4 marks)
4. Outline and evaluate the theory of planned behaviour as it relates to the reduction of addiction. (16 marks)

Prochaska's six-stage model of behaviour change

Prochaska's six-stage model highlights what many other models tend to ignore, i.e. that overcoming addiction is rarely the result of one single decision to change. James Prochaska believes that change comes about through a subtle and often complex progression, as the individual thinks, hesitates, moves forward, perhaps stumbles backwards and occasionally starts all over again. On the final spread of this chapter, we examine the six stages that make up positive behaviour change away from the misery of addiction.

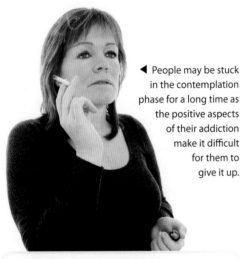

◀ People may be stuck in the contemplation phase for a long time as the positive aspects of their addiction make it difficult for them to give it up.

The processes of change

The 'stages of change' describe *when* shifts in intention or behaviour change but do not tell us *how* these changes occur. Prochaska *et al.* (1992) describe a number of activities and experiences that individuals engage in to help move them from one stage to the next. For example, movement from the precontemplation stage to the contemplation stage may involve the use of *consciousness raising* and *environmental re-evaluation*. In consciousness raising, the individual learns new facts and ideas that would support the recommended behaviour change. In environmental re-evaluation, the individual may come to realise the negative impact his or her behaviour has on others and the positive impact that behaviour change would have. To maintain the positive behaviour change, they may use *stimulus control*, removing any cues to engage in the problem behaviour, and *helping relationships*, seeking and using social support to help them 'stay clean'.

An overview of the model

Instead of viewing behaviour change (such as giving up gambling) as a single 'event' that happens when the individual is sufficiently motivated, stage theories emphasise the gradual nature of such change, and assume a transition through a fixed series of discrete stages. Prochaska's model sees people passing through six stages when attempting to change a problematic behaviour such as smoking or gambling.

The first three of the stages represent variations in a person's *intention* to change their behaviour, and therefore might be regarded as 'pre-action'. The latter three stages are all 'post-action' stages and represent the duration of the change. These post-action stages cover the first hesitant steps toward recovery through to long-term behaviour change. Individuals move through these stages in order, but may, on occasion, relapse and revert to an earlier stage before repeating the cycle again.

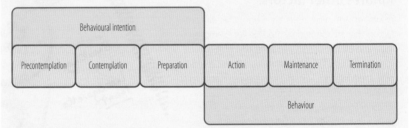

▲ The first three stages represent the 'pre-action' stages, and the latter three stages the 'post-action' stages.

The six stages of change

Stage 1: Precontemplation
Individuals who currently have no intention to change their behaviour in the near future are in the 'Precontemplation' stage. They may be unaware that their behaviour is becoming problematic and may only seek help because of pressure from others. For example, a person may threaten to leave their partner because of their partner's gambling habits.

Stage 2: Contemplation
In this stage, the person may be aware that a problem exists but have yet to make a commitment to doing anything about it. The positive aspects of their addiction (e.g. the 'buzz' they get from gambling) and the amount of effort it will take to give it up present significant barriers for them in changing it. People may be stuck in this stage for a long time.

Stage 3: Preparation
This stage combines *intention* to change with actual *behavioural* change. Individuals who are prepared to change their problem behaviour report small behavioural changes, such as gambling less frequently or smoking fewer cigarettes, but have yet to reduce their addictive behaviour to a point of complete abstinence.

Stage 4: Action
In this stage individuals modify their behaviour in order to overcome their problems. This stage involves the most overt behavioural changes and requires considerable commitment on the part of the individual. Individuals are classified as being in this stage when they have successfully altered their problem behaviour for a period between one day and six months.

Stage 5: Maintenance
The individual in this stage works to consolidate the gains attained during the previous stage and to prevent relapse. The individual is classified as being in this stage when they have stayed free of the previously addictive behaviour for a period of six months or more.

Stage 6: Termination
The individual is no longer tempted to revert to the former behaviour and is completely confident that they are able to maintain the change. People in this stage often keep building on their initial change, adding new goals and achieving even more success. According to Prochaska, only about one in five ever make it to this stage.

Usefulness of the model

The stage model has been shown to be useful because it suggests that the most effective strategy to use in reducing addiction is determined by the current stage the individual is in. For example, Haslam and Draper (2000) found that women further along the cycle of change were more convinced about the dangers of smoking during pregnancy. Women in the first stage of change were most resistant to engaging in positive health behaviour during pregnancy, whereas pregnant women further along the cycle of change were more convinced about the health risks of smoking during pregnancy. This suggests that interventions need to be tailored to an individual's particular stage of change in order to maximise their effectiveness.

Evidence does not always demonstrate *behavioural* outcomes

In a critical review of Prochaska's model, Whitelaw *et al.* (2000) conclude that there is a paucity of empirical studies that have used behavioural outcomes as a way of measuring the usefulness of this model. Much of the research evidence has tended to focus on what Whitelaw *et al.* refer to as 'softer' indications of effectiveness, such as stage progression within the model. However, stage progression does not necessarily equate to subsequent behaviour change. For example, it may be the *intention* to quit smoking that changes and not the behaviour itself. This led Whitelaw *et al.* to conclude that the popularity of the model had 'little to do with its scientific support', as the strength of the evidence base tends to be overstated.

Design weaknesses in supporting studies

Whitelaw *et al.* highlight another issue with the research support for this model. Few studies have included all the characteristics associated with a robust experimental design. For example, some studies have not used control groups (e.g. Marcus *et al.*, 1996), whereas others have used only self-selected samples (e.g. Campbell *et al.*, 1997). Other studies have used a variety of interventions as part of any treatment. For example, Steptoe *et al.* (1999) used nicotine replacement therapy alongside behavioural counselling. As a result, it becomes difficult to disentangle the specific effects of a 'stages of change' approach from the more generalised effects of intervention.

Research fails to support the effectiveness of the model

More recent research that does employ a robust experimental protocol has cast doubts about the effectiveness of staged intervention in the treatment of addiction. For example, Baumann *et al.* (2015) randomly allocated problem drinkers (i.e. people not intending to change) to either an experimental group, who received an intervention tailored to their motivational stage, and a control group, who received minimal intervention only. Only a very few participants subsequently gave up drinking completely (2%), although 35% decreased the quantity and frequency of their drinking. However, there was no significant difference in beneficial effects between the staged intervention group and the control group, suggesting that the advantages of Prochaska's model may have been overstated.

Social norms may influence progression through the stages of change

A limitation of the 'stages of change' approach is that it fails to acknowledge the importance of social norms in changing behaviour. For example, Daoud *et al.* (2015) found that, in Arab cultures, social smoking, where cigarettes are distributed during social events such as weddings and funerals, makes it more difficult to quit. In a study of Arab male smokers, they found that 62% were still in the precontemplation stage and only 14% at the preparation stage, compared to studies in the US and Europe which have found that 40% of smokers are in the precontemplation stage and 20% in the preparation stage. These findings indicate that a lower readiness to quit smoking in some cultures may be a product of social norms and pressures that limit the effectiveness of therapeutic interventions.

▲ In Arab cultures, the widespread use of cigarettes at social occasions makes it more difficult for individuals to quit.

MEET THE RESEARCHER

James Prochaska
After his father died from alcoholism, James Prochaska resolved to find a way to help people break their addictive habits. His approach was simple: he found people who had beaten addiction on their own and asked them how they had managed it. After years of studying these successful changers, he soon detected a pattern, and came up with the six-stage model described on this spread. Named one of the five most influential authors in psychology by the American Psychological Society, he now serves as Director of the Cancer Prevention Research Center and Professor of Clinical and Health Psychology at the University of Rhode Island. He was the first psychologist to win a Medal of Honor for Clinical Research from the American Cancer Society.

🐾 APPLY YOUR KNOWLEDGE

Matt and Gareth like to gamble. It started when they would meet once a week with friends for a friendly game of poker. They then started going to casinos and more recently have got into online gambling in a big way. Both of them now spend a lot of time gambling or thinking about gambling. Matt has lost his job at a local mobile phone shop and Gareth, who is a research scientist, has found that he is struggling to concentrate at work, and has recently lost a large research grant because he spends time online gambling when he should be working.

Matt understands that his gambling is an issue, particularly now that he has to borrow money to keep gambling. However, he doesn't feel ready to stop and says he will miss the buzz he gets from gambling if he were to give it up.

Gareth had a real wake-up call when he lost the research grant, and has taken steps to curb his problem gambling. With help from his family, he has now managed to abstain from any form of gambling for just over three months.

Using your knowledge of Prochaska's six-stage model of behaviour change, identify which stage each of these two friends are at and explain what features of their current behaviour would place them at that stage.

CAN YOU?   No. 11.12

1. Briefly explain **one** stage of Prochaska's six-stage model of behaviour change. (2 marks)
2. Briefly outline and give **one** limitation of Prochaska's six-stage model of behaviour change. (4 marks)
3. Outline and evaluate Prochaska's six-stage model of behaviour change. (16 marks)

We have identified here the key points of the topics on the AQA A level specification, i.e. the bare minimum that you need to know. You may want to fill in further details to elaborate and personalise this material.

DESCRIBING ADDICTION

CHARACTERISTICS OF ADDICTION

- Physical dependence associated with long-term use of drugs – withdrawal symptoms and increased tolerance.
- Psychological dependence associated with cravings when abstaining from drug use.
- Psychological dependence arises because experiential system takes priority over rational system.
- Tolerance – larger doses of drug are necessary for the same effect.
- Metabolic and learned tolerance in use of alcohol (Isbell *et al.*).
- Withdrawal syndrome follows discontinuation of drug use.
- Two phases of withdrawal: Acute and post-acute withdrawal.

RISK FACTORS IN ADDICTION

GENETICS, STRESS AND PERSONALITY

GENETIC VULNERABILITY, STRESS AND PERSONALITY

- Slutske *et al.* high level of heritability for gambling addiction in MZ twins.
- Dopamine receptor gene – individuals vulnerable to addiction low levels of dopamine (Blum and Payne).
- Self-medication model (Gelkopf *et al.*) e.g. stress predicts relapse (Dawes *et al.*)
- Traumatic stress increases vulnerability to addictions (e.g. Robins *et al.*).
- Personality e.g. sensation seeking and impulsivity associated with addiction (Krueger *et al.*).
- Addiction-prone personality predicts different types of addictive behaviour (Barnes *et al.*).
- Personality disorders associated with e.g. polydrug use (Verhheul *et al.*).

EVALUATION

- Gender differences in genetic vulnerability to addiction –inconsistent findings with women (McGue).
- Genetics and the diathesis-stress model – people with A1 variant of dopamine-receptor gene more likely to develop addiction.
- If stress leads to addiction, does coping lead to abstinence? – stress coping resources helps smoking cessation (Matheny and Weatherman).
- The role of stress varies by type of addiction – e.g. not shown in alcohol addiction (Arévalo *et al.*).
- Support for the role of impulsivity – e.g. Labouvie and McGee.
- Personality: Implications of an addiction-prone personality – enables identification of vulnerable individuals.

FAMILY INFLUENCES AND PEERS

FAMILY INFLUENCES

- Importance of family in transmission of gambling behaviour (Reith and Dobbie).
- Parental influences – through provision of models e.g. Biederman *et al.*
- Parental influence through parenting styles, e.g. authoritative parenting = lower levels of substance abuse (Fletcher *et al.*).
- XINFO – sibling influence through modelling from older siblings (Windle).

EVALUATION OF FAMILY INFLUENCES

- Support for the role of family influences – tolerant parental attitudes and sibling substance use led to substance abuse (Bahr *et al.*).
- Substance abuse may be due to a *lack* of parental influence – e.g. of parental monitoring (Stattin and Kerr).
- Intervention studies tend to ignore sibling influences (Kim *et al.*).

PEERS

- Peers exert influence through peer pressure to engage in risky behaviours.
- Social networks e.g. smokers befriend smokers (Eiser *et al.*).
- XINFO – peer influences may be expressed through indirect parent influence (Shakya *et al.*).

EVALUATION OF PEER INFLUENCES

- Support for peer influences through social media – e.g. Moreno *et al.* MySpace study.
- Peer influences may be overstated – similarity may be more due to friendship selection (De Vries *et al.*).
- Reducing peer influences through social norms interventions.

EXPLANATIONS FOR NICOTINE ADDICTION

BRAIN NEUROCHEMISTRY

- Nicotine addictive because of dopamine release.
- Glutamate speeds up activity of dopamine neurons (Zickler).
- GABA slows down activity. Nicotine inhibits GABA action.
- Cigarette smoke inhibits MAO to produce higher dopamine levels.
- Nicotine causes neuronal changes that stimulate cravings (DiFranza).

EVALUATION

- Support for the nicotine-dopamine link – GVG reduces surge of dopamine and addictive qualities of nicotine (Paterson and Markou).
- Support for the role of glutamate and GABA – D'Souza and Markou study of rats.
- Nicotine and Parkinson's disease (PD) – improves symptoms (Fagerstrom *et al.*)
- Nicotine addiction and depression – long-term smoking may alter brain neurochemistry (e.g. Khaled *et al.* Canadian study).
- Nicotine affects men and women differently – nicotine affects different areas of the brain in men and women (Cosgrove *et al.*).

LEARNING THEORY

- Initiation phase – smoking increases because rewarding properties of nicotine.
- Maintenance – smoking avoids withdrawal symptoms (negative reinforcement).
- Cue reactivity – smoking eventually leads to a strong conditioned association between sensory aspects of smoking and reinforcing effects of nicotine.
- Nicotine effect when brain lowers dopamine levels in presence of smoking-related cues.
- XINFO – FDA suggested other ingredients in cigarette smoke increase appeal.

EVALUATION

- Support for social learning explanations of smoking initiation – e.g. DiBlasio and Benda peer group influences.
- Support for smoking and mood manipulation – negative mood increases nicotine craving (Shiffman and Waters).
- Support for the role of cue reactivity – Wiers *et al.* conditioned cues in nicotine cravings.
- Gender differences in patterns of nicotine addiction (López *et al.*).
- Implications for treatment – e.g. use of cue exposure therapy (Unrod *et al.*).

EXPLANATIONS FOR GAMBLING ADDICTION

LEARNING THEORY

LEARNING THEORY AND GAMBLING ADDICTION
- Behaviour that produces rewarding consequence becomes more frequent.
- Behaviour acquired through partial reinforcement slower to extinguish.
- Variable reinforcement – only a proportion of gambler's responses are rewarded.
- Gambling may produce rewards e.g. the 'big win hypothesis' and the 'near miss'.
- The gambling environment may also be reinforcing by increasing arousal.
- XINFO – gambling legislation specifies RTP rates (minimum is 70%).

EVALUATION
- Learning theory can't explain all forms of gambling, e.g. long time periods.
- Fails to explain why only some people become addicted – suggests other factors are involved.
- Support for the influence of partial reinforcement – gamblers responded for longer (Horsley et al.).
- Reinforcement schedules may lead to irrational beliefs – wins earlier in session lead to winning expectations (Sharpe).
- Different pathways to gambling addiction – 'behaviourally conditioned' and 'emotionally vulnerable'.

COGNITIVE THEORY

COGNITIVE THEORY AND GAMBLING ADDICTION
- Cognitive biases include 'the gambler's fallacy', 'illusions of control'.
- Key study: Griffiths – Cognitive bias in fruit machine gambling.
- Procedure – regular and non-regular gamblers given £3 to spend on fruit machine and verbalisations noted.
- Findings – Regular gamblers more likely to make irrational statements (e.g. illusion of control) and explain 'near misses' as 'near wins'.
- XINFO – pathological gamblers have deficits in executive cognitive functions.

EVALUATION
- Research support for the role of cognitive biases – e.g. 80% of verbalisations of gamblers irrational (Ladouceur et al.).
- Implications for treatment – Echeburúa et al. CBT effective with gamblers.
- Irrational thinking varies with type of gambling – more likely in gambling machines than sports betting (Lund).
- Awareness does not decrease susceptibility to cognitive bias – statistics students still prone to cognitive biases (Benhsain and Ladouceur).
- Cognitive biases may have a biological bias – Clark et al. identified insula.

REDUCING ADDICTION

DRUG THERAPY

- NRT releases nicotine into the bloodstream at lower levels than cigarettes.
- Varenicline and Bupropion reduce craving.
- Opiod antagonists reduce reinforcing properties of gambling by targeting dopamine pathways.
- Gamblers treated with SSRIs show improvements because reduces depression and impulsivity.
- Xinfo – Methadone mimics effects of heroin but lasts longer and less addictive.

EVALUATION
- Support for the effectiveness of NRT – 70% more effective than placebo (Stead et al.).
- Lack of blinding in NRT studies – patients receiving nicotine recognise sensation (Mooney et al.).
- Naltrexone can make fun activities seem 'uninspiring'.
- Methodological issues in drug therapies for gambling addiction – e.g. small sample sizes.
- Support for the effectiveness of drug treatments for gambling – SSRIs (Grant and Potenza).

BEHAVIOURAL INTERVENTIONS

- Change motivations for addictive behaviour.
- Aversion therapy – addictive behaviours are associated with unpleasant sensations.
- Patient engages in the behaviour while at the same time being exposed to something unpleasant.
- Treatment of gambling addiction – small shock when exposed to gambling stimuli.
- Covert sensitisation – unpleasant stimulus is imagined by the individual.

EVALUATION
- Research support for aversion therapy – urges to use drugs eliminated (Smith and Frawley).
- Ethical problems with aversion therapy – uncomfortable consequences.
- Support for covert sensitisation (Kraft and Kraft).
- Covert sensitisation a more ethical form of treatment – no physical risks involved.
- Problems with behaviour modification of addiction – fails to address other factors.

COGNITIVE BEHAVIOURAL THERAPY

- Changes way people think about addiction.
- Used to help gamblers identify triggers to their behaviour and challenge irrational thinking.
- Young used CB-IA to reduce Internet addiction.
- CBT sessions focus on how individual thinks or feels when they engage in a behaviour.
- After 'cognitive restructuring', encouraged to practise these changes in their daily life.
- CBT relapse prevention techniques.

EVALUATION
- Supporting evidence for the role of CBT in treating addiction – drug addiction (Magill and Ray).
- Support for CBT in the treatment of Internet addiction – adolescents online gaming (Kim et al.).
- Advantages of CBT as a treatment for addiction – not overwhelmed, able to resist peer pressure.
- Irrational thinking or irrational environment?
- Making the transition from use to non-use – a sense of belonging to the substance use culture.

BEHAVIOUR CHANGE

THE THEORY OF PLANNED BEHAVIOUR

THE THEORY OF PLANNED BEHAVIOUR
- Individual's decision to engage in a behaviour directly predicted by intention.
- Intention is a function of three factors: behavioural attitude, subjective norms and perceived behavioural control.
- ONDCP campaign successful in changing attitudes toward marijuana use.
- Anti-drug campaigns attempt to change subjective norms.
- Perceived behavioural control important predictor of smoking cessation (Godin et al.).
- XINFO – self-efficacy important in many aspects of addiction prevention.

EVALUATION
- TPB is too rational – fails to take into account emotions (Armitage et al.)
- Ignores other factors – e.g. identification with peers and motivation to recover.
- Methodological issues with the TPB – questionnaires fail to address intention and behaviour in the behavioural situation (where peer influences may occur).
- Predicts intention rather than behaviour change – successful in predicting intention to change rather than behavioural change (Armitage and Conner).
- The influence of alcohol and drugs – can produce a discrepancy between measured intention and actual behaviour.

PROCHASKA'S MODEL OF BEHAVIOUR CHANGE

THE 'STAGES OF CHANGE' MODEL
- Gradual nature of change, and transition through series of discrete stages.
- Precontemplation – Individuals who have no intention to change behaviour.
- Contemplation – aware problem exists but yet to make commitment.
- Preparation – small behavioural changes but not total abstinence.
- Action – individuals modify behaviour to overcome their problems.
- Maintenance – works to consolidate gains attained during previous stage.
- Termination – no longer tempted to revert to former behaviour.
- XINFO – Activities e.g. *consciousness raising* and *environmental re-evaluation*.

EVALUATION
- Usefulness of the model – most effective strategy determined by current stage.
- Evidence does not demonstrate *behavioural* outcomes (Whitelaw et al.).
- Design weaknesses in supporting studies – e.g. difficult to disentangle specific effects of this approach from other aspects of intervention (e.g. NRT).
- Research fails to support the effectiveness of the model (e.g. Baumann et al.).
- Social norms may influence progression through the stages of change – in Arab cultures, social smoking makes it more difficult to quit (Daoud et al.).

0 1 Read the item below and answer the question that follows.

> Ewan is addicted to alcohol. He drinks at the end of every day, and says the alcohol makes him feel calm. His family have noticed that he does not appear to 'get drunk' anymore despite his high intake. Ewan has tried to stop drinking on occasions, but when he does he becomes agitated and very bad tempered.

Describe what is meant by addiction, using the case of Ewan as part of your answer. **[6 marks]**

0 2 Explain what is meant by withdrawal syndrome in relation to addiction. **[2 marks]**

0 3 Which one of the following is *not* a trait used in Eysenck's theory of the criminal personality? Write the letter of your chosen answer in your answer booklet. **[1 mark]**

A. extraversion

B. hostility

C. neuroticism

D. psychoticism

0 4 Explain how **one** research study has investigated the genetic vulnerability in relation to addiction. **[3 marks]**

0 5 Evaluate the view that stress is a risk factor in developing an addiction. **[6 marks]**

0 6 Using an example, outline how peers may increase the risk of developing an addiction. **[3 marks]**

0 7 Outline and discuss **at least two** risk factors associated with the development of addiction. Refer to research evidence as part of your answer. **[16 marks]**

0 8 Outline and evaluate **one** research study which investigated the role of dopamine in nicotine addiction. **[5 marks]**

0 9 Read the item below and answer the question that follows.

> Amber is only 15 years old but has been a persistent smoker for over a year. She is often in trouble for smoking on the school grounds, where she 'hangs out' with a gang of older girls who supply her with cigarettes. Despite being punished many times, she says she cannot stop herself from smoking.

Using your knowledge of **both** brain neurochemistry **and** learning theory, outline reasons why Amber is addicted to smoking. **[6 marks]**

1 0 Describe and briefly evaluate the role of cue reactivity in smoking behaviour. **[6 marks]**

1 1 Discuss brain neurochemistry as an explanation of nicotine addiction. **[16 marks]**

1 2 Read the item below and answer the question that follows.

> Asif is addicted to gambling, and especially the game of roulette. Although he loses a lot of money at the casino, he hangs on and hangs on for a big win – which occasionally does happen. Asif knows the laws of probability are against him but he cannot resist the 'buzz' he gets when he is handed a lot of money, even though he ends up losing it all over again.

Using your knowledge of partial and variable reinforcement, explain how Asif may have learned to become an addictive gambler. **[4 marks]**

1 3 Using an example of gambling behaviour, explain the role of cognitive bias in addiction. **[3 marks)**

1 4 Discuss **one or more** explanations of gambling addiction. Refer to research evidence as part of your answer. [16 marks]

1 5 Which one of the following reduces addiction by changing thought processes. Write the letter of your chosen answer in your answer booklet. [1 mark]

    A. aversion therapy

    B. cognitive behaviour therapy

    C. covert sensitisation

    D. drug therapy

1 6 Using an example, outline the difference between aversion therapy and covert sensitisation as ways of reducing addiction. [3 marks]

1 7 Evaluate the use of drug therapy as a way of reducing addiction. [6 marks]

1 8 Describe and briefly evaluate **one** research study which has investigated the use of cognitive behaviour therapy to reduce addiction. [6 marks]

1 9 Read the item below and answer the question that follows.

> Dylan is concerned about his growing addiction to computer games. He is worried that it is in danger of getting out of control. He knows it is not normal to play computer games for as many hours as he does and thinks it is best that he stops altogether. However, he does not think he has the ability to do this without the help of others.

Explain how the theory of planned behaviour could be applied to Dylan to help him to change his addictive behaviour. [6 marks]

2 0 Which one of the following stages comes before the 'action' stage in Prochaska's six-stage model of behaviour change. Write the letter of your chosen answer in your answer booklet. [1 mark]

    A. contemplation

    B. maintenance

    C. preparation

    D. termination

2 1 Identify **one** stage of Prochaska's six-stage model of behaviour change and explain how it relates to changing addictive behaviour. [3 marks]

2 2 Discuss the application of **both** the theory of planned behaviour **and** Prochaska's six-stage model of behaviour change to addiction. [16 marks]

2 3 Read the item below and answer the questions that follow.

> A psychologist used a volunteer sample to collect a group of 23 people who were addicted to using their mobile phones. At the start of the study, each participant was rated for their addiction. This rating was based on each person's own judgement plus the judgement of two other close relatives or friends. Each participant then took part in ten sessions of cognitive behaviour therapy. At the end of this time, the same rating system was used. Findings showed that the median rating for addiction was significantly lower after therapy than before.

    (i) Give **one** advantage and **one** disadvantage of using a volunteer sample in this study. [2 marks]

    (ii) Explain why close relative and friends were used for the addiction ratings. [3 marks]

    (iii) The psychologist analysed the data using the Wilcoxon test.

        Outline **two** reasons why the psychologist used the Wilcoxon test for this study. [4 marks)

    (iv) Explain how the psychologist would identify the critical value for this test. [3 marks]

The exam questions on addiction will be varied but are likely to involve some short answer questions (AO1), some application of knowledge questions (AO2), research methods questions and possibly an extended writing question (AO1 + AO3). We've provided answers to some additional questions together with comments from an examiner about how well they've each done.

---

02 Using an example, distinguish between physical and psychological dependence in addiction. *(3 marks)*

Maisie's answer

Physical dependence is when an addict is physically dependent on a drug so that they cannot do without it. If a person is psychologically dependent on something, they feel better when they do it (for example when they gamble) and can't give it up because it would make them anxious without it.

Ciaran's answer

When a person abstains from taking a substance on which they are physically dependent, they experience withdrawal symptoms, e.g. people who are physically dependent on caffeine must drink coffee to feel 'normal'. Psychological dependence, on the other hand, does not involve physical changes, but the person's thoughts and activities revolve excessively round a particular substance or activity, such as gambling. When gamblers abstain from gambling they experience strong cravings to gamble again, and feel anxious if they don't indulge.

Examiner's comments

Maisie's answer is worth only 1 mark. She has not really defined physical dependence just reused the words again. 'Can't do without it' implies dependence but does not address the physical aspect. Her explanation of psychological dependence is clearer and includes psychological ideas (feelings, anxious). However, briefly referencing gambling does not constitute use of an example – it needs to be more developed.

Examiner's comments

Ciaran earns 3 marks here. Initially he struggles to find new words to describe physical dependence but the point of distinction (where he says 'on the other hand') he does draw out the difference between physical and psychological dependence as required by the question. It might have been better to use an example of one addictive behaviour to clearly illustrate the distinction but the question equally invites two separate examples which is how Ciaran has decided to approach it.

---

07 Explain one criticism of the idea that personality is a risk factor in developing an addiction. *(3 marks)*

Maisie's answer

One criticism of the idea that personality is a risk factor in developing an addiction is that research has shown it is more likely to be genetic. For example, drug abuse and nicotine dependence have both been shown to be a product of a person's genetics. Explanations based on personality alone tend to ignore the role of genetics, therefore this is a weakness of this sort of explanation.

Ciaran's answer

Evidence (e.g Barnes et al., 2000) supports the claim that an individual's personality predicts the likelihood of them developing addictive behaviours. An implication of this supporting evidence is that it gives the possibility that individuals who are more vulnerable to developing an addiction can be identified in advance by measuring their personality. As a result, these individuals can then be given help to stop their potentially harmful behaviours developing into an addiction.

Examiner's comments

Maisie's answer is worth 1 mark as essentially the criticism is that other factors are ignored – a rather simplistic approach to criticising a theory. She describes the role of alternative factors rather than using them in a more analytical way. It is also complicated by the fact that personality traits can be genetically determined anyway.

Examiner's comments

Ciaran earns no marks for this answer. The response is supporting rather than criticising the idea that personality factors impact on addictive behaviour and actually goes on to consider how this may be applied to prevention.

09 Read the item below and answer the question that follows.

> Christian is a teenager with a heroin addiction. His older brother is addicted too. Christian blames their problems on his father Len. Although Len has never been addicted to drugs, he has had a life-long problem with smoking.

Discuss **both** genetic vulnerability **and** family influences as explanations of addictive behaviours. Refer to Christian's addiction as part of your discussion. *(16 marks)*

Maisie's answer

It is possible to explain Christian's heroin addiction in terms of genetics. This is because his older brother, with whom he shares 50% of his genes is also addicted to heroin. The stimulus material also mentions that Christian and his brother blame their problems on their father, which could be a reference to their genetic inheritance of their addictive behaviour. Smoking is another behaviour that has been shown to have a genetic component. Vink et al. found that the likelihood of becoming addicted to nicotine was mostly caused by genetic factors.

There are problems with a genetic explanation of addictive behaviour, particularly Christian's addictive behaviour. For example, genetic explanations largely ignore the role of environmental factors. Christian blames his father for his addictive behaviour, but this could be because of the environment that his father had brought him up in rather than the genes that he received from his father. Some critics of genetic explanations of addictive behaviour claim that most of the research has concentrated only on males, such as Christian, therefore research has not told us much about the importance of genetics in the addictive behaviour of females.

There may well have been certain family influences that contributed to Christian's addictive behaviour. Parents may model particular behaviours, which are then imitated by their children. It is possible that Christian's father also had a heroin addiction, and that Christian and his brother learned their addictive behaviour from observing him. The stimulus material mentions that Christian blames his father for his addictive behaviour, so this may be a reference to a lack of warmth in his father's behaviour that pushed Christian to start abusing heroin as a form of compensation.

A problem with family influence explanations of addictive behaviour is that they ignore the important role that siblings play in the development of addictive behaviour. Kim et al. claim that brothers and sisters play an important role in the development of substance abuse, particularly if older brothers and sisters use substances. As Christian's older brother also uses heroin, this supports the claim that sibling influences may be more important than parental influences. Other critics claim that rather than substance abuse being a consequence of specific family influences it may be due to parents not being sufficiently involved in their children's upbringing, or not wanting to know what their children are up to. As a result they stop checking what their children are doing so that they become more vulnerable to the influence of others, particularly other substance abusers. 418 words

Examiner's comments

Maisie addresses all three skills tested in this essay to good effect: she demonstrates knowledge and understanding of the relevant explanations; she uses this item to illustrate her points; she evaluates both theories. A real strength of the essay is the way that Maisie includes the stimulus materials when evaluating as well as describing – and this partially compensates for quite brief coverage of the actual explanations themselves and a relatively limited range of evaluation points. Maisie does not go much beyond the nature/nurture debate – for example, she could have considered more philosophical points (e.g. genetic explanations being too reductionist) or implications (e.g. if addictive behaviour is learned it can be potentially unlearned). Because the application is so strong throughout the essay, Maisie has done just enough to qualify for a level 4 mark.

---

22 Describe and evaluate **two** techniques used to reduce addiction. *(16 marks)*

Ciaran's answer

Drug therapies involve the use of medications that interact with receptors in the brain's reward system and reduce cravings to engage in a particular behaviour. Drug treatments for nicotine addiction involve the use of nicotine replacement therapy (NRT) or drugs that reduce withdrawal symptoms when the person tries to quit. NRT works by releasing nicotine into the bloodstream at much lower levels than with cigarettes, gradually reducing the cravings for cigarettes. Drugs such as bupropion inhibit the re-uptake of dopamine, improving mood and reducing the likelihood of relapse in people trying to quit smoking.

There is research support for the effectiveness of NRT in reducing nicotine addiction. Stead et al. (2012) analysed the results of 150 interventions where NRT was compared to a placebo. They concluded that NRT was 70% more effective than the placebo in reducing the desire to smoke. The effectiveness of NRT was independent of any other types of support, which suggests that it was the drug alone that reduced addiction. A problem for studies comparing NRT to a placebo is that patients are often able to recognise whether they are in the NRT or placebo condition. For example, Mooney et al. (2004) found that two-thirds of patients in the placebo condition were confident they had not received the drug. This means that drawing conclusions about the effectiveness of NRT compared to placebo is more difficult than generally believed.

Cognitive-behaviour therapy (CBT) reduces addiction by changing the way that people think about their addiction. Gamblers can learn to challenge their irrational thinking about being able to control random events and to cope with the urges that lead them to gamble. During therapy, a gambler can be re-educated about the nature of randomness and challenged about how effective their own strategy has been so far. After any cognitive biases have been corrected, patients practice these changes in their daily life, keeping a diary to record any triggers to gambling (e.g. places or emotions), and so prevent relapse.

CBT has been shown to be effective in reducing a number of different addictions. For example, Petry et al. (2006) found that CBT was more effective at reducing gambling behaviour than being referred to 'Gamblers Anonymous,' and Ravindran et al. (2006) found CBT was more effective than drug therapy in the treatment of gambling addiction. There are advantages of using CBT in the treatment of addiction. For example, addicts often engage in addictive take drugs or gamble because of peer pressure. CBT gives addicts new and effective ways of resisting these pressures and so reduces the temptation to engage in the addictive behaviour. A problem with this, however is that over time, addicts associate more and more with other addicts and less with the mainstream culture, so changing the way people think about their behaviour may be insufficient motivation for them to change their lives completely. 475 words

Examiner's comments

Ciaran's answer is shows sound knowledge of his two chosen techniques and related research through his clear and accurate description. Research is used to good effect and presented in a way that also earns AO3 marks as it contributes to the general discussion. Ciaran could have included more limitations of the two techniques in order to broaden the evaluation. The points made are generally well developed but there are not enough of them to gain full credit. The essay could be improved by ending with a conclusion – possibly one that draws the comparison between the two techniques to give the essay better coherency. Ciaran's answer is just about good enough to be awarded a level 3 mark.

References

Aasved, M. (2003). *The Sociology of Gambling* (Vol. 2). Springfield, IL. Charles C Thomas Publisher.

Aboujaoude, E., Koran, L.M. and Gamel, N. (2006). Potential markers for problematic Internet use: a telephone survey of 2,513 adults. *CNS Spectrums, 11*(10), 750–5.

Abraham, C., Sheeran, P. and Johnston, M. (1998). From health beliefs to self-regulation: Theoretical advances in the psychology of action control. *Psychology and Health, 13*, 569–91.

Abramson, L.Y., Metalsky, F.I. and Alloy, L.B. (1989). Hopelessness depression: A theory- based subtype of depression. *Psychological Review, 96*(2), 358–72.

Adachi, P.J. and Willoughby, T. (2013). Demolishing the competition: The longitudinal link between competitive video games, competitive gambling, and aggression. *Journal of Youth and adolescence, 42*(7), 1090–104.

Adams, D.B. (1983). Why there are so few women warriors. *Cross-Cultural Research, 18*(3), 196–212.

Addington, J. and Addington, D. (2005). Patterns of premorbid functioning in first episode psychosis: Relationship to 2-year outcome. *Acta Psychiatrica Scandinavica, 112*, 40–6.

Ajzen, I. (1989). Attitude structure and behavior. In A.R. Pratkanis, S.J. Beckler and A.G. Greenwald (eds), *Attitude Structure and Function*. Hillsdale, NJ: Lawrence Erlbaum.

Ajzen, I. and Fishbein, M. (2005). The influence of attitudes on behavior. In D. Albarracín, B.T. Johnson, and M.P. Zanna (eds), *The Handbook of Attitudes* (pp. 173–221). Mahwah, NJ: Erlbaum.

Akers, R.L., Krohn, M.D., Lanza-Kaduce, L. and Radosewich, M. (1979). Social learning and deviant behaviour: A specific test of a general theory. *American Sociological Review, 44*, 636–655.

Albarracín, D., Gillette, J.C., Earl, A.N., Glasman, L.R., Durantini, M.R. and Ho, M.H. (2005). A test of major assumptions about behavior change: A comprehensive look at the effects of passive and active HIV-prevention interventions since the beginning of the epidemic. *Psychological Bulletin, 131*(6), 856–97.

Albert, D.J., Walsh, M.L. and Jonik, R.H. (1994). Aggression in humans: What is its biological foundation? *Neuroscience and Biobehavioral Reviews, 17*(4), 405–25.

Aleman, A. (2001). Hallucinations and the cerebral hemispheres. *Journal of Psychiatry and Neuroscience, 26*(1), 64.

Alison, L.J., Smith, M.D. and Morgan, K. (2003). Interpreting the accuracy of offender profiles. *Psychology, Crime and Law, 9*, 185–95.

Allen, K. (2003). Are pets a healthy pleasure? The influence of pets on blood pressure. *Current Directions of Psychological Science, 12*(6), 236–9.

Allender, D.M. and Marcell, F. (2003). Career criminals, security threat groups, and prison gangs: An interrelated threat. *FBI Law Enforcement Bulletin, 72*(6), 8–12.

Alleye, R. (2011). British men sharing the burden of household chores. *The Telegraph*, July. *See* www.telegraph.co.uk/women/mother-tongue/8673420/British-men-sharing-the-burden-of-household-chores.html (accessed September 2015).

Allport, G.W. (1961). *Pattern and Growth in Personality*. New York: Holt, Rinehart and Winston.

Allport, G.W. (1965). *Letters from Jenny*. New York: Harcourt, Brace and World.

Altorfer, A., Kasermann, M.L. and Hirsbrunner, H. (1998). Arousal and communication: I. The relationship between nonverbal, behavioral, and physiological indices of the stress response. *Journal of Psychophysiology, 12*, 40–59.

Amnesty Innternational (2015). *See* www.amnestyusa.org/our-work/issues/death-penalty/us-death-penalty-facts (accessed September 2015).

Anderson, C.A. and Dill, K.E. (2000). Video games and aggressive thoughts, feelings, and behavior in the laboratory and in life. *Journal of Personality and Social Psychology, 78*(4), 772–90.

Anderson, C.A., Gentile, D.A. and Buckley, K.E. (2007). *Violent Video Game Effects on Children and Adolescents*. New York: Oxford University Press.

Appell, G.N. (1984). Freeman's refutation of Mead's coming of age in Samoa: The implications for anthropological inquiry. *The Eastern Anthropologist, 37*, 183–214.

Archer, J. (2009). The nature of human aggression. *International Journal of Law and Psychiatry, 32*(4), 202–8.

Archer, J. (2013). Can evolutionary principles explain patterns of family violence? *Psychological Bulletin, 139*(2), 403–40.

Arevalo, S., Prado, G. and Amaro, H. (2008). Spirituality, sense of coherence, and coping responses in women receiving treatment for alcohol and drug addiction. *Evaluation and program planning, 31*(1), 113–23.

Armitage, C.J. and Conner, M. (2001). Efficacy of the theory of planned behaviour: A meta-analytic review. *British Journal of Social Psychology, 40*(4), 471–99.

Armitage, C.J., Armitage, C.J., Conner, M., Loach, J. and Willetts, D. (1999). Different perceptions of control: Applying an extended theory of planned behavior to legal and illegal drug use. *Basic and Applied Social Psychology, 21*(4), 301–16.

Ashe, D.D. and McCutcheon, L.E. (2001). Shyness, loneliness, and attitude toward celebrities. *Current Research in Social Psychology, 6*(9), 124–33.

Ashton, H. (1997). Benzodiazepine dependency. In A. Baum, S. Newman, J. Weinman, R. West, and C. McManus (eds), *Cambridge Handbook of Psychology, Health and Medicine*. Cambridge: Cambridge University Press.

Atkin, C. (1983). Effects of realistic TV violence vs. fictional violence on aggression. *Journalism Quarterly, 60*(4), 615–21.

Atlas, J.G., Smith, G.T., Hohlstein, L.A., McCarthy, D.M. and Kroll, L.S. (2002). Similarities and differences between Caucasian and African American college women on eating and dieting expectancies, bulimic symptoms, dietary restraint, and disinhibition. *International Journal of Eating Disorders, 32*(3), 326–34.

Atwell, P. (2015). Personal communication.

Aumer-Ryan, P. (2006). Visual rating system for HFES graphics: Design and analysis. In *Proceedings of the Human Factors and Ergonomics Society Annual Meeting* (Vol. 50, No. 18, October, pp. 2124–8). SAGE.

Ayllon, T. and Azrin, N. (1968). *The Token Economy: A Motivation System for Therapy and Rehabilitation*. New York: Appleton-Century-Crofts, Educational Division, Meredith Corporation.

Azrin, N.H. and Foxx, R.M. (orig. 1974, reprinted 1989). *Toilet Training in Less Than a Day*. New York: Pocketbook.

Baerwert, A. (2014). Nicotine addiction discriminates between men and women. *See* www.thefix.com (accessed February 2016).

Bahr, S.J., Hoffmann, J.P. and Yang, X. (2005). Parental and peer influences on the risk of adolescent drug use. *Journal of Primary Prevention, 26*(6), 529–51.

Bailer, U.F., Frank, G.K., Henry, S.E., Price, J.C., Meltzer, C.C., Mathis, C.A., Wagner, A., Thornton, L., Hoge, J., Ziolko, S.K. and Becker, C.R. (2007). Exaggerated 5-HT1A but normal 5-HT2A receptor activity in individuals ill with anorexia nervosa. *Biological Psychiatry, 61*(9), 1090–9.

Bailey, A.A. and Hurd, P.L. (2005). Finger length ratio (2D:4D) correlates with physical aggression in men but not in women. *Biological Psychology, 68*(3), 215–22.

Bailey, F.J. and Dua, J. (1999). Individualism-collectivism, coping styles, and stress in international and Anglo-Australian students: A comparative study. *Australian Psychologist, 34*(3), 177–82.

Baillargeon, R. (1994). How do infants learn about the physical world? *Current Directions in Psychological Science, 3*(5), 133–40.

Baillargeon, R. and DeVos, J. (1991). Object permanence in infants: Further evidence. *Child Development, 62*, 1227–46.

Baillargeon, R., Wu, D., Yuan, S., Li, J. and Luo, Y. (2009). Young infants' expectations about self-propelled objects. In B.M. Hood and L.R. Santos (eds), *The Origins of Object Knowledge*. Oxford: Oxford University Press.

Baker, C.A. and Morrison, A.P. (1998). Cognitive processes in auditory hallucinations: Attributional biases and metacognition. *Psychological Medicine, 28*(5), 1199–208.

Baker, L. and Oswald, D. (2010). Shyness and online social networking services. *Journal of Social and Personal Relationships, 27*(7), 873–89.

Bandura, A. (1961). Psychotherapy as a learning process. *Psychological Bulletin, 58*(2), 143–59.

Bandura, A. (1973). *Aggression: A Social Learning Analysis*. Englewood Cliffs, NJ: Prentice-Hall.

Bandura, A. (1977). Self-efficacy: Toward a unifying theory of behavioral change. *Psychological Review, 84*(2), 191–215.

Bandura, A. (1986). *Social Foundations of Thought and Action: A Social Cognitive Theory*. Englewood Cliffs, NJ: Prentice-Hall.

Bandura, A. (1991). Social cognitive theory of self-regulation. *Organizational Behavior and Human Decision Processes, 50*, 248–87.

Bandura, A. and Bussey, K. (2004). On broadening the cognitive, motivational, and sociostructural scope of theorizing about gender development and functioning: Comment on Martin, Ruble, and Szkrybalo (2002). *Psychological Bulletin, 130*, 690–701.

Bandura, A. and Walters, R.H. (1963). *Social Learning and Personality Development*. New York: Holt, Rinehart and Winston.

Bandura, A., Ross, D. and Ross, S.A. (1961). Transmission of aggression through imitation of aggressive models. *Journal of Abnormal Social Psychology, 63*, 575–82.

Bandura, A., Ross, D. and Ross, S.A. (1963). Imitation of film-mediated aggressive models. *Journal of Abnormal and Social Psychology, 66*, 3–11.

Barbato, G., Fichele, M., Senatore, I., Casiello, M. and Muscettola, G. (2006). Increased dopaminergic activity in restricting-type anorexia nervosa. *Psychiatry Research*, *142*(2), 253–5.

Barber, B.K. and Buehler, C. (1996). Family cohesion and enmeshment: Different constructs, different effects. *Journal of Marriage and the Family*, 433–41.

Barelds-Dijkstra, P. and Barelds, D.P. (2008). Positive illusions about one's partner's physical attractiveness. *Body Image*, *5*(1), 99–108.

Barnes, A. (2004). Race, schizophrenia, and admission to state psychiatric hospitals. *Administration and Policy in Mental Health*, *31*(3), 241–52.

Barnes, G.E., Barnes, M.D. and Patton, D. (2005). Prevalence and predictors of 'heavy' marijuana use in a Canadian youth sample. *Substance Use and Abuse*, *40*(12), 1849–63

Barnes, G.E., Murray, R.P., Patton, D., Bentler, P.M. and Anderson, R.E. (2000). *The Addiction Prone Personality: Longitudinal Research in the Social Sciences: An Interdisciplinary Series*. New York: Springer.

Baron-Cohen, S. (1995). *Mindblindness: An Essay on Autism and Theory of Mind*. Cambridge, MA: MIT Press.

Baron-Cohen, S., Jolliffe, T., Mortimore, C. and Robertson, M. (1997). Another advanced test of theory of mind: Evidence from very high functioning adults with autism or Asperger Syndrome. *Journal of Child Psychology and Psychiatry*, *38*, 813–22.

Baron-Cohen, S., Leslie, A.M. and Frith, U. (1985). Does the autistic child have a 'theory of mind'? *Cognition*, *21*, 37–46.

Bassett, J.E. and Blanchard, E.B. (1977). The effects of the absence of close supervision on the use of response cost in a prison token economy. *Journal of Applied Behaviour Analysis*, *10*, 375–9.

Bates, S.H. and Myers, M.G. (2003). The role of leptin receptor signaling in feeding and neuroendocrine function. *Trends in Endocrinology & Metabolism*, *14*(10), 447–52.

Bateson, G., Jackson, D., Haley, J. and Weakland, J. (1956). Toward a theory of schizophrenia. *Behavioural Science*, *1*, 251–64.

Bateson, G., Jackson, D.D., Haley, J. and Weakland, J. (1956). Toward a theory of schizophrenia. *Klassiekers van de kinder-en jeugdpsychiatrie II*, 300.

Baumann, S., Gaertner, B., Schnuerer, I., Haberecht, K., John, U. and Freyer-Adam, J. (2015). Belief incongruence and the intention-behavior gap in persons with at-risk alcohol use. *Addictive Behaviours*, *48*, 5–11.

Beck, A.T. (1976). *Cognitive Therapy and the Emotional Disorders*. New York: International Universities Press.

Beck, A.T. and Rector, N.A. (2005). Cognitive approaches to schizophrenia: Theory and therapy. *Annual Review of Clinical Psychology*, *1*, 577–606.

Becker, A.E., Burwell, R.A., Herzog, D.B., Hamburg, P. and Gilman, S.E. (2002). Eating behaviours and attitudes following prolonged exposure to television among ethnic Fijian adolescent girls. *The British Journal of Psychiatry*, *180*(6), 509–14.

Becona, E., Lorenzo, M.D.C. and Fuentes, M.J. (1996). Pathological gambling and depression. *Psychological Reports*, *78*(2), 635–40.

Bell, R.R., Draper, H.H. and Bergan, J.G. (1973). Sucrose, lactose, and glucose tolerance in northern Alaskan Eskimos. *The American Journal of Clinical Nutrition*, *26*(11), 1185–90.

Bellisle, F., Clément, K., Barzic, M., Gall, A., Guy-Grand, B. and Basdevant, A. (2004). The Eating Inventory and body adiposity from leanness to massive obesity: a study of 2509 adults. *Obesity Research*, *12*(12), 2023–30.

Bem, S.L. (1981). *Bem Sex-Role Inventory: Professional Manual*. Palo Alto, CA: Consulting Psychologists Press.

Bem, S.L. (1983). Gender schema theory and its implications for child development: Raising gender-aschematic children in a gender-schematic society. *Signs: Journal of Women in Culture and Society*, *8*, 598–616.

Bem, S.L. (1989). Genital knowledge and gender constancy in preschool children. *Child Development*, *60*, 649–62.

Ben-Tovim, D.I., Walker, M.K., Fok, D. and Yap, E. (1989). An adaptation of the Stroop test for measuring shape and food concerns in eating disorders: A quantitative measure of psychopathology? *International Journal of Eating Disorders*, *8*(6), 681–7.

Benhsain, K. and Ladouceur, R. (2004). Knowledge in statistics and erroneous perceptions in gambling. *Gambling Research*, *16*(1), 25–31.

Bennett, N. (1976). *Teacher Styles and Pupil Progress*. London: Open Books.

Benton, D. (2004). Role of parents in the determination of the food preferences of children and the development of obesity. *International Journal of Obesity* *28*, 858–69.

Berenbaum, S.A. and Bailey, J.M. (2003). Effects on gender identity of prenatal androgens and genital appearance: Evidence from girls with congenital adrenal hyperplasia. *The Journal of Clinical Endocrinology and Metabolism*, *88*(3), 1102–6.

Berg, J.H. and Archer, R.L. (1980). Disclosure or concern: A second look at liking for the norm breaker. *Journal of Personality*, *48*(2), 245–57.

Berger, A. (1965). A test of the doublebind hypothesis of schizophrenia. *Family Process*, *4*, 198–205.

Berkowitz, L. (1984). Some effects of thoughts on anti- and prosocial influences of media events: A cognitive-neoassociation analysis. *Psychological Bulletin*, *95*(3), 410.

Berkowitz, L. (1989). Frustration–aggression hypothesis: Examination and reformulation. *Psychological Bulletin*, *106*(1), 59.

Bernstein, I.L. and Webster, M.M. (1980). Learned taste aversions in humans. *Physiology & Behavior*, *25*(3), 363–6.

Berry, J.W., Poortinga, Y.H., Segall, M.H. and Dasen, P.R. (2002). *Cross-cultural Psychology* (2nd edition). Cambridge: Cambridge University Press.

Berscheid, E. and Walster, E.H. (1969). *Interpersonal Attraction*. Reading, Mass: Addison-Wesley.

Berscheid, E., Dion, K., Walster, E. and Walster, G.W. (1971). Physical attractiveness and dating choice: A test of the matching hypothesis. *Journal of Experimental Social Psychology*, *7*, 173–89.

Biederman, J., Mick, E. and Faraone, S.V. (2000). Age-dependent decline of symptoms of attention deficit hyperactivity disorder: Impact of remission definition and symptom type. *American Journal of Psychiatry*, *157*(5), 816–8.

Binkofski, F., Amunts, K., Stephan, K.M., Posse, S., Schormann, T., Freund, H.-J., Zilles, K. and Seitz, R.J. (2000). Broca's region subserves imagery of motion: A combined cytoarchitectonic and fMRI study. *Human Brain Mapping*, *11*, 273–85.

Birch, L.L. (1980). Effects of peer models' food choices and eating behaviors on preschoolers' food preferences. *Child Development*, *51*, 489–96.

Birch, L.L., Marlin, D. and Rotter, J. (1984). Eating as the 'means' activity in a contingency: effects on young children's food preference. *Child Development*, *55*, 431–9.

Birch, L.L., McPhee, L., Shoba, B.C., Pirok, E. and Steinberg, L. (1987). What kind of exposure reduces children's food neophobia? Looking vs. tasting. *Appetite*, *9*(3), 171–8.

Bjorkqvist, K. (1985). *Violent Films, Anxiety and Aggression*. Helsinki: Finnish Society of Sciences and Letters.

Blacker, J., Watson, A. and Beech, A.R. (2008). A combined drama-based and CBT approach to working with self-reported anger aggression. *Criminal Behaviour and Mental Health*, *18*, 129–37.

Blakemore, C. and Cooper, G.F. (1970). Development of the brain depends on the visual environment. *Nature*, *228*, 477–8.

Blanchard, R. (1985). Typology of male-to-female transsexualism. *Archives of Sexual Behavior*, *14*, 247–61.

Blanco, C., Ibáñez, A., Sáiz-Ruiz, J., Blanco-Jerez, C. and Nunes, E.V. (2000). Epidemiology, pathophysiology and treatment of pathological gambling. *CNS Drugs*, *13*(6), 397–407.

Blasio, F.A. and Benda, B.B. (1993). Adolescent sexual intercourse: Family and peer influences. *School Social Work Journal*, *18*, 17–31.

Blaszczynski, A. and Nower, L. (2002). A pathways model of problem and pathological gambling. *Addiction*, *97*(5), 487–99.

Blonigen, D.M., Hicks, B.B., Krueger, R.F., Patrick, C.J. and Iancano, W.G. (2005). Psychopathic personality traits: Heritability and genetic overlap with internalizing and externalising psychopathology. *Psycho-logical Medicine*, *35*, 637–48.

Blonigen, D.M., Timko, C., Finney, J.W., Moos, B.S. and Moos, R.H. (2011). Alcoholics Anonymous attendance, decreases in impulsivity and drinking and psychosocial outcomes over 16 years: moderated-mediation from a developmental perspective. *Addiction*, *106*(12), 2167–77.

Blum, K. and Payne, J.E. (1991). *Alcohol and the Addictive Brain*. New York: Free Press.

Blum, K., Noble, E.P., Sheridan, P.J., Montgomery, A., Ritchie, T., Jagadeeswaran, P. and Cohn, J.B. (1990). Allelic association of human dopamine D2 receptor gene in alcoholism. *Jama*, *263*(15), 2055–60.

BMA (2000). *Eating Disorders, Body Image and the Media*. London: British Medical Association.

Boccardi, M., Ganzola, R., Rossi, R., Sabattoli, F., Laakso, M.P., Repo-Tiihonen, E., Vaurio, O., Könönen, M., Aronen, H.J., Thompson, P.M., Frisoni, G.B. and Tiihonen, J. (2010). Abnormal hippocampal shape in offenders with psychopathy. *Human Brain Mapping*, *31*(3), 438–47.

Bond, M.J., McDowell, A.J. and Wilkinson, J.Y. (2001). The measurement of dietary restraint, disinhibition and hunger: An examination of the factor structure of the Three Factor Eating Questionnaire (TFEQ). *International Journal of Obesity and Related Metabolic Disorders: Journal of the International Association for the Study of Obesity*, *25*(6), 900–6.

Børglum, A.D., Demontis, D., Grove, J., Pallesen, J., Hollegaard, M.V., Pedersen, C.B. and Mors, O. (2014). Genome-wide study of association and interaction with maternal cytomegalovirus infection suggests new schizophrenia loci. *Molecular Psychiatry*, *19*(3), 325–33.

Bortolozzi, A., Masana, M., Díaz-Mataix, L., Cortés, R., Scorza, M.C., Gingrich, J.A., Toth, M. and Artigas, F. (2010). Dopamine release induced by atypical antipsychotics in prefrontal cortex requires 5-HT1A receptors but not 5-HT2A receptors. *International Journal of Neuropsychopharmacology*, *13*(10), 1299–314.

Bouteyre, E., Maurel, M. and Bernaud, J.-L. (2007). Daily hassles and depressive symptoms among first year psychology students in France: The role of coping and social support. *Stress and Health*, *23*(2), 93.

Bowlby, J. (1944). Forty-four juvenile thieves: Their characters and their home life. *International Journal of Psychoanalysis, 25*, 1–57, 207–28.

Bowlby, J. (1951). *Maternal Care and Mental Health*. Geneva: World Health Organization.

Bowlby, J. (1953). *Child Care and the Growth of Love*. Harmondsworth: Penguin.

Bowlby, J. (1969). *Attachment and Loss. Vol. 1: Attachment*. London: Hogarth Press.

Bown, W. (1992). Sex-test confusion could create havoc at Olympics. *New Scientist*, *133*(1804), 14.

Boyland, E.J. and Halford, J.C.G. (2013). Television advertising and branding. Effects on eating behaviour and food preferences in children. *Appetite*, *62*, 236–41.

Bradbard, M.R., Martin, C.L., Endsley, R.C. and Halvesron, C.F. (1986). Influence of sex stereotypes on children's exploration and memory: A competence versus performance distinction. *Developmental Psychology*, *22*, 481–6.

Bradley, G.M., Couchman, G.M., Perlesz, A., Nguyen, A.T. and Riess, C. (2006). Multiple-family group treatment for English- and Vietnamese-speaking families living with schizophrenia. *Psychiatric Services*, *57*(4), 521–30.

Bradley, L.A. (1995). Chronic benign pain. In D. Wedding (ed.), *Behaviour and Medicine* (2nd edition). St Louis, MO: Mosby-Year Book.

Brekke, J.S. and Barrio, C. (1997). Cross-ethnic symptom differences in schizophrenia: The influence of culture and minority status. *Schizophrenia Bulletin*, *23*(2), 305–16.

Bremner, J.G. (2013). From perception to action: The early development of knowledge. In F. Simion and G. Butterworth (eds), *The Development of Sensory, Motor and Cognitive Capacities in Early Infancy*. Hove: Psychology Press.

Brewer, K. (2000). *Psychology and Crime*. London: Heinemann.

British Medical Association, BMA (2000). *Eating Disorders, Body Image and the Media*. British Medical Association.

Brockner, J., Pressman, B., Cabitt, J. and Moran, P. (1982). Nonverbal intimacy, sex, and compliance: a field study. *Journal of Nonverbal Behavior*, *6*, 253–8.

Brosnan, M. (2008). Digit ratio as an indicator of numeracy relative to literacy in 7-year-old British school children. *British Journal of Psychology*, *99*, 75–85.

Brosnan, S.F. and De Waal, F.B. (2003). Monkeys reject unequal pay. *Nature*, *425*(6955), 297–9.

Brosnan, S.F., Schiff, H.C. and De Waal, F.B. (2005). Tolerance for inequity may increase with social closeness in chimpanzees. *Proceedings of the Royal Society of London B: Biological Sciences*, *272*(1560), 253–8.

Broverman, I.K., Broverman, D.M., Clarkson, F.E., Rosenkrantz, P.S. and Vogel, S.R. (1970). Sex-role stereotypes and clinical judgments of mental health. *Journal of Consulting and Clinical Psychology*, *34*(1), 1.

Brown, G.W. (1974). Meaning, measurement and stress of life events. In B.S. Dohrenwend and B.P. Dohrenwend (eds), *Stressful Life Events: Their Nature and Effects*. New York: Wiley.

Brown, G.W. and Harris, T. (1978). *Social Origins of Depression*. London: Tavistock.

Brown, R. (1986). *Social Psychology: The Second Edition*. New York: The Free Press.

Brown, R. and Ogden, J. (2004). Children's eating attitudes and behaviour: A study of the modeling and control theories of parental influence. *Health Education Research*, *19*(3), 261–71.

Brown, R., Maras, P., Masser, B., Vivian, J. and Hewstone, M. (2001). Life on the ocean wave: Testing some intergroup hypotheses in a naturalistic setting. *Group Processes & Intergroup Relations*, *4*(2), 81–97.

Brunner, H.G., Nelen, M., Breakefield, X.O., Ropers, H.H. and Van Oost, B.A. (1993). Abnormal behavior associated with a point mutation in the structural gene for monoamine oxidase A. *Science*, *262*(5133), 578–80.

Brunner, H.G., Nelen, M., Breakefield, X.O., Ropers, H.H. and van Oost, B.A. (1993). Abnormal behavior associated with a point mutation in the structural gene for Monoamine Oxidase A. *Science*, *262*(5133), 578–80.

Brunstrom, J.M., Yates, H.M. and Witcomb, G.L. (2004). Dietary restraint and heightened reactivity to food. *Physiology & Behavior*, *81*(1), 85–90.

Bryant, E.J., King, N.A. and Blundell, J.E. (2008). Disinhibition: Its effects on appetite and weight regulation. *Obesity Reviews*, *9*(5), 409–19.

Bryant, P. (1995). Jean Piaget. In R. Fuller (ed.), *Seven Pioneers of Psychology*. London: Routledge.

Bryant, P.E. and Trabasso, T. (1971). Transitive inferences and memory in young children. *Nature*, *232*, 456–8.

Buckley, P.F., Miller, B.J., Lehrer, D.S. and Castle, D.J. (2009). Psychiatric comorbidities and schizophrenia. *Schizophrenia Bulletin*, *35*(2), 383–402.

Bulik, C., Sullivan, P., Tozzi, F., Furberg, H., Lichtenstein, P. and Pedersen N. (2006). Prevalence, heritability and prospective risk factors for anorexia nervosa. *Archives of General Psychiatry, 63*, 305–12.

Bulik, C.M. (2004). Genetic and Biological Risk Factors. In J.K. Thompson (ed.), *Handbook of Eating Disorders and Obesity*. Hoboken, NJ: John Wiley & Sons, Inc.

Buller, D.J. (2005). *Adapting Minds: Evolutionary Psychology and the Persistent Quest for Human Nature*. New York: Bradford Books.

Burchard, J.D. and Lane, T.W. (1982). Crime and delinquency. In A.S. Bellack, M. Hersen and A.E. Kazdin (eds), *International Handbook of Behavior Modification and Therapy*. New York: Plenum Press.

Bushman, B.J. (1998). Priming effects of media violence on the accessibility of aggressive constructs in memory. *Personality and Social Psychology Bulletin*, *24*, 537–45.

Bushman, B.J. (2002). Does venting anger feed or extinguish the flame? Catharsis, rumination, distraction, anger, and aggressive responding. *Personality and Social Psychology Bulletin*, *28*(6), 724–731.

Bushman, B.J. and Anderson, C.A. (2009). Comfortably numb desensitizing effects of violent media on helping others. *Psychological Science*, *20*(3), 273–7.

Bushman, B.J. and Huesmann, L.R. (2006). Short-term and long-term effects of violent media on aggression in children and adults. *Archives of Pediatrics & Adolescent Medicine*, *160*(4), 348–52.

Buss, D.M. (1988). From vigilance to violence: Tactics of mate retention in American undergraduates. *Ethology and Sociobiology*, *9*(5), 291–317.

Buss, D.M. (1989). Sex differences in human mate preferences: Evolutionary hypotheses tested in 37 cultures. *Behavioral and Brain Sciences*, *12*, 1–49.

Buss, D.M. (2003). *The Evolution of Desire: Strategies of Human Mating*. New York: Basic Books.

Buss, D.M. (ed.) (2005). *The Handbook of Evolutionary Psychology*. Hoboken, NJ: John Wiley and Sons.

Bussey, K. and Bandura, A. (1992). Self-regulatory mechanisms governing gender development. *Child Development*, *63*, 1236–50.

Bussey, K. and Bandura, A. (1999). Social cognitive theory of gender development and differentiation. *Psychological Review*, *106*, 676–713.

Button, E.J., Sonuga-Barke, E.J.S., Davies, J. and Thompson, M. (1996). A prospective study of self-esteem in the prediction of eating problems in adolescent schoolgirls: Questionnaire findings. *British Journal of Clinical Psychology*, *35*(2), 193–203.

Byers, E.S., Wang, A., Harvey, J.H., Wenzel, A. and Sprecher, S. (2004). Understanding sexuality in close relationships from the social exchange perspective. *The Handbook of Sexuality in Close Relationships*, 203–34.

Byrne, D., Ervin, C. and Lamberth, J. (1970). Continuity between the experimental study of attraction and real-life computer dating. *Journal of Personality and Social Psychology*, *16*, 157–65.

Cairns, G., Angus, K., Hastings, G. and Caraher, M. (2013). Systematic reviews of the evidence of the nature, extent and effects of food marketing to children. A retrospective summary. *Appetite, 62*, 209–15.

Calhoun, J.B. (1962). Population density and social pathology. *Scientific American*, *206*(2), 139–48.

Campbell, A. (1993). *Men, Women and Aggression: From Rage in Marriage to Violence in the Streets. How Gender Affects the Way We Act*. New York: Basic Books.

Campbell, W. (1997). Evaluation of a residential program using the Addiction Severity Index and Stages of Change. *Journal of Addictive Diseases*, *16*, 27–39.

Cannavale, F.J., Scarr, H.A. and Pepitone, A. (1970). Deindividuation in the small group: Further evidence. *Journal of Personality and Social Psychology*, *16*(1), 141.

Canter , D. (2010). *Forensic Psychology: A very short introduction*. Oxford: OUP.

Canter, D. and Larkin, P. (1993). The environmental range of serial rapists. *Journal of Environmental Psychology*, *13*, 63–69.

Canter, D., Alison, A.J., Alison, E. and Wentink, N. (2004). The organized/disorganized typologies of Serial Murder: Myth or Model? *Psychology, Public Policy and Law*, *10*(3), 293–320.

Carmichael, L., Hogan, P. and Walter, A. (1932). An experimental study of the effect of language on the reproduction of visually perceived forms. *Journal of Experimental Psychology*, *15*, 73–86.

Carnagey, N.L., Anderson, C.A. and Bushman, B.J. (2007). The effect of video game violence on physiological desensitization to real-life violence. *Journal of Experimental Social Psychology*, *43*(3), 489–96.

Carpenter, M., Pennington, B.F. and Rogers, S.J. (2001). Understanding of others' intentions in children with autism. *Journal of Autism and Developmental Disorders, 31*(6), 589–99.

Carr, A. (2009). The effectiveness of family therapy and systemic interventions for adult-focused problems. *Journal of Family Therapy, 31*(1), 46–74.

Carrabine, E., Cox, P., Fussey, P., Hobbs, D., South, N., Thiel, D. and Turton, J. (2014). *Criminology: A sociological introduction* (3rd edition). London: Routledge.

Carré, J.M. and Olmstead, N.A. (2015). Social neuroendocrinology of human aggression: Examining the role of competition-induced testosterone dynamics. *Neuroscience, 286,* 171–86.

Carroll, D. (1992). *Health Psychology: Stress, Behaviour and Disease*. London: Falmer Press.

Casey, D.E. (1995). Neuroleptic-induced acute extrapyramidal syndromes and tardive dyskinesia. In S.R. Hirsch and D.R. Weinberger (eds), *Schizophrenia*. Oxford: Blackwell Science Ltd.

Cash, T.F. (1995). Developmental teasing about physical appearance: Retrospective descriptions and relationships with body image. *Social Behavior and Personality: An international journal, 23*(2), 123–30.

Caspi, A., McClay, J., Moffitt, T.E., Mill, J., Martin, J., Craig, I.W., Taylor, A. and Poulton, R. (2002). Role of genotype in the cycle of violence in maltreated children. *Science, 297*(5582), 851–4.

Cavedini, P., Riboldi, G., Keller, R., D'Annucci, A. and Bellodi, L. (2002). Frontal lobe dysfunction in pathological gambling patients. *Biological Psychiatry, 51*(4), 334–41.

Chagnon, N. (1992). *Yanomamö*. Fort Worth, TX: Harcourt, Brace, Jovanovich.

Chagnon, N.A. (1988). Life histories, blood revenge, and warfare in a tribal population. *Science, 239*(4843), 985–92.

Charles, S.T., Piazza, J.R., Mogle, J., Sliwinski, M.J. and Almeida, D.M. (2013). The wear-and-tear of daily stressors on mental health. *Psychological Science, 24*(5), 733–41.

Charlton, T., Gunter, B. and Hannan, A. (eds) (2000). *Broadcast Television Effects in a Remote Community*. Hillsdale, NJ: Lawrence Erlbaum.

Charlton, T., Gunter, B. and Hannan, A. (eds) (2002). *Broadcast Television Effects in a Remote Community*. London: Routledge.

Chen, C.-A. and and Howitt, D. (2007). Different crime types and moral reasoning development in young offenders compared with non-offender controls. *Psychology, Crime and Law, 13,* 405–16.

Chen, G. (1995). Differences in self-disclosure patterns among Americans versus Chinese: A comparative study. *Journal of Cross-Cultural Psychology, 26,* 84–91.

Chen, X. and Yang, X. (2014). Does food environment influence food choices? A geographical analysis through 'tweets'. *Applied Geography, 51,* 82–9.

Cheung, Y., Lee, P.-L., Yang, C.-Y., Lin, C.-P., Hung, D. and Decety, J. (2009). Gender differences in the mu rhythm of the human mirror-neuron system. *PLoS ONE, 3,* e2113. *See* www.ncbi.nlm.nih.gov/pmc/articles/PMC2361218 (accessed June 2015).

Chodorow, N. (1994). *Femininities, Masculinities, Sexualities: Freud and Beyond*. Lexington, KY: University Press of Kentucky.

Chory-Assad, R.M. and Yanen, A. (2005). Hopelessness and loneliness as predictors of older adults' involvement with favorite television performers. *Journal of Broadcasting & Electronic Media, 49*(2), 182–201.

Christensen, A., Atkins, D.C., Berns, S., Wheeler, J., Baucom, D.H. and Simpson, L.E. (2004). Traditional versus integrative behavioral couple therapy for significantly and chronically distressed married couples. *Journal of Consulting and Clinical Psychology, 72,* 176–91.

Chung, W.C., De Vries, G.J. and Swaab, D.F. (2002). Sexual differentiation of the bed nucleus of the stria terminalis in humans may extend into adulthood. *The Journal of Neuroscience, 22*(3), 1027–33.

Churchland, P.S. (2011). *Braintrust: What Neuroscience Tells Us About Morality*. Princeton, NJ: Princeton University Press.

Clark, L., Studer, B., Bruss, J., Tranel, D. and Bechara, A. (2014). Damage to insula abolishes cognitive distortions during simulated gambling. *Proceedings of the National Academy of Sciences, 111*(16), 6098–103.

Clark, M. S. (1984). A distinction between two types of relationships and its implications for development. In J.C. Masters and K. Yarin-Levin (eds). *Boundary Areas in Social and Developmental Psychology*, New York: Academic Press.

Clarke, D., Abbott, M., DeSouza, R. and Bellringer, M. (2007). An overview of help seeking by problem gamblers and their families including barriers to and relevance of services. *International Journal of Mental Health and Addiction, 5*(4), 292–306.

Claussnitzer, M., Dankel, S.N., Kim, K.H., Quon, G., Meuleman, W., Haugen, C., Glunk, V., Sousa, I.S., Beaudry, J.L., Puviindran, V. and Abdennur, N.A. (2015). FTO obesity variant circuitry and adipocyte browning in humans. *New England Journal of Medicine, 373*(10), 895–907.

Coates, S., Friedman, R.C. and Wolfe, S. (1991). The etiology of boyhood gender identity disorder: A model for integrating temperament, development, and psychodynamics. *Psychological Dialogues, 1,* 481–523.

Coccaro, E.F., Berman, M.E. and Kavoussi, R.J. (1997). Assessment of life history of aggression: development and psychometric characteristics. *Psychiatry Research, 73*(3), 147–57.

Cohen, H.L. and Filipcjak, F. (1971). *A New Learning Environment: What's new and what isn't*. San Francisco, CA: Jossey-Bass Inc.

Cohen, J. (2004). Parasocial break-up from favorite television characters: The role of attachment styles and relationship intensity. *Journal of Social and Personal Relationships, 2,* 187–202.

Cohen, S., Tyrrell, D.A. and Smith, A.P. (1993). Negative life events, perceived stress, negative affect, and susceptibility to the common cold. *Journal of Personality and Social Psychology, 64,* 131–40.

Cohen, S., Tyrrell, D.A. and Smith, A.P. (1991). Psychological stress and susceptibility to the common cold. *New England Journal of Medicine, 325,* 606–12.

Colapinto, J. (2000). *As Nature Made Him: The Boy Who was Raised as a Girl*. New York: Quartet Books.

Colby, A. and Kohlberg, L. (1987). *The Measurement of Moral Judgement: Vol. 1: Theoretical foundations and research validation*. Cambridge: Cambridge University Press.

Colby, A., Kohlberg, L., Gibbs, J., and Lieberman, M. (1983). A longitudnal study of moral judgement. *Monographs of the Society for Research in Child Development, 48,* nos. 1–2.

Cole, C.M., O'Boyle, M., Emory, L.E. and Meyer III, W.J. (1997). Co-morbidity of gender dysphoria and other major psychiatric diagnoses. *Archives of Sexual Behaviour, 26,* 13–26.

Cole, P. (1986). Children's spontaneous expressive control of facial expression. *Child Development, 57,* 1309–21.

Cole, T. and Leets, L. (1999). Attachment styles and intimate television viewing: insecurely forming relationships in a parasocial way. *Journal of Social and Personal Relationships, 16*(4), 495–511.

Collins, J.J. (1989). Alcohol and interpersonal violence: Less than meets the eye. In N.A. Weiner, M.E. Wolfgang (eds), *Pathways to Criminal Violence*. Newbury Park, CA: SAGE.

Collins, N.L. and Miller, L.C. (1994). Self-disclosure and liking: A meta-analytic review. *Psychological Bulletin, 116*(3), 457–75.

Colman, A.M. (1991). Crowd psychology in South African murder trials. *American Psychologist, 46*(10), 1071–9.

Comer, R.J. (2013). *Fundamentals of Abnormal Psychology* (7th edition). New York: Worth Publishers.

Conley, T.D. and Ramsey, L.R. (2011). Killing us softly? Investigating portrayals of women and men in contemporary magazine advertisements. *Psychology of Women* Quarterly, *35*(3), 469–478.

Connor, J.P., Young, R.M., Lawford, B.R., Saunders, J.B., Ritchie, T.L. and Noble, E.P. (2007). Heavy nicotine and alcohol use in alcohol dependence is associated with D2 dopamine receptor (DRD2) polymorphism. *Addictive Behaviors, 32*(2), 310–19.

Contrada, R.J. (1989). Type A behavior, personality hardiness, and cardiovascular responses to stress. *Journal of Personality and Social Psychology, 57*(5), 895–903.

Cooke, D.J., Wozniak, E. and Johnstone, L. (2008). Casting light on prison violence in scotland evaluating the impact of situational risk factors. *Criminal Justice and Behavior, 35*(8), 1065–78.

Coolican, H. (1996). *Introduction to Research Methods and Statistics in Psychology*. London: Hodder and Stoughton.

Coolican, H. (2004). Personal communication.

Cooney, E.W. and Selman, R.L. (1978). Children's use of social conceptions: Toward a dynamic model of social cognition. *New Directions for Child Development: Social Cognition, 1,* 22–44.

Cooper, A. and Sportolari, L. (1997). Romance in cyberspace: Understanding online attraction. *Journal of Sex Education and Therapy, 22*(1), 7–14.

Cooper, M. (1997). Cognitive theory in anorexia nervosa and bulimia nervosa: A review, *Behavioural and Cognitive Psychotherapy, 25*(2), 113–45.

Copeland, J.R.M., Cooper, J.E., Kendell, R.E. and Gourlay, A.J. (1971). Differences in usage of diagnostic labels amongst psychiatrists in the British Isles. *The British Journal of Psychiatry, 118*(547), 629–40.

Copson, G. (1995). *Coals to Newcastle? Part 1: A study of offender profiling*. London: Home Office, Police Research Group.

Cornwell, C., Mustard, D.B. and Van Parys, J. (2013). Non-cognitive skills and the gender disparities in test scores and teacher assessments: Evidence from primary school. *Journal of Human Resources, 48,* 236–64.

Corrigan, P.W. (1991). Strategies that overcome barriers to token economies in community programs for severe mentally ill adults. *Community Mental Health Journal, 27*(1), 17–30.

Cosgrove, K.P., Wang, S., Kim, S.J., McGovern, E., Nabulsi, N., Gao, H. and Morris, E.D. (2014). Sex Differences in the Brain's Dopamine Signature of Cigarette Smoking. *The Journal of Neuroscience, 34*(50), 16851–5.

Cosmides, L. (1989). The logic of social exchange: Has natural selection shaped how humans reason? Studies with the Wason selection task. *Cognition, 31,* 187–276.

Costa-Font, J. and Jofre-Bonet, M. (2013). Anorexia, body image and peer effects: evidence from a sample of European women. *Economica, 80*(317), 44–64.

Cox, S.M., Allen, J.M., Hanser, R.H. and Conrad, J.J. (2014). *Juvenile Justice: A guide to theory, policy, and practice*. Thousand Oaks, CA: SAGE.

Coyne, S.M., Manning, J.T., Ringer, L. and Bailey, L. (2007). Directional asymmetry (right–left differences) in digit ratio (2D:4D) predict indirect aggression in women. *Personality and Individual Differences*, *43*(4), 865–72.

Craik, F.I.M. and Tulving, E. (1975). Depth of processing and the retention of words in episodic memory. *Journal of Experimental Psychology*, *104*, 268–94.

Crossley, N.A., Constante, M., McGuire, P. and Power, P. (2010). Efficacy of atypical v. typical antipsychotics in the treatment of early psychosis: Meta-analysis. *The British Journal of Psychiatry*, *196*(6), 434–9.

Crowe, R.R. (1972). The adopted offspring of women criminal offenders. *Archives of General Psychiatry*, *27*, 600–3.

Csikszentmihalyi, M. and LeFevre, J. (1989). Optimal experience in work and leisure. *Journal of Personality and Social Psychology*, *56*, 815–22.

Cullen, J.E. and Seddon, J.W. (1981). Application of a behavioural regime to disturbed young offenders. *Personality and Individual Differences*, *2*(4), 285–92.

Curran, D.J. and Renzetti, C.M. (2001). *Theories of Crime* (2nd edition). Boston, MA: Alleyn & Bacon.

D'Entremont, B., Hains, S.M.J. and Muir, D.W. (1997). A demonstration of gaze following in 3- to 6-month-olds. *Infant Behavior and Development*, *20*, 569–72.

D'Souza, M.S. and Markou, A. (2013). The 'stop' and 'go' of nicotine dependence: Role of GABA and glutamate. *Cold Spring Harbor perspectives in medicine*, *3*(6), a012146.

Dabbs Jr, J.M., Frady, R.L., Carr, T.S. and Besch, N.F. (1987). Saliva testosterone and criminal violence in young adult prison inmates. *Psychosomatic medicine*, *49*(2), 174–182.

Dabbs, J.M. (1990). Salivary testosterone measurements: Reliability across hours, days, and weeks. *Physiology & Behavior*, *48*(1), 83–6.

Daly, M. and Wilson, M. (1988). *Homicide*. Piscataway, NJ: Transaction Publishers.

Daly, M. and Wilson, M. (1998). *The Truth about Cinderella: A Darwinian View of Parental Love*. Yale University Press.

Danner, F.W. and Day, M.C. (1977). Eliciting formal operations. *Child Development*, *48*, 1600–6.

Daoud, N., Hayek, S., Muhammad, A.S., Abu-Saad, K., Osman, A., Thrasher, J.F. and Kalter-Leibovici, O. (2015). Stages of change of the readiness to quit smoking among a random sample of minority Arab-male smokers in Israel. *BMC Public Health*, *15*(1), 672.

Dapretto, M., Davies, M.S., Pfeifer, J.H., Scott, A.A., Sigman, M., Bookheimer, S.Y. and Iacoboni, M. (2006). Understanding emotions in others: Mirror neuron dysfunction in children with autism spectrum disorders. *Nature Neuroscience*, *9*(1), 28–30.

Darwin, C. (1871). *The Descent of Man and Selection in Relation to Sex*. London: Murray.

Dasen, B. (1994). Culture and cognitive development from a Piagetian perspective. In W.J. Lonner and R. Malpass (eds), *Psychology and Culture*. Boston: Allyn & Bacon.

Davies, A., Wittebrod, K. and Jackson, J.L. (1997). Predicting the antecedents of a stranger rapist from his offence behaviour. *Science and Justice*, *37*, 161–170.

Davis, K.L. and Kahn, R.S. (1991). Dopamine in schizophrenia: A review and reconceptualization. *The American Journal of Psychiatry*, *148*(11), 1474.

Dawes, M.A., Antelman, S.M., Vanyukov, M.M., Giancola, P., Tarter, R.E., Susman, E.J. and Clark, D.B. (2000). Developmental sources of variation in liability to adolescent substance use disorders. *Drug and Alcohol Dependence*, *61*(1), 3–14.

De Vries, H., Candel, M., Engels, R. and Mercken, L. (2006). Challenges to the peer influence paradigm: results for 12–13 year olds from six European countries from the European Smoking Prevention Framework Approach study. *Tobacco Control*, *15*(2), 83–9.

Decety, J. (2007). A social cognitive neuroscience model of human empathy. In E. Harmon-Jones and P. Winkielman (eds), *Social Neuroscience: Integrating Biological and Psychological Explanations of Social Behavior*. New York: Guilford Publications.

DeJong, C.A., Van den Brink, W., Harteveld, F.M. and van der Wielen, E.G.M. (1993). Personality disorders in alcoholics and drug addicts. *Comprehensive psychiatry*, *34*(2), 87–94.

Delfabbro, P., Lahn, J. and Grabosky, P. (2006). It's not what you know, but how you use it: Statistical knowledge and adolescent problem gambling. *Journal of Gambling Studies*, *22*(2), 179–93.

Delfabbro, P.H. and Winefield, A.H. (1999). Poker-machine gambling: An analysis of within session characteristics. *British Journal of Psychology*, *90*(3), 425–39.

DeLisi, M., Berg, M.T. and Hochstetler, A. (2004). Gang members, career criminals and prison violence: Further specification of the importation model of inmate behavior. *Criminal Justice Studies*, *17*(4), 369–83.

DeLisi, M., Hochstetler, A. and Murphy, D.S. (2003). Self-control behind bars: A validation study of the Grasmick *et al*. scale. *Justice Quarterly*, *20*(2), 241–63.

Dell, S. (1984). *Murder into Manslaughter: The Diminished Responsibility Defence in Practice*. Oxford: Oxford University Press.

DeLongis, A., Folkman, S. and Lazarus, R.S. (1988). The impact of daily stress on health and mood: Psychological and social resources as mediators. *Journal of Personality and Social Psychology*, *54*, 486–95.

DeMaris, A., Mahoney, A. and Pargament, K.I. (2010). Sanctification of marriage and general religiousness as buffers of the effects of marital inequity. *Journal of Family Issues*, *31*(10), 1255–78.

Dennett, D.C. (2003). *Freedom Evolves*. New York: Penguin.

Derlega, V.J. and Grzelak, J. (1979). Appropriateness of self-disclosure. In G.J. Chelune (ed.), *Self-disclosure: Origins, Patterns, and Implications of Openness in Interpersonal Relationships*. San Francisco, CA: Jossey-Bass.

Dewe, P.J. (1989). Examining the nature of work stress: Individual evaluations of stressful experiences and coping. *Human Relations*, *42*, 993–1013.

Dickerson, F.B., Tenhula, W.N. and Green-Paden, L.D. (2005). The token economy for schizophrenia: review of the literature and recommendations for future research. *Schizophrenia Research*, *75*(2), 405–16.

Dickinson, W.J., Potter, G.G., Hybels, C.F., McQuoid, D.R. and Steffens, D.C. (2011). Change in stress and social support as predictors of cognitive decline in older adults with and without depression. *International Journal of Geriatric Psychiatry*, *26*(12), 1267–74.

Dickson, F.C. (1995). The best is yet to be: Research on long-lasting marriages. *Understudied relationships: Off the beaten track*, 22–50.

Diener, E. (1973). Deindividuating Effects of Group Presence and Arousal on Stealing by Halloween Trick-or-Treaters.

Diener, E. (1980). Deindividuation: The absence of self-awareness and self-regulation in group members. *The Psychology of Group Influence*, *209242*.

Difranza, J.R. (2008). Nicotine withdrawal in subthreshold smokers. *Addiction*, *103*(3), 511–2.

DiFranza, J.R. and Ursprung, W.S.A. (2008). The latency to the onset of nicotine withdrawal: a test of the Sensitization-Homeostasis Theory. *Addictive behaviors*, *33*(9), 1148–53.

Dignan, J. (2005). *Understanding Victims and Restorative Justice*. Maidenhead: Open University Press.

Dijkstra, P. and Barelds, D.P. (2008). Do people know what they want: A similar or complementary partner? *Evolutionary Psychology*, *6*(4), 595–602.

Dobash, R.E. and Dobash, R.P. (1984). The nature and antecedents of violent events. *The British Journal of Criminology*, 269–88.

Dollard, J., Doob, L., Miller, N.M., Mowrer, O.O. and Sears, R. (1939). *Frustration and Aggression*. New Haven, CT: Yale University Press.

Donoghue, J. and Lader, M. (2010). Usage of benzodiazepines: A review. *International Journal of Clinical Practice*, *14*(2), 78–87.

Doob, L.W. and Sears, R.R. (1939). Factors determining substitute behavior and the overt expression of aggression. *The Journal of Abnormal and Social Psychology*, *34*(3), 293.

Douglas, J.E., Burgess, A.W., Burgess, A.G. and Ressler, R.K. (1992). *Crime Classification Manual: A standard system for investigating and classifying violent crime*. New York: Simon & Schuster.

Douglas, J.E., Ressler, R.K., Burgess, A.W. and Hartman, C.R. (2006). Criminal profiling from crime scene analysis. *Behavioural Sciences and the Law*, *4*(4), 401–21.

Dovey, T.M., Staples, P.A., Gibson, E.L. and Halford, J.C. (2008). Food neophobia and 'picky/fussy' eating in children: A review. *Appetite*, *50*(2), 181–93.

Drummond, D.C., Cooper, T. and Glautier, S.P. (1990). Conditioned learning in alcohol dependence: implications for cue exposure treatment. *British Journal of Addiction*, *85*(6), 725–43.

Drury, A.J. and DeLisi, M. (2011). Gangkill: An exploratory empirical assessment of gang membership, homicide offending, and prison misconduct. *Crime & Delinquency*, *57*, 130–46.

Duck, S. (1982). A topography of relationship disengagement and dissolution. In S. Duck (ed.), *Personal Relationships*, *4*. London: Academic Press.

Duck, S. (2005). How do you tell someone you're letting go? *The Psychologist*, *18*(4), 210–13.

Duck, S. W. (1973). *Personal Relationships and Personal Constructs. A study of friendship formation*. New York: John Wiley.

Duke, A.A., Bègue, L., Bell, R. and Eisenlohr-Moul, T. (2013). Revisiting the serotonin–aggression relation in humans: A meta-analysis. *Psychological Bulletin*, *139*(5), 1148–72.

Dunbar, R.I.M., Baron, R., Frangou, A., Pearce, E., van Leeuwen, E.J.C., Stow, J., Partridge, G., MacDonald, I., Barra, V. and van Vught, M. (2011). Social laughter is correlated with an elevated pain threshold. *Proceedings of the Royal Society*, *279*(1373), 1161–7.

Dunlop, P.D., Morrison, D.L., Koenig, J. and Silcox, B. (2012). Comparing the Eysenck and HEXACO models of personality in the prediction of adult delinquency. *European Journal of Personality*, *26*(3), 194–202.

Duntley, J.D. and Buss, D.M. (2004). The evolutionary psychology of good and evil. In A. Miller, A. (ed.), *The Social Psychology of Good and Evil*. New York: Guilford.

Eagly, A. H. (2013). Women as leaders: Leadership style versus leaders' values and attitudes. In Ely, R.J. and Cuddy, A.J.C. (eds), *Gender and Work: Challenging Conventional Wisdom*. Boston, MA: Harvard Business School Press.

Eagly, A.H. (1978). Sex differences in influenceability. *Psychological Bulletin*, 85, 86–116.

Eagly, A.H. and Carli, L.L. (1981). Sex of researchers and sex-typed communications as determinants of sex differences in influenceability: A meta-analysis of social influence studies. *Psychological Bulletin*, 90, 1–20.

Eagly, A.H. and Johnson, B.T. (1990). Gender and leadership style: A meta-analysis. *Psychological Bulletin*, 108, 233–56.

Eagly, A.H. and Wood, W. (1999). The origins of sex differences in human behavior: Evolved dispositions versus social roles. *American Psychologist*, 54, 408–23.

Eastwick, P.W. and Finkel E.J. (2008). Sex differences in mate preferences revisited: Do people know what they initially desire in a romantic partner? *Journal of Personality and Social Psychology*, 94(2), 245–64.

Eastwick, P.W., Eagly, A.H., Finkel, E.J. and Johnson, S.E. (2011). Implicit and explicit preferences for physical attractiveness in a romantic partner: A double dissociation in predictive validity. *Journal of Personality and Social Psychology*, 101, 993–1011.

Echeburúa, E., Báez, C. and Fernández-Montalvo, J. (1996). Comparative effectiveness of three therapeutic modalities in the psychological treatment of pathological gambling: Long-term outcome. *Behavioural and Cognitive Psychotherapy*, 24(01), 51–72.

Edgar, P.M. (1977). *Children and Screen Violence*. Brisbane: University of Queensland Press.

Eibl-Eibesfeldt, I. (1972). Similarities and differences between cultures in expressive movements. In R.A. Hinde (ed.), *Nonverbal Communication*. Cambridge: Cambridge University Press.

Eisenberg, M.E., Neumark-Sztainer, D., Story, M. and Perry, C. (2005). The role of social norms and friends' influences on unhealthy weight-control behaviors among adolescent girls. *Social Science & Medicine*, 60(6), 1165–73.

Eisenberg, N. (2000). Emotion, regulation and moral development. *Annual Review of Psychology*, 51, 665–97.

Eisenegger, C., Haushofer, J. and Fehr, E. (2011). The role of testosterone in social interaction. *Trends in Cognitive Sciences*, 15(6), 263–71.

Eisenegger, C., Naef, M., Snozzi, R., Heinrichs, M. and Fehr, E. (2010). Prejudice and truth about the effect of testosterone on human bargaining behaviour. *Nature*, 463, 356–9.

Eiser, J.R., Morgan, M., Gammage, P., Brooks, N. and Kirby, R. (1991). Adolescent health behaviour and similarity-attraction: Friends share smoking habits (really), but much else besides. *British Journal of Social Psychology*, 30(4), 339–48.

Elks, C.E., den Hoed, M., Zhao, J.H., Sharp, S.J., Wareham, N.J. and Loos, R.J. (2012). Variability in the heritability of body mass index: a systematic review and meta-regression. *Frontiers in Endocrinology (Lausanne)*, 3(29).

Ellason, J.W. and Ross, C.A. (1995). Positive and negative symptoms in dissociative identity disorder and schizophrenia: A comparative analysis. *Journal of Nervous and Mental Disease*, 183(4), 236–41.

Endler, N.S. and Parker, J.D.A. (1994). Assessment of multidimensional coping: Task, emotion, and avoidance strategies. *Psychological Assessment*, 6(1), 50–60.

Epstein, S. (1994). An integration of the cognitive and psychodynamic unconscious. *American Psychologist*, 49, 709–24.

Evans, P., Bristow, M., Hucklebridge, F., Clow, A. and Pang, F.-Y. (1994). Stress, arousal, cortisol and secretory immunoglobulin A in students undergoing assessment. *British Journal of Clinical Psychology*, 33, 575–6.

Evans, P., Clow, A. and Hucklebridge, F. (1997). Stress and the immune system. *The Psychologist*, 10(7), 303–7.

Eyal, K. and Cohen, J. (2006). When good friends say goodbye: A parasocial breakup study. *Journal of Broadcasting & Electronic Media*, 50(3), 502–23.

Eysenck, H. J. (1982). *Personality, Genetics, and Behavior: Selected papers*. New York: Praeger.

Eysenck, H.J. (1947). *Dimensions of Personality*. London: Routledge and Kegan Paul.

Eysenck, H.J. (1967). *The Biological Basis of Personality*. Springield, ILL: C.C. Thomas.

Eysenck, H.J. (1978). Superfactors P, E and N in a comprehensive factor space. *Multivariate Behavioural Research*, 13, 475–82.

Fagerström, K.O., Pomerleau, O., Giordani, B. and Stelson, F. (1994). Nicotine may relieve symptoms of Parkinson's disease. *Psychopharmacology*, 116(1), 117–9.

Fairburn, C.G., Bailey-Straebler, S., Basden, S., Doll, H.A., Jones, R., Murphy, R., O'Connor, M.E. and Cooper, Z. (2015). A transdiagnostic comparison of enhanced cognitive behaviour therapy (CBT-E) and interpersonal psychotherapy in the treatment of eating disorders. *Behaviour Research and Therapy*, 70, 64–71.

Fairburn, C.G., Cooper, Z. and Shafran, R. (2003). Cognitive behaviour therapy for eating disorders: A 'transdiagnostic' theory and treatment. *Behaviour Research and Therapy*, 41, 509–28.

Fairburn, C.G., Cooper, Z., Doll, H.A. and Welch, S.L. (1999). Risk factors for anorexia nervosa: Three integrated case-control comparisons. *Archives of General Psychiatry*, 56(5), 468–76.

Fantz, R.L. (1961). The origin of form perception. *Scientific American, 204*(5), 66–72.

Farrell, G. and Pease, K. (2007). Crime in England Wales: More violence and more chronic victims. *Civitas Review, 4*(2). See www.civitas.org.uk/pdf/CivitasReviewJun07.pdf (accessed September 2015).

Farrington, D.P., Coid, J.W. and Murray, J. (2009). Family factors in intergenerational transmission of offending. *Criminal Behaviour and Mental Health, 19*, 109–24.

FDA (1995). Regulations restricting the sale and distribution of cigarettes and smokeless tobacco products to protect children and adolescents; proposed rule analysis regarding FDA's jurisdiction over nicotine-containing cigarettes and smokeless tobacco products; notice. *Federal Register, 60*, 41314–792.

Feinberg, M.E., Solmeyer, A.R. and McHale, S.M. (2012). The third rail of family systems: Sibling relationships, mental and behavioral health, and preventive intervention in childhood and adolescence. *Clinical Child and Family Psychology Review, 15*(1), 43–57.

Ferguson, C.J. and Kilburn, J. (2009). The public health risks of media violence: A meta-analytic review. *The Journal of Pediatrics, 154*(5), 759–63.

Ferguson, C.J., San Miguel, C. and Hartley, R.D. (2009). A multivariate analysis of youth violence and aggression: the influence of family, peers, depression, and media violence. *The Journal of Pediatrics, 155*(6), 904–8.

Ferguson, C.P., La Via, M.C., Crossan, P.J. and Kaye, W.H. (1999). Are serotonin selective reuptake inhibitors effective in underweight anorexia nervosa? *International Journal of Eating Disorders, 25*(1), 11–7.

Fessler, D.M. (2002, September). Dimorphic foraging behaviors and the evolution of hominid hunting. *Rivista Di Biologia Biology Forum, 95*(3), 429–54.

Festinger, L., Pepitone, A. and Newcomb, T. (1952). Some consequences of deindividuation in a group. *Journal of Abnormal and Social Psychology, 47*, 382–9.

Findlay, L. (2011). *Theories of Offending*. Fraserborough: Banff and Buchan College.

Fischer, D.R. (2001). Arizona Department of Corrections: Security Threat Group (STG) Program Evaluation, Final Report.

FitzGerald, D.P. and White, K.J. (2003). Linking children's social worlds: Perspective-taking in parent–child and peer contexts. *Social Behavior & Personality: An International Journal, 31*(5), 509–22.

Fletcher, A.C., Darling, N. and Steinberg, L. (1995). Parental monitoring and peer influences on adolescent substance use. In J. McCord (ed.), *Coercion and Punishment in Long-term Perspectives*. New York: Cambridge University Press, 259–71.

Flett, G.L., Blankstein, K.R., Hichen, J. and Watson, M.S. (1995). Social support and help-seeking in daily hassles versus major life events stress. *Journal of Applied Social Psychology, 25*, 49–58.

Fox, R. (1978). *The Tory Islanders: A People of the Celtic Fringe*. Notre Dame, IL: University of Notre Dame Press.

Frankenhauser, M. (1983). The sympathetic-adrenal and pituitary-adrenal response to challenge: Comparison between the sexes. In T.M. Dembroski, T.H. Schmidt and G. Blumchen (eds), *Biobehavioural Biases in Coronary Heart Disease*. Basel: Karger.

Franklin, T.W., Franklin, C.A. and Pratt, T.C. (2006). Examining the empirical relationship between prison crowding and inmate misconduct: A meta-analysis of conflicting research results. *Journal of Criminal Justice, 34*(4), 401–12.

Freeman, D. (1984). *Margaret Mead and Samoa: The Making and Unmaking of an Anthropological Myth*. Cambridge, MA: Harvard University Press.

Freeman, D., Dunn, G., Garety, P., Weinman, J., Kuipers, E., Fowler, D., Jolley, S. and Bebbington, P. (2013). Patients' beliefs about the causes, persistence and control of psychotic experiences predict take-up of effective cognitive behaviour therapy for psychosis. *Psychological Medicine, 43*(2), 269–77.

Freud, S. (1905). *Three Essays on the Theory of Sexuality*, trans. James Strachey. New York: Basic Books.

Freud, S. (1909). *Analysis of a Phobia of a Five-Year-Old Boy*. The Pelican Freud Library (1997), Vol. 8, Case Histories, pp. 169–306.

Friedman, M. and Rosenman, R.H. (1959). Association of specific overt behaviour pattern with blood and cardiovascular findings. *Journal of the American Medical Association, 169*, 1286–96.

Friedman, M. and Rosenman, R.H. (1974). *Type A Behaviour and Your Heart*. New York: Knopf.

Friedman, M., Thoresen, C.E., Gill, J.J., Ulmer, D., Powell, L.H., Powell, H., Price, V.A., Brown, B., Thompson, L., Rabin, D.D., Breall, W.S., Bourg, E., Levy, R. and Dixon, T. (1986). Alteration of type A behavior and its effect on cardiac recurrences in post myocardial infarction patients: Summary results of the recurrent coronary prevention project. *American Heart Journal, 112*(4), 653–65.

Funk, S.C. (1992). Hardiness: A review of theory and research. *Health Psychology, 11*, 335–45.

Furlong, C. (2011). A fresh look at the London riots. www.thesaint-online.com/2011/12/a-fresh-look-at-the-london-riots (accessed January 2012).

Furuhashi, T. (2011). Biological male 'Gender Identity Disorder' is composed of essentially distinguishable core and periphery groups. *Ethical Human Psychology and Psychiatry, 13*(1), 64–75.

Gallese, V. and Goldman, A. (1998). Mirror neurons and the simulation theory of mind-reading. *Trends in Cognitive Sciences, 12*, 493–501.

Garcia, J., Kimeldorf, D.J. and Koelling, R.A. (1955). Conditioned aversion to saccharin resulting from exposure to gamma radiation. *Science, 122*(3160), 157–8.

Gardner, R. and Heider, K.G. (1968). *Gardens of War*. New York: Random House.

Garety, P., Fowler, D., Freeman, D., Bebbington, P., Dunn, G. and Kuipers, E. (2008). A randomised controlled trial of cognitive behavioural therapy and family intervention for the prevention of relapse and reduction of symptoms in psychosis. *The British Journal of Psychiatry, 192*, 412–23.

Garner, D.M. and Bemis, K.M. (1982). A cognitive-behavioral approach to anorexia nervosa. *Cognitive Therapy and Research, 6*(2), 123–50.

Gazzola, V., Aziz-Zadeh, L. and Keysers, C. (2006). Empathy and the somatotopic auditory mirror system in humans. *Current Biology, 16*(18), 1824–9.

Gee, C.J. and Leith, L.M. (2007). Aggressive behavior in professional ice hockey: A cross-cultural comparison of North American and European born NHL players. *Psychology of Sport and Exercise, 8*(4), 567–83.

Gelkopf, M., Levitt, S. and Bleich, A. (2002). An integration of three approaches to addiction and methadone maintenance treatment: The self-medication hypothesis, the disease model and social criticism. *The Israel journal of psychiatry and related sciences, 39*(2), 140.

Gentile, D.A. and Anderson, C.A. (2003). Violent video games: The newest media violence hazard. *Media Violence and Children*, 131–52.

Gentile, D.A. and Stone, W. (2005). Violent video game effects on children and adolescents: A review of the literature. *Minerva Pediatrica, 57*(6), 337–58.

George, S. and Murali, V. (2005). Pathological gambling: an overview of assessment and treatment. *Advances in Psychiatric Treatment, 11*(6), 450–6.

Gibson, W.T., Farooqi, I.S., Moreau, M., DePaoli, A.M., Lawrence, E., O'Rahilly, S. and Trussell, R.A. (2004). Congenital leptin deficiency due to homozygosity for the Δ133G mutation: Report of another case and evaluation of response to four years of leptin therapy. *The Journal of Clinical Endocrinology & Metabolism, 89*(10), 4821–26.

Giles, D. and Maltby, J. (2006). Praying at the altar of the stars. *The Psychologist, 19*, 82–5.

Gilligan, C. (1982). In a different voice: Psychological theory and women's development. Cambridge, MA: Harvard University Press.

Gilligan, C. (1982). *In a Different Voice: Psychological Theory and Women's Development*. Cambridge, MA: Harvard University Press.

Gilligan, C. and Attanucci, J. (1988). Two moral orientations: Gender differences and similarities. *Merrill-Palmer Quarterly, 34*, 223–37.

Gillman, M.W., Rifas-Shiman, S.L., Frazier, A.L., Rockett, H.R., Camargo Jr, C.A., Field, A.E., Berkey, C.S. and Colditz, G.A. (2000). Family dinner and diet quality among older children and adolescents. *Archives of Family Medicine, 9*(3), 235–40.

Giraldi, T., Rodani, M., Cartei, G. and Grassi, L. (1997). Psychosocial factors and breast cancer: A 6-year Italian follow-up study. *Psychotherapy and Psychosomatics, 66*, 229–36.

Glassman, N. (1999). All things being equal: The two roads of Piaget and Vygotsky. In P. Lloyd and C. Fernyhough (eds), *Lev Vygotsky: Critical Assessments: Vygotsky's Theory* (vol. I). New York: Routledge.

Glover, J. (2009). Every night you cry. *See* www.barnardos.org.uk/191009_every_night_you_cry.pdf (accessed November 2015).

Glueck, S. and Glueck, E. (1970). *Toward a Typology of Juvenile Delinquency*. London: Routledge & Kegan Paul.

Godden, D. and Baddeley, A. (1975). Context-dependent memory in two natural environments. *British Journal of Psychology, 66*, 325–31.

Godden, D. and Baddeley, A. (1980). When does context influence recognition memory? *British Journal of Experimental Psychology, 71*, 99–104.

Godin, G., Lévy, J.J. and Trottier, G. (2002). *Vulnérabilités et Prévention VIH/SIDA: Enjeux Contemporains*. Presses Université Laval.

Gold, R.M. (1973). Hypothalamic Obesity: The myth of the ventromedial nucleus. Science, 182: 488–90.

Goldberg, S. and Lewis, M. (1969). Play behaviour in the year-old infant: Early sex differences. *Child Development, 40*, 21–31.

Goldhagen, D.J. (1996). *Hitler's Willing Executioners: Ordinary Germans and the Holocaust*. New York: Alfred A. Knopf.

Goldstein, J.M. and Kreisman, D. (1988). Gender, family environment and schizophrenia. *Psychological Medicine, 18*(4), 861–72.

Goodfriend, W. and Agnew, C.R. (2008). Sunken costs and desired plans: Examining different types of investments in close relationships. *Personality and Social Psychology Bulletin, 34*, 1639–52.

Goranson, R.E. (1969). A review of recent literature on psychological effects of media portrayals of violence. *Mass Media and Violence: A Staff Report to the National Commission on the Causes and Prevention of Violence, 9*, 395–413.

Goren, C.C., Sart, M. and Wu, P.Y.K. (1975). Visual following and pattern discrimination of face-like stimuli by newborn infants. *Pediatrics, 56*(4), 544–9.

Goring, C. (1913). *The English Convict: A statistical study*. London: HMSO.

Gottesman, I.I. (1991). *Schizophrenia Genesis: The Origins of Madness*. New York: WH Freeman/Times Books/Henry Holt & Co.

Gottman, J.M. and Levenson, R.W. (1992). Marital processes predictive of later dissolution: behavior, physiology and health. *Journal of Personality and Social Psychology, 63*, 221–33.

Goudriaan, E., Oosterlaan, J., DeBeurs, E. and van den Brink, W. (2006). Psychophysiological determinants and concomitants of deficient decision making in pathological gamblers. *Drug and Alcohol Dependence, 84*, 231–9.

Gould, S.J. (1981). *The Mismeasure of Man*. Harmondsworth, Middlesex: Penguin.

Grant, J.E. and Potenza, M.N. (2006). Escitalopram Treatment of Pathological Gambling with Co-Occurring Anxiety: An Open-Label Pilot Study with Double-Blind Discontinuation. *International Clinical Psychopharmacology, 21*, 203–9.

Gravener, J.A., Haedt, A.A., Heatherton, T.F. and Keel, P.K. (2008). Gender and age differences in associations between peer dieting and drive for thinness. *International Journal of Eating Disorders, 41*, 57–63.

Gredler, M. (1992). *Learning and Instruction: Theory into Practice*. New York: Macmillan Publishing.

Greenhalgh, J., Dowey, A.J., Horne, P.J., Lowe, C.F., Griffiths, J.H. and Whitaker, C.J. (2009). Positive- and negative peer modelling effects on young children's consumption of novel blue foods. *Appetite, 52*, 646–53.

Greenwood, D.N. and Long, C.R. (2009). Mood specific media use and emotion regulation: Patterns and individual differences. *Personality and Individual Differences, 46*(5), 616–21.

Greer, S., Morris, T. and Pettingale, K.W. (1979). Psychological response to breast cancer: Effect on outcome. *Lancet, 2*(8146), 785–7.

Greitemeyer, T. and Mügge, D.O. (2014). Video games do affect social outcomes: A meta-analytic review of the effects of violent and prosocial video game play. *Personality and Social Psychology Bulletin, 40*(5), 578–89.

Gremillion, H. (2003). *Feeding Anorexia: Gender and Power at a Treatment Center*. Durham, NC: Duke University Press.

Griffin, K.W., Botvin, G.J., Scheier, L.M. and Nichols, T.R. (2002). Factors associated with regular marijuana use among high school students: A long-term follow-up study. *Substance Use and Misuse, 37*(2), 225–38.

Griffiths, M.D. (1991). The psychobiology of the near miss in fruit machine gambling. *Journal of Psychology, 125*, 347–57.

Griffiths, M.D. (1993). Fruit machine addiction in adolescence: A case study. *Journal of Gambling Studies, 9*, 387–99.

Griffiths, M.D. (1994). The role of cognitive bias and skill in fruit machine gambling. *British Journal of Psychology, 85*, 351–69.

Griffiths, M.D. (2009). Understanding gaming floor influences on player behaviour. *Casino and Gaming International, 5*(1), 21–6.

Griffitt, W. and Veitch, R. (1971). Hot and crowded: Influences of population density and temperature on interpersonal affective behavior. *Journal of Personality and Social Psychology, 17*, 92–8.

Grill, H.J. and Norgren, R. (1978). The taste reactivity test. I. Mimetic responses to gustatory stimuli in neurologically normal rats. *Brain Research, 143*(2), 263–79.

Grilly, D.M. (2002). *Drugs and Human Behavior*. Needham Heights, MA: Allyn & Bacon.

Gruber, B.L. and Taub, E. (1998). Thermal and EMG biofeedback learning in nonhuman primates. *Applied Psychophysiological Biofeedback, 23*(1), 1–12.

Gudjonsson, G.H. and Sigurdsson, J.F. (2007). Motivation for offending and personality. A study among offenders on probation. *Personality and Individual Differences, 42*, 1243–53.

Gunnar, M.R., Kryzer, E., Van Ryzin, M.J. and Phillips, D.A. (2010). The rise in cortisol in family daycare: Associations with aspects of care quality, child behaviour and child sex. *Child Development, 81*(3), 851–69.

Gurucharri, C. and Selman, R.L. (1982). The development of interpersonal understanding during childhood, preadolescence, and adolescence: A longitudinal follow-up. *Child Development, 53*, 924–7.

Haddock, G., Eisner, E., Davies, G., Coupe, N. and Barrowclough, C. (2013). Psychotic symptoms, self-harm and violence in individuals with schizophrenia and substance misuse problems. *Schizophrenia Research, 151*(1), 215–20.

Hales, J., Nevill, C., Pudney, S. and Tipping, S. (2007). Research report 19: Longitudinal analysis of the Offending, Crime and Justice Survey 2003–6. *See* www.gov.uk/government/uploads/system/uploads/attachment_data/file/116611/horr19-report.pdf (accessed September 2015).

Hall, C.S. and Lindzey, G. (1970). *Theories of Personality*. London: Wiley.

Hall, J. (1979). Token economy strategies in criminal institutions. *British Journal of Criminology, 19*(4), 373–83.

Hall, J.A. and Levin, S. (1980). Affect and verbal non-verbal discrepancy in schizophrenic and non-schizophrenic family communication. *British Journal of Psychiatry, 137*, 78–92.

Hamilton, S. and Fagot, B.I. (1988). Chronic stress and coping styles: A comparison of male and female undergraduates. *Journal of Personality and Social Psychology, 55*(5), 819–23.

Hammen, C. (1992). Cognitive, life stress, and interpersonal approaches to a developmental psychopathology model of depression. *Development and Psychopathology, 4*(1), 189–206.

Hardt, J., Sidor, A., Bracko, M. and Egle, U. (2006). Reliability of retrospective assessments of childhood experiences in Germany. *Journal of Nervous and Mental Disease, 194*(9), 676–83.

Hare-Mustin, R.T. and Marcek, J. (1988). The meaning of difference: Gender theory, post-modernism and psychology. *American Psychologist, 43*, 455–64.

Hare, L., Bernard, P., Sanchez, F., Baird, P., Vilain, E., Kennedy, T. and Harley, V. (2009). Androgen receptor repeat length polymorphism associated with male-to-female transsexualism. *Biological Psychiatry, 65*(1), 93–6.

Harer, M.D. and Steffensmeier, D.J. (1996). Race and prison violence. *Criminology, 34*(3), 323–55.

Harlow, H.F (1959). Love in infant monkeys. *Scientific American, 200*(6), 68–74.

Harmon, K. (2012). Brain injury rate 7 times greater among U.S. prisoners. Scientific American, 4 February. *See* www.scientificamerican.com/article.cfm?id=traumatic-brain-injury-prison (accessed September 2015).

Harrison, G., Hopper, K. and Craig, T. (2001). Recovery from psychotic illness: a 15- and 25-year international follow-up study. *British Journal of Psychiatry, 178*, 506–17.

Harrison, K. and Cantor, J. (1997). The relationship between media consumption and eating disorders. *Journal of Communication, 47*, 40–67.

Haslam, C. and Draper, E. (2000). Stage of change is associated with assessment of the health risks of maternal smoking among pregnant women. *Social Science and Medicine, 51*(8), 1189–96.

Hatfield, E. and Rapson, R.L. (2011). Equity theory in close relationships. *Handbook of Theories of Social Psychology, 2*, 200–17.

Hawkins, N.G., Davies, R. and Holmes, T.H. (1957). Evidence of psychosocial factors in the development of pulmonary tuberculosis. *American Review of Tuberculosis and Pulmonary Diseases, 75*, 768–80.

Hays, N.P. and Roberts, S.B. (2008). Aspects of eating behaviors 'disinhibition' and 'restraint' are related to weight gain and BMI in women. *Obesity, 16*(1), 52–8.

Heath, L., Bresolin, L.B. and Rinaldi, R.C. (1989). Effects of media violence on children. *Archives of General Psychiatry, 46*, 376–9.

Heather, N. (1976). *Radical Perspectives in Psychology*. London: Methuen.

Heikkinen, M.E. and Lönnqvist, J.K. (1995). Recent life events in elderly suicide: A nationwide study in Finland. *International Psychogeriatrics, 7*, 287–300.

Heller, S.B., Pollack, H., Ander, R. and Ludwig, J. (2013). Preventing youth violence and dropout: A randomized field experiment. NBER Working Paper 19104. *See* http://sites.sas.upenn.edu/hellersa/publications/preventing-youth-violence-and-dropout-randomized-field-experiment (accessed September 2015).

Henrich, J., Heine, S.J. and Norensayan, A. (2010). The weirdest people in the world? *Behavioural and Brain Science, 33*(2–3), 61–83.

Herman, C.P. and Mack, D. (1975). Restrained and unrestrained eating. *Journal of Personality, 43*, 647–60.

Herman, C.P. and Polivy, J. (1984). A boundary model for the regulation of eating. In A.J. Stunkard and E. Stellar (eds). *Eating and its Disorders*, pp. 141–56. New York: Raven.

Herrnstein, R.J. and Murray, C.A. (1994). *The Bell Curve: Intelligence and Class Structure in American Life*. New York: Free Press.

Heyes, C. (2009). Where do mirror neurons come from? *Neuroscience and Biobehavioral Review, 34*(4), 575–83.

Heymsfield, S.B., Greenberg, A.S., Fujioka, K., Dixon, R.M., Kushner, R., Hunt, T., Lubina, J.A., Patane, J., Self, B., Hunt, P. and McCamish, M. (1999). Recombinant leptin for weight loss in obese and lean adults: A randomized, controlled, dose-escalation trial. *Jama, 282*(16), 1568–75.

Hickok, G. (2009). Eight problems for the mirror neuron theory of action understanding in monkeys and humans. *Journal of Cognitive Neuroscience, 7*, 1229–43.

Higgins, L. and Gray, W. (1999). What do anti-dieting programs achieve? A review of research. *Australian Journal of Nutrition and Dietetics, 56*(3), 128–36.

Hildebrandt, D.E., Feldman, S.E. and Ditrichs, R.A. (1973). Rules, models, and self-reinforcement in children. *Journal of Personality and Social Psychology, 25*, 1–5.

Hill, A.J., Weaver, C. and Blundell, J.E. (1990). Dieting concerns of 10 year old girls and their mothers. *British Journal of Clinical Psychology, 29*, 346–8.

Hill, J.O. and Peters, J.C. (1998). Environmental contributions to the obesity epidemic. *Science, 280*(5368), 1371–4.

Hill, L., Craig, I.W., Chorney, M.J., Chorney, K. and Plomin, R. (1999). IGF2R and cognitive ability in children. *Molecular Psychiatry, 4*(suppl. 108).

Hilts, P. (1995). *Memory's Ghost: The Strange Tale of Mr. M. and the Nature of Memory*. New York: Simon & Schuster.

Hobbs, T.R. and Holt, M. (1976). The effects of token reinforcement on the behavior of delinquents in cottage settings. *Journal of Applied Behavioural Analysis, 9*(2), 189–98.

Hodges, K.K., Brandt, D.A. and Kline, J. (1981). Competence, guilt and victimization: Sex differences in ambition of causality in television dramas. *Sex Roles, 7*, 537–46.

Hoebel, E.A. (1967). Song duels among the Eskimo. In P. Bohannan (ed.). *Law and Warfare*. New York: The Natural History Press.

Hoffman, L. (1998). The effects of mother's employment on the family and the child. *See* http://parenthood.library.wisc.edu/Hoffman/Hoffman.html (accessed June 2012).

Hoffman, R.M. and Borders, L.D. (2001). Twenty-five years after the Bem Sex-Role Inventory: A reassessment and new issues regarding classification variability. *Measurement and Evaluation in Counseling and Development, 34*, 39–55.

Hollin, C.R., Browne, D. and Palmer, E.J. (2002). *Delinquency and Young Offenders*. Oxford: Blackwell Publishing.

Holmes, T.H. and Rahe, R.H. (1967). The Social Readjustment Rating Scale. *Journal of Psychosomatic Research, 11*, 213–18.

Holt, R.R. (1967). Individuality and generalisation in the psychology of personality. In R.S. Lazarus and E.M. Opton (eds) *Personality*. Harmondsworth: Penguin.

Home Office (2005). *See* http://webarchive.nationalarchives.gov.uk/20110220105210/rds.homeoffice.gov.uk/rds/pdfs05/hosb2505.pdf (accessed September 2015).

Horsley, R.R., Osborne, M., Norman, C. and Wells, T. (2012). High-frequency gamblers show increased resistance to extinction following partial reinforcement. *Behavioural Brain Research, 229*(2), 438–42.

House, J.S. (1981). *Work Stress and Social Support*. Boston, MA: Addison-Wesley.

Howells, K. and Day, A. (2003). Readiness for anger management: Clinical and; theoretical Issues. *Clinical Psychology Review, 23*, 319–37.

Howells, K., Day, A., Williamson, P., Bubner, S., Jauncey, S., Parker, A. and Heseltine, K. (2005). Brief anger management programs with offenders: Outcomes and predictors of change. *The Journal of Forensic Psychiatry & Psychology, 16*(2), 296–311.

Howes, O.D. and Murray, R.M. (2014). Schizophrenia: An integrated sociodevelopmental-cognitive model. *The Lancet, 383*(9929), 1677–87.

Hoyle, R.H. (1993). Interpersonal attraction in the absence of explicit attitudinal information. *Social Cognition, 11*, 309–20.

Huesmann, L.R., Moise-Titus, J., Podolski, C.L. and Eron, L.D. (2003). Longitudinal relations between children's exposure to TV violence and their aggressive and violent behavior in young adulthood: 1977–1992. *Developmental Psychology, 39*(2), 201–21.

Hughes, J.R., Keely, J. and Naud, S. (2004). Shape of the relapse curve and long-term abstinence among untreated smokers. *Addiction, 99*(1), 29–38.

Hughes, M. (1975). *Egocentrism in Preschool Children*. Unpublished PhD thesis, University of Edinburgh.

Hulshoff Pol, H.E., Cohen-Kettenis, P.T., Van Haren, E.N., Peper, J.S., Brans, R.G., Cahn, W., Schnack, H.G., Gooren, L.J. and Kahn, R.S. (2006). Changing your sex changes your brain: Influences of testosterone and estrogen on adult human brain structure. *European Journal of Endocrinology, 155*(suppl. 1), S107–S114.

Huseman, R.C., Hatfield, J.D. and Miles, E.W. (1987). A new perspective on equity theory: The equity sensitivity construct. *Academy of Management Review, 12*(2), 222–34.

Huston, A.C. (1985). The development of sex typing: Themes from recent research. *Developmental Review, 5*, 1–17.

Hutchings, B. and Mednick, S.A. (1975). Registered criminality in the adoptive and biological parents of registered male criminal adoptees. In *Proceedings of the Annual Meeting of the American Psychopathological Association* (No. 63, 105).

Iacoboni, M., Molnar-Szakacs, I., Gallese, V., Buccino, G., Mazziotta, J.C. and Rizzolatti, G. (2005). Grasping the intentions of others with one's own mirror neuron system. *PLoS Biology 3*, e79, 1–7.

Imperato-McGinley, J., Guerro, L., Gautier, T. and Peterson, R.E. (1974). Steroid 5-reductase deficiency in man: An inherited form of male pseudohermaphroditism. *Science, 186*, 1213–16.

Inhelder, B., Sinclair, H. and Bovet, M. (1974). *Learning and the Development of Cognition*. London: Routledge.

Ireland, J. (2004). Anger management therapy with young male offenders: An evaluation of treatment outcome. *Aggressive Behaviour, 30*(2), 174–85.

Irwin, J. and Cressey, D.R. (1962). Thieves, convicts and the inmate culture. *Social Problems*, 142–55.

Isbell, H., Fraser, H.F., Wikler, A., Belleville, R.E. and Eiserman, A.J. (*1955*). An experimental study of the etiology of 'rum fits' and delirium tremens. *Quarterly Journal of Studies on Alcohol, 16*, 1–33.

Itula-Abumere, F. (2013). With reference to empirical work, discuss why some people get stressed more than others? *Psychology and Social Behavior Research, 1*(2), 18–24.

Jackson, J.L. and Bekerian, D.A. (1997). Does offender profiling have a role to play? In J. L. Jackson and D. B. Bekerian (eds) *Offender profiling: Theory, research, and practice*. Chichester: Wiley.

James, L.E. (2004). Meeting Mr Farmer versus meeting a farmer: Specific effects of ageing on learning proper names. *Psychology and Aging, 19*(3), 515–22.

James, W. (1890). *Principles of Psychology*. New York: Holt.

Jansen, A. and Tenney, N. (2001). Seeing mum drinking a 'light' product: is social learning a stronger determinant of taste preference acquisition than caloric conditioning? *European Journal of Clinical Nutrition, 55*(6), 418–22.

Jaremko, M.E. (1980). The use of stress inoculation training in the reduction of public speaking anxiety. *Journal of Clinical Psychology, 36*(3), 735–38.

Jarvis, M.J. (2004). Why people smoke. *British Medical Journal, 328*(7434), 277–9.

Jauhar, S., McKenna, P.J., Radua, J., Fung, E., Salvador, R. and Laws, K.R. (2014). Cognitive-behavioural therapy for the symptoms of schizophrenia: Systematic review and meta-analysis with examination of potential bias. *The British Journal of Psychiatry, 204*(1), 20–9.

Jay, S.M. and Elliott, C.H. (1990). A stress inoculation program for parents whose children are undergoing painful medical procedures. *Journal of Consulting and Clinical Psychology, 58*, 799–804.

Johansson, G., Aronsson, G. and Lindström, B.O. (1978). Social psychological and neuro-endocrine stress reactions in highly mechanised work. *Ergonomics, 21*, 583–99.

Jones, A.M. and Buckingham, J.T. (2005). Self–esteem as a moderator of the effect of social comparison on women's body image. *Journal of Social and Clinical Psychology, 24*(8), 1164–87.

Jones, D. and Elcock, J. (2001). *History and Theories of Psychology: A critical perspective*. London: Hodder.

Jones, D. and Hollin, C. R. (2004). Managing Problematic Anger: The Development of a Treatment Program for Personality Disordered Patients in High Security. *The International Journal of Forensic Mental Health, 3*(2), 197–210.

Jones, D.C. and Crawford, J.K. (2006). The peer appearance culture during adolescence: Gender and body mass variations. *Journal of Youth and Adolescence, 35*(2), 257–69.

Jones, F. and Bright, J. (2001). *Stress, Myth, Theory and Research*. London: Prentice Hall.

Joronen, K. and Åstedt-Kurki, P. (2005). Familial contribution to adolescent subjective well-being. *International Journal of Nursing Practice, 11*(3), 125–33.

Joseph, J. (2004). Schizophrenia and heredity: Why the emperor has no genes. In J. Read, L. Mosher and R. Bentall (eds), *Models of Madness: Psychological, Social and Biological Approaches to Schizophrenia*. London: Taylor & Francis.

Joseph, J. (2004). *The Gene Illusion: Genetic Research in Psychiatry and Psychology under the Microscope*. New York: Algora Publishing.

Josselson, R. (1988). *Finding Herself: Pathways to Identity Development in Women*. New York: Jossey Bass.

Jourard, S.M. (1971). *Self-disclosure: An Experimental Analysis of the Transparent Self*. Princeton, NJ: VanNostrand.

Jung, C. (1913). *The Theory of Psychoanalysis*, vol. 4, trans. R.F.C. Hull. London and Henley: Routledge and Kegan Paul, 1961.

Jüni, P., Altman, D.G. and Egger, M. (2001). Assessing the quality of controlled clinical trials. *British Medical Journal, 323*(7303), 42–6.

Kahn, R.J., McNair, D.M., Lipman, R.S., Covi, L., Rickels, K., Downing, R., Fisher, S. and Frankenthaler, L.M. (1986). Imipramine and chlordiazepoxide in depressive and anxiety disorders. II. Efficacy in anxious outpatients. *Archives of General Psychiatry, 43*, 79.

Kamarck, T.W., Manuck, S.B. and Jennings, J.R. (1990). Social support reduces cardiovascular reactivity to psychological challenge: A laboratory model. *Psychosomatic Medicine, 52*, 42–58.

Kandel, D.B. and Wu, P. (1995). The contributions of mothers and fathers to the intergenerational transmission of cigarette smoking in adolescence. *Journal of Research on Adolescence, 5*(2), 225–52.

Kandel, E.R. (1979). *Behavioural Biology of Aplysia*. San Francisco: W.H. Freeman and Co.

Kanner, A.D., Coyne, J.C., Schaefer, C. and Lazarus, R.S. (1981). Comparison of two modes of stress measurement: Daily hassles and uplifts versus major life events. *Journal of Behavioral Medicine, 4*, 187–212.

Kapur, S., Zipursky, R., Jones, C., Remington, G. and Houle, S. (2000). Relationship between dopamine D2 occupancy, clinical response, and side effects: A double-blind PET study of first-episode schizophrenia. *The American Journal of Psychiatry, 157*(4), 514–52.

Karcher, M.J. and Finn, L. (2005). How connectedness contributes to experimental smoking among rural youth: Developmental and ecological analyses. *Journal of Primary Prevention, 26*(1), 25–36.

Kasser, T. and Sharma, Y.S. (1999). Reproductive freedom, educational equality, and females' preference for resource-acquisition characteristics in mates. *Psychological Science, 10*(4), 374–7.

Kaye, W. (2008). Neurobiology of anorexia and bulimia nervosa. *Physiology & Behavior, 94*(1), 121–35.

Kaye, W.H., Frank, G., Bailer, U.F. and Henry, S. (2005). Neurobiology of anorexia nervosa: clinical implications of alterations of the function of serotonin and other neuronal systems. *International Journal of Eating Disorders, 37*, S15–S19.

Kaye, W.H., Nagata, T., Weltzin, T.E., Hsu, L.G., Sokol, M.S., McConaha, C., Plotnicov, K.H., Weise, J. and Deep, D. (2001). Double-blind placebo-controlled administration of fluoxetine in restricting-and restricting-purging-type anorexia nervosa. *Biological Psychiatry, 49*(7), 644–52.

Kazdin, A.E. (1977). *The Token Economy*. New York, The Plenum Press.

Keating, D. and Clark, L.V. (1980). Development of physical and social reasoning in adolescence. *Developmental Psychology, 16*, 23–30.

Keenan, A. and Newton, T.J. (1989). Stressful events, stressors and psychological strains in young professional engineers. *Human Relations, 42*(11), 993–1013.

Kennedy, H.G. and Grubin, D.H. (1992). Patterns of of denial in sex offenders. *Psychological Medicine, 22*(01), 191–6.

Kenny P.J., Gasparini, F. and Markou, A. (2003). Group II metabotropic and alpha-amino-3-hydroxy-5-methyl-4-isoxazole propionate (AMPA)/kainate glutamate receptors regulate the deficit in brain reward function associated with nicotine withdrawal in rats. *Journal of Pharmacology and Experimental Therapeutics 306*(3), 1068–76.

Kerckhoff, A.C. and Davis, K.E. (1962). Value consensus and need complementarity in mate selection. *American Sociological Review*, 295–303.

Kern, P.A., Martin, R.A., Carty, J., Goldberg, I.J. and Ong, J.M. (1990). Identification of lipoprotein lipase immunoreactive protein in pre-and postheparin plasma from normal subjects and patients with type I hyperlipoproteinemia. *Journal of Lipid Research, 31*(1), 17–26.

Kessler, R.C., Sonnega, A., Bromet, E., Hughes, M. and Nelson, C.B. (1995). Posttraumatic stress disorder in the National Comorbidity Survey. *Archives of General Psychiatry, 52*, 1048–60.

Khaled, S.M., Bulloch, A., Exner, D.V. and Patten, S.B. (2009). Cigarette smoking, stages of change, and major depression in the Canadian population. *Canadian Journal of Psychiatry. Revue Canadienne de Psychiatrie, 54*(3), 204–8.

Kiecolt-Glaser, J.K. and Newton, T.L. (2001). Marriage and health: His and hers. *Psychological Bulletin, 127*(4), 472–503.

Kiecolt-Glaser, J.K., Garner, W., Speicher, C.E., Penn, G.M., Holliday, J. and Glaser, R. (1984). Psychosocial modifiers of immunocompetence in medical students. *Psychosomatic Medicine, 46*, 7–14.

Kiecolt-Glaser, J.K., Loving, T.J., Stowell, J.R., Malarkey, W.B., Lemeshow, S., Dickinson, S.L. and Glaser, R. (2005). Hostile marital interactions, proinflammatory cytokine production, and wound healing. *Archives of General Psychiatry, 62*, 1377–84.

Kim, J.Y., McHale, S.M., Crouter, A.C. and Osgood, D.W. (2007). Longitudinal linkages between sibling relationships and adjustment from middle childhood through adolescence. *Developmental Psychology, 43*, 960–73.

Kim, L.S., Sandler, I.N. and Tein, J.Y. (1997). Locus of control as a stress moderator and mediator in children of divorce. *Journal of Abnormal Child Psychology, 25*(2), 145–55.

Kim, S.M., Han, D.H., Lee, Y.S. and Renshaw, P.F. (2012). Combined cognitive behavioural therapy and bupropion for the treatment of problematic online game play. *Computers in Human Behaviour, 28*, 954–9.

Kim, S.W., Grant, J.E. and Adson, D.E. (2002). A double blind, placebo-controlled study of the efficacy and safety of paroxetine in the treatment of pathological gambling. *Journal of Clinical Psychiatry, 63*, 501–7.

Kimmett, E., O'Donnell, I. and Martin, C. (2002). *Prison Violence: The Dynamics of Conflict, Fear and Power*. Cullompton: Willan Publishing.

Kinard, B. and Webster, C. (2010). The effects of advertising, social influences, and self-efficacy on adolescence tobacco use and alcohol consumption. *The Journal of Consumer Affairs, 44*(1), 24–43.

Kivimäki, M., Leino-Arjas, P., Luukkonen, R., Riihimäki, H., Vahtera, J. and Kirjonen, J. (2002). Work stress and risk of cardiovascular mortality: Prospective cohort study of industrial employees. *BMJ, 325*(7369), 857.

Klag, S.M. (2006). Self-determination theory and the theory of planned behaviour applied to substance abuse treatment in a therapeutic community setting. Doctoral dissertation, Griffith University.

Klein, N.C., Alexander, J.F. and Parsons, B.V. (1977). Impact of family systems intervention on recidivism and sibling delinquency: A model of primary prevention and program evaluation. *Journal of Consulting and Clinical Psychology, 45*, 469–74.

Klintworth, G.K. (2014). *Giants, Crooks and Jerks in Science*. Bloomington, IN: Xlibris Corporation.

Klump, K.L., Suisman, J.L., Burt, S.A., McGue, M. and Iacono, W.G. (2009). Genetic and environmental influences on disordered eating: An adoption study. *Journal of Abnormal Psychology*, 118(4), 797–805.

Kluver, H. and Bucy, P.C. (1937). Psychic blindness and other symptoms following bilateral temporal lobectomy in rhesus monkeys. *American Journal of Physiology, 119*, 352–3.

Knaapila, A., Tuorila, H., Silventoinen, K., Keskitalo, K., Kallela, M., Wessman, M. and Perola, M. (2007). Food neophobia shows heritable variation in humans. *Physiology & Behavior*, 91(5), 573–78.

Knop, K., Öncü, J.S., Penzel, J., Abele, T.S., Brunner, T., Vorderer, P. and Wessler, H. (2016). Offline time is quality time. Comparing within-group self-disclosure in mobile messaging applications and face-to-face interactions. *Computers in Human Behavior*, 55, 1076–84.

Kobasa, S.C. (1979). Stressful life events, personality, and health: An inquiry into hardiness. *Journal of Personality and Social Psychology*, 37, 1–11.

Kobasa, S.C. and Maddi, S.R. (1977). Existential personality theory. In R. Corsini (ed.), *Current Personality Theories*. Itasca, IL.: Peacock.

Kobasa, S.C., Maddi, S.R., Puccetti, M.C. and Zola, M.A. (1985). Effectiveness of hardiness, exercise and social support as resources against illness. *Journal of Psychosomatic Research*, 29(5), 525–33.

Kog, E. and Vandereycken, W. (1989). Family interaction in eating disordered patients and normal controls. *International Journal of Eating Disorders, 8*, 11–23.

Kohlberg, L. (1966). A cognitive-developmental analysis of children's sex-role concepts and attitudes. In E.E. Maccoby (ed.), *The Development of Sex Differences*. Stanford, CA: Stanford University Press.

Kohlberg, L. (1969). Stage and sequence: the cognitive-developmental approach to socialisation. In D.A. Goslin (ed.), *Handbook of Socialisation Theory and Practice*. Skokie, IL: Rand McNally.

Kotovsky, L. and Baillargeon, R. (1995). Should a stationary object be displaced when hit by a moving object? Reasoning about collision events in 2.5-month-old infants. Manuscript submitted for publication. Cited in C. Rovee-Collie and L.P. Lipsitt (eds), *Advances in Infancy Research*, Vol. 9. Norwood, NJ: Ablex Publishing.

Kraft, T. and Kraft, D. (2005). Covert sensitization revisited: Six case studies. *Contemporary Hypnosis*, 22(4), 202–9.

Krebs, D.L. and Denton, K. (2005). Toward a more pragmatic approach to morality: A critical evaluation of Kohlberg's model. *Psychological Review, 112*, 629–49.

Krebs, J.R. (2009). The gourmet ape: evolution and human food preferences. *The American Journal of Clinical Nutrition*, 90(3), 707–11.

Kretschmer, E. (1921). *Korperbau und Charakter*, English translation published 1931: *Physique and Character*. London: Routledge.

Krueger, R.F., Caspi, A., Moffitt, T.E. and Silva, P.A. (1998). The structure and stability of common mental disorders (DSM-III-R): a longitudinal-epidemiological study. *Journal of Abnormal Psychology*, 107(2), 216–27.

Kruijver, F.P.M., Zhou, J.N., Pool, C.W., Hofman, M.A., Gooren, L.J. and Swaab, D.F. (2000). Male-to-female transsexuals have female neuron numbers in a limbic nucleus. *Journal of Clinical Endocrinology & Metabolism*, 85(5), 2034–41.

Kuhn, T.S. (1962). *The Structure of Scientific Revolutions*. Chicago, IL: University of Chicago Press.

Kuipers, L., Sturgeon, D., Berkowitz, R. and Leff, J. (1983). Characteristics of expressed emotion: Its relationship to speech and looking in schizophrenic patients and their relatives. *British Journal of Clinical Psychology*, 22(4), 257–64.

Kunzig, R. (2004). Autism: what's sex got to do with it? *Psychology Today*, Jan/Feb (full text at www.psychologytoday.com/articles/200401/autism-whats-sex-got-do-it, accessed September 2015).

Kurdek, L. A. (1993). Predicting marital dissolution: A 5-year prospective longitudinal study of newlywed couples. *Journal of Personality and Social Psychology*, 64(2), 221–42.

Kurdek, L.A. and Schmitt, J.P. (1986). Relationship quality of partners in heterosexual married, heterosexual cohabiting, and gay and lesbian relationships. *Journal of Personality and Social Psychology*, 51(4), 711.

La Gaipa, J.J. (1982). Rules and rituals in disengaging from relationships. *Personal relationships*, 4, 189–210.

Labouvie, E.W. and McGee, C.R. (1986). Relation of personality to alcohol and drug use in adolescence. *Journal of Consulting and Clinical Psychology. 54*, 289–93.

Lacan, J. (1966). *The Four Fundamental Concepts of Psychoanalysis*. London: Hogarth.

Ladouceur, R., Sylvain, C., Boutin, C. and Doucet, C. (2002). *Understanding and treating the pathological gambler*. Ontario: John Wiley & Sons.

Ladouceur, R., Sylvain, C., Boutin, C., Lachance, S., Doucet, C., Leblond, J. and Jacques, C. (2001). Cognitive treatment of pathological gambling. *Journal of Nervous and Mental Disease, 189*, 774–80.

Lamb, M.E. and Roopnarine, J.L. (1979). Peer influences on sex-role development in preschoolers. *Child Development*, 50, 1219–22.

Landenberger, N.A. and Lipsey, M.W. (2005). The positive effects of cognitive-behavioural programs for offenders: A meta-analysis of factors associated with effective treatment. *Journal of Experimental Criminology*, 1, 451–476.

Lang, K., Lloyd, S., Khondoker, M., Simic, M., Treasure, J. and Tchanturia, K. (2015). Do Children and Adolescents with Anorexia Nervosa Display an Inefficient Cognitive Processing Style? *PloS one*, 10(7), e0131724.

Lang, S. (1998). *Men as Women, Women as Men: Changing Gender in Native American Cultures*. Austin, TX: University of Texas Press.

Langlois, J.H. and Downs, A.C. (1980). Mothers, fathers, peers as socialization agents of sex-stereotyped play behaviours in young children. *Child Development*, 51, 1217–47.

Lassek, W.D. and Gaulin, S.J. (2009). Costs and benefits of fat-free muscle mass in men: Relationship to mating success, dietary requirements, and native immunity. *Evolution and Human Behavior*, 30(5), 322–8.

Latessa, E.J. and Lowenkamp, C.T. (2006). What works in reducing recidivism? *St. Thomas Law Journal*, 3(3), 521–35.

Latkin, C.A., Hua, W. and Tobin, K. (2004). Social network correlates of self-reported non-fatal overdose. *Drug and Alcohol Dependence*, 73(1), 61–7.

Latzer, Y. and Gaber, L.B. (1998). Pathological conflict avoidance in anorexia nervosa: Family perspectives. *Contemporary Family Therapy*, 20(4), 539–51.

Law, K. (1997). Further evaluation of anger-management courses at HMP Wakefield: an examination of behavioural change. *Inside Psychology: The Journal of Prison Service Psychology*, 3, 91–95.

Lawrence, A.A. (2003). Factors associated with satisfaction or regret following male-to-female sex reassignment surgery. *Archives of Sexual Behavior, 32*, 299–315.

Lazarus, R.S. (1990). Theory-based stress measurement and reply to commentators. *Psychological Inquiry*, 1, 3–51.

Lazarus, R.S. (1992). Can we demonstrate important psychosocial influences on health? With commentaries. *Advances, 8*, 5–45.

Lazarus, R.S. (1995). Vexing research problems inherent in cognitive-mediational theories of emotion, and some solutions. *Psychological Inquiry*, 6, 183–265.

Lazarus, R.S. (1999). *Stress and Emotion: A New Synthesis*. London: Free Association Books.

Lazarus, R.S. and Folkman, S. (1984). *Stress, Appraisal, and Coping*. New York: Springer.

Lazarus, R.S., Cohen, J.B., Folkman, S., Kanner, A. and Schaefer, C. (1980). Psychological stress and adaptation: Some unresolved issues. In H. Selye (ed.), *Selye's Guide to Stress Research, Vol. 1*. New York: Van Nostrand Reinhold.

Le Bon, G. (1960). *The Crowd*. New York: Viking.

Le Bon, G. (1995). *The crowd: A study of the popular mind*. London: Transaction Publishers. (Original work published in 1895.)

le Grange, D. and Eisler, I. (2009). Family interventions in adolescent anorexia nervosa. *Child and Adolescent Psychiatric Clinics of North America, 18*(1), 159–73.

Le, B. and Agnew, C.R. (2003). Commitment and its theorized determinants: A meta–analysis of the Investment Model. *Personal Relationships*, 10(1), 37–57.

Le, B., Dove, N.L., Agnew, C.R., Korn, M.S. and Mutso, A.A. (2010). Predicting nonmarital romantic relationship dissolution: A meta-analytic synthesis. *Personal Relationships, 17*(3), 377–90.

Lea, S.E.G. (1984). *Instinct, Environment and Behaviour*. London: Methuen.

Lebell, M.B., Marder, S.R., Mintz, J., Mintz, L.I., Tompson, M., Wirshing, W., Johnston-Cronk, K. and McKenzie, J. (1993). Patients' perceptions of family emotional climate and outcome in schizophrenia. *The British Journal of Psychiatry, 162*(6), 751–4.

Leets, L., De Becker, G. and Giles, H. (1995). Fans exploring expressed motivations for contacting celebrities. *Journal of Language and Social Psychology, 14*(1–2), 102–23.

Lehrman, D.S. (1953). A critique of Konrad Lorenz's theory of instinctive behavior. *Quarterly Review of Biology*, 337–63.

Lemaire, J.B., Wallace, J.E., Lewin, A.M., de Grood, J. and Schaefer, J.P. (2011). The effect of a biofeedback-based stress management tool on physician stress: a randomized controlled clinical trial. *Open Medicine*, 5(4), e154–e165.

Leucht, S., Cipriani, A., Spineli, L., Mavridis, D., Örey, D., Richter, F. *et al.* (2013). Comparative efficacy and tolerability of 15 antipsychotic drugs in schizophrenia: A multiple-treatments meta-analysis. *The Lancet*, 382(9896), 951–62.

Leucht, S., Tardy, M., Komossa, K., Heres, S., Kissling, W., Salanti, G. and Davis, J.M. (2012). Antipsychotic drugs versus placebo for relapse prevention in schizophrenia: A systematic review and meta-analysis. *The Lancet*, 379(9831), 2063–71.

Levin, H.L. (1921). On the prognostic significance of the mental content in manic-depressive psychosis. *The State Hospital Quarterly, VII*: 594–95.

Levinger, G., Senn, D.J. and Jorgensen, B.W. (1970). Progress toward permanence in courtship: A test of the Kerckhoff–Davis hypotheses. *Sociometry*, *33*, 427–43.

Lewis, G.F., Hourani, L., Tueller, S., Kizakevich, P., Bryant, S., Weimer, B. and Strange, L. (2015). Relaxation training assisted by heart rate variability biofeedback: Implication for a military predeployment stress inoculation protocol. *Psychophysiology*, 11 June. doi:10.1111/psyp.12455. (Epub ahead of print.)

Lhermitte, F., Pillon, B. and Serdaru, M. (1986). Human autonomy and the frontal lobes. Part I: imitation and utilization behavior: a neuropsychological study of 75 patients. *Annals of Neurology*, *19*(4), 326–34.

Li, X., Lu, Q. and Miller, R. (2008). Self-medication versus pure pleasure seeking compulsive consumption. In A.Y. Lee and D. Soman (eds), *Advances in Consumer Research*, *35*, 845–6.

Liberman, D. and Gaa, J.P. (1986). The effect of response style on the validity of the BSRI. *Journal of Clinical Psychology*, *42*(6), 905–8.

Libet, B., Gleason, C.A., Wright, E.W. and Pearl, D.K. (1983). Time of conscious intention to act in relation to onset of cerebral activity (readiness-potential). The unconscious initiation of a freely voluntary act. *Brain*, *106*, 623–42.

Liem, J.H. (1974). Effects of verbal communications of parents and children: A comparison of normal and schizophrenic families. *Journal of Consulting and Clinical Psychology*, *42*(3), 438.

Lifton, D., Seay, S., McCarly, N., Olive-Taylor, R., Seeger, R. and Bigbee, D. (2006). Correlating hardiness with graduation persistence. *Academic Exchange Quarterly*, *10*(3), 277–83.

Lindblom, J. and Ziemke, T. (2003). Social situatedness of natural and artificial intelligence: Vygotsky and beyond. *Adaptive Behaviour*, *11*(2), 79–96.

Linszen, D.H., Dingemans, P.M., Nugter, M.A., Van der Does, A., Scholte, W.F. and Lenior, M.A. (1997). Patient attributes and expressed emotion as risk factors for psychotic relapse. *Schizophrenia Bulletin*, *23*(1), 119.

Linz, D., Donnerstein, E. and Penrod, S. (1984). The effects of multiple exposures to filmed violence against women. *Journal of Communication*, *34*(3), 130–47.

Lipsman, N., Woodside, D.B. and Lozano, A.M. (2015). Neurocircuitry of limbic dysfunction in anorexia nervosa. *Cortex*, *62*, 109–18.

Lipsman, N., Woodside, D.B., Giacobbe, P., Hamani, C., Carter, J.C., Norwood, S.J. and Smith, G.S. (2013). Subcallosal cingulate deep brain stimulation for treatment-refractory anorexia nervosa: a phase 1 pilot trial. *The Lancet*, *381*(9875), 1361–70.

Litt, D.M. and Stock, M.L. (2011). Adolescent alcohol-related risk cognitions: The roles of social norms and social networking sites. *Psychology of Addictive Behaviors*, *25*(4), 708–13.

Littlejohn, S.W. (1989). *Theories of Human Communication* (3rd edition). Belmont, CA: Wadsworth Publishing Company.

Liu, D., Wellman, H.M., Tardif, T. and Sabbagh, M.A. (2004). *Development of Chinese and North American Children's Theory of Mind*. Paper presented at the 28th International Congress of Psychology, Beijing, China.

Livingstone Smith, D. (2007). *The Most Dangerous Animal: Human Nature and the Origins of War*. New York: St Martin's Press.

Livingstone, S. (1996). On the continuing problems of media effects research. *Mass Media and Society*, *2*, 305–24.

Lobban, F., Glentworth, D., Chapman, L., Wainwright, L., Postlethwaite, A., Dunn, G., Pinfold, V., Larkin, W. and Haddock, G. (2013). Feasibility of a supported self-management intervention for relatives of people with recent-onset psychosis: REACT study. *The British Journal of Psychiatry*, *203*(5), 366–72.

Lockwood, A.H. (1989). Medical problems of musicians. *New England Journal of Medicine*, *320*, 221–7.

Loftus, E.F. and Palmer, J.C. (1974). Reconstruction of automobile destruction: An example of the interaction between language and memory. *Journal of Verbal Learning and Verbal Behavior*, *13*, 585–9.

Loftus, E.F. and Palmer, J.C. (1974). Reconstruction of automobile destruction: An example of the interaction between language and memory. *Journal of Verbal Learning and Verbal Behavior*, *13*, 585–589.

Lombroso, C. (1897). L'Uomo Delinquente studiato in rapporto alla antropologia, alla medecina legale, ed alle discipline carcerarie (5th edition). Milan: Hoepli.

Lombroso, C. and Ferrero, G. (1893). *La donna delinquente, la prostituta e la donna normale*. Turin: Roux.

Lopez, A.D., Collishaw, N.E. and Piha, T. (1994). A descriptive model of the cigarette epidemic in developed countries. *Tobacco Control*, *3*(3), 242–7.

Lorenz, K. (1950). The comparative method in studying innate behavior patterns. *Symposia of the Society for Experimental Biology*, *4*, 221–68.

Lorenz, K. (1952). *King Solomon's Ring: New Light on Animal Ways*. New York: Crowell.

Loring, M. and Powell, B. (1988). Gender, race, and DSM-III: A study of the objectivity of psychiatric diagnostic behavior. *Journal of Health and Social Behavior*, *29*, 1–22.

Loro, A.D. and Orleans, C.S. (1981). Binge eating in obesity: Preliminary findings and guidelines for behavioral analysis and treatment. *Addictive Behaviors*, *6*, 155–66.

Loza, W. and Loza-Fanous, A. (1999). Anger and prediction of violent and nonviolent offenders' recidivism. *Journal of Interpersonal Violence*, *14*, 1014–29.

Lucknow, A., Reifman, A. and McIntosh, D.N. (1998). Gender differences in coping: A meta-analysis. Poster presented to the annual meeting of the American Psychological Association, San Francisco, CA.

Luhrmann, T.M., Padmavati, R., Tharoor, H. and Osei, A. (2015). Differences in voice-hearing experiences of people with psychosis in the USA, India and Ghana: interview-based study. *The British Journal of Psychiatry*, *206*(1), 41–4.

Luk, J.W. and Tsoh, J.Y. (2010). Moderation of gender on smoking and depression in Chinese Americans. *Addictive behaviors*, *35*(11), 1040–3.

Lund, I. (2011). Irrational beliefs revisited: Exploring the role of gambling preferences in the development of misconceptions in gamblers. *Addiction Research and Theory*, *19*(1), 40–6.

Maccoby, E.E. (1998). *The Two Sexes: Growing up Apart, Coming Together*. Cambridge, MA: Belknap Press.

MacDonald, T.K., Zanna, M.P. and Fong, G.T. (1996). Why common sense goes out the window: Effects of alcohol on intentions to use condoms. *Personality and Social Psychology Bulletin*, (22), 763–75.

Macintyre, S., Reilly, J., Miller, D. and Eldridge, J. (1998). Food Choice, food scares, and health: the role of the media. In A. Murcott (Ed), *The Nation's Diet: the social science of food choice*. Harlow: Addison Wesley Longman.

Maddi, S.R. (1987). Hardiness training at Illinois Bell Telephone. In J.P. Opatz (ed.), *Health Promotion Evaluation*. Stevens Point, WI: National Wellness Institute.

Maddi, S.R. (1997). Personal views survey II: A measure of dispositional hardiness. In C.P. Zalaquett and R.J. Wood (eds), *Evaluating Stress: A Book of Resources*. Lanham, MD: Scarecrow Press, Inc.

Maddi, S.R. (1999). The personality construct of Hardiness: I. Effects on experiencing, coping, and strain. *Consulting Psychology Journal: Practice and Research*, *51*(2).

Maddi, S.R., Kahn, S. and Maddi, L.K. (1998). The effectiveness of hardiness training. *Consulting Psychology Journal*, *50*, 78–86.

Maes, H.H., Neale, M.C. and Eaves, L.J. (1997). Genetic and environmental factors in relative body weight and human adiposity. *Behavior Genetics*, *27*(4), 325–51.

Maguire, C. (2013). Autism on the rise: A global perspective. *See* www.hcs. harvard.edu/hghr/online/autism-on-the-rise-a-global-perspective (accessed April 2015).

Maguire, E.A., Gadian, D.G., Johnsrude, I.S., Good, C.D., Ashburner, J., Frackowiak, R.S. and Frith, C.D. (2000). Navigation-related structural change in the hippocampi of taxi drivers. *Proceedings of the National Academy of Science*, *97*(8), 4398–403.

Maguire, E.R., Burgoine, T. and Monsivais, P. (2015). Area deprivation and the food environment over time: A repeated cross-sectional study on takeaway outlet density and supermarket presence in Norfolk, UK, 1990–2008. *Health & Place*, *33*, 142–7.

Majer, J.M., Jason, L.A. and Olson, B.D. (2004). Optimism, abstinence self-efficacy and self-mastery: a comparative analysis of cognitive resources. *Assessment*, *11*(1), 57–63.

Mäkinen, J., Miettunen, J., Isohanni, M. and Koponen, H. (2008). Negative symptoms in schizophrenia – a review. *Nordic Journal of Psychiatry*, *62*(5), 334–41.

Malmberg, A., Lewis, G., David, A. and Allebeck, P. (1998). Premorbid adjustment and personality in people with schizophrenia. *The British Journal of Psychiatry*, *172*(4), 308–13.

Maltby, J., Houran, M.A. and McCutcheon, L.E. (2003). A clinical interpretation of attitudes and behaviors associated with celebrity worship. *Journal of Nervous and Mental Disease*, *191*, 25–9.

Mann, J., Arango, V. and Underwood, M. (1990). Serotonin and suicidal behaviour. *Annals of the New York Academy of Science*, *600*, 476–84.

Mann, L. (1981). The baiting crowd in episodes of threatened suicide. *Journal of Personality and Social Psychology*, *41*(4), 703–9.

Manstead, A.R. and McCulloch, C. (1981). Sex-role stereotyping in British television advertisements. *British Journal of Social Psychology, 20*, 171–80.

Manzi, C., Vignoles, V.L., Regalia, C. and Scabini, E. (2006). Cohesion and enmeshment revisited: Differentiation, identity, and well-being in two European cultures. *Journal of Marriage and Family*, *68*(3), 673–89.

Marcus, B., Simkin, L., Rossi, J. and Pinto, B. (1996). Longitudinal shifts in employees' stages and processes of exercise behaviour change. *American Journal of Health Promotion*, *10*, 195–201.

Marmot, M., Bosma, H., Hemingway, H., Brunner, E. and Stansfield, S. (1997). Contribution of job control and other risk factors to social variation in health disease incidence. *The Lancet*, *350*, 235–9.

Martin, C.L. (1991). Children's use of gender-related information in making social judgements. *Developmental Psychology*, 25, 80–8.

Martin, C.L. and Halverson, C.F. (1981). A schematic processing model of sex typing and stereotyping in children. *Child Development*, 52, 1119–34.

Martin, C.L. and Halverson, C.F. (1983). The effects of sex-typing schemas on young children's memory. *Child Development*, 54, 563–74.

Martin, C.L. and Little, J.K. (1990). The relation of gender understanding to children's sex-typed preferences and gender stereotypes. *Child Development*, 61, 1427–39.

Martin, C.L., Eisenbud, L. and Rose, H. (1995). Children's gender-based reasoning about toys. *Child Development*, 66, 1453–71.

Martin, S.D., Martin, E., Santoch, S.R., Richardson, M.A. and Rovall, R. (2001). Brain blood flow changes in depressed patients treated with interpersonal psychotherapy or venlafaxine hydrochloride. *Archives of General Psychiatry, 58*, 641–8.

Martins, Y., Pelchat, M.L. and Pliner, P. (1997). 'Try it; it's good and it's good for you': Effects of taste and nutrition information on willingness to try novel foods. *Appetite*, 28(2), 89–102.

Maruna, S. and Mann, R. (2006). A fundamental attribution error? Rethinking cognitive distortions. *Legal and Criminological Psychology, 11*, 155–77.

Maslach, C., Schaufeli, W.B. and Leiter, M.P. (2001). Job burnout. *Annual Review of Psychology*, 52(1), 397–422.

Matheny, K.B. and Weatherman, K.E. (1998). Predictors of smoking cessation and maintenance. *Journal of Clinical Psychology*, 54(2), 223–35.

Matud, M.P. (2004). Gender differences in stress and coping styles. *Personality and Individual Differences*, 37(7), 1401–15.

Maude-Griffin, P. and Tiffany, S.T. (1996). Production of smoking urges through imagery: The impact of affect and smoking abstinence. *Experimental and Clinical Psychopharmacology*, 4(2), 198–208.

Mazur, A. (1985). A biosocial model of status in face-to-face primate groups. *Social Forces*, 64(2), 377–402.

McConaghy, M.J. (1979). Gender permanence and the genital basis of gender: Stages in the development of constancy of gender identity. *Child Development*, 50, 1223–6.

McCorkle, R.C., Miethe, T.D. and Drass, K.A. (1995). The roots of prison violence: A test of the deprivation, management, and 'not-so-total' institution models. *Crime and Delinquency*, 41(3), 317–31.

McCutcheon, L.E., Lange, R. and Houran, J. (2002). Conceptualization and measurement of celebrity worship. *British Journal of Psychology*, 93, 67–87.

McDermott, R., Tingley, D., Cowden, J., Frazzetto, G. and Johnson, D.D. (2009). Monoamine oxidase A gene (MAOA) predicts behavioral aggression following provocation. *Proceedings of the National Academy of Sciences*, 106(7), 2118–23.

McGarrigle, J. and Donaldson, M. (1974). Conservation accidents. *Cognition*, 3, 341–50.

McGhee, P. and Frueh, T. (1980). Television viewing and the learning of sex-role stereotypes. *Sex Roles*, 6, 179–88.

McGue, M., Slutske, W., Taylor, J. and Iacono, W.G. (1997). Personality and substance use disorders: I. Effects of gender and alcoholism subtype. *Alcoholism: Clinical and Experimental Research*, 21(3), 513–20.

McGuire, J. (2008). A review of effective interventions for reducing aggression and violence. *Philosophical Transaction of the Royal Society B, 363*, 2577–97.

McHugh, R.K., Hearon, B.A. and Otto, M.W. (2010). Cognitive-behavioral therapy for substance use disorders. *Psychiatric Clinics of North America, 33*(3), 511–25.

McMonagle, T. and Sultana, A. (2000). Token economy for schizophrenia. *Cochrane Database of Systematic Reviews*, 3.

McNaughton, S. and Leyland, J. (1990). Maternal regulation of children's problem-solving behaviour and its impact on children's performance. *Child Development*, 61, 113–26.

Mead, M. (1935). *Sex and Temperament in Three Primitive Societies*. New York: Morrow.

Mears, D.P., Stewart, E.A., Siennick, S.E. and Simons, R.L. (2013). The code of the street and inmate violence: Investigating the salience of imported belief systems. *Criminology*, 51(3), 695–728.

Mednick, S., Parnas, J. and Schulsinger, F. (1987). The Copenhagen High-Risk project, 1962–86. *Schizophrenia Bulletin*, 13(3), 485–95.

Meichenbaum, D. (1977). *Cognitive-Behaviour Modification: An Integrative Approach*. New York: Plenum Press.

Meichenbaum, D. (1985). *Stress Inoculation Training*. New York: Pergamon.

Meichenbaum, D. (2007). Stress inoculation training: A preventative and treatment approach. In P.M. Lehrer, R.L. Woolfolk and W.S. Sime (eds), *Principles and Practice of Stress Management* (3rd edition). New York: Guilford Press.

Meltzer, A.L., McNulty, J.K., Jackson, G.L. and Karney, B.R. (2014). Sex differences in the implications of partner physical attractiveness for the trajectory of marital satisfaction. *Journal of Personality and Social Psychology*, 106(3), 418.

Meltzoff, A. and Moore, M. (1983). New born infants imitate adult facial gestures. *Child Development*, 54, 702–9.

Meltzoff, A.N. and Moore, M.K. (1977). Imitation of facial and manual gestures by human neonates. *Science*, 198, 75–8.

Mennella, J.A. (2014). Ontogeny of taste preferences: basic biology and implications for health. *The American Journal of Clinical Nutrition*, 99(3), 704–11.

Meredith, S.E., Juliano, L.M., Hughes, J.R. and Griffiths, R.R. (2013). Caffeine use disorder: A comprehensive review and research agenda. *Journal of Caffeine Research*, 3(3), 114–30.

Milan, M.A. and McKee, J.M. (1976). The cellblock token economy: Token reinforcement procedures in a maximum security correctional institution for adult male felons. *Journal of Applied Behavioural Analysis*, 9(3), 253–75.

Miles, D.R. and Carey, G. (1997). Genetic and environmental architecture on human aggression. *Journal of Personality and Social Psychology*, 72(1), 207–17.

Milev, P., Ho, B.C., Arndt, S. and Andreasen, N.C. (2005). Predictive values of neurocognition and negative symptoms on functional outcome in schizophrenia: a longitudinal first-episode study with 7-year follow-up. *American Journal of Psychiatry*, 162(3), 495–506.

Miller, D., Staats, S. and Partlo, C. (1992). Discriminating positive and negative aspects of pet interaction: Sex differences in the older population. *Social Indicators Research, 27*, 363–74.

Miller, L. (1994). *See* www.radix.net/~reimann/enet/VC94/Msg/msg34.html (accessed March 2003).

Miller, N. and DiCara, L. (1967). Instrumental learning of heart rate changes in curarised rats: Shaping and specificity to discriminative stimulus. *Journal of Comparative and Physiological Psychology*, 63, 12–19.

Millon, T. and Davis, R.D. (1996). *Disorders of Personality: DSM-IV and Beyond* (2nd edition). New York: John Wiley & Sons.

Milton, K. (2008). Back to basics: Why foods of wild primates have relevance for modern human health. *Nutrition*, 16(7–8), 480–3.

Ministry of Justice (2012). *See* www.bbc.co.uk/news/uk-23923321 (accessed September 2015).

Ministry of Justice (2014). Safety in Custody Statistics. England and Wales Deaths in Custody to September 2014, Assaults and Self-harm to June 2014. *Ministry of Justice Statistics Bulletin*.

Minuchin, S., Rosman, B.L., Baker, L. and Minuchin, S. (2009). *Psychosomatic Families: Anorexia nervosa in context*. Cambridge, MA: Harvard University Press.

Minuchin, S., Rosman, B.L. and Baker, L. (1978). *Psychosomatic Families: Anorexia Nervosa in Context*. Cambridge, MA: Harvard University Press.

Mischel, W. and Ayduk, O. (2004). Willpower in a cognitive-affective processing system: The dynamics of delay of gratification. In K.D. Vohs and R.F. Baumeister (eds), *Handbook of Self-regulation: Research, Theory, and Applications*, (pp. 99–129). New York: Guilford Press.

Mischel, W. and Peake, P.K. (1982). Beyond deja vu in the search for cross-situational consistency. *Psychological Review*, 89, 730–55.

Mojtabi, R. and Nicholson, R. (1995). Interrater reliability of ratings of delusions and bizarre delusions. *American Journal of Psychiatry*, 152, 1804–8.

Moncrieff, J. (2009). A critique of the dopamine hypothesis of schizophrenia and psychosis. *Harvard Review of Psychiatry*, 17(3), 214–25.

Money, J. and Ehrhardt, A.A. (1972). *Man and Woman, Boy and Girl*. Baltimore, MD: Johns Hopkins University Press.

Monroe, S.M., Rohde, P., Seeley, J.R. and Lewinsohn, P.M. (1999). Life events and depression in adolescence: relationship loss as a prospective risk factor for first onset of major depressive disorder. *Journal of Abnormal Psychology*, 108(4), 606.

Montague, C.T., Farooqi, I.S., Whitehead, J.P., Soos, M.A., Rau, H., Wareham, N.J., Sewter, C.P., Digby, J.E., Mohammed, S.N., Hurst, J.A., Cheetham, C.H., Earley, A.R., Barnett, A.H., Prins, J.B. and O'Rahilly, S. (1997). Congenital leptin deficiency is associated with severe early-onset obesity in humans. *Nature, 387*, 903–8.

Mooney, M., White, T. and Hatsukami, D. (2004). The blind spot in the nicotine replacement therapy literature: Assessment of the double-blind in clinical trials. *Addictive Behaviors*, 29(4), 673–84.

Moos, R.H. and Swindle, R.W., Jnr (1990). Stressful life circumstances: Concepts and measures. *Stress Medicine*, 6, 171–8.

Moreno, M.A., Brockman, L., Rogers, C.B. and Christakis, D.A. (2010). An evaluation of the distribution of sexual references among 'Top 8' MySpace friends. *Journal of Adolescent Health*, 47(4), 418–20.

Morris, T., Greer, S., Pettingale, K.W. and Watson, M. (1981). Patterns of expression of anger and their psychological correlates in women with breast cancer. *Journal of Psychosomatic Research*, 25(2), 111–17.

Moyes, T., Tennent, T.G. and Bedford, A.P. (1985). Long-term follow-up study of a ward-based behaviour modification programme for adolescents with acting-out and conduct problems. *British Journal of Psychiatry*, 147, 300–5.

Mukamel, R., Ekstrom, A.D., Kaplan, J., Iacoboni, M. and Fried, I. (2010). Single-neuron responses in humans during execution and observation of actions. *Current Biology*, 20, 750–6.

Mullen, B. (1986). Atrocity as a function of lynch mob composition: A self-attention perspective. *Personality and Social Psychology Bulletin*, 12(2), 187–97.

Mullin, C.R. and Linz, D. (1995). Desensitization and resensitization to violence against women: Effects of exposure to sexually violent films on judgments of domestic violence victims. *Journal of Personality and Social Psychology*, 69(3), 449–59.

Myrtek, M. (2001). Meta-analyses of prospective studies on coronary heart disease, type A personality, and hostility. *International Journal of Cardiology*, 79, 245–51.

Nabi, R.L., Prestin, A. and So, J. (2013). Facebook friends with (health) benefits? Exploring social network site use and perceptions of social support, stress, and well-being. *CyberPsychology, Behaviour and Social Networking*, 16(10), 721–7.

Nakanishi, M. (1986). Perceptions of self-disclosure in initial interaction: A Japanese sample. *Human Communication Research,13*, 167–90.

Nakonezny, P.A. and Denton, W.H. (2008). Marital relationships: A social exchange theory perspective. *The American Journal of Family Therapy*, 36(5), 402–12.

National Collaborating Centre for Mental Health (NCCMH). (2009). *Core Interventions in the Treatment and Management of Schizophrenia in Adults in Primary and Secondary Care*. London: National Institute for Health and Care Excellence.

National Institute for Health and Care Excellence (NICE). (2014). *Psychosis and Schizophrenia in Adults: Treatment and Management*. London: National Institute for Health and Care Excellence.

Neel, J.V. (1962). Diabetes mellitus: A 'thrifty' genotype rendered detrimental by 'progress'? *American Journal of Human Genetics*, 14(4), 353–62.

Nemeroff, C.B. and Musselman, D.L. (2000). Are platelets the link between depression and ischemic heart disease? *American Heart Journal*, 140(4), 57–62.

Nettle, D. and Clegg, H. (2006). Schizotypy, creativity and mating success in humans. *Proceedings of the Royal Society of London B: Biological Sciences*, 273(1586), 611–15.

Newburn, T. (2002). Young people, crime and youth justice. In M. Maguire, R. Morgan and R. Reiner (eds), *The Oxford Handbook of Criminology*. Oxford: Oxford University Press.

Newton, A. (1980). The effects of imprisonment. *Criminal Justic Abstracts*, 12, 134–51.

Ng, M., Fleming, T., Robinson, M., Thomson, B., Graetz, N., Margono, C. *et al.* (2014). Global, regional, and national prevalence of overweight and obesity in children and adults during 1980–2013: A systematic analysis for the Global Burden of Disease Study 2013. *The Lancet*, 384(9945), 766–81.

NHS (2012). *See* www.nhs.uk/conditions/gender-dysphoria/Pages/Introduction.aspx (accessed June 2012).

Niehoff, D. (2014). Not hardwired: The complex neurobiology of sex differences in violence. *Violence and Gender*, 1(1), 19–24.

Nietzel, M.T. (1979). *Crime and its Modification: A social learning perspective*. Oxford: Pergamon Press.

Noble, E.P., Blum, K., Khalsa, M.E., Ritchie, T., Montgomery, A., Wood, R.C. and Sparkes, R.S. (1993). Allelic association of the D 2 dopamine receptor gene with cocaine dependence. *Drug and Alcohol Dependence*, 33(3), 271–85.

Noll, R. (2009). *The Encyclopedia of Schizophrenia and Other Psychotic Disorders*. New York: Infobase Publishing.

Novaco, R.W. (1975). *Anger Control: The development and evaluation of an experimental treatment*. Lexington, MA: Lexington Books, D.C. Heath.

Novaco, R.W. (1977). Stress inoculation: A cognitive therapy for anger. *Journal of Consulting and Clinical Psychology*, 45, 600–8.

Novaco, R.W. (2011). Perspectives on anger treatment: Discussion and commentary. *Cognitive and behavioral practice, 18*, 251–55.

Novaco, R.W. (2013). Reducing anger-related offending: What works? In L. Craig, L. Dixon and T. Gannon (eds) *What works in offender rehabilitation: An evidence-based approach to assessment and treatment*. Chichester: John Wiley & Sons.

Ogden, J. and Steward, J. (2000). The role of the mother-daughter relationship in explaining weight concern. *International Journal of Eating Disorders, 28*(1), 78–83.

Ogden, J. and Wardle, J. (1991). Cognitive and emotional responses to food. *International Journal of Eating Disorders, 10*, 297–311.

Okami, P., Olmstead, R., Abramson, P.R. and Pendleton, L. (1998). Early childhood exposure to parental nudity and scenes of parental sexuality ('primal scenes'): An 18-year longitudinal study of outcome. *Archives of Sexual Behavior*, 27(4), 361–84.

Olweus, D., Mattsson, A., Schalling, D. and Loew, H. (1988). Circulating testosterone levels and aggression in adolescent males: A causal analysis. *Psychosomatic Medicine*, 50(3), 261–72.

ONS (2015). *See* www.ons.gov.uk/ons/publications/re-reference-tables.html?edition=tcm%3A77-373433 (accessed September 2015).

Osborn, S.G. and West, D.J. (1979). Conviction records of fathers and sons compared. *The British Journal of Criminology*, 19(2), 120–33.

Oshumi, T. and Ohira, H. (2010). The positive side of psychopathy: Emotional detachment in psychopathy and rational decision-making in the ultimatum game. *Personality and Individual Differences*, 49, 451–6.

Owen-Anderson, A.F.H., Bradley, S.J. and Zucker, K.J. (2010). Expressed emotion in mothers of boys with gender identity disorder. *Journal of Sex & Marital Therapy*, 36, 327–45.

Owen, P.R. (2012). Portrayals of schizophrenia by entertainment media: A content analysis of contemporary movies. *Psychiatric Services*, 63(7), 655–9.

Pardini, D.A., Raine, A., Erickson, K. and Loeber, R. (2014). Lower amygdala volume in men is associated with childhood aggression, early psychopathic traits, and future violence. *Biological Psychiatry*, 75(1), 73–80.

Pasch, L.A. and Bradbury, T.N. (1998). Social support, conflict, and the development of marital dysfunction. *Journal of Consulting and Clinical Psychology*, 66(2), 219–30.

Pastore, N. (1952). The role of arbitrariness in the frustration–aggression hypothesis. *The Journal of Abnormal and Social Psychology*, 47(3), 728–31.

Patel, N.H., Vyas, N.S., Puri, B.K., Nijran, K.S. and Al-Nahhas, A. (2010). Positron emission tomography in schizophrenia: A new perspective. *Journal of Nuclear Medicine*, 51(4), 511–20.

Paterline, B.A. and Petersen, D.M. (1999). Structural and social psychological determinants of prisonization. *Journal of Criminal Justice*, 27(5), 427–41.

Paterson, N.E. and Markou, A. (2002). Increased GABA neurotransmission via administration of gamma-vinyl GABA decreased nicotine self-administration in the rat. *Synapse*, 44(4), 252–53.

Patterson, C.J. (2004). Lesbian and gay parents and their children: Summary of research findings. In *Lesbian and Gay Parenting: A Resource for Psychologists*. Washington, DC: American Psychological Association.

Paykel, E.S., Abbott, R., Jenkins, R., Brugha, T.S. and Meltzer, H. (2000). Urban–rural mental health differences in Great Britain: Findings from the National Morbidity Survey. *Psychological Medicine*, 30(02), 269–80.

Penton-Voak, I.S., Perrett, D.I., Castles, D.L., Kobayashi, T., Burt, D.M. and Murray, L.K. (1999). Menstrual cycle alters face preference. *Nature*, 399, 741–2.

Perner, J., Ruffman, T. and Leekam, S. (1994). Theory of mind is contagious: You catch it from your sibs. *Child Development*, 65, 1228–38.

Perry, D.G. and Bussey, K. (1979). The social learning theory of sex differences: Imitation is alive and well. *Journal of Personality and Social Psychology*, 37, 1699–712.

Perry, R.A., Mallan, K.M., Koo, J., Mauch, C.E., Daniels, L.A. and Magarey, A.M. (2015). Food neophobia and its association with diet quality and weight in children aged 24 months: A cross sectional study. *International Journal of Behavioral Nutrition and Physical Activity*, 12(1),13.

Peterson, B.D., Newton, C.R., Rosen, K.H. and Skaggs, G.E. (2006). Gender differences in how men and women who are referred for IVF cope with infertility stress. *Human Reproduction*, 21(9), 2443–9.

Petherick, W. (ed) (2006). *Serial crime: Theoretical and practical issues in behavioural profiling*. London: Elsevier.

Petry, N. (2005). *Pathological Gambling: Etiology, comorbidity and treatment*. Washington, DC: American Psychological Association.

Petry, N.M., Ammerman, Y., Bohl, J., Doersch, A., Gay, H., Kadden, R. and Steinberg, K. (2006). Cognitive-behavioral therapy for pathological gamblers. *Journal of Consulting and Clinical Psychology*, 74(3), 555–67.

Pharoah, F., Mari, J., Rathbone, J. and Wong, W. (2010). Family intervention for schizophrenia. *Cochrane Database of Systematic Reviews*, 12.

Piaget, J. (1926). *The Language and Thought of the Child*. New York: Harcourt Brace Jovanovich.

Piaget, J. (1954). *The Construction of Reality in the Child*. New York: Basic Books.

Piaget, J. (1970). *Main Trends in Psychology*. London: George Allen & Unwin.

Pike, K.M. and Rodin, J. (1991). Mothers, daughters, and disordered eating. *Journal of Abnormal Psychology*, 100(2), 198–204.

Piliavin, I.M., Rodin, J. and Piliavin, J.A. (1969). Good Samaritanism: An underground phenomenon. *Journal of Personality and Social Psychology, 13*, 1200–13.

Pingree, S. (1978). The effects of nonsexist television commercials and perceptions of reality on children's attitudes about women. *Psychology of Women Quarterly*, 2, 262–77.

Pinker, S. (2003). *The Blank Slate*. London: Penguin Books.

Pitkänen, T., Lyyra, A.L. and Pulkkinen, L. (2005). Age of onset of drinking and the use of alcohol in adulthood: A follow-up study from age 8–42 for females and males. *Addiction*, 100(5), 652–61.

Pliner, P. (1994). Development of measures of food neophobia in children. *Appetite, 23*(2), 147–63.

Plomin, R., DeFries, J.C. and Loehlin, J.C. (1977). Genotype–environment interaction and correlation in the analysis of human behavior. *Psychological Bulletin, 84*(2), 309–22.

Plomin, R., Foch, T.T. and Rowe, D.C. (1981). Bobo clown aggression in childhood: Environment, not genes. *Journal of Research in Personality, 15*(3), 331–42.

Plowden Report (1967). *Children and their Primary Schools*. London: HMSO.

Poole, E.D. and Regoli, R.M. (1983). Professionalism, role conflict, work alienation, and anomia: A look at prison management. *The Social Science Journal, 20*(1), 63–70.

Popper, K.R. (1934). *The Logic of Scientific Discovery*. English translation, 1959. London: Hutchinson.

Porter, G. and Starcevic, V. (2007). Are violent video games harmful? *Australasian Psychiatry, 15*(5), 422–6.

Postmes, T. and Spears, R. (1998). Deindividuation and antinormative behavior: A meta-analysis. *Psychological Bulletin, 123*(3), 238–59.

Prakash, J., Kotwal, A.S.M., Ryali, V.S.S.R., Srivastava, K., Bhat, P.S. and Shashikumar, R. (2010). Does androgyny have psychoprotective attributes? A cross-sectional community-based study. *Industrial Psychiatry Journal, 19*, 119–24.

Pranis, K., Stewart, B. and Wedge, M. (2003). *Peacemaking Circles from Crime to Community*. St. Paul, MN: Living Justice Press.

Prescott, J. (2013). *Taste Matters: Why we like the foods we do*. London: Reaktion Books.

Priks, M. (2010). Does frustration lead to violence? Evidence from the Swedish hooligan scene. *Kyklos, 63*(3), 450–60.

Prinz, J.J. (2012). *Beyond Human Nature: How Culture and Experience Shape our Lives*. London: Penguin.

Prison Reform Trust (2014). *See* www.prisonreformtrust.org.uk/Portals/0/Documents/Prison%20the%20facts%20May%202014.pdf (accessed September 2015).

Pritkin, M.H. (2009). Is prison increasing crime? *Wisconsin Law Review, 2*, 1049–108.

Prochaska, J.O. and DiClemente, C.C. (1992). Stages of change in the modification of problem behaviors. *Progress in Behavior Modification, 28*, 183–218.

Provencher, V., Drapeau, V., Tremblay, A., Després, J.P. and Lemieux, S. (2003). Eating behaviors and indexes of body composition in men and women from the Quebec family study. *Obesity Research, 11*(6), 783–92.

Przybylski, A.K., Deci, E.L., Rigby, C.S. and Ryan, R.M. (2014). Competence-impeding electronic games and players' aggressive feelings, thoughts, and behaviors. *Journal of Personality and Social Psychology, 106*(3), 441–57.

Putnam, R.D. (2000). *Bowling Alone: The Collapse and Revival of American Community*. New York: Simon & Schuster.

Puts, D.A. (2010). Beauty and the beast: Mechanisms of sexual selection in humans. *Evolution and Human Behavior, 31*(3), 157–75.

Quadagno, D.M., Briscoe, R. and Quadagno, R.S. (1977). Effect of perinatal gonadal hormones on selected nonsexual behavior patterns: A critical assessment of the non-human and human literature. *Psychological Bulletin, 84*, 62–80.

Ragland, D.R. and Brand, R.J. (1988). Type A behaviour and mortality from coronary heart disease. *New England Journal of Medicine, 318*(2), 65–9.

Rahe, R.H. (1974). The pathway between subjects' recent life changes and their near-future illness reports: Representative results and methodological issues. In B.S. Dohrenwend and B.P. Dohrenwend (eds), *Stressful Life Events: Their Nature and Effects*. New York: Wiley.

Rahe, R.H., Mahan, J. and Arthur, R. (1970). Prediction of near-future health-change from subjects' preceding life changes. *Journal of Psychosomatic Research, 14*, 401–6.

Raine, A. (1993). *The Psychopathology of Crime*. San Diego, CA: Academic.

Raine, A. (2004). Unlocking Crime: The Biological Key, BBC News, December. *See* http://news.bbc.co.uk/1/hi/programmes/if/4102371.stm (accessed September 2015).

Raine, A., Buchsbaum, M. and LaCasse, L. (1997). Brain abnormalities in murderers indicated by positron emission tomography. *Biological Psychiatry, 42*, 495–508.

Raine, A., Mellingen, K., Liu, J., Venables, P. and Mednick, S.A. (2014). Effects of environmental enrichment at ages 3–5 years on schizotypal personality and antisocial behavior at ages 17 and 23 years. *American Journal of Psychiatry, 135*(2), 255–63.

Raleigh, M.J., McGuire, M.T., Brammer, G.L., Pollack, D.B. and Yuwiler, A. (1991). Serotonergic mechanisms promote dominance acquisition in adult male vervet monkeys. *Brain Research, 559*(2), 181–90.

Ramachandran, V.S. (2000). Mirror neurons and imitation learning as the driving force behind 'the great leap forward' in human evolution. *See* www.edge.org/3rd_culture/ ramachandran/ramachandran_p1.html (accessed November 2008).

Ramachandran, V.S. (2008). Phantom penises in transsexuals. *Journal of Consciousness Studies, 15*(1), 5–16.

Ramachandran, V.S. and McGeoch, P.D. (2007). Occurrence of phantom genitalia after gender reassignment surgery. *Medical Hypotheses, 69*, 1001–3.

Ramachandran, V.S. and McGeoch, P.D. (2008). Phantom penises in transsexuals: Evidence of an innate gender-specific body image in the brain. *Journal of Consciousness Studies, 15*, 5–16.

Ramachandran, V.S., Rogers-Ramachandran, D.C. and Cobb, S. (1995). Touching the phantom. *Nature, 377*(6549), 489–90.

Rametti, G., Carrillo, B., Gómez-Gil, E., Junque, C., Segovia, S., Gomez, A. and Guillamon, A. (2011). White matter microstructure in female to male transsexuals before cross-sex hormonal treatment: A diffusion tensor imaging study. *Journal of Psychiatric Research, 45*(2), 199–204.

Ratcliffe, J.M., Fenton, M.B. and Galef, B.G. (2003). An exception to the rule: common vampire bats do not learn taste aversions. *Animal Behaviour, 65*(2), 385–9.

Ravindran, A.V., Telner, J., Bhatla, R., Cameron, C., Horn, E. *et al.* (2006). Pathological gambling: Treatment correlates. *European Neuropsychpharmacology, 16*(4), S506.

Read, J. (2004). Poverty, ethnicity and gender. In J. Read, L. Mosher and R. Bentall (eds), *Models of Madness: Psychological, Social and Biological Approaches to Schizophrenia*. London: Brunner-Routledge.

Read, J. and Haslam, N. (2004). Public opinion: Bad things happen and can drive you crazy. In J. Read, L. Mosher and R. Bentall (eds), *Models of Madness: Psychological, Social and Biological Approaches to Schizophrenia*. London: Brunner-Routledge.

Redden, J.P. (2008). Reducing satiation: The role of categorization level. *Journal of Consumer Research, 34*(5), 624–34.

Regier, D.A., Narrow, W.E., Clarke, D.E., Kraemer, H.C., Kuramoto, S.J., Kuhl, E.A. and Kupfer, D.J. (2013). DSM-5 field trials in the United States and Canada, Part II: test-retest reliability of selected categorical diagnoses. *American Journal of Psychiatry, 170*(1), 59–70.

Rehm, J., Steinleitner, M. and Lilli, W. (1987). Wearing uniforms and aggression – A field experiment. *European Journal of Social Psychology, 17*(3), 357–60.

Reicher, S. and Stott, C. (2011). *Mad Mobs and Englishmen? Myths and Realities of the 2011 Riots*. Kindle edition: Robinson.

Reid, R. L. (1986). The psychology of the near miss. *Journal of Gambling Behavior, 2*(1), 32–39.

Reifman, A., Larrick, R. and Fein, S. (1991). Temper and temperature on the diamond: The heat–aggression relationship in Major League Baseball. *Personality and Social Psychology Bulletin, 17*, 580–5.

Reiner, W.G. and Gearhart, M.D. (2004). Discordant sexual identity in some genetic males with cloacal exstrophy assigned to female sex at birth. *New England Journal of Medicine, 350*, 333–41.

Reith, G. and Dobbie, F. (2011). Beginning gambling: The role of social networks and environment. *Addiction Research and Theory, 19*(6), 483–93.

Reynolds, J. and Wickens, J.R. (2000). Substantia nigra dopamine regulates synaptic plasticity and membrane potential fluctuations in the rat neostriatum, in vivo. *Neuroscience, 99*, 199–203.

Rhee, S.H. and Waldman, I.D. (2002). Genetic and environmental influences on antisocial behavior: A meta-analysis of twin and adoption studies. *Psychological Bulletin, 128*(3), 490–529.

Rice, M.E., Quinsey, V.L. and Houghton, R. (1990). Predicting treatment outcome and recidivism among patients in a maximum security token economy. *Behavioural Sciences and the Law, 8*, 313–26.

Riska, E. (2002). From Type A man to the hardy man: Masculinity and health. *Sociology of Health and Illness, 24*(3), 347–58.

Rizzolatti, G. and Arbib, M.A. (1998). Language within our grasp. *Trends in Neuroscience, 21*, 188–94.

Rizzolatti, G., Fadiga, L., Fogassi, L. and Gallese, V. (1996). Premotor cortex and the recognition of motor actions. *Cognitive Brain Research, 3*, 131–41.

Robins, L.N. (1974). *The Vietnam drug user returns: final report, September 1973* (No. 2). Special Action Office Monograph, Series A(2).

Robinson, T.N., Kierman, M., Matheson, D.M. and Haydel, K.F. (2001). Is parental control over children's eating associated with childhood obesity? *Obesity Research, 9*, 306–312.

Rogers, C.R. (1959). A theory of therapy, personality, and interpersonal relationships as developed in the client-centred framework. In S. Koch (ed.), *Psychology: A Study of a Science*. New York: McGraw-Hill.

Rollie, S.S. and Duck, S.W. (2006). Stage theories of marital breakdown. In J.H. Harvey and M.A. Fine (eds), *Handbook of Divorce and Dissolution of Romantic Relationships*. Hillsdale, NJ: Lawrence Erlbaum.

Romans-Clarkson, S.E., Walton, V.A., Herbison, G.P. and Mullen, P.E. (1990). Psychiatric morbidity among women in urban and rural New Zealand: psycho-social correlates. *The British Journal of Psychiatry, 156*(1), 84–91.

Romer, D., Betancourt, L.M., Brodsky, N.L., Giannetta, J.M., Yang, W. and Hurt, H. (2011). Does adolescent risk taking imply weak executive function? A prospective study of relations between working memory performance, impulsivity, and risk taking in early adolescence. *Developmental Science*, *14*(5), 1119–33.

Rosado, B., García-Belenguer, S., León, M., Chacón, G., Villegas, A. and Palacio, J. (2010). Blood concentrations of serotonin, cortisol and dehydroepiandrosterone in aggressive dogs. *Applied Animal Behaviour Science*, *123*(3), 124–30.

Rose, J.E. (2006). Nicotine and non-nicotine factors in cigarette addiction. *Psychopharmacology (Berl)*, *184*(3–4), 274–85.

Rosenfeld, M.J. and Thomas, R.J. (2012). Searching for a mate: The rise of the Internet as a social intermediary. *American Sociological Review*, *77*(4), 523–47.

Rosenhan, D.L. (1973). On being sane in insane places. *Science*, *179*, 250–8.

Rosenthal, R. (1966). *Experimenter Effects in Behaviour Research*. New York: Appleton.

Ross, C.A. and Read, J. (2004). Antipsychotic medication: Myths and facts. In J. Read, L. Mosher and R. Bentall (eds), *Models of Madness: Psychological, Social and Biological Approaches to Schizophrenia*. London: Brunner-Routledge.

Rossmo, D.K. (1999). *Geographic profiling*. Boca Raton, FL: CRC Press.

Rotter, J.B. (1966). Generalised expectancies for internal versus external control of reinforcement. *Psychological Monographs*, *30*(1), 1–26.

Rozanski, A., Blumental, J.A. and Kaplan, J. (1999). Impact of psychological factors on the pathogenisis of cardiovascular disease and implications for therapy. *Circulatrion*, *99*, 2192–217.

Rozin, P. (1976). The selection of foods by rats, humans and other animals. *Advances in the Study of Behavior*, *6*, 21–6.

Rozin, P. (1997). The use of characteristic flavoring in human culinary practice. In C.M. Apt (ed.) *Flavor: Its Chemical, Behavioral and Commercial Aspects*. Boulder, CO: Westview Press.

Rubin, Z. (1975). Disclosing oneself to a stranger: Reciprocity and its limits. *Journal of Experimental Social Psychology*, *11*(3), 233–60.

Ruffin, C.L. (1993). Stress and health: Little hassles vs major life events. *Australian Psychologist*, *28*, 201–8.

Rusbult, C. (1980). Commitment and satisfaction in romantic associations: A test of the investment model. *Journal of Experimental Social Psychology*, *16*, 172–86.

Rusbult, C.E. and Martz, J.M. (1995). Remaining in an abusive relationship: An investment model analysis of non-voluntary commitment. *Personality and Social Psychology Bulletin*, 21, 558–71.

Rusbult, C.E., Martz, J.M. and Agnew, C.R. (1998). The investment model scale: Measuring commitment level, satisfaction level, quality of alternatives, and investment size. *Personal relationships*, *5*(4), 357–87.

Russell, C.G., Worsley, A. and Campbell, K.J. (2015). Strategies used by parents to influence their children's food preferences. *Appetite*, *90*, 123–30.

Russell, G.F.M., Treasure, J. and Eisler, I. (1998). Mothers with anorexia nervosa who underfeed their children: their recognition and management. *Psychological Medicine*, *28*(1), 93–108.

Rutter, M. and Sonuga-Barke, E.J. (2010). X. Conclusions: Overview of findings from the era study, inferences, and research implications. *Monographs of the Society for Research in Child Development*, *75*(1), 212–29.

Rymer, R. (1993). *Genie: Escape from a Silent Childhood*. London: Michael Joseph.

Sabbagh, M.A. and Callanan, M.A. (1998). Metarepresentation in action: Children's theories of mind developing and emerging in parent–child conversations. *Developmental Psychology*, *34*, 491–502.

Saha, S., Chant, D., Welham, J., McGrath, J. (2005). A systematic review of the prevalence of schizophrenia. *PLoS Med*, *2*(5): e141.

Sakurai, T., Amemiya, A., Ishii, M., Matsuzaki, I., Chemelli, R.M., Tanaka, H. and Arch, J.R. (1998). Orexins and orexin receptors: a family of hypothalamic neuropeptides and G protein-coupled receptors that regulate feeding behavior. *Cell*, *92*(4), 573–85.

Salfati, C.G. and Canter, D.V. (1999). Differentiating stranger murders: Profiling offender characteristics from behavioural styles. *Behavioural Science and the Law*, *17*, 391–406.

Samuel, J. and Bryant, P. (1984). Asking only one question in the conservation experiment. *Journal of Child Psychology and Psychiatry*, *25*(2), 315–18.

Sandvik, A.M., Bartone, P.T., Hystad, S.W., Phillips, T.M., Thayer, J.F. and Johnsen, B.H. (2013). Psychological hardiness predicts neuroimmunology response. *Psychology, Health & Medicine*, *18*(6), 705–13.

Sapolsky, R. (1998). *The Trouble with Testosterone: And other essays on the biology of the human predicament*. New York: Scribner.

Sarin, F. and Wallin, L. (2014). Cognitive model and cognitive behavior therapy for schizophrenia: An overview. *The Nordic Journal of Psychiatry*, *68*(3), 145–53.

Sarkar, S., Praharaj, S.K., Chaudhury, S. and Das, B. (2010). Anhedonia in acute schizophrenia: Scientific letter. *African Journal of Psychiatry*, *13*(3), 226–7.

Sato, T. (2005). The Eysenck Personality questionnaire brief version: Facto structure and reliability. *Journal of Psychology*, *139*(6), 545–52.

Savage-Rumbaugh, E.S. (1991). Language learning in the bonobo: How and why they learn. In N.A. Krasnegor, D.M. Rumbaugh, R.L. Schiefelbusch and M. Studdert-Kennedy (eds), *Biological and Behavioural Determinants of Language Development*. Hillsdale, NJ: Lawrence Erlbaum Associates.

Scarr, S. and McCartney, K. (1983). How people make their own environments: A theory of genotype-environment effects. *Child Development*, *54*, 424–35.

Schaefer, C., Coyne, J.C. and Lazarus, R.S. (1981). The health related functions of social support. *Journal of Behavioral Medicine*, *4*, 381–406.

Schafer, R.B. and Keith, P.M. (1980). Equity and depression among married couples. *Social Psychology Quarterly*, 430–5.

Schaubroeck, J., Jones, J.R. and Xie, J.L. (2001). Individual differences in utilizing control to cope with job demands: Effects on susceptibility to infectious disease. *Journal of Applied Psychology*, *86*(2), 265–78.

Scherer, J.A. and Jarvis, J.P. (2014). Criminal investigative analysis: Measuring success (part three of four). FBI Law Enforcements Bulletin, August. *See* https://leb.fbi.gov/2014/august/criminal-investigative-analysis-practicioner-perspectives-part-three-of-four (accessed September 2015).

Schiappa, E., Allen, M. and Gregg, P.B. (2007). Parasocial relationships and television: A meta-analysis of the effects. In R.W. Preiss, B.M. Gayle, N. Burrell, M. Allen and J. Bryant (eds), *Mass Media Effects Research* (pp. 301–14). New York: Erlbaum.

Schlesinger, M. and Casey, P. (2003). Where infants look when impossible things happen: Simulating and testing a gaze-direction model. *Connection Science*, *15*, 271–80.

Schmid, H. and Klimmt, C. (2011). A magically nice guy: Parasocial relationships with harry potter across different cultures. *International Communication Gazette*, *73*(3), 252–69.

Schönenberg, M. and Aiste, J. (2014). Investigation of the hostile attribution bias toward ambiguous facial cues in antisocial violent offenders. *European Archives of Psychiatry and Clinical Neuroscience*, *64*(1), 61–9.

Schweizer, R., Roth, W.T. and Elbert, T. (1991). Effect of two beta-blockers on stress during mental arithmetic. *Psychopharmacology*, *105*(4), 573–7.

Sears, D.O. (1986). College sophomores in the laboratory: Influences of a narrow data base on psychology's view of human nature. *Journal of Personality and Social Psychology*, *51*, 515–30.

Segerstrom, S.C. and Miller, G.E. (2004). Psychological stress and the human immune system: A meta-analytic study of 30 years of inquiry. *Psychological Bulletin*, *130*, 601–30.

Selman, R. (1976). Social cognitive understanding. In T. Lickona (ed.), *Moral Development and Behavior*. New York: Holt, Rinehart and Winston.

Selman, R. (2003). Teaching social awareness: An interview with Larsen Professor Robert Selman by A. Bucuvalas. *See* www.gse.harvard.edu/news/features/selman02012003.html (accessed November 2008).

Selman, R.L. (1971). Taking another's perspective: Role-taking development in early childhood. *Child Development*, *42*, 1721–34.

Selman, R.L. (1977). A structural-developmental model of social cognition: Implications for intervention research. *The Counseling Psychologist*, *6*(4), 3–6.

Selman, R.L., Jacquette, D. and Lavin, D.R. (1977). Interpersonal awareness in children: Toward an integration of developmental and clinical child psychology. *American Journal of Orthopsychiatry*, *47*, 264–74.

Selye, H. (1936). A syndrome produced by diverse nocuous agents. *Nature*, *138*, 32.

Seo, D., Patrick, C.J. and Kennealy, P.J. (2008). Role of serotonin and dopamine system interactions in the neurobiology of impulsive aggression and its comorbidity with other clinical disorders. *Aggression and Violent Behavior*, *13*, 383–95.

Shakya, H.B., Christakis, N.A. and Fowler, J.H. (2012). Parental influence on substance use in adolescent social networks. *Archives of Pediatrics and Adolescent Medicine*, *166*(12), 1132–9.

Sharpe, L. (2002). A reformulated cognitive-behavioral model of problem gambling: A biopsychosocial perspective. *Clinical Psychology Review*, *22*, 1–25.

Shearer, N. (2013). As work related stress costs UK economy nearly £6.5bn each year, what steps should businesses and employees be taking? *See* www.huffingtonpost.co.uk/natasha-shearer/work-related-stress-business_b_3545476.html (accessed January 2016).

Sheehy, R.S. and Horan, J.J. (2004). The effects of stress-inoculation training for first year law students. *International Journal of Stress Management*, *11*, 44–55.

Sheldon, W.H. (1949). *Varieties of Delinquent Youth*. New York: Harper and Brothers.

Sheps, D.S., McMahon, R.P., Becker, L., Carney, R.M., Freedland, K.E., Cohen, J.D., Sheffield, D., Goldberg, A.D., Ketterer, M.W., Pepine, C.J., Raczynski, J.M., Light, K., Krantz, D.S., Stone, P.H., Knatterud, G.L. and Kaufmann, P.G. (2002). Mental stress-induced ischemia and all-cause mortality in patients with coronary artery disease: Results from the Psychophysiological Investigations of Myocardial Ischemia Study. *Circulation, 105*, 1780–4.

Sheridan, C.L. and Radmacher, S.A. (1992). *Health Psychology*. Chichester: Wiley.

Sherman, L.W. and Strang, H. (2007). *Restorative Justice: The evidence*. London: The Smith Institute.

Shi, L., Lin, Q. and Su, B. (2015). Estrogen regulation of microcephaly genes and evolution of brain sexual dimorphism in primates. *BMC Evolutionary Biology, 15*, 127.

Shiffman, S. and Waters, A.J. (2004). Negative affect and smoking lapses: A prospective analysis. *Journal of Consulting and Clinical Psychology, 72*(2), 192–201.

Shroff, H. and Thompson, J.K. (2006). Peer influences, body-image dissatisfaction, eating dysfunction and self-esteem in adolescent girls. *Journal of Health Psychology, 11*(4), 533–51.

Shultz, K.S., Wang, M. and Olson, D.A. (2010). Role overload and underload in relation to occupational stress and health. *Stress and Health, 26*, 99–111.

Sieber, J.E. and Stanley, B. (1988). Ethical and professional dimensions of socially sensitive research. *American Psychologist, 43*, 49–55.

SIGN (2013). *The Management of Schizophrenia*. Scottish Intercollegiate Guidelines Network. Edinburgh.

Signorelli, N. and Bacue, A. (1999). Recognition and respect: A content analysis of prime-time television characters across three decades. *Sex Roles, 40*, 527–44.

Simpson, J.A., Gangestad, S. and Lerma, M. (1990). Perception of physical attractiveness: Mechanisms involved in the maintenance of romantic relationships. *Journal of Personality and Social Psychology, 59*, 1192–201.

Sinclair-de-Zwart, H. (1969). Developmental psycholinguistics. In D. Elkind and J. Flavell (eds), *Studies in Cognitive Development*. Oxford: Oxford University Press.

Sinha, R., Fuse, T., Aubin, L.R. and O'Malley, S.S. (2000). Psychological stress, drug-related cues and cocaine craving. *Psychopharmacology, 152*(2),140–8.

Skinner, B.F. (1953). Some contributions of an experimental analysis of behavior to psychology as a whole. *American Psychologist, 8*(2), 69–78.

Slaby, R.G. and Frey, K.S. (1975). Development of gender constancy and selective attention to same-sex models. *Child Development, 46*, 849–56.

Slack, G. (2007). Source of human empathy found in brain. *New Scientist, 12 November*, 2629.

Slater, M.D., Kelly, K.J., Lawrence, F.R., Stanley, L.R. and Comello, M.L.G. (2011). Assessing media campaigns linking marijuana non-use with autonomy and aspirations:'Be Under Your Own Influence' and ONDCP's 'Above the Influence'. *Prevention Science, 12*(1), 12–22.

Slutske, W.S., Zhu, G., Meier, M.H. and Martin, N.G. (2010). Genetic and environmental influences on disordered gambling in men and women. *Archives of General Psychiatry, 67*(6), 624–30.

Smetana, J.G. (1989). Adolescents' and parents' reasoning about actual family conflict. *Child Development, 60*, 1052–67.

Smith, C. and Lloyd, B. (1978). Maternal behaviour and perceived sex of infant: Revisited. *Child Development, 49*, 1263–5.

Smith, J.W. and Frawley, P.J. (1993). Treatment outcome of 600 chemically dependent patients treated in a multimodal inpatient program including aversion therapy and pentothal interviews. *Journal of Substance Abuse Treatment, 10*(4), 359–69.

Smith, L.B. (1999). Do infants possess innate knowledge structures? The con side. *Developmental Scie*nce, 2, 133–44.

Smith, P. and Bond, M.H. (1998). *Social Psychology Across Cultures: Analysis and perspectives* (2nd edition). New York: Harvester Wheatsheaf.

Smith, P.K. and Pellegrini, A. (2008). Learning through play. *See* www.child-encyclopedia.com/Pages/PDF/Smith-PellegriniANGxp.pdf (accessed September 2015).

Smith, S.S., O'Hara, B.F., Persico, A.M., Gorelick, D.A., Newlin, D.B., Vlahov, D., Solomon, L., Pickens, R. and Uhl, G.R. (1992). Genetic vulnerability to drug abuse: The D2 dopamine receptor Taq I B1 restriction fragment length polymorphism appears more frequently in polysubstance abusers. *Archives of General Psychiatry, 49*(9), 723–7.

Smolak, L., Levine, M.P. and Schermer, F. (1999). Parental input and weight concerns among elementary school children. *International Journal of Eating Disorders, 25*(3), 263–71.

Snarey, J.R. (1985). Cross-cultural universality of social-moral development: A critical review of Kohlbergian research. *Psychological Bulletin, 97*, 202–32.

Snook, B., Cullen, R.M., Bennell, C., Taylor, P.J. and Gendreau, P. (2008). The criminal profiling illusion: what's behind the smoke and mirrors? *Criminal Justice and Behavior, 35*(10), 1257–76.

Snyder, J., Bank, L. and Burraston, B. (2005).The consequences of antisocial behavior in older male siblings for younger brothers and sisters. *Journal of Family Psychology, 19*, 643–53.

Soetens, B., Braet, C., Dejonckheere, P. and Roets, A. (2006). 'When Suppression Backfires': The ironic effects of suppressing eating-related thoughts. *Journal of Health Psychology, 11*(5), 655–68.

Song, H. and Baillargeon, R. (2008). Infants' reasoning about others' false perceptions. *Developmental Psychology, 44*, 1789–95.

Soon, C., Brass, M., Heinze, H. and Haynes, J. (2008). Unconscious determinants of free decisions in the human brain. *Nature Neuroscience, 11*(5), 543–5.

Soper, W.B. and Miller, M.J. (1983). Junk-time junkies: An emerging addiction among students. *The School Counselor, 31*(1), 40–3.

Speakman, J.R. (2008). Thrifty genes for obesity, an attractive but flawed idea, and an alternative perspective: The 'drifty gene' hypothesis. *International Journal of Obesity, 32*(11), 1611–7.

Speisman, J.C., Lazarus, R.S., Mordkoff, A.M. and Davidson, L.A. (1964). The experimental reduction of stress based on ego defence theory. *Journal of Abnormal and Social Psychology, 68*, 397–8.

Spelke, E.S., Breinlinger, K., Macomber, J. and Jacobson, K. (1992). Origins of knowledge. *Psychological Review, 99*, 605–32.

Spence, J.T., Helmreich, R.L. and Stapp, J. (1975). Ratings of self and peers on sex-role attributes and their relation to self-esteem and conceptions of masculinity and femininity. *Journal of Personality and Social Psychology, 32*, 29–39.

Spivey, C.B. and Prentice-Dunn, S. (1990). Assessing the directionality of deindividuated behavior: Effects of deindividuation, modeling, and private self-consciousness on aggressive and prosocial responses. *Basic and Applied Social Psychology, 11*(4), 387–403.

Sprecher, S. (1987). The effects of self-disclosure given and received on affection for an intimate partner and stability of the relationship. *Journal of Social and Personal Relationships, 4*(2), 115–27.

Sprecher, S. (1992). How men and women expect to feel and behave in response to inequity in close relationships. *Social Psychology Quarterly, 55*(1), 57–69.

Sprecher, S. (2001). Equity and social exchange in dating couples: Associations with satisfaction, commitment and stability. *Journal of Marriage and the Family, 63*, 599–613.

Sprecher, S. and Hatfield, E. (2009). Matching hypothesis. In H. Reis and S. Sprecher (eds), *Encyclopedia of Human Relationships*. New York: SAGE.

Sprecher, S., Treger, S., Wondra, J. D., Hilaire, N. and Wallpe, K. (2013). Taking turns: Reciprocal self-disclosure promotes liking in initial interactions. *Journal of Experimental Social Psychology, 49*(5), 860–6.

Sprecher, S., Treger, S., Wondra, J.D., Hilaire, N. and Wallpe, K. (2013). Taking turns: Reciprocal self-disclosure promotes liking in initial interactions. *Journal of Experimental Social Psychology, 49*(5), 860–6.

Sran, S.K. and Borrero, J.C. (2010). Assessing the value of choice in a token system. *Journal of Applied Behavior Analysis, 43*(3), 553–7.

Stafford, L. and Canary, D.J. (2006). Equity and interdependence as predictors of relational maintenance strategies. *The Journal of Family Communication, 6*(4), 227–54.

Stanley, B.G., Kyrkouli, S.E., Lampert, S. and Leibowitz, S.F. (1986). Neuropeptide Y chronically injected into the hypothalamus: A powerful neurochemical inducer of hyperphagia and obesity. *Peptides, 7*(6), 1189–92.

Stattin, H. and Kerr, M. (2000). Parental monitoring: A reinterpretation. *Child Development, 71*(4), 1072–85.

Staub, E. (1996). Cultural-societal roots of violence: The examples of genocidal violence and of contemporary youth violence in the United States. *American Psychologist, 51*(2), 117.

Stead, L.F., Perera, R., Bullen, C., Mant, D., Hartmann-Boyce, J., Cahill, K. and Lancaster, T. (2012). Nicotine replacement therapy for smoking cessation. *Cochrane Database Syst Rev, 11*(11).

Steele, C.M. and Josephs, R.A. (1990). Alcohol myopia: Its prized and dangerous effects. *American Psychologist, 45*(8), 921–33.

Steiner, B. (2009). Assessing static and dynamic influences on inmate violence levels. *Crime & Delinquency, 55*(1), 134–61.

Stephens, R., Atkins, J. and Kingston, A. (2009). Swearing as a response to pain. *Neuroreport, 20*(12), 1056–60.

Steptoe, A., Day, S., Doherty, S., Rink, E., Kerry, S., Kendrick, T. and Hilton, S. (1999). Behavioural counselling in general practice for the promotion of healthy behaviour among adults at increased risk of coronary heart disease: randomised trial commentary: Treatment allocation by the method of minimisation. *British Medical Journal, 319*(7215), 943–8.

Stern, M., Norman, S. and Komm, C. (1993). Medical students' differential use of coping strategies as a function of stressor type, year of training, and gender. *Behavioural Medicine, 18*(4), 173–80.

Stever, G. (2009). Parasocial and social interaction with celebrities: Classification of Media fans. *Journal of Media Psychology, 14*(3), 1–39.

Stocks, J.T., Thyer, B.A. and Kearsley, M. (1987). Using a token economy in a community-based residential program for disabled adults: An empirical evaluation leads to program modification. *Behavioral Residential Treatment*, 1, 173–85.

Stoller, R.J. (1975). *Sex and Gender. Vol. 2: The Transsexual Experiment*. London: Hogarth.

Strober, M., Freeman, R., Lampert, C., Diamond, J. and Kaye W. (2000). Controlled family study of anorexia and bulimia nervosa: evidence of shared liability and transmission of partial syndromes. *American Journal of Psychiatry, 157*, 393–401.

Stroebe, W., Mensink, W., Aarts, H., Schut, H. and Kruglanski, A.W. (2008). Why dieters fail: Testing the goal conflict model of eating. *Journal of Experimental Social Psychology*, 44(1), 26–36.

Stunkard, A.J., Harris, J.R., Pedersen, N.L. and McClearn, G.E. (1990). The body-mass index of twins who have been reared apart. *New England Journal of Medicine*, 322(21), 1483–7.

Stunkard, A.J., Sørensen, T.I., Hanis, C., Teasdale, T.W., Chakraborty, R., Schull, W.J. and Schulsinger, F. (1986). An adoption study of human obesity. *New England Journal of Medicine*, 314(4), 193–8

Sutherland, E.H. (1939). *Principles of Criminology* (3rd edition). Philadelphia: Lippincott.

Sutherland, E.H. (1983). *White Collar Crime: The uncut version*. New Haven, CT: Yale University Press.

Swets, M., Dekker, J., van Emmerik-van Oortmerssen, K., Smid, G.E., Smit, F., de Haan, L. and Schoevers, R.A. (2014). The obsessive compulsive spectrum in schizophrenia: A meta-analysis and meta-regression exploring prevalence rates. *Schizophrenia Research*, 152(2), 458–68.

Sykes, G. (1958). The pains of imprisonment. *The Society of Captives: A Study of a Maximum Security Prison*, 63–78.

Tajfel, H. and Turner, J.C. (1986). The social identity theory of intergroup behaviour. In S. Worchel and W.G. Austin (eds), *Psychology of Intergroup Relations* (2nd edition). Chicago, IL: Nelson-Hall.

Takano, Y. and Osaka, E. (1999). An unsupported common view: Comparing Japan and the U.S. on individualism/collectivism. *Asian Journal of Social Psychology*, 2(3), 311–41.

Tal-Or, N. and Hershman-Shitrit, M. (2015). Self-disclosure and the liking of participants in reality TV. *Human Communication Research*, 41(2), 245–67.

Tamir, D.I. and Mitchell, J.P. (2012). Disclosing information about the self is intrinsically rewarding. *PNAS*, 109(21), 8038–43.

Tarbox, R.S.F., Ghezzi, P.M. and Wilson, G. (2006). The effects of token reinforcement on attending in a young child with autism. *Behavioural Interventions*, 21(3), 155–64.

Tashiro, T. and Frazier, P. (2003). 'I'll never be in a relationship like that again': Personal growth following romantic relationship breakups. *Personal Relationships, 10*(1), 113–128.

Taylor, J.L. and Novaco, R.W. (2006). *Anger Treatment for People with Developmentl Disabilities: A theory, evidence and manual-based approach*. Chichester: Wiley.

Taylor, L.S., Fiore, A.T., Mendelsohn, G.A. and Cheshire, C. (2011). 'Out of my league': A real-world test of the matching hypothesis. *Personality and Social Psychology Bulletin*, 37(7), 942–54.

Taylor, M. and Perera, U. (2015). NICE CG178 Psychosis and schizophrenia in adults: Treatment and management – an evidence-based guideline? *The British Journal of Psychiatry*, 206(5), 357–9.

Taylor, S.E., Klein, L.C., Lewis, B.P., Gruenewald, T.L., Gurung, R.A. and Updegraff, J.A. (2000). Biobehavioral responses to stress in females: Tend-and-befriend, not fight-or-flight. *Psychological Review*, 107(3), 411–29.

Temoshok, L. (1987). Personality, coping style, emotion and cancer: Towards an integrative model. *Cancer Surveys*, 6(3), 545–67.

The Plowden Report (1967). *Children and their Primary Schools*. London: HMSO.

Thibaut, J.W. and Kelley, H.H. (1959). *The Social Psychology of Groups*. New York: Wiley.

Thiessen, D., Young, R.K. and Burroughs, R. (1993). Lonely hearts advertisements reflect sexually dimorphic mating strategies. *Ethology and Sociobiology*, 14(3), 209–29.

Thompson, S.K. (1975). Gender labels and early sex-role development. *Child Development*, 46, 336–421.

Thornton, A. and Young-DeMarco, L. (2001). Four decades of trends in attitudes toward family issues in the United States: The 1960s through the 1990s. *Journal of Marriage and Family*, 63(4), 1009–37.

Thorton, L.M, Mazzeo, S.E. and Bulik, C.M. (2010). The heritability of eating disorders: Methods and current findings. In R.A.H. Adan and W.H. Kaye (eds), *Behavioural Neurobiology of Eating Disorders*. Berlin: Springer Verlag.

Tidwell, N.D., Estwick, P.W. and Finkel, E.J. (2013). Perceived, not actual, similarity predicts initial attraction in a live romantic context: Evidence from the speed-dating paradigm. *Personal Relationships*, 20, 199–215.

Tienari, P., Wynne, L.C. and Moring, J. (1994). The Finnish adoptive family study of schizophrenia: implications for family research. *British Journal of Psychiatry*, 163(23), 20–6.

Tienari, P., Wynne, L.C., Sorri, A., Lahti, I., Läksy, K., Moring, J., Naarala, M., Nieminen, P. and Wahlberg, K.E. (2004). Genotype–environment interaction in schizophrenia-spectrum disorder Long-term follow-up study of Finnish adoptees. *The British Journal of Psychiatry*, 184(3), 216–22.

Tiihonen, J., Lehti, M., Aaltonen, M., Kivivuori, J., Kautiainen, H., Virta, L., Hoti, F., Tanskanen, A. and Korhonen, P. (2015). Psychotropic drugs and homicide: a prospective cohort study from Finland. *World Psychiatry*, 14(2), 245–7.

Tiihonen, J., Lehti, M., Aaltonen, M., Kivivuori, J., Kautiainen, H., Virta, L.J., Hoti, F., Tanskanen, A. and Korhonen, P. (2015). Psychotropic drugs and homicide: A prospective cohort study from Finland. *World Psychiatry*, 14(2), 245–7.

Time magazine (2012). Parents who hid child's gender for five years now face backlash. *See* http://newsfeed.time.com/2012/01/24/parents-who-hid-childs-gender-for-five-years-now-face-backlash (accessed July 2015).

Tinbergen, N. (1951). *The Study of Instinct*. New York: Oxford University Press.

Tomiyama, A.J., Mann, T. and Comer, L. (2009). Triggers of eating in everyday life. *Appetite*, 52(1), 72–82.

Topa, G. and Moriano, J.A. (2010). Theory of planned behavior and smoking: Meta-analysis and SEM model. *Substance abuse and rehabilitation*, 1, 23–33.

Tozzi, F. Thornton, L., Klump, K.L., Bulik, C.M., Fichter, M.M. and Halmi, K. (2005). Symptom fluctuation in eating disorders: correlates of diagnostic crossover. *American Journal of Psychiatry*, 162(4), 732–40.

Tranel, D., Kemmerer, D., Adolphs, R., Damasio, H. and Damasio, A.R. (2003). Neural correlates of conceptual knowledge for actions. *Cognitive Neuropsychology*, 20(3), 409–32.

Trevena, J. and Miller, J. (2009). Brain preparation before a voluntary action: Evidence against unconscious movement initiation. *Consciousness and Cognition*, 19(1), 447–56.

Trimble, T.J., Shevlin, M., Egan, V., O'Hare, G., Rogers, D. and Hannigan, B. (2015). An evaluation of a brief anger management programme for offenders managed in the community using cross-lagged panel models. *Journal of Criminal Psychology*, 5(2), 124.

Turner, S.L., Hamilton, H., Jacobs, M., Angood, L.M. and Dwyer, D.H. (1997). The influence of fashion magazines on the body image satisfaction of college women: An exploratory analysis. *Adolescence*, 32(127), 603–14.

Turvey, B. (1999). *Criminal Profiling: An introduction to behavioral evidence analysis*. San Diego, CA: Academic Press.

Turvey, B.E. (2011). *Criminal Profiling: An Introduction to Behavioral Evidence Analysis* (4th edition). London: Elsevier Science.

UK Restorative Justice Council (2015). *See* www.restorativejustice.org.uk/resources/evidence-supporting-use-restorative-justice (accessed September 2015).

Unrod, M., Drobes, D.J., Stasiewicz, P.R., Ditre, J.W., Heckman, B., Miller, R.R. and Brandon, T.H. (2014). Decline in cue-provoked craving during cue exposure therapy for smoking cessation. *Nicotine and Tobacco Research*, 16(3), 306–15.

Valentine, E.R. (1992). *Conceptual Issues in Psychology* (2nd edition). London: Routledge.

Van Dam, C., De Bruyn, E.E.J. and Janssens, J.M.A. (2007). Personality, delinquency and criminal recidivism, *Adolescence*, 42(168), 763–77.

Van Yperen, N.W. and Buunk, B.P. (1990). A longitudinal study of equity and satisfaction in intimate relationships. *European Journal of Social Psychology*, 20(4), 287–309.

Varese, F., Smeets, F., Drukker, M., Lieverse, R., Lataster, T., Viechtbauer, W., Read, J., van Os, J. and Bentall, R.P. (2012). Childhood adversities increase the risk of psychosis: A meta-analysis of patient-control, prospective and cross-sectional cohort studies. *Schizophrenia Bulletin*, 38(4), 661–71.

Vassos, E., Pedersen, C.B., Murray, R.M., Collier, D.A. and Lewis, C.M. (2012). Meta-analysis of the association of urbanicity with schizophrenia. *Schizophrenia Bulletin*, 38(6), 1118–23.

Vaughan, K.K. and Fouts, G.T. (2003). Changes in television and magazine exposure and eating disorder symptomatology. *Sex Roles*, 49(7–8), 313–20.

Verdoux, H., Van Os, J., Maurice-Tison, S., Gay, B., Salamon, R. and Bourgeois, M. (1998). Is early adulthood a critical developmental stage for psychosis proneness? A survey of delusional ideation in normal subjects. *Schizophrenia Research*, 29(3), 247–54.

Verheul, R., van den Brink, W. and Hartgers, C. (1995). Prevalence of personality disorders among alcoholics and drug addicts: an overview. *European Addiction Research*, 1, 166–77.

Vernimmen, T. (2015). Damsels in control. *New Scientist*, 226(3027), 34–7.

Viken, R.J., Treat, T.A., Nosofsky, R.M., McFall, R.M. and Palmeri, T.J. (2002). Modeling individual differences in perceptual and attentional processes related to bulimic symptoms. *Journal of Abnormal Psychology*, 111(4), 598–609.

Vink, J.M., Willemsen, G. and Boomsma, D.I. (2005). Heritability of smoking initiation and nicotine dependence. *Behavior Genetics, 35*(4), 397–406.

von Holst, E. (1954). Relations between the central nervous system and the peripheral organs. *British Journal of Animal Behaviour, 2*, 89–94.

Vreugdenhil, H.J.I., Slijper, F.M.E., Mukder, P.G.H. and Weisglas-Kuperus, N. (2002). Effects of perinatal exposure to PCBs and dioxins on play behaviour in Dutch children at school age. *Environmental Health Perspectives, 110*(10), A593–A598.

Vygotsky, L.S. (orig. 1934, reprinted 1962). *Thought and Language*. Cambridge, MA: MIT Press.

Wachtel, T. and McCold, P. (2003). In pursuit of paradigm: A theory of restorative justice. Paper presented at the XIII World Congress of Criminology, 10–15 August 2003, Rio de Janeiro. *See* www.iirp.edu/article_detail.php?article_id=NDI0 (accessed September 2015).

Wade, T.D., Bulik, C.M., Neale, M. and Kendler, K.S. (2000). Anorexia nervosa and major depression: shared genetic and environmental risk factors. *American Journal of Psychiatry, 157*(3), 469–71.

Walker, A., Kershaw, C. and Nicholas, A. (2006). *Crime in England and Wales 2005/2006*. London: Home Office.

Walker, N., Farrington D.P. and Tucker, G. (1981). Reconviction Rates of Adult Males After Different Sentences. *British Journal of Criminology, 21*(4), 357–60.

Walster, E. and Walster, G. W. (1969). The matching hypothesis. *Journal of Personality and Social Psychology, 6*, 248–53.

Walster, E., Aronson, V., Abrahams, D. and Rottman, L. (1966). Importance of physical attractiveness in dating behavior. *Journal of Personality and Social Psychology, 4*(5), 508–16.

Wang, E.W. and Diamond, P.M. (1999). Empirically identifying factors related to violence risk in corrections. *Behavioral Sciences & the Law, 17*(3), 377–89.

Wang, H.D. and Deutch, A.Y. (2008). Dopamine depletion of the prefrontal cortex induces dendritic spine loss: Reversal by atypical antipsychotic drug treatment. *Neuropsychopharmacology, 33*(6), 1276–86.

Wardle, J. and Beales, S. (1988). Control and loss of control over eating: An experimental investigation. *Journal of Abnormal Psychology, 97*(1), 35–40.

Wardle, J., Carnell, S. and Cooke, L. (2005). Parental control over feeding and children's fruit and vegetable intake: How are they related? *Journal of the American Dietetic Association, 105*(2), 227–32.

Warr, P. (1987). *Work, Unemployment, and Mental Health*. Oxford: Clarendon Press.

Wason, P.C. and Shapiro, D. (1971). Natural and contrived experience in reasoning problems. *Quarterly Journal of Experimental Psychology, 23*, 63–71.

Watson, D. and Clark, L.A. (1984). Negative affectivity: The disposition to experience aversive emotional states. *Psychological Bulletin, 96*, 465–90.

Watson, J.B. and Rayner, R. (1920). Conditioned emotional reactions. *Journal of Experimental Psychology, 3*, 1–14.

Watson, R.I., Jr (1973). Investigation into deindividuation using a cross-cultural survey technique. *Journal of Personality and Social Psychology*, 25, 342–5.

Waynforth, D. and Dunbar R.I.M. (1995). Conditional mate choice strategies in humans: Evidence from 'lonely hearts' advertisements. *Behaviour*, 132, 755–79.

Wearing, D. (2005). *Forever Today: A Memoir of Love and Amnesia*. London: Corgi.

Weatherly, J.N., Sauter, J.M. and King, B.M. (2004). The 'big win' and resistance to extinction when gambling. *The Journal of Psychology, 138*(6), 495–504.

Weber, N.S., Cowan, D.N., Millikan, A.M. and Niebuhr, D.W. (2009). Psychiatric and general medical conditions comorbid with schizophrenia in the National Hospital Discharge Survey. *Psychiatric Services, 60*(8), 1059–67.

Wegner, D.M. (1994). Ironic processes of mental control. *Psychological Review*, 101, 34–52.

Wegner, D.M., Schneider, D.J., Carter, S.R. and White, T.L. (1987). Paradoxical effects of thought suppression. *Journal of Personality and Social Psychology*, 53, 5–13

Weiss, R.S. (1991). The attachment bond in childhood and adulthood. In C.M. Parkes, J. Stevenson-Hinde and P. Marris (eds), *Attachment across the Life Cycle*. New York: Tavistock/Routledge.

Wellman, H.M. and Woolley, J.D. (1990). From simple desires to ordinary beliefs: The early development of everyday psychology. *Cognition, 35*, 245–75.

West, S.L., Garbutt, J.C., Carey, T.S., Lux, L.J., Jackman, A.M. and Tolleson-Rinehart, S. (1999). *Pharmacotherapy for Alcohol Dependence*. Rockville, MD: U.S. Department of Health and Human Services; Public Health Service; Agency for Health Care Policy and Research.

Westcott, M.R. (1982). Quantitative and qualitative aspects of experienced freedom. *Journal of Mind and Behavior, 3*, 99–126.

Westenhoefer, J., Broeckmann, P., Münch, A.K. and Pudel V. (1994). Cognitive control of eating behavior and the disinhibition effect. *Appetite, 23*, 27–41.

Weymouth, L.A. and Howe, T.R. (2011). A multi-site evaluation of Parents Raising Safe Kids violence prevention program. *Children and Youth Services Review, 33*(10), 1960–67.

Whaley, A.L. (2001). Cultural mistrust and clinical diagnosis of paranoid schizophrenia in African-American patients. *Journal of Psychopathology and Behavioral Assessment, 23*, 93–100.

White, G.L., Fishbein, S. and Rutstein, J. (1981). Passionate love and the misattribution of arousal. *Journal of Personality and Social Psychology, 41*, 56–62.

Whitelaw, S., Baldwin, S., Bunton, R. and Flynn, D. (2000). The status of evidence and outcomes in Stages of Change research. *Health Education Research, 15*(6), 707–18.

Whiteman, S.D. and Christiansen, A.E. (2008). Processes of sibling influence in adolescence: Individual and family correlates. *Family Relations, 57*, 24–34.

Wicker, B., Keysers, C., Plailly, J., Royet, J.P., Gallese, V. and Rizzolatti, G. (2003). Both of us disgusted in my insula: The common neural basis of seeing and feeling disgust. *Neuron, 40*, 655–64.

Wiers, C.E., Kühn, S., Javadi, A.H., Korucuoglu, O., Wiers, R.W., Walter, H. and Bermpohl, F. (2013). Automatic approach bias towards smoking cues is present in smokers but not in ex-smokers. *Psychopharmacology, 229*(1), 187–97.

Wilkinson, L.L., Rowe, A.C., Bishop, R.J. and Brunstrom, J.M. (2010). Attachment anxiety, disinhibited eating, and body mass index in adulthood. *International Journal of Obesity, 34*(9), 1442–5.

Williams, J.E., Paton, C.C., Siegler, I.C., Eigenbrodt, M.L., Nieto, F.J. and Tyroler, H.A. (2000). Anger proneness predicts coronary heart disease risk: Prospective analysis from the atherosclerosis risk in communities (ARIC) study. *Circulation, 101*(17), 2034–9.

Williams, J.H.G., Whiten, A., Suddendorf, T. and Perrett, D.I. (2001). Imitation, mirror neurons and autism. *Neuroscience and Biobehavioral Reviews, 25*(4), 287–95.

Williams, T.M. (1985). Implications of a natural experiment in the developed world for research on television in the developing world. Special issue: Television in the developing world. *Journal of Cross-cultural Psychology, 16*(3), 263–87.

Wilson, D. (2010). Institutional aggression. *Psychology Review, 15*(4), 2–4.

Wilson, D. (2014). *Pain and Retribution: A short history of British prisons 1066 to the present*. London: Reaktion Books.

Wilson, R.J., Picheca, J.E. and Prinzo, M (2007). Evaluating the effectiveness of professionally facilitated volunteerism in the community management of high risk sexual offenders. *The Howard Journal of Criminal Justice, 46*, 289–302.

Wilson, R.W. and Kolander, C.A. (2003). *Drug Abuse Prevention: A School and Community Partnership*. Burlington, MA: Jones and Bartlett Learning.

Wimmer, H. and Perner, J. (1983). Beliefs about beliefs: Representation and constraining function of wrong beliefs in young children's understanding of deception. *Cognition, 13*, 103–28.

Winch, R.F. (1958). *Mate-Selection: A Study of Complementary Needs*, New York: Harper.

Windle, M. (2000). Parental, sibling, and peer influences on adolescent substance use and alcohol problems. *Applied Developmental Science, 4*(2), 98–110.

Wober, M. (1974). Towards an understanding of the Kiganda concept of intelligence. In J.W. Berry and P. Dasen (eds), *Culture and Cognition: Readings in Cross-cultural Psychology*. London: Methuen.

Wolpe, J. (1973). *The Practice of Behavior Therapy*. New York: Pergamon Press.

Wood, D.J. and Middleton, D.J. (1975). A study of assisted problem-solving. *British Journal of Psychology, 66*, 181–91.

Wood, D.J., Bruner, J.S. and Ross, G. (1976). The role of tutoring in problem-solving. *Journal of Child Psychology and Psychiatry, 17*, 89–100.

Wren, A.M., Seal, L.J., Cohen, M.A., Brynes, A.E., Frost, G.S., Murphy, K.G., Dhillo, W.S., Ghatei, M.A. and Bloom, S.R. (2001). Ghrelin enhances appetite and increases food intake in humans. *Journal of Clinical Endocrinology and Metabolism, 86*(12), 5992.

Wright, J.P., Stephen, G. and Tibbetts, L.E. (2015). *Criminals in the Making: Criminality across the life course* (2nd edition). Thousand Oaks, CA: SAGE.

Wu, T., Li, Y., Liu, G., Bian, Z., Li, J., Zhang, J., Xie, L. and Ni, J. (2006). Investigation of authenticity of 'claimed' randomized controlled trials (RCTs) and quality assessment of RCT reports published in China. *Proceedings of the 14th Cochrane Colloquium*; Dublin. 2006.

Wykes, T., Steel, C., Everitt, B. and Tarrier, N. (2008). Cognitive behavior therapy for schizophrenia: effect sizes, clinical models, and methodological rigor. *Schizophrenia Bulletin, 34*(3), 523–37.

Yamamiya, Y., Cash, T.F., Melnyk, S.E., Posavac, H.D. and Posavac, S.S. (2005). Women's exposure to thin-and-beautiful media images: Body image effects of media-ideal internalization and impact-reduction interventions. *Body Image, 2*(1), 74–80.

Young K.S. (2011). CBT-IA: The first treatment model to address Internet addiction. *Journal of Cognitive Therapy*, 25, 304–12.

Young, K.S. (1999). Internet Addiction: Symptoms, Evaluation and Treatment. In L. VandeCreek and T.L. Jackson (eds). *Innovations in Clinical Practice* (Vol 17), Sarasota, FL: Professional Resource Press.

Yuille, J.C. and Cutshall, J.L. (1986). A case study of eyewitness testimony of a crime. *Journal of Applied Psychology*, *71*, 291–301.

Yuma, Y. (2010). [The effect of prison crowding on prisoners' violence in Japan: Testing with cointegration regressions and error correction models]. *Shinrigaku kenkyu: The Japanese Journal of Psychology*, *81*(3), 218–25.

Yurchisin, J., Watchravesringkan, K. and McCabe, D.B. (2005). An exploration of identity re-creation in the context of Internet dating. *Social Behavior and Personality*, *33*(8), 735–50.

Zajonc, R.B. (1968). Attitudinal effects of mere exposure. *Journal of Personality and Social Psychology (Monograph)*, *9*, 1–29.

Zehr, H. (2002). *Little Book of Restorative Justice and Peacebuilding*. Intercourse, PA: Good Books.

Zelli, A., Huesmann, L.R. and Cervone, D. (1995). Social inference and individual differences in aggression: Evidence for spontaneous judgments of hostility. *Aggressive Behavior*, 21, 405–17.

Zhao, S., Grasmuck, S. and Martin, J. (2008). Identity construction on Facebook: Digital empowerment in anchored relationships. *Computers in Human Behavior*, *24*(5), 1816–36.

Zhong, C.B., Bohns, V.K. and Gino, F. (2010). Good lamps are the best police: Darkness increases dishonesty and self-interested behavior. *Psychological science*, *21*(3), 311–14.

Zhou, J.-N., Hofman, M.A., Gooren, L.J. and Swaab, D.F. (1995). A sex difference in the human brain and its relation to transsexuality. *Nature*, *378*, 68–70.

Zickler, P. (2003). Nicotine's multiple effects on the brain's reward system drive addiction. *NIDA Notes*, *17*(6), 1–6.

Zimbardo, P.G. (1969). The human choice: Individuation, reason, and order versus deindividuation, impulse, and chaos. In *Nebraska Symposium on Motivation*. University of Nebraska Press.

Zimbardo, P.G., Banks, P.G., Haney, C. and Jaffe, D. (1973). Pirandellian prison: The mind is a formidable jailor. *New York Times Magazine*, 8 April, 38–60.

Zimbardo, P.G., Haney, C., Curtis Banks, W. and Jaffe, D. (1972). *Stanford Prison Experiment: A Simulation Study of the Psychology of Imprisonment*. Philip G. Zimbardo, Incorporated.

Zosuls, K.M., Ruble, D.N., Tamis-LeMonda, C.S., Shrout, P.E., Bornstein, M.H. and Greulich, F.K. (2009). The acquisition of gender labels in infancy: Implications for sex-typed play. *Developmental Psychology*, *45*(3), 688–701.

Zucker, K.J. (2004). Gender identity development and issues. *Child and Adolescent Psychiatric Clinics of North America*, *13*(3), 551–68.

Zucker, K.J., Bradley, S.J. and Lowry Sullivan, C.B. (1996). Traits of separation anxiety in boys with gender identity disorder. *Journal of the American Academy of Child and Adolescent Psychiatry*, *35*(6), 791–8.

Zuckerman, M. (1987). All parents are environmentalists until they have their second child. *Behavioural and Brain Sciences*, *10*, 42–3.

Glossary/Index

bottom-up approach A data-driven approach where statistical techniques are used to produce predictions about the likely characteristics of an offender. 260, 282

boundary model 180

buffering hypothesis 216

Bundy, T. 258

Buss, D. 64, 234, 235
mate preferences across cultures study 45, 64, 65, 66, 84
'butterfly effect' 47

C

Cadherin 13 (CDH13) 231, 264

caffeine dependency 292

calculated value The value of a test statistic calculated for a particular data set. 25

Canary, D.J. 74, 85

Canter, D. 259, 260, 261, 263

cardiovascular disorder Refers to any disorder of the heart (such as coronary heart disease, CHD) and circulatory system (such as hypertension, commonly known as high blood pressure) as well as strokes (restricted blood flow to parts of the brain). 194, 195
studies of link between Type A behaviour and CHD 204, 205, 219
study of links between anger and 194, 218

carrot task (Baillargeon and DeVos) 122, 130

case study A research method that involves a detailed study of a single individual, institution or event. Case studies provide a rich record of human experience but are hard to generalise from. 14, 34

chance 23

chaos theory 47

chi-squared test 32, 35

chromosomes The X-shaped bodies that carry all the genetic information (*DNA*) for an organism. 94, 108

circle theory 260, 261

class inclusion The relation between two classes where all members of one class are included in the other. 118

coding The process of placing quantitative or qualitative data in categories. 12

cognition and development 114–35
Baillargeon's explanation of early infant abilities 122–3, 130
carrot task 122, 130
exam practice questions 132–3
exam questions with answers 134–5
logical thinking 115
Maxi false belief study 126, 131
mirror neuron system 128–9, 131
Piaget's stages of intellectual development 118–19, 130
Piaget's theory of cognitive development 116–17, 123, 130
Sally-Anne test 126, 127, 131
Selman's theory of development of social cognition 124–5, 131
summary 130–1
theory of mind 126–7, 128, 131
Vygotsky's theory of cognitive development 120–1, 130

cognitive behavioural therapy (CBT) A combination of cognitive therapy (a way of changing maladaptive thoughts and beliefs) and behavioural therapy (a way of changing behaviour in response to these thoughts and beliefs). 149, 278, 310
addiction 310–11, 317
anger management 278, 279
eating disorders 177

psychosis 148–9, 157

fruit machine gambling study 304, 316

Piaget's theory of 116–19, 130

Vygotsky's theory of 120–1, 130

cognitive biases are irrational beliefs that are unhelpful, illogical and inconsistent with our social reality, and which can lead us to behave in inappropriate ways. 304, 305, 310

cognitive development The process by which our mental processes change as we age. 116

cognitive distortion Thinking that has a bias, such that what is perceived by a person does not match reality. 268, 269, 284

cognitive explanations of mental disorders propose that abnormalities in cognitive function are a key component of schizophrenia. 144
gender development 96–9, 108
offending behaviour 268–9, 284
schizophrenia 144, 145, 156

cognitive priming refers to a temporary increase in the accessibility of thoughts and ideas. For example, violent media activates thoughts or ideas about violence, which activate other aggressive thoughts through their association in memory pathways. 246, 247, 249

cognitive theory When applied to disorders, this is any explanation about the way in which a person processes information that affects their feelings and their behaviour. 176
anorexia nervosa and 176–7, 185
gambling addiction and 304–5, 316
collision phenomenon study (Kotovsky and Baillargeon) 123

Columbine murders 268

commitment The likelihood that an individual will persist with their current relationship. It is a product of high satisfaction and investment in the relationship and low quality of alternatives. 76, 77

co-morbidity refers to the extent that two (or more) conditions or diseases occur simultaneously in a patient, for example schizophrenia and depression. 140, 141

complementarity of needs refers to how well two people fit together as a couple and meet each other's needs. 70, 71

computer dance study (Walster *et al.*) 66, 67, 84

computer games, studies of violent 244, 245, 249

concurrent validity A means of establishing validity by comparing an existing test or questionnaire with the one you are interested in. 19

conformity research 45

congenital adrenal hyperplasia (CAH) 95

conservation The ability to distinguish between reality and appearance, for example to understand that quantity is not changed even when a display is transformed. 96, 118, 119

content analysis A kind of observational study in which behaviour is observed indirectly in visual, written or verbal material. May involve either qualitative or quantitative analysis, or both. 12, 34

control is to direct or to exercise authoritative influence over events or behaviours. 172, 173

correlation coefficient A number between −1 and +1 that tells us how closely the co-variables in a correlational analysis are related. 30

correlation, tests of 30–1, 35

cortisol A hormone produced as a result of chronic stress, with both positive and negative effects (e.g. burst of energy and reduced immune response). 192, 193, 194, 202

counting system, Papua New Guinea 121

covert sensitisation involves eliminating an unwanted behaviour by creating an imaginary association between the behaviour and an unpleasant stimulus or consequence. 308, 309

crime refers to any behaviour that is unlawful and punished by the state. It is an act that is harmful to an individual, group or society as a whole. 256
defining and measuring 256–7, 282
criminal geographic targeting (CGT) 260

criminal personality
Eysenck's theory of 266–7, 284
types 262–3, 283

critical value In a statistical test the value of the test statistic that must be reached to show significance. 25

cue reactivity Objects and environments associated with a drug or behaviour become conditioned stimuli, so people experience greater craving and physiological arousal when exposed to the objects and environments associated with their addiction. 300, 301

cult group behaviour 15

cultural bias The tendency to judge all people in terms of your own cultural assumptions. This distorts or biases your judgement. 44–5, 56, 119, 127

cultural differences
aggression 239
coping with stress 217
diagnosis of schizophrenia 140, 141
gender roles 104
importance of equity 75
Mead's classic study in Papua New Guinea 44, 103, 104, 105
in response to de-individuation conditions 241
self-disclosure patterns 69

cultural influences
defining crime 256
food preferences 166, 167, 184
gender development 95
gender roles 104, 105, 109

cultural relativism The view that behaviour cannot be judged properly unless it is viewed in the context of the culture in which it originates. 44

culture The rules, customs, morals and ways of interacting that bind together members of a society or some other collection of people. 44, 104, 141
in psychology 44–5, 56
role in cognitive development 121
custodial sentencing 274–5, 285
restorative justice compared with 281

D

daily hassles are the 'irritating, frustrating, distressing demands that to some degree characterise everyday transactions with the environment' (Kanner *et al.*, 1981). 197, 198–9, 219

daily uplifts are the opposite – they are the minor positive experiences of everyday life, for example receiving a compliment at work or feeling good about one's appearance. 198, 199

dating couples study (Kerckhoff and Davis) 70, 71, 84

Davis, K. 70, 71, 84

degrees of freedom The number of values that are free to vary given that the overall total values are known. 25

stress inoculation therapy A type of CBT which trains people to cope with anxiety and stressful situations more effectively by learning skills to 'inoculate' themselves against the damaging effects of future stressors. 210–11, 220

superego Part of Freud's conception of the structure of the personality. The superego embodies our conscience and sense of right and wrong, as well as notions of the ideal self. It develops between the ages of 3 and 6. 272, 273, 285

sympathomedullary pathway The parts of the body involved in the immediate response to stress (fight-or-flight) involving adrenaline. 192, 214

symptom overlap refers to the fact that symptoms of a disorder may not be unique to that disorder but may also be found in other disorders, making accurate diagnosis difficult. 140, 141

T

taste aversion is a learned response to eating toxic, spoiled or poisonous food, which results in the animal avoiding eating the food that made it ill in the future. 164, 165

temporal validity Concerning the ability to generalise a research effect beyond the particular time period of the study. 19, 93

tend-and-befriend response An adaptive response to stress in female animals, related to protecting offspring (tend) and relying on the social group for mutual defence (befriending). 214, 215

testosterone A hormone produced mainly by the testes in males, but also occurring in females. It is associated with the development of secondary sexual characteristics in males (e.g. body hair), but has also been implicated in aggression and dominance behaviours. 94, 95, 214, 228, 229

test–retest reliability The same test or interview is given to the same participants on two occasions to see if the same results are obtained. 16, 17

test statistic A statistical test is used to calculate a numerical value. For each test this value has a specific name such as S for the sign test. 25

thematic analysis A technique used when analysing qualitative data. Themes or categories are identified and then data is organised according to these themes. 12, 13

theory of mind An individual's understanding that other people have separate mental states (beliefs, intentions, emotions) and that others see the world from a different point of view to their own. 126–7, 128, 131

theory of planned behaviour An individual's decision to engage in a particular behaviour can be directly predicted by their intention to engage in that behaviour, which in turn is determined by their behavioural attitude, subjective norms and perceived behavioural control. 312–13, 317

token economy A form of therapy where desirable behaviours are encouraged by the use of selective reinforcements. Rewards (tokens) are given as *secondary reinforcers* when individuals engage in correct/socially desirable behaviours. The tokens can then be exchanged for *primary reinforcers* – food or privileges. 153, 277
  dealing with offending behaviour 276–7, 285
  ethical issues 277
  and management of schizophrenia 152–3, 157
  study in training school for delinquents 276

tolerance means that an individual no longer responds to a drug in the same way, with the result that larger and larger doses are needed in order to experience the same effects as before. 292, 293

top-down approach (also called crime scene analysis) An analysis of previous crimes creates a profile of a likely offender. A profiler uses this knowledge to narrow the field of possible suspects. Unlike the bottom-up approach, the top-down approach relies on the intuition and beliefs of the profiler. 258–9, 282

two-tailed test Form of test used with a non-directional hypothesis. 25

Type A personality is characterised as someone who experiences constant time pressure, competitiveness in work and social situations, and anger, i.e. being easily frustrated by other people. 204, 205

Type B personality is characterised by an easygoing, relaxed and patient approach to life. 204

Type C personality is characterised by extreme emotional suppression and a desire to please others. 204, 205

type I error occurs when a researcher *rejects* a null hypothesis that is true. 22, 23

type II error occurs when a researcher *accepts* a null hypothesis that was not true. 22, 23

typical antipsychotics are dopamine *antagonists* in that they bind to but do not stimulate dopamine receptors and so reduce the symptoms of schizophrenia. 146, 147

U

universality The aim to develop theories that apply to all people, which may include real differences. 42

V

validity Refers to whether an observed effect is a genuine one. 18–19, 34, 140, 141
  of workplace stress studies 201

variable reinforcement A response is reinforced after an unpredictable number of responses. In variable ratio reinforcement, the delivery of reinforcement is unpredictable but averages out at a specific rate. 302, 303

violation of expectation research A method of conducting research with infants using their surprise as a measure of whether what they see is not what they expect to see. Thus we know what their expectations are. 122, 123

virtual relationships are relationships that are conducted through the Internet rather than face to face, for example through social media. 80–1, 85

W

withdrawal syndrome can occur when a drug on which an individual is physically dependent is discontinued. In such situations, withdrawal symptoms, such as shaking and anxiety, can occur, as the body attempts to deal with the absence of a drug's effects. 292, 293

workload The amount of effort and/or activity involved in a job. It is quite often discussed as 'job demand', i.e. the amount required for a person to do during their working day. 200, 201

workplace stress Aspects of our working environment (such as work overload or impending deadlines) that we experience as stressful, and which cause a stress reaction in our body. 200–1, 219

Y

Z

zone of proximal development In Vygotsky's theory of cognitive development, the 'region' between a person's current abilities, which they can perform with no assistance, and their potential capabilities, which they can be helped to achieve with the assistance of 'experts'. 120, 121

Appendix: Research methods terms from the Year 1 and AS Student Book

Aims A statement of what the researcher intends to find out in an investigation.

Bar chart A graph used to represent the frequencies of nominal (category) or discrete (discontinuous) data.

Behavioural categories A way of operationalising behaviour by defining specific, objective, mutually exclusive observable components.

Bias A systematic distortion.

Calculated value The value of a test statistic calculated for a particular data set.

Case study A detailed study of a single individual, institution or event.

Closed questions Questions that have a predetermined set of answers from which respondents select one. Tend to produce quantitative data.

Content analysis A kind of observational study in which behaviour is observed indirectly in written or verbal material such as interviews, conversations, books, diaries or TV programmes.

Co-variables The two measured variables in a correlational analysis. They must be continuous.

Confederate An individual in a study who is not a real participant and has been instructed how to behave by the investigator.

Confidentiality Concerns the communication of personal information and the trust that the information will be protected.

Confounding variable A variable in a study which is not the IV but which also affects the DV.

Continuous variable A variable that can take on any value within a certain range.

Control The extent to which any variable is held constant or regulated by a researcher.

Controlled observation A form of investigation in which behaviour is observed under conditions where certain variables have been organised by the researcher.

Correlation Determining the extent of an association between two variables. The co-variables may not be linked at all (zero correlation) or may both increase together (positive correlation), or as one variable increases the other decreases (negative correlation).

Correlation coefficient A number between -1 and +1 that describes the strength of the association between two co-variables in a correlational analysis.

Cost-benefit analysis A systematic approach to estimating the negative and positive impact of any research.

Counterbalancing Used to overcome order effects when using a repeated measures experimental design. Ensures that each condition is tested first or second in equal amounts.

Covert observations Observing people without their knowledge. Knowing that behaviour is being observed is likely to alter a participant's behaviour.

Critical value In an inferential test, the value of the test statistic that must be reached to show significance.

Curvilinear correlation A non-linear relationship between co-variables, that does not fall on a straight line.

Debriefing A post-research interview designed to inform participants of the true nature of the study and to restore them to the physical and psychological state they were in at the start of the study.

Deception A participant is not told the true aim of the study and thus cannot give truly informed consent.

Demand characteristics A cue that makes participants unconsciously aware of the aims of a study or causes them to change their behaviour to match what they think is expected.

Descriptive statistics A way of summarising a data set using measures of central tendency and dispersion.

Directional hypothesis States the direction of the predicted difference between the two conditions or two groups of participants.

Effect size A measure of the strength of the relationship between two variables.

Ethical guidelines (code of conduct) A set of principles designed to help professionals behave honestly and with integrity.

Ethical issues Concern questions of right and wrong. They arise in research where there are conflicting sets of values between researchers and participants.

Ethics committee A group of people within a research institution that must approve a study before it begins.

Event sampling An observational technique in which a count is kept of the number of times a certain behaviour occurs.

Experiment A research method in which causal conclusions can be drawn because an independent variable is deliberately manipulated to observe the effect on the dependent variable.

Experimental design A set of procedures used to control the influence of factors such as participant variables in an experiment. How the participants are allocated to the different conditions of the IV.

External validity The degree to which a research finding can be generalised to other settings (ecological validity); to other groups of people (population validity); over time (historical validity).

Extraneous variable Any variable, other than the IV, which may affect the DV and therefore affect validity of the findings. Extraneous variables need to be controlled in an experiment wherever possible.

Field experiment A controlled experiment conducted outside a laboratory. The IV is manipulated by the experimenter, but participants are usually unaware that they are being studied.

Fraction, percentage, decimal, ratio Methods of expressing parts of a whole.

Generalisation Applying the findings of a study to the population, or to situations beyond the research context.

Heuristic A mental rule or short-cut allowing for more efficient decision making, but often leading to cognitive biases.

Histogram A graph showing the frequency distribution of continuous data.

Hypothesis A precise and testable statement about the predicted relationship between the variables. Should be operationalised.

Independent groups design Participants are allocated to different groups, representing different conditions of the IV, preferably by random allocation.

Independent variable (IV) The condition that is directly manipulated by an experimenter in order to test its effect on the DV.

Inter-observer reliability The extent to which there is agreement between two or more observers involved in observations of a behaviour.

Intervening variables Variables that come in between two other variables and can explain their association.

Dependent variable The variable that is being measured in an experiment.

Inferential statistics Statistical tests to find out the likelihood that a result could have occurred simply by chance in a sample.

Informed consent Participants must be given comprehensive information concerning the nature and purpose of the research and their role in it, in order that they can make an informed decision about whether to participate.

Internal validity The degree to which an observed effect was due to the experimental manipulation rather than other factors such as confounding or extraneous variables.

Interview A research method that involves a face-to-face, real-time interaction with another individual in order to collect data.

Interviewer bias The effect of an interviewer's expectations, communicated unconsciously, on a respondent's behaviour.

Investigator effect Anything that an investigator does that affects a participants' performance in a study, directly (through interaction with the participant) or indirectly (through bias in the study design).

Laboratory experiment An experiment carried out in a controlled setting.

Linear correlation A systematic relationship between co-variables that fits a straight line.

Level of significance The level of error we are prepared to accept, for example $p < 0.05$ means there is less than 5% chance that the difference or association occurred by chance in a sample.

Matched pairs design Pairs of participants are matched on key variables. One member of each pair is randomly allocated to each experimental condition.

Mean The arithmetic average of a data set.

Measure of central tendency A descriptive statistic that provides information about a 'typical' value in a data set.

Measure of dispersion A descriptive statistic that provides information about how spread out the data are in a data set.

Median The middle value of a data set when the items are placed in rank order.

Meta-analysis A research method in which a researcher statistically analyses the findings of a number of different studies to investigate the overall effect.

Mode The most frequently occurring value or category in a data set.

Mundane realism The degree to which experiences encountered in the research environment mirror those in the real world.

Natural experiment A research method in which the experimenter has not manipulated the IV directly for ethical or practical reasons.

Naturalistic observation An observation carried out in an everyday setting, in which the investigator does not interfere in any way but merely observes the behaviour(s) in question.

Negatively skewed distribution Most of the scores are bunched to the right. The mean is affected by extreme scores in the long tail to the left, so the mean is to the left of the mode.

Non-directional hypothesis Predicts that there is a difference between two conditions without stating the direction of the difference.

Non-participant observation The observer is separate from the people being observed.

Normal distribution A symmetrical bell-shaped frequency distribution curve. The mean, median and mode are at the mid-point.

Observer bias Observers' expectations affect what they see or hear. This reduces the validity of the observations.

One-tailed test Form of test used with a directional hypothesis.

Open questions Questions that invite respondents to provide their own answers. Tends to produce qualitative data.

Operationalise Ensuring that variables are in a form that can be easily tested.

Opportunity sample A sample of participants produced by selecting people who are most easily available at the time of the study.

Order effect In a repeated measures design, an extraneous variable arising from the order in which conditions are presented, e.g. a practice effect or fatigue effect.

Order of magnitude A means of comparing numbers by focussing on the overall size (magnitude). This may be done by expressing the number in standard form (powers of 10).

Overt observation Observational studies where participants are aware that their behaviour is being studied.

Participant observation Observations made by someone who is also participating in the activity being observed, which may affect their objectivity.

Peer review The practice of using independent experts to assess the quality and validity of scientific research and academic reports.

Presumptive consent Dealing with lack of informed consent or deception, by asking people who are similar to the participants whether they would agree to take part in the study. If they consent, it is presumed that the real participants would also agree.

Pilot study A small scale trial run of a study to test any aspects of the procedure, with a view to making improvements.

Population The group of people that the researcher is interested in studying, from whom a sample is drawn, and about whom generalisations can be made.

Positively skewed distribution Most of the scores are bunched to the left. The mean is to the right of the mode because it is affected by the long tail on the right.

Primary data Information observed or collected directly from first-hand experience.

Privacy A person's right to control the flow of information about themselves.

Probability (*p*) A measure of the likelihood or chance that certain events will occur.

Protection from harm During a research study, participants should not experience negative physical or psychological effects, such as physical injury, lowered self-esteem or embarrassment.

Qualitative data Non-numerical data.

Quantitative data Data measured in numbers.

Quasi-experiment A research method in which the independent variable is a characteristic of the individual, and cannot be manipulated by the experimenter.

Questionnaire Data are collected through the use of written questions.

Random allocation Allocating participants to experimental conditions or groups using random techniques.

Random sample A sample of participants produced by using a random technique so that every member of the target population has an equal chance of being selected.

Range The difference between the highest and lowest item in a data set. Usually 1 is added as a correction.

Reciprocity A sense of fairness, a social rule that people should repay acts of kindness.

Repeated measures design Each participants takes part in every condition of the experiment, i.e. every level of the IV.

Review A consideration of many of studies that have investigated the same topic in order to reach a general conclusion.

Right to withdraw Participants can stop participating in a study if they are uncomfortable in any way. This is especially important in cases where it was not possible to give fully informed consent. Participants should also have the right to refuse permission for the researcher to use any data they produced.

Sampling The method used to select participants for a study. Sampling also refers to the method of recording behaviours in an observation such as event or time sampling.

Scattergram A graphical representation of the association (i.e. the correlation) between two co-variables.

Secondary data Information used in a research study that was collected by someone else or for a purpose other than the current one, such as published data or data collected in the past.

Sign test An inferential statistical test to determine the significance of a difference in scores in a sample of related items.

Significance A statistical term indicating that the association between variables is sufficiently strong for us to accept the research hypothesis under test.

Significant figures The number of single digits (other than zero) used to represent a number. The zeros exist as place holders, to maintain the correct order of magnitude.

Skewed distribution A frequency distribution in which the scores are not evenly distributed either side of the median.

Social desirability bias A distortion in the way people answer questions – they tend to answer questions in such a way that presents themselves in a better light.

Standard deviation The spread of data around the mean.

Standard form (or scientific notation) A way of expressing any number in two parts, in the form $A \times 10^n$. A is a number between 1 and 10, and n can be positive (for very large numbers) or negative (for very small numbers).

Standardised procedures A set of procedures that are the same for all participants in order to be able to repeat the study.

Stratified sample A sample of participants produced by identifying subgroups and selecting participants randomly from these subgroups, in the same proportion as their occurrence in the population.

Structured interview Any interview in which the questions are decided in advance.

Structured observation The use of systems such as behavioural categories and sampling procedures to organise an observation.

Systematic sample A sample obtained by selecting every *n*th person (where *n* is a number).

Table of critical values A table of numbers used to judge significance. The calculated value of the test statistic is compared to the relevant number in the table (the critical value) to see if the calculated value is significant.

Test statistic The number calculated in statistical testing. For the sign test, the test statistic is known as *S*.

Time sampling An observational technique in which the observer records behaviours at regular intervals, e.g. every 20 seconds.

Two-tailed test Form of test used with a non-directional hypothesis.

Unstructured interview The interview starts out with some general aims and initial questions, then lets the interviewee's answers guide subsequent questions.

Validity Whether an observed effect is a genuine one.

Volunteer bias A form of sampling bias arising because volunteers have special characteristics such as higher than average motivation.

Volunteer sample A sample of participants that relies on self-selected volunteers.

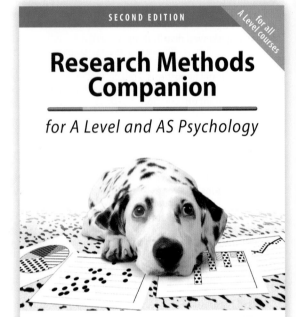
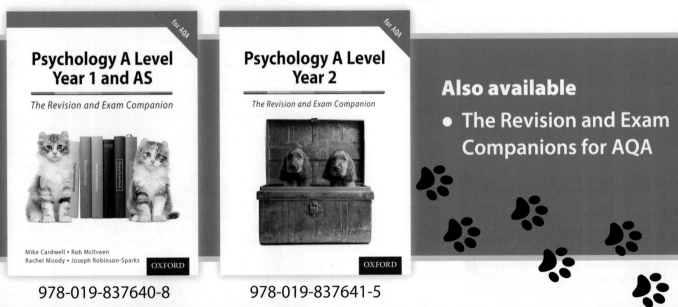